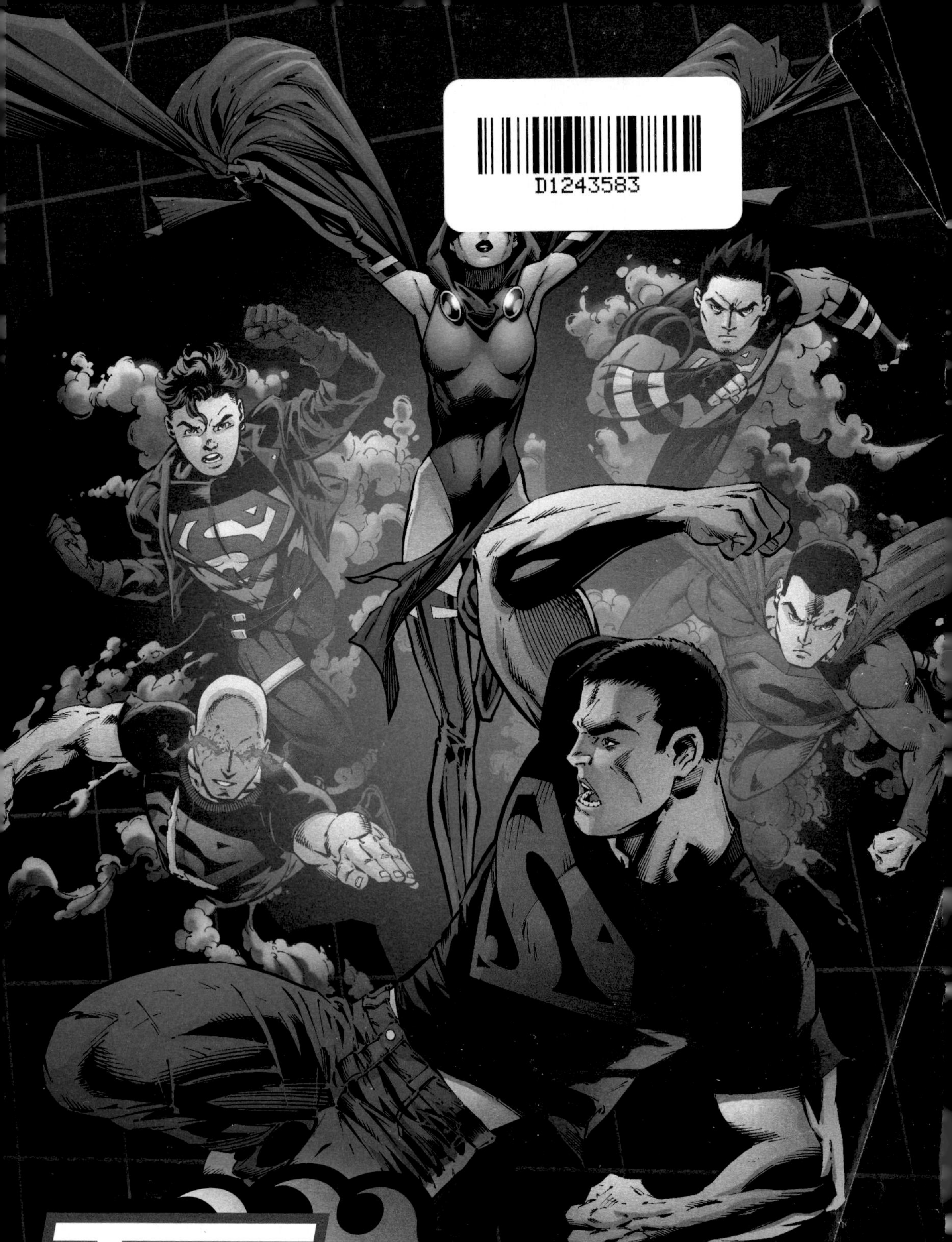

Teen Titans

BY **GEOFF JOHNS**

BOOK THREE

Teen Titans

BY **GEOFF JOHNS**

BOOK THREE

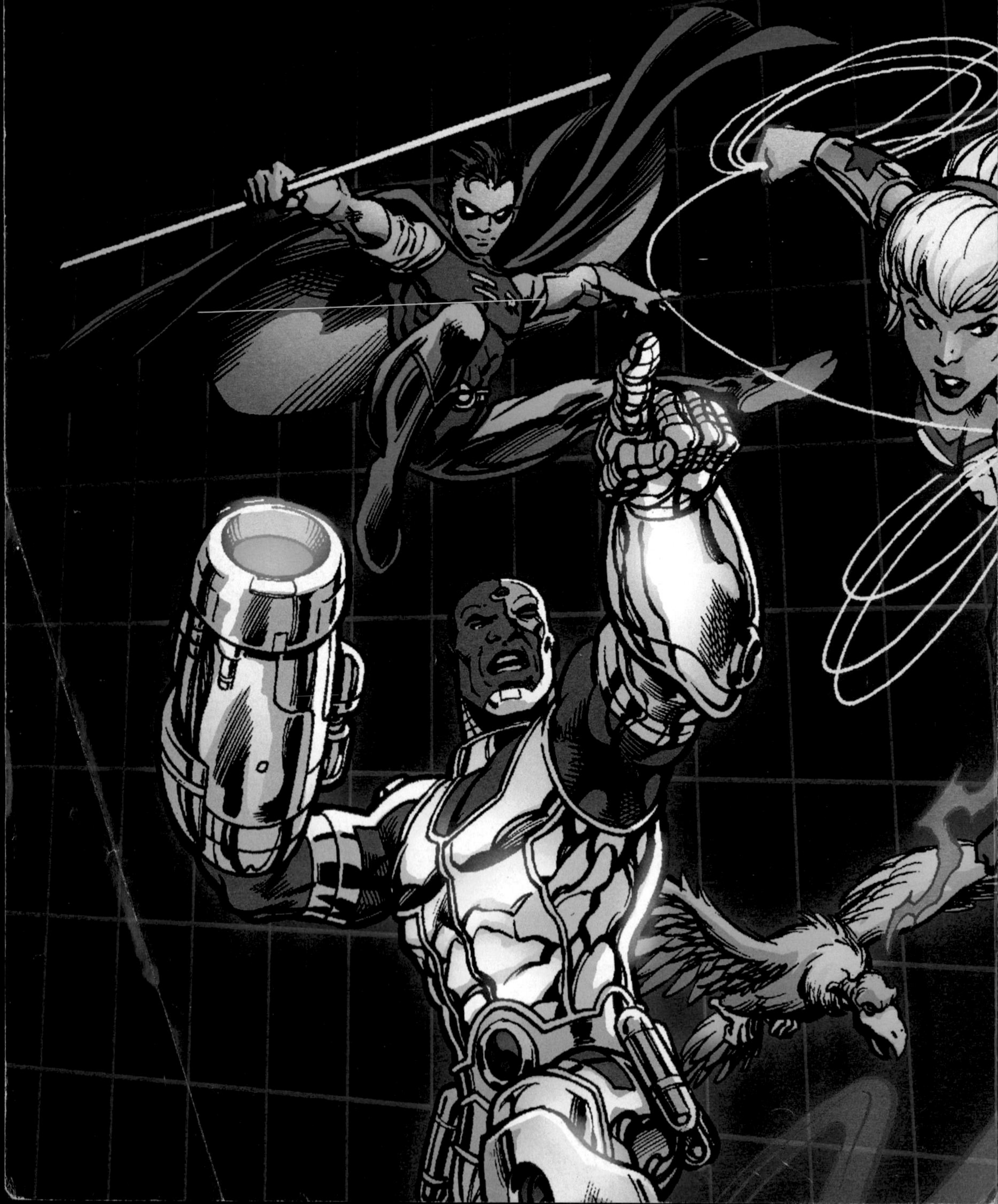

GEOFF JOHNS
JUDD WINICK
WRITERS

MIKE McKONE MARLO ALQUIZA
TOM GRUMMETT MATTHEW CLARK
ART THIBERT TONY S. DANIEL
CARLOS D'ANDA SCOTT SHAW
SCOTT ROBERTS NELSON
RICHARD BONK TODD NAUCK
ARTISTS

JEROMY COX
GUY MAJOR
TANYA & RICHARD HORIE
COLORISTS

COMICRAFT
PHIL BALSMAN
LETTERERS

MIKE McKONE,
MARLO ALQUIZA
and JEROMY COX
COLLECTION COVER ARTISTS

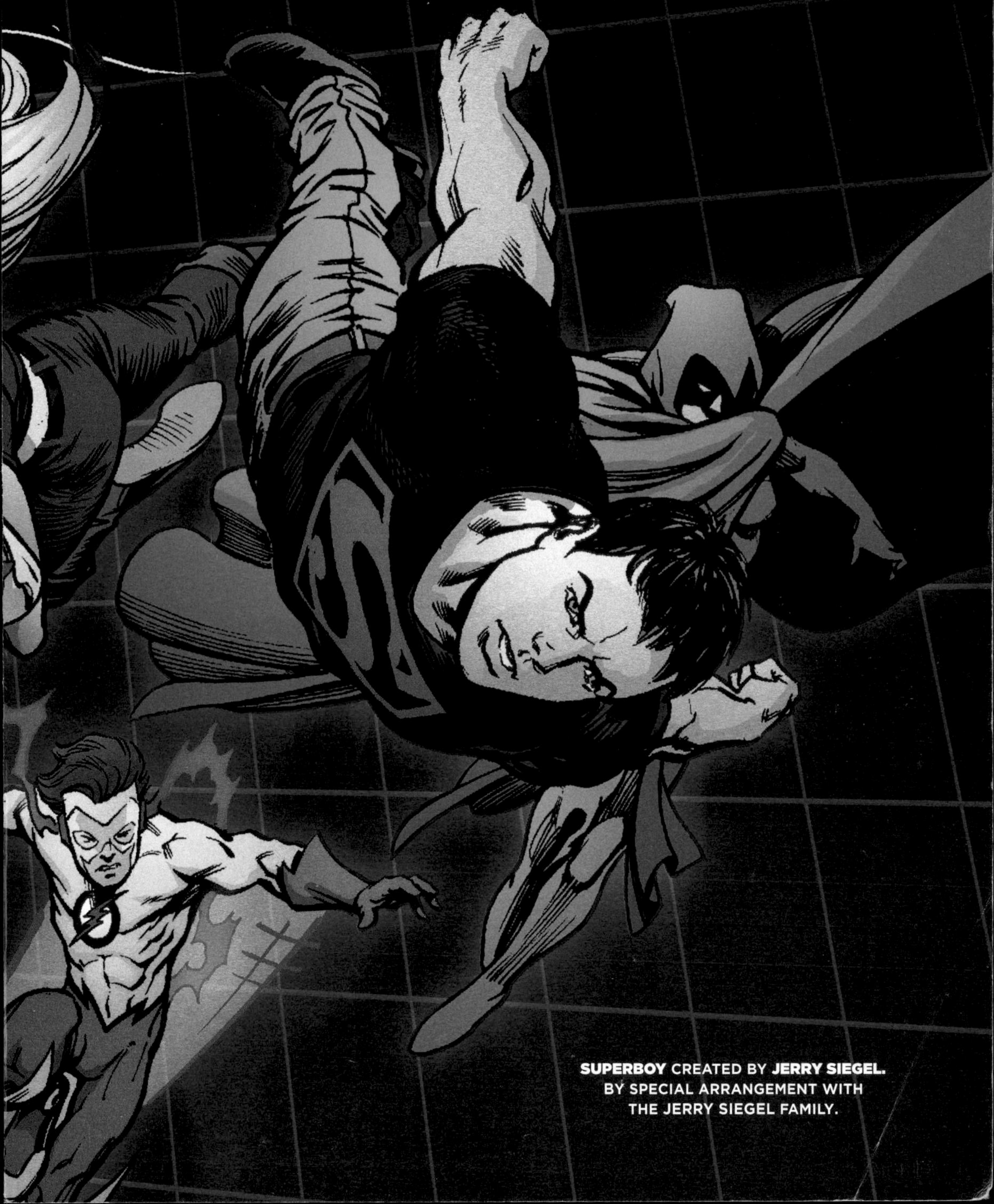

SUPERBOY CREATED BY **JERRY SIEGEL.**
BY SPECIAL ARRANGEMENT WITH
THE JERRY SIEGEL FAMILY.

TEEN TITANS BY GEOFF JOHNS BOOK THREE

Published by DC Comics. Compilation and all new material Copyright © 2019 DC Comics. All Rights Reserved.
Originally published in single magazine form in TEEN TITANS 20-26, 29-31 and OUTSIDERS 24-25. Copyright © 2005, 2006
DC Comics. All Rights Reserved. All characters, their distinctive likenesses and related elements featured in this publication
are trademarks of DC Comics. The stories, characters and incidents featured in this publication are entirely fictional.
DC Comics does not read or accept unsolicited submissions of ideas, stories or artwork.

DC Comics, 2900 West Alameda Ave., Burbank, CA 91505
Printed by LSC Communications, Kendallville, IN, USA.
4/12/19. First Printing. ISBN: 978-1-4012-8952-2.
Library of Congress Cataloging-in-Publication Data is available.

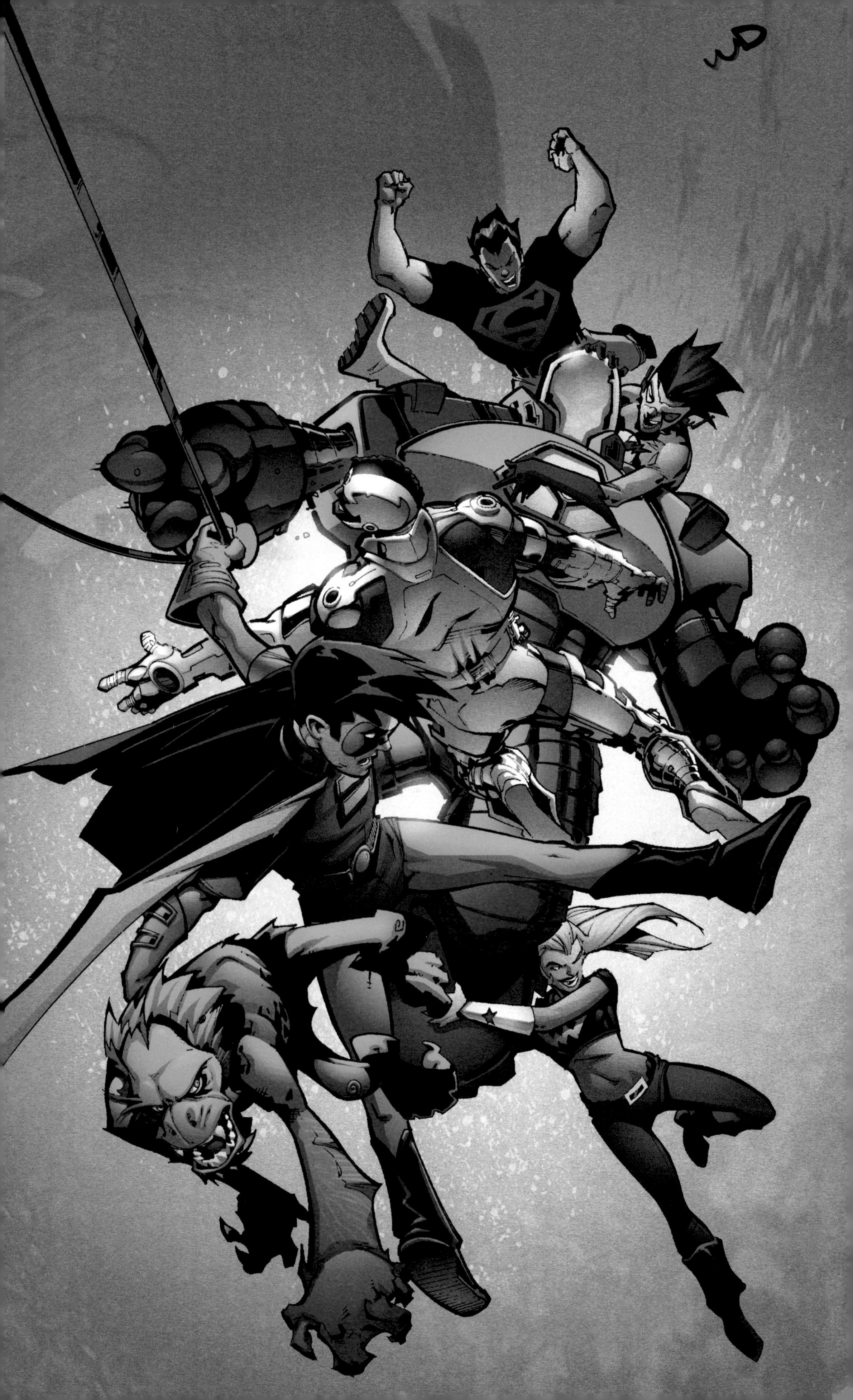

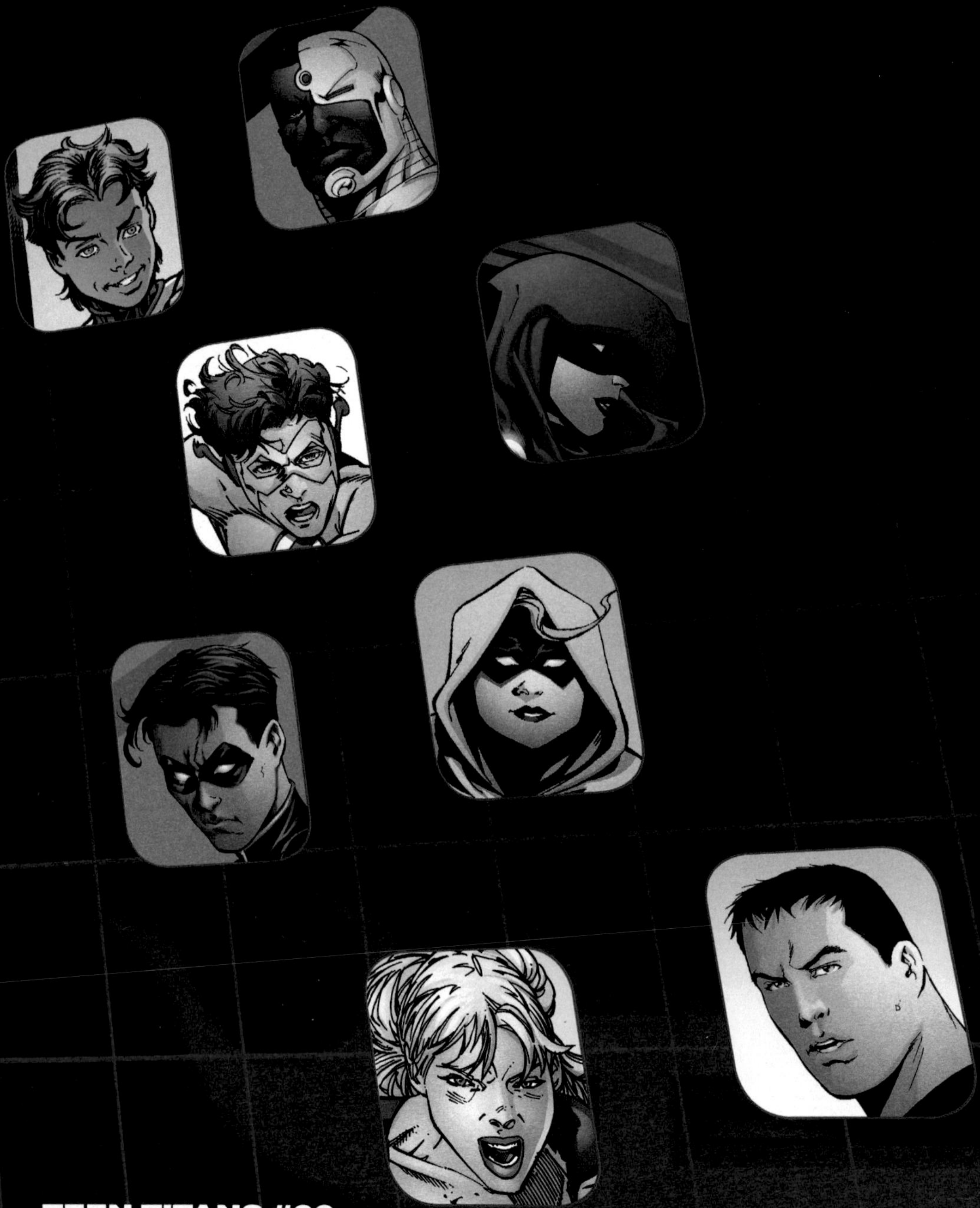

TEEN TITANS #20

GEOFF JOHNS
Writer

TOM GRUMMETT
Penciller

NELSON
Inker

JEROMY COX
Colorist

COMICRAFT
Letterer

DUNCAN ROULEAU & JEROMY COX
Cover Artists

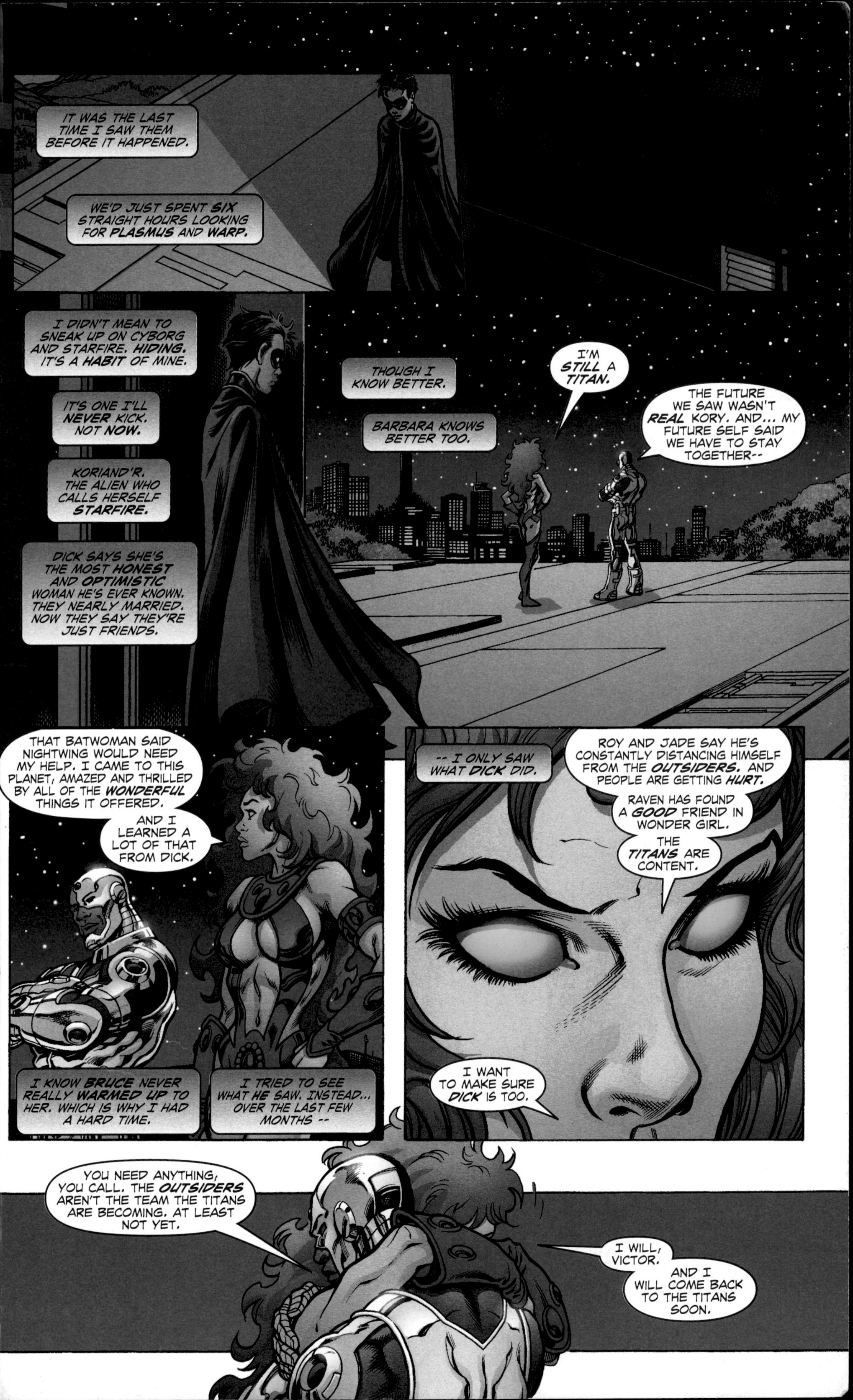

IT WAS THE LAST TIME I SAW THEM BEFORE IT HAPPENED.
WE'D JUST SPENT SIX STRAIGHT HOURS LOOKING FOR PLASMUS AND WARP.
I DIDN'T MEAN TO SNEAK UP ON CYBORG AND STARFIRE. HIDING. IT'S A HABIT OF MINE.
IT'S ONE I'LL NEVER KICK. NOT NOW.
KORIAND'R. THE ALIEN WHO CALLS HERSELF STARFIRE.
DICK SAYS SHE'S THE MOST HONEST AND OPTIMISTIC WOMAN HE'S EVER KNOWN. THEY NEARLY MARRIED. NOW THEY SAY THEY'RE JUST FRIENDS.
THOUGH I KNOW BETTER.
BARBARA KNOWS BETTER TOO.
I'M STILL A TITAN.
THE FUTURE WE SAW WASN'T REAL KORY. AND... MY FUTURE SELF SAID WE HAVE TO STAY TOGETHER--
THAT BATWOMAN SAID NIGHTWING WOULD NEED MY HELP. I CAME TO THIS PLANET, AMAZED AND THRILLED BY ALL OF THE WONDERFUL THINGS IT OFFERED.
AND I LEARNED A LOT OF THAT FROM DICK.
I KNOW BRUCE NEVER REALLY WARMED UP TO HER. WHICH IS WHY I HAD A HARD TIME.
I TRIED TO SEE WHAT HE SAW. INSTEAD... OVER THE LAST FEW MONTHS --
-- I ONLY SAW WHAT DICK DID.
ROY AND JADE SAY HE'S CONSTANTLY DISTANCING HIMSELF FROM THE OUTSIDERS. AND PEOPLE ARE GETTING HURT.
RAVEN HAS FOUND A GOOD FRIEND IN WONDER GIRL.
THE TITANS ARE CONTENT.
I WANT TO MAKE SURE DICK IS TOO.
YOU NEED ANYTHING, YOU CALL. THE OUTSIDERS AREN'T THE TEAM THE TITANS ARE BECOMING. AT LEAST NOT YET.
I WILL, VICTOR.
AND I WILL COME BACK TO THE TITANS SOON.

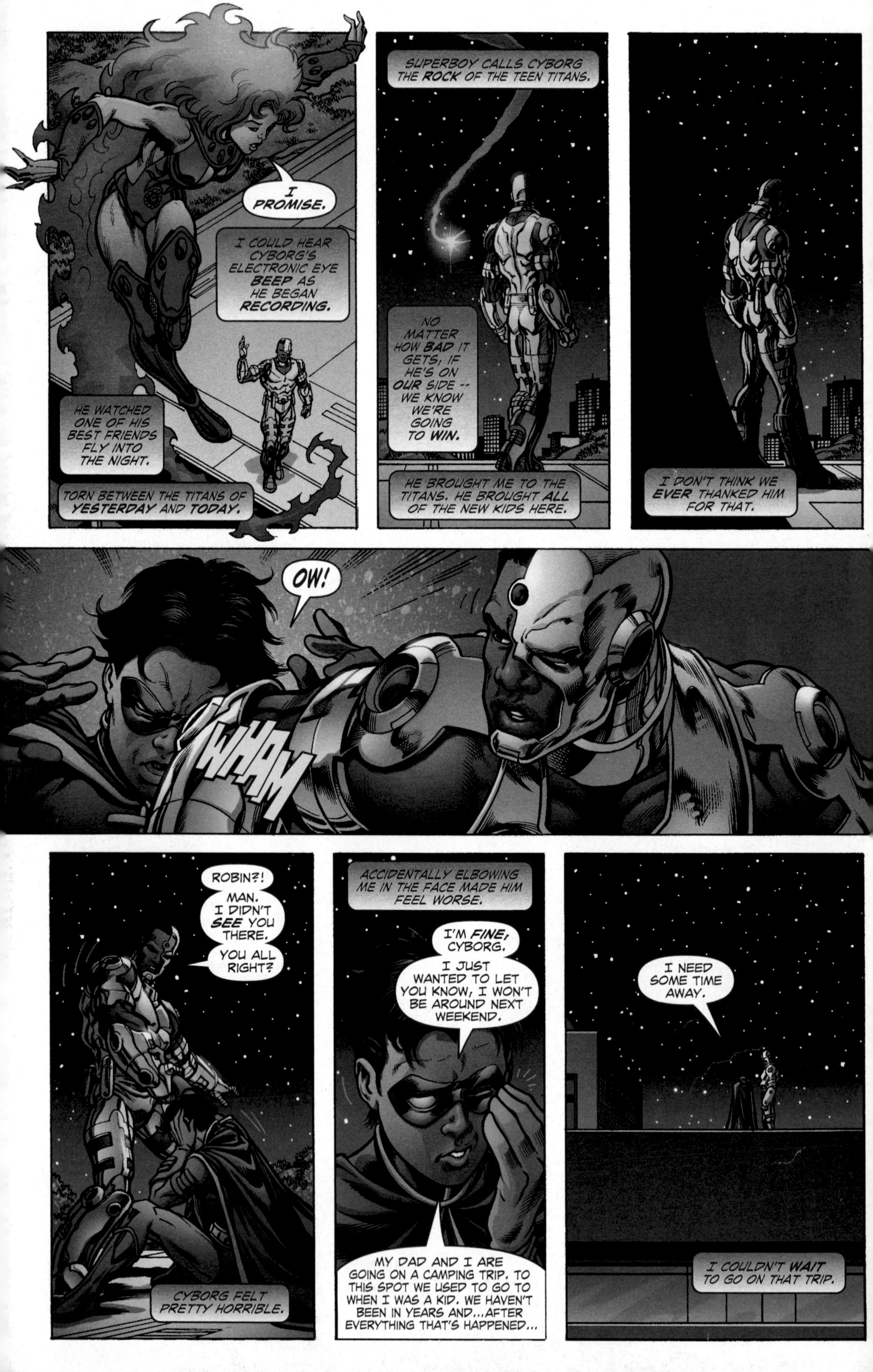
I PROMISE.
I COULD HEAR CYBORG'S ELECTRONIC EYE BEEP AS HE BEGAN RECORDING.
HE WATCHED ONE OF HIS BEST FRIENDS FLY INTO THE NIGHT.
TORN BETWEEN THE TITANS OF YESTERDAY AND TODAY.
SUPERBOY CALLS CYBORG THE ROCK OF THE TEEN TITANS.
NO MATTER HOW BAD IT GETS, IF HE'S ON OUR SIDE -- WE KNOW WE'RE GOING TO WIN.
HE BROUGHT ME TO THE TITANS. HE BROUGHT ALL OF THE NEW KIDS HERE.
I DON'T THINK WE EVER THANKED HIM FOR THAT.
OW!
WHAM
ROBIN?!
MAN. I DIDN'T SEE YOU THERE.
YOU ALL RIGHT?
CYBORG FELT PRETTY HORRIBLE.
ACCIDENTALLY ELBOWING ME IN THE FACE MADE HIM FEEL WORSE.
I'M FINE, CYBORG.
I JUST WANTED TO LET YOU KNOW, I WON'T BE AROUND NEXT WEEKEND.
MY DAD AND I ARE GOING ON A CAMPING TRIP. TO THIS SPOT WE USED TO GO TO WHEN I WAS A KID. WE HAVEN'T BEEN IN YEARS AND...AFTER EVERYTHING THAT'S HAPPENED...
I NEED SOME TIME AWAY.
I COULDN'T WAIT TO GO ON THAT TRIP.

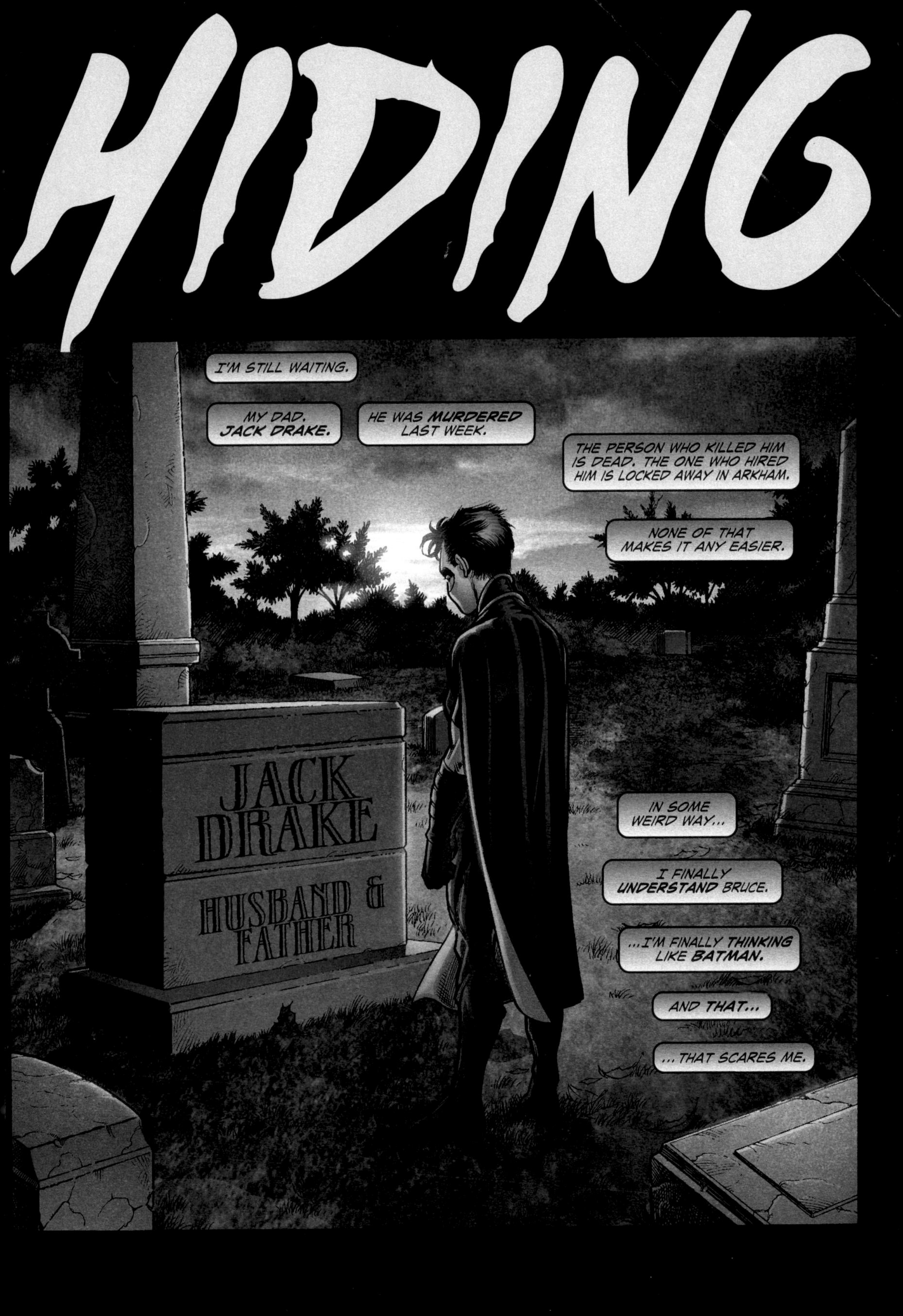
HIDING
I'M STILL WAITING.
MY DAD. JACK DRAKE.
HE WAS MURDERED LAST WEEK.
THE PERSON WHO KILLED HIM IS DEAD. THE ONE WHO HIRED HIM IS LOCKED AWAY IN ARKHAM.
NONE OF THAT MAKES IT ANY EASIER.
JACK DRAKE
HUSBAND & FATHER
IN SOME WEIRD WAY...
I FINALLY UNDERSTAND BRUCE.
...I'M FINALLY THINKING LIKE BATMAN.
AND THAT...
...THAT SCARES ME.

GUY'S LUCKY HE'S STILL ALIVE, THE WAY HE *TOOK* THOSE BULLETS.

-- SUPPOSED TO COME PICK HIM UP IN A FEW HOURS. HE'S GONNA BE EXTRADITED TO LOS ANGELES FOR OVER A *DOZEN* COUNTS OF *MURDER.*

WHO'S PICKIN' HIM UP ANYWAY?

THAT *STUNT* MAN TURNED DEMON HUNTER. *BLUE DEVIL.*

BLUE *DEVIL?* I THINK MY KID HAS HIS ACTION FIGURE. MAYBE I CAN GET AN AUTOGRAPH--

LARRY BOLATINKSY, A.K.A. BOLT - Suffered multiple gunshot wounds to the chest; rhabdomyolysis due to unknown meta-human biology. Condition: Stable.

HEY, YOU SEE THAT?

VZZTTT

LIGHTS JUST *FLICKERED.* AND THE AIR... FEELS LIKE I'M COVERED IN STATIC--

LARRY BOLATINKSY, A.K.A. BOLT - Suffered multiple gunshot wounds to the chest; rhabdomyolysis due to unknown meta-human biology. Condition: Stable.

--WHAT THE *HELL?*

STOP RIGHT THERE! DON'T *MOVE!* DON'T--

LARRY BOLATINKSY, A.K.A. BOLT - Suffered multiple gunshot wounds to the chest; rhabdomyolysis due to unknown meta-human biology. Condition: Stable.

KRRAZZZTTT

LARRY BOLATINKSY, A.K.A. BOLT - Suffered multiple gunshot wounds to the chest; rhabdomyolysis due to unknown meta-human biology. Condition: Stable.

LARRY BOLATINKSY, A.K.A. BOLT - Suffered multiple gunshot wounds to the chest; rhabdomyolysis due to unknown meta-human biology. Condition: Stable.

EVENING, BOLT.

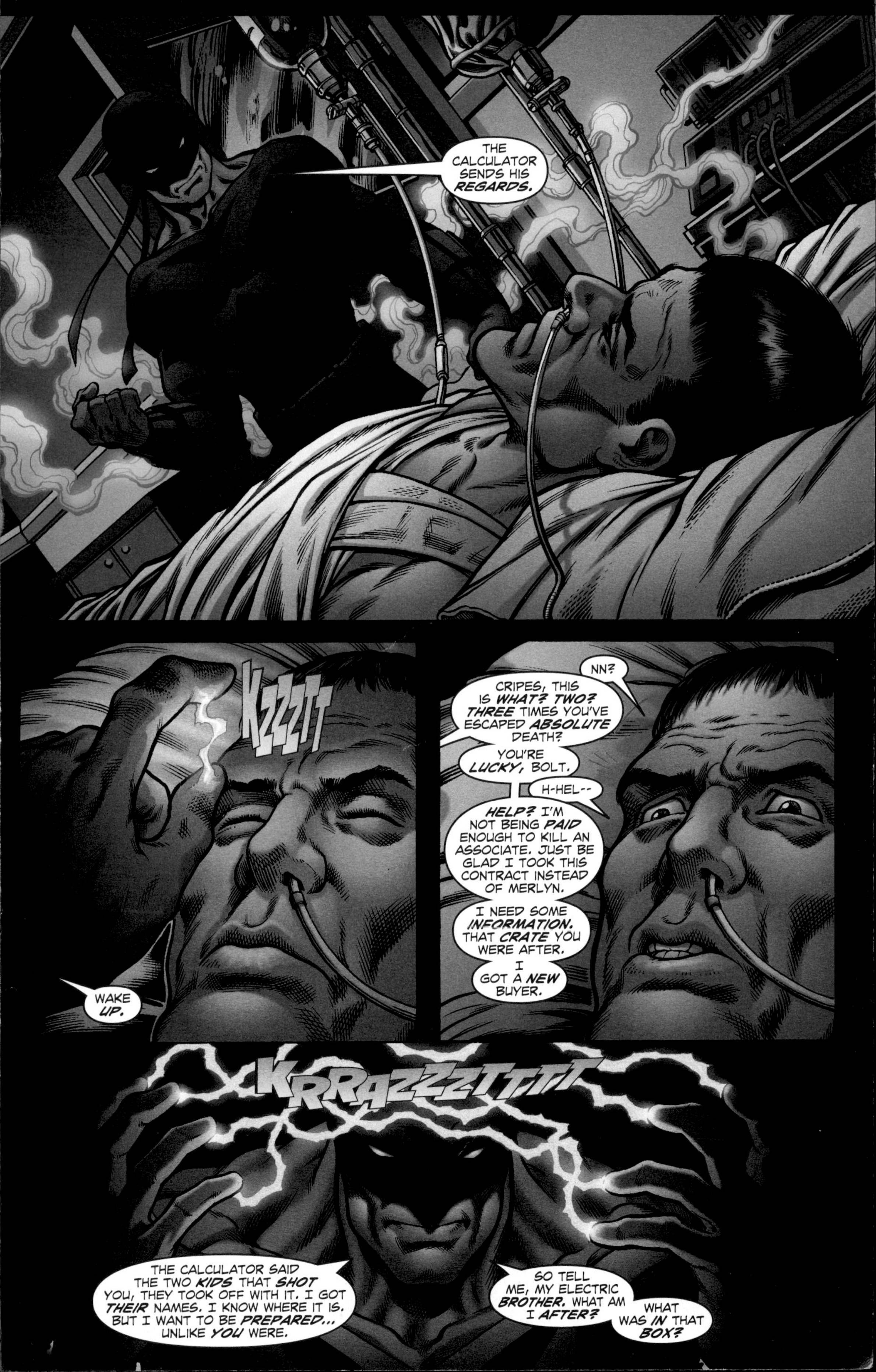
THE CALCULATOR SENDS HIS REGARDS.
KZZZTT
WAKE UP.
NN?
CRIPES, THIS IS WHAT? TWO? THREE TIMES YOU'VE ESCAPED ABSOLUTE DEATH?
YOU'RE LUCKY, BOLT.
H-HEL--
HELP? I'M NOT BEING PAID ENOUGH TO KILL AN ASSOCIATE. JUST BE GLAD I TOOK THIS CONTRACT INSTEAD OF MERLYN.
I NEED SOME INFORMATION. THAT CRATE YOU WERE AFTER.
I GOT A NEW BUYER.
KRRAZZZZTTTTT
THE CALCULATOR SAID THE TWO KIDS THAT SHOT YOU, THEY TOOK OFF WITH IT. I GOT THEIR NAMES. I KNOW WHERE IT IS. BUT I WANT TO BE PREPARED... UNLIKE YOU WERE.
SO TELL ME, MY ELECTRIC BROTHER. WHAT AM I AFTER?
WHAT WAS IN THAT BOX?

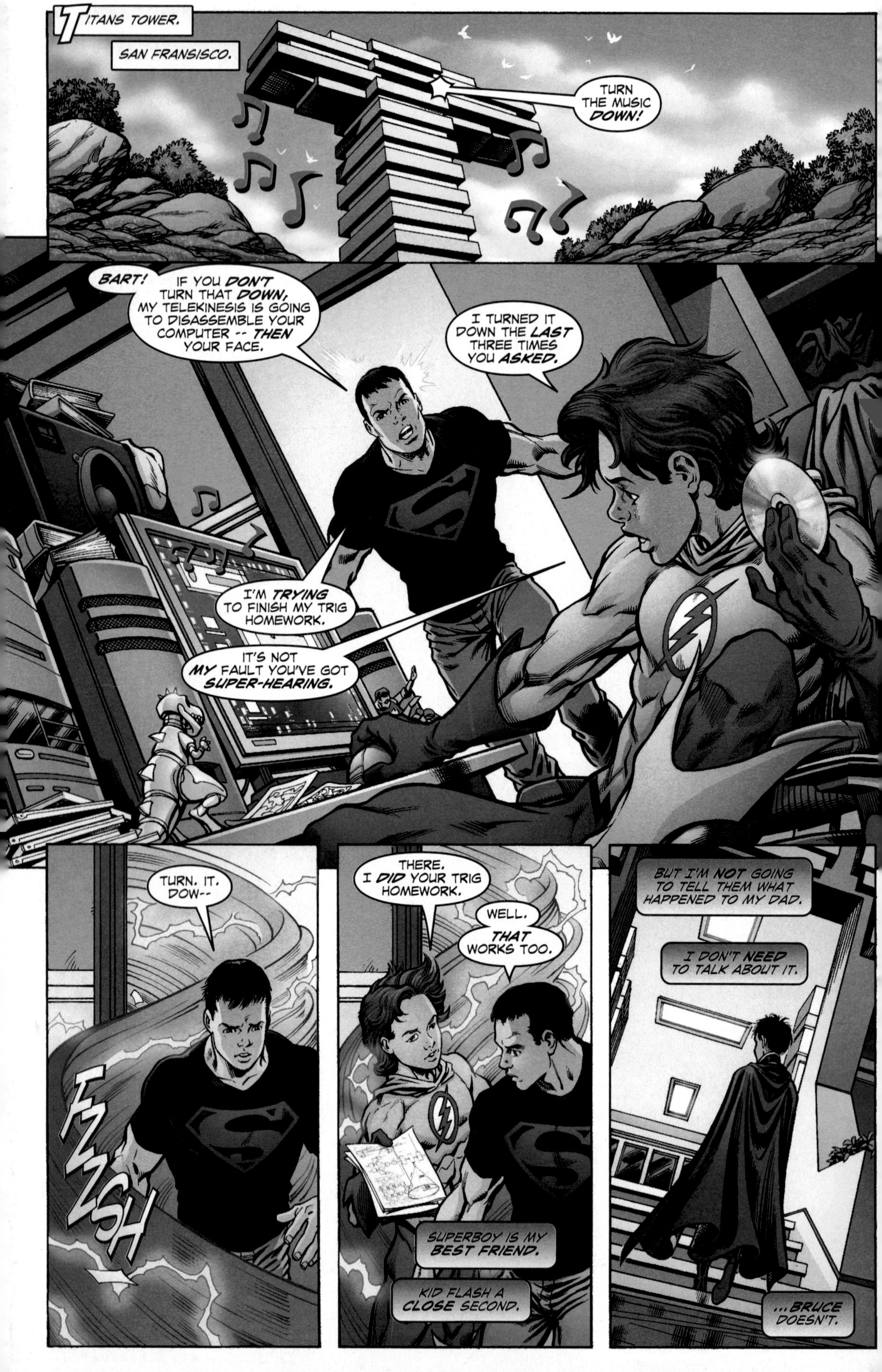
TITANS TOWER.
SAN FRANSISCO.
TURN THE MUSIC DOWN!
BART!
IF YOU DON'T TURN THAT DOWN, MY TELEKINESIS IS GOING TO DISASSEMBLE YOUR COMPUTER -- THEN YOUR FACE.
I TURNED IT DOWN THE LAST THREE TIMES YOU ASKED.
I'M TRYING TO FINISH MY TRIG HOMEWORK.
IT'S NOT MY FAULT YOU'VE GOT SUPER-HEARING.
TURN. IT. DOW--
FZZSH
THERE. I DID YOUR TRIG HOMEWORK.
WELL. THAT WORKS TOO.
SUPERBOY IS MY BEST FRIEND.
KID FLASH A CLOSE SECOND.
BUT I'M NOT GOING TO TELL THEM WHAT HAPPENED TO MY DAD.
I DON'T NEED TO TALK ABOUT IT.
...BRUCE DOESN'T.

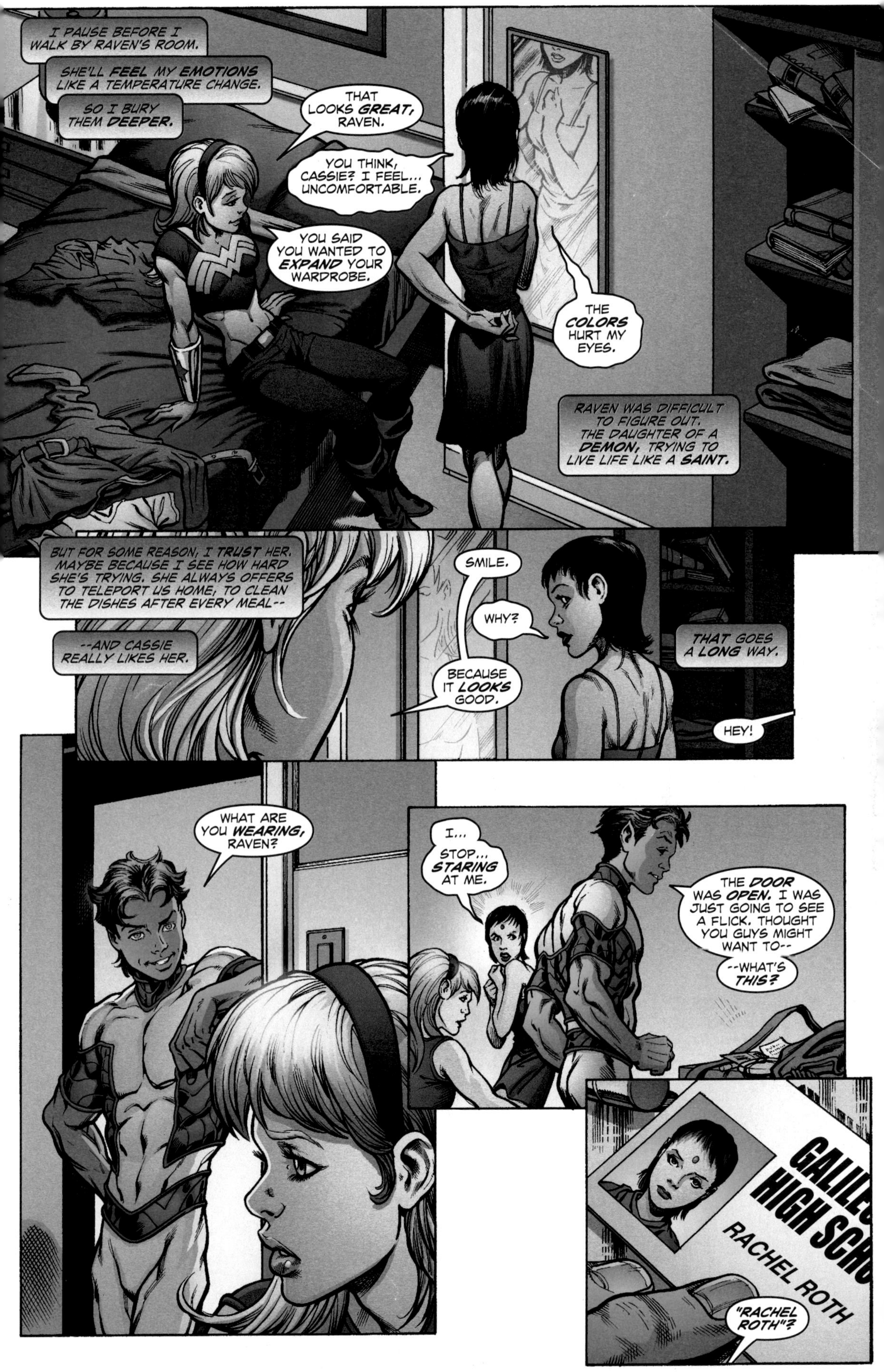
I PAUSE BEFORE I WALK BY RAVEN'S ROOM.
SHE'LL FEEL MY EMOTIONS LIKE A TEMPERATURE CHANGE.
SO I BURY THEM DEEPER.
THAT LOOKS GREAT, RAVEN.
YOU THINK, CASSIE? I FEEL... UNCOMFORTABLE.
YOU SAID YOU WANTED TO EXPAND YOUR WARDROBE.
THE COLORS HURT MY EYES.
RAVEN WAS DIFFICULT TO FIGURE OUT. THE DAUGHTER OF A DEMON, TRYING TO LIVE LIFE LIKE A SAINT.
BUT FOR SOME REASON, I TRUST HER. MAYBE BECAUSE I SEE HOW HARD SHE'S TRYING. SHE ALWAYS OFFERS TO TELEPORT US HOME, TO CLEAN THE DISHES AFTER EVERY MEAL--
--AND CASSIE REALLY LIKES HER.
SMILE.
WHY?
BECAUSE IT LOOKS GOOD.
THAT GOES A LONG WAY.
HEY!
WHAT ARE YOU WEARING, RAVEN?
I...
STOP... STARING AT ME.
THE DOOR WAS OPEN. I WAS JUST GOING TO SEE A FLICK. THOUGHT YOU GUYS MIGHT WANT TO--
--WHAT'S THIS?
GALILEO HIGH SCHO
RACHEL ROTH
"RACHEL ROTH"?

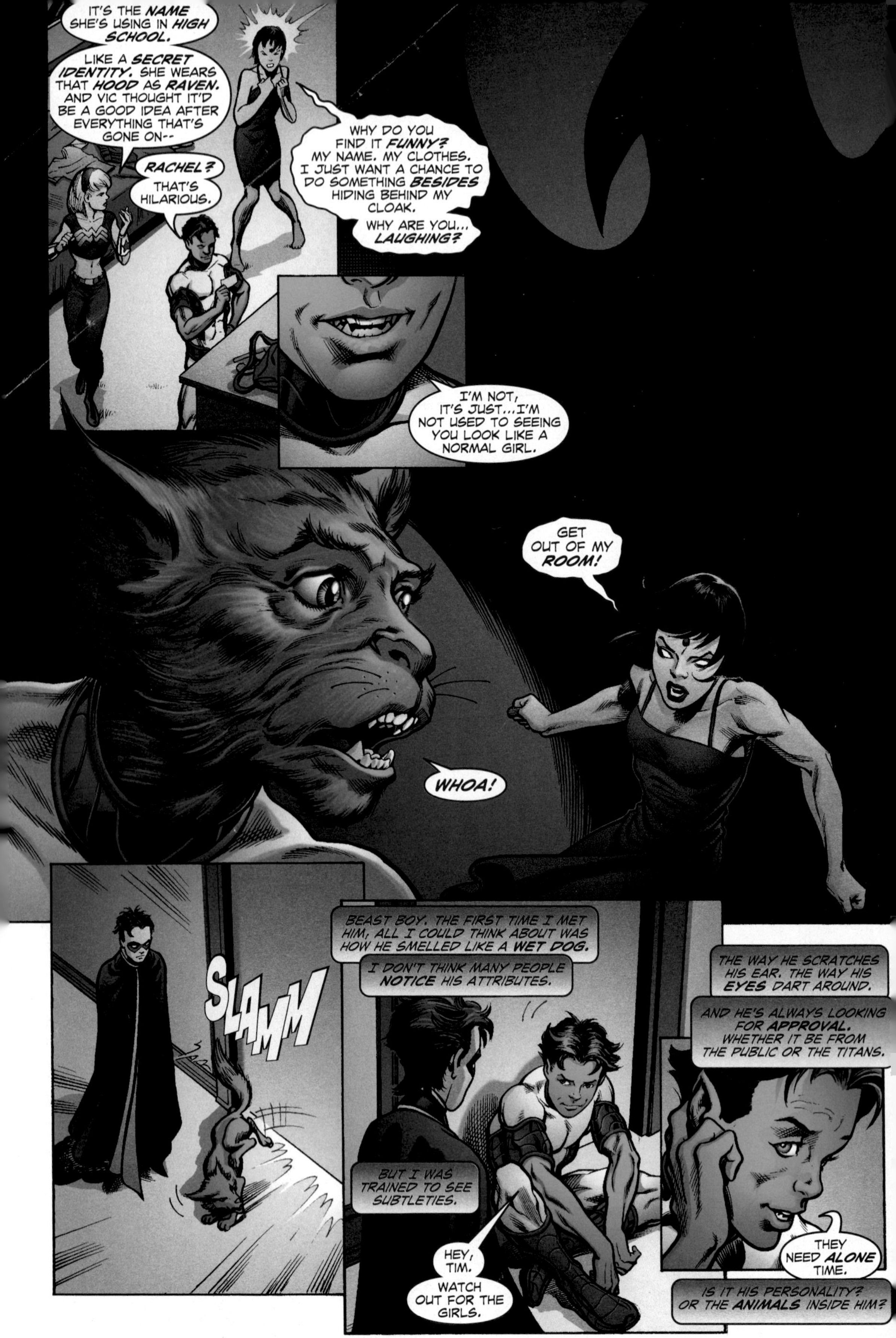

IT'S THE NAME SHE'S USING IN HIGH SCHOOL.
LIKE A SECRET IDENTITY. SHE WEARS THAT HOOD AS RAVEN. AND VIC THOUGHT IT'D BE A GOOD IDEA AFTER EVERYTHING THAT'S GONE ON--
RACHEL? THAT'S HILARIOUS.
WHY DO YOU FIND IT FUNNY? MY NAME. MY CLOTHES. I JUST WANT A CHANCE TO DO SOMETHING BESIDES HIDING BEHIND MY CLOAK.
WHY ARE YOU... LAUGHING?
I'M NOT, IT'S JUST...I'M NOT USED TO SEEING YOU LOOK LIKE A NORMAL GIRL.
GET OUT OF MY ROOM!
WHOA!
SLAMM
BEAST BOY. THE FIRST TIME I MET HIM, ALL I COULD THINK ABOUT WAS HOW HE SMELLED LIKE A WET DOG.
I DON'T THINK MANY PEOPLE NOTICE HIS ATTRIBUTES.
BUT I WAS TRAINED TO SEE SUBTLETIES.
HEY, TIM.
WATCH OUT FOR THE GIRLS.
THE WAY HE SCRATCHES HIS EAR. THE WAY HIS EYES DART AROUND.
AND HE'S ALWAYS LOOKING FOR APPROVAL. WHETHER IT BE FROM THE PUBLIC OR THE TITANS.
THEY NEED ALONE TIME.
IS IT HIS PERSONALITY? OR THE ANIMALS INSIDE HIM?

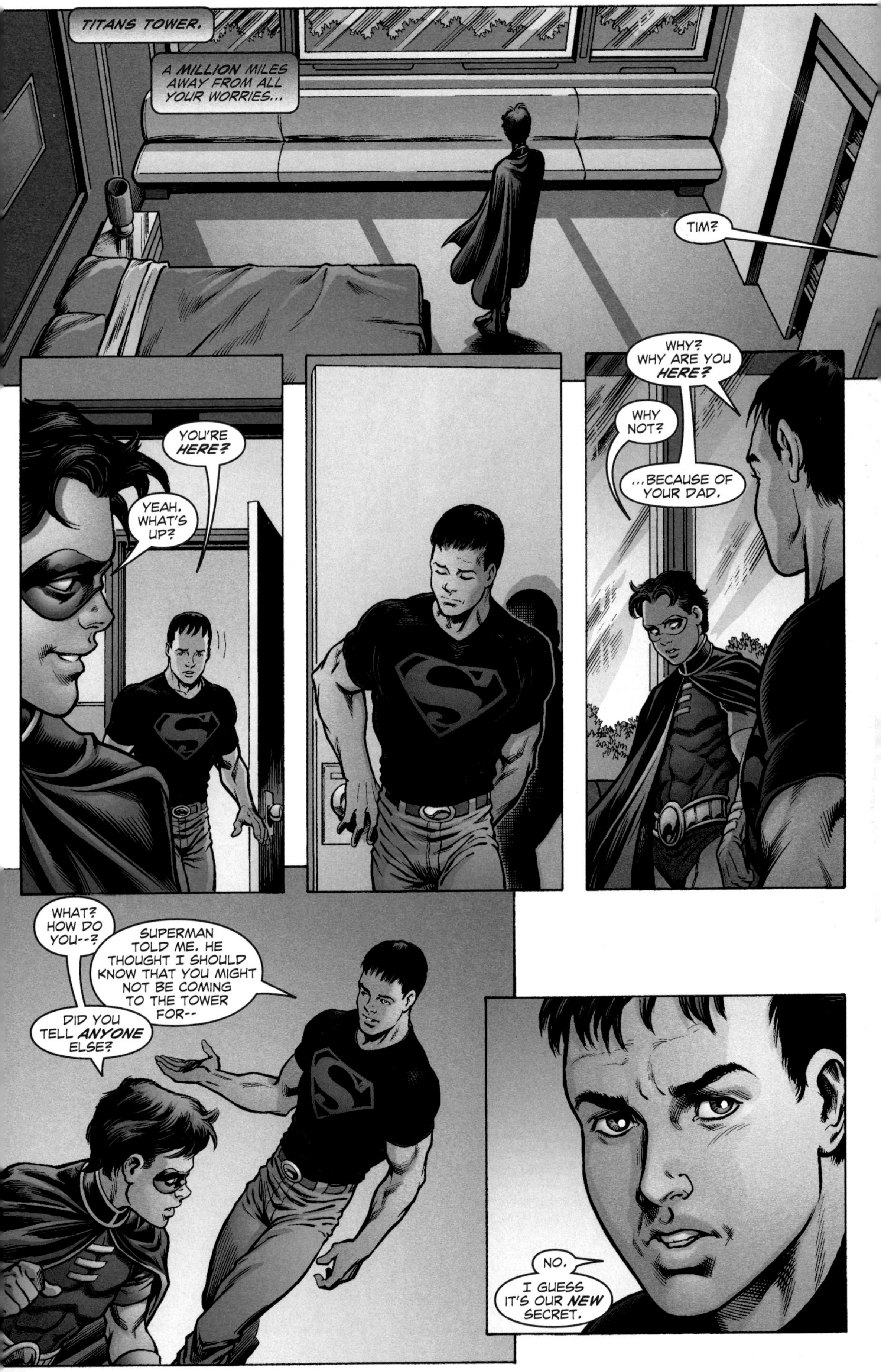

TITANS TOWER.
A MILLION MILES AWAY FROM ALL YOUR WORRIES...
TIM?
YOU'RE HERE?
YEAH. WHAT'S UP?
WHY? WHY ARE YOU HERE?
WHY NOT?
...BECAUSE OF YOUR DAD.
WHAT? HOW DO YOU--?
SUPERMAN TOLD ME. HE THOUGHT I SHOULD KNOW THAT YOU MIGHT NOT BE COMING TO THE TOWER FOR--
DID YOU TELL ANYONE ELSE?
NO.
I GUESS IT'S OUR NEW SECRET.

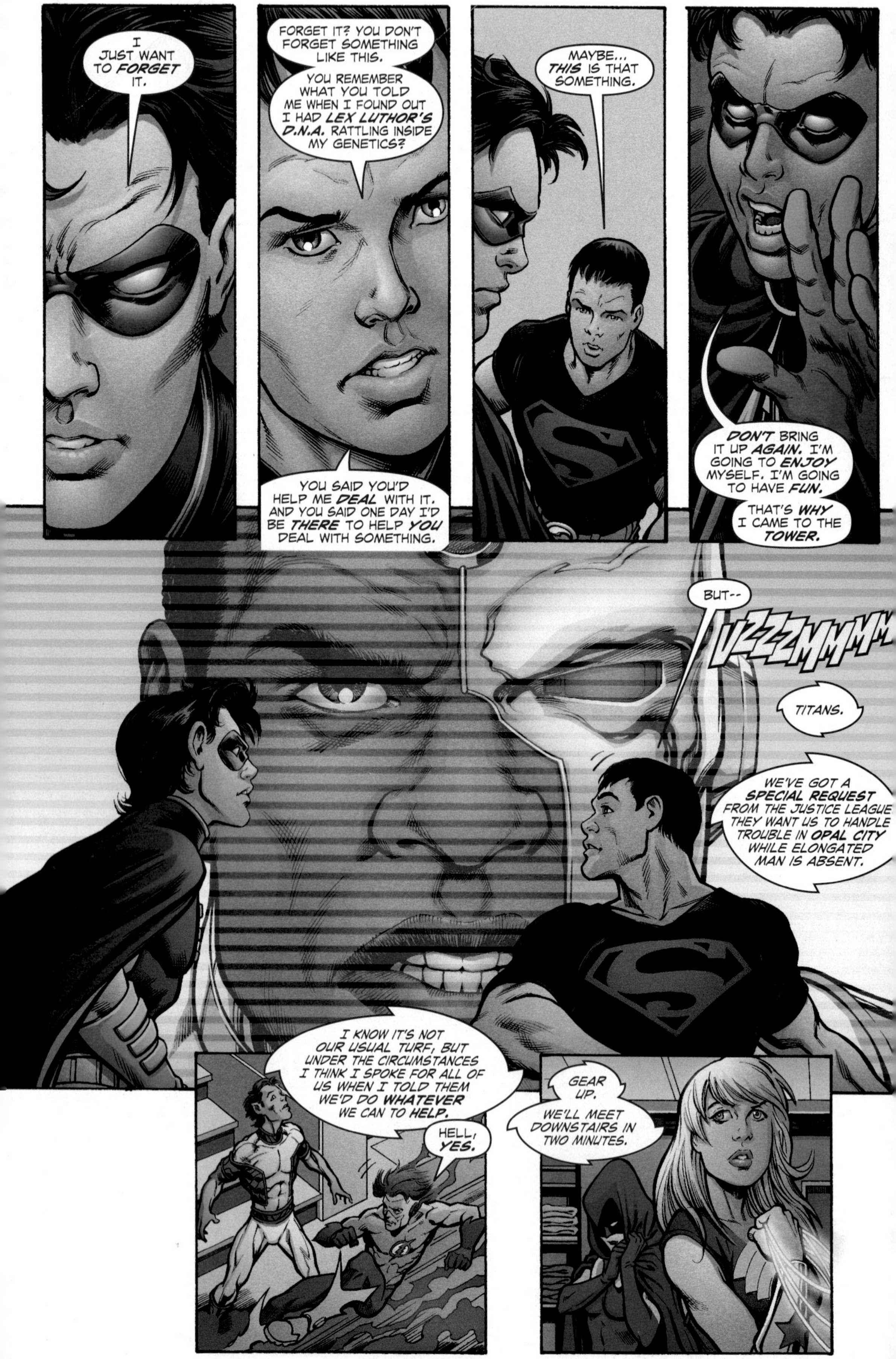
I JUST WANT TO FORGET IT.
FORGET IT? YOU DON'T FORGET SOMETHING LIKE THIS.
YOU REMEMBER WHAT YOU TOLD ME WHEN I FOUND OUT I HAD LEX LUTHOR'S D.N.A. RATTLING INSIDE MY GENETICS?
YOU SAID YOU'D HELP ME DEAL WITH IT. AND YOU SAID ONE DAY I'D BE THERE TO HELP YOU DEAL WITH SOMETHING.
MAYBE... THIS IS THAT SOMETHING.
DON'T BRING IT UP AGAIN. I'M GOING TO ENJOY MYSELF. I'M GOING TO HAVE FUN.
THAT'S WHY I CAME TO THE TOWER.
BUT--
VZZZMMMM
TITANS.
WE'VE GOT A SPECIAL REQUEST FROM THE JUSTICE LEAGUE. THEY WANT US TO HANDLE TROUBLE IN OPAL CITY WHILE ELONGATED MAN IS ABSENT.
I KNOW IT'S NOT OUR USUAL TURF, BUT UNDER THE CIRCUMSTANCES I THINK I SPOKE FOR ALL OF US WHEN I TOLD THEM WE'D DO WHATEVER WE CAN TO HELP.
HELL, YES.
GEAR UP.
WE'LL MEET DOWNSTAIRS IN TWO MINUTES.

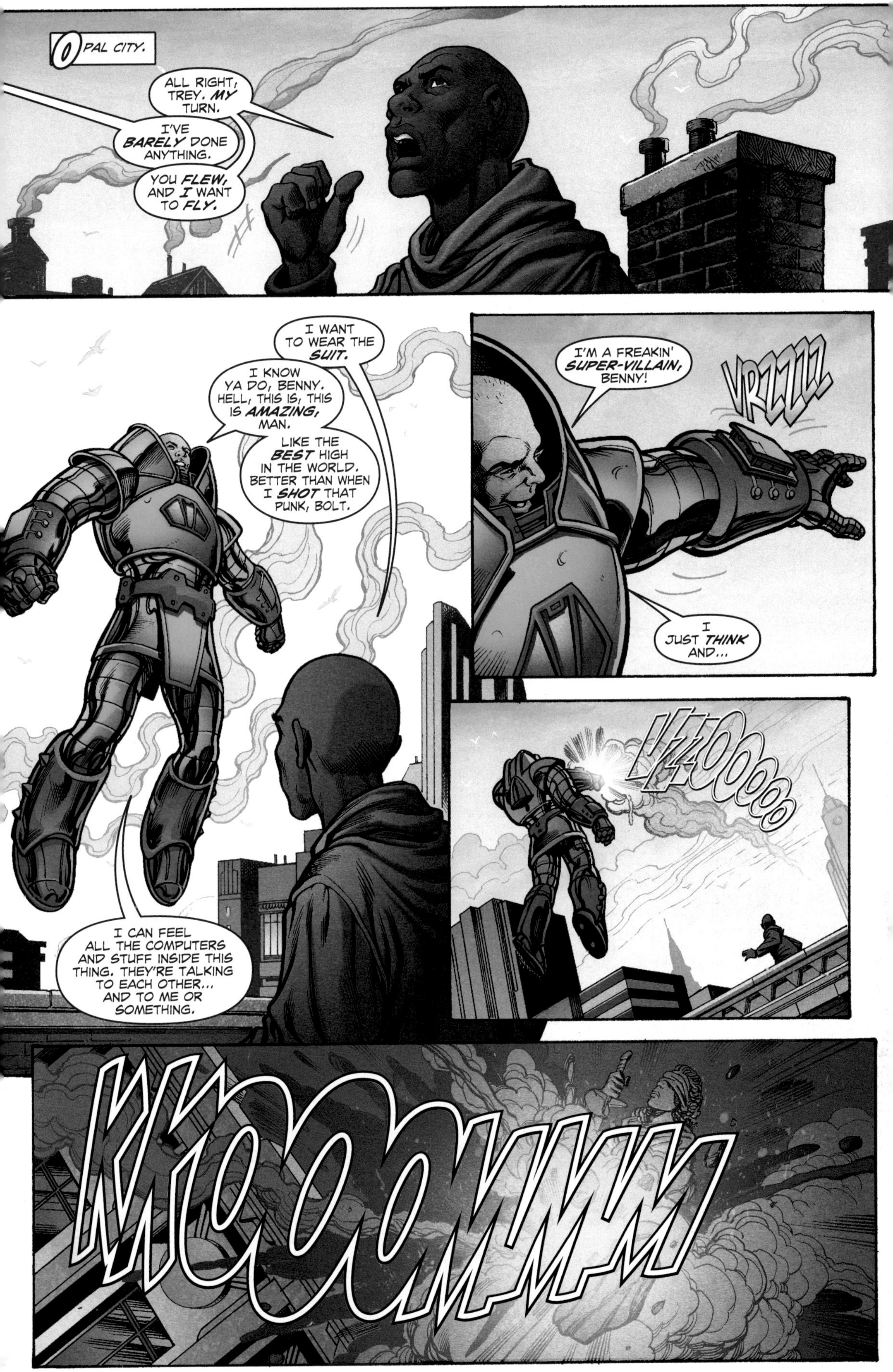
OPAL CITY.
ALL RIGHT, TREY. MY TURN.
I'VE BARELY DONE ANYTHING.
YOU FLEW, AND I WANT TO FLY.
I WANT TO WEAR THE SUIT.
I KNOW YA DO, BENNY. HELL, THIS IS, THIS IS AMAZING, MAN.
LIKE THE BEST HIGH IN THE WORLD. BETTER THAN WHEN I SHOT THAT PUNK, BOLT.
I CAN FEEL ALL THE COMPUTERS AND STUFF INSIDE THIS THING. THEY'RE TALKING TO EACH OTHER... AND TO ME OR SOMETHING.
I'M A FREAKIN' SUPER-VILLAIN, BENNY!
VRZZZZ
I JUST THINK AND...
VZZOOOOOO
KRoooMMMM

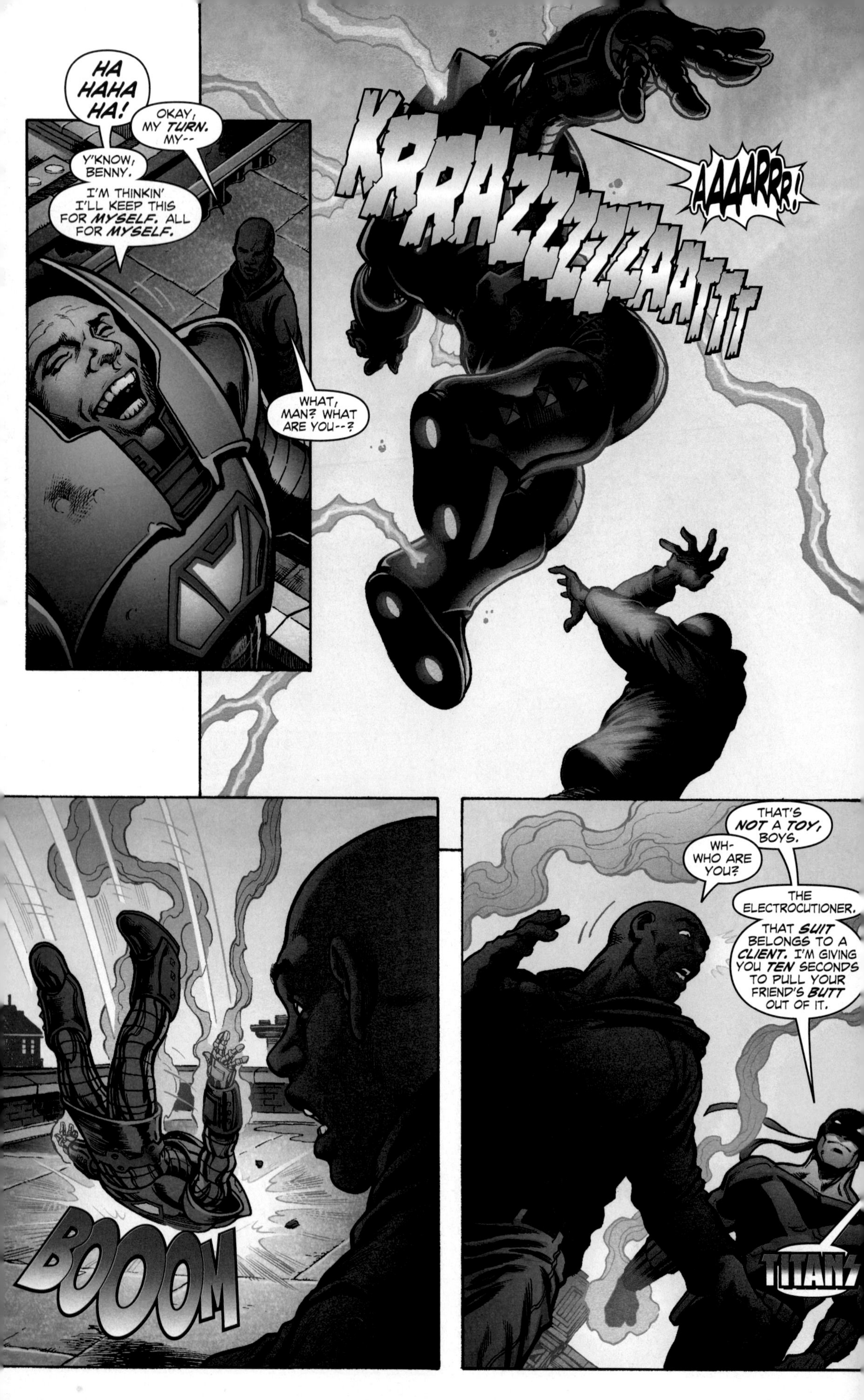

HA HAHA HA!
Y'KNOW, BENNY.
I'M THINKIN' I'LL KEEP THIS FOR MYSELF. ALL FOR MYSELF.
OKAY, MY TURN. MY--
WHAT, MAN? WHAT ARE YOU--?
KRRAZZZZZAATTT
AAAARRR!
BOOOM
WH- WHO ARE YOU?
THAT'S NOT A TOY, BOYS.
THE ELECTROCUTIONER.
THAT SUIT BELONGS TO A CLIENT. I'M GIVING YOU TEN SECONDS TO PULL YOUR FRIEND'S BUTT OUT OF IT.
TITANS

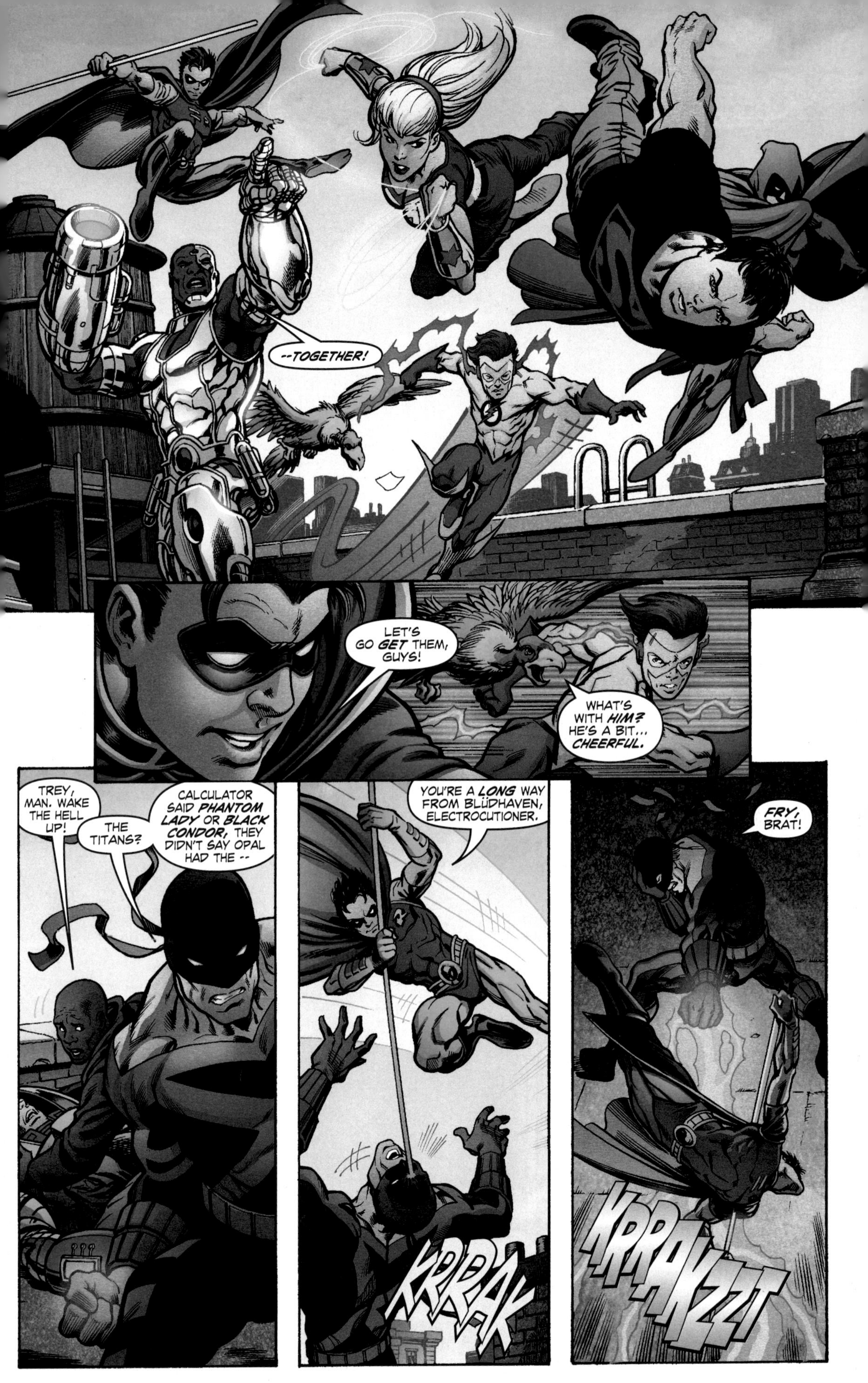
--TOGETHER!
LET'S GO GET THEM, GUYS!
WHAT'S WITH HIM? HE'S A BIT... CHEERFUL.
TREY, MAN. WAKE THE HELL UP!
THE TITANS?
CALCULATOR SAID PHANTOM LADY OR BLACK CONDOR, THEY DIDN'T SAY OPAL HAD THE --
YOU'RE A LONG WAY FROM BLÜDHAVEN, ELECTROCUTIONER.
KRRAK
FRY, BRAT!
KRRAKZZT

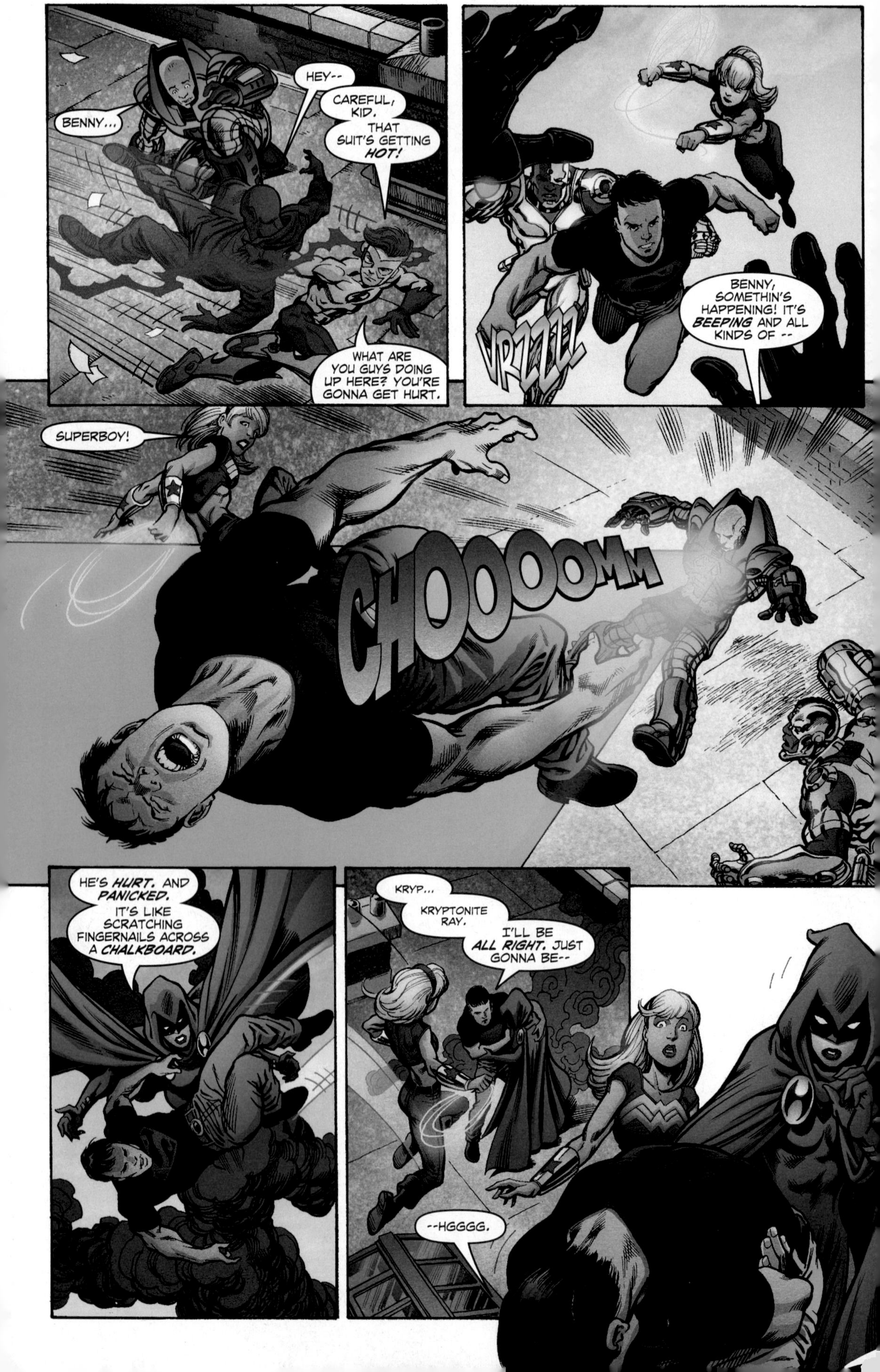
BENNY...
HEY--
CAREFUL, KID. THAT SUIT'S GETTING *HOT!*
WHAT ARE YOU GUYS DOING UP HERE? YOU'RE GONNA GET HURT.
VRZZZZ
BENNY, SOMETHIN'S HAPPENING! IT'S *BEEPING* AND ALL KINDS OF --
SUPERBOY!
CHOOOOMM
HE'S *HURT.* AND *PANICKED.* IT'S LIKE SCRATCHING FINGERNAILS ACROSS A *CHALKBOARD.*
KRYP...
KRYPTONITE RAY.
I'LL BE *ALL RIGHT.* JUST GONNA BE--
--HGGGG.

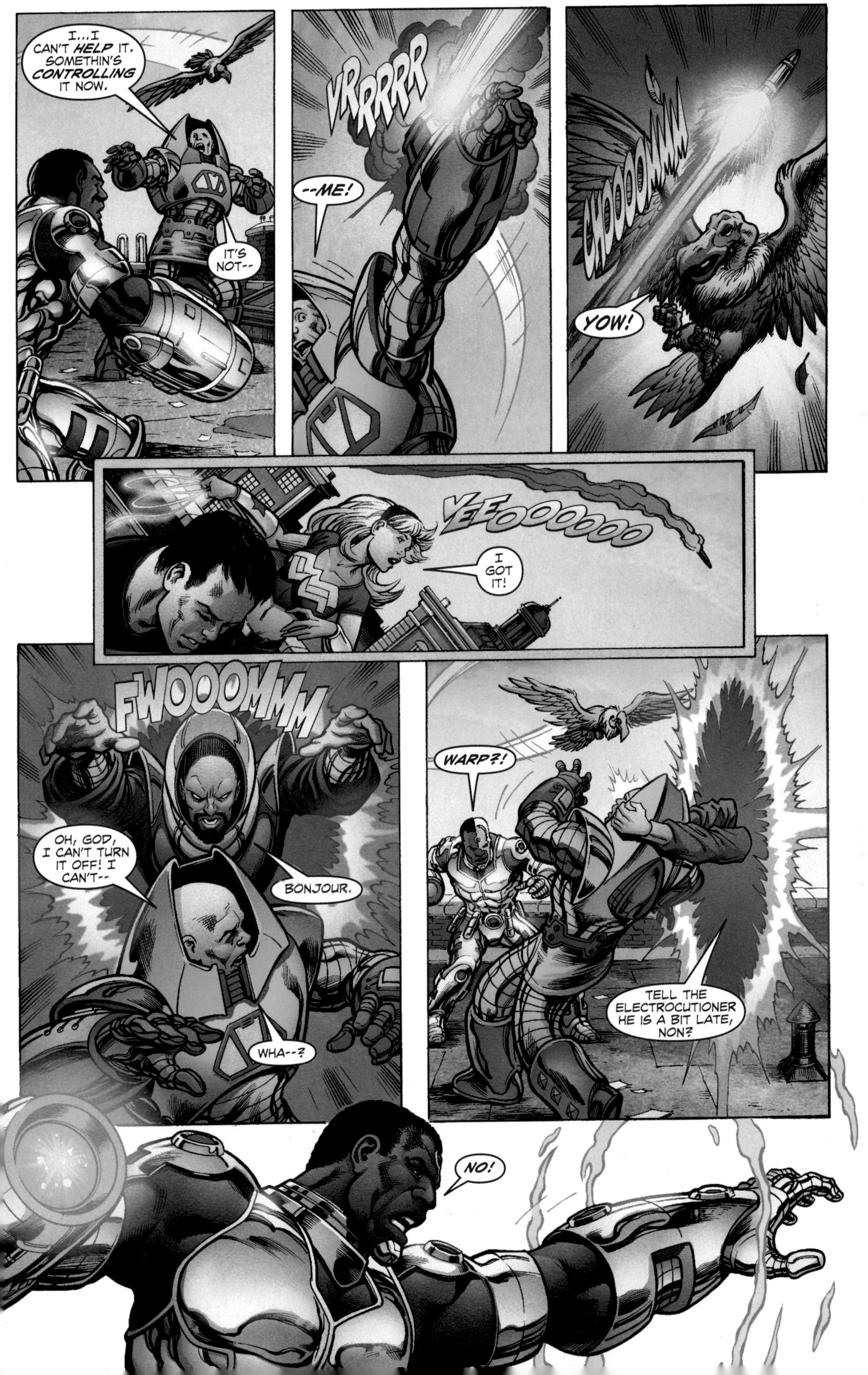
I...I CAN'T HELP IT. SOMETHIN'S CONTROLLING IT NOW.
IT'S NOT--
VRRRRR
--ME!
CHOOOMMM
YOW!
VEEOOOOOOO
I GOT IT!
FWOOOMMM
OH, GOD, I CAN'T TURN IT OFF! I CAN'T--
BONJOUR.
WHA--?
WARP?!
TELL THE ELECTROCUTIONER HE IS A BIT LATE, NON?
NO!

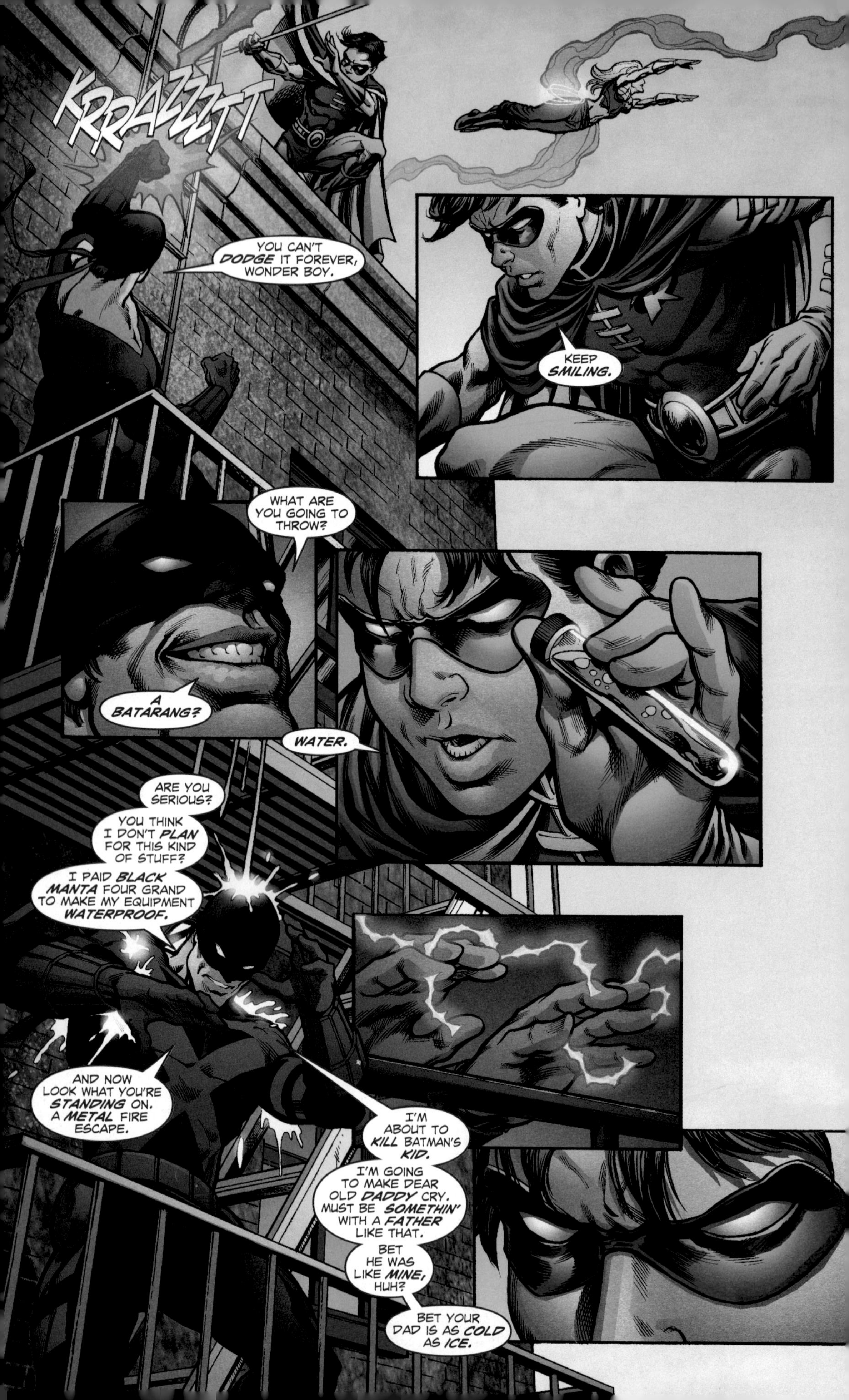
KRRAZZZTT
YOU CAN'T DODGE IT FOREVER, WONDER BOY.
KEEP SMILING.
WHAT ARE YOU GOING TO THROW?
A BATARANG?
WATER.
ARE YOU SERIOUS?
YOU THINK I DON'T PLAN FOR THIS KIND OF STUFF?
I PAID BLACK MANTA FOUR GRAND TO MAKE MY EQUIPMENT WATERPROOF.
AND NOW LOOK WHAT YOU'RE STANDING ON. A METAL FIRE ESCAPE.
I'M ABOUT TO KILL BATMAN'S KID.
I'M GOING TO MAKE DEAR OLD DADDY CRY. MUST BE SOMETHIN' WITH A FATHER LIKE THAT.
BET HE WAS LIKE MINE, HUH?
BET YOUR DAD IS AS COLD AS ICE.

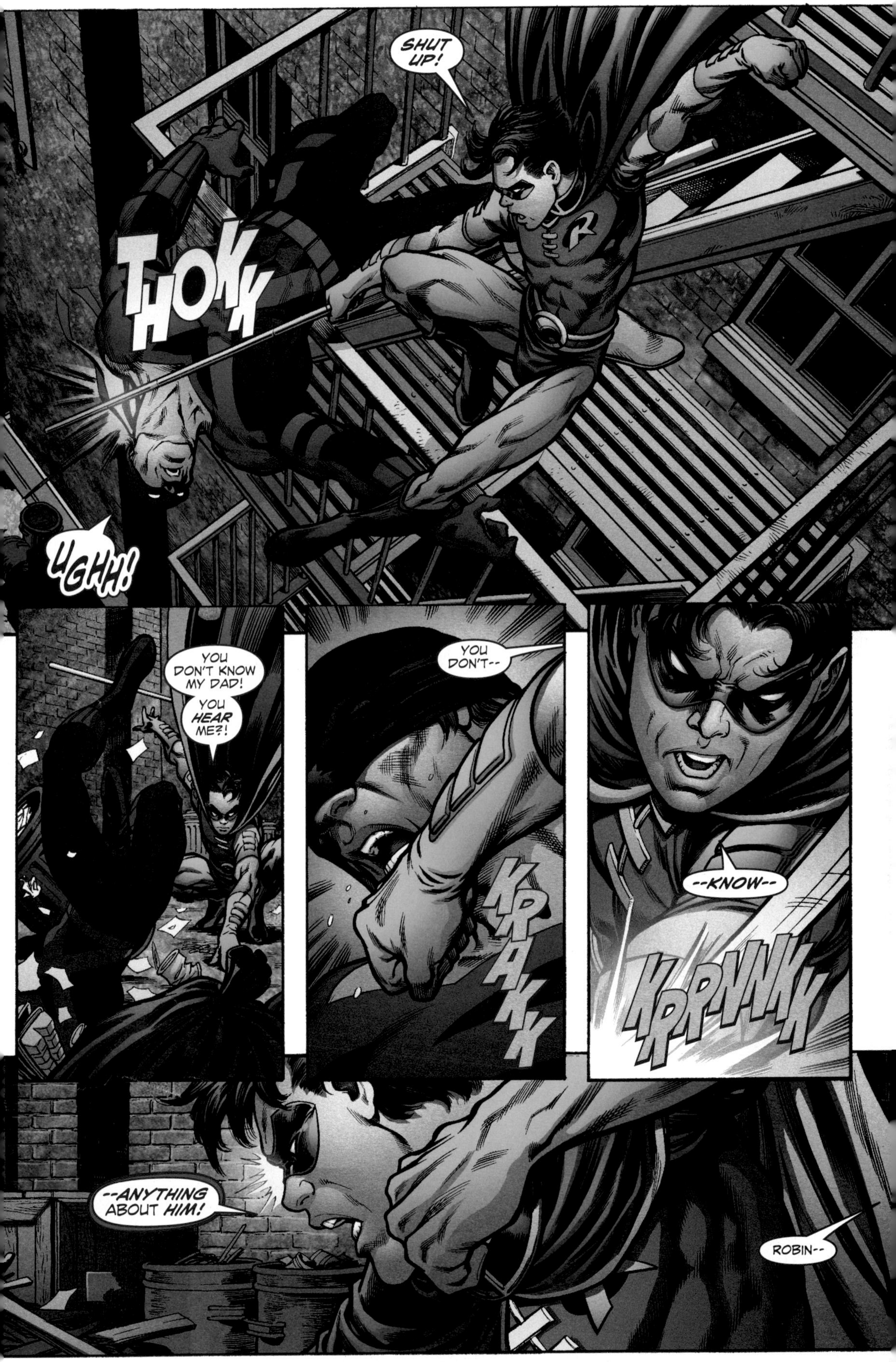
SHUT UP!
THOKK
UGHH!
YOU DON'T KNOW MY DAD!
YOU HEAR ME?!
YOU DON'T--
KRAKK
--KNOW--
KRRNNKK
--ANYTHING ABOUT HIM!
ROBIN--

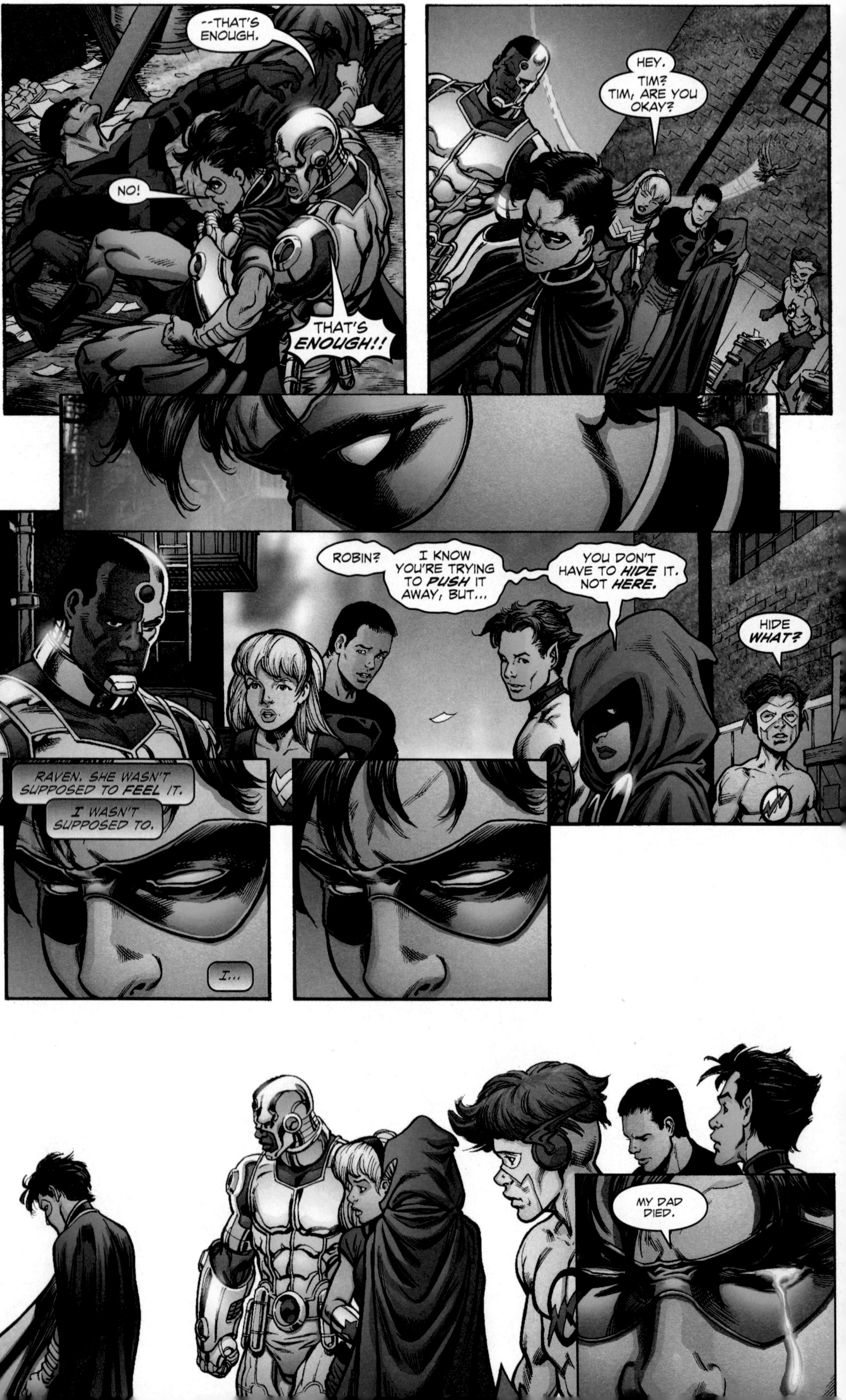
--THAT'S ENOUGH.
NO!
THAT'S ENOUGH!!
HEY.
TIM?
TIM, ARE YOU OKAY?
ROBIN?
I KNOW YOU'RE TRYING TO PUSH IT AWAY, BUT...
YOU DON'T HAVE TO HIDE IT. NOT HERE.
HIDE WHAT?
RAVEN. SHE WASN'T SUPPOSED TO FEEL IT.
I WASN'T SUPPOSED TO.
I...
MY DAD DIED.

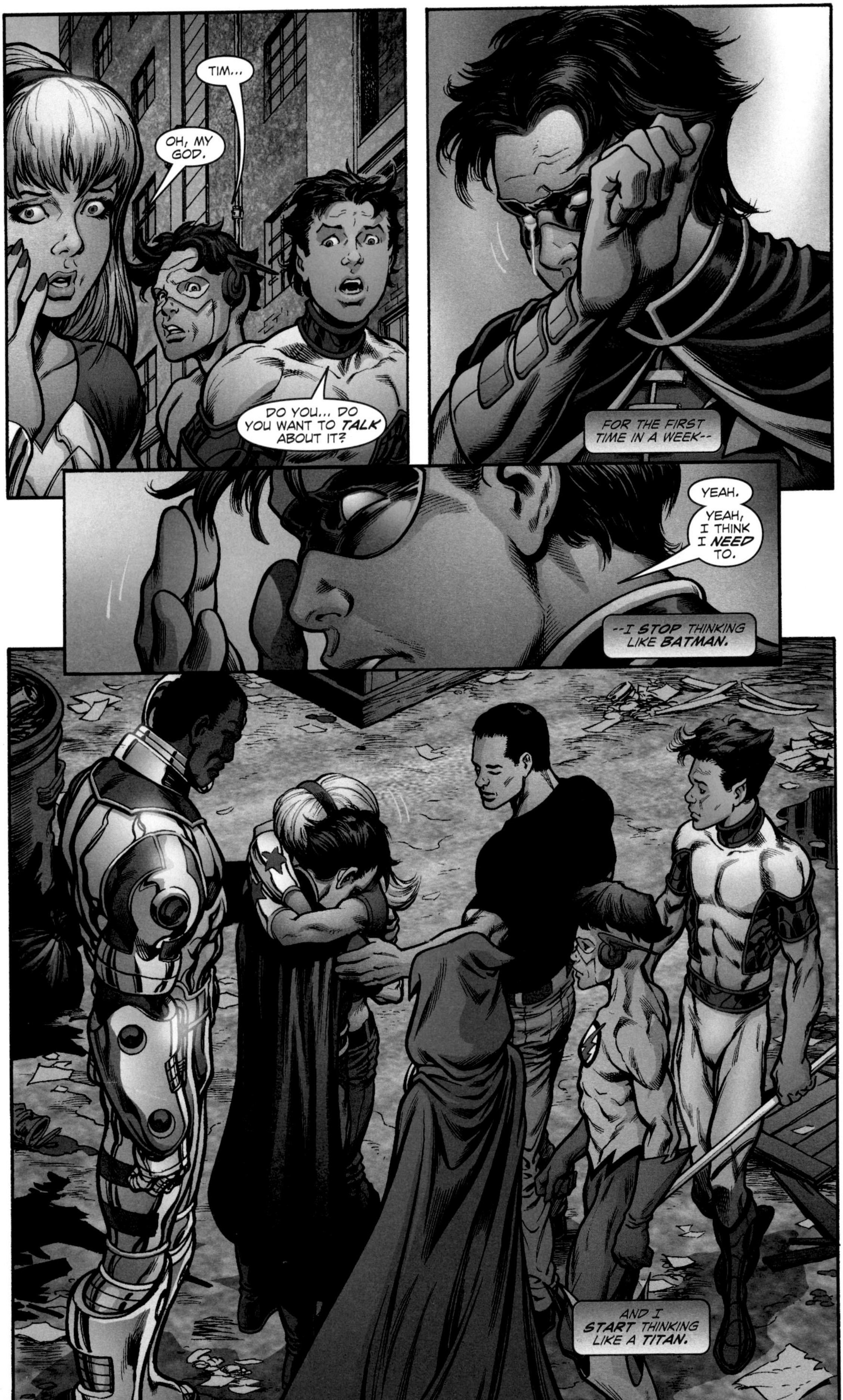
TIM...
OH, MY GOD.
DO YOU... DO YOU WANT TO TALK ABOUT IT?
FOR THE FIRST TIME IN A WEEK--
YEAH.
YEAH, I THINK I NEED TO.
--I STOP THINKING LIKE BATMAN.
AND I START THINKING LIKE A TITAN.

EPILOGUE ONE

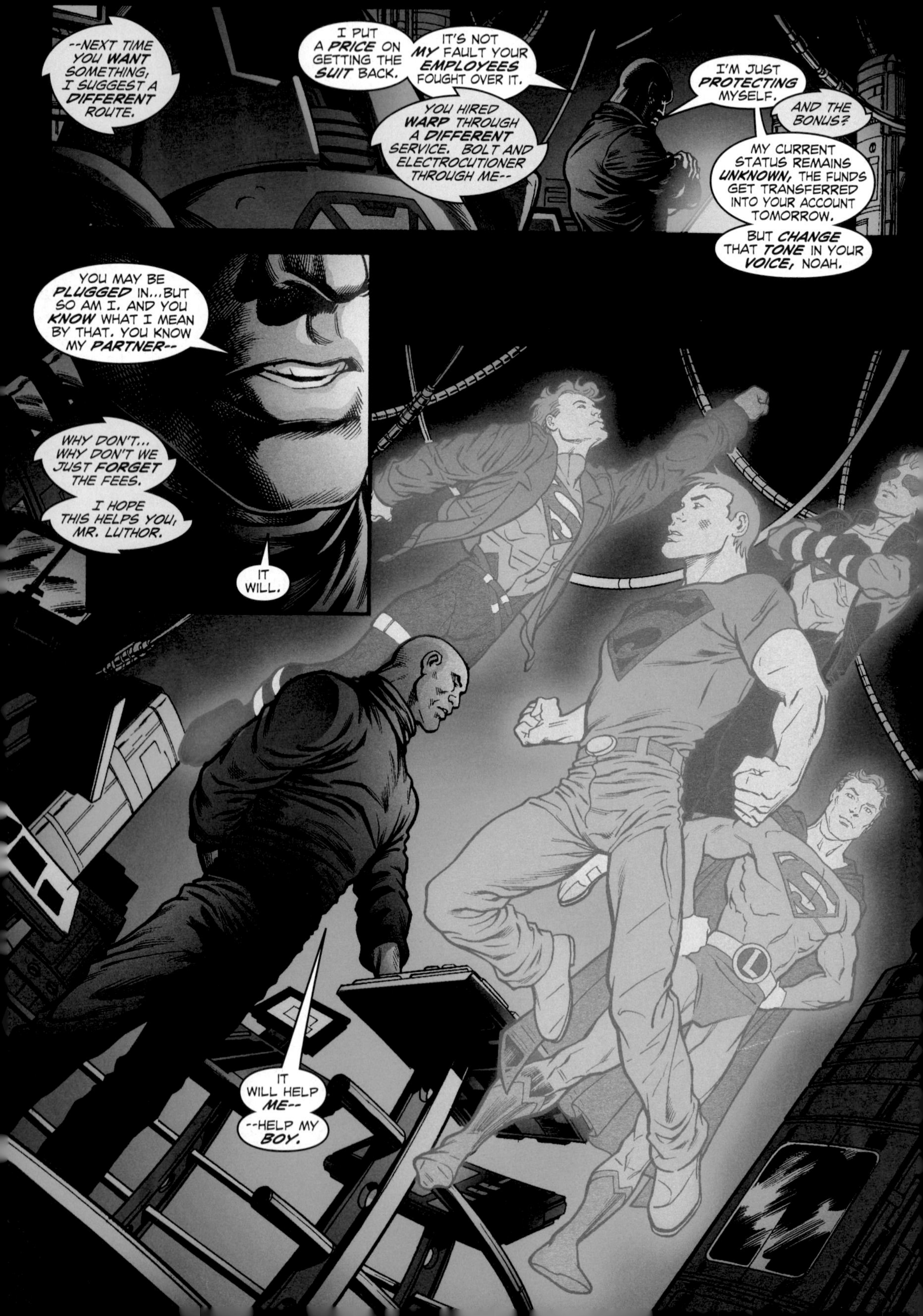
--NEXT TIME YOU WANT SOMETHING, I SUGGEST A DIFFERENT ROUTE.
I PUT A PRICE ON GETTING THE SUIT BACK.
IT'S NOT MY FAULT YOUR EMPLOYEES FOUGHT OVER IT.
YOU HIRED WARP THROUGH A DIFFERENT SERVICE. BOLT AND ELECTROCUTIONER THROUGH ME--
I'M JUST PROTECTING MYSELF.
AND THE BONUS?
MY CURRENT STATUS REMAINS UNKNOWN, THE FUNDS GET TRANSFERRED INTO YOUR ACCOUNT TOMORROW.
BUT CHANGE THAT TONE IN YOUR VOICE, NOAH.
YOU MAY BE PLUGGED IN...BUT SO AM I. AND YOU KNOW WHAT I MEAN BY THAT. YOU KNOW MY PARTNER--
WHY DON'T... WHY DON'T WE JUST FORGET THE FEES.
I HOPE THIS HELPS YOU, MR. LUTHOR.
IT WILL.
IT WILL HELP ME--
--HELP MY BOY.

EPILOGUE TWO

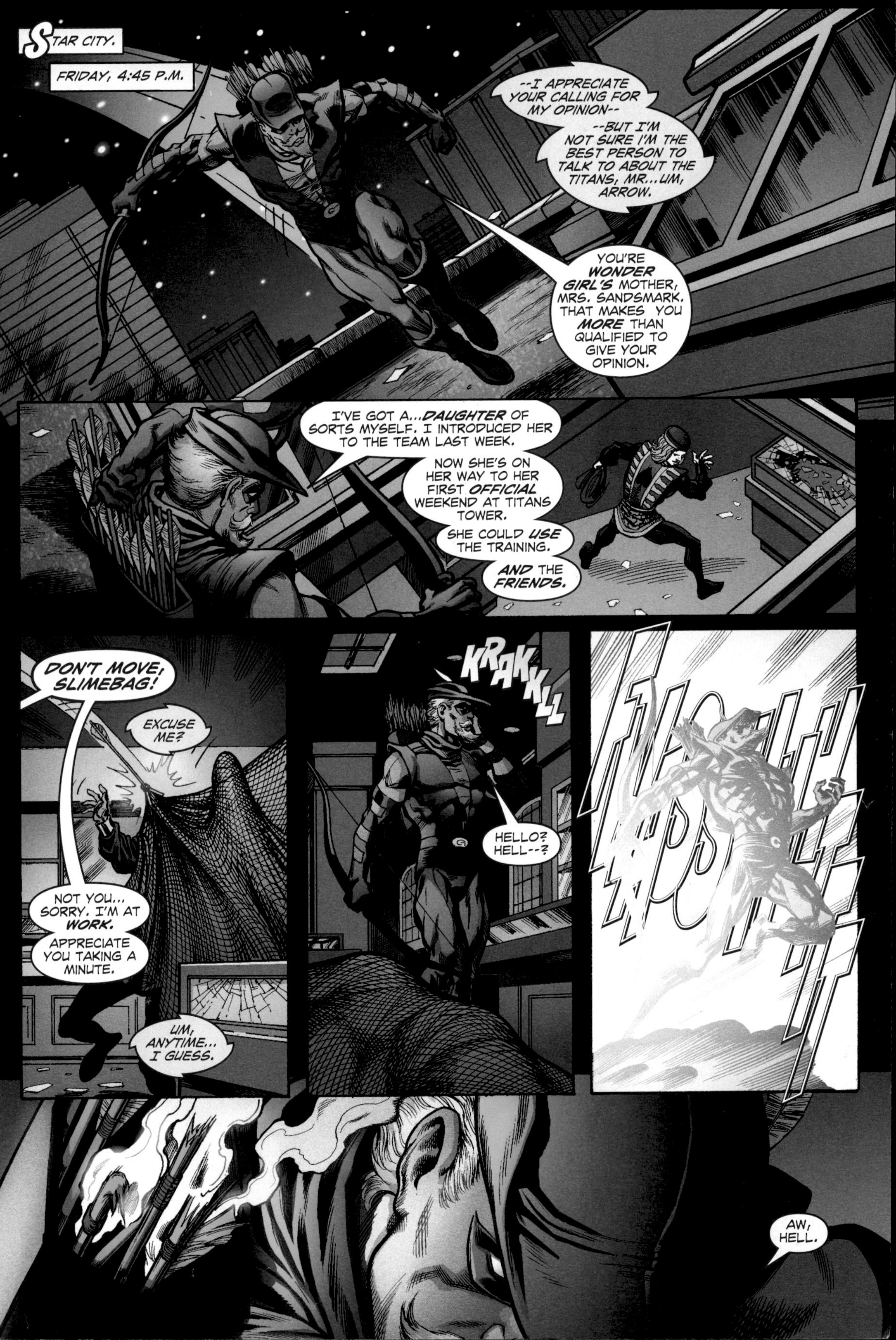
STAR CITY.
FRIDAY, 4:45 P.M.
--I APPRECIATE YOUR CALLING FOR MY OPINION--
--BUT I'M NOT SURE I'M THE BEST PERSON TO TALK TO ABOUT THE TITANS, MR...UM, ARROW.
YOU'RE WONDER GIRL'S MOTHER, MRS. SANDSMARK. THAT MAKES YOU MORE THAN QUALIFIED TO GIVE YOUR OPINION.
I'VE GOT A...DAUGHTER OF SORTS MYSELF. I INTRODUCED HER TO THE TEAM LAST WEEK.
NOW SHE'S ON HER WAY TO HER FIRST OFFICIAL WEEKEND AT TITANS TOWER.
SHE COULD USE THE TRAINING.
AND THE FRIENDS.
DON'T MOVE, SLIMEBAG!
EXCUSE ME?
NOT YOU... SORRY. I'M AT WORK.
APPRECIATE YOU TAKING A MINUTE.
UM, ANYTIME... I GUESS.
KRAKKLL
HELLO? HELL--?
AW, HELL.

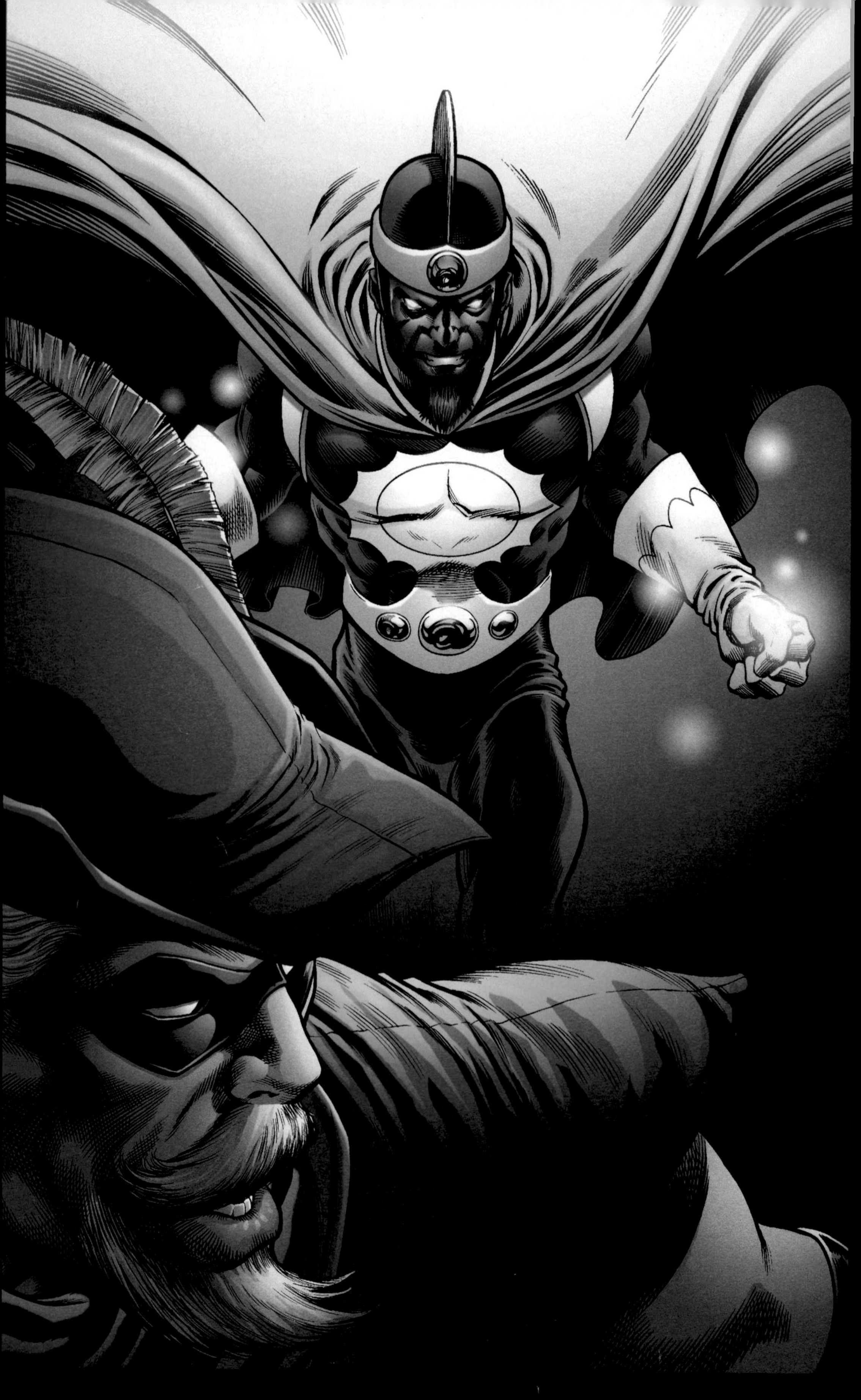

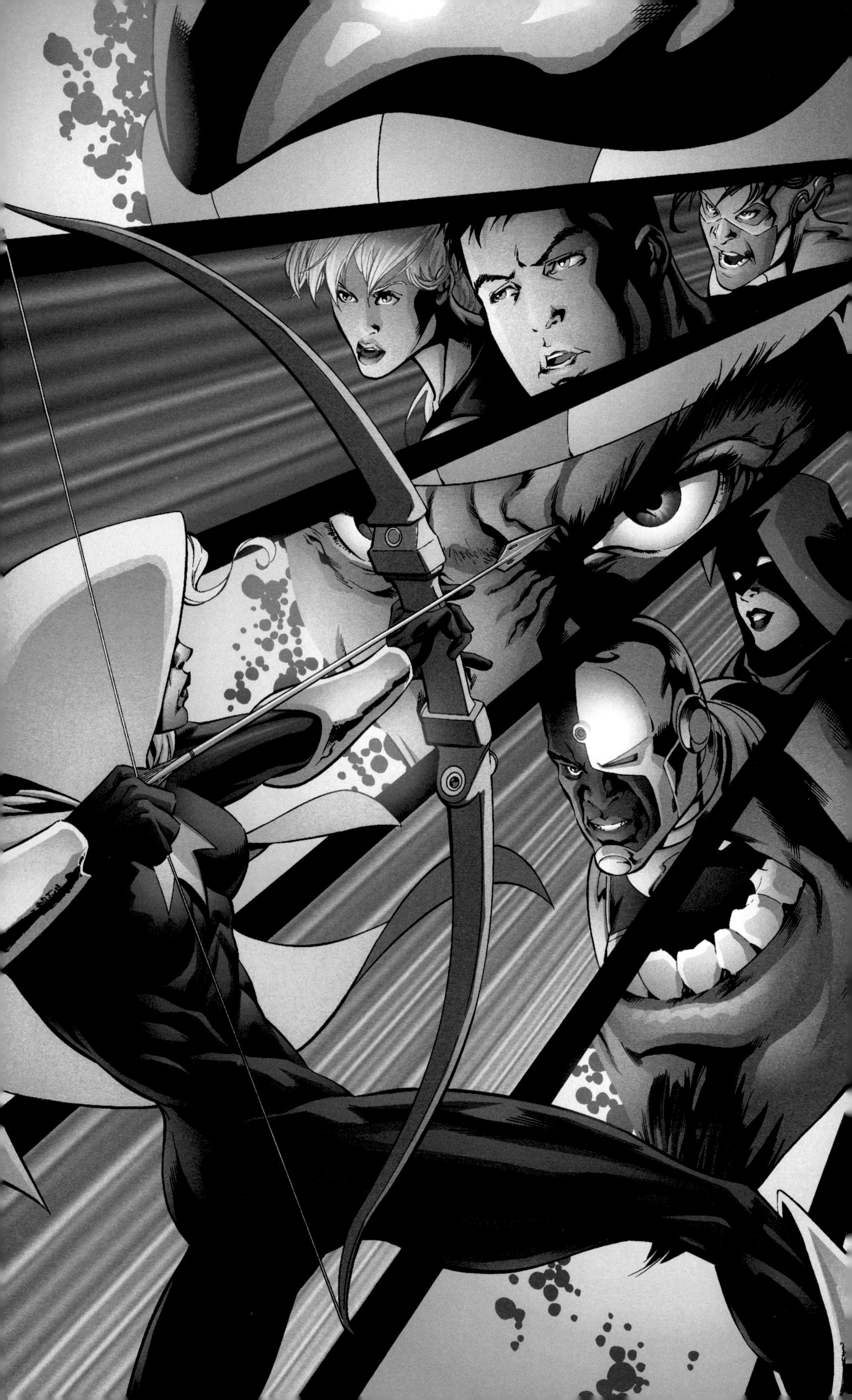

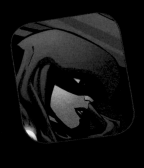

TEEN TITANS #21

GEOFF JOHNS
Writer

MIKE McKONE
Penciller

MARLO ALQUIZA
Inker

JEROMY COX
Colorist

COMICRAFT
Letterer

**MIKE McKONE,
MARLO ALQUIZA & JEROMY COX**
Cover Artists

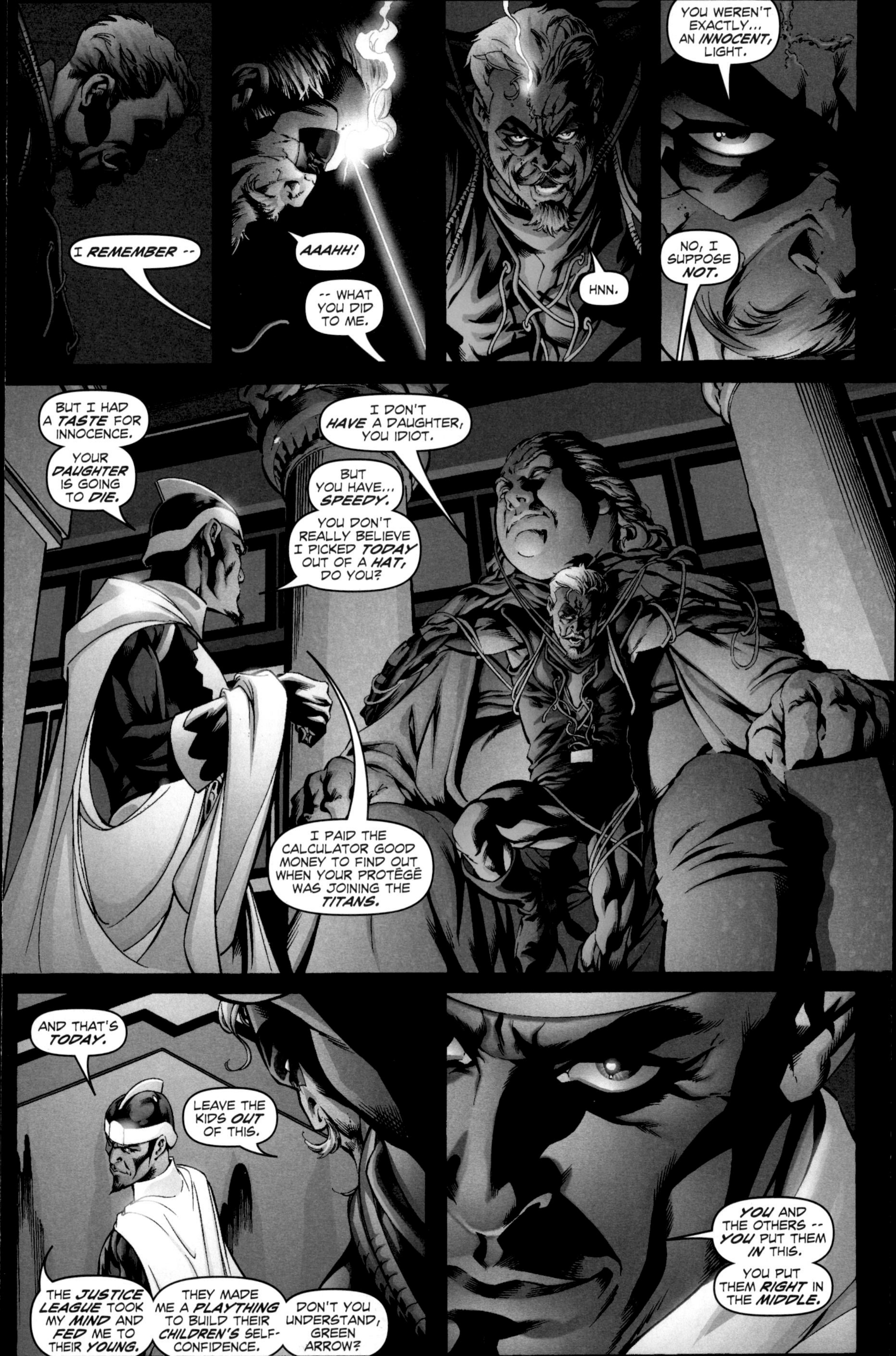
I REMEMBER --
AAAHH!
-- WHAT YOU DID TO ME.
HNN.
YOU WEREN'T EXACTLY... AN INNOCENT, LIGHT.
NO, I SUPPOSE NOT.
BUT I HAD A TASTE FOR INNOCENCE.
YOUR DAUGHTER IS GOING TO DIE.
I DON'T HAVE A DAUGHTER, YOU IDIOT.
BUT YOU HAVE... SPEEDY.
YOU DON'T REALLY BELIEVE I PICKED TODAY OUT OF A HAT, DO YOU?
I PAID THE CALCULATOR GOOD MONEY TO FIND OUT WHEN YOUR PROTÉGÉ WAS JOINING THE TITANS.
AND THAT'S TODAY.
LEAVE THE KIDS OUT OF THIS.
THE JUSTICE LEAGUE TOOK MY MIND AND FED ME TO THEIR YOUNG.
THEY MADE ME A PLAYTHING TO BUILD THEIR CHILDREN'S SELF-CONFIDENCE.
DON'T YOU UNDERSTAND, GREEN ARROW?
YOU AND THE OTHERS -- YOU PUT THEM IN THIS.
YOU PUT THEM RIGHT IN THE MIDDLE.

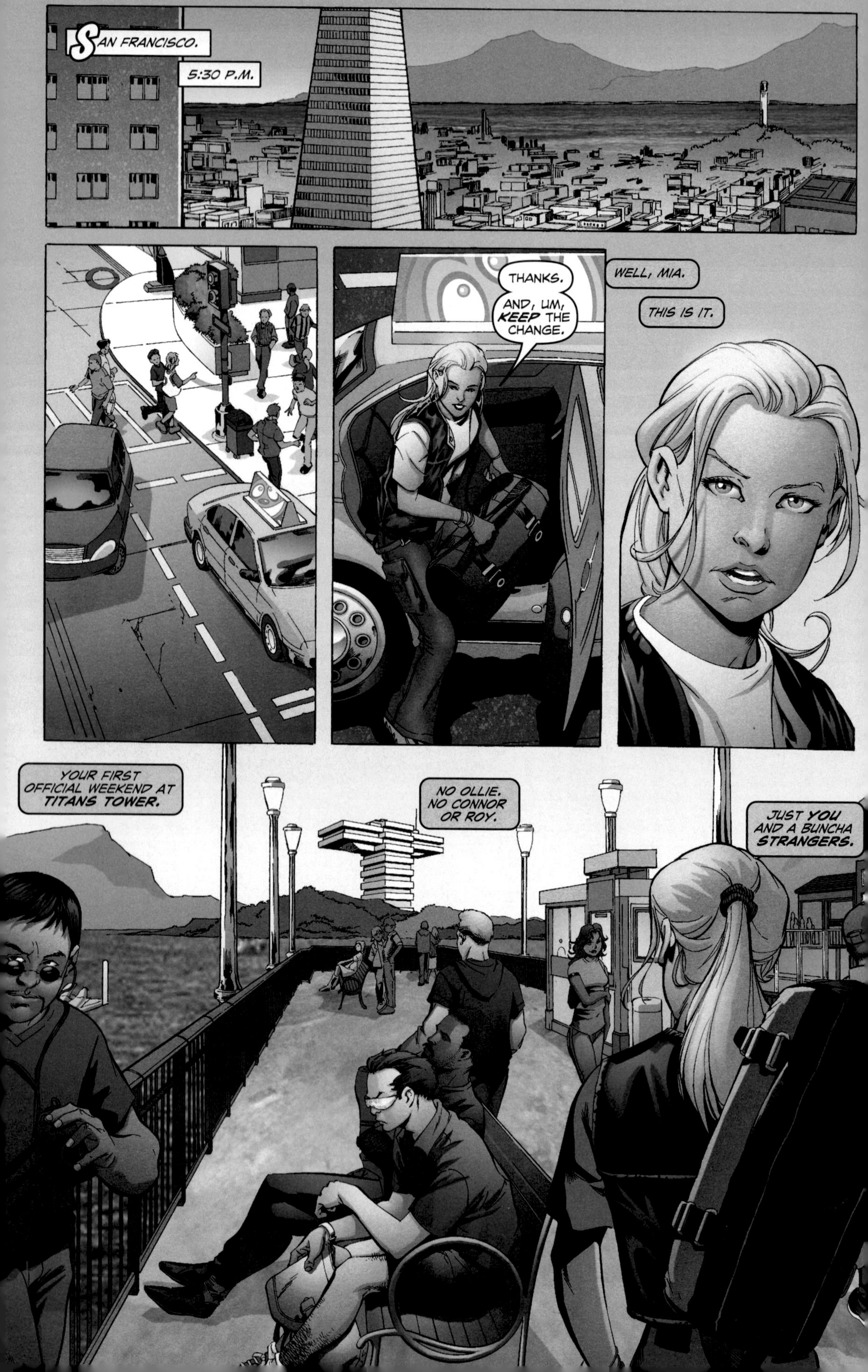
SAN FRANCISCO.
5:30 P.M.
THANKS.
AND, UM, KEEP THE CHANGE.
WELL, MIA.
THIS IS IT.
YOUR FIRST OFFICIAL WEEKEND AT TITANS TOWER.
NO OLLIE. NO CONNOR OR ROY.
JUST YOU AND A BUNCHA STRANGERS.

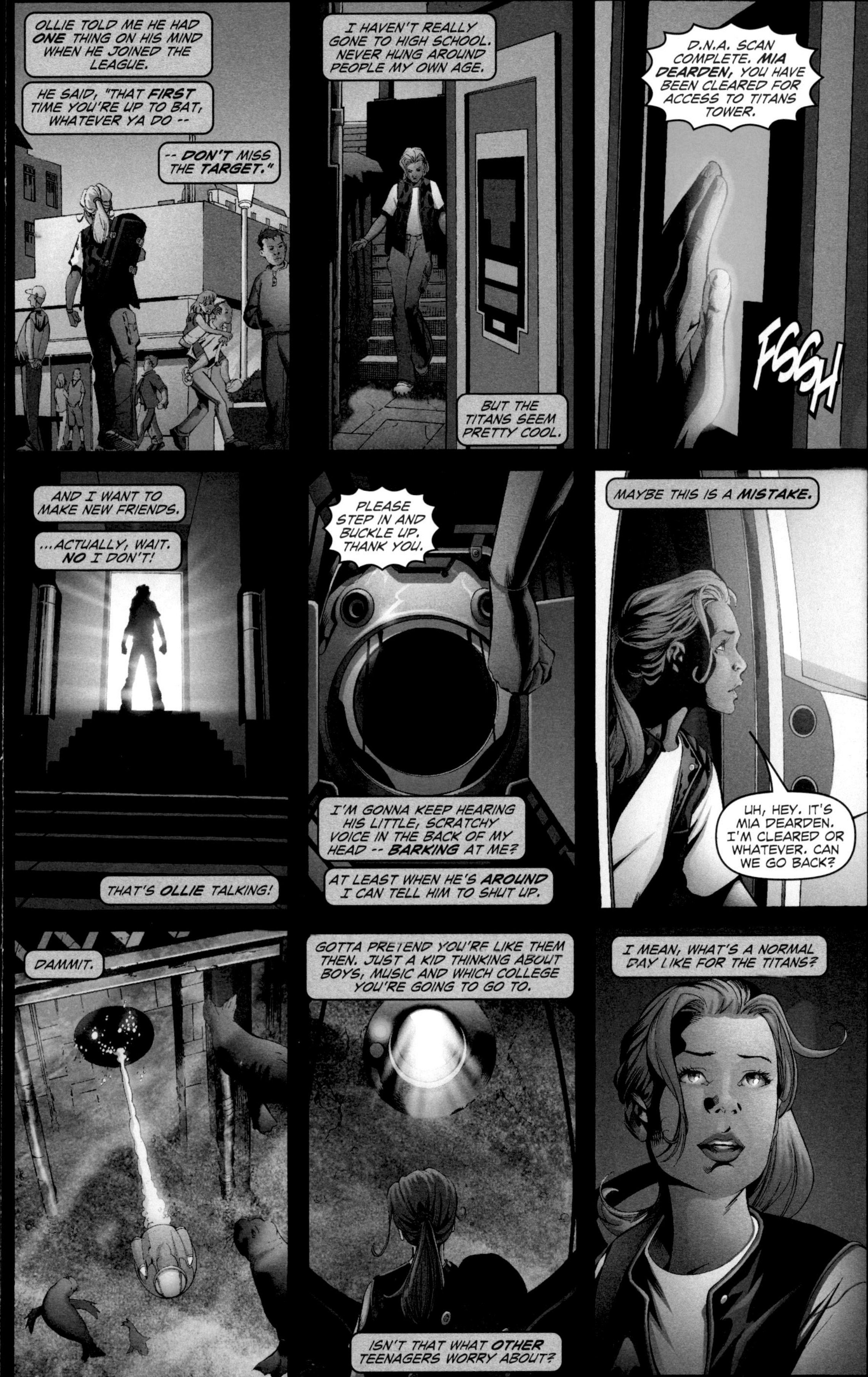
OLLIE TOLD ME HE HAD ONE THING ON HIS MIND WHEN HE JOINED THE LEAGUE.
HE SAID, "THAT FIRST TIME YOU'RE UP TO BAT, WHATEVER YA DO --
-- DON'T MISS THE TARGET."
I HAVEN'T REALLY GONE TO HIGH SCHOOL. NEVER HUNG AROUND PEOPLE MY OWN AGE.
BUT THE TITANS SEEM PRETTY COOL.
D.N.A. SCAN COMPLETE. MIA DEARDEN, YOU HAVE BEEN CLEARED FOR ACCESS TO TITANS TOWER.
FSSH
AND I WANT TO MAKE NEW FRIENDS.
...ACTUALLY, WAIT. NO I DON'T!
THAT'S OLLIE TALKING!
PLEASE STEP IN AND BUCKLE UP. THANK YOU.
I'M GONNA KEEP HEARING HIS LITTLE, SCRATCHY VOICE IN THE BACK OF MY HEAD -- BARKING AT ME?
AT LEAST WHEN HE'S AROUND I CAN TELL HIM TO SHUT UP.
MAYBE THIS IS A MISTAKE.
UH, HEY. IT'S MIA DEARDEN. I'M CLEARED OR WHATEVER. CAN WE GO BACK?
DAMMIT.
GOTTA PRETEND YOU'RE LIKE THEM THEN. JUST A KID THINKING ABOUT BOYS, MUSIC AND WHICH COLLEGE YOU'RE GOING TO GO TO.
ISN'T THAT WHAT OTHER TEENAGERS WORRY ABOUT?
I MEAN, WHAT'S A NORMAL DAY LIKE FOR THE TITANS?

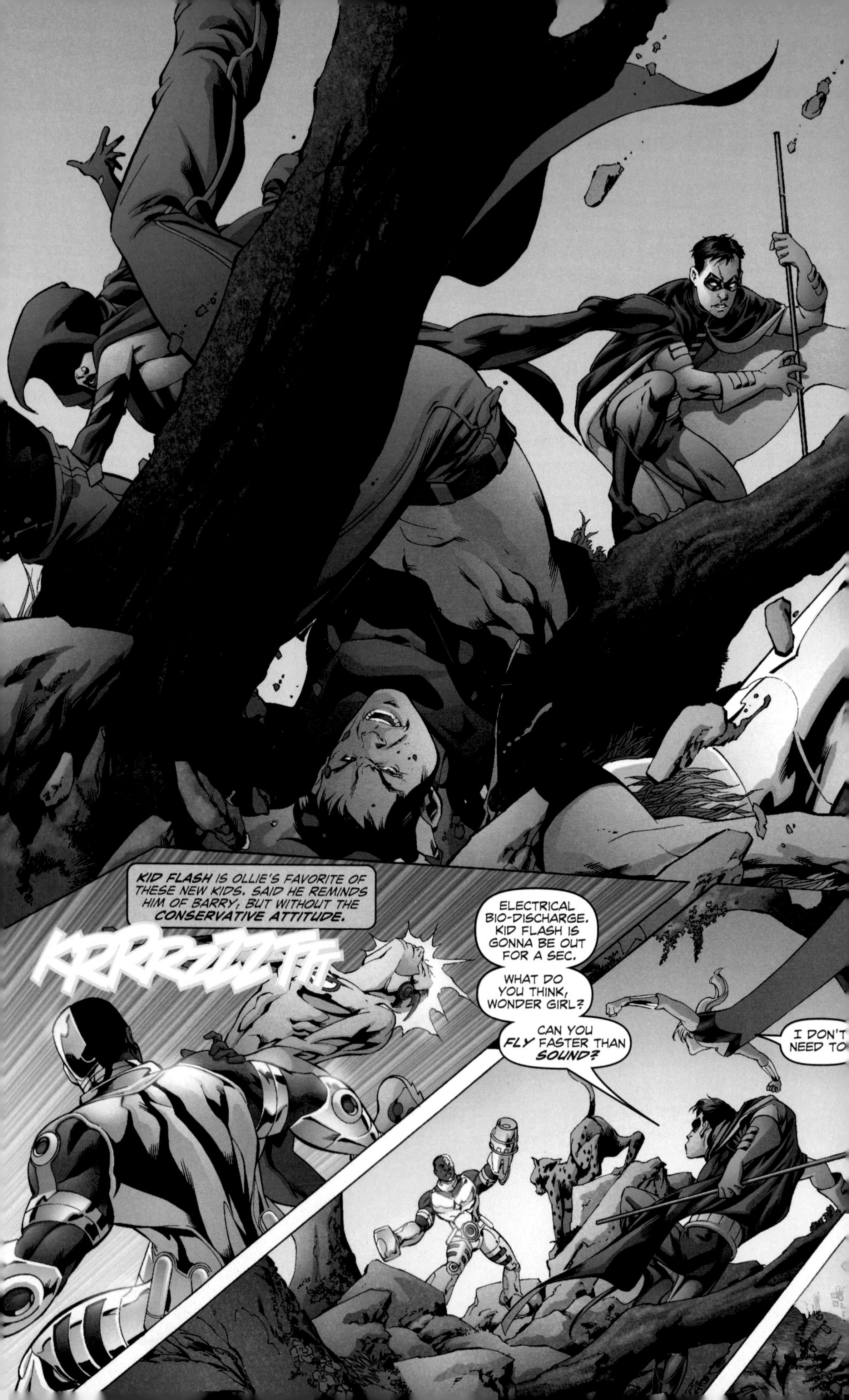
KID FLASH IS OLLIE'S FAVORITE OF THESE NEW KIDS. SAID HE REMINDS HIM OF BARRY, BUT WITHOUT THE CONSERVATIVE ATTITUDE.
KRRRZZZTT!
ELECTRICAL BIO-DISCHARGE. KID FLASH IS GONNA BE OUT FOR A SEC.
WHAT DO YOU THINK, WONDER GIRL?
CAN YOU FLY FASTER THAN SOUND?
I DON'T NEED TO

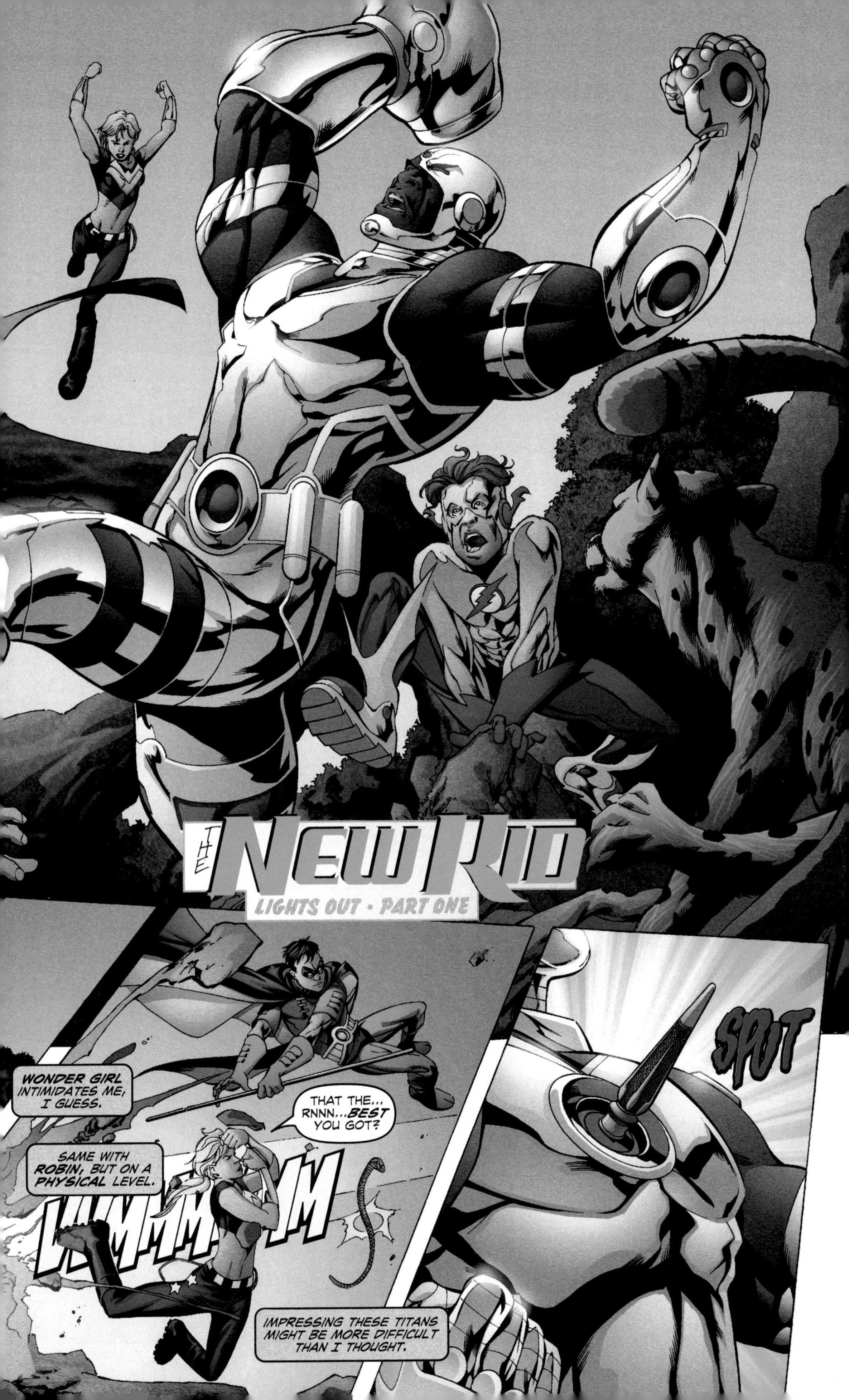
THE NEW KID
LIGHTS OUT · PART ONE
WONDER GIRL INTIMIDATES ME, I GUESS.
THAT THE... RNNN...BEST YOU GOT?
SAME WITH ROBIN, BUT ON A PHYSICAL LEVEL.
SPUT
IMPRESSING THESE TITANS MIGHT BE MORE DIFFICULT THAN I THOUGHT.

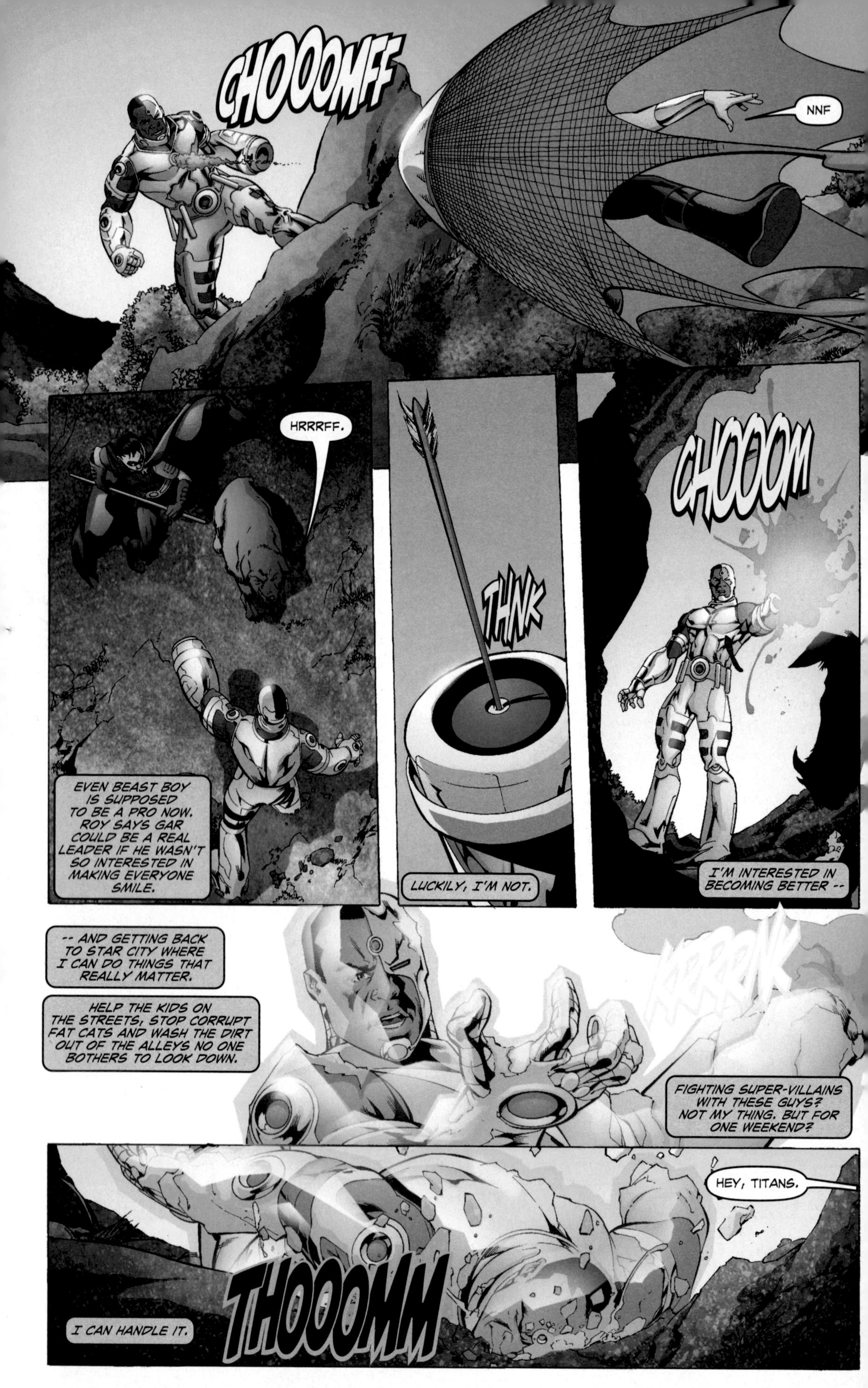
CHOOOMFF
NNF
HRRRFF.
EVEN BEAST BOY IS SUPPOSED TO BE A PRO NOW. ROY SAYS GAR COULD BE A REAL LEADER IF HE WASN'T SO INTERESTED IN MAKING EVERYONE SMILE.
THNK
LUCKILY, I'M NOT.
CHOOOM
I'M INTERESTED IN BECOMING BETTER --
-- AND GETTING BACK TO STAR CITY WHERE I CAN DO THINGS THAT REALLY MATTER.
HELP THE KIDS ON THE STREETS, STOP CORRUPT FAT CATS AND WASH THE DIRT OUT OF THE ALLEYS NO ONE BOTHERS TO LOOK DOWN.
FIGHTING SUPER-VILLAINS WITH THESE GUYS? NOT MY THING. BUT FOR ONE WEEKEND?
HEY, TITANS.
I CAN HANDLE IT.
THOOOMM

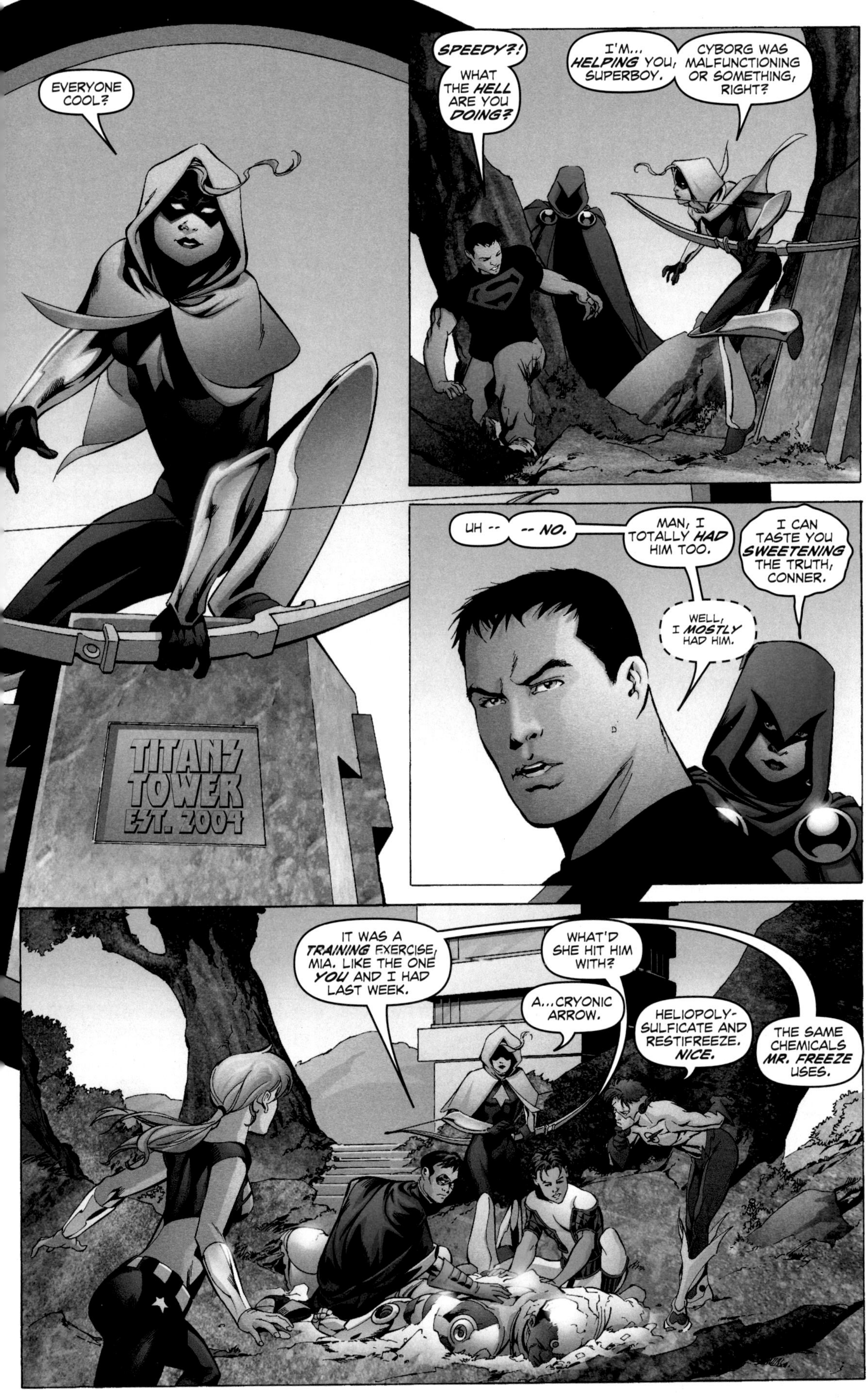
EVERYONE COOL?
TITANS TOWER EST. 2004
SPEEDY?! WHAT THE HELL ARE YOU DOING?
I'M... HELPING YOU, SUPERBOY.
CYBORG WAS MALFUNCTIONING OR SOMETHING, RIGHT?
UH --
-- NO.
MAN, I TOTALLY HAD HIM TOO.
WELL, I MOSTLY HAD HIM.
I CAN TASTE YOU SWEETENING THE TRUTH, CONNER.
IT WAS A TRAINING EXERCISE, MIA. LIKE THE ONE YOU AND I HAD LAST WEEK.
WHAT'D SHE HIT HIM WITH?
A...CRYONIC ARROW.
HELIOPOLY-SULFICATE AND RESTIFREEZE. NICE.
THE SAME CHEMICALS MR. FREEZE USES.

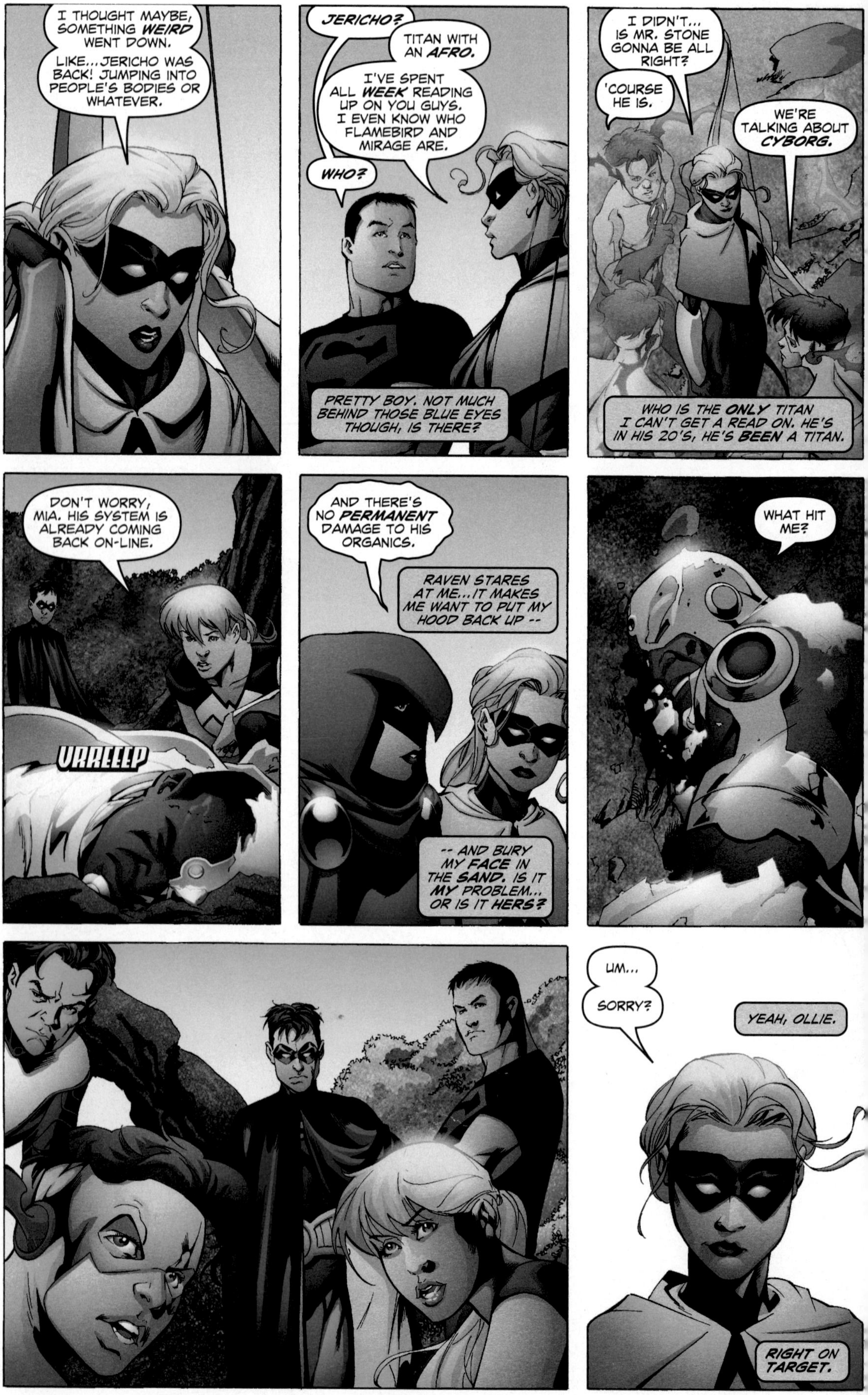
I THOUGHT MAYBE, SOMETHING WEIRD WENT DOWN.
LIKE...JERICHO WAS BACK! JUMPING INTO PEOPLE'S BODIES OR WHATEVER.
JERICHO?
TITAN WITH AN AFRO.
I'VE SPENT ALL WEEK READING UP ON YOU GUYS. I EVEN KNOW WHO FLAMEBIRD AND MIRAGE ARE.
WHO?
PRETTY BOY. NOT MUCH BEHIND THOSE BLUE EYES THOUGH, IS THERE?
I DIDN'T... IS MR. STONE GONNA BE ALL RIGHT?
'COURSE HE IS.
WE'RE TALKING ABOUT CYBORG.
WHO IS THE ONLY TITAN I CAN'T GET A READ ON. HE'S IN HIS 20'S; HE'S BEEN A TITAN.
DON'T WORRY, MIA. HIS SYSTEM IS ALREADY COMING BACK ON-LINE.
VRRREEEP
AND THERE'S NO PERMANENT DAMAGE TO HIS ORGANICS.
RAVEN STARES AT ME...IT MAKES ME WANT TO PUT MY HOOD BACK UP --
-- AND BURY MY FACE IN THE SAND. IS IT MY PROBLEM... OR IS IT HERS?
WHAT HIT ME?
UM...
SORRY?
YEAH, OLLIE.
RIGHT ON TARGET.

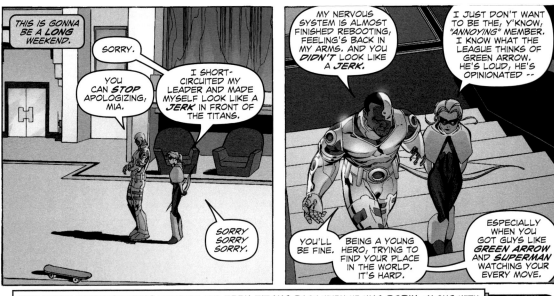

THIS IS GONNA BE A **LONG** WEEKEND.

SORRY.

YOU CAN **STOP** APOLOGIZING, MIA.

I SHORT-CIRCUITED MY LEADER AND MADE MYSELF LOOK LIKE A **JERK** IN FRONT OF THE TITANS.

SORRY SORRY SORRY.

MY NERVOUS SYSTEM IS ALMOST FINISHED REBOOTING, FEELING'S BACK IN MY ARMS. AND YOU **DIDN'T** LOOK LIKE A **JERK**.

I JUST DON'T WANT TO BE THE, Y'KNOW, "ANNOYING" MEMBER. I KNOW WHAT THE LEAGUE THINKS OF GREEN ARROW. HE'S LOUD, HE'S OPINIONATED --

YOU'LL BE FINE. BEING A YOUNG HERO, TRYING TO FIND YOUR PLACE IN THE WORLD. IT'S HARD.

ESPECIALLY WHEN YOU GOT GUYS LIKE **GREEN ARROW** AND **SUPERMAN** WATCHING YOUR EVERY MOVE.

"BUT THAT'S WHY **NIGHTWING** FOUNDED THE **TEEN TITANS** BACK WHEN HE WAS **ROBIN.** ALONG WITH ARSENAL WHEN **HE** WAS SPEEDY, THE FIRST KID FLASH, THE ORIGINAL WONDER GIRL AND AQUALAD."

"THEY MADE THE TEAM A PLACE THEY COULD BE THEMSELVES, INSTEAD OF HAVING TO STAND UP **STRAIGHT** AND WATCH **EVERY** WORD THEY SAID."

YEARS LATER, **RAVEN** HELPED GET THE TEAM BACK TOGETHER TO FIGHT HER FATHER, **TRIGON.** BROUGHT NEW MEMBERS IN LIKE **ME,** KORY AND GAR.

IT WAS AN AMAZING TIME.

"BUT NOW, IT'S A **NEW** GENERATION'S TEAM. A **NEW** TEEN TITANS.

"AND YOU'RE WELCOME TO BE A PART OF IT, MIA."

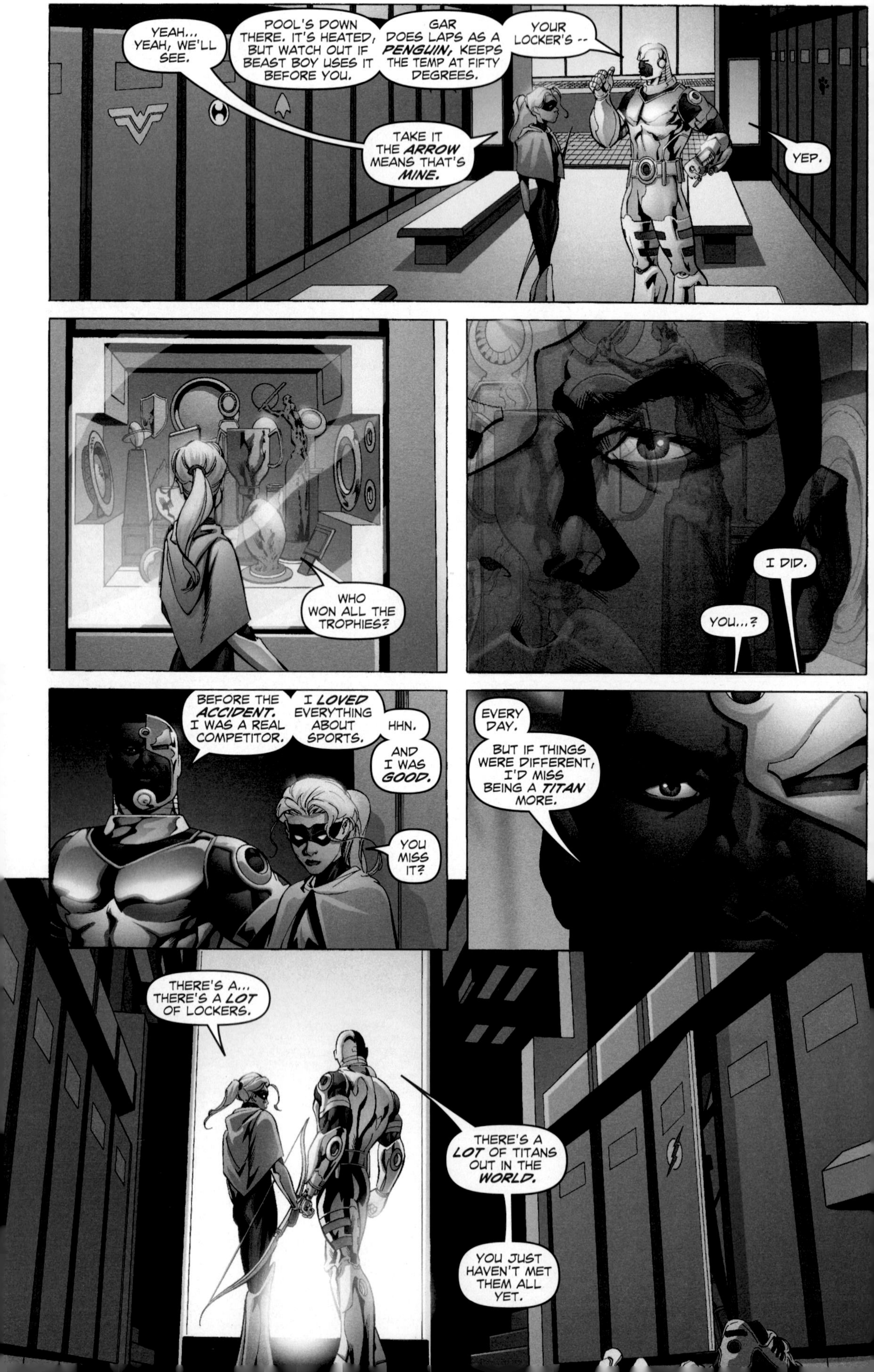
YOUR LOCKER'S --
GAR DOES LAPS AS A PENGUIN, KEEPS THE TEMP AT FIFTY DEGREES.
POOL'S DOWN THERE. IT'S HEATED, BUT WATCH OUT IF BEAST BOY USES IT BEFORE YOU.
YEAH... YEAH, WE'LL SEE.
TAKE IT THE ARROW MEANS THAT'S MINE.
YEP.
WHO WON ALL THE TROPHIES?
I DID.
YOU...?
BEFORE THE ACCIDENT. I WAS A REAL COMPETITOR.
I LOVED EVERYTHING ABOUT SPORTS.
HHN.
AND I WAS GOOD.
YOU MISS IT?
EVERY DAY.
BUT IF THINGS WERE DIFFERENT, I'D MISS BEING A TITAN MORE.
THERE'S A... THERE'S A LOT OF LOCKERS.
THERE'S A LOT OF TITANS OUT IN THE WORLD.
YOU JUST HAVEN'T MET THEM ALL YET.

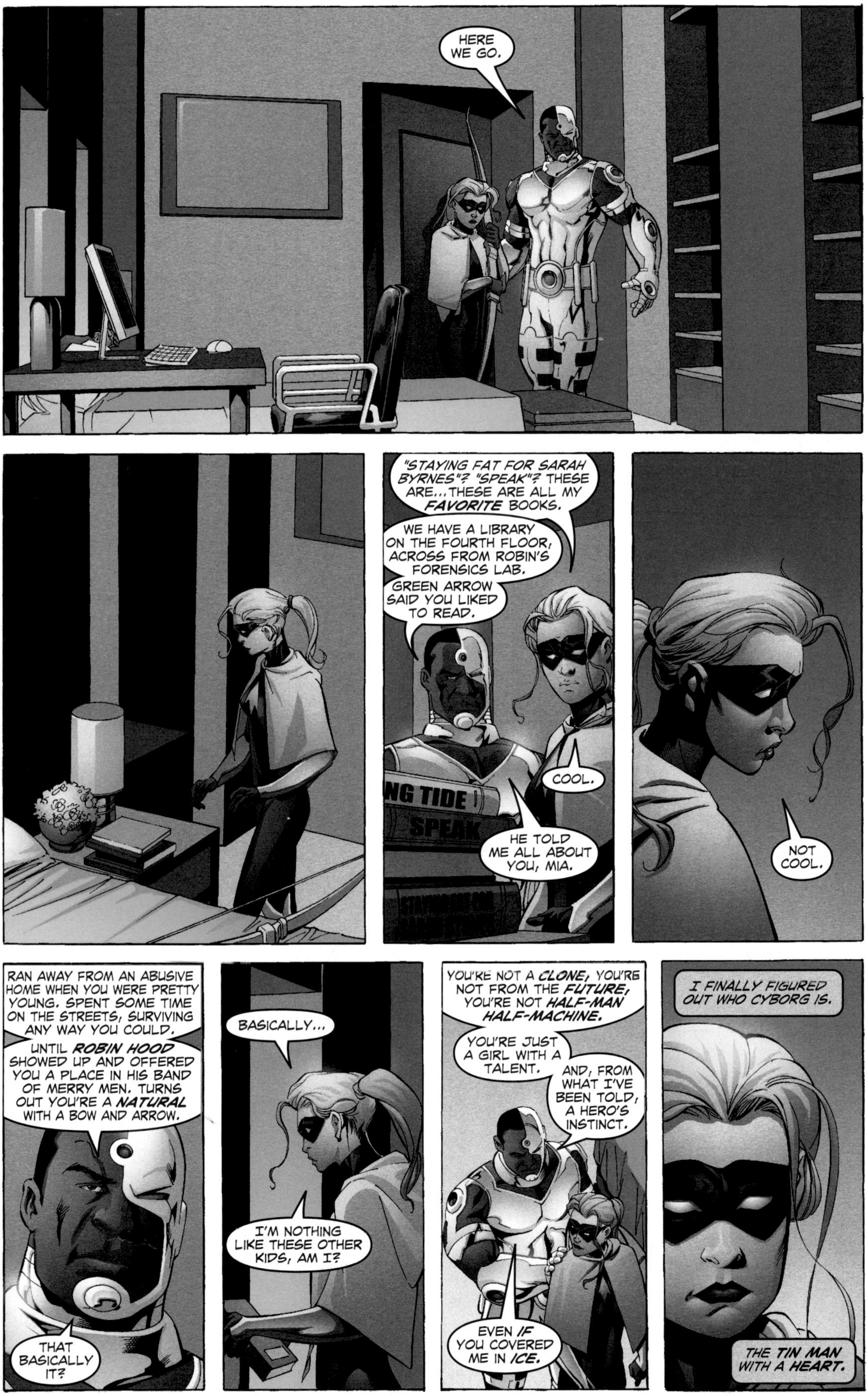

HERE WE GO.
"STAYING FAT FOR SARAH BYRNES"? "SPEAK"? THESE ARE... THESE ARE ALL MY FAVORITE BOOKS.
WE HAVE A LIBRARY ON THE FOURTH FLOOR, ACROSS FROM ROBIN'S FORENSICS LAB.
GREEN ARROW SAID YOU LIKED TO READ.
COOL.
NG TIDE
SPEAK
HE TOLD ME ALL ABOUT YOU, MIA.
NOT COOL.
RAN AWAY FROM AN ABUSIVE HOME WHEN YOU WERE PRETTY YOUNG. SPENT SOME TIME ON THE STREETS, SURVIVING ANY WAY YOU COULD.
UNTIL ROBIN HOOD SHOWED UP AND OFFERED YOU A PLACE IN HIS BAND OF MERRY MEN. TURNS OUT YOU'RE A NATURAL WITH A BOW AND ARROW.
THAT BASICALLY IT?
BASICALLY...
I'M NOTHING LIKE THESE OTHER KIDS, AM I?
YOU'RE NOT A CLONE, YOU'RE NOT FROM THE FUTURE, YOU'RE NOT HALF-MAN HALF-MACHINE.
YOU'RE JUST A GIRL WITH A TALENT.
AND, FROM WHAT I'VE BEEN TOLD, A HERO'S INSTINCT.
EVEN IF YOU COVERED ME IN ICE.
I FINALLY FIGURED OUT WHO CYBORG IS.
THE TIN MAN WITH A HEART.

I GOT SOMETHIN' FOR YOU.

WHAT ARE--?

THEY BELONGED TO SPEEDY BEFORE HE TRADED IN THE *TRICK ARROWS* FOR HIS *ARSENAL* IDENTITY.

ROY WANTED YOU TO HAVE THEM. SAID HE MISSED YOUR SEVENTEENTH BIRTHDAY.

IT WAS, UH, LAST WEEK.

HE MENTIONED THE MAGNESIUM FLARES WERE PROBABLY EXPIRED. WHICHEVER ONES THOSE ARE.

THESE. WITH THE GLASS BULBS ON THE END.

HEY.

WHAT'S THE *BLUE* ONE FOR?

DON'T KNOW.

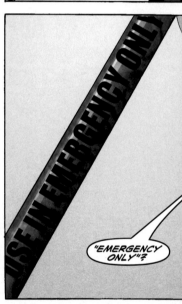

USE IN EMERGENCY ONLY

"EMERGENCY ONLY"?

CYBORG. I ALSO... I NEED TO TELL YOU ALL SOMETHING ELSE--

YO!

AAAA!

SORRY, SPEEDY, BUT... YOU GUYS BETTER *SEE* THIS.

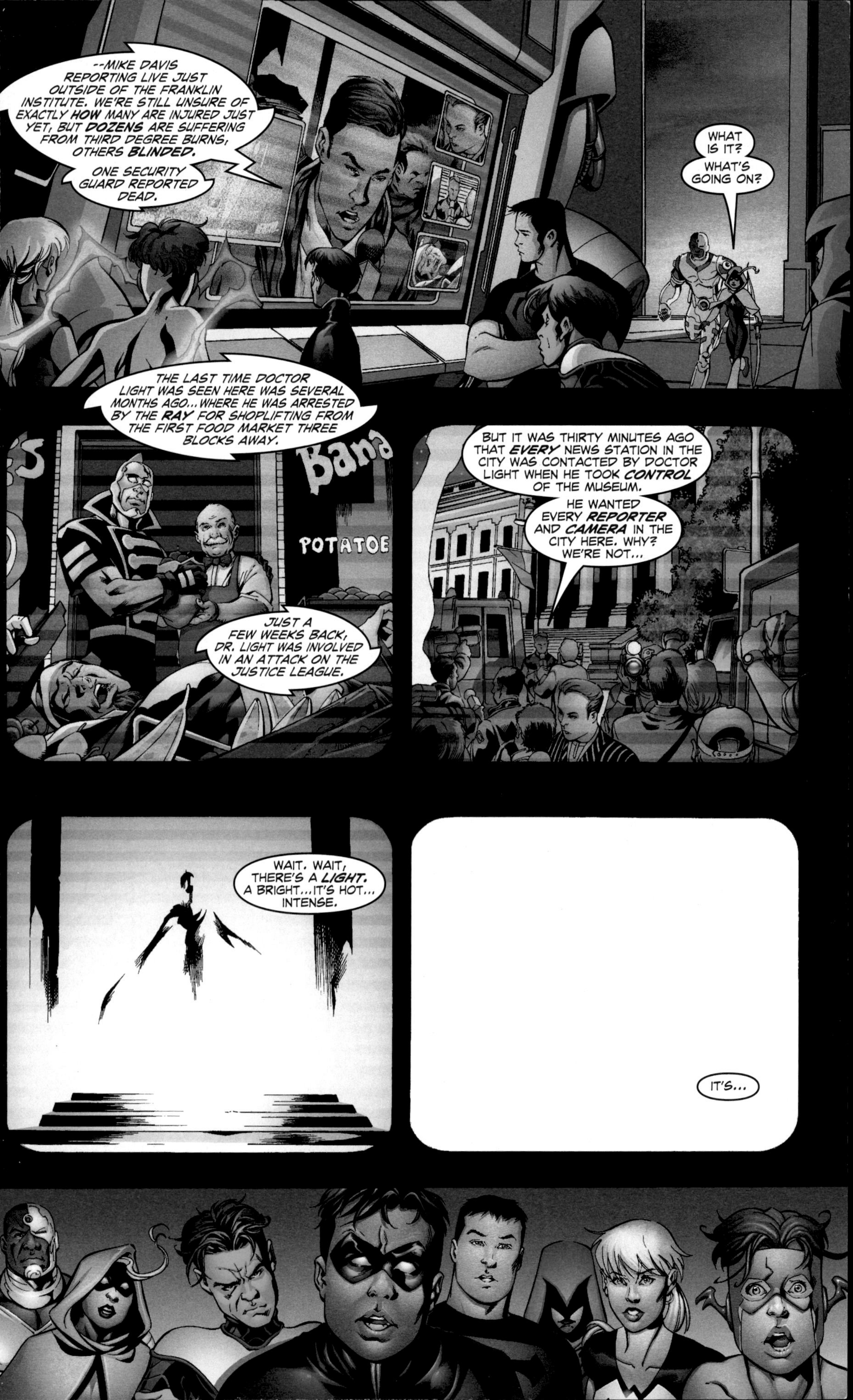
--MIKE DAVIS REPORTING LIVE JUST OUTSIDE OF THE FRANKLIN INSTITUTE. WE'RE STILL UNSURE OF EXACTLY HOW MANY ARE INJURED JUST YET, BUT DOZENS ARE SUFFERING FROM THIRD DEGREE BURNS, OTHERS BLINDED.
ONE SECURITY GUARD REPORTED DEAD.
WHAT IS IT? WHAT'S GOING ON?
THE LAST TIME DOCTOR LIGHT WAS SEEN HERE WAS SEVERAL MONTHS AGO...WHERE HE WAS ARRESTED BY THE RAY FOR SHOPLIFTING FROM THE FIRST FOOD MARKET THREE BLOCKS AWAY.
POTATOE
JUST A FEW WEEKS BACK, DR. LIGHT WAS INVOLVED IN AN ATTACK ON THE JUSTICE LEAGUE.
BUT IT WAS THIRTY MINUTES AGO THAT EVERY NEWS STATION IN THE CITY WAS CONTACTED BY DOCTOR LIGHT WHEN HE TOOK CONTROL OF THE MUSEUM.
HE WANTED EVERY REPORTER AND CAMERA IN THE CITY HERE. WHY? WE'RE NOT...
WAIT. WAIT, THERE'S A LIGHT. A BRIGHT...IT'S HOT... INTENSE.
IT'S...

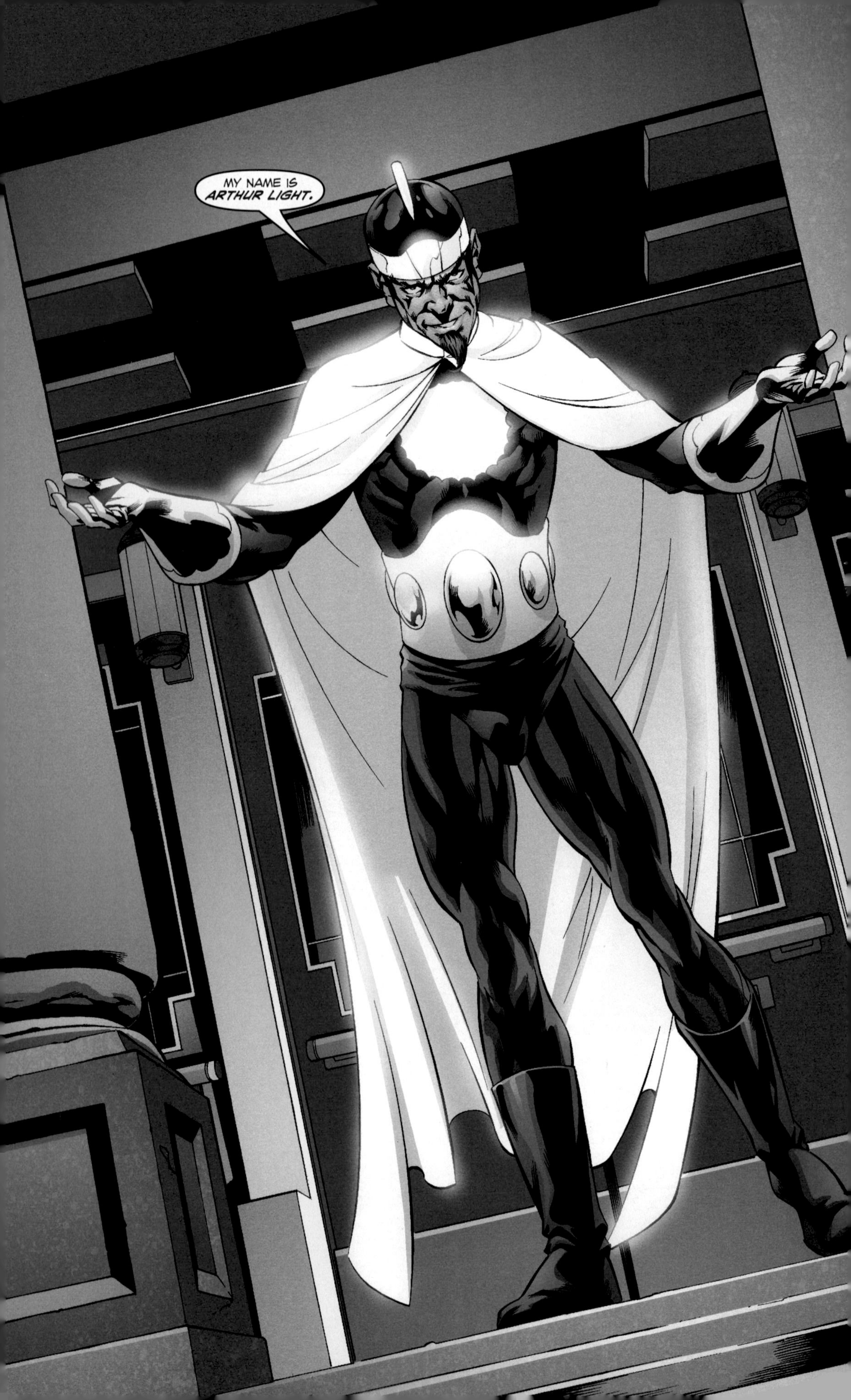
MY NAME IS ARTHUR LIGHT.

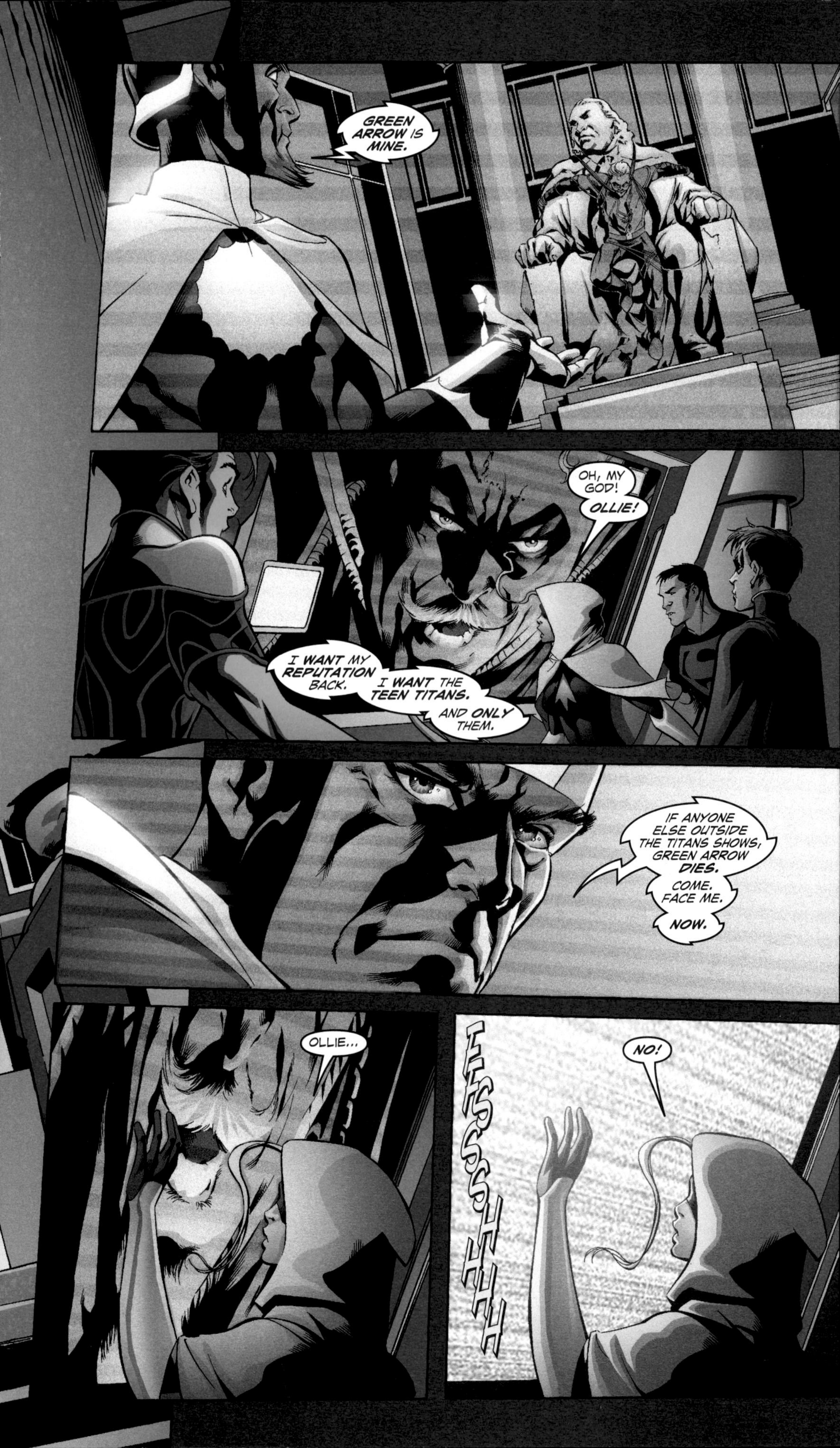
GREEN ARROW IS MINE.
OH, MY GOD! OLLIE!
I WANT MY REPUTATION BACK.
I WANT THE TEEN TITANS.
AND ONLY THEM.
IF ANYONE ELSE OUTSIDE THE TITANS SHOWS, GREEN ARROW DIES.
COME. FACE ME.
NOW.
OLLIE...
FFSSSHHHH
NO!

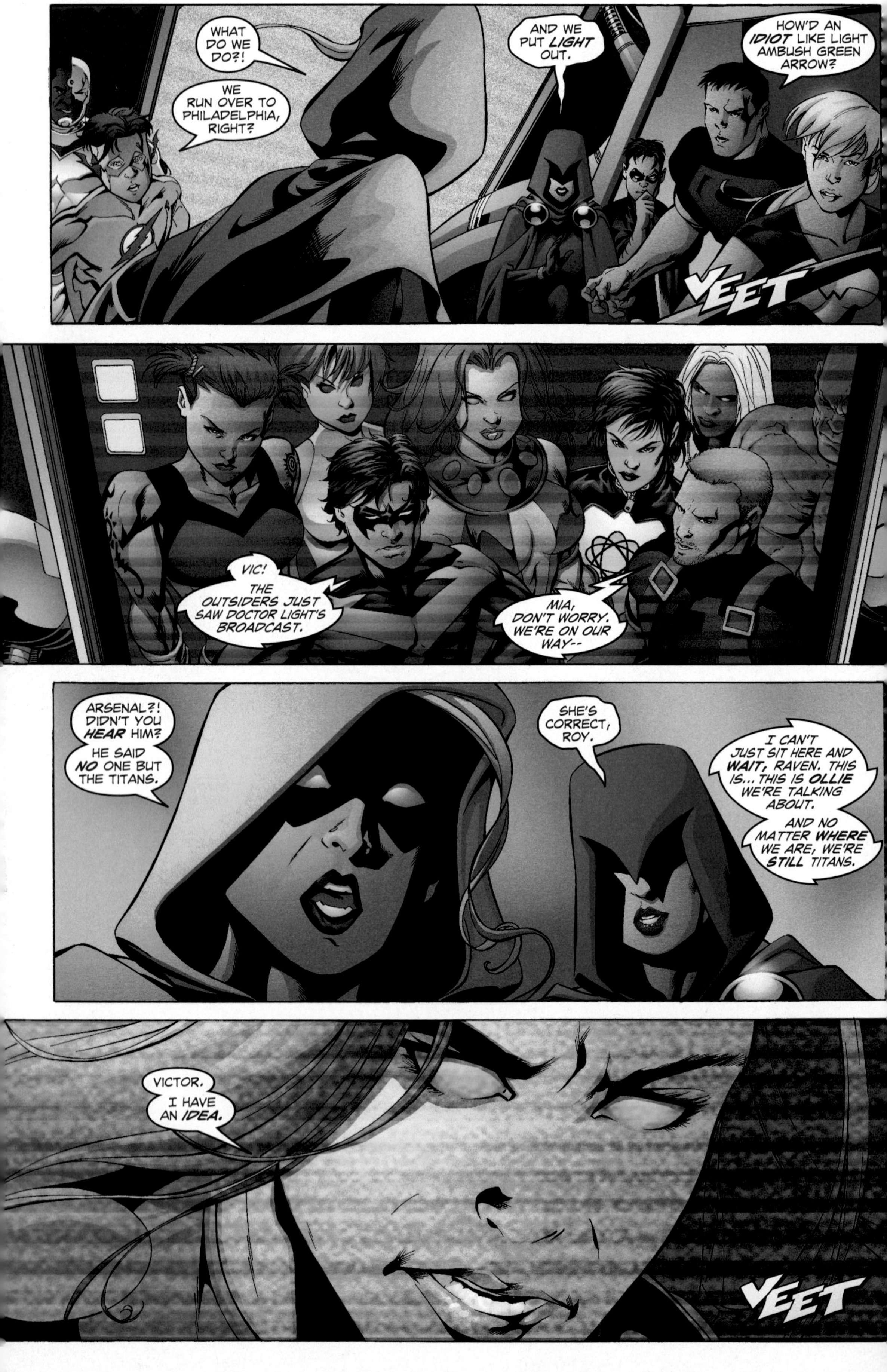
WHAT DO WE DO?!
WE RUN OVER TO PHILADELPHIA, RIGHT?
AND WE PUT LIGHT OUT.
HOW'D AN IDIOT LIKE LIGHT AMBUSH GREEN ARROW?
VEET
VIC! THE OUTSIDERS JUST SAW DOCTOR LIGHT'S BROADCAST.
MIA, DON'T WORRY. WE'RE ON OUR WAY--
ARSENAL?! DIDN'T YOU HEAR HIM? HE SAID NO ONE BUT THE TITANS.
SHE'S CORRECT, ROY.
I CAN'T JUST SIT HERE AND WAIT, RAVEN. THIS IS... THIS IS OLLIE WE'RE TALKING ABOUT.
AND NO MATTER WHERE WE ARE, WE'RE STILL TITANS.
VICTOR. I HAVE AN IDEA.
VEET

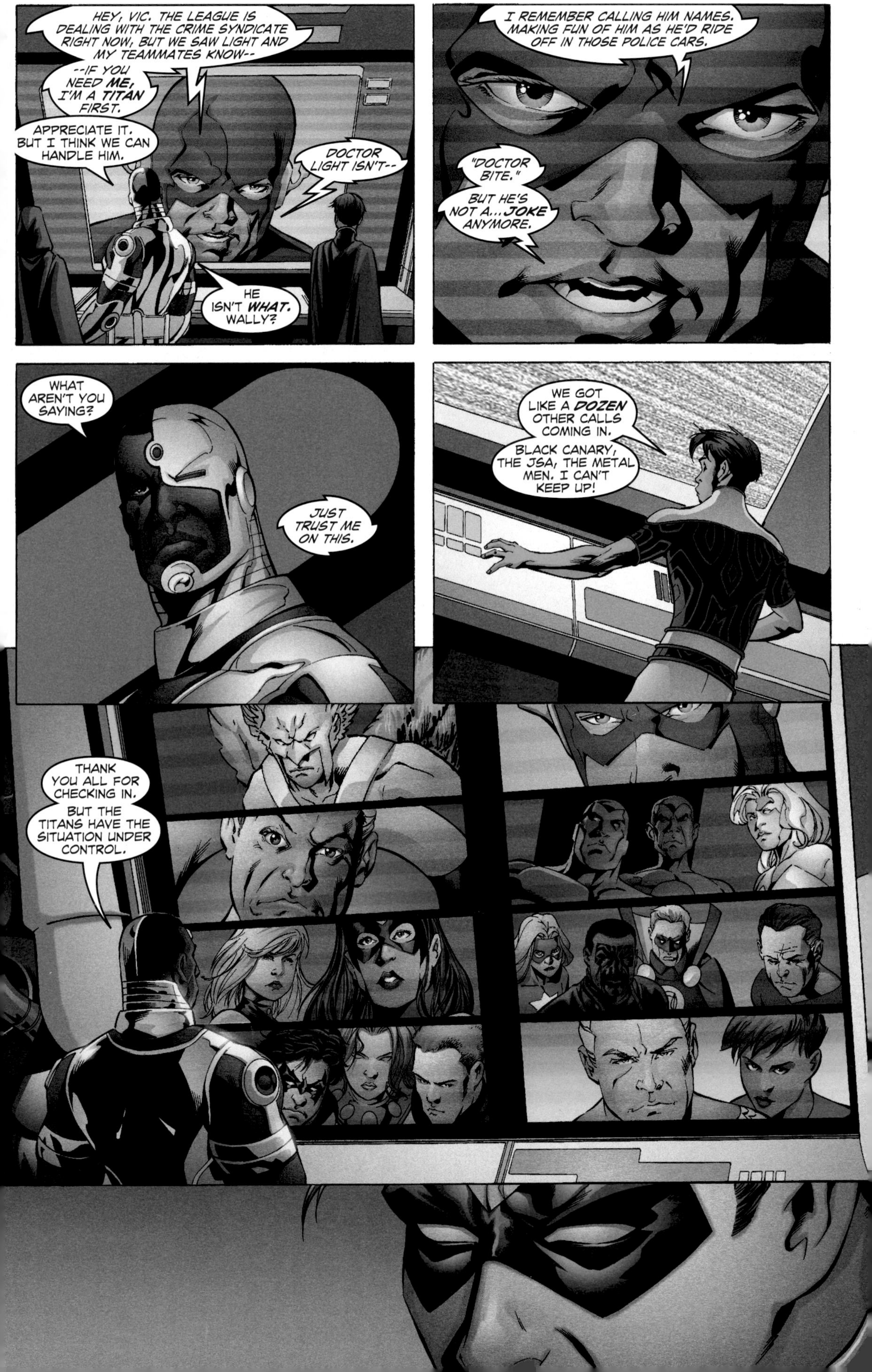
HEY, VIC. THE LEAGUE IS DEALING WITH THE CRIME SYNDICATE RIGHT NOW, BUT WE SAW LIGHT AND MY TEAMMATES KNOW--
--IF YOU NEED ME, I'M A TITAN FIRST.
APPRECIATE IT. BUT I THINK WE CAN HANDLE HIM.
DOCTOR LIGHT ISN'T--
HE ISN'T WHAT. WALLY?
I REMEMBER CALLING HIM NAMES. MAKING FUN OF HIM AS HE'D RIDE OFF IN THOSE POLICE CARS.
"DOCTOR BITE."
BUT HE'S NOT A...JOKE ANYMORE.
WHAT AREN'T YOU SAYING?
JUST TRUST ME ON THIS.
WE GOT LIKE A DOZEN OTHER CALLS COMING IN.
BLACK CANARY, THE JSA, THE METAL MEN. I CAN'T KEEP UP!
THANK YOU ALL FOR CHECKING IN.
BUT THE TITANS HAVE THE SITUATION UNDER CONTROL.

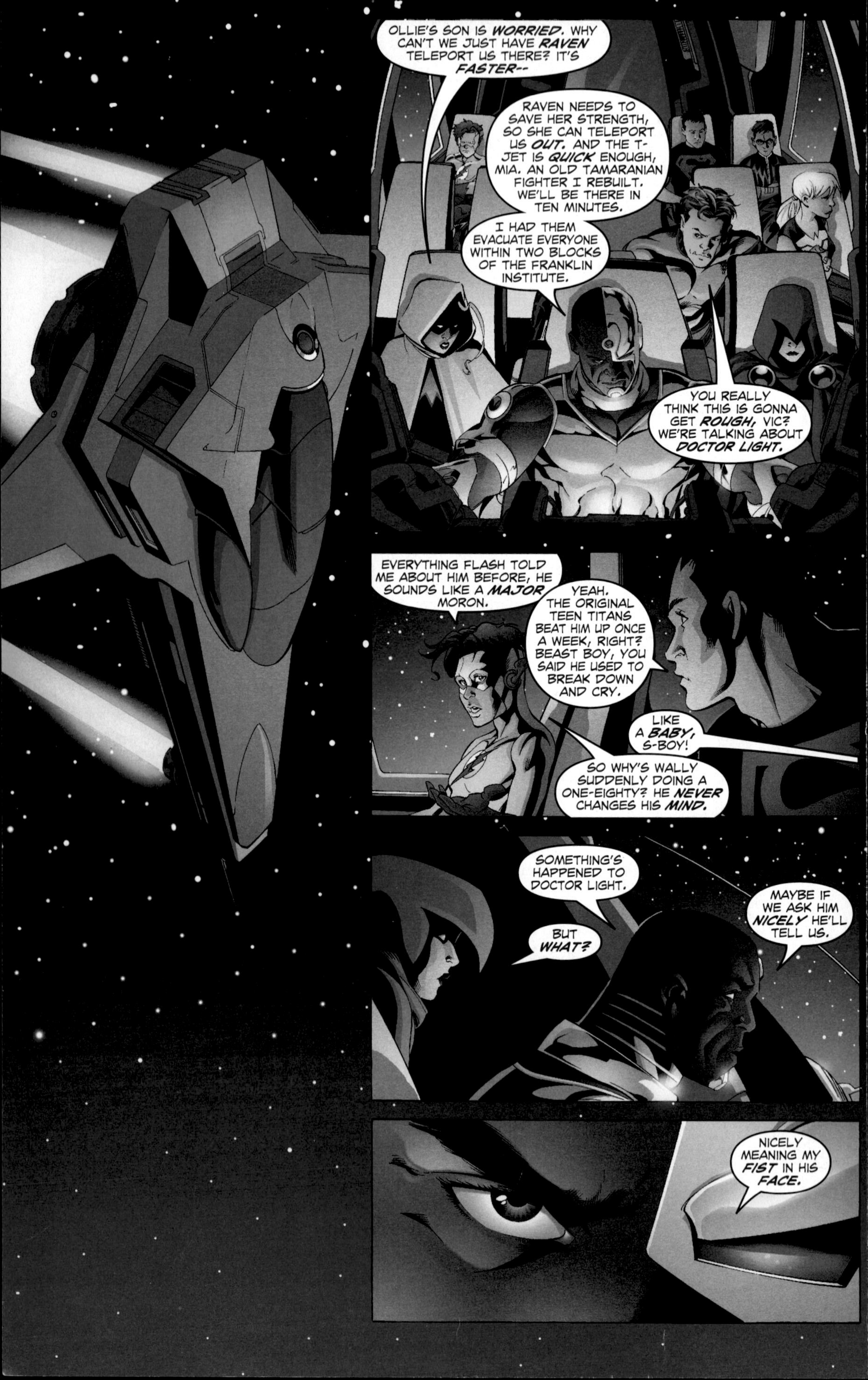

OLLIE'S SON IS WORRIED. WHY CAN'T WE JUST HAVE RAVEN TELEPORT US THERE? IT'S FASTER--
RAVEN NEEDS TO SAVE HER STRENGTH, SO SHE CAN TELEPORT US OUT. AND THE T-JET IS QUICK ENOUGH, MIA. AN OLD TAMARANIAN FIGHTER I REBUILT. WE'LL BE THERE IN TEN MINUTES.
I HAD THEM EVACUATE EVERYONE WITHIN TWO BLOCKS OF THE FRANKLIN INSTITUTE.
YOU REALLY THINK THIS IS GONNA GET ROUGH, VIC? WE'RE TALKING ABOUT DOCTOR LIGHT.
EVERYTHING FLASH TOLD ME ABOUT HIM BEFORE, HE SOUNDS LIKE A MAJOR MORON.
YEAH. THE ORIGINAL TEEN TITANS BEAT HIM UP ONCE A WEEK, RIGHT? BEAST BOY, YOU SAID HE USED TO BREAK DOWN AND CRY.
LIKE A BABY, S-BOY!
SO WHY'S WALLY SUDDENLY DOING A ONE-EIGHTY? HE NEVER CHANGES HIS MIND.
SOMETHING'S HAPPENED TO DOCTOR LIGHT.
BUT WHAT?
MAYBE IF WE ASK HIM NICELY HE'LL TELL US.
NICELY MEANING MY FIST IN HIS FACE.

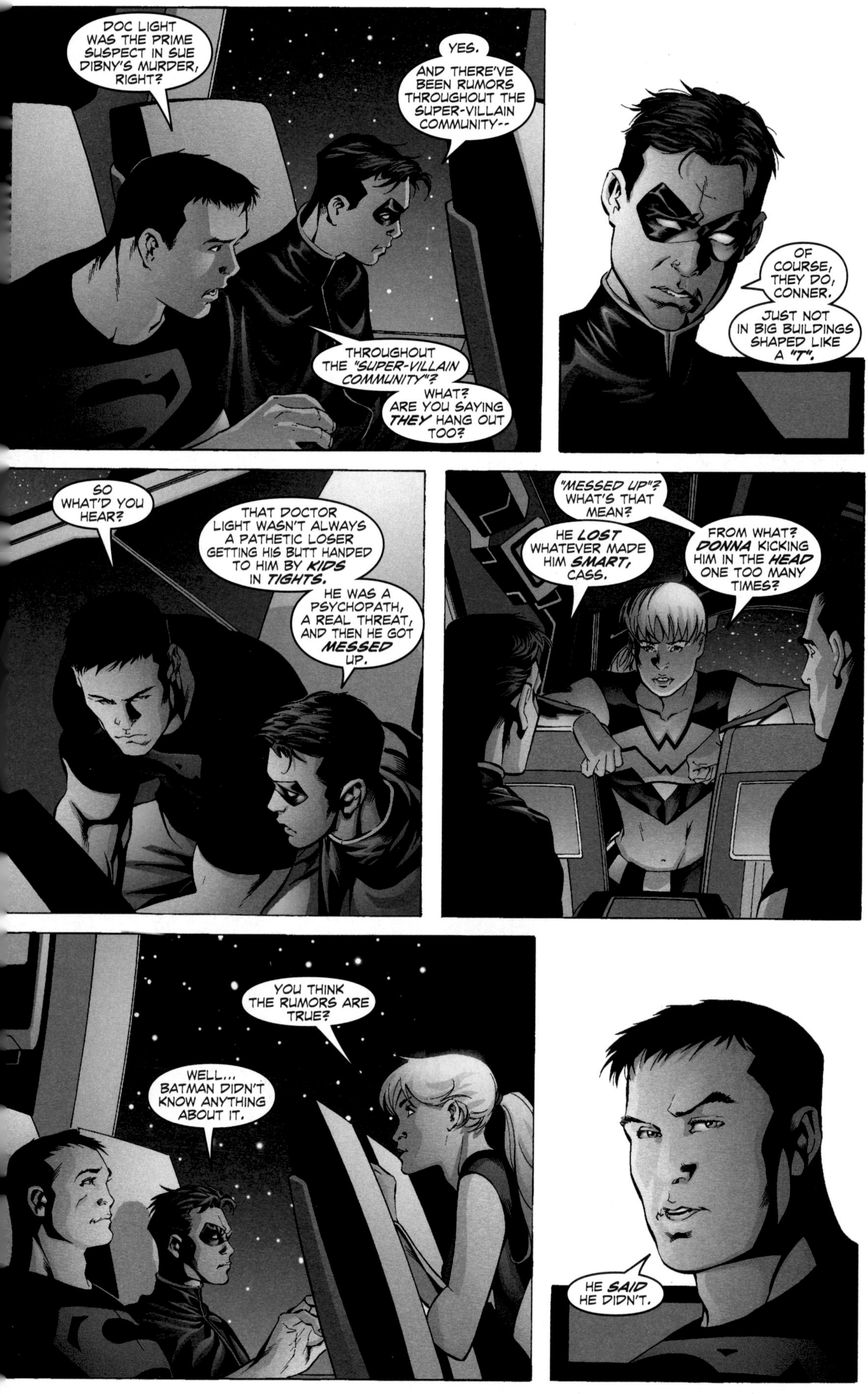
DOC LIGHT WAS THE PRIME SUSPECT IN SUE DIBNY'S MURDER, RIGHT?
YES.
AND THERE'VE BEEN RUMORS THROUGHOUT THE SUPER-VILLAIN COMMUNITY--
THROUGHOUT THE "SUPER-VILLAIN COMMUNITY"?
WHAT? ARE YOU SAYING THEY HANG OUT TOO?
OF COURSE, THEY DO, CONNER.
JUST NOT IN BIG BUILDINGS SHAPED LIKE A "T".
SO WHAT'D YOU HEAR?
THAT DOCTOR LIGHT WASN'T ALWAYS A PATHETIC LOSER GETTING HIS BUTT HANDED TO HIM BY KIDS IN TIGHTS.
HE WAS A PSYCHOPATH, A REAL THREAT, AND THEN HE GOT MESSED UP.
"MESSED UP"? WHAT'S THAT MEAN?
HE LOST WHATEVER MADE HIM SMART, CASS.
FROM WHAT? DONNA KICKING HIM IN THE HEAD ONE TOO MANY TIMES?
YOU THINK THE RUMORS ARE TRUE?
WELL... BATMAN DIDN'T KNOW ANYTHING ABOUT IT.
HE SAID HE DIDN'T.

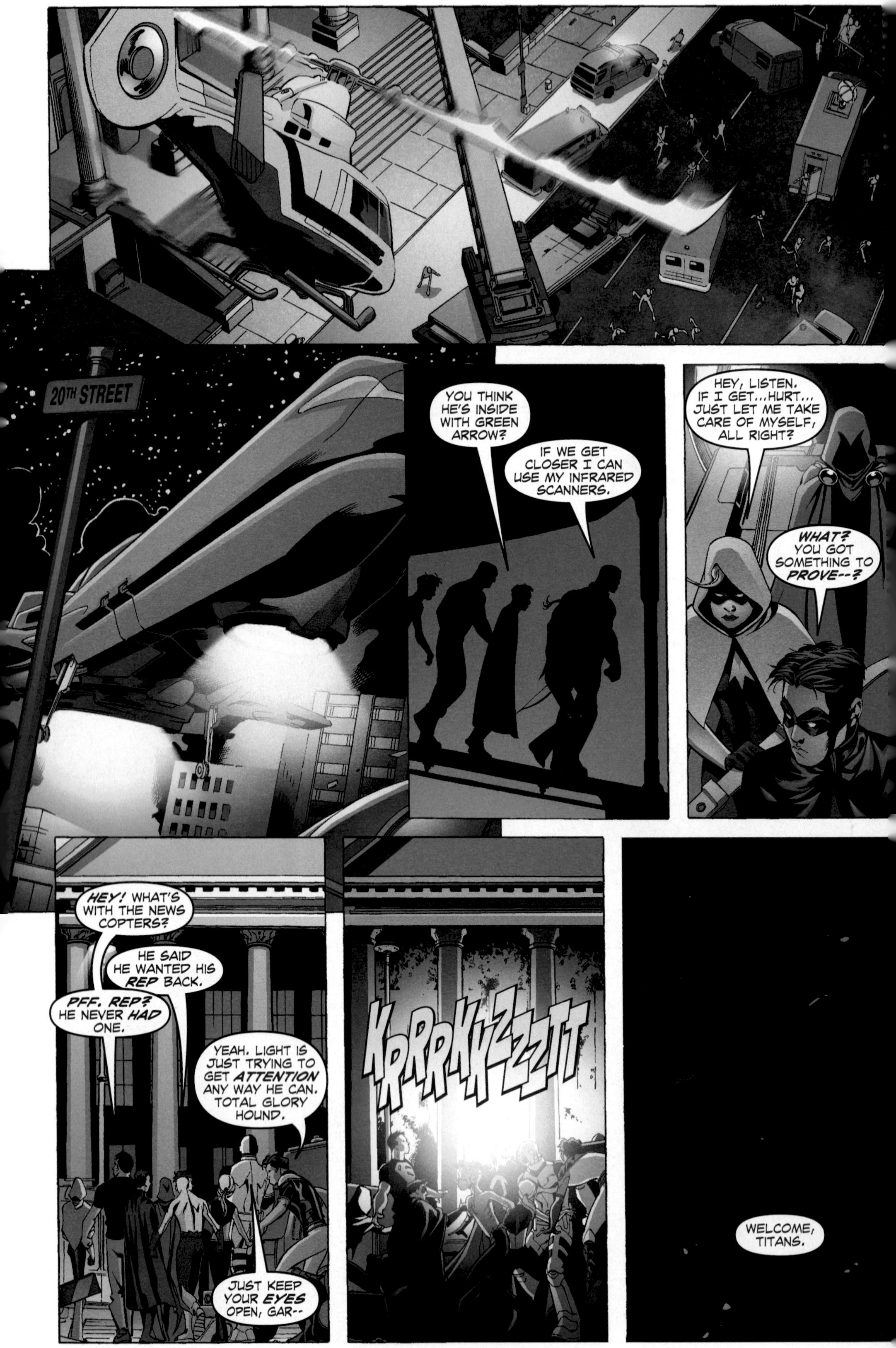
20TH STREET
YOU THINK HE'S INSIDE WITH GREEN ARROW?
IF WE GET CLOSER I CAN USE MY INFRARED SCANNERS.
HEY, LISTEN. IF I GET...HURT... JUST LET ME TAKE CARE OF MYSELF, ALL RIGHT?
WHAT? YOU GOT SOMETHING TO PROVE--?
HEY! WHAT'S WITH THE NEWS COPTERS?
HE SAID HE WANTED HIS REP BACK.
PFF. REP? HE NEVER HAD ONE.
YEAH. LIGHT IS JUST TRYING TO GET ATTENTION ANY WAY HE CAN. TOTAL GLORY HOUND.
JUST KEEP YOUR EYES OPEN, GAR--
KRRRKKZZZZTT
WELCOME, TITANS.

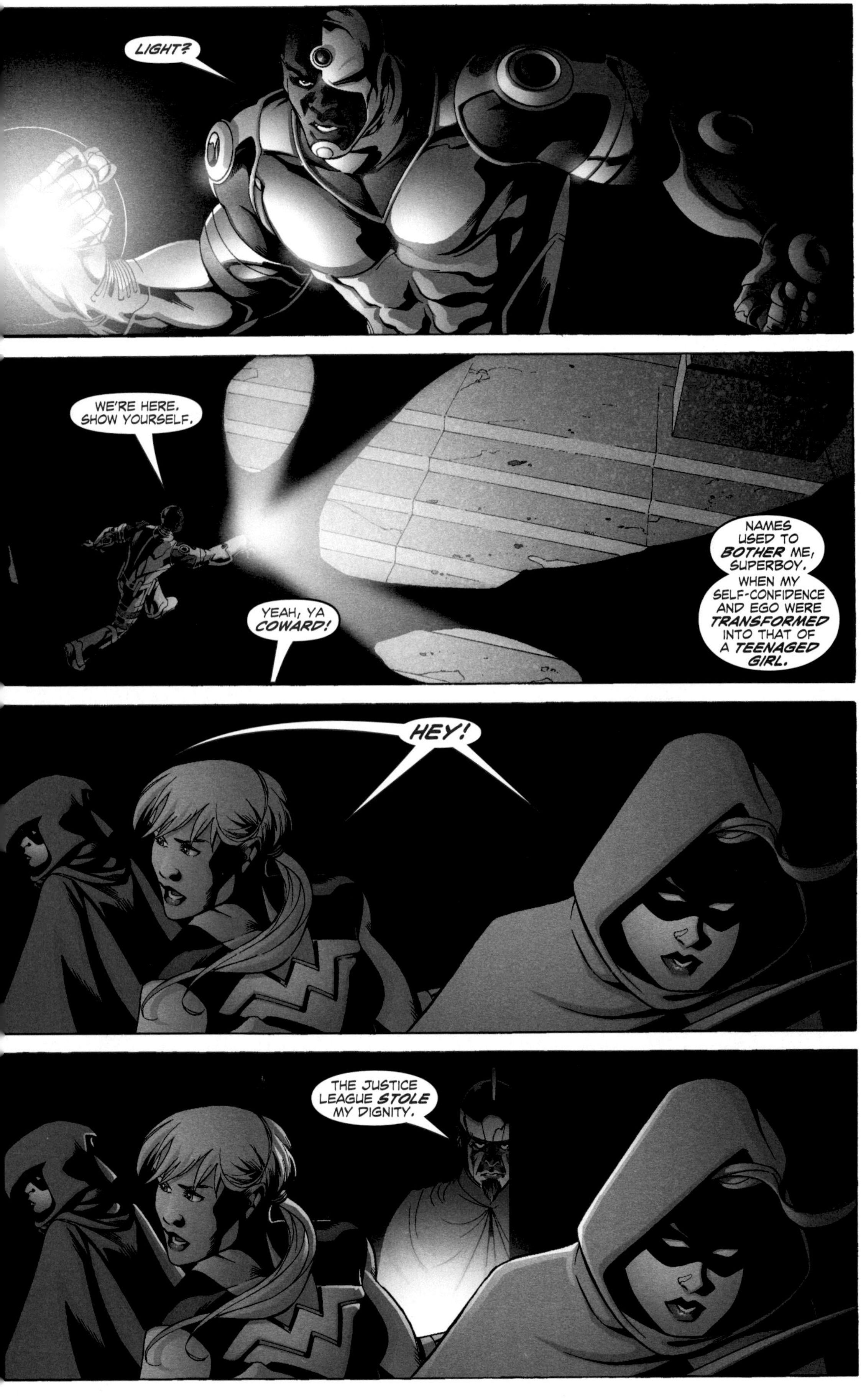
LIGHT?
WE'RE HERE. SHOW YOURSELF.
YEAH, YA COWARD!
NAMES USED TO BOTHER ME, SUPERBOY.
WHEN MY SELF-CONFIDENCE AND EGO WERE TRANSFORMED INTO THAT OF A TEENAGED GIRL.
HEY!
THE JUSTICE LEAGUE STOLE MY DIGNITY.

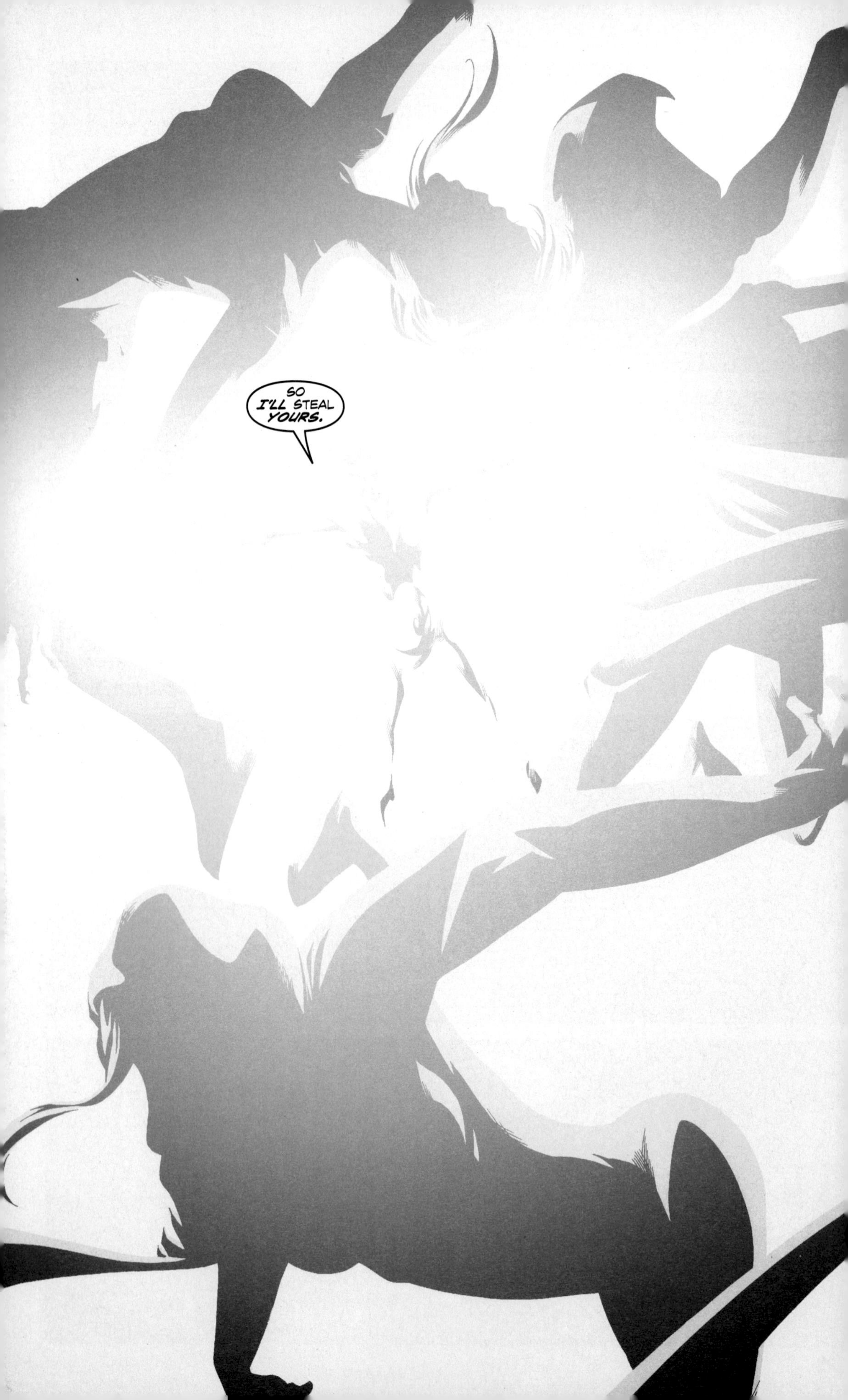
SO I'LL STEAL YOURS.

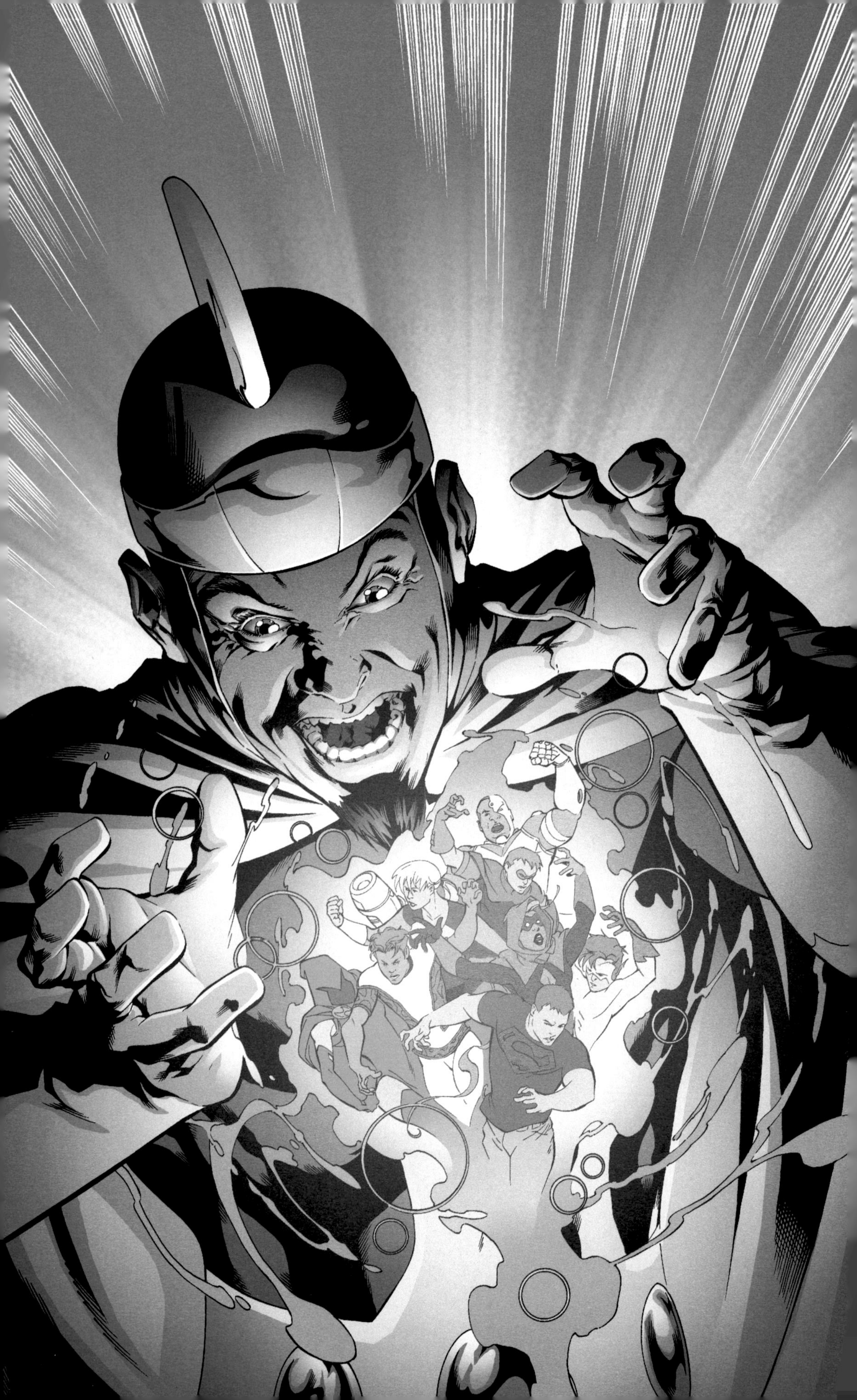

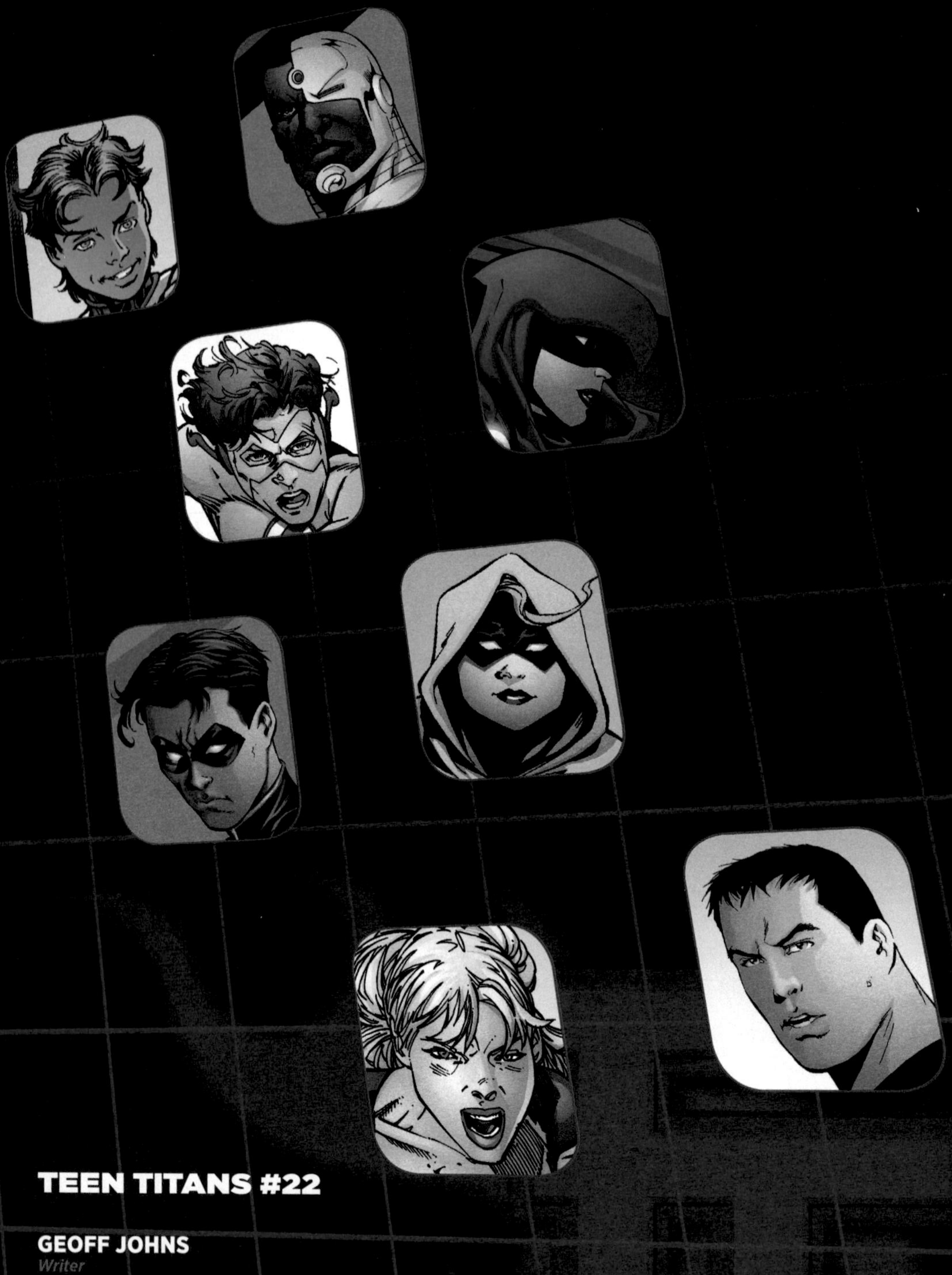

TEEN TITANS #22

GEOFF JOHNS
Writer

MIKE McKONE
Penciller

MARLO ALQUIZA
Inker

JEROMY COX
Colorist

COMICRAFT
Letterer

MIKE McKONE, MARLO ALQUIZA & JEROMY COX
Cover Artists

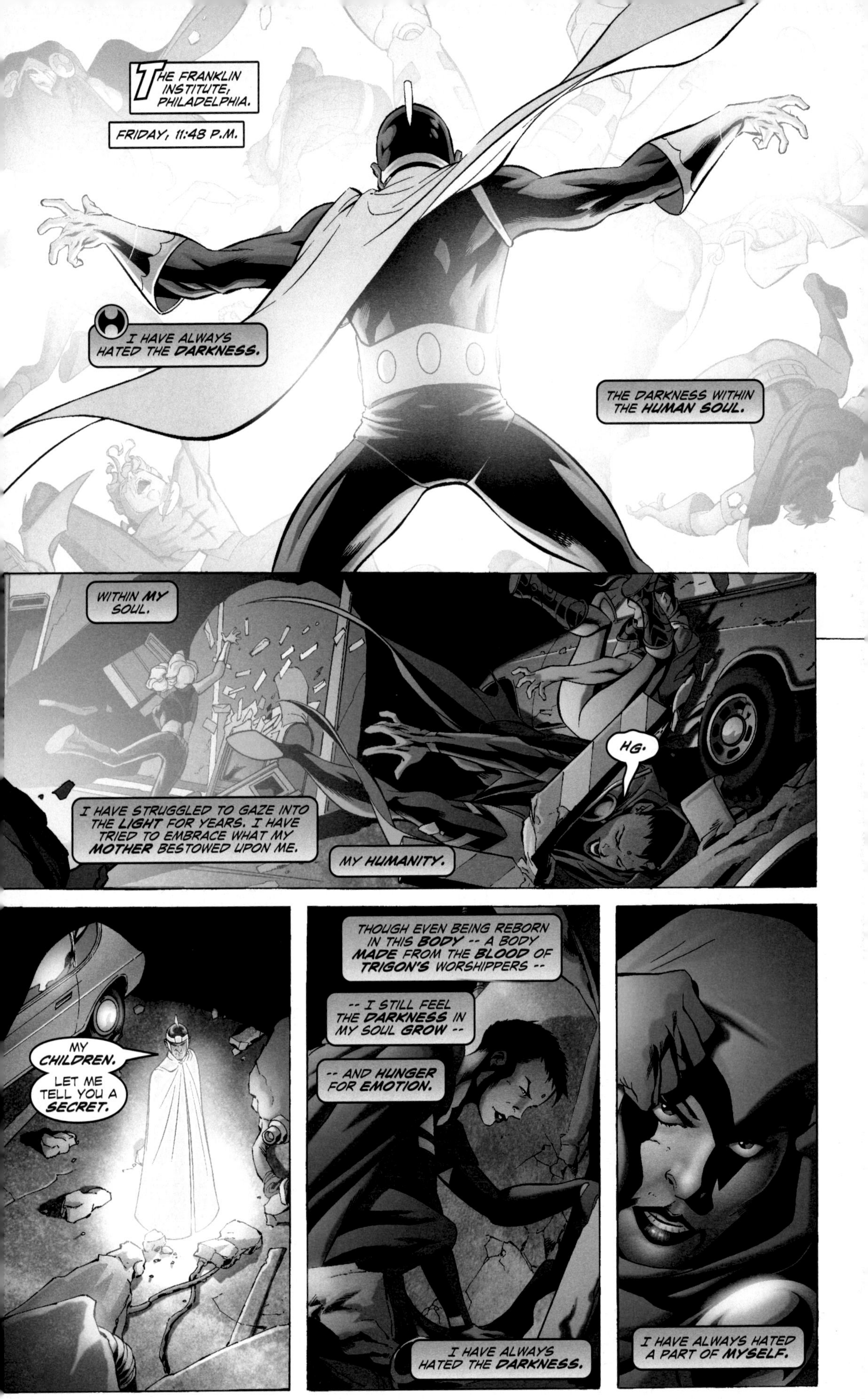
THE FRANKLIN INSTITUTE, PHILADELPHIA.
FRIDAY, 11:48 P.M.
I HAVE ALWAYS HATED THE DARKNESS.
THE DARKNESS WITHIN THE HUMAN SOUL.
WITHIN MY SOUL.
HG.
I HAVE STRUGGLED TO GAZE INTO THE LIGHT FOR YEARS. I HAVE TRIED TO EMBRACE WHAT MY MOTHER BESTOWED UPON ME.
MY HUMANITY.
MY CHILDREN.
LET ME TELL YOU A SECRET.
THOUGH EVEN BEING REBORN IN THIS BODY -- A BODY MADE FROM THE BLOOD OF TRIGON'S WORSHIPPERS --
-- I STILL FEEL THE DARKNESS IN MY SOUL GROW --
-- AND HUNGER FOR EMOTION.
I HAVE ALWAYS HATED THE DARKNESS.
I HAVE ALWAYS HATED A PART OF MYSELF.

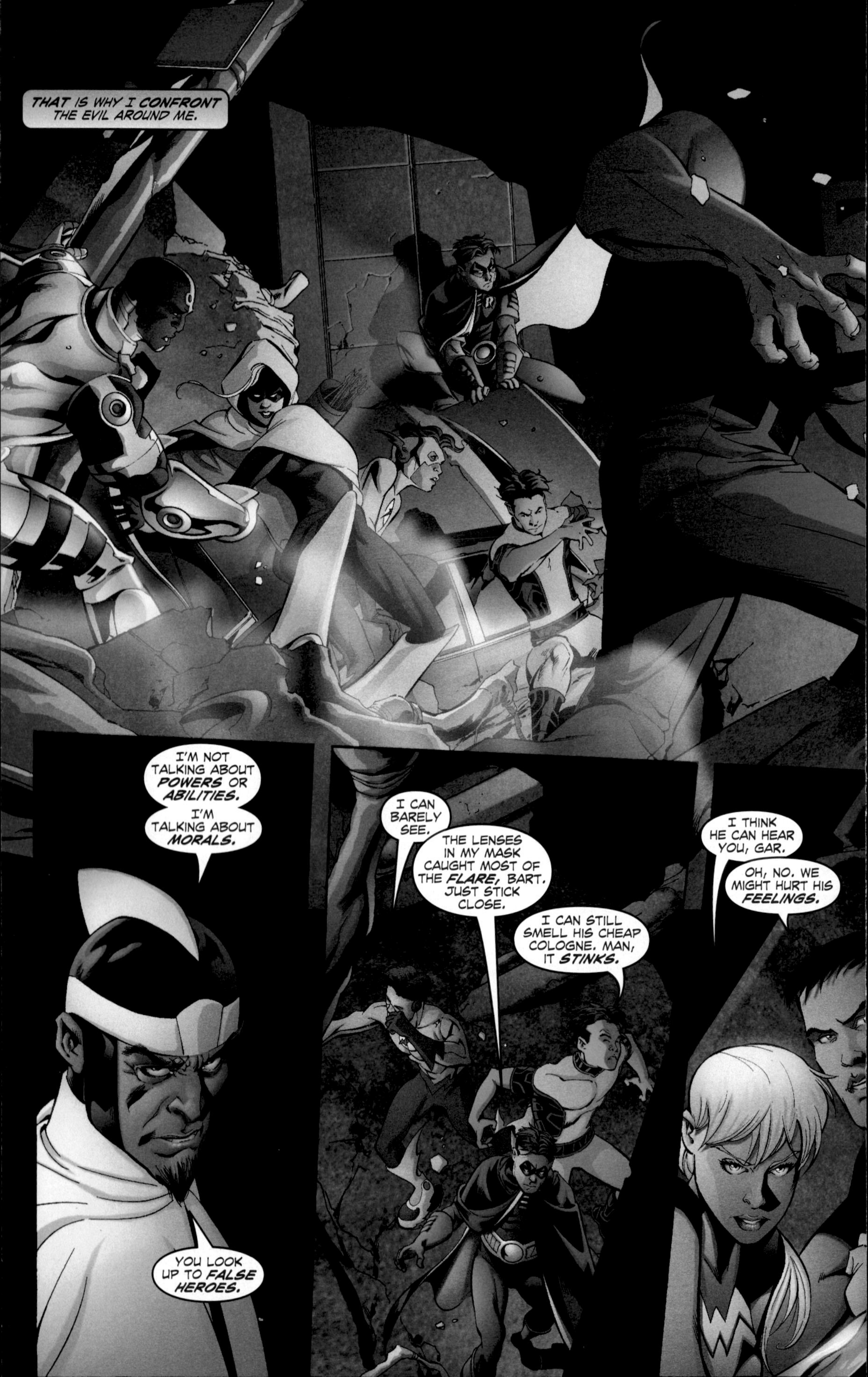
THAT IS WHY I CONFRONT THE EVIL AROUND ME.
I'M NOT TALKING ABOUT POWERS OR ABILITIES.
I'M TALKING ABOUT MORALS.
YOU LOOK UP TO FALSE HEROES.
I CAN BARELY SEE.
THE LENSES IN MY MASK CAUGHT MOST OF THE FLARE, BART. JUST STICK CLOSE.
I CAN STILL SMELL HIS CHEAP COLOGNE. MAN, IT STINKS.
I THINK HE CAN HEAR YOU, GAR.
OH, NO. WE MIGHT HURT HIS FEELINGS.

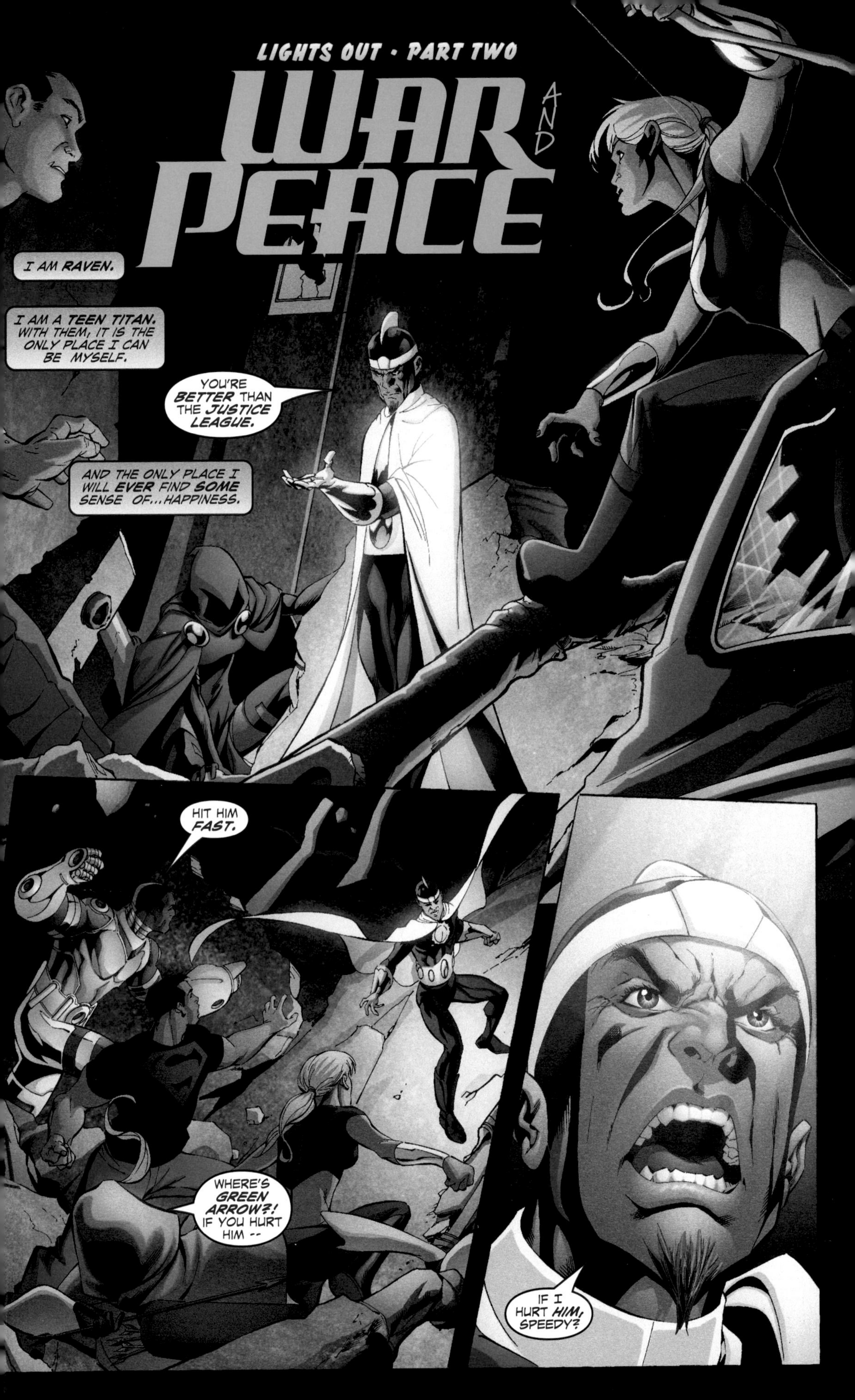

LIGHTS OUT · PART TWO
WAR AND PEACE
I AM RAVEN.
I AM A TEEN TITAN. WITH THEM, IT IS THE ONLY PLACE I CAN BE MYSELF.
YOU'RE BETTER THAN THE JUSTICE LEAGUE.
AND THE ONLY PLACE I WILL EVER FIND SOME SENSE OF...HAPPINESS.
HIT HIM FAST.
WHERE'S GREEN ARROW?! IF YOU HURT HIM --
IF I HURT HIM, SPEEDY?

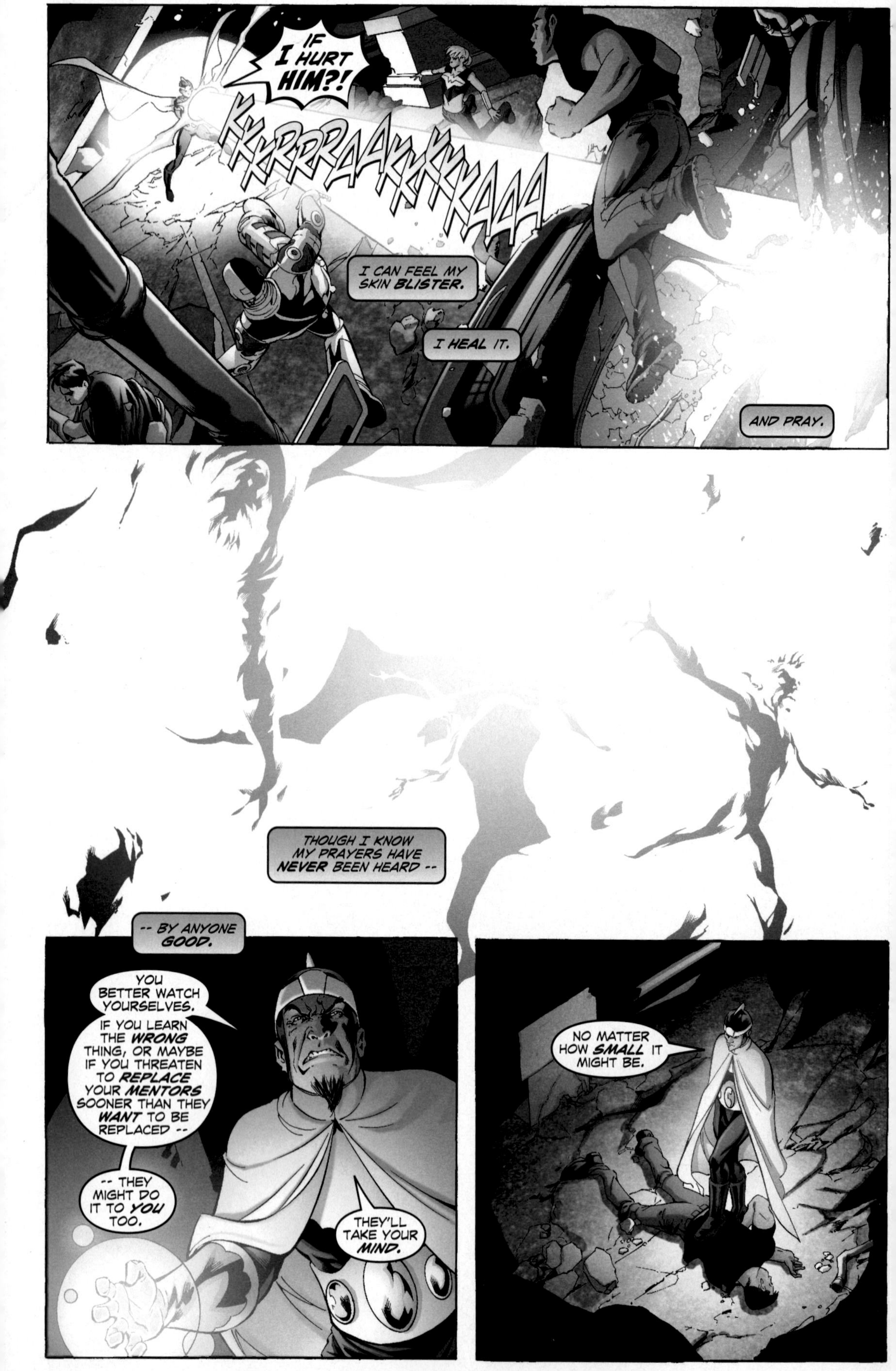
IF I HURT HIM?!
KKKRRRAAKKKKKAAAA
I CAN FEEL MY SKIN BLISTER.
I HEAL IT.
AND PRAY.
THOUGH I KNOW MY PRAYERS HAVE NEVER BEEN HEARD --
-- BY ANYONE GOOD.
YOU BETTER WATCH YOURSELVES.
IF YOU LEARN THE WRONG THING, OR MAYBE IF YOU THREATEN TO REPLACE YOUR MENTORS SOONER THAN THEY WANT TO BE REPLACED --
-- THEY MIGHT DO IT TO YOU TOO.
THEY'LL TAKE YOUR MIND.
NO MATTER HOW SMALL IT MIGHT BE.

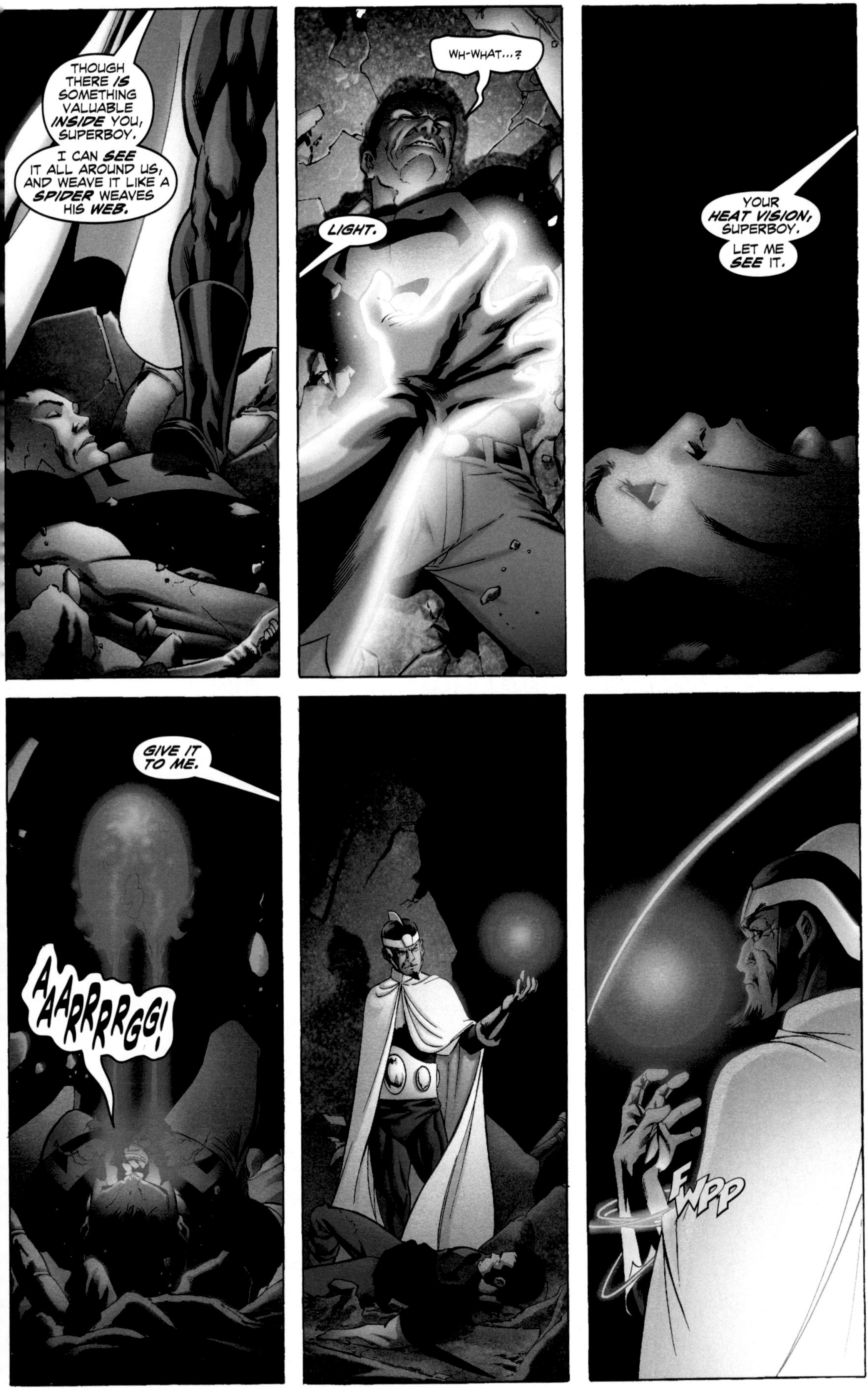

THOUGH THERE *IS* SOMETHING VALUABLE *INSIDE* YOU, SUPERBOY.
I CAN *SEE* IT ALL AROUND US, AND WEAVE IT LIKE A *SPIDER* WEAVES HIS *WEB*.
WH-WHAT...?
LIGHT.
YOUR *HEAT VISION*, SUPERBOY.
LET ME *SEE* IT.
GIVE IT TO ME.
AAARRRRGG!
FWPP

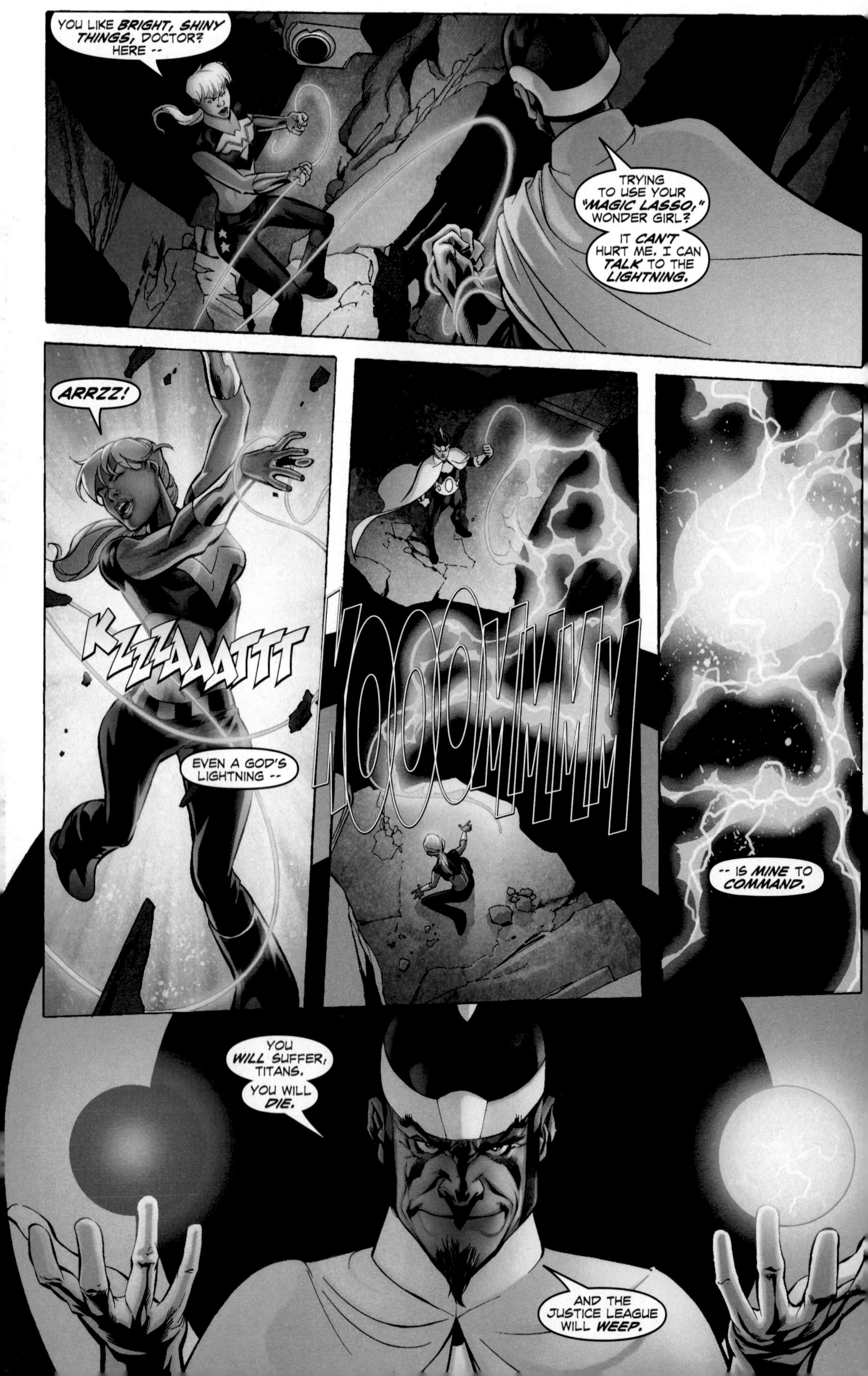
YOU LIKE BRIGHT, SHINY THINGS, DOCTOR? HERE --
TRYING TO USE YOUR "MAGIC LASSO," WONDER GIRL?
IT CAN'T HURT ME. I CAN TALK TO THE LIGHTNING.
ARRZZ!
KZZZAAATTT
EVEN A GOD'S LIGHTNING --
-- IS MINE TO COMMAND.
YOU WILL SUFFER, TITANS.
YOU WILL DIE.
AND THE JUSTICE LEAGUE WILL WEEP.

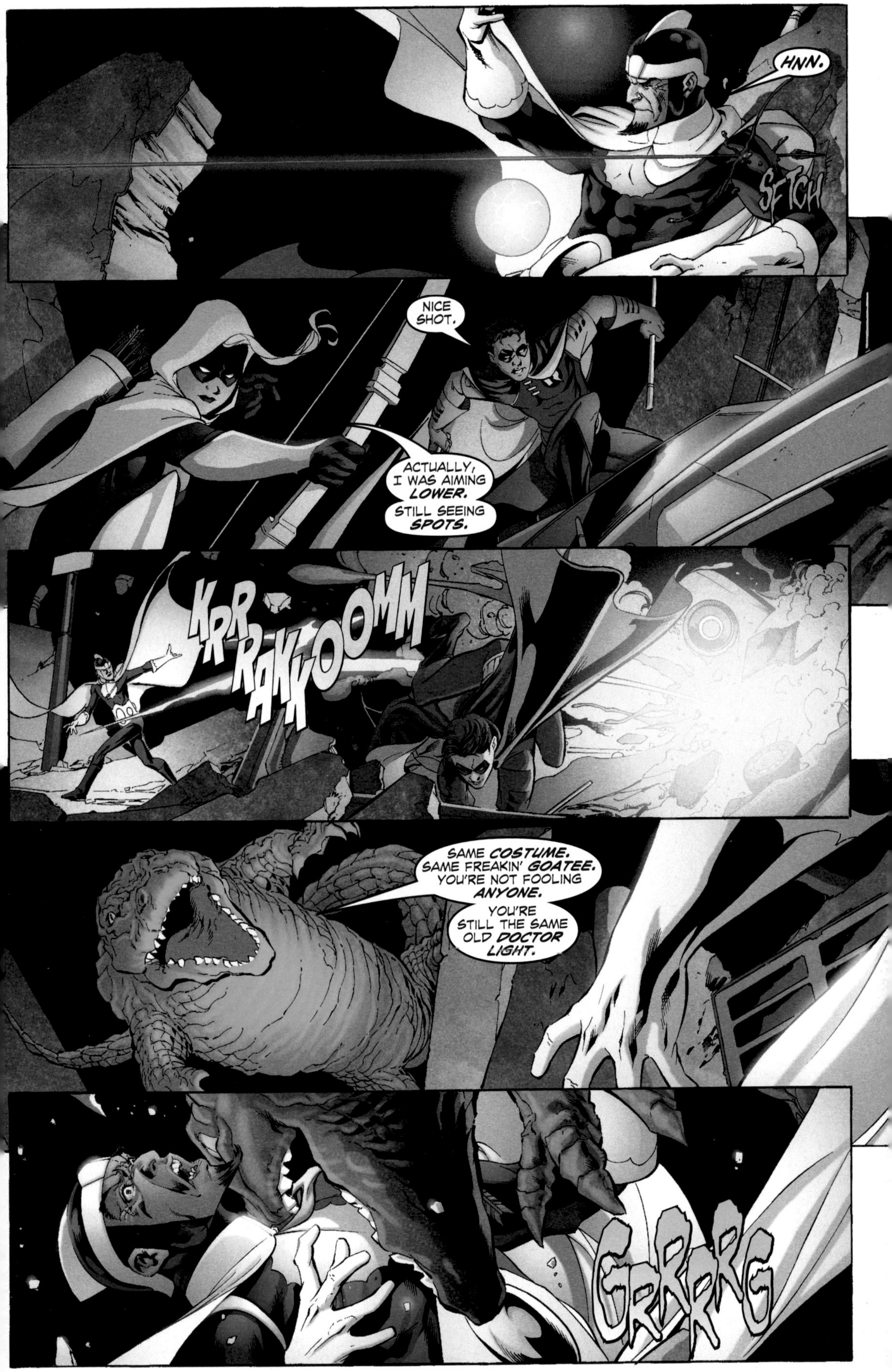
HNN.
SFTCH
NICE SHOT.
ACTUALLY, I WAS AIMING LOWER.
STILL SEEING SPOTS.
KRRRAKKOOMM
SAME COSTUME. SAME FREAKIN' GOATEE. YOU'RE NOT FOOLING ANYONE.
YOU'RE STILL THE SAME OLD DOCTOR LIGHT.
GRRRRG

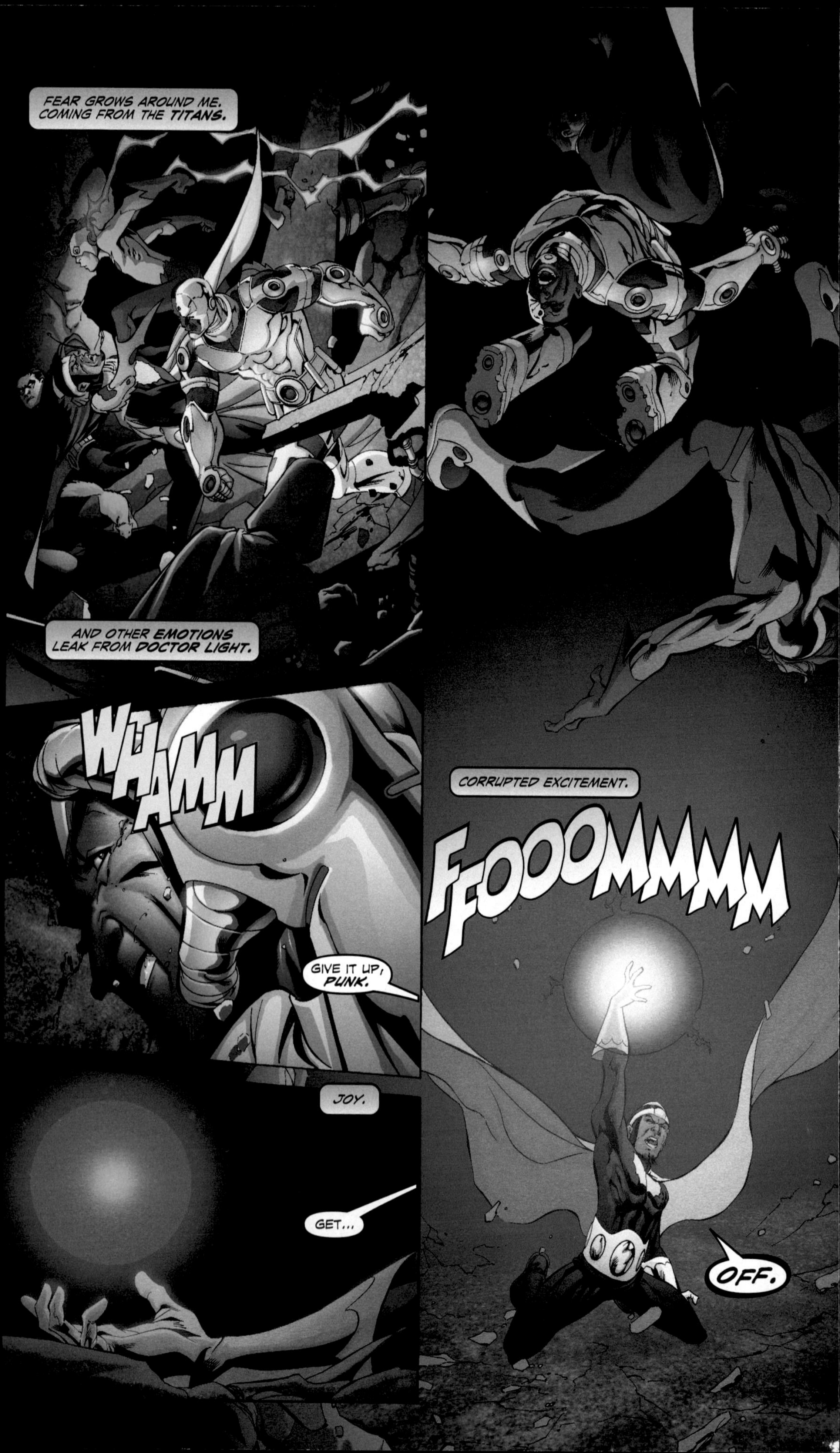
FEAR GROWS AROUND ME. COMING FROM THE TITANS.
AND OTHER EMOTIONS LEAK FROM DOCTOR LIGHT.
WHAMM
GIVE IT UP, PUNK.
JOY.
GET...
CORRUPTED EXCITEMENT.
FFOOOMMMMM
OFF.

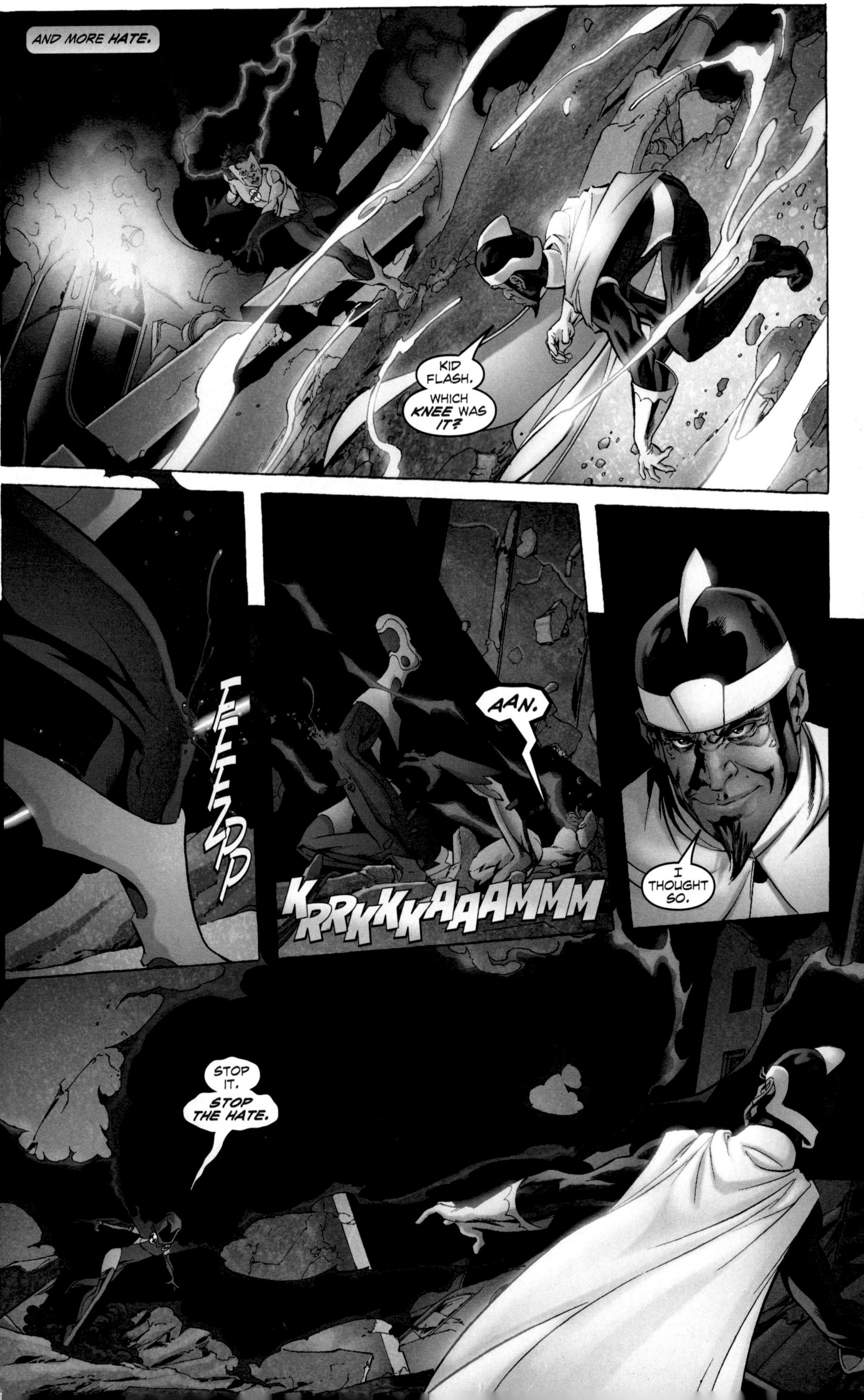
AND MORE HATE.
KID FLASH. WHICH KNEE WAS IT?
FZZZZPP
AAN.
KRRKKKAAAAMMMM
I THOUGHT SO.
STOP IT. STOP THE HATE.

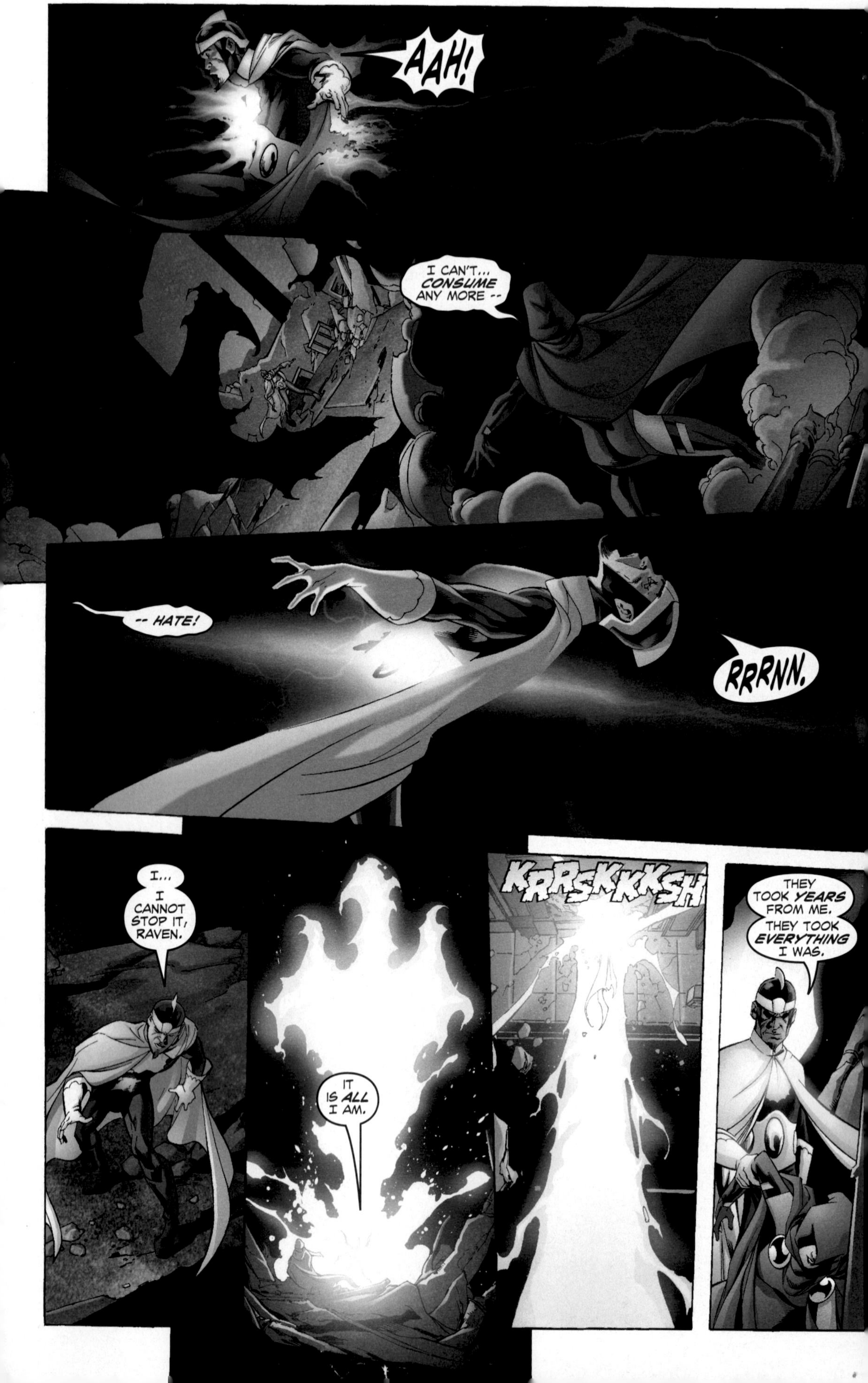
AAH!
I CAN'T... CONSUME ANY MORE --
-- HATE!
RRRNN.
I... I CANNOT STOP IT, RAVEN.
IT IS ALL I AM.
KRRSKKKSH
THEY TOOK YEARS FROM ME. THEY TOOK EVERYTHING I WAS.

SO TASTE IT. TASTE MY HATRED.

IT'S AS BRIGHT AS DAY.

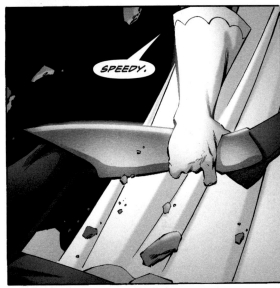

SPEEDY.

COME.

-- FIGHTING SEEMS TO HAVE STOPPED FOR THE MOMENT, THE DEVASTATION NOW COVERING OVER A CITY BLOCK. THE SMOKE IS OBSCURING THE VIEW BUT WHAT WE DO KNOW IS THAT SOMEHOW...

DOCTOR LIGHT IS STILL STANDING.

OFFICIALS CONTINUE TO EXTEND THE EVACUATION ANOTHER SIX SQUARE BLOCKS, BUT WITH THE POWER STILL OUT AND NIGHT FALLING, THERE HAVE BEEN REPORTS OF RIOTING AND UNREST --

WPHL - LIVE

STARFIRE'S PLAN IS ALREADY IN MOTION.

AND DOCTOR LIGHT?

WHEN THIS IS FINISHED...

SHNNGG

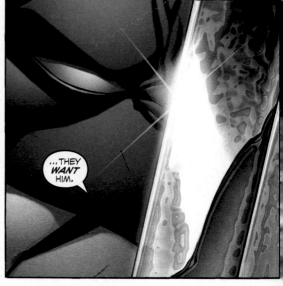

...THEY WANT HIM.

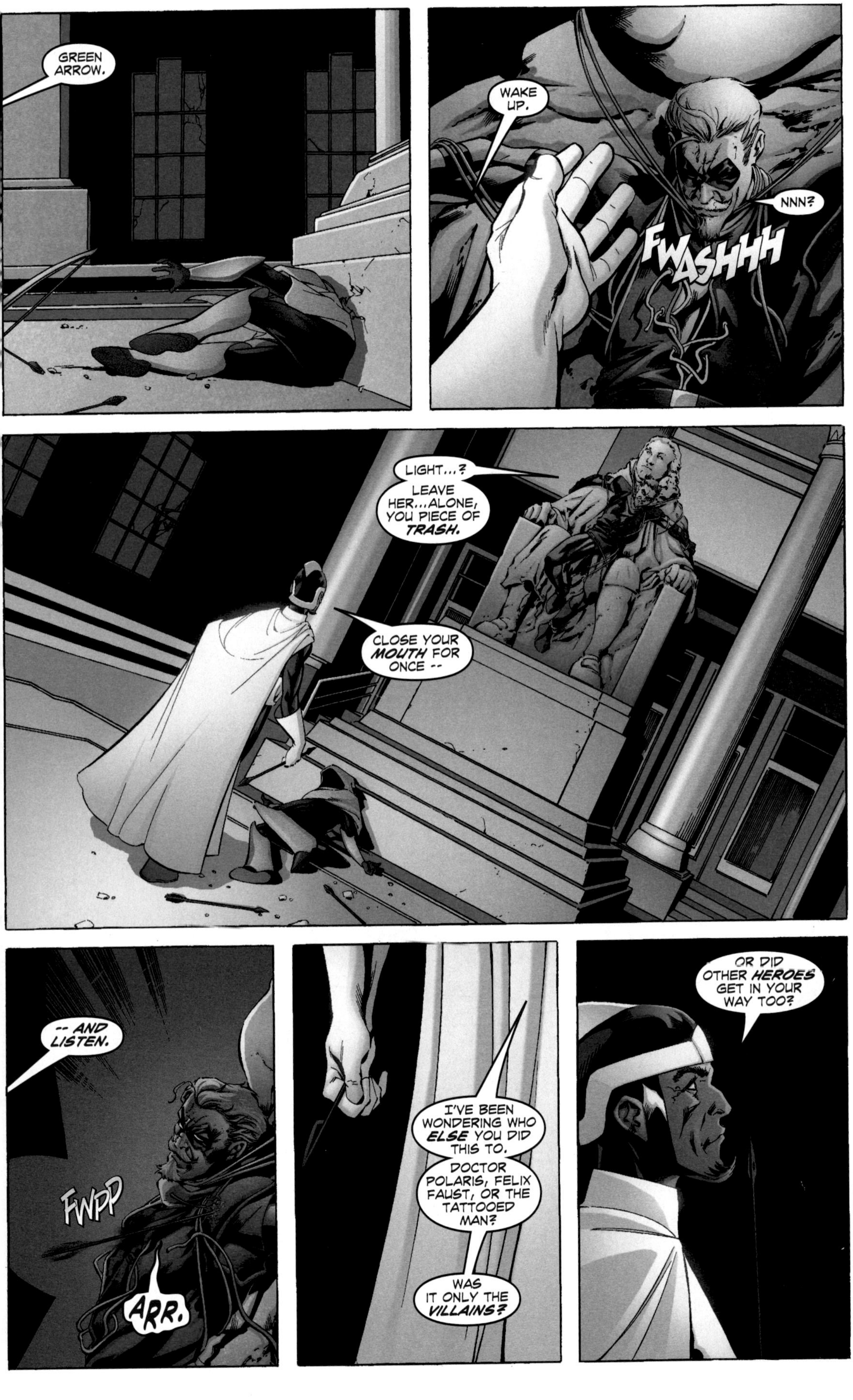
GREEN ARROW.
WAKE UP.
NNN?
FWASHHH
LIGHT...?
LEAVE HER...ALONE, YOU PIECE OF TRASH.
CLOSE YOUR MOUTH FOR ONCE --
-- AND LISTEN.
FWPP
ARR.
I'VE BEEN WONDERING WHO ELSE YOU DID THIS TO.
DOCTOR POLARIS, FELIX FAUST, OR THE TATTOOED MAN?
WAS IT ONLY THE VILLAINS?
OR DID OTHER HEROES GET IN YOUR WAY TOO?

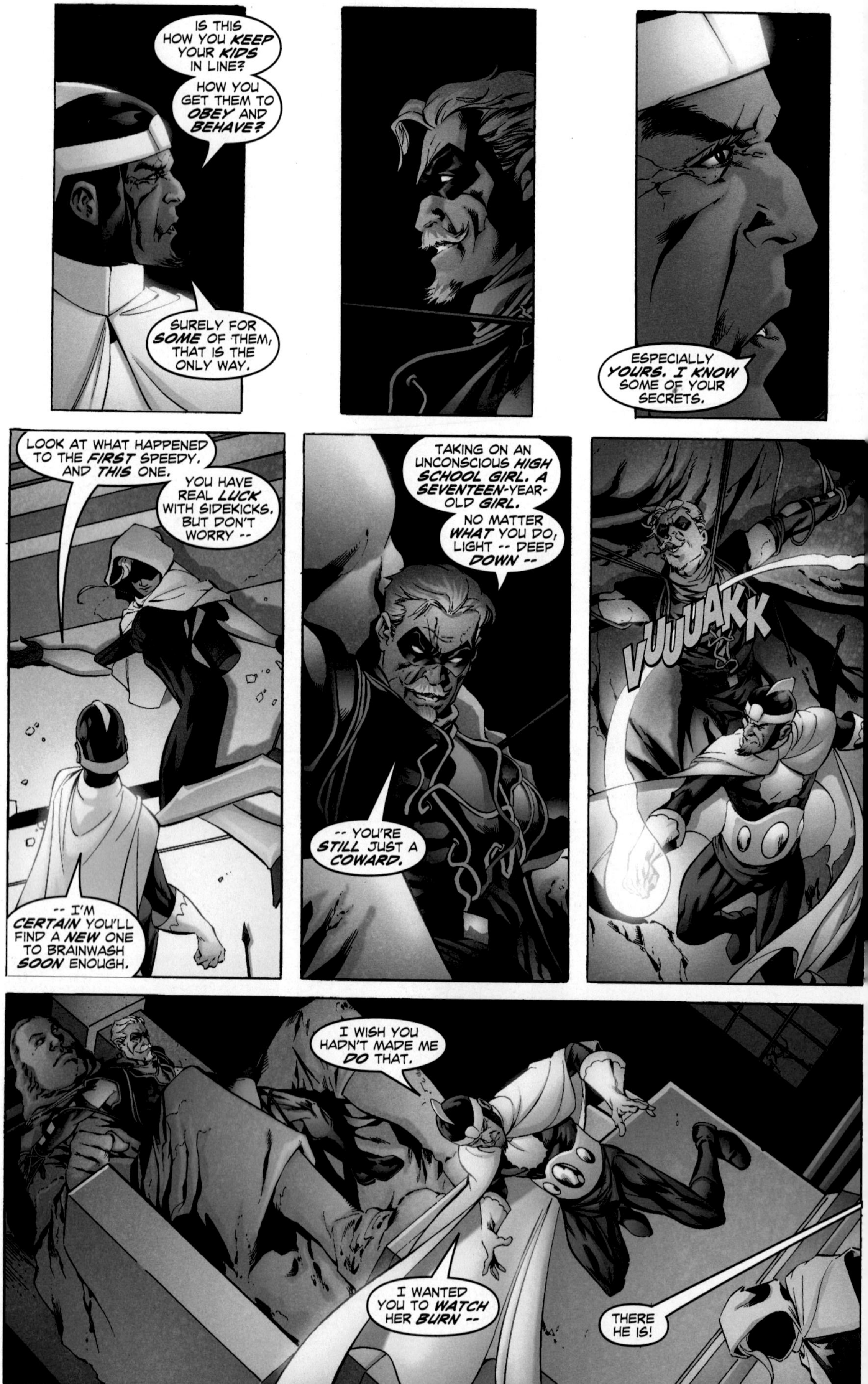
IS THIS HOW YOU KEEP YOUR KIDS IN LINE?
HOW YOU GET THEM TO OBEY AND BEHAVE?
SURELY FOR SOME OF THEM, THAT IS THE ONLY WAY.
ESPECIALLY YOURS. I KNOW SOME OF YOUR SECRETS.
LOOK AT WHAT HAPPENED TO THE FIRST SPEEDY. AND THIS ONE.
YOU HAVE REAL LUCK WITH SIDEKICKS. BUT DON'T WORRY --
-- I'M CERTAIN YOU'LL FIND A NEW ONE TO BRAINWASH SOON ENOUGH.
TAKING ON AN UNCONSCIOUS HIGH SCHOOL GIRL. A SEVENTEEN-YEAR-OLD GIRL.
NO MATTER WHAT YOU DO, LIGHT -- DEEP DOWN --
-- YOU'RE STILL JUST A COWARD.
VUUUAKK
I WISH YOU HADN'T MADE ME DO THAT.
I WANTED YOU TO WATCH HER BURN --
THERE HE IS!

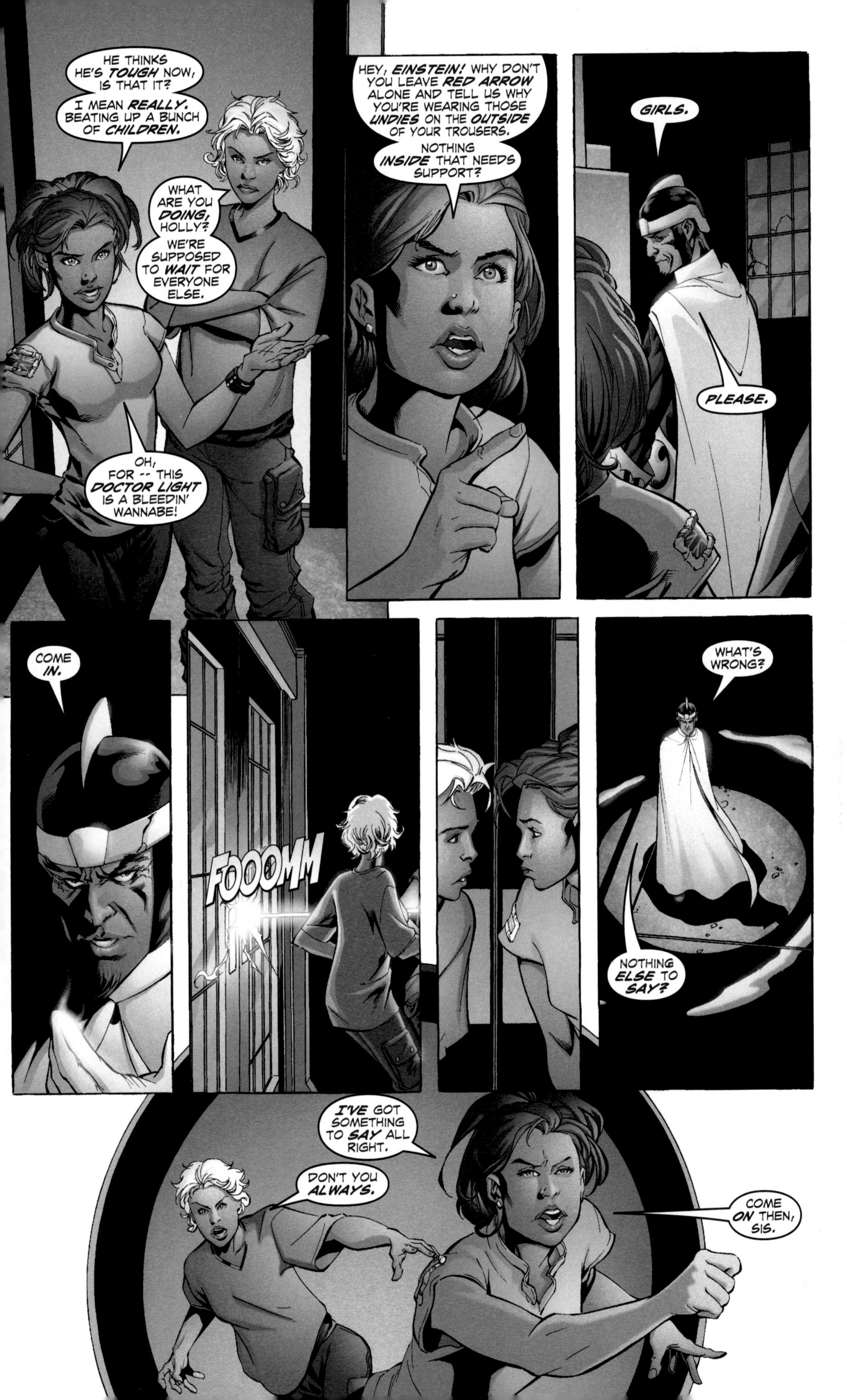
HE THINKS HE'S TOUGH NOW, IS THAT IT?
I MEAN REALLY. BEATING UP A BUNCH OF CHILDREN.
WHAT ARE YOU DOING, HOLLY?
WE'RE SUPPOSED TO WAIT FOR EVERYONE ELSE.
OH, FOR -- THIS DOCTOR LIGHT IS A BLEEDIN' WANNABE!
HEY, EINSTEIN! WHY DON'T YOU LEAVE RED ARROW ALONE AND TELL US WHY YOU'RE WEARING THOSE UNDIES ON THE OUTSIDE OF YOUR TROUSERS.
NOTHING INSIDE THAT NEEDS SUPPORT?
GIRLS.
PLEASE.
COME IN.
FOOOMM
WHAT'S WRONG?
NOTHING ELSE TO SAY?
I'VE GOT SOMETHING TO SAY ALL RIGHT.
DON'T YOU ALWAYS.
COME ON THEN, SIS.

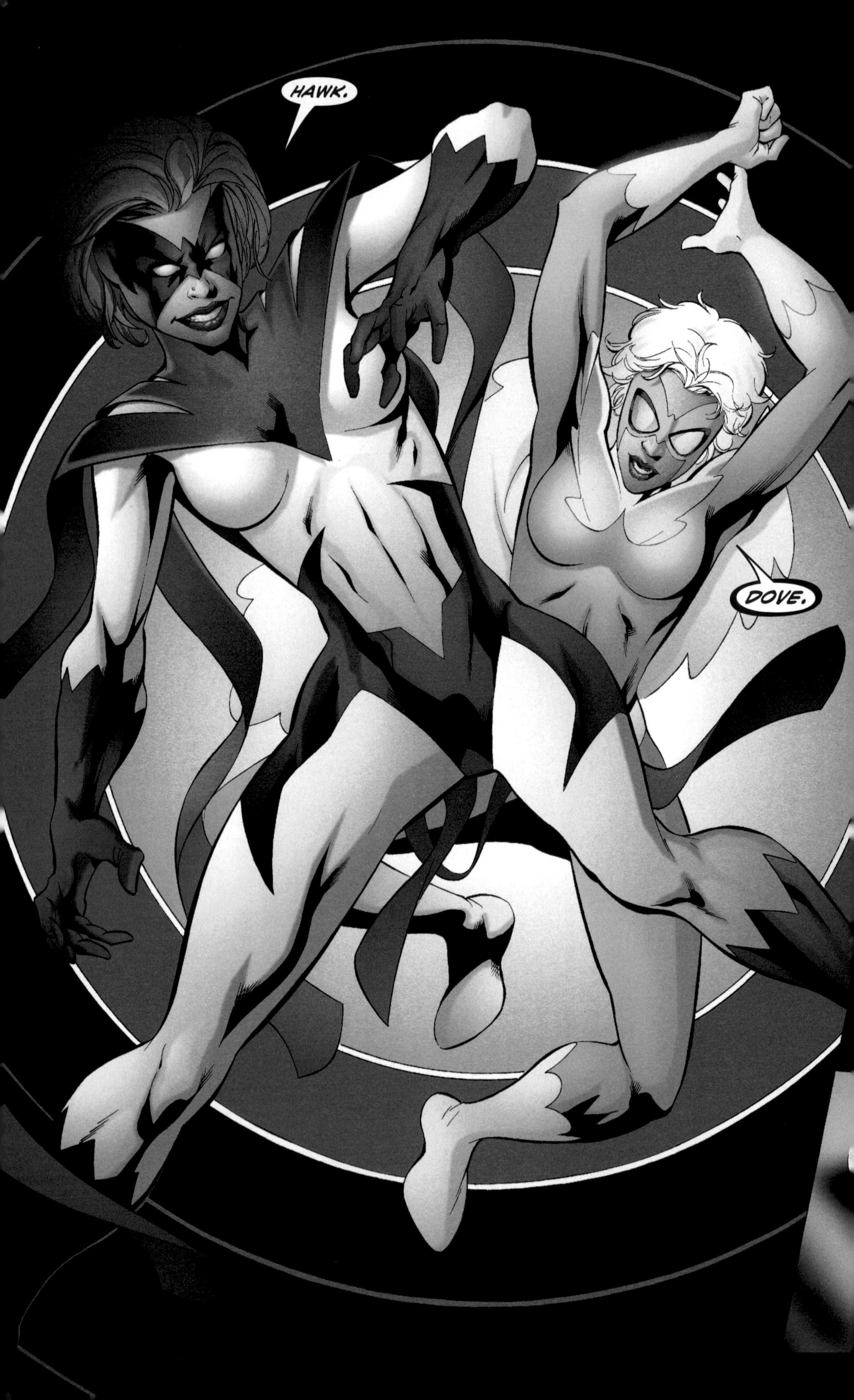
HAWK.
DOVE.

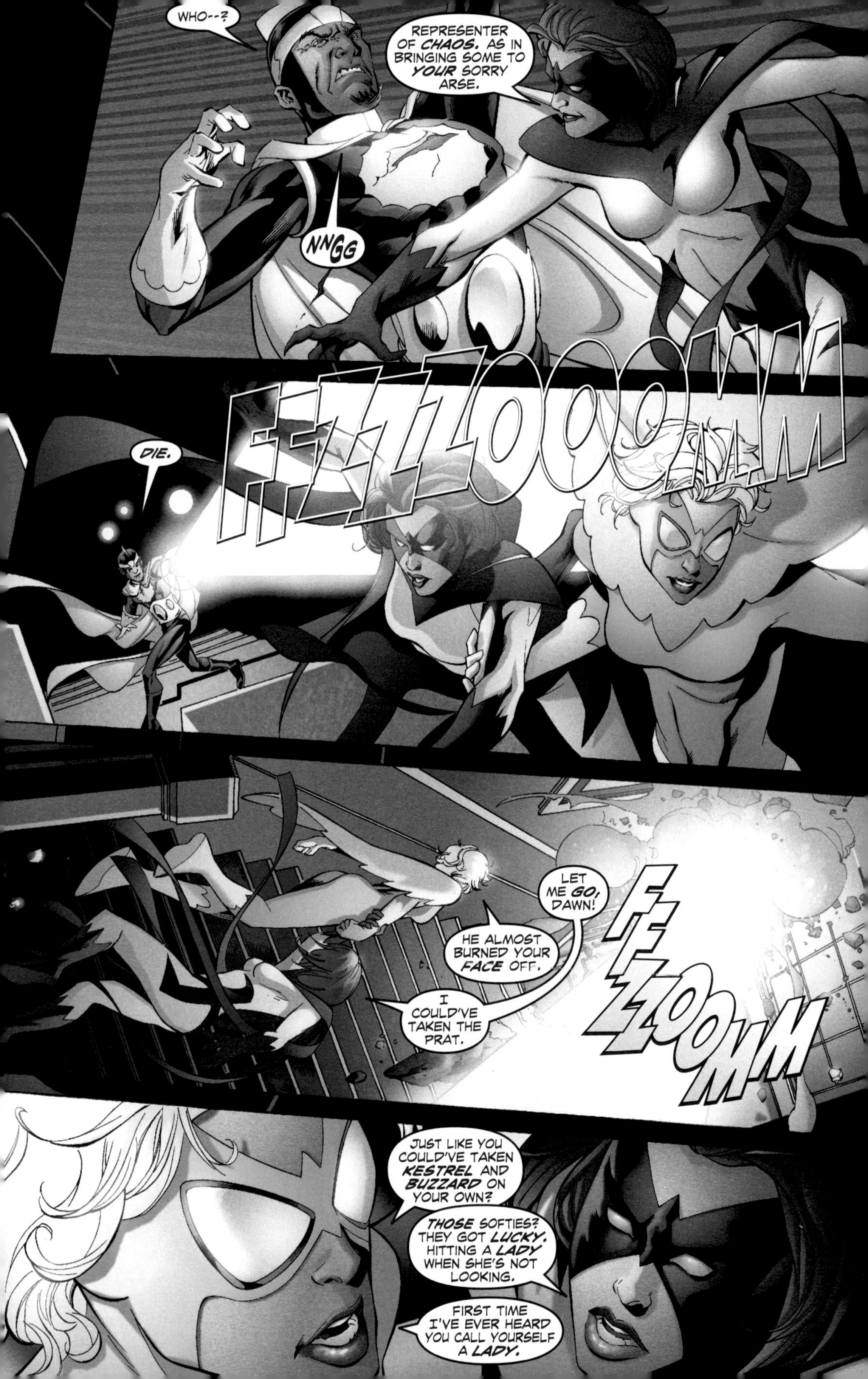
WHO--?
REPRESENTER OF CHAOS. AS IN BRINGING SOME TO YOUR SORRY ARSE.
NNGG
DIE.
FFZZZLOOOOMM
LET ME GO, DAWN!
HE ALMOST BURNED YOUR FACE OFF.
I COULD'VE TAKEN THE PRAT.
FFZZOOMM
JUST LIKE YOU COULD'VE TAKEN KESTREL AND BUZZARD ON YOUR OWN?
THOSE SOFTIES? THEY GOT LUCKY. HITTING A LADY WHEN SHE'S NOT LOOKING.
FIRST TIME I'VE EVER HEARD YOU CALL YOURSELF A LADY.

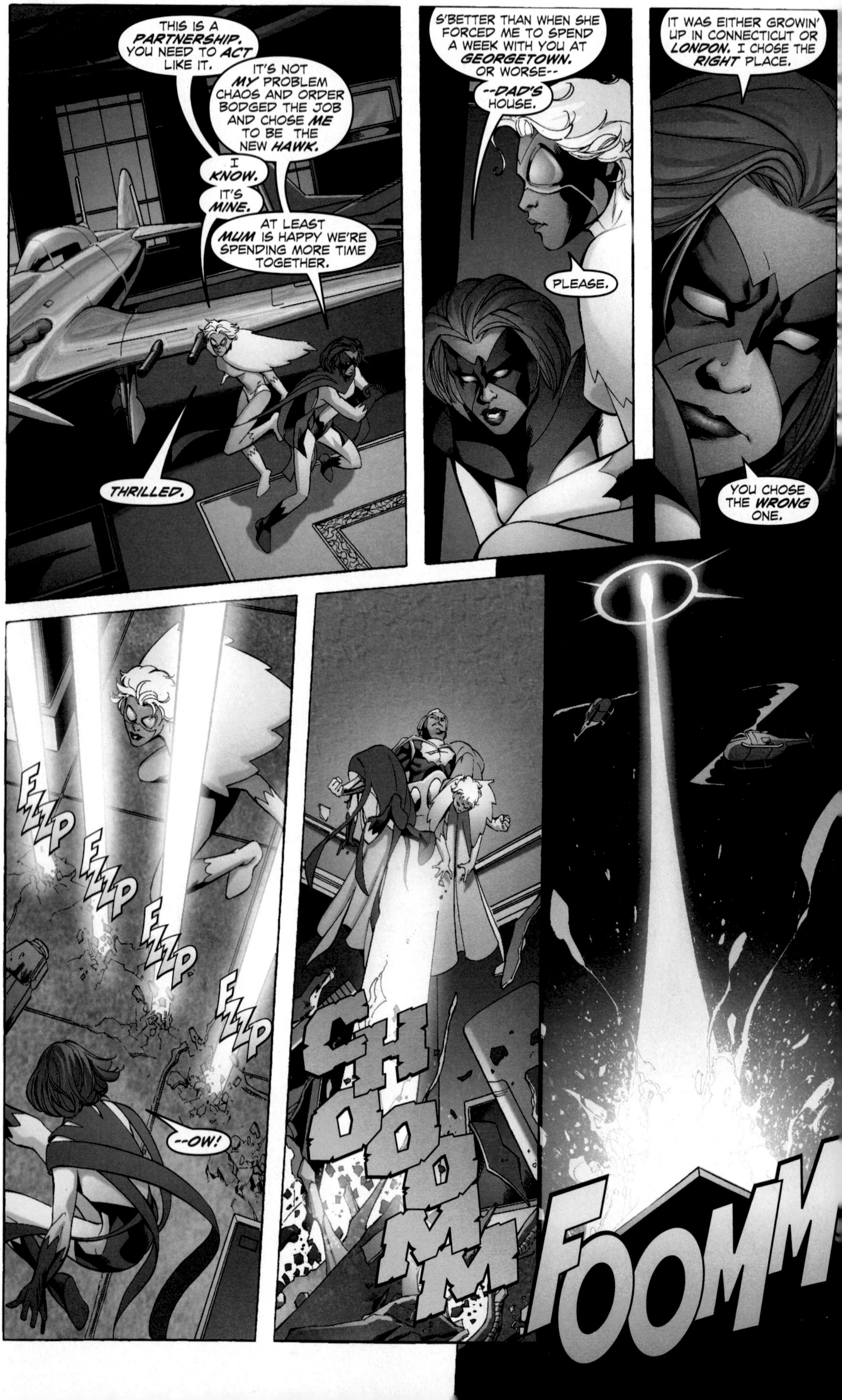

THIS IS A PARTNERSHIP. YOU NEED TO ACT LIKE IT.
IT'S NOT MY PROBLEM CHAOS AND ORDER BODGED THE JOB AND CHOSE ME TO BE THE NEW HAWK.
I KNOW.
IT'S MINE.
AT LEAST MUM IS HAPPY WE'RE SPENDING MORE TIME TOGETHER.
THRILLED.
S'BETTER THAN WHEN SHE FORCED ME TO SPEND A WEEK WITH YOU AT GEORGETOWN. OR WORSE--
--DAD'S HOUSE.
PLEASE.
IT WAS EITHER GROWIN' UP IN CONNECTICUT OR LONDON. I CHOSE THE RIGHT PLACE.
YOU CHOSE THE WRONG ONE.
FZZP
FZZP
FZZP
FZZP
--OW!
CHOOOMM
FOOMM

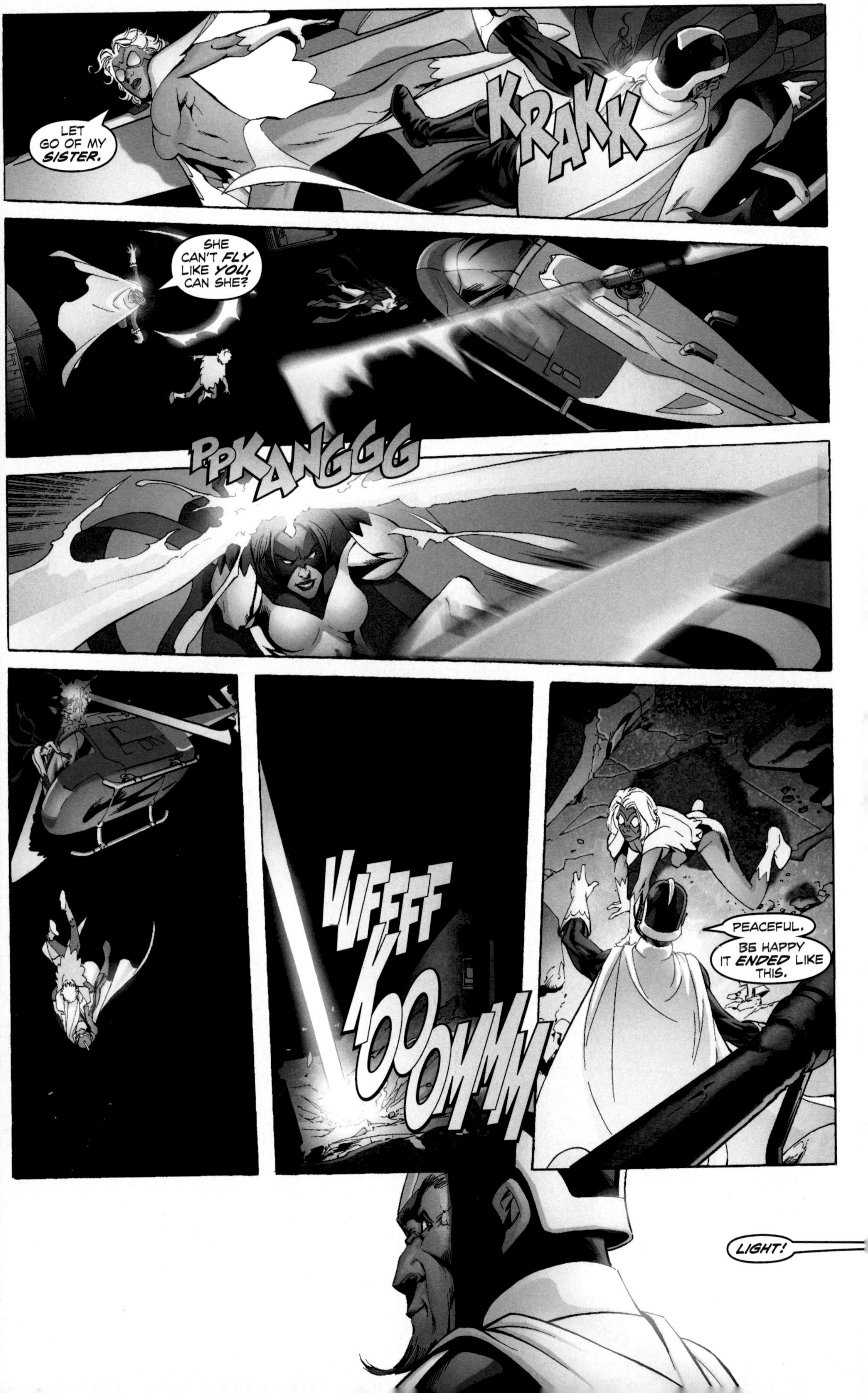
LET GO OF MY SISTER.
KRAKK
SHE CAN'T FLY LIKE YOU, CAN SHE?
PPKANGGG
VUFFFF
KOOOMMM
PEACEFUL. BE HAPPY IT ENDED LIKE THIS.
LIGHT!

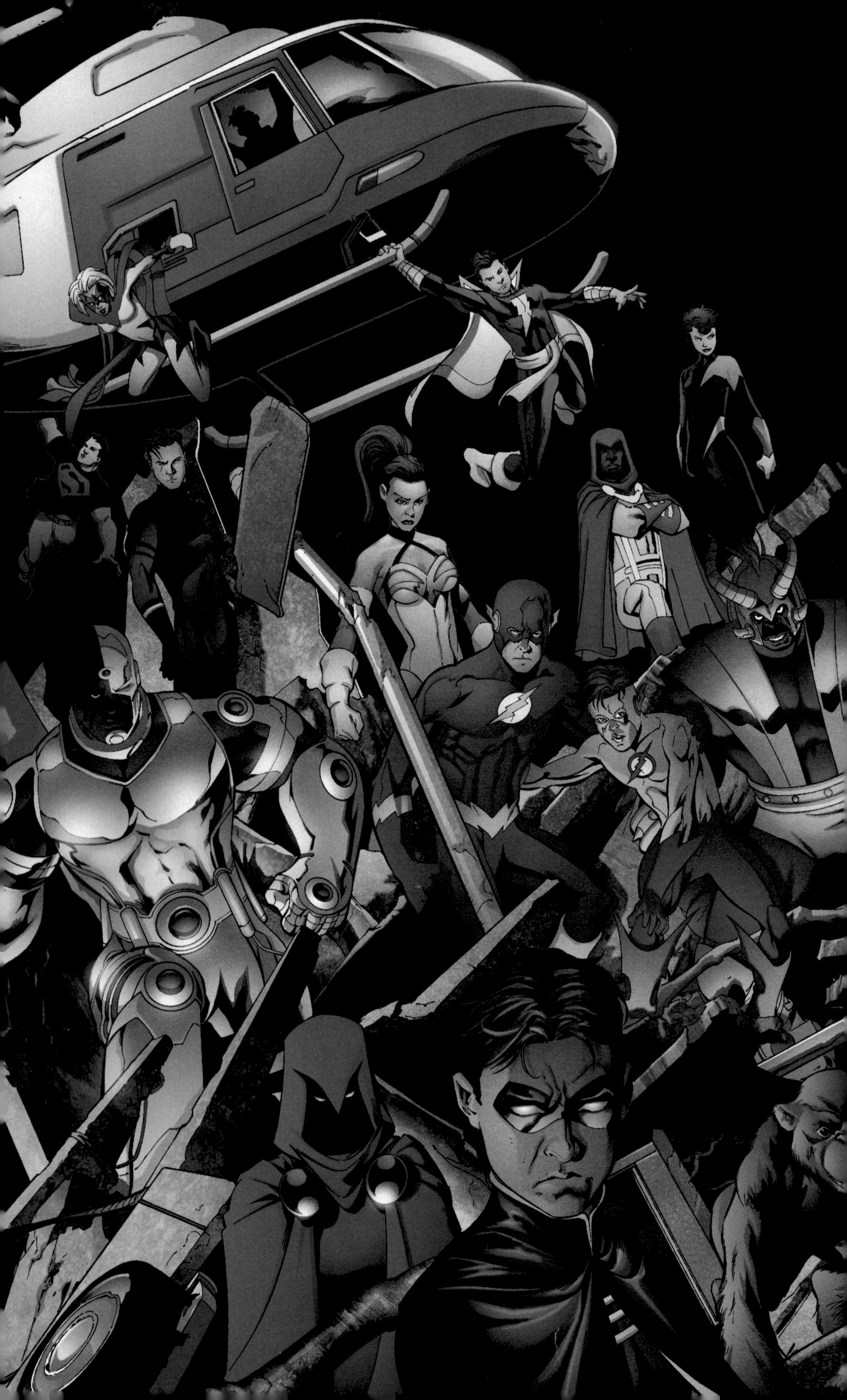

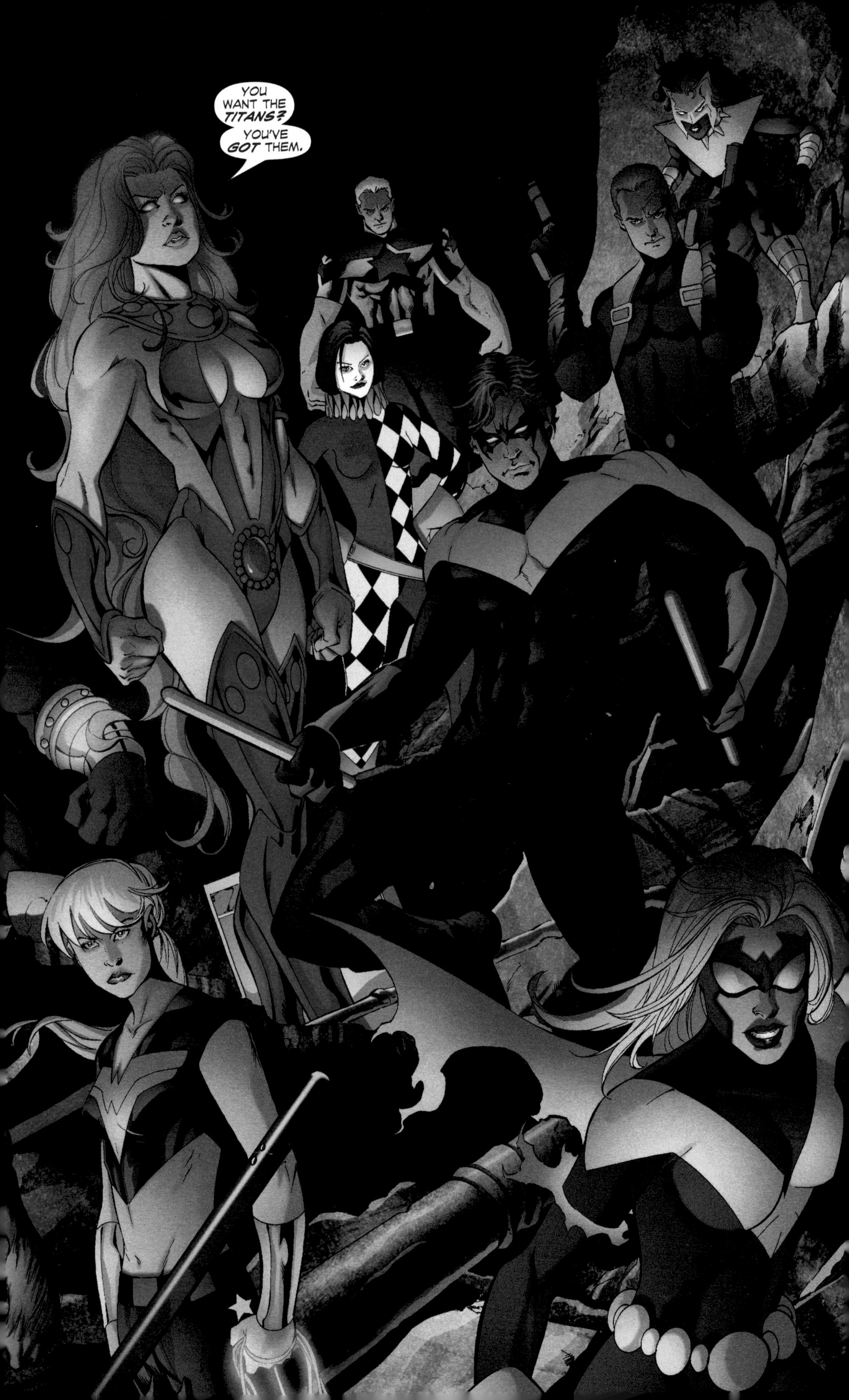
YOU WANT THE *TITANS?* YOU'VE *GOT* THEM.

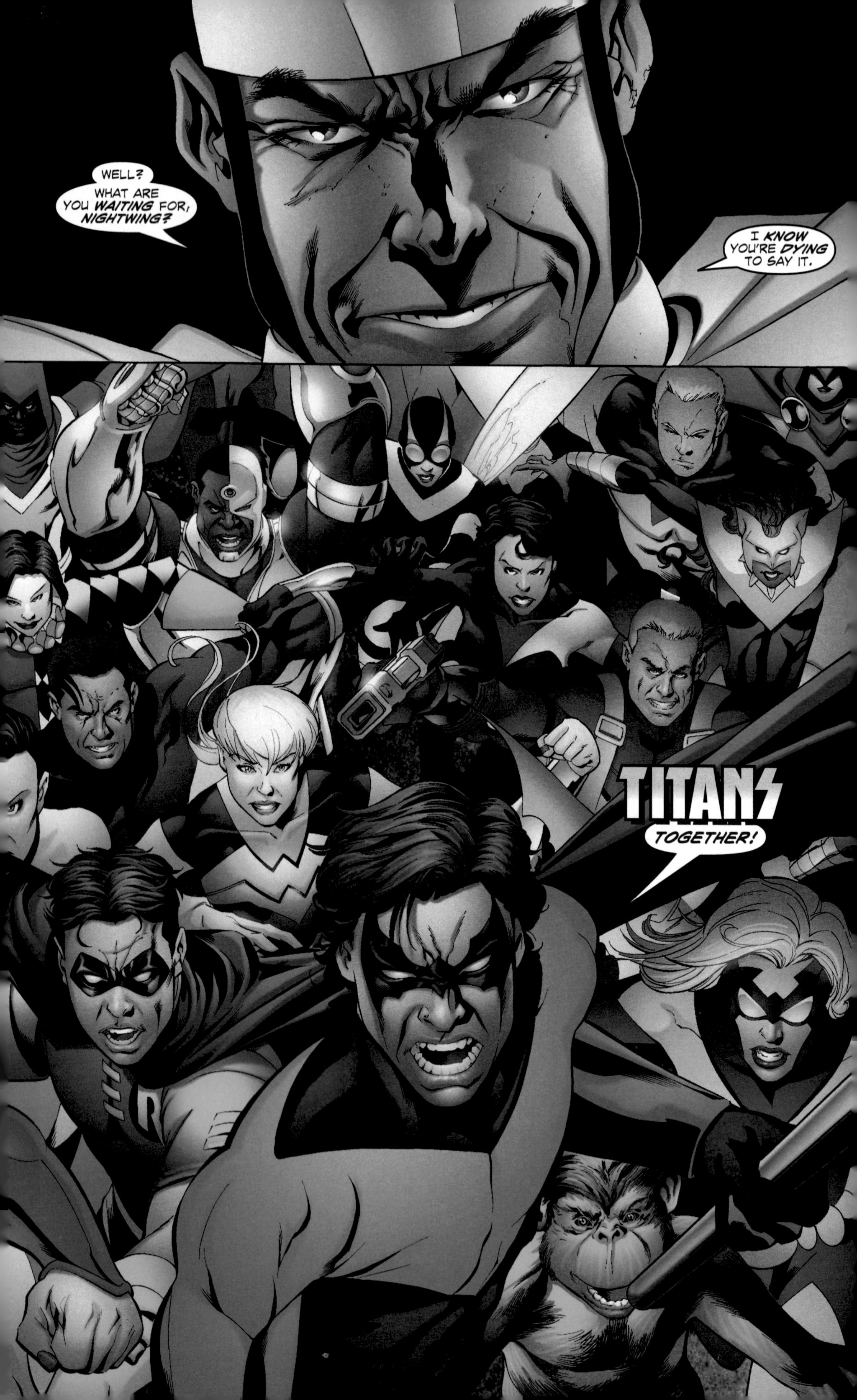
WELL? WHAT ARE YOU WAITING FOR, NIGHTWING?
I KNOW YOU'RE DYING TO SAY IT.
TITANS TOGETHER!

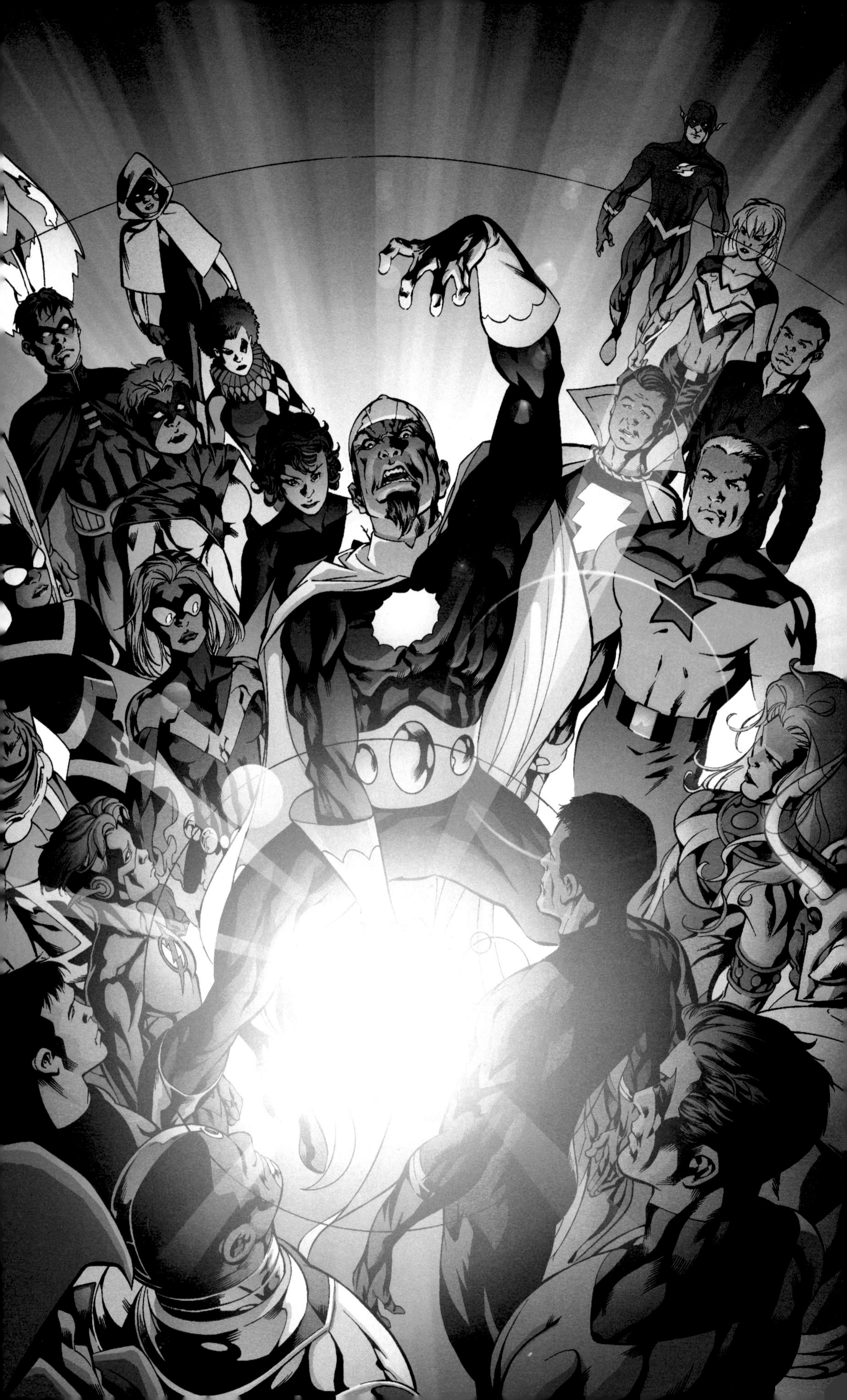

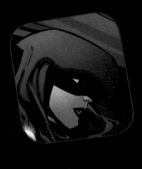

TEEN TITANS #23

GEOFF JOHNS
Writer

MIKE McKONE
Penciller

MARLO ALQUIZA
Inker

JEROMY COX
Colorist

COMICRAFT
Letterer

**MIKE McKONE,
MARLO ALQUIZA & JEROMY COX**
Cover Artists

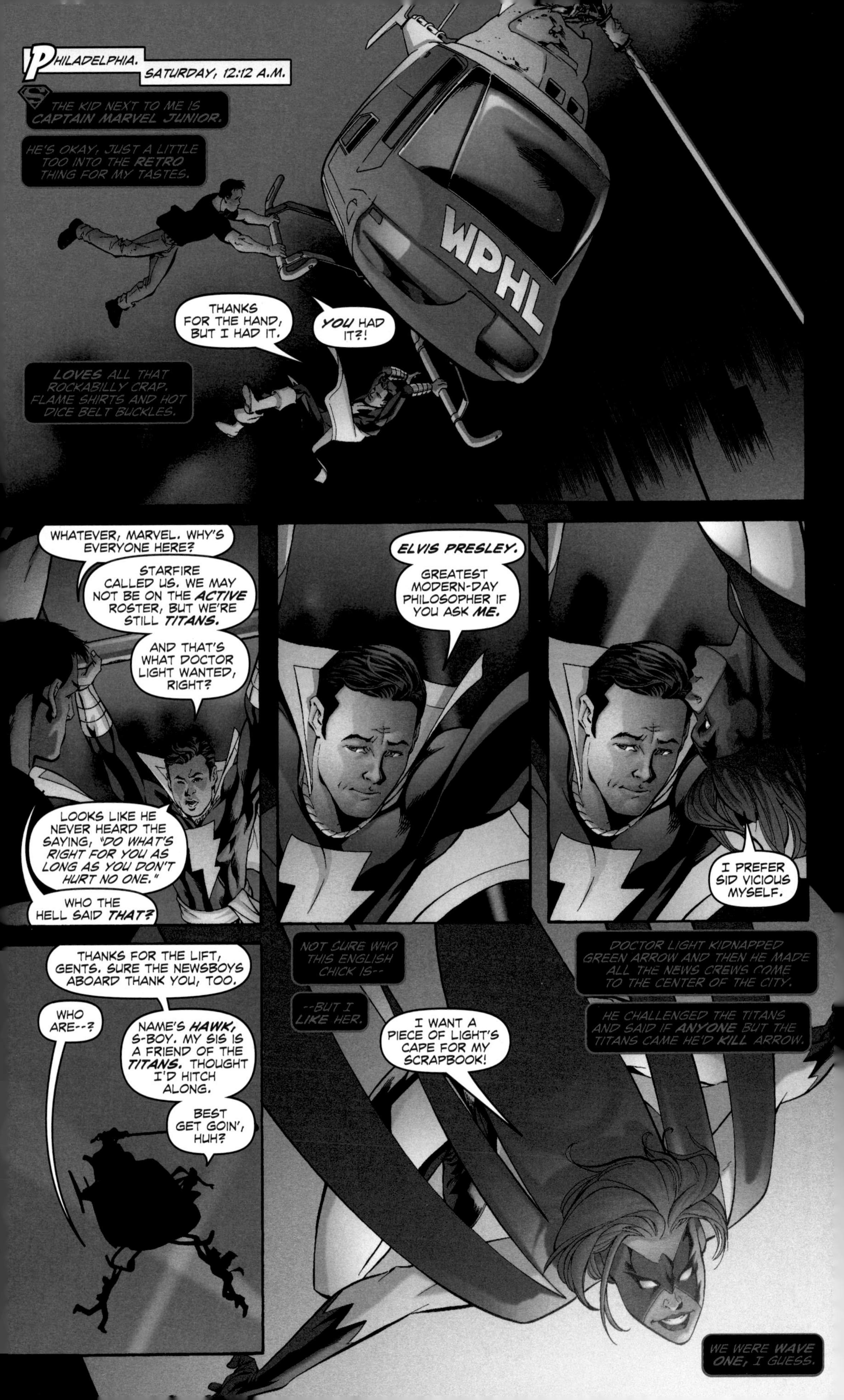
PHILADELPHIA.
SATURDAY, 12:12 A.M.
THE KID NEXT TO ME IS CAPTAIN MARVEL JUNIOR.
HE'S OKAY, JUST A LITTLE TOO INTO THE RETRO THING FOR MY TASTES.
THANKS FOR THE HAND, BUT I HAD IT.
YOU HAD IT?!
LOVES ALL THAT ROCKABILLY CRAP. FLAME SHIRTS AND HOT DICE BELT BUCKLES.
WPHL
WHATEVER, MARVEL. WHY'S EVERYONE HERE?
STARFIRE CALLED US. WE MAY NOT BE ON THE ACTIVE ROSTER, BUT WE'RE STILL TITANS.
AND THAT'S WHAT DOCTOR LIGHT WANTED, RIGHT?
LOOKS LIKE HE NEVER HEARD THE SAYING, "DO WHAT'S RIGHT FOR YOU AS LONG AS YOU DON'T HURT NO ONE."
WHO THE HELL SAID THAT?
ELVIS PRESLEY.
GREATEST MODERN-DAY PHILOSOPHER IF YOU ASK ME.
I PREFER SID VICIOUS MYSELF.
THANKS FOR THE LIFT, GENTS. SURE THE NEWSBOYS ABOARD THANK YOU, TOO.
WHO ARE--?
NAME'S HAWK, S-BOY. MY SIS IS A FRIEND OF THE TITANS. THOUGHT I'D HITCH ALONG.
BEST GET GOIN', HUH?
NOT SURE WHO THIS ENGLISH CHICK IS--
--BUT I LIKE HER.
I WANT A PIECE OF LIGHT'S CAPE FOR MY SCRAPBOOK!
DOCTOR LIGHT KIDNAPPED GREEN ARROW AND THEN HE MADE ALL THE NEWS CREWS COME TO THE CENTER OF THE CITY.
HE CHALLENGED THE TITANS AND SAID IF ANYONE BUT THE TITANS CAME HE'D KILL ARROW.
WE WERE WAVE ONE, I GUESS.

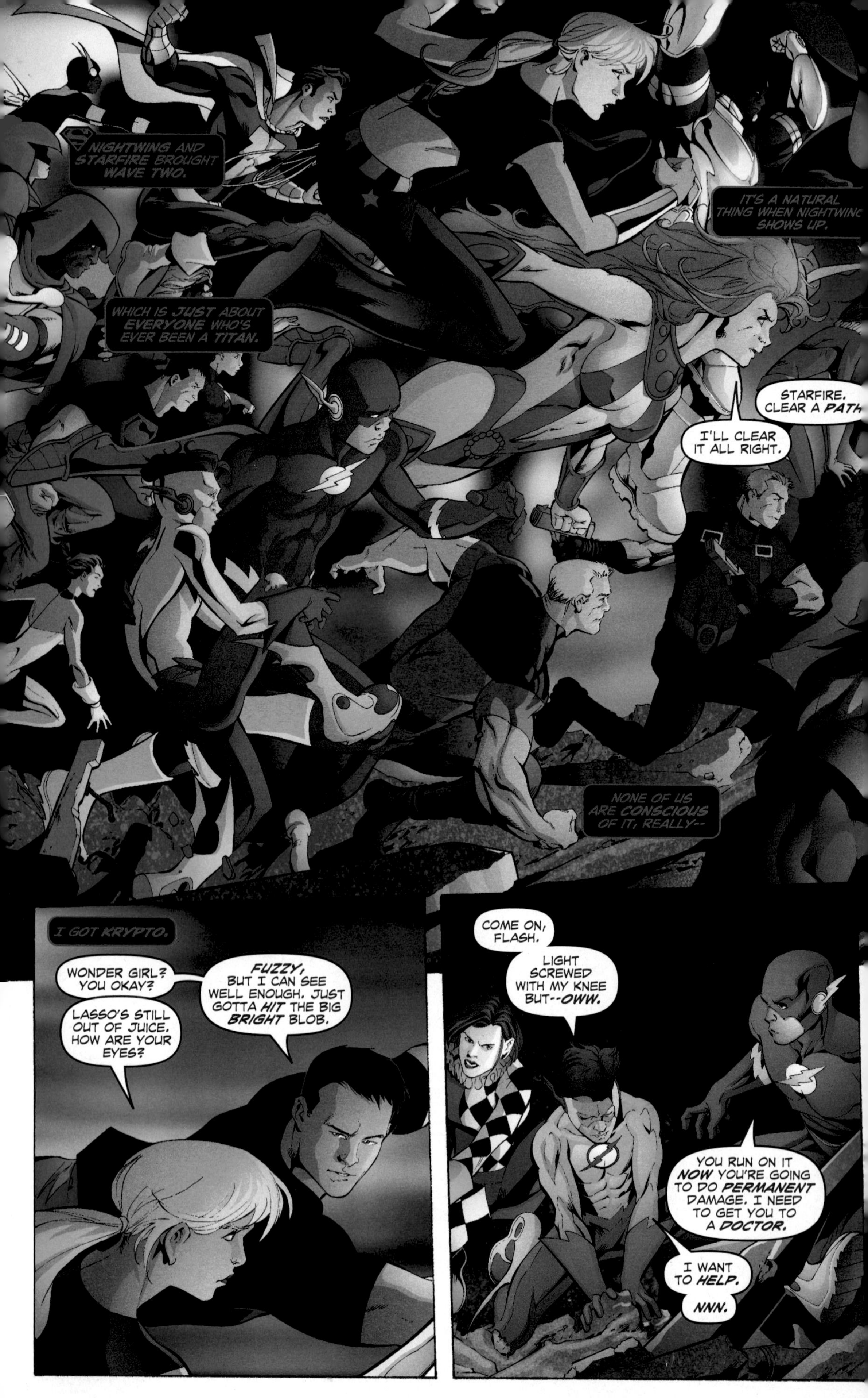
NIGHTWING AND STARFIRE BROUGHT WAVE TWO.
IT'S A NATURAL THING WHEN NIGHTWING SHOWS UP.
WHICH IS JUST ABOUT EVERYONE WHO'S EVER BEEN A TITAN.
STARFIRE. CLEAR A PATH
I'LL CLEAR IT ALL RIGHT.
NONE OF US ARE CONSCIOUS OF IT, REALLY--
I GOT KRYPTO.
WONDER GIRL? YOU OKAY?
LASSO'S STILL OUT OF JUICE. HOW ARE YOUR EYES?
FUZZY, BUT I CAN SEE WELL ENOUGH. JUST GOTTA HIT THE BIG BRIGHT BLOB.
COME ON, FLASH.
LIGHT SCREWED WITH MY KNEE BUT--OWW.
YOU RUN ON IT NOW YOU'RE GOING TO DO PERMANENT DAMAGE. I NEED TO GET YOU TO A DOCTOR.
I WANT TO HELP.
NNN.

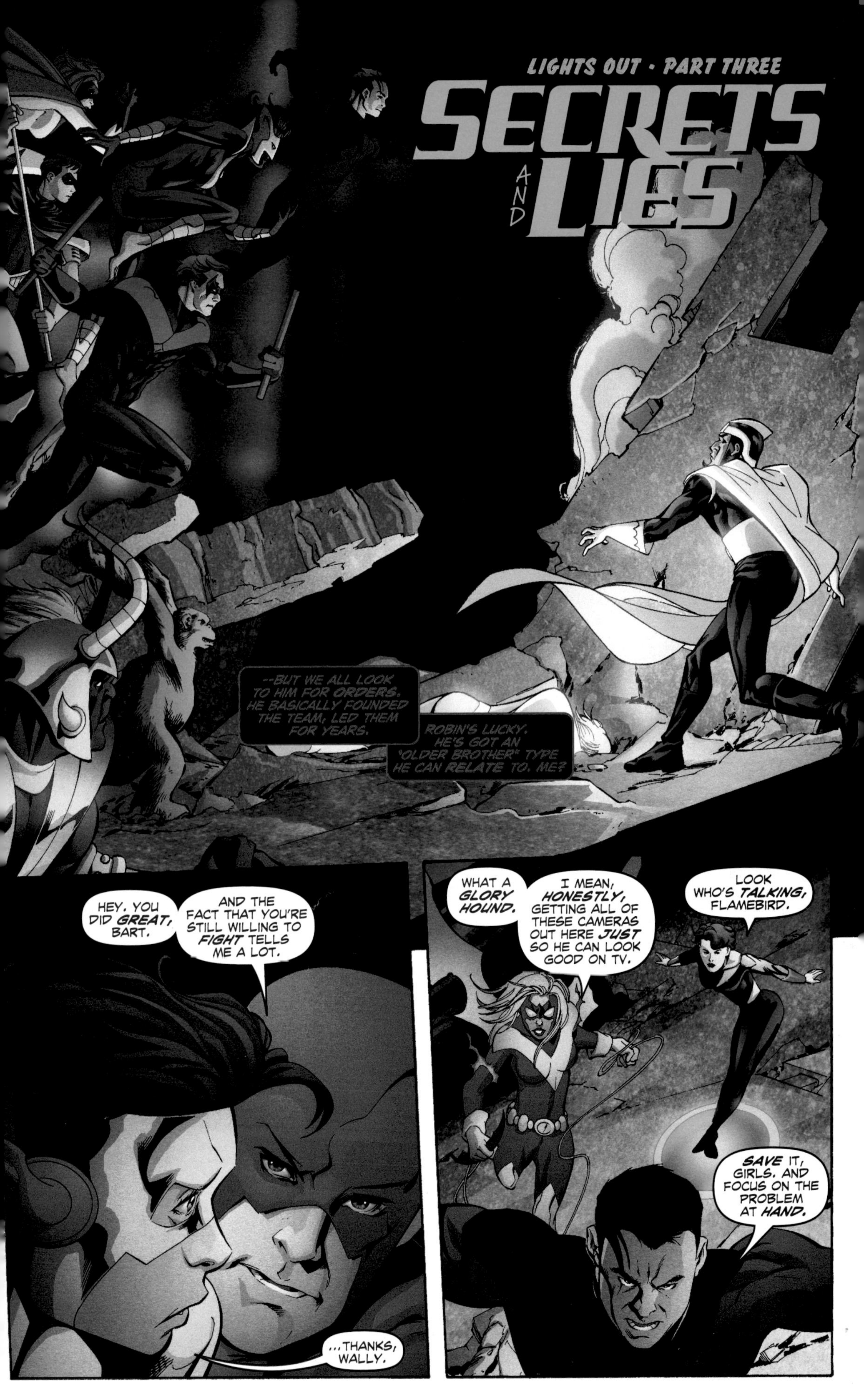
LIGHTS OUT · PART THREE
SECRETS AND LIES
--BUT WE ALL LOOK TO HIM FOR ORDERS. HE BASICALLY FOUNDED THE TEAM, LED THEM FOR YEARS.
ROBIN'S LUCKY. HE'S GOT AN "OLDER BROTHER" TYPE HE CAN RELATE TO. ME?
HEY. YOU DID GREAT, BART.
AND THE FACT THAT YOU'RE STILL WILLING TO FIGHT TELLS ME A LOT.
...THANKS, WALLY.
WHAT A GLORY HOUND.
I MEAN, HONESTLY, GETTING ALL OF THESE CAMERAS OUT HERE JUST SO HE CAN LOOK GOOD ON TV.
LOOK WHO'S TALKING, FLAMEBIRD.
SAVE IT, GIRLS. AND FOCUS ON THE PROBLEM AT HAND.

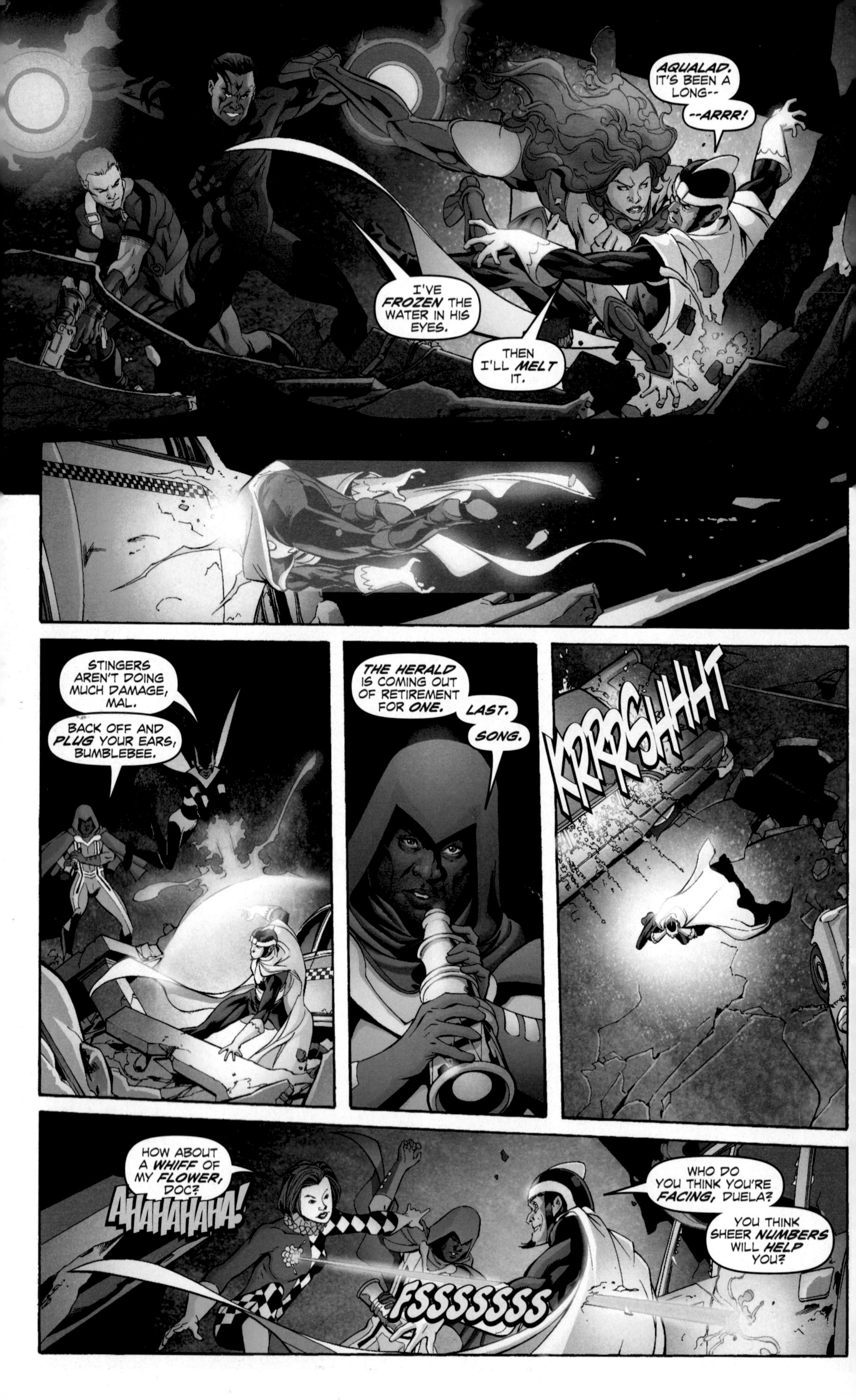
AQUALAD. IT'S BEEN A LONG--
--ARRR!
I'VE FROZEN THE WATER IN HIS EYES.
THEN I'LL MELT IT.
STINGERS AREN'T DOING MUCH DAMAGE, MAL.
BACK OFF AND PLUG YOUR EARS, BUMBLEBEE.
THE HERALD IS COMING OUT OF RETIREMENT FOR ONE.
LAST.
SONG.
KRRRSHHHT
HOW ABOUT A WHIFF OF MY FLOWER, DOC?
AHAHAHAHA!
WHO DO YOU THINK YOU'RE FACING, DUELA?
YOU THINK SHEER NUMBERS WILL HELP YOU?
FSSSSSSS

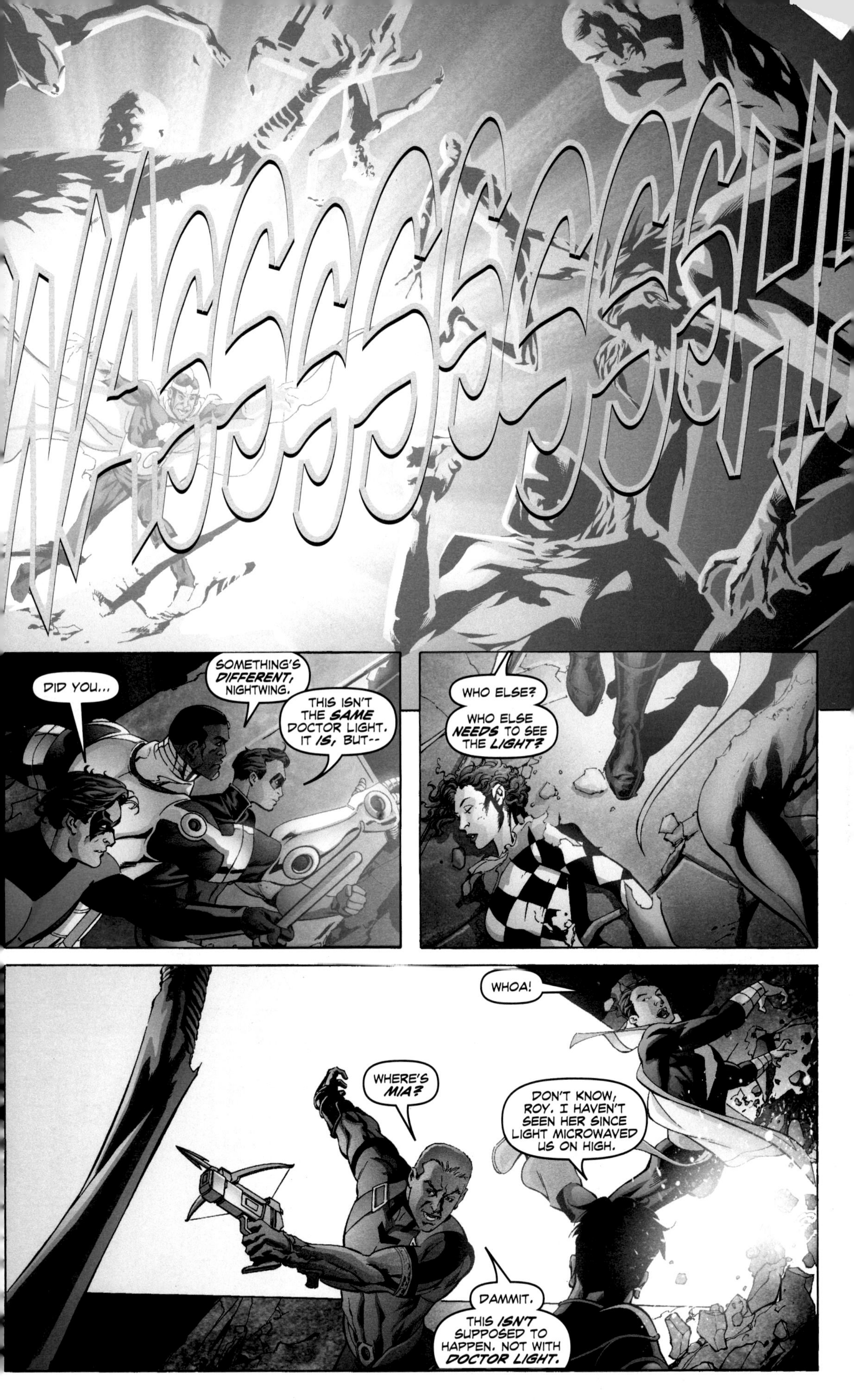

DID YOU...
SOMETHING'S *DIFFERENT*, NIGHTWING.
THIS ISN'T THE *SAME* DOCTOR LIGHT. IT *IS*, BUT--
WHO ELSE?
WHO ELSE *NEEDS* TO SEE THE *LIGHT?*
WHOA!
WHERE'S *MIA?*
DON'T KNOW, ROY. I HAVEN'T SEEN HER SINCE LIGHT MICROWAVED US ON HIGH.
DAMMIT.
THIS *ISN'T* SUPPOSED TO HAPPEN. NOT WITH *DOCTOR LIGHT.*

DOVE, WE'RE MISSIN' THE BLEEDIN' *FUN!*

COME ON! WE...

DAWN?

SHE IS... WOUNDED.

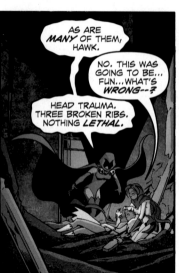

AS ARE *MANY* OF THEM, HAWK.

NO. THIS WAS GOING TO BE... FUN...WHAT'S *WRONG*--?

HEAD TRAUMA. THREE BROKEN RIBS. NOTHING *LETHAL.*

MEANING I CAN *HEAL* HER.

GIVE UP AND YOU DON'T GET *HURT,* LIGHT.

I CAN *SEE* RIGHT *THROUGH* IT.

BOOM

YOU THINK YOUR *ILLUSION-WEAVING* FOOLS *ME,* MIRAGE?

SEE THROUGH *THIS.*

KRRSHHT

FRRZZZZZ

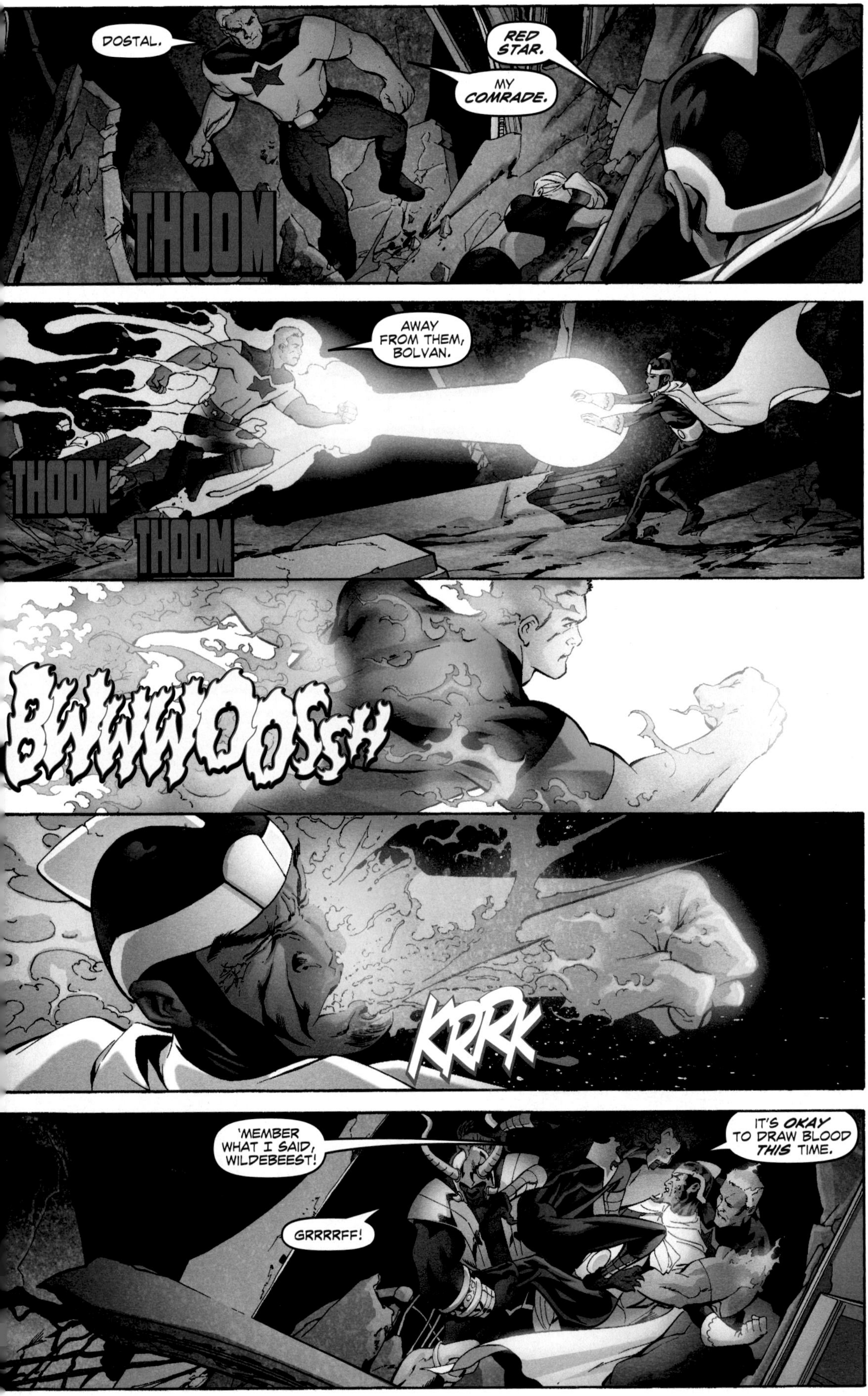
DOSTAL.
RED STAR.
MY COMRADE.
THOOM
AWAY FROM THEM, BOLVAN.
THOOM
THOOM
BWWOOSSH
KRRK
'MEMBER WHAT I SAID, WILDEBEEST!
IT'S OKAY TO DRAW BLOOD THIS TIME.
GRRRRFF!

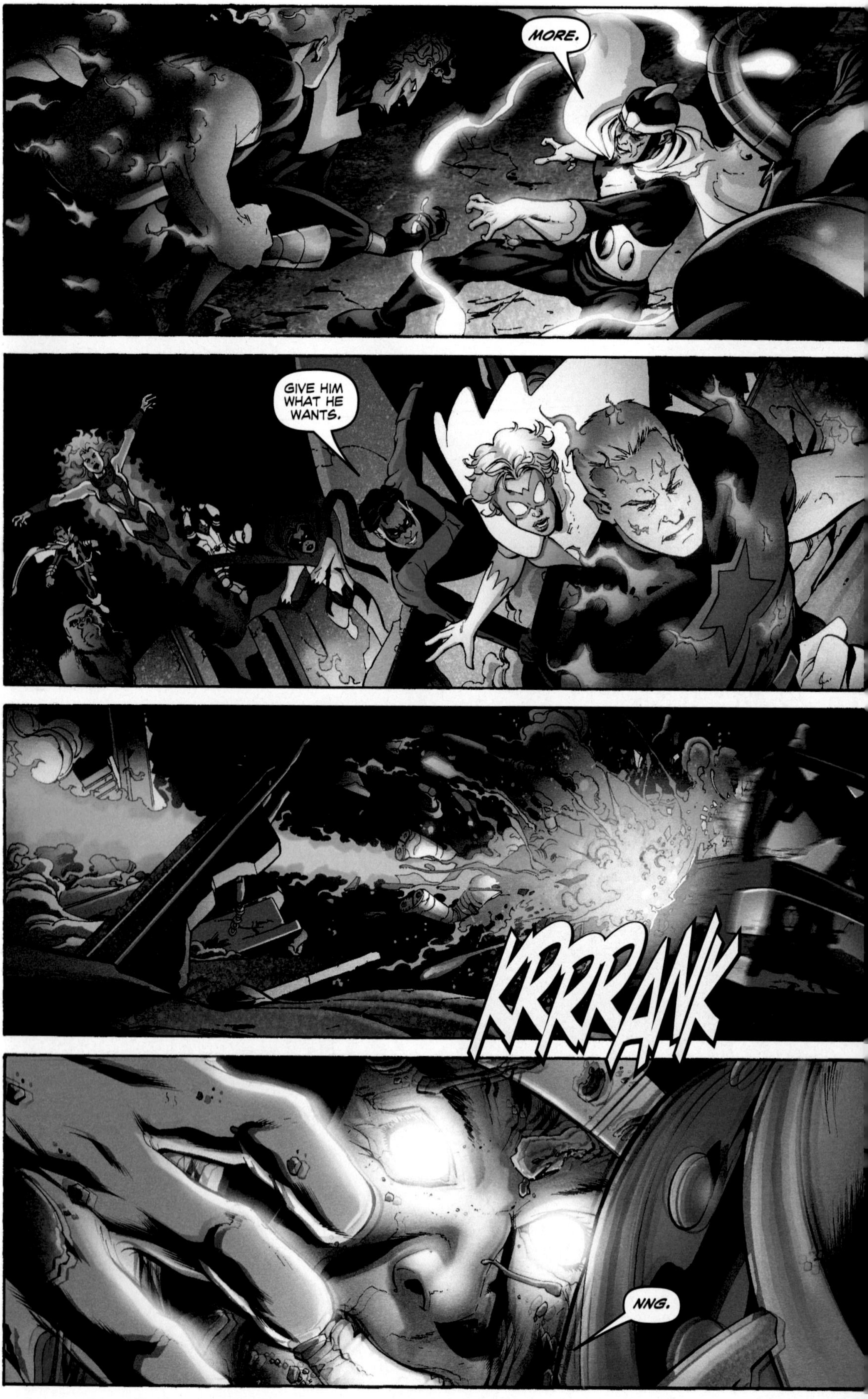
MORE.
GIVE HIM WHAT HE WANTS.
KRRRANK
NNG.

IS IT GETTING *DARKER?*

HE'S *POWERING* UP. HE'S *SUCKING* IN ALL THE *AMBIENT* LIGHT.

TITANS! GET--

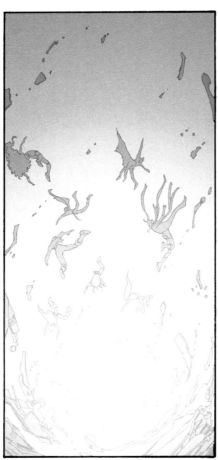

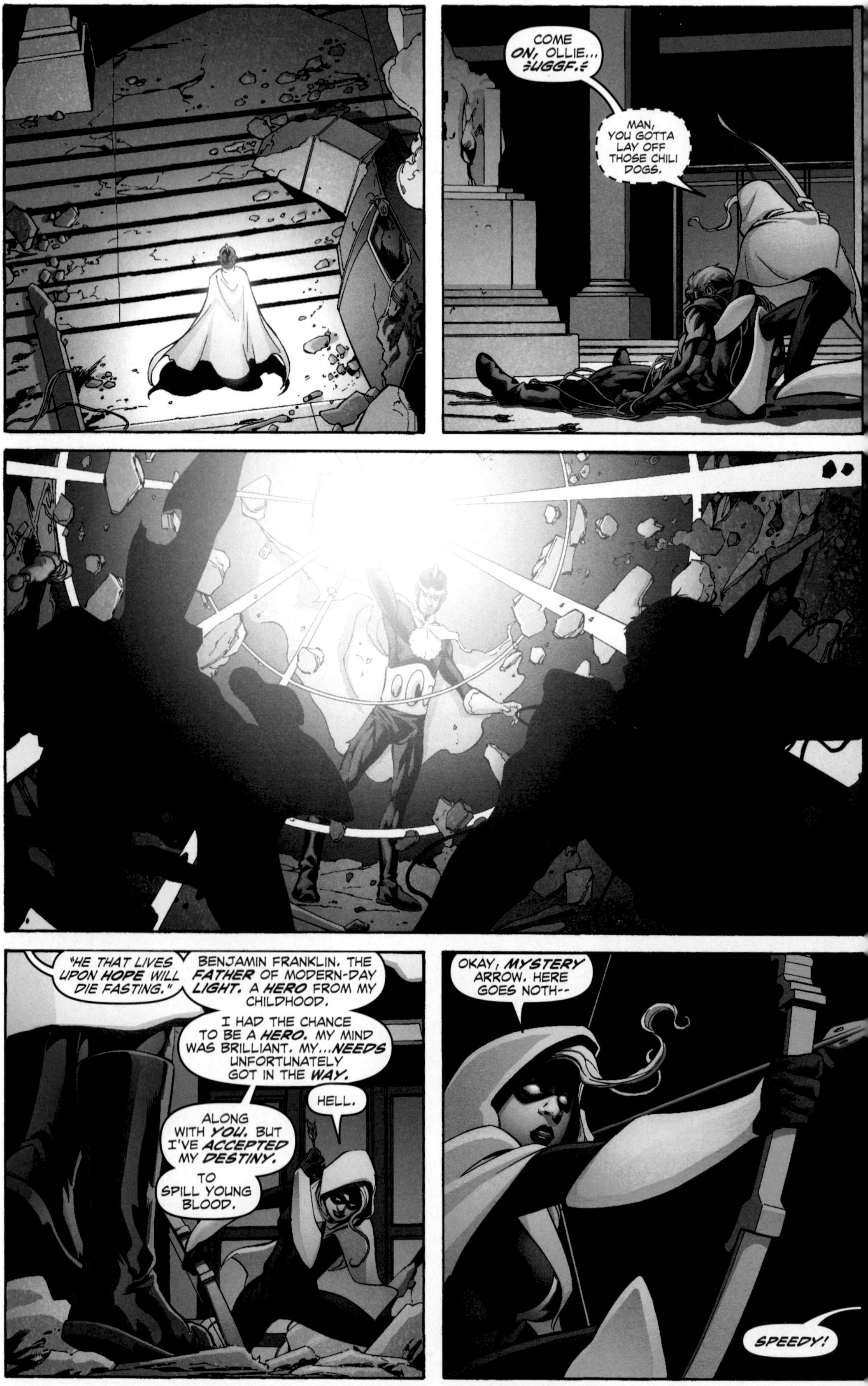
COME ON, OLLIE... UGGF.
MAN, YOU GOTTA LAY OFF THOSE CHILI DOGS.
"HE THAT LIVES UPON HOPE WILL DIE FASTING."
BENJAMIN FRANKLIN. THE FATHER OF MODERN-DAY LIGHT. A HERO FROM MY CHILDHOOD.
I HAD THE CHANCE TO BE A HERO. MY MIND WAS BRILLIANT. MY...NEEDS UNFORTUNATELY GOT IN THE WAY.
ALONG WITH YOU. BUT I'VE ACCEPTED MY DESTINY.
TO SPILL YOUNG BLOOD.
HELL.
OKAY, MYSTERY ARROW. HERE GOES NOTH--
SPEEDY!

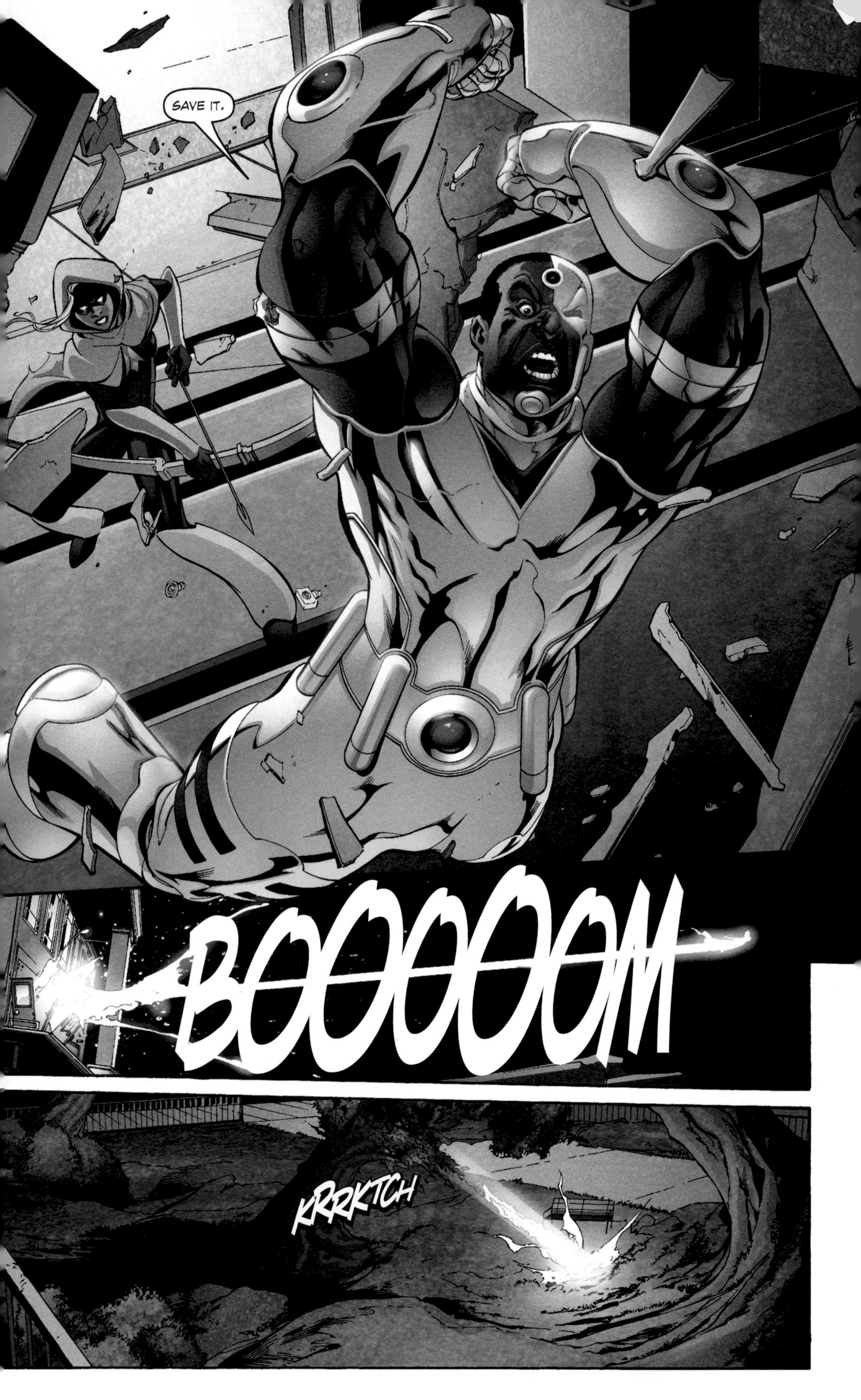

SAVE IT.
BOOOOOM
KRRKTCH

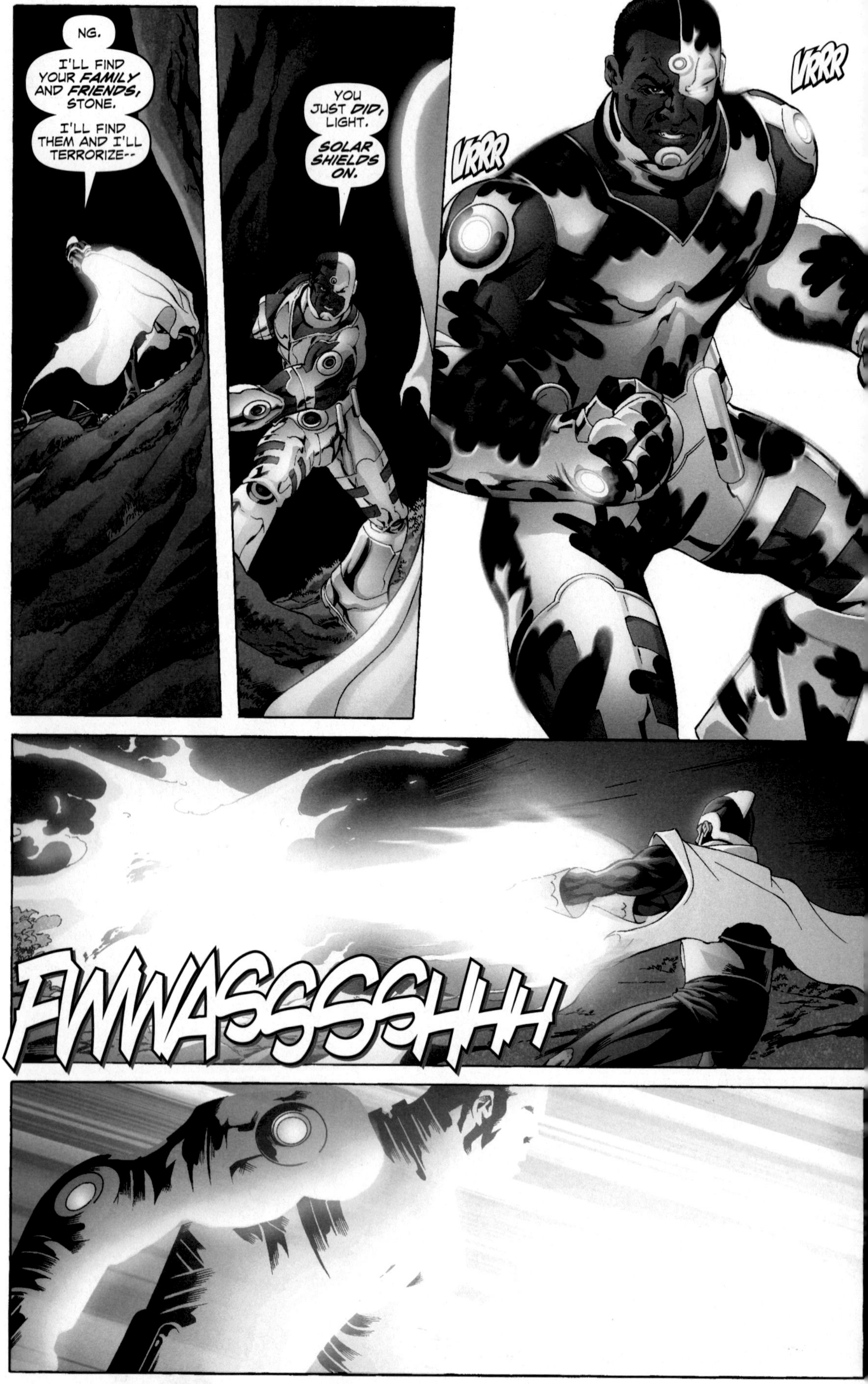
NG.
I'LL FIND YOUR FAMILY AND FRIENDS, STONE.
I'LL FIND THEM AND I'LL TERRORIZE--
YOU JUST DID, LIGHT.
SOLAR SHIELDS ON.
VRRR
VRRR
FWWASSSSHHH

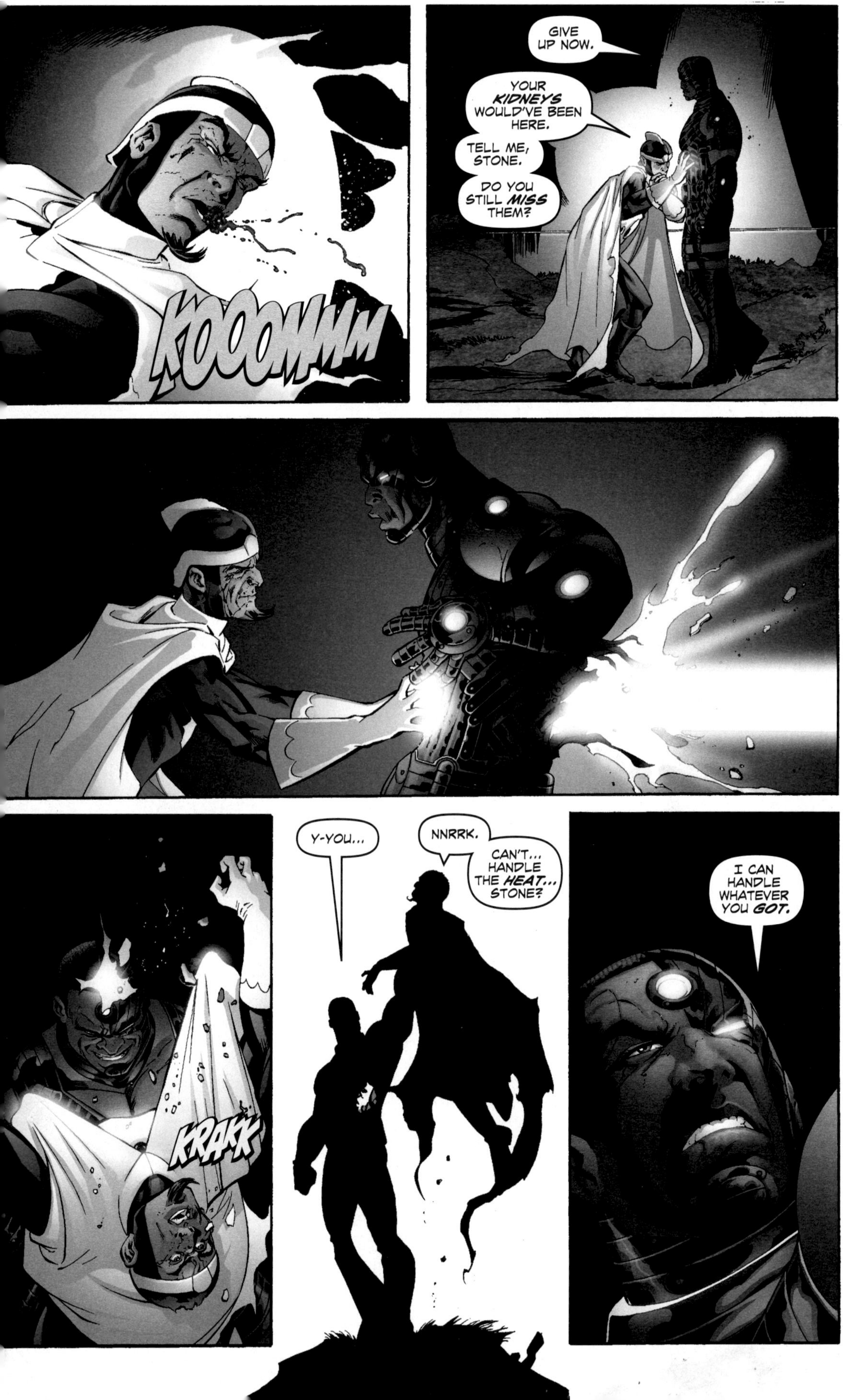
KOOOMMM
GIVE UP NOW.
YOUR KIDNEYS WOULD'VE BEEN HERE.
TELL ME, STONE.
DO YOU STILL MISS THEM?
KRAKK
Y-YOU...
NNRRK.
CAN'T... HANDLE THE HEAT... STONE?
I CAN HANDLE WHATEVER YOU GOT.

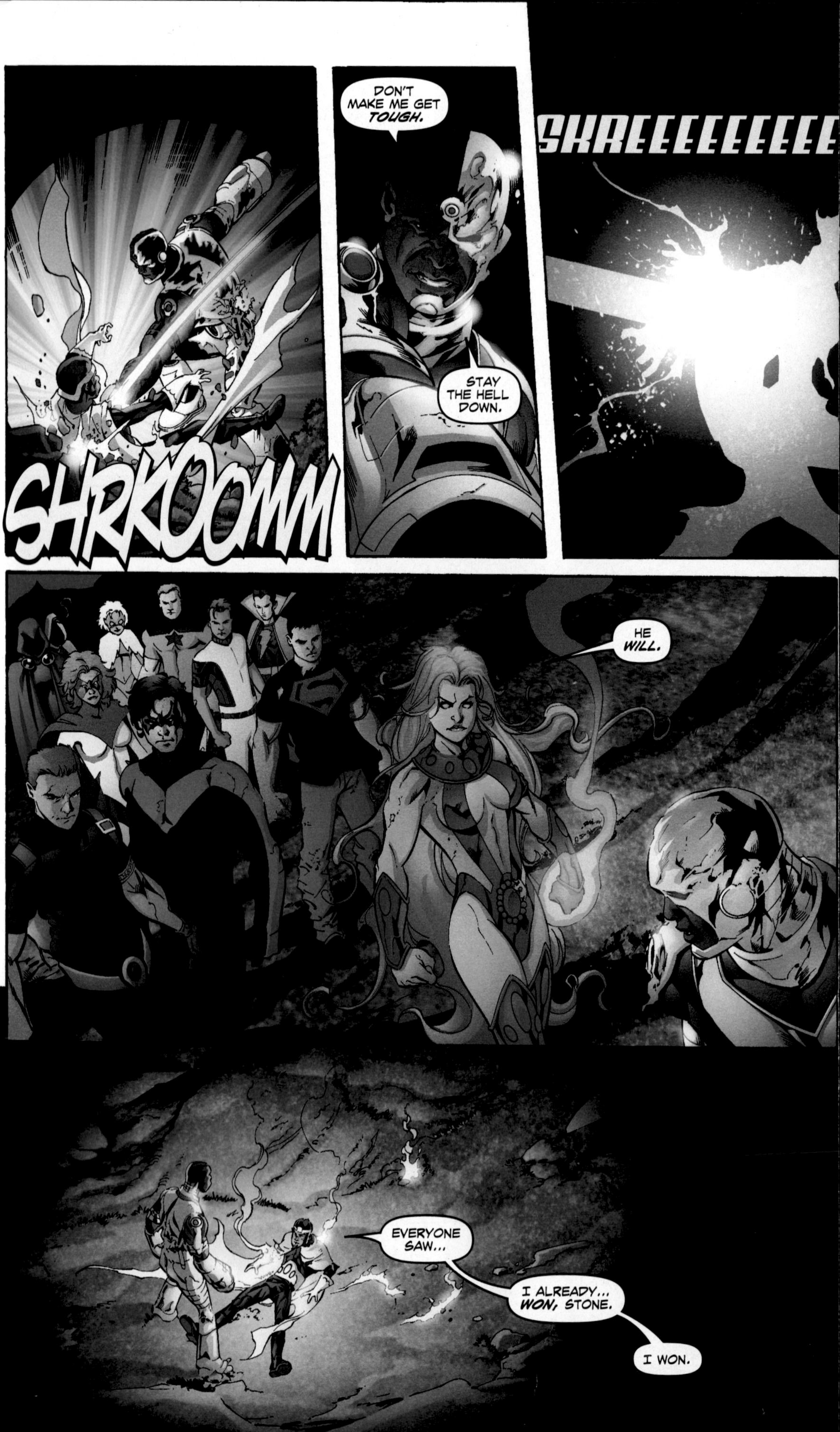
SHRKOOMM
DON'T MAKE ME GET TOUGH.
STAY THE HELL DOWN.
SKREEEEEEEEEE
HE WILL.
EVERYONE SAW...
I ALREADY... WON, STONE.
I WON.

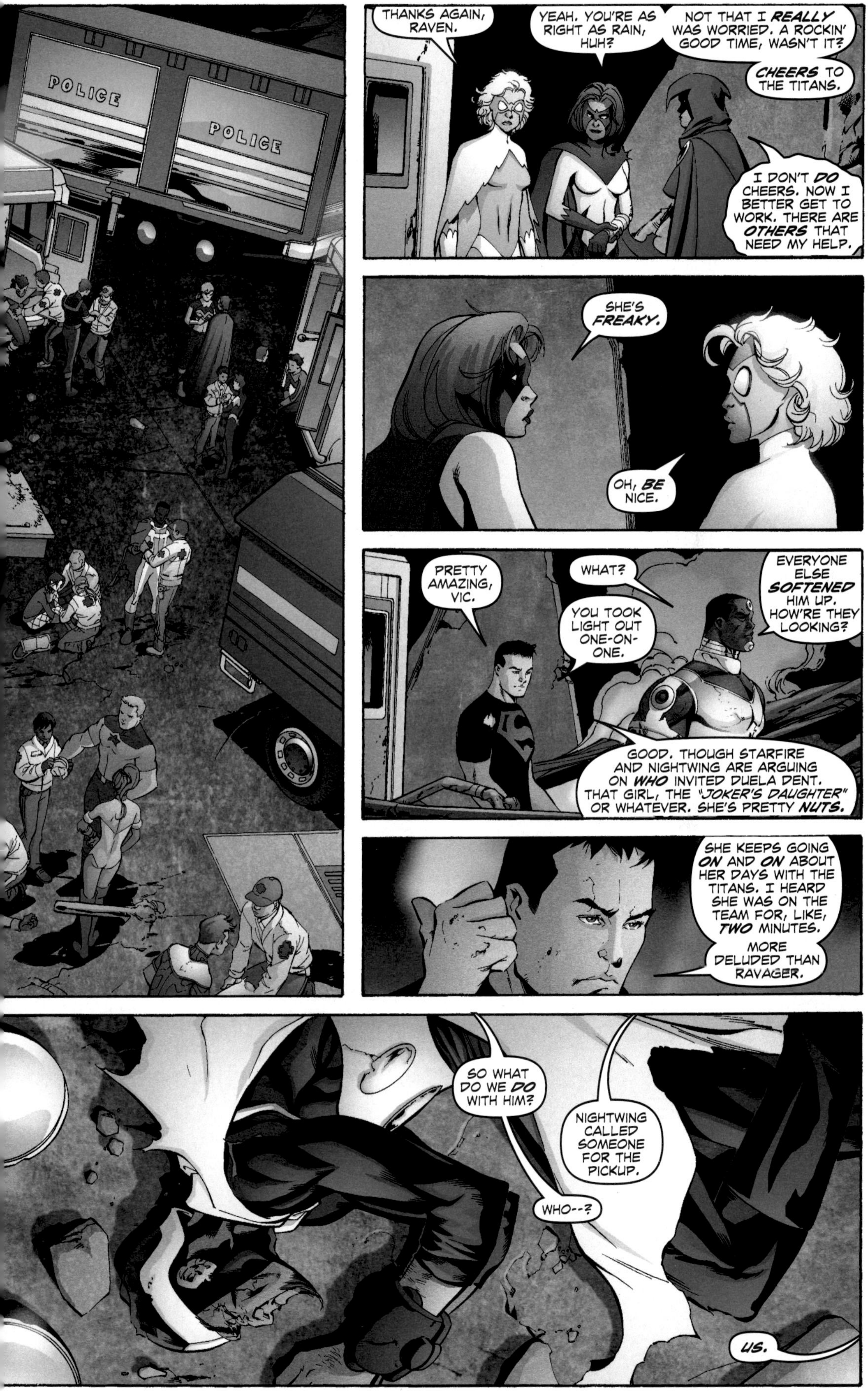
POLICE
POLICE
THANKS AGAIN, RAVEN.
YEAH. YOU'RE AS RIGHT AS RAIN, HUH?
NOT THAT I REALLY WAS WORRIED. A ROCKIN' GOOD TIME, WASN'T IT?
CHEERS TO THE TITANS.
I DON'T DO CHEERS. NOW I BETTER GET TO WORK. THERE ARE OTHERS THAT NEED MY HELP.
SHE'S FREAKY.
OH, BE NICE.
PRETTY AMAZING, VIC.
WHAT?
YOU TOOK LIGHT OUT ONE-ON-ONE.
EVERYONE ELSE SOFTENED HIM UP. HOW'RE THEY LOOKING?
GOOD. THOUGH STARFIRE AND NIGHTWING ARE ARGUING ON WHO INVITED DUELA DENT. THAT GIRL, THE "JOKER'S DAUGHTER" OR WHATEVER. SHE'S PRETTY NUTS.
SHE KEEPS GOING ON AND ON ABOUT HER DAYS WITH THE TITANS. I HEARD SHE WAS ON THE TEAM FOR, LIKE, TWO MINUTES.
MORE DELUDED THAN RAVAGER.
SO WHAT DO WE DO WITH HIM?
NIGHTWING CALLED SOMEONE FOR THE PICKUP.
WHO--?
US.

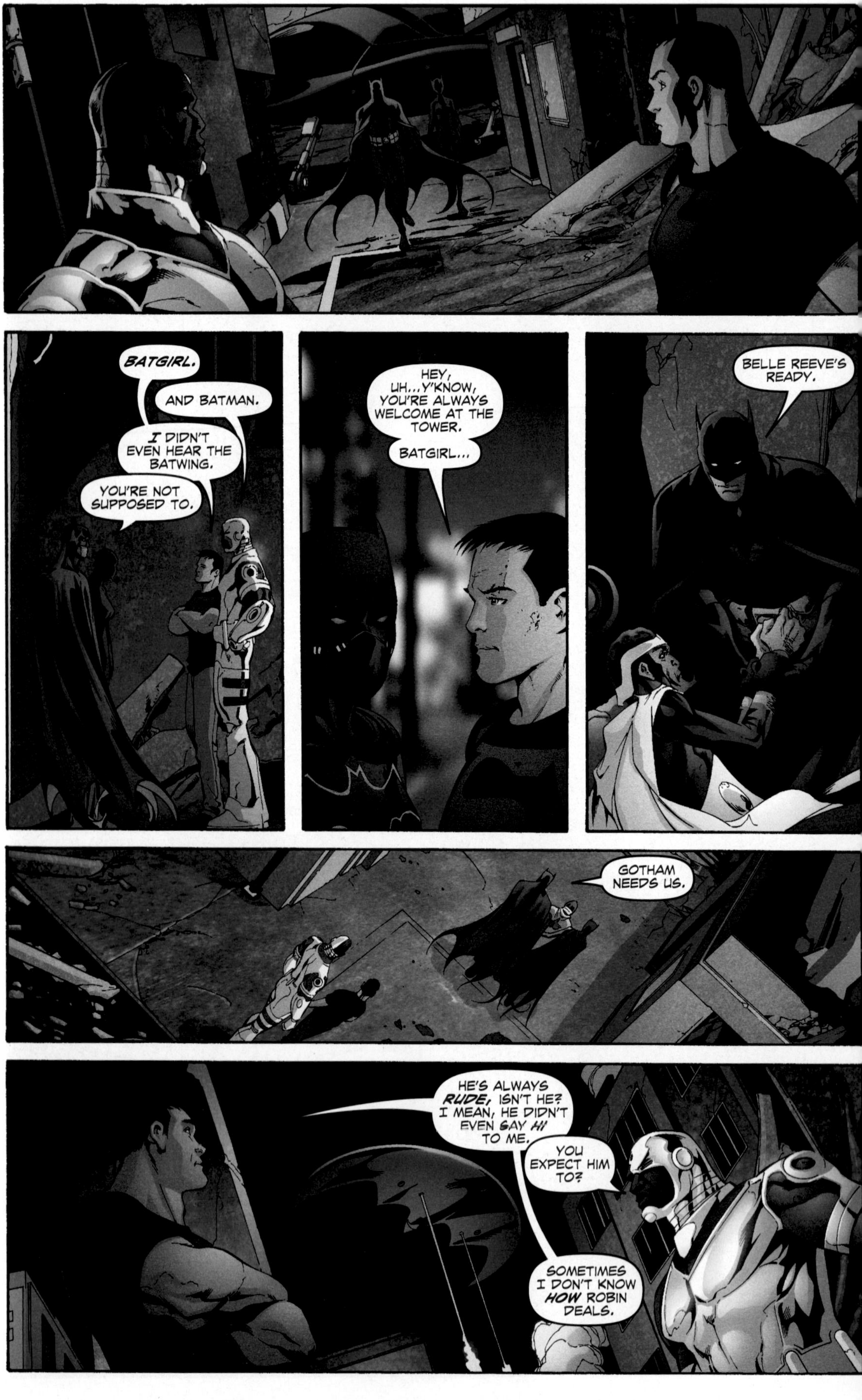
BATGIRL.
AND BATMAN.
I DIDN'T EVEN HEAR THE BATWING.
YOU'RE NOT SUPPOSED TO.
HEY, UH...Y'KNOW, YOU'RE ALWAYS WELCOME AT THE TOWER.
BATGIRL...
BELLE REEVE'S READY.
GOTHAM NEEDS US.
HE'S ALWAYS RUDE, ISN'T HE? I MEAN, HE DIDN'T EVEN SAY HI TO ME.
YOU EXPECT HIM TO?
SOMETIMES I DON'T KNOW HOW ROBIN DEALS.

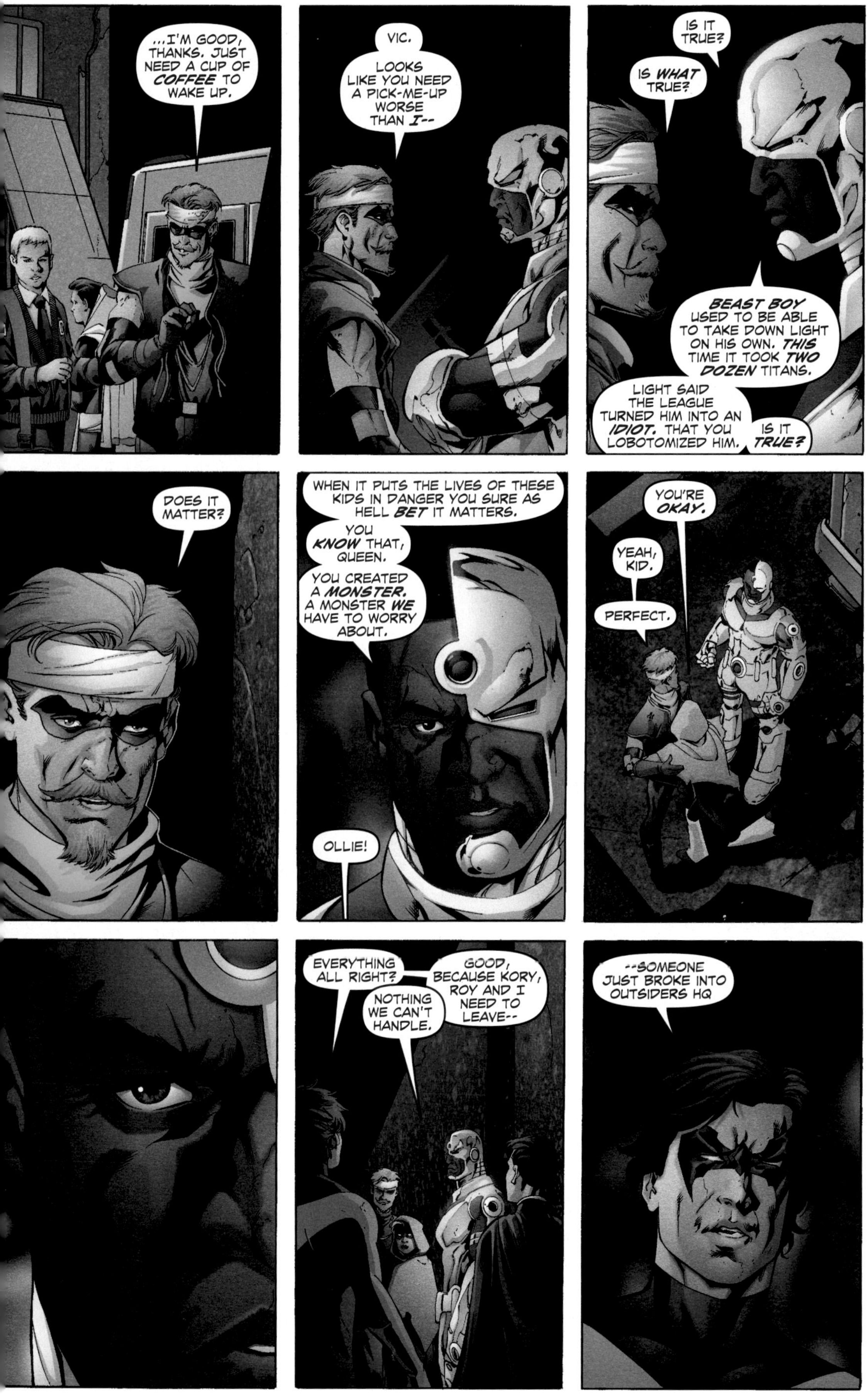
...I'M GOOD, THANKS. JUST NEED A CUP OF COFFEE TO WAKE UP.
VIC.
LOOKS LIKE YOU NEED A PICK-ME-UP WORSE THAN I--
IS IT TRUE?
IS WHAT TRUE?
BEAST BOY USED TO BE ABLE TO TAKE DOWN LIGHT ON HIS OWN. THIS TIME IT TOOK TWO DOZEN TITANS.
LIGHT SAID THE LEAGUE TURNED HIM INTO AN IDIOT. THAT YOU LOBOTOMIZED HIM.
IS IT TRUE?
DOES IT MATTER?
WHEN IT PUTS THE LIVES OF THESE KIDS IN DANGER YOU SURE AS HELL BET IT MATTERS.
YOU KNOW THAT, QUEEN.
YOU CREATED A MONSTER. A MONSTER WE HAVE TO WORRY ABOUT.
OLLIE!
YOU'RE OKAY.
YEAH, KID.
PERFECT.
EVERYTHING ALL RIGHT?
NOTHING WE CAN'T HANDLE.
GOOD, BECAUSE KORY, ROY AND I NEED TO LEAVE--
--SOMEONE JUST BROKE INTO OUTSIDERS HQ

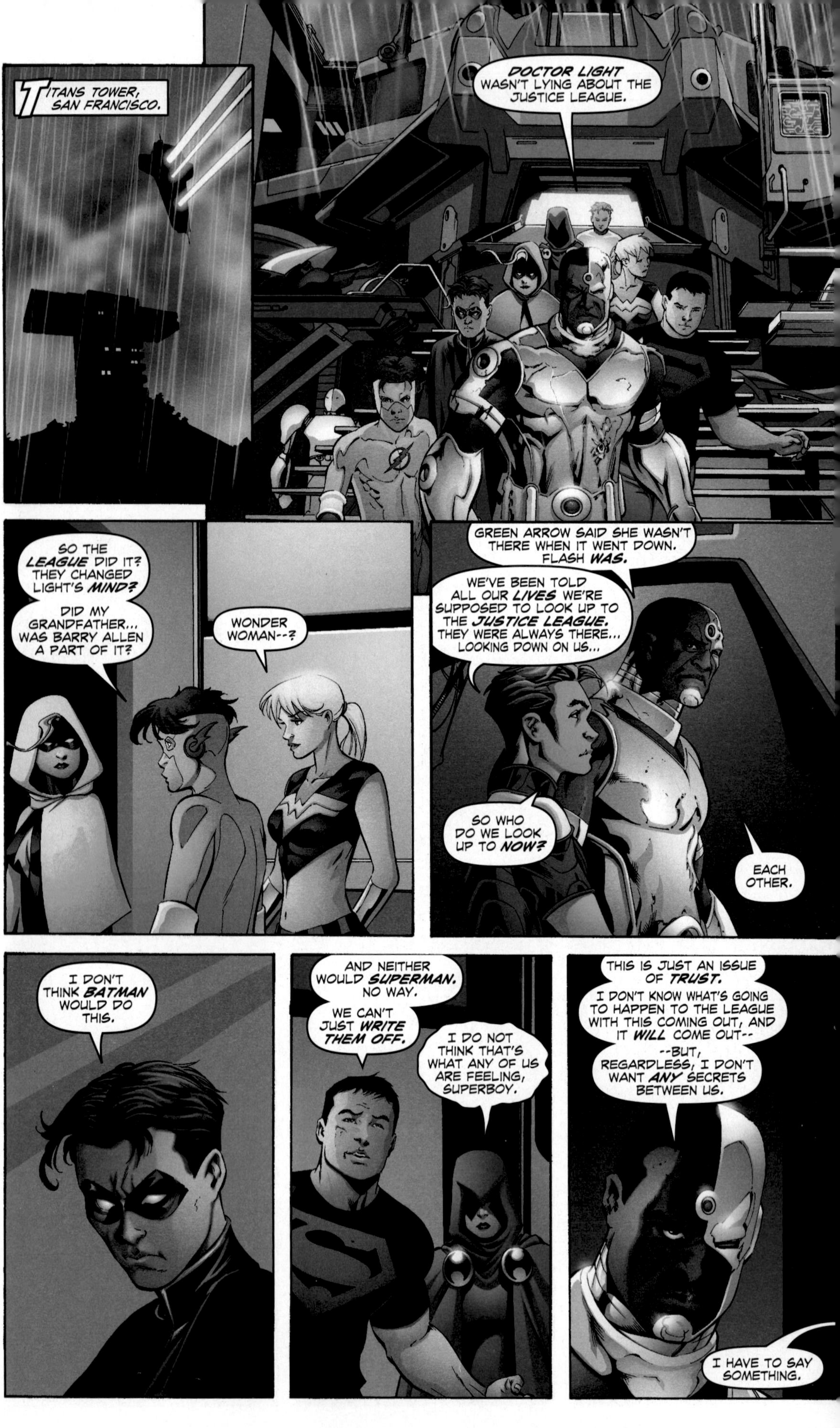
TITANS TOWER, SAN FRANCISCO.
DOCTOR LIGHT WASN'T LYING ABOUT THE JUSTICE LEAGUE.
SO THE LEAGUE DID IT? THEY CHANGED LIGHT'S MIND?
DID MY GRANDFATHER... WAS BARRY ALLEN A PART OF IT?
WONDER WOMAN--?
GREEN ARROW SAID SHE WASN'T THERE WHEN IT WENT DOWN. FLASH WAS.
WE'VE BEEN TOLD ALL OUR LIVES WE'RE SUPPOSED TO LOOK UP TO THE JUSTICE LEAGUE. THEY WERE ALWAYS THERE... LOOKING DOWN ON US...
SO WHO DO WE LOOK UP TO NOW?
EACH OTHER.
I DON'T THINK BATMAN WOULD DO THIS.
AND NEITHER WOULD SUPERMAN. NO WAY.
WE CAN'T JUST WRITE THEM OFF.
I DO NOT THINK THAT'S WHAT ANY OF US ARE FEELING, SUPERBOY.
THIS IS JUST AN ISSUE OF TRUST.
I DON'T KNOW WHAT'S GOING TO HAPPEN TO THE LEAGUE WITH THIS COMING OUT, AND IT WILL COME OUT--
--BUT, REGARDLESS, I DON'T WANT ANY SECRETS BETWEEN US.
I HAVE TO SAY SOMETHING.

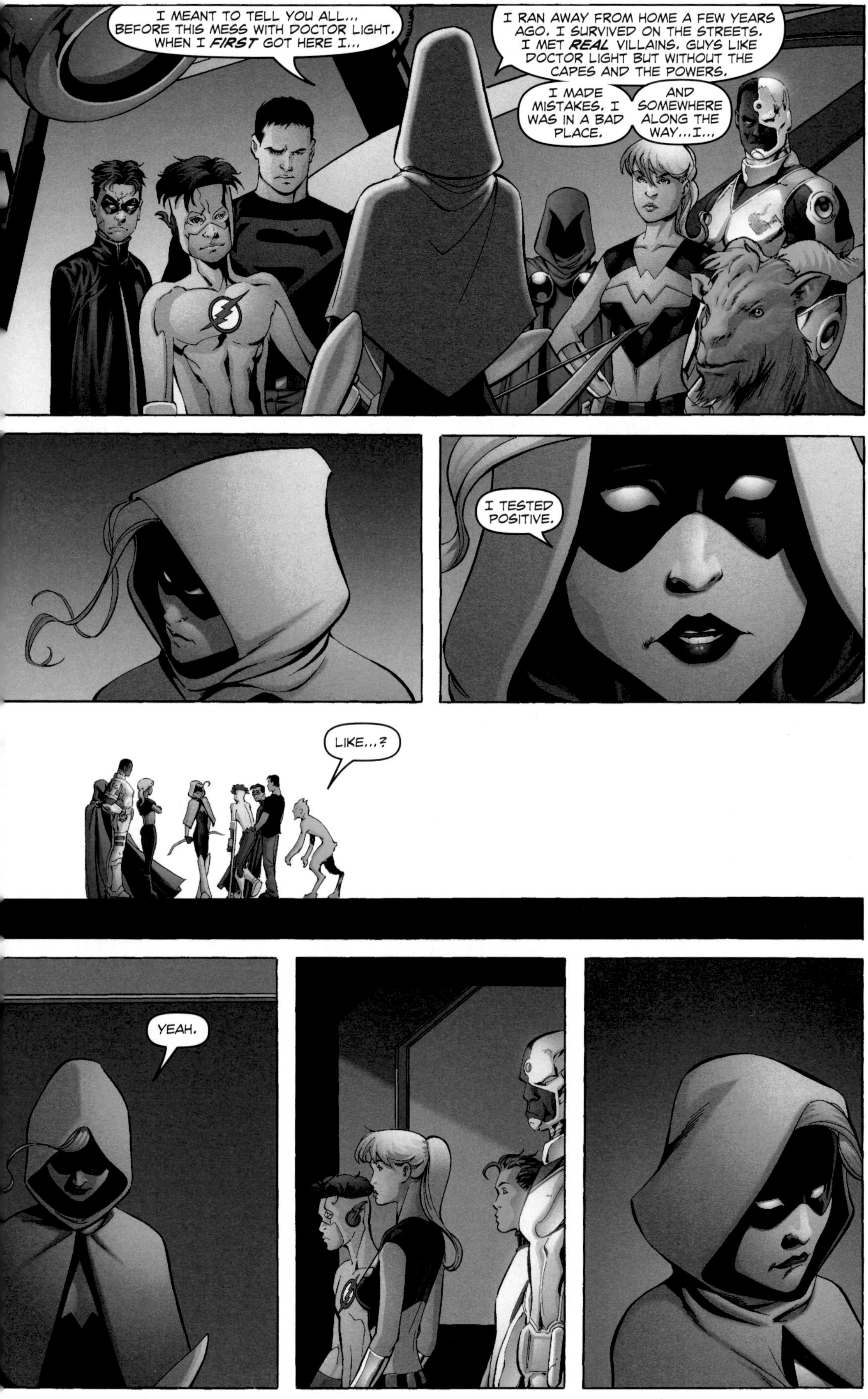
I MEANT TO TELL YOU ALL... BEFORE THIS MESS WITH DOCTOR LIGHT. WHEN I FIRST GOT HERE I...
I RAN AWAY FROM HOME A FEW YEARS AGO. I SURVIVED ON THE STREETS. I MET REAL VILLAINS. GUYS LIKE DOCTOR LIGHT BUT WITHOUT THE CAPES AND THE POWERS.
I MADE MISTAKES. I WAS IN A BAD PLACE.
AND SOMEWHERE ALONG THE WAY...I...
I TESTED POSITIVE.
LIKE...?
YEAH.

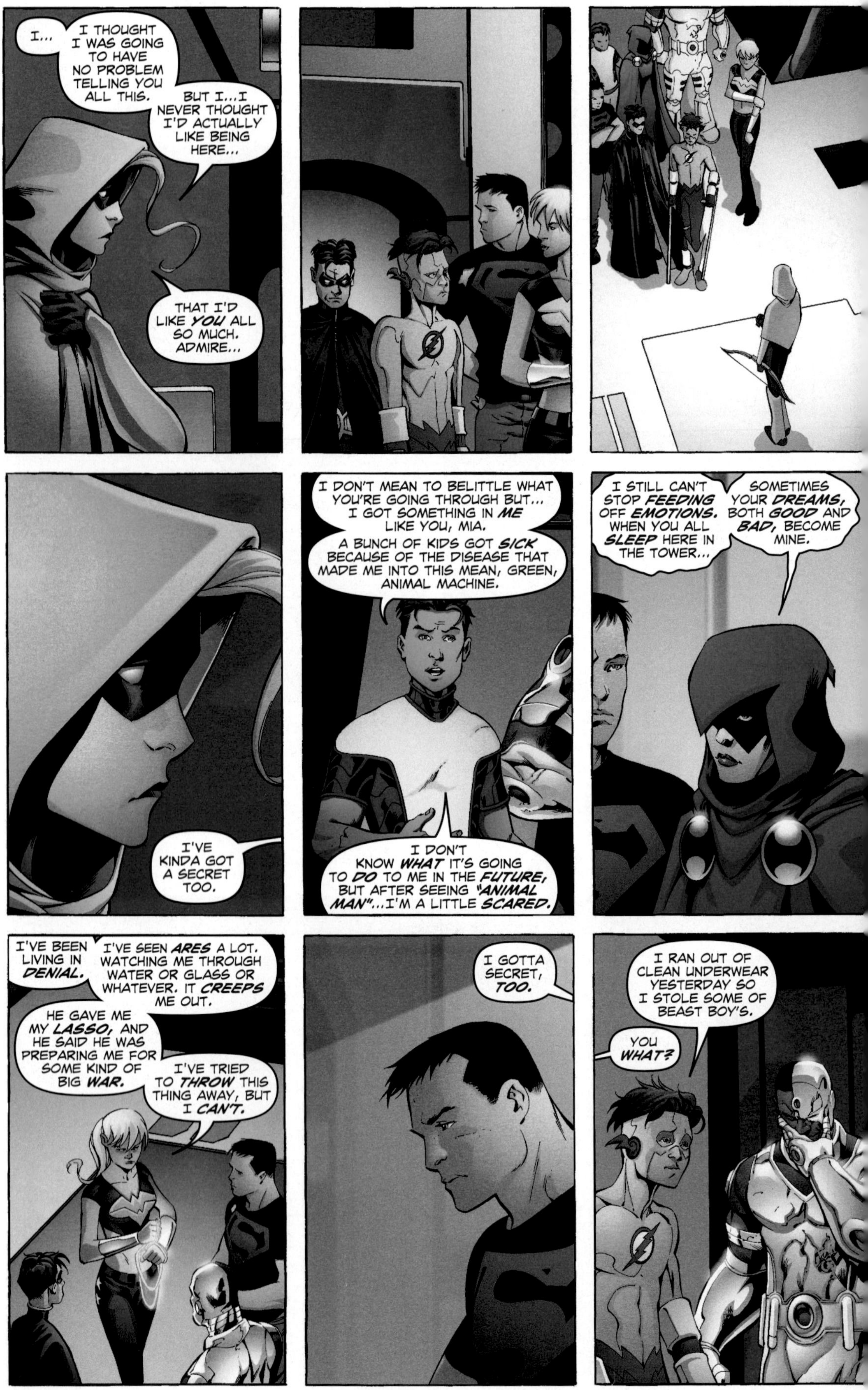
I...
I THOUGHT I WAS GOING TO HAVE NO PROBLEM TELLING YOU ALL THIS.
BUT I...I NEVER THOUGHT I'D ACTUALLY LIKE BEING HERE...
THAT I'D LIKE YOU ALL SO MUCH. ADMIRE...
I'VE KINDA GOT A SECRET TOO.
I DON'T MEAN TO BELITTLE WHAT YOU'RE GOING THROUGH BUT... I GOT SOMETHING IN ME LIKE YOU, MIA.
A BUNCH OF KIDS GOT SICK BECAUSE OF THE DISEASE THAT MADE ME INTO THIS MEAN, GREEN, ANIMAL MACHINE.
I DON'T KNOW WHAT IT'S GOING TO DO TO ME IN THE FUTURE, BUT AFTER SEEING "ANIMAL MAN"...I'M A LITTLE SCARED.
I STILL CAN'T STOP FEEDING OFF EMOTIONS. WHEN YOU ALL SLEEP HERE IN THE TOWER...
SOMETIMES YOUR DREAMS, BOTH GOOD AND BAD, BECOME MINE.
I'VE BEEN LIVING IN DENIAL.
I'VE SEEN ARES A LOT. WATCHING ME THROUGH WATER OR GLASS OR WHATEVER. IT CREEPS ME OUT.
HE GAVE ME MY LASSO, AND HE SAID HE WAS PREPARING ME FOR SOME KIND OF BIG WAR.
I'VE TRIED TO THROW THIS THING AWAY, BUT I CAN'T.
I GOTTA SECRET, TOO.
I RAN OUT OF CLEAN UNDERWEAR YESTERDAY SO I STOLE SOME OF BEAST BOY'S.
YOU WHAT?

AREN'T ANY OF YOU...WEIRDED OUT OR --?

UNCOMFORTABLE? SOME OF US, SURE.

BUT HOW *ELSE* DID YOU EXPECT US TO *REACT?* YOU THINK WE'RE GOING TO *KICK* YOU OUT?

WE WANT TO BE *SMART* ABOUT THIS. WE WANT TO TAKE ANY NECESSARY PRECAUTIONS TO KEEP YOU AND THE TITANS *SAFE.*

AND I'M SURE WE'LL HAVE QUESTIONS. MAYBE A *LOT* OF THEM.

I'LL ANSWER ANY YOU HAVE. IT WON'T BE EASY BUT...

WE KNOW WHAT IT'S LIKE TO BE DIFFERENT, MIA.

THAT'S *WHY* WE ALL COME TO THE TOWER.

AND ME AND VIC ARE HERE *SEVEN* DAYS A *WEEK.* YOU NEED ANYTHING, YOU JUST SWING BY.

LIKE ALL THOSE OTHER GUYS THAT SHOWED UP. YOU'RE A *TITAN,* SPEEDY! NOW AND FOREVER!

I'M A TITAN...?

I'M A TITAN.

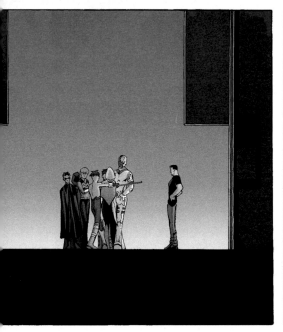

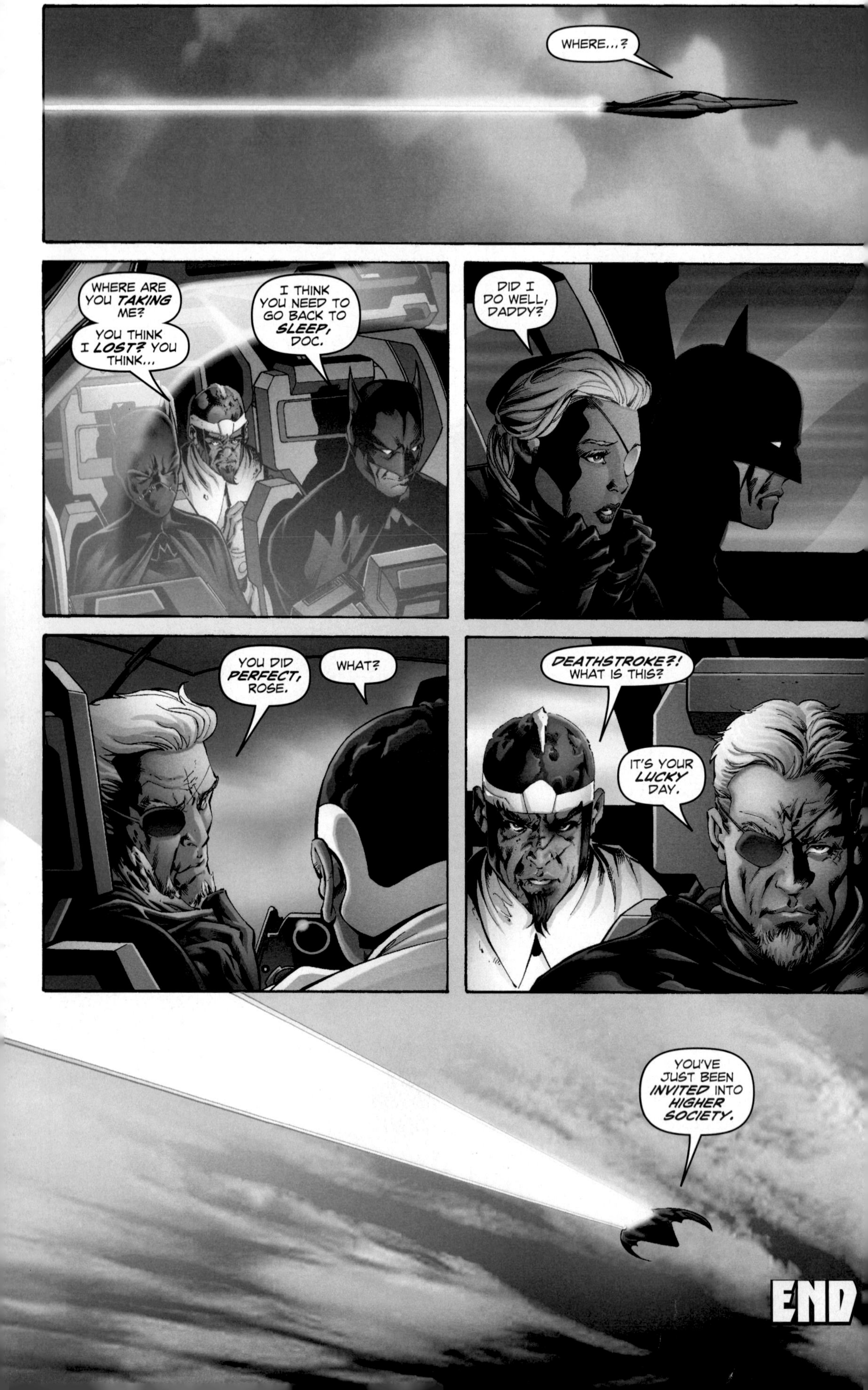
WHERE...?
WHERE ARE YOU TAKING ME?
YOU THINK I LOST? YOU THINK...
I THINK YOU NEED TO GO BACK TO SLEEP, DOC.
DID I DO WELL, DADDY?
YOU DID PERFECT, ROSE.
WHAT?
DEATHSTROKE?! WHAT IS THIS?
IT'S YOUR LUCKY DAY.
YOU'VE JUST BEEN INVITED INTO HIGHER SOCIETY.
END

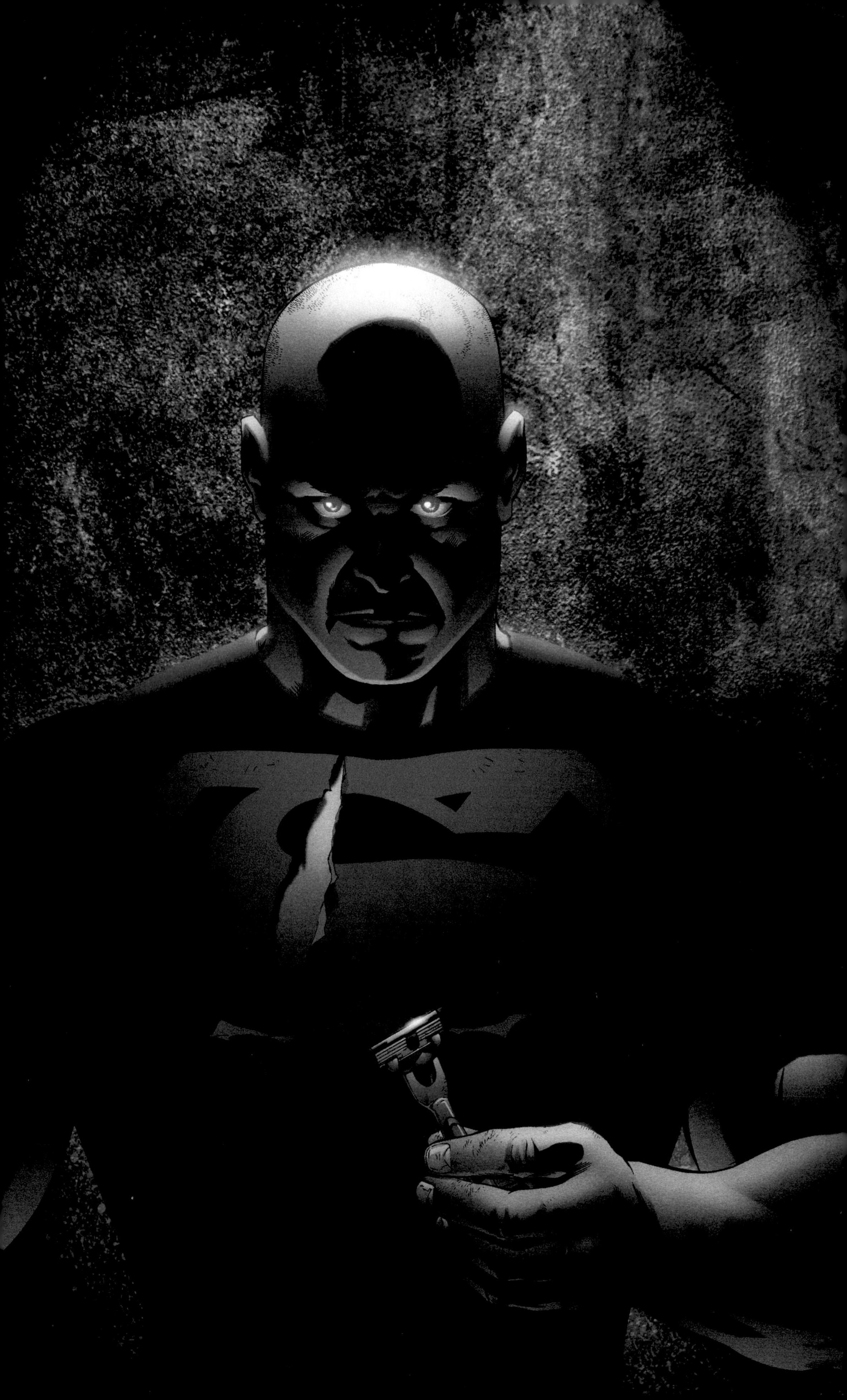

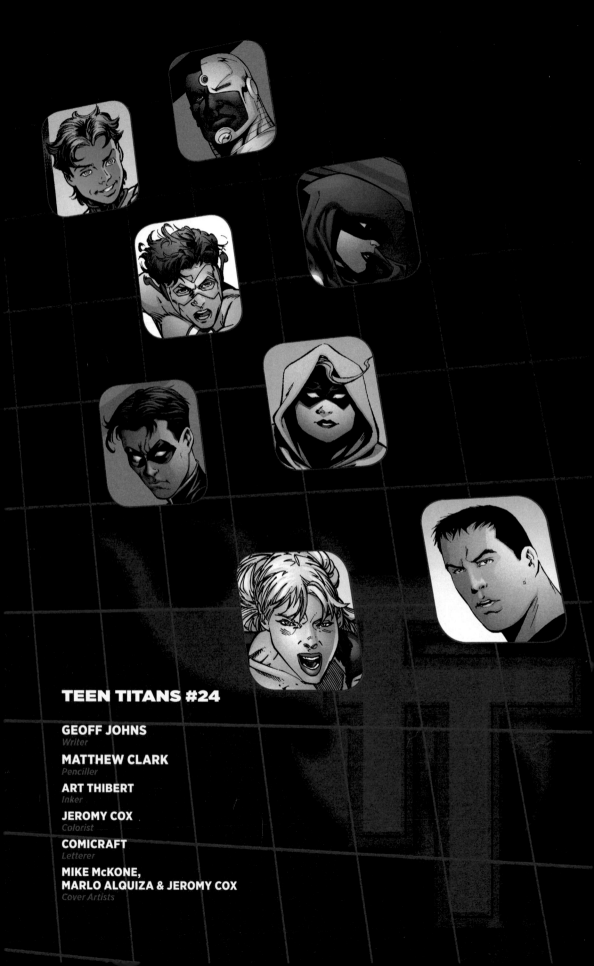

TEEN TITANS #24

GEOFF JOHNS
Writer

MATTHEW CLARK
Penciller

ART THIBERT
Inker

JEROMY COX
Colorist

COMICRAFT
Letterer

**MIKE McKONE,
MARLO ALQUIZA & JEROMY COX**
Cover Artists

SAN FRANCISCO.

SATURDAY, 9:24 A.M.

I WAS SUPPOSED TO BE *SUPERMAN*.

THE JOURNEY OF MAN

INHERITING MEMORIES

HUMAN GENETICS:
CONCEPTS AND APPLICATIONS

LEX LUTHOR
THE UNAUTHORIZED BIO

BUT I DON'T DESERVE IT.

I'M NOT A MAN OF STEEL.

I'M A FAKE.

MY REAL NAME WAS ON A TEST TUBE.

I'D GUESS IT WAS SOMETHING LIKE *SUBJECT SIXTEEN* OR *PROJECT: SUPERMAN*.

BUT AFTER I ESCAPED FROM CADMUS LABS, THE *PRESS* LABELED ME *SUPERBOY*.

SUPERMAN CALLED ME *KON-EL*.

MY FRIENDS CALL ME--

CONNER.

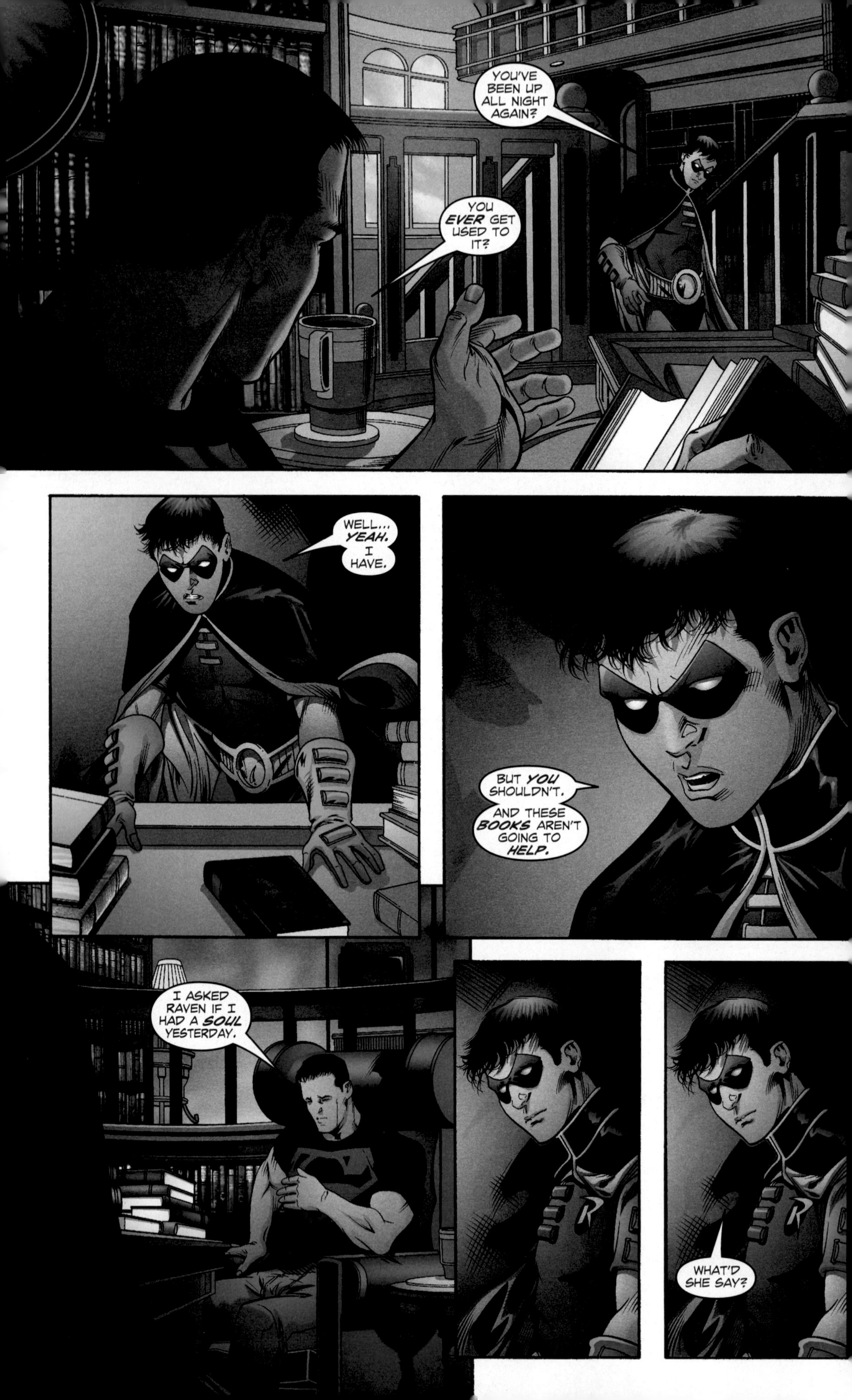
YOU'VE BEEN UP ALL NIGHT AGAIN?
YOU EVER GET USED TO IT?
WELL... YEAH. I HAVE.
BUT YOU SHOULDN'T.
AND THESE BOOKS AREN'T GOING TO HELP.
I ASKED RAVEN IF I HAD A SOUL YESTERDAY.
WHAT'D SHE SAY?

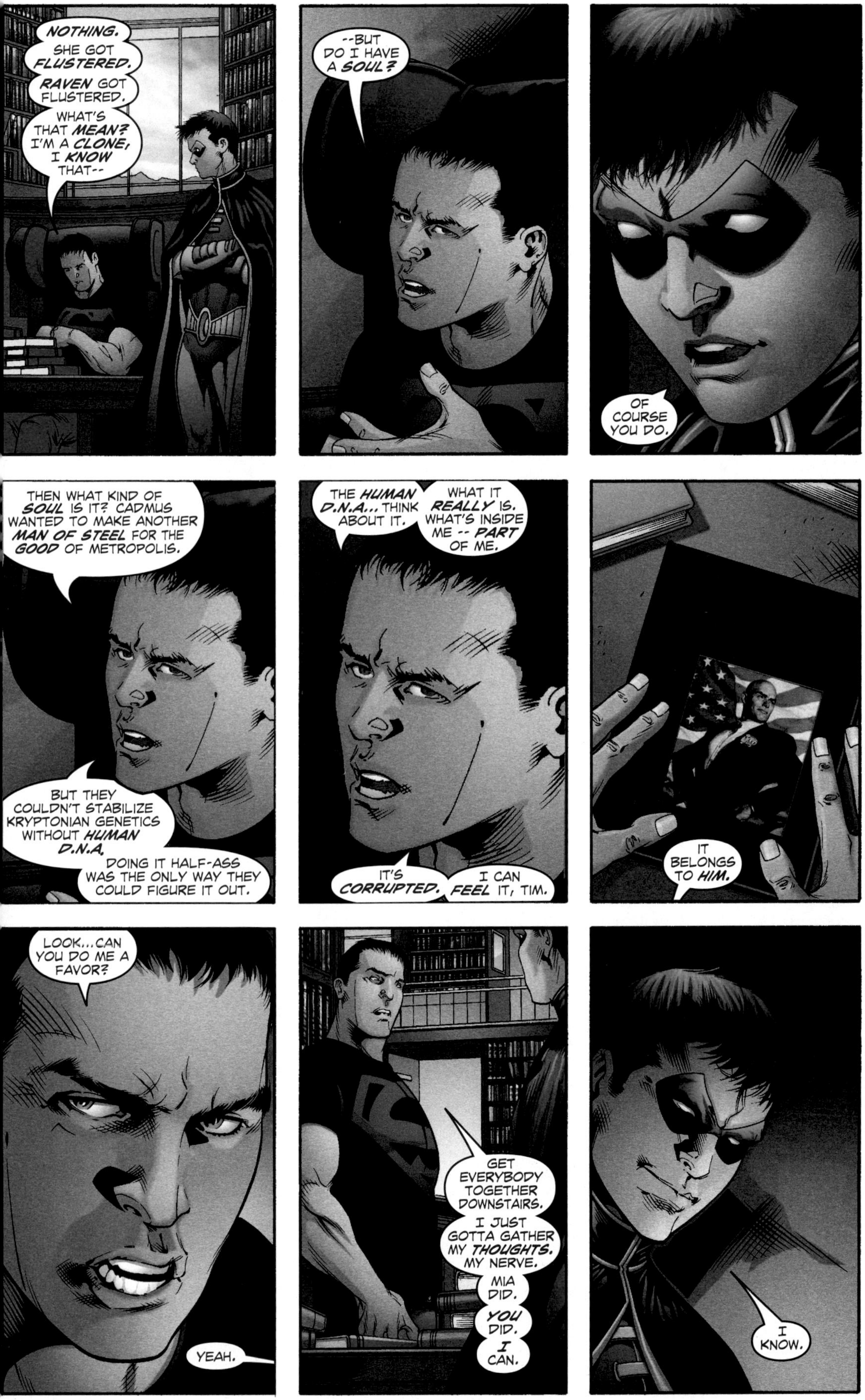

NOTHING.
SHE GOT FLUSTERED.
RAVEN GOT FLUSTERED.
WHAT'S THAT MEAN? I'M A CLONE, I KNOW THAT--
--BUT DO I HAVE A SOUL?
OF COURSE YOU DO.
THEN WHAT KIND OF SOUL IS IT? CADMUS WANTED TO MAKE ANOTHER MAN OF STEEL FOR THE GOOD OF METROPOLIS.
BUT THEY COULDN'T STABILIZE KRYPTONIAN GENETICS WITHOUT HUMAN D.N.A.
DOING IT HALF-ASS WAS THE ONLY WAY THEY COULD FIGURE IT OUT.
THE HUMAN D.N.A... THINK ABOUT IT.
WHAT IT REALLY IS. WHAT'S INSIDE ME -- PART OF ME.
IT'S CORRUPTED.
I CAN FEEL IT, TIM.
IT BELONGS TO HIM.
LOOK...CAN YOU DO ME A FAVOR?
YEAH.
GET EVERYBODY TOGETHER DOWNSTAIRS.
I JUST GOTTA GATHER MY THOUGHTS. MY NERVE.
MIA DID.
YOU DID.
I CAN.
I KNOW.

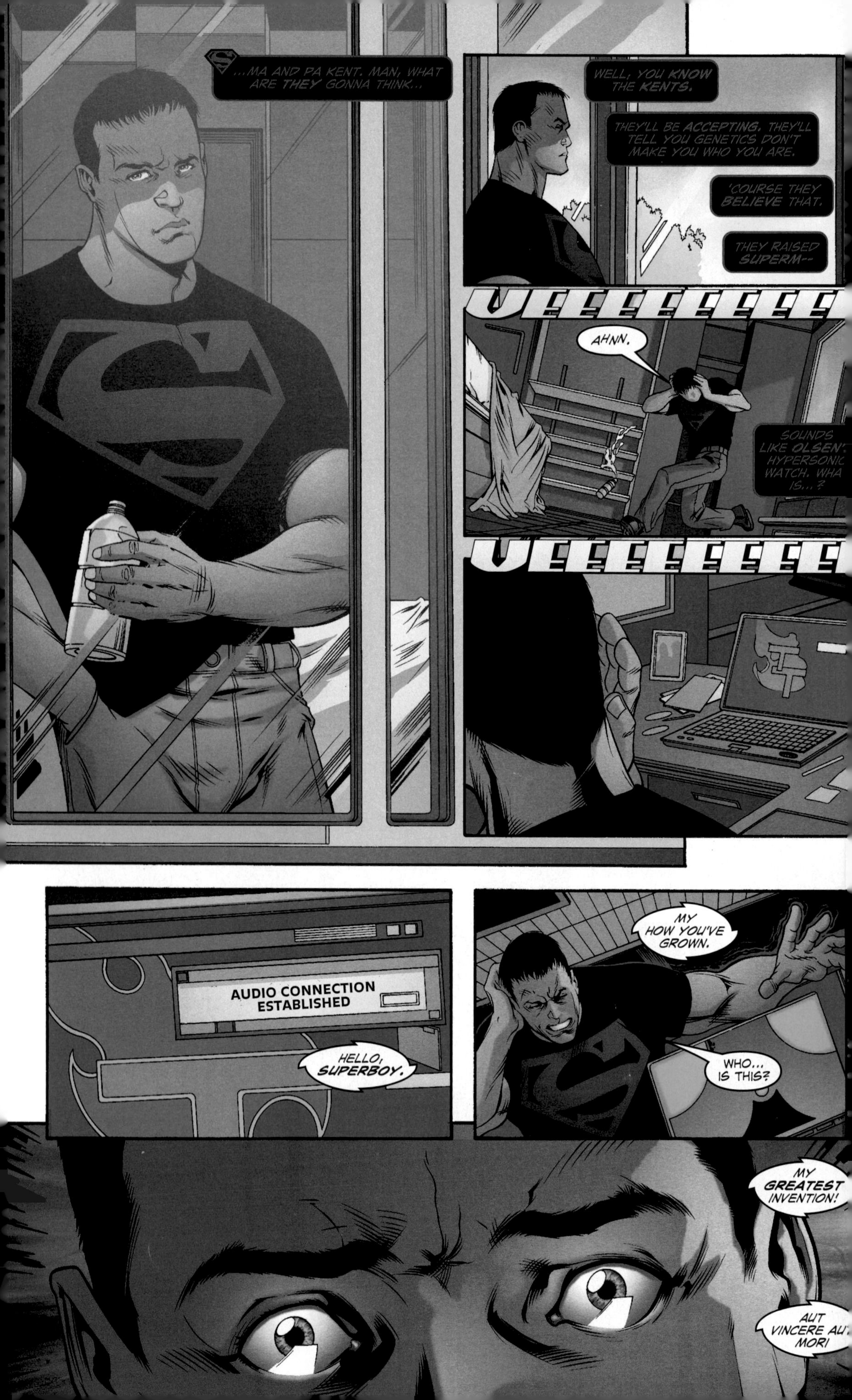
...MA AND PA KENT. MAN, WHAT ARE THEY GONNA THINK...
WELL, YOU KNOW THE KENTS.
THEY'LL BE ACCEPTING. THEY'LL TELL YOU GENETICS DON'T MAKE YOU WHO YOU ARE.
'COURSE THEY BELIEVE THAT.
THEY RAISED SUPERM--
VEEEEEEEEE
AHNN.
SOUNDS LIKE OLSEN'S HYPERSONIC WATCH. WHAT IS...?
VEEEEEEEEE
AUDIO CONNECTION ESTABLISHED
HELLO, SUPERBOY.
MY HOW YOU'VE GROWN.
WHO... IS THIS?
MY GREATEST INVENTION!
AUT VINCERE AUT MORI

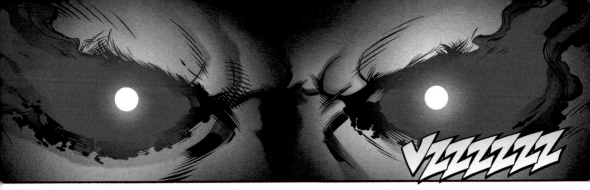

VZZZZZZ

AUDIO CONNECTION
TERMINATED

SKKKT

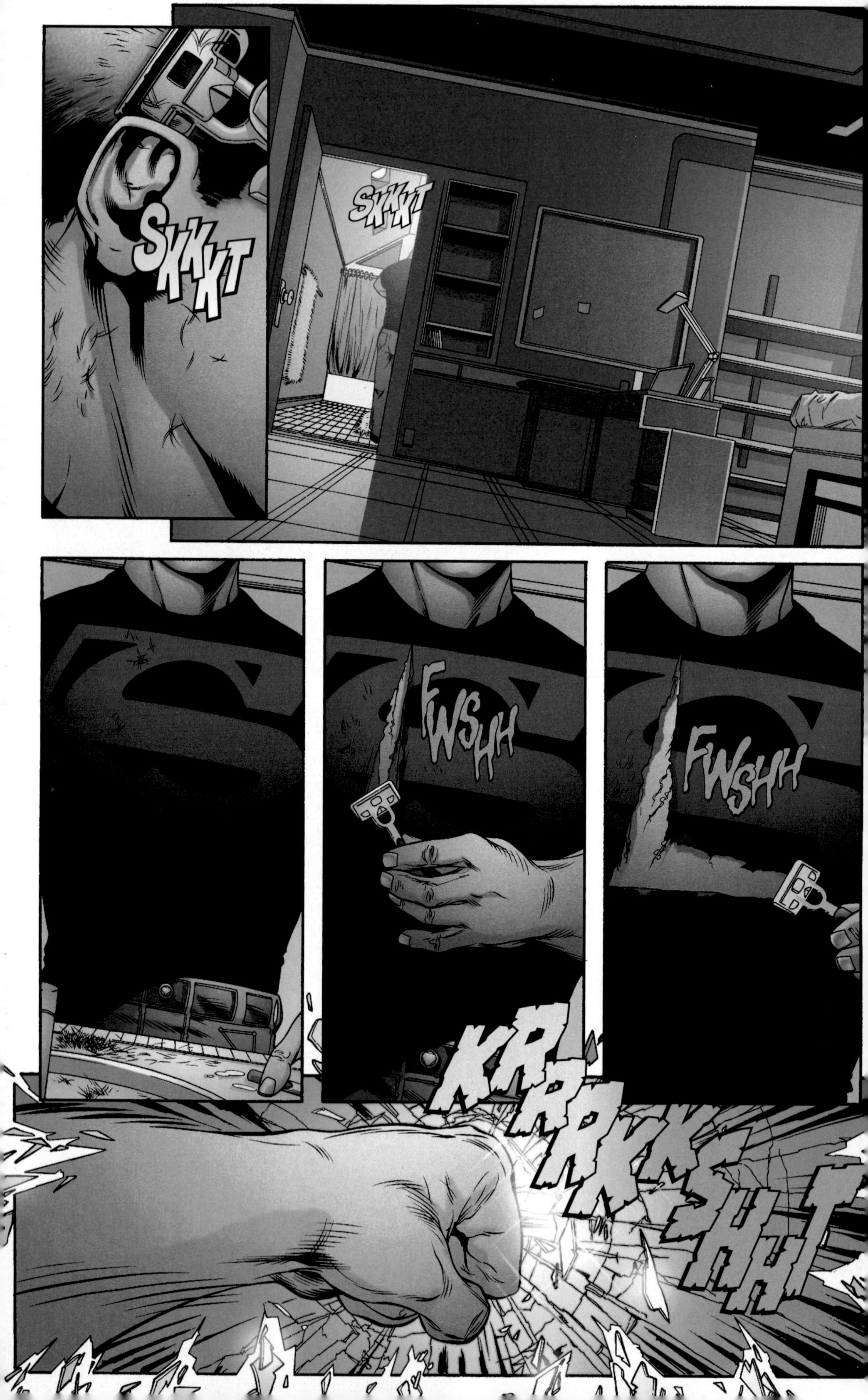
SKKKT
SKKKT
FWSHH
FWSHH
KRRRKKSHHT

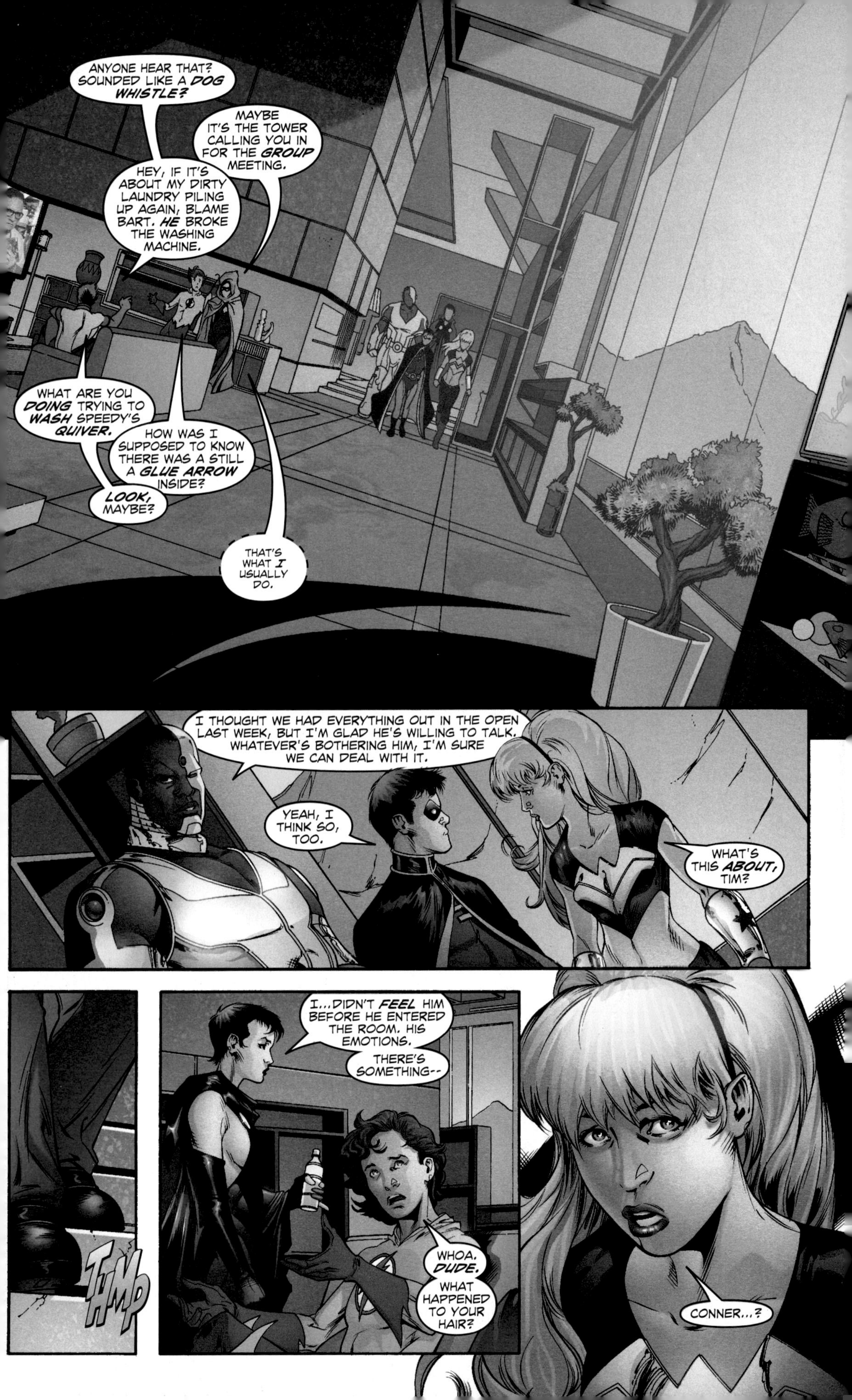
ANYONE HEAR THAT? SOUNDED LIKE A *DOG WHISTLE?*
MAYBE IT'S THE TOWER CALLING YOU IN FOR THE *GROUP* MEETING.
HEY, IF IT'S ABOUT MY DIRTY LAUNDRY PILING UP AGAIN, BLAME BART. *HE* BROKE THE WASHING MACHINE.
WHAT ARE YOU *DOING* TRYING TO *WASH* SPEEDY'S *QUIVER.*
HOW WAS I SUPPOSED TO KNOW THERE WAS A STILL A *GLUE ARROW* INSIDE?
LOOK, MAYBE?
THAT'S WHAT *I* USUALLY DO.
I THOUGHT WE HAD EVERYTHING OUT IN THE OPEN LAST WEEK, BUT I'M GLAD HE'S WILLING TO TALK. WHATEVER'S BOTHERING HIM, I'M SURE WE CAN DEAL WITH IT.
YEAH, I THINK SO, TOO.
WHAT'S THIS *ABOUT,* TIM?
THMP
I...DIDN'T *FEEL* HIM BEFORE HE ENTERED THE ROOM. HIS EMOTIONS.
THERE'S SOMETHING--
WHOA. *DUDE.* WHAT HAPPENED TO YOUR HAIR?
CONNER...?

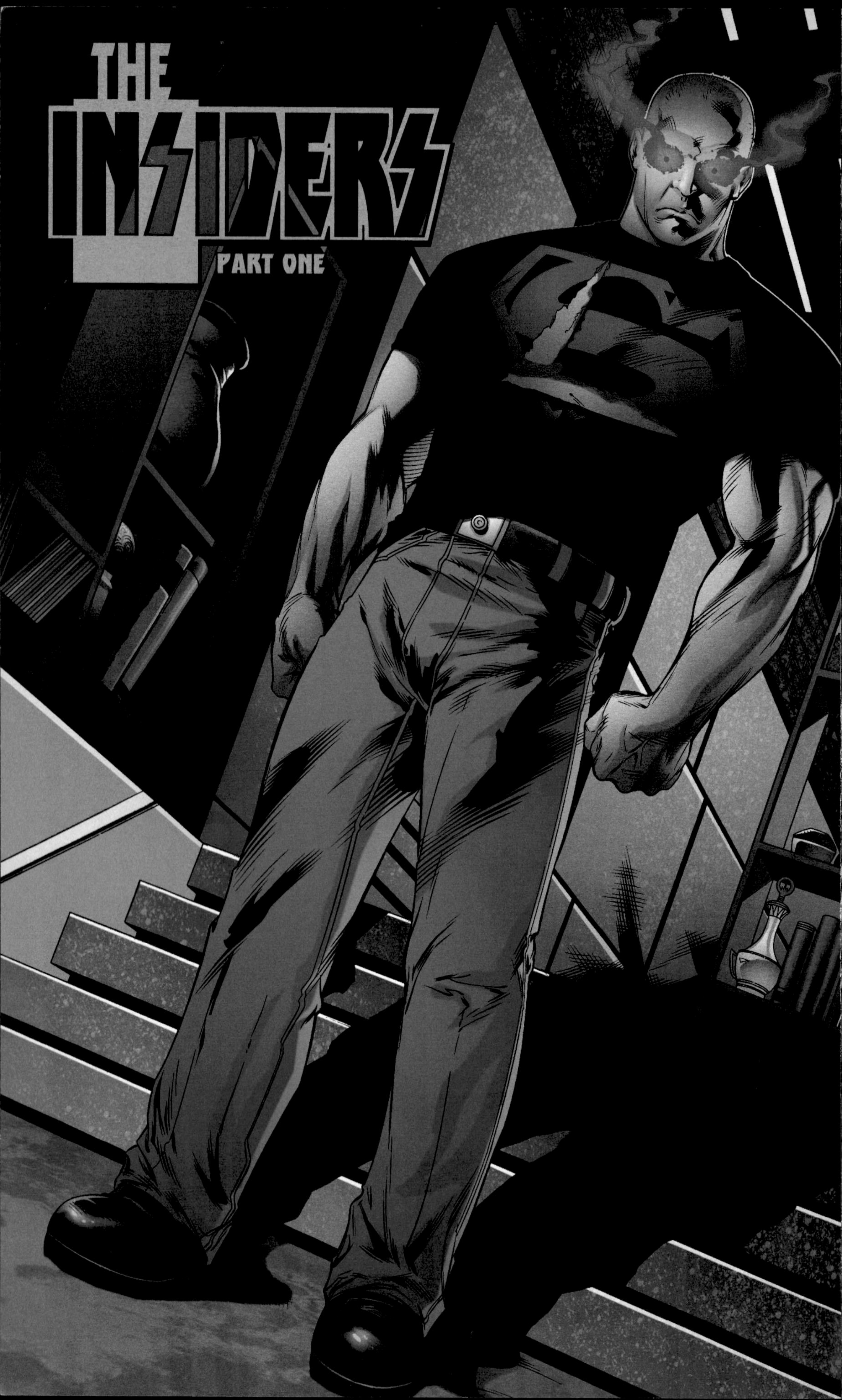
THE INSIDERS
PART ONE

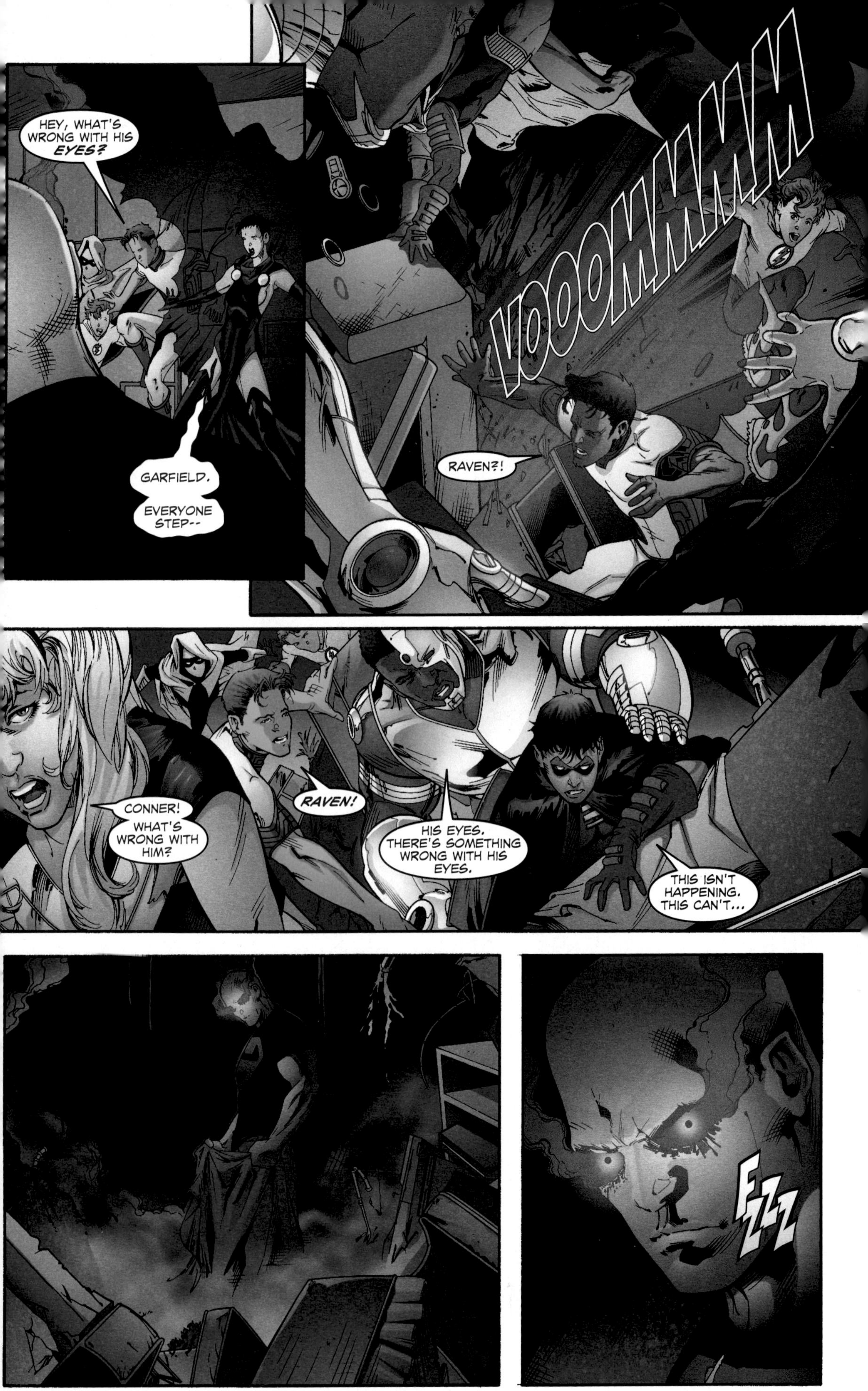
HEY, WHAT'S WRONG WITH HIS EYES?
GARFIELD.
EVERYONE STEP--
VOOOMMMMM
RAVEN?!
CONNER! WHAT'S WRONG WITH HIM?
RAVEN!
HIS EYES. THERE'S SOMETHING WRONG WITH HIS EYES.
THIS ISN'T HAPPENING. THIS CAN'T...
FZZZ

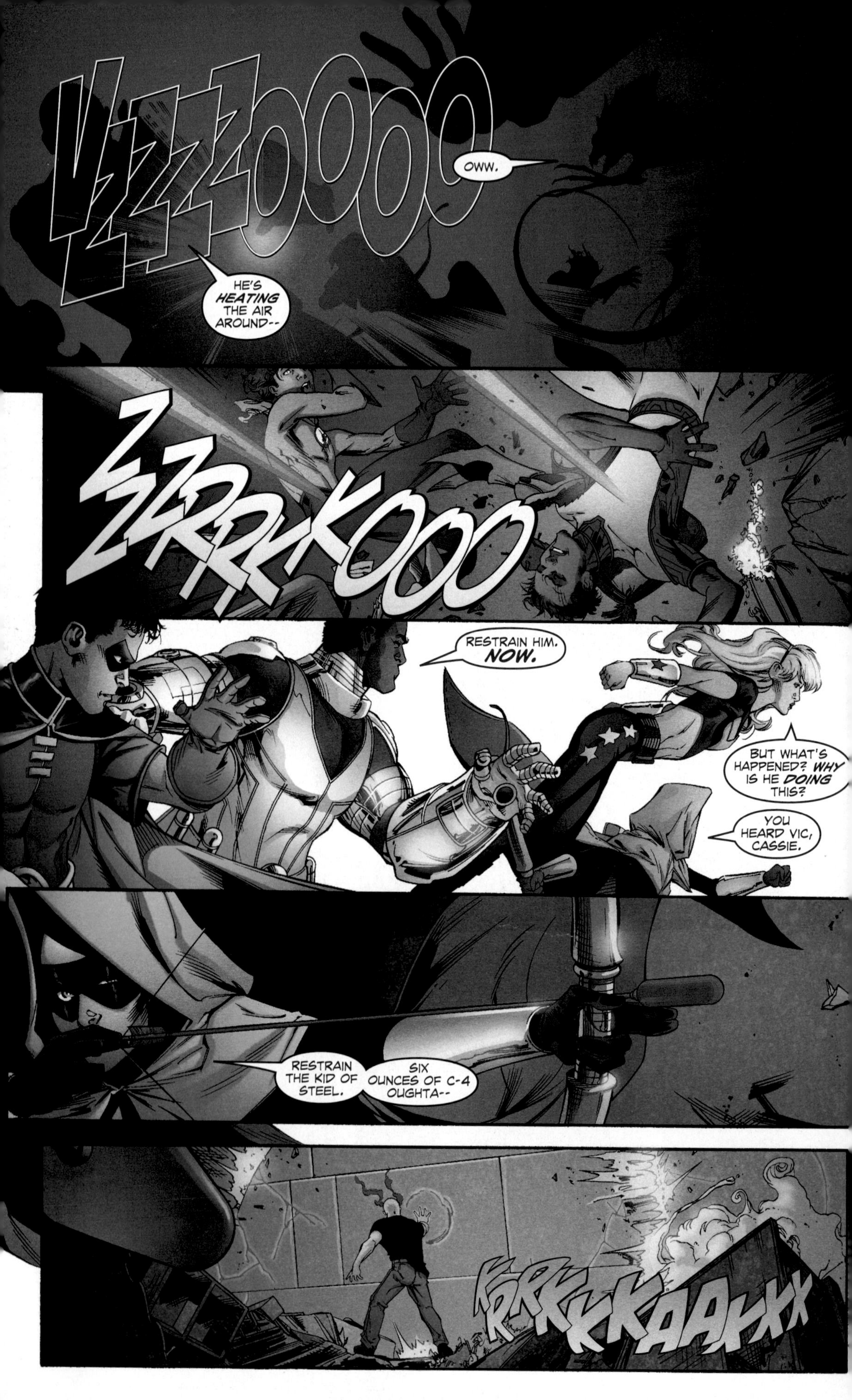
VZZZZOOOO
OWW.
HE'S HEATING THE AIR AROUND--
ZZRRKOOO
RESTRAIN HIM. NOW.
BUT WHAT'S HAPPENED? WHY IS HE DOING THIS?
YOU HEARD VIC, CASSIE.
RESTRAIN THE KID OF STEEL.
SIX OUNCES OF C-4 OUGHTA--
KRRKKAAKKK

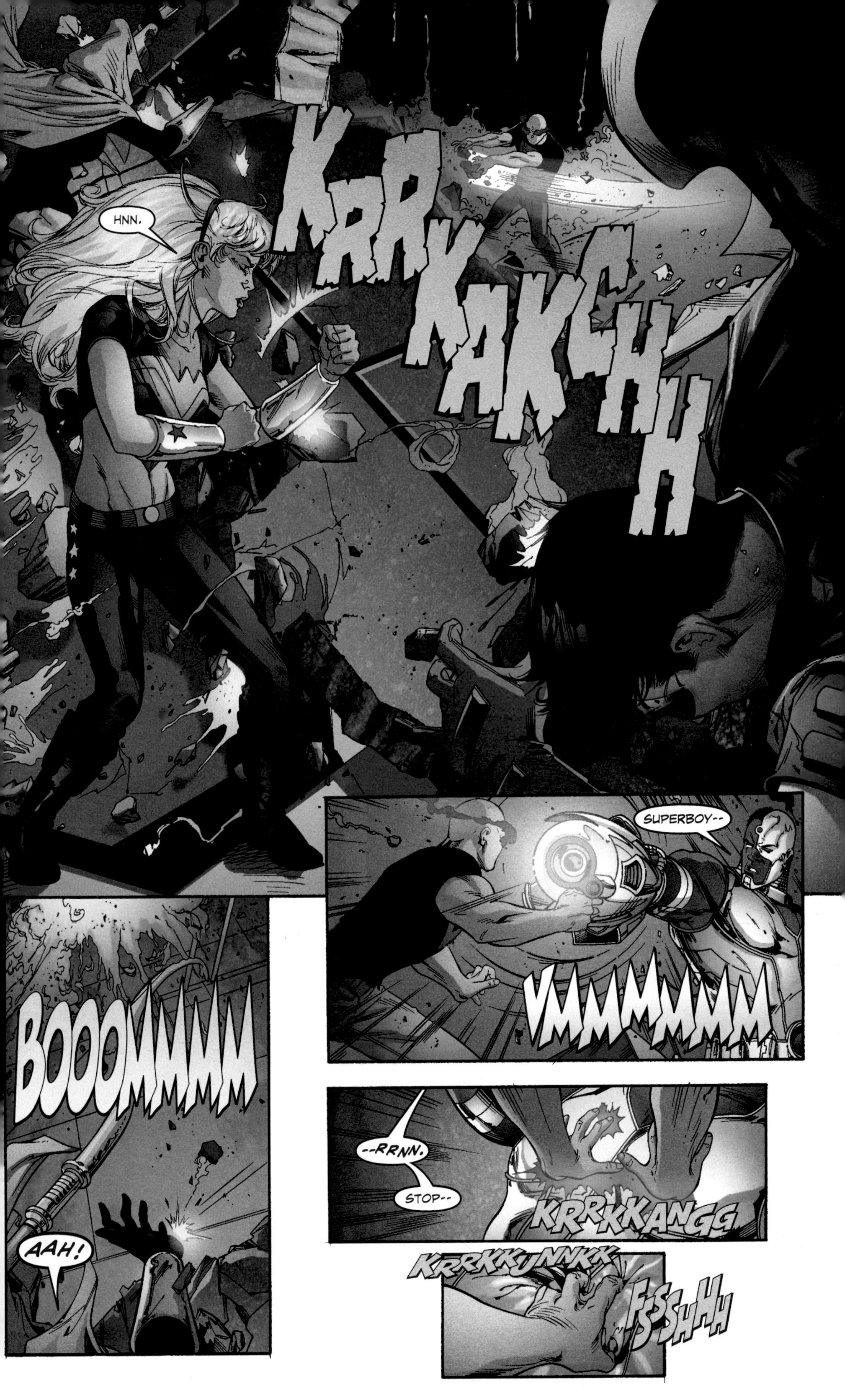
HNN.
KRRKAKCHHH
SUPERBOY--
VMMMMMM
BOOOMMMM
AAH!
--RRNN.
STOP--
KRRKKANGG
KRRKKUNNKK
FSSSHHH

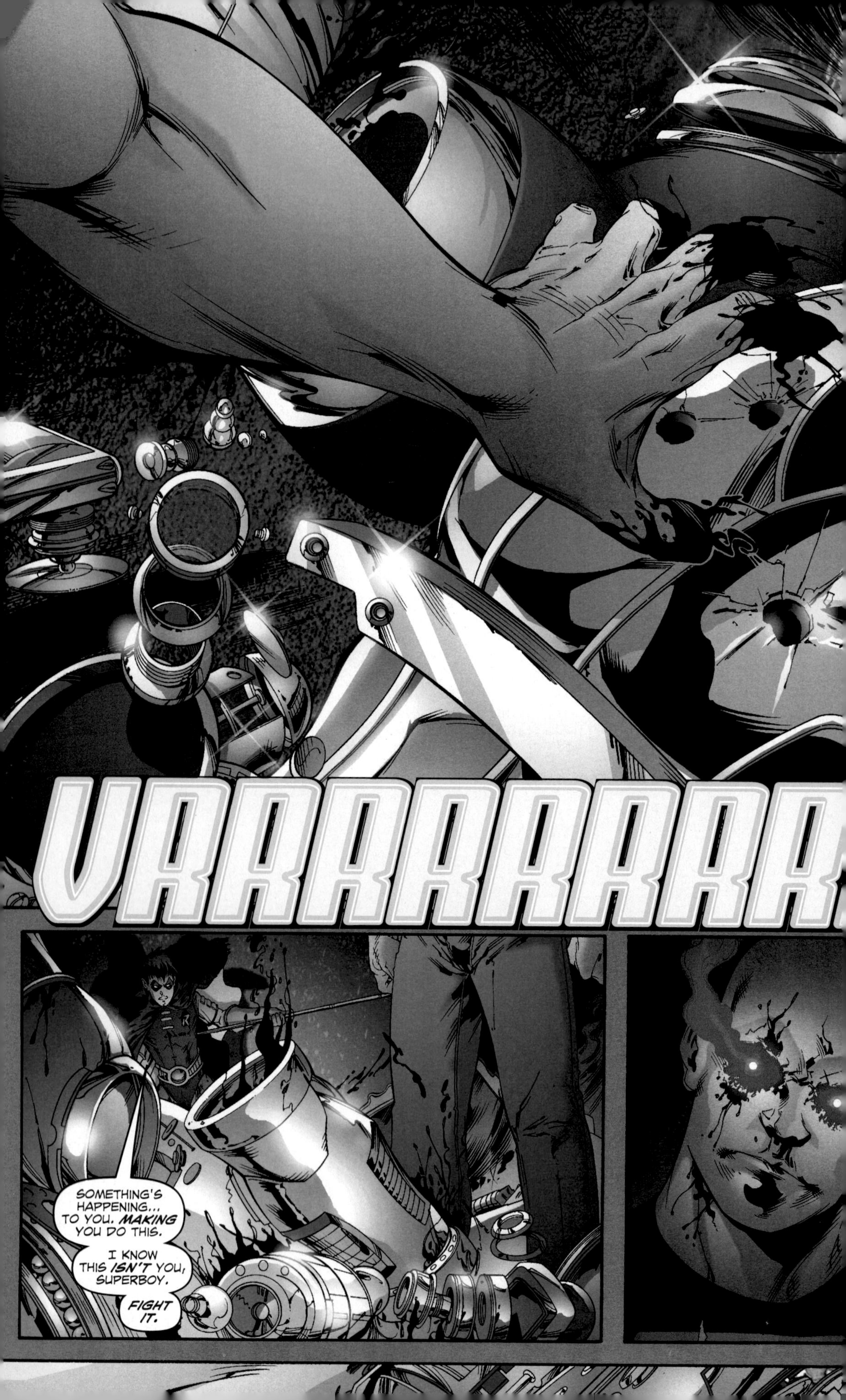
VRRRRRRRRRR
SOMETHING'S HAPPENING... TO YOU. *MAKING* YOU DO THIS.
I KNOW THIS *ISN'T* YOU, SUPERBOY.
FIGHT IT.

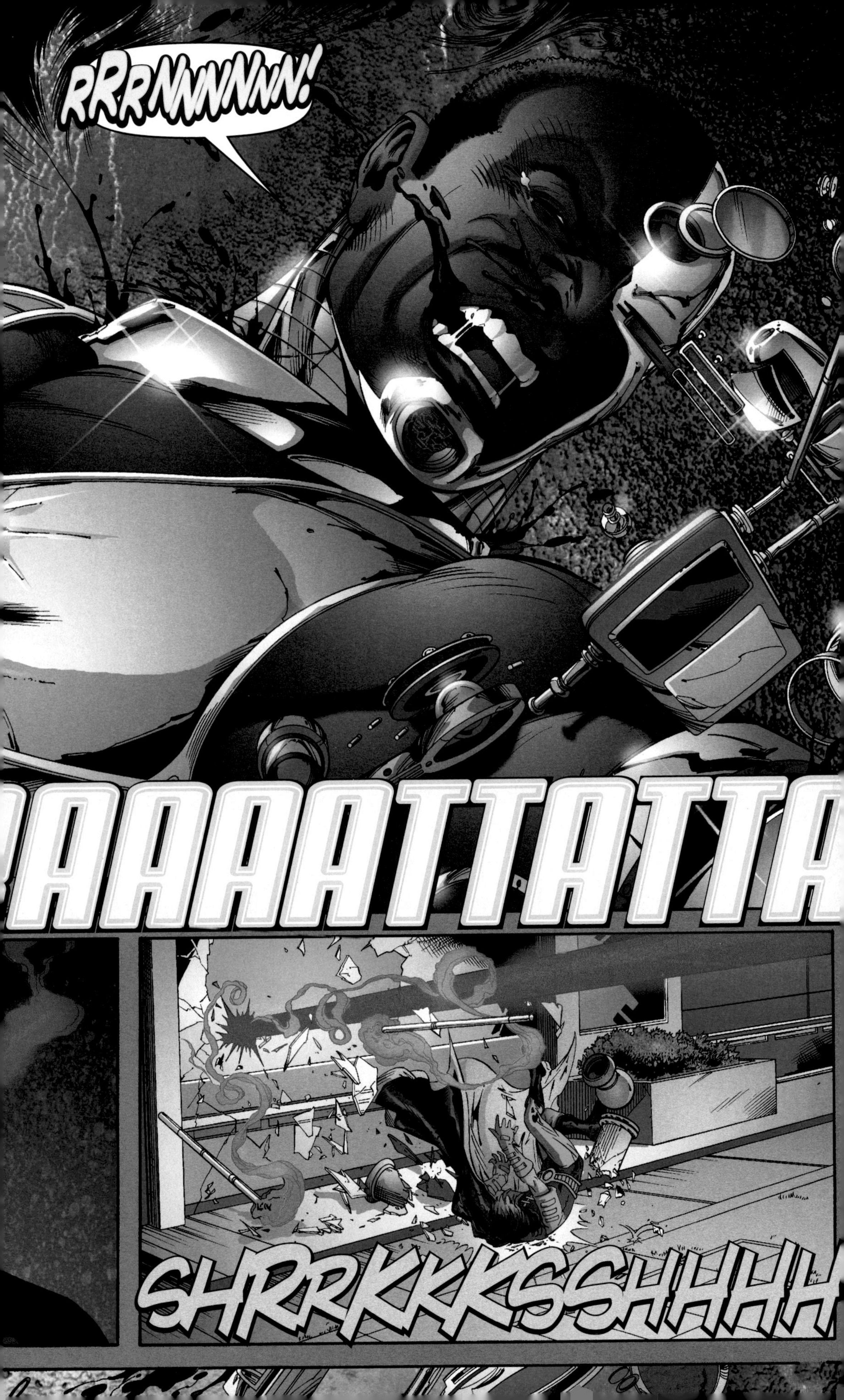
RRRNNNNNN!
AAAAATTATTA
SHRRKKKSSHHHH

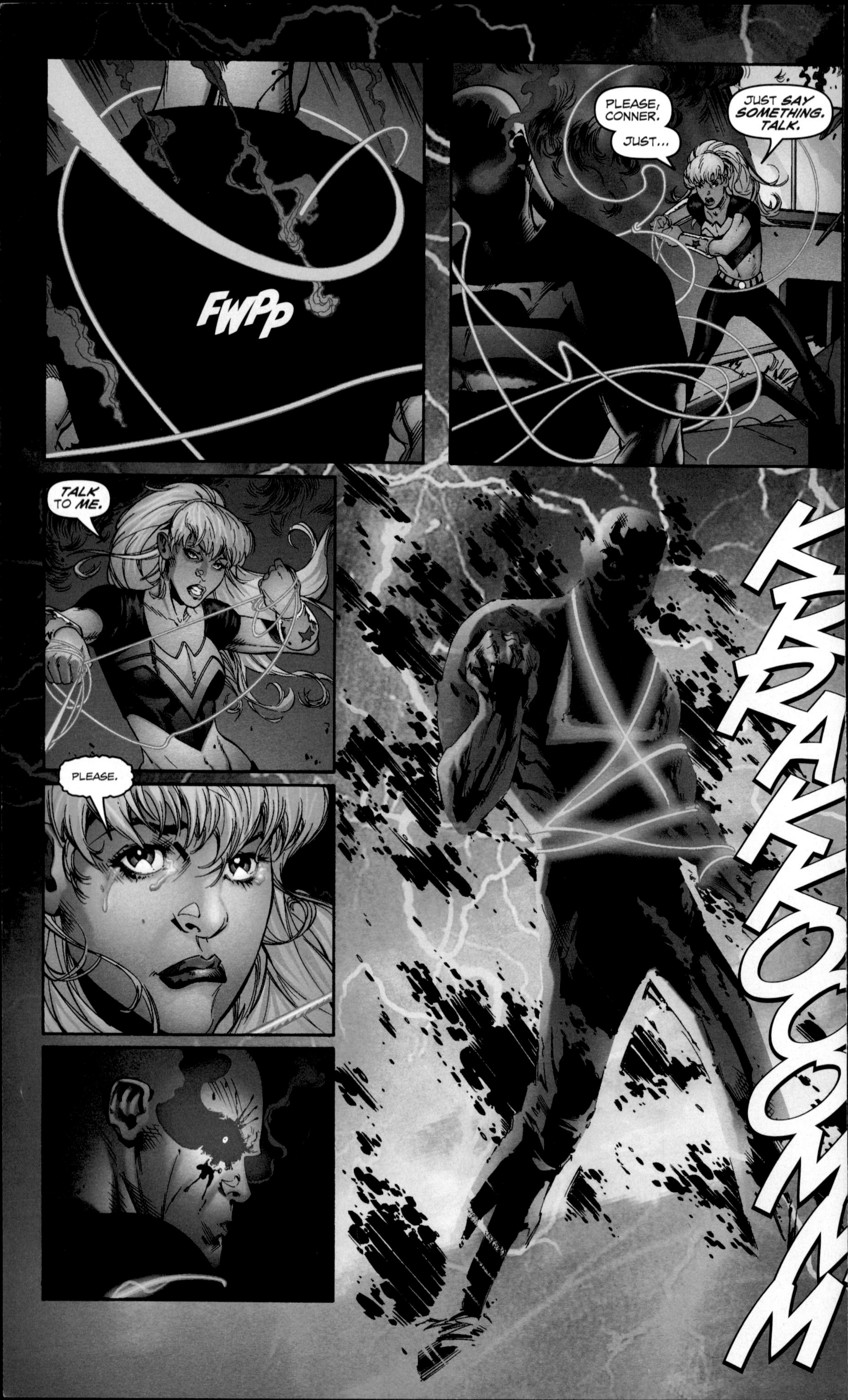
FWPP
PLEASE, CONNER.
JUST...
JUST SAY SOMETHING. TALK.
TALK TO ME.
PLEASE.
KRAKOOOOMM

WAKE UP, OKAY? WAKE UP AND I DON'T HAVE TO DO IT AGAI--

FSSSSSSS

FWP

KKKRRKKRKKKKKRKKRKKKRKRK

I... DON'T WANT TO FIGHT... YOU...

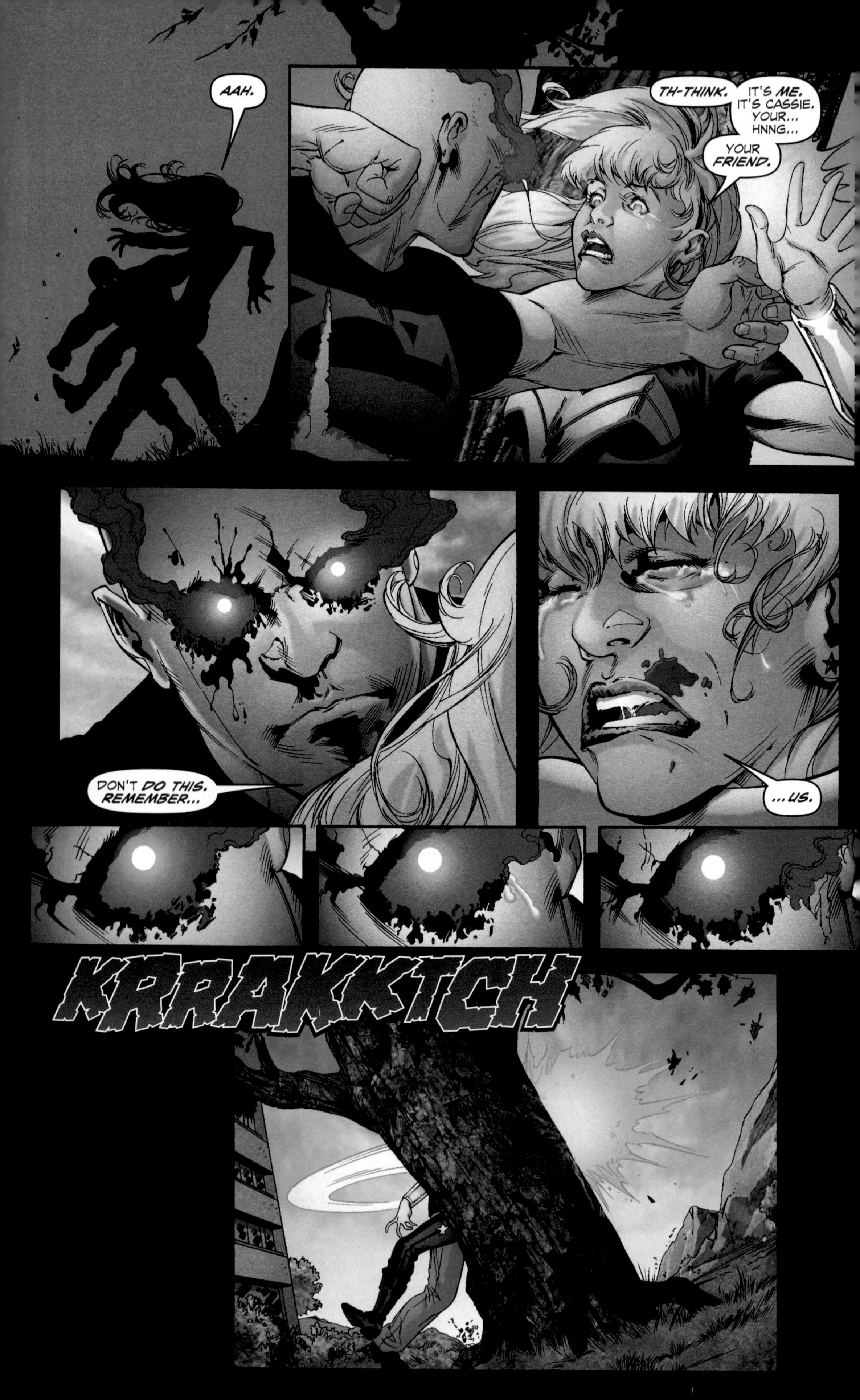
AAH.
TH-THINK.
IT'S ME. IT'S CASSIE. YOUR... HNNG...
YOUR FRIEND.
DON'T DO THIS. REMEMBER...
...US.
KRRAKKTCH

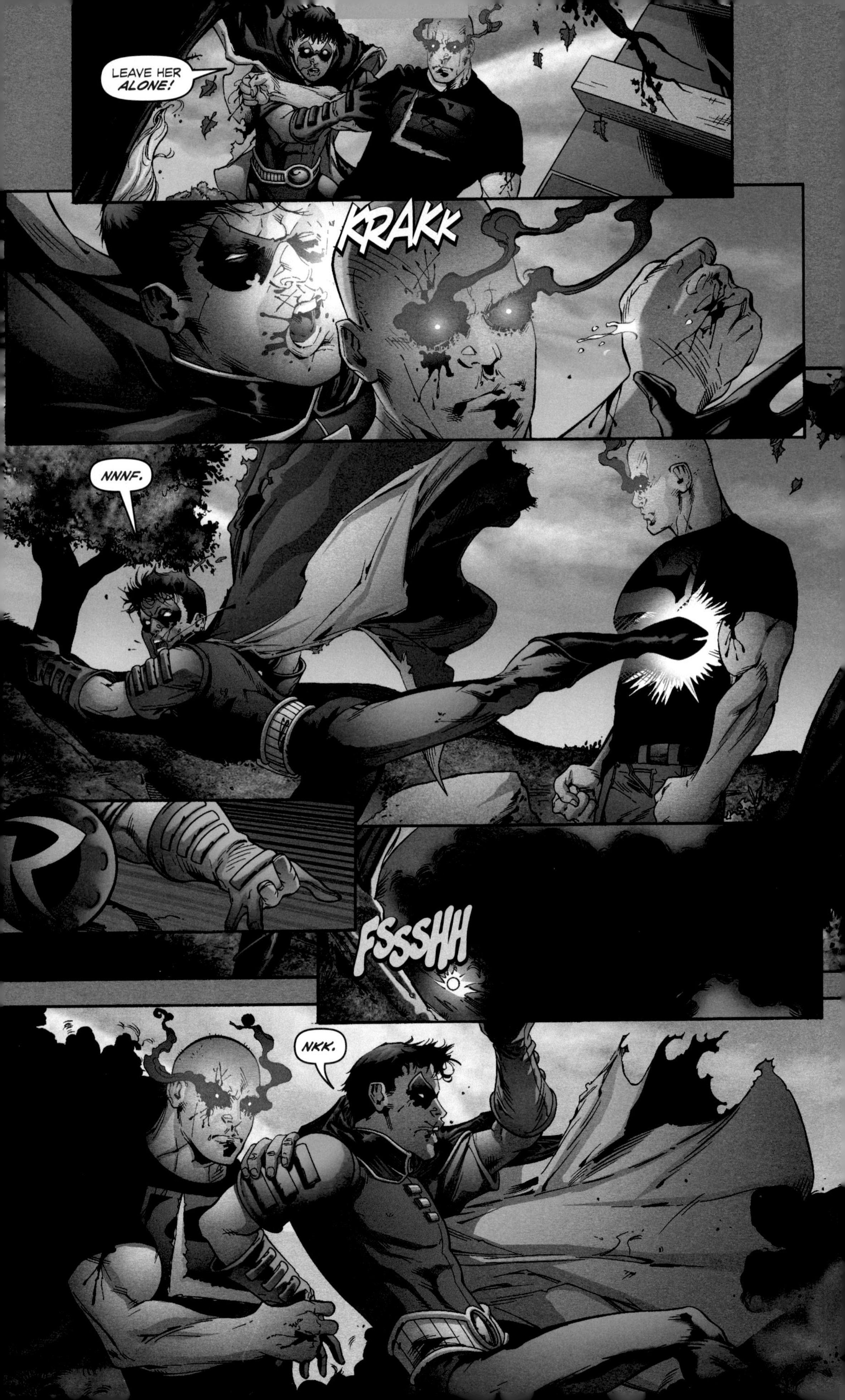
LEAVE HER ALONE!
KRAKK
NNNF.
FSSSHH
NKK.

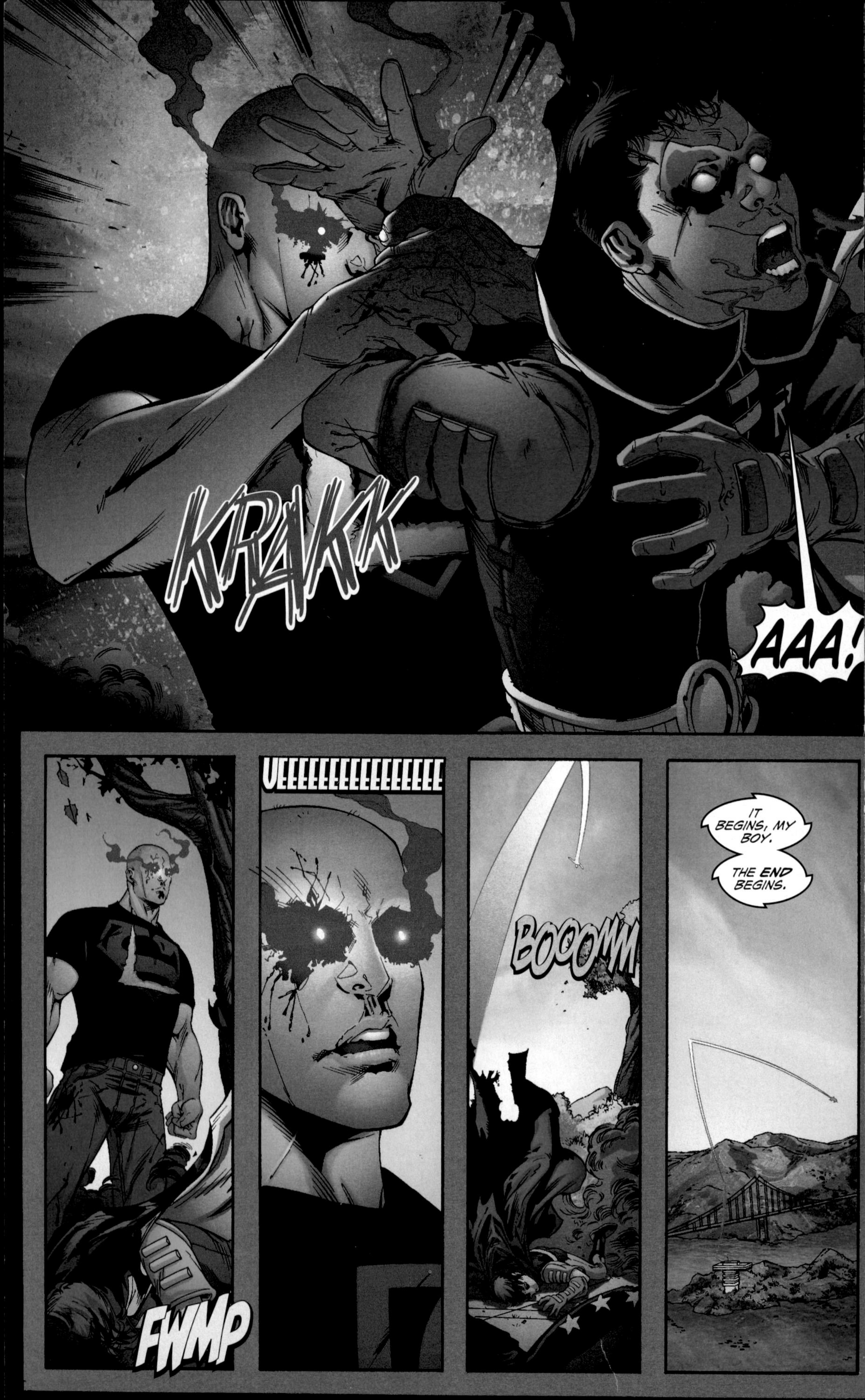
KRAKK
AAA!
FWMP
UEEEEEEEEEEEEEEE
BOOOMM
IT BEGINS, MY BOY.
THE END BEGINS.

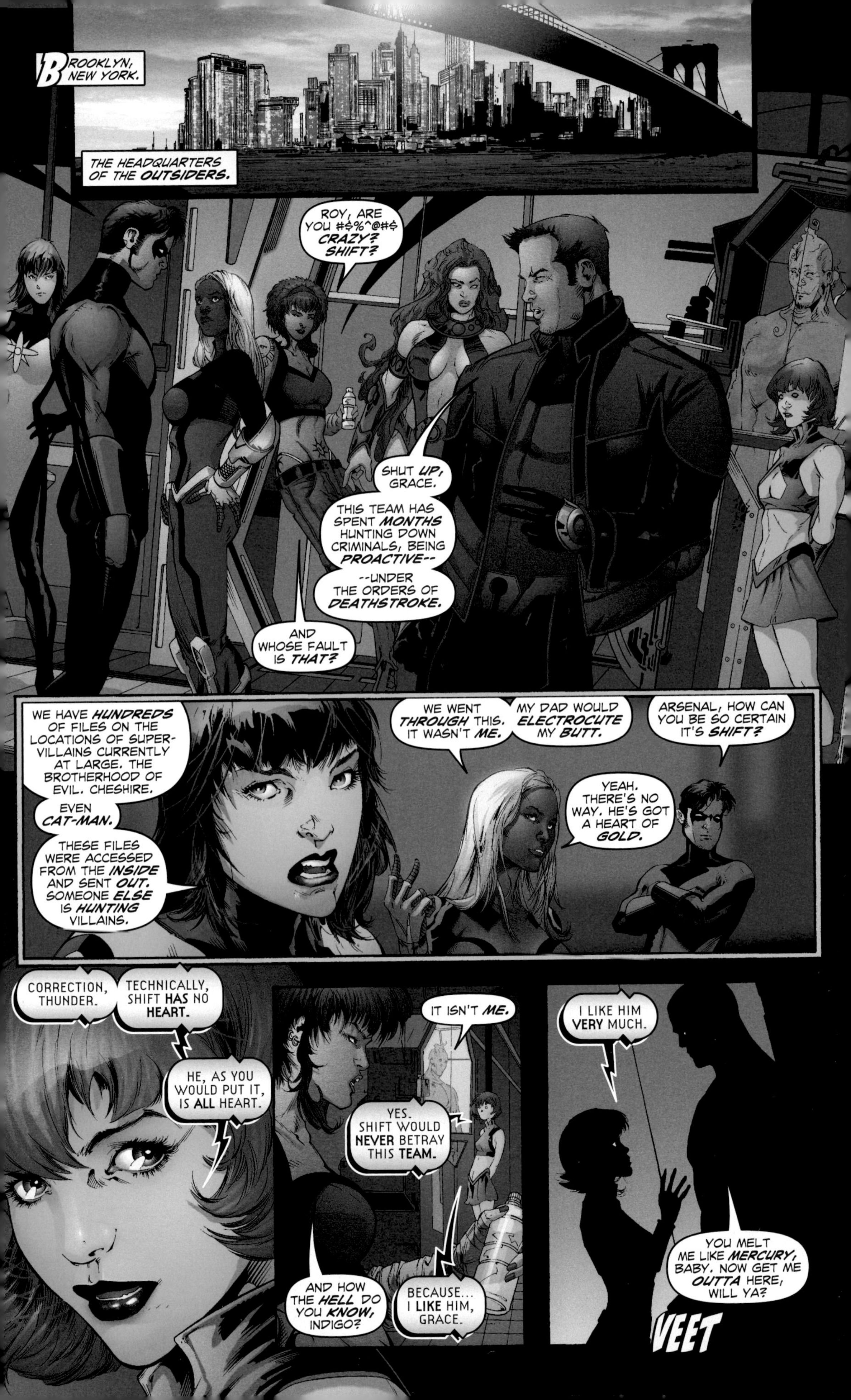
BROOKLYN, NEW YORK.
THE HEADQUARTERS OF THE OUTSIDERS.
ROY, ARE YOU #$%^@#$ CRAZY? SHIFT?
SHUT UP, GRACE.
THIS TEAM HAS SPENT MONTHS HUNTING DOWN CRIMINALS, BEING PROACTIVE--
--UNDER THE ORDERS OF DEATHSTROKE.
AND WHOSE FAULT IS THAT?
WE HAVE HUNDREDS OF FILES ON THE LOCATIONS OF SUPER-VILLAINS CURRENTLY AT LARGE. THE BROTHERHOOD OF EVIL. CHESHIRE.
EVEN CAT-MAN.
THESE FILES WERE ACCESSED FROM THE INSIDE AND SENT OUT. SOMEONE ELSE IS HUNTING VILLAINS.
WE WENT THROUGH THIS. IT WASN'T ME.
MY DAD WOULD ELECTROCUTE MY BUTT.
ARSENAL, HOW CAN YOU BE SO CERTAIN IT'S SHIFT?
YEAH. THERE'S NO WAY. HE'S GOT A HEART OF GOLD.
CORRECTION, THUNDER.
TECHNICALLY, SHIFT HAS NO HEART.
HE, AS YOU WOULD PUT IT, IS ALL HEART.
IT ISN'T ME.
YES. SHIFT WOULD NEVER BETRAY THIS TEAM.
AND HOW THE HELL DO YOU KNOW, INDIGO?
BECAUSE... I LIKE HIM, GRACE.
I LIKE HIM VERY MUCH.
YOU MELT ME LIKE MERCURY, BABY. NOW GET ME OUTTA HERE, WILL YA?
VEET

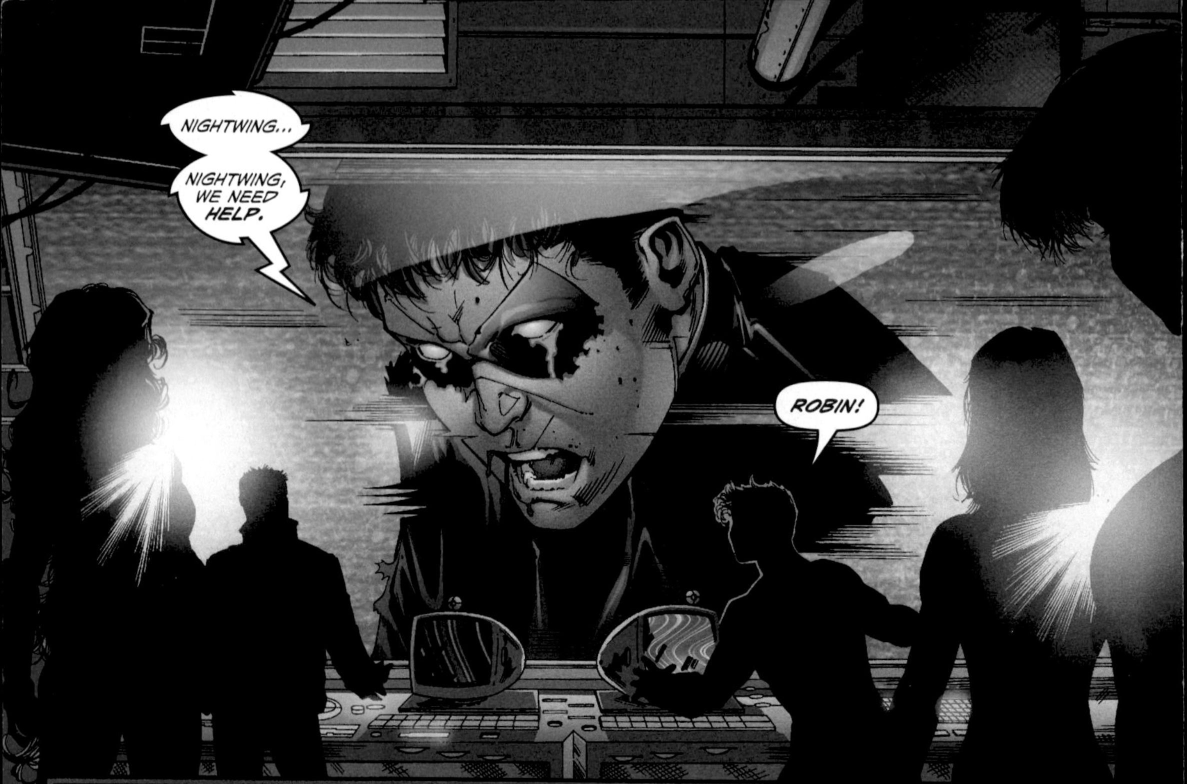
NIGHTWING...
NIGHTWING, WE NEED HELP.
ROBIN!

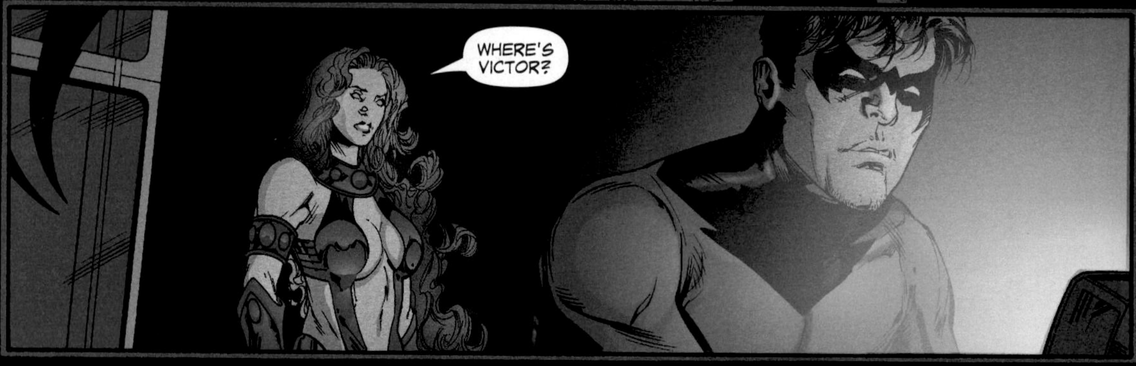
WHERE'S VICTOR?

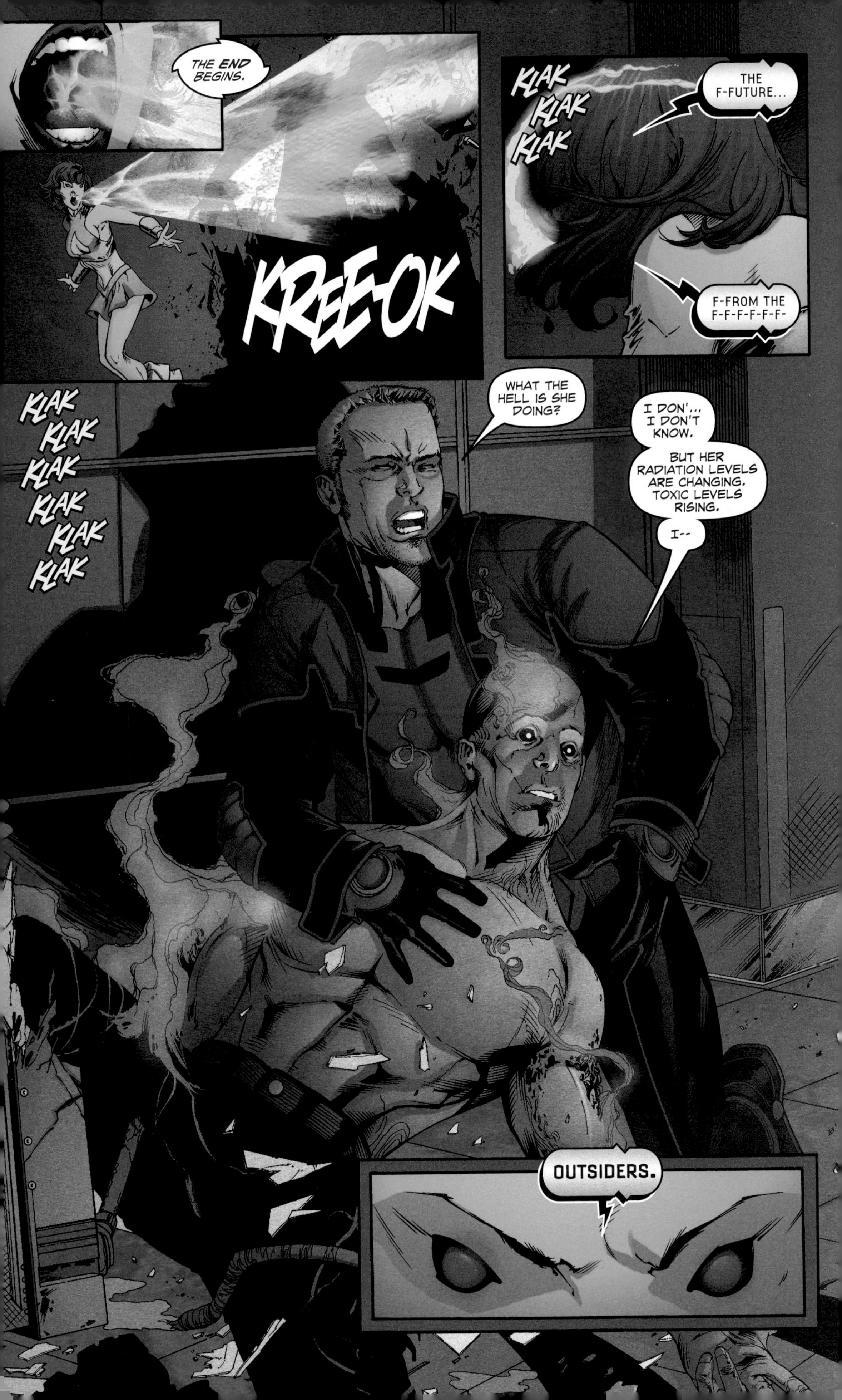

THE END BEGINS.
KREE-OK
KLAK KLAK KLAK
THE F-FUTURE...
F-FROM THE F-F-F-F-F-F-
KLAK KLAK KLAK KLAK KLAK KLAK
WHAT THE HELL IS SHE DOING?
I DON'... I DON'T KNOW.
BUT HER RADIATION LEVELS ARE CHANGING. TOXIC LEVELS RISING.
I--
OUTSIDERS.

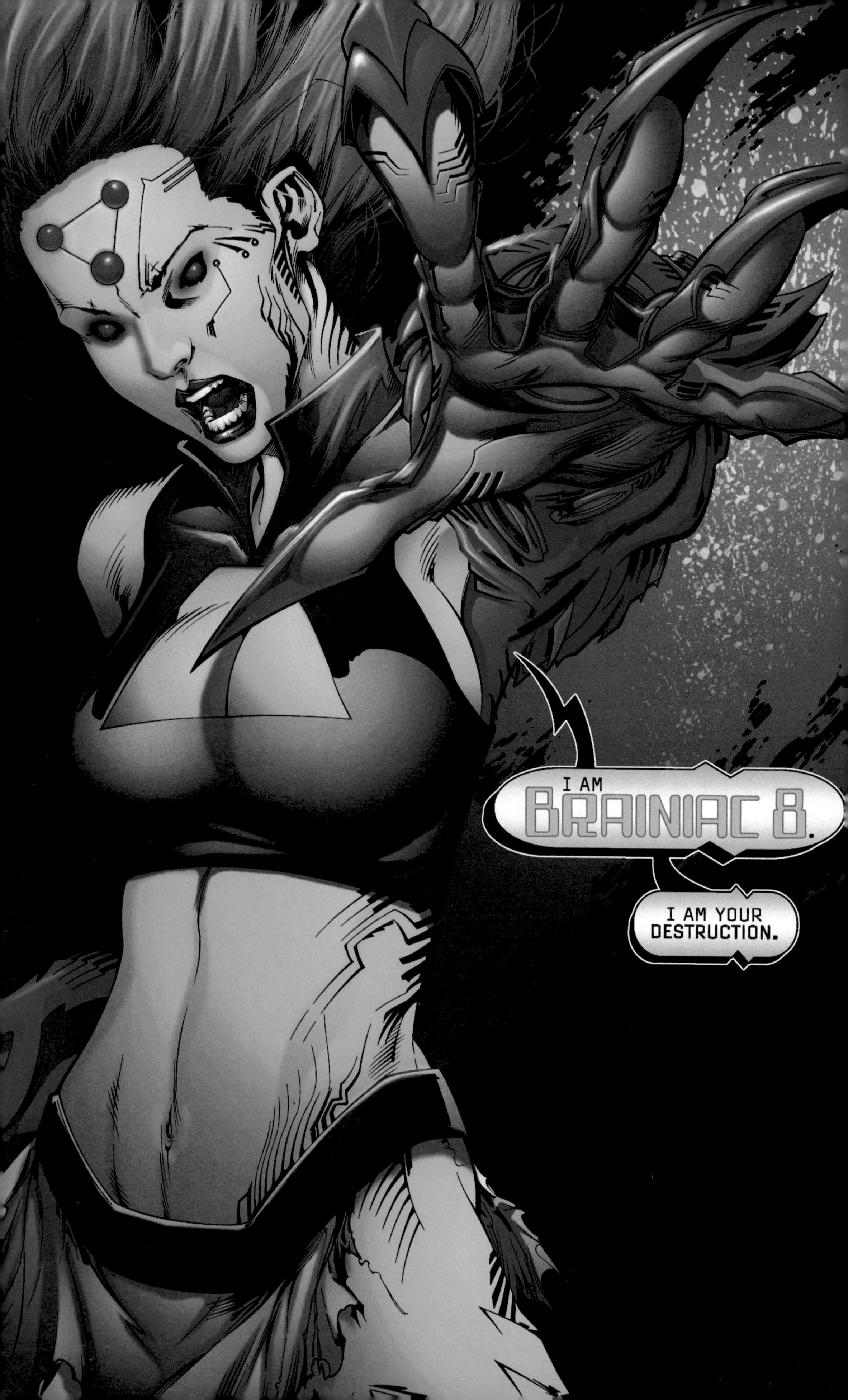
I AM BRAINIAC 8.
I AM YOUR DESTRUCTION.

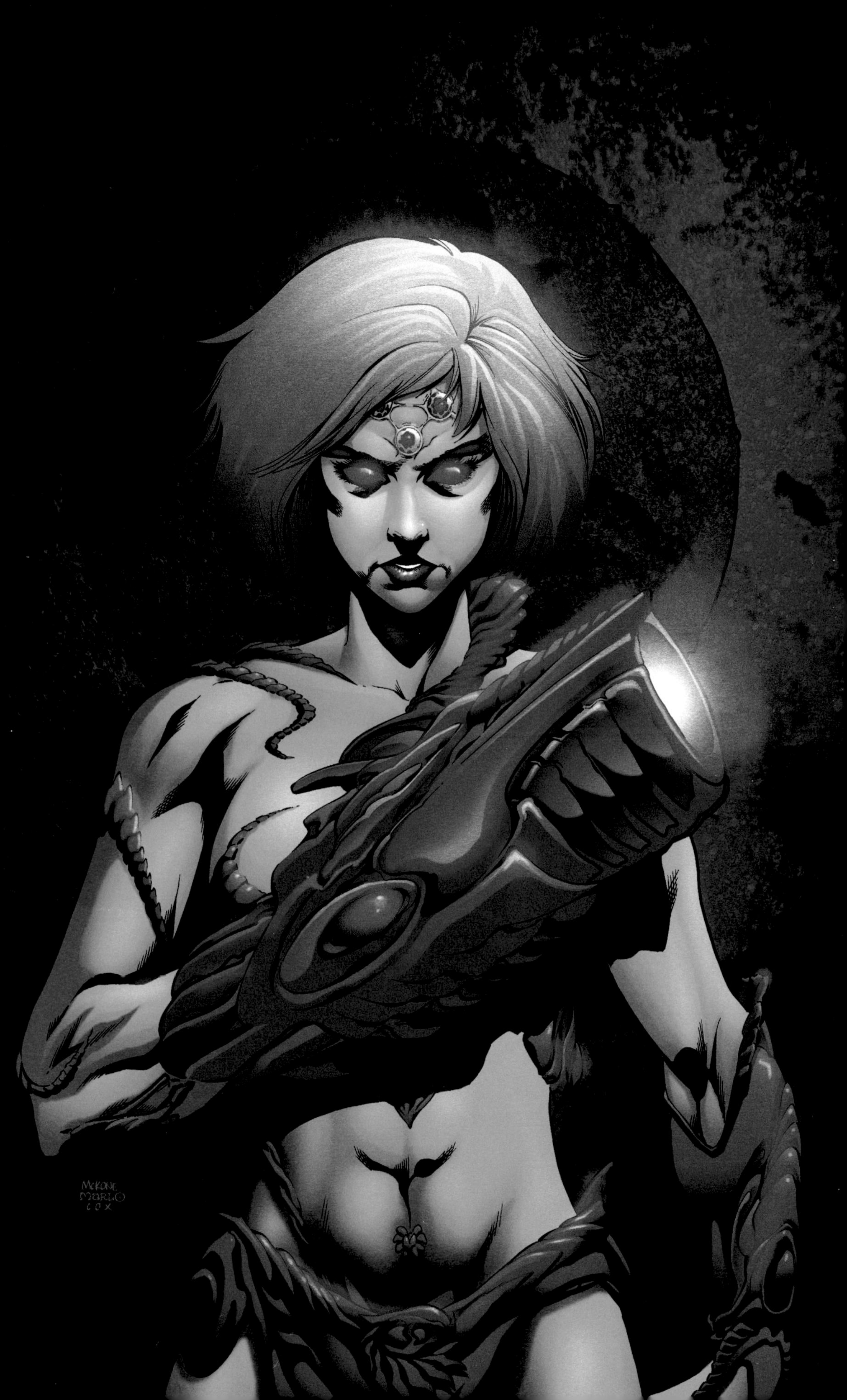

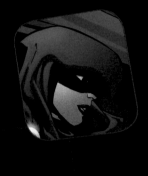

OUTSIDERS #24

JUDD WINICK
Writer

CARLOS D'ANDA
Artist

GUY MAJOR
Colorist

PHIL BALSMAN
Letterer

**MIKE McKONE,
MARLO ALQUIZA & JEROMY COX**
Cover Artists

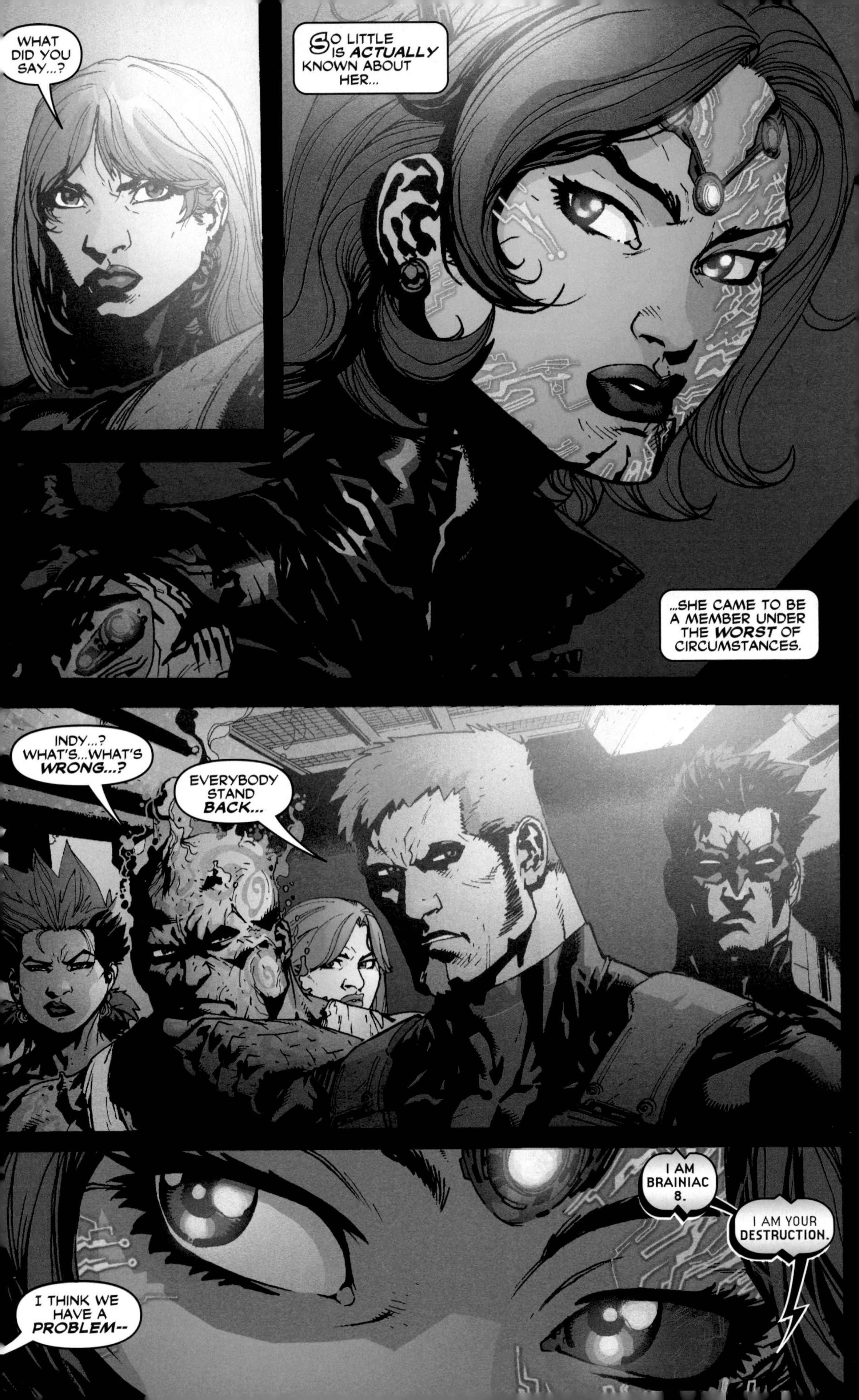
WHAT DID YOU SAY...?
SO LITTLE IS ACTUALLY KNOWN ABOUT HER...
...SHE CAME TO BE A MEMBER UNDER THE WORST OF CIRCUMSTANCES.
INDY...? WHAT'S...WHAT'S WRONG...?
EVERYBODY STAND BACK...
I AM BRAINIAC 8.
I AM YOUR DESTRUCTION.
I THINK WE HAVE A PROBLEM--

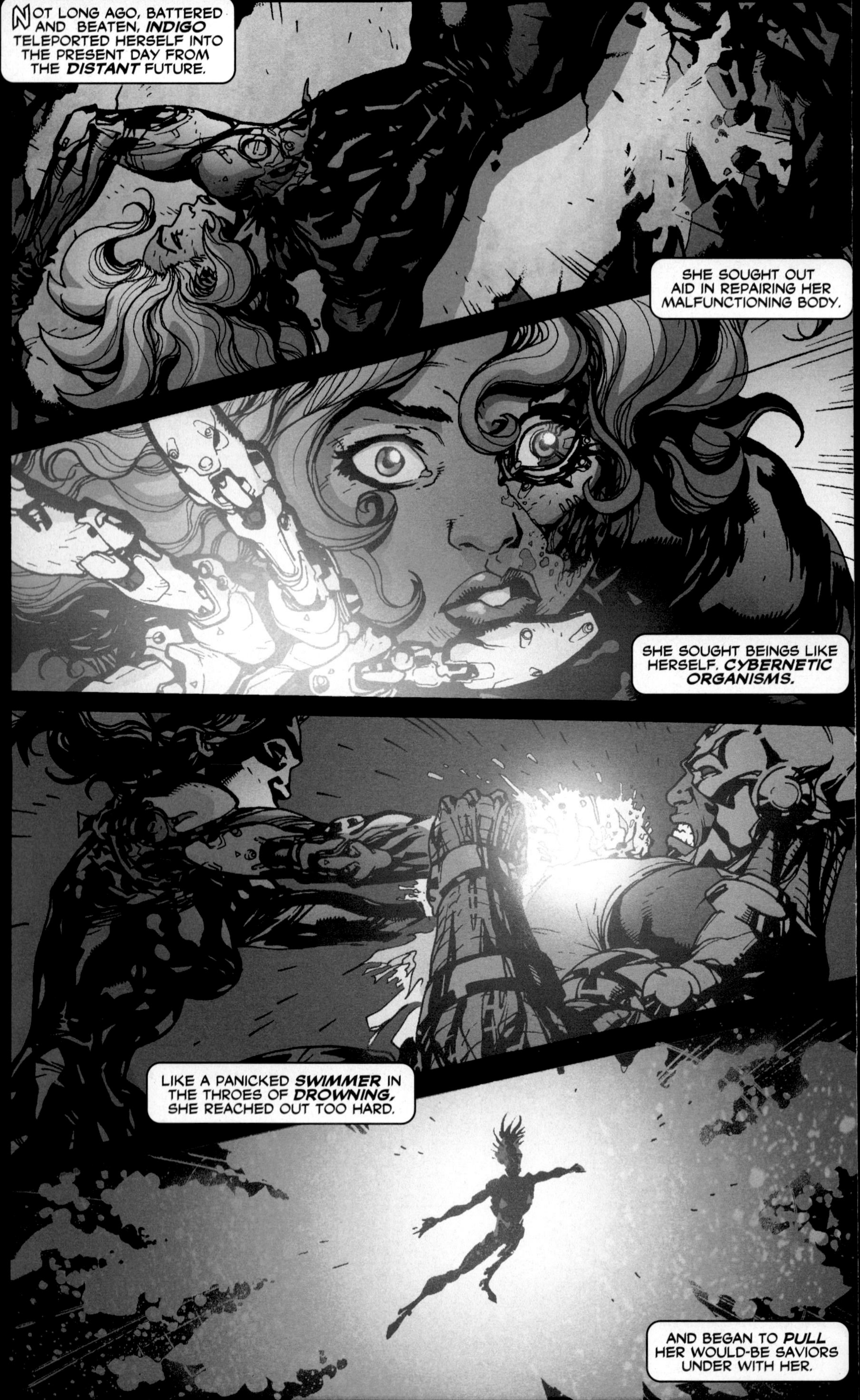
NOT LONG AGO, BATTERED AND BEATEN, INDIGO TELEPORTED HERSELF INTO THE PRESENT DAY FROM THE DISTANT FUTURE.
SHE SOUGHT OUT AID IN REPAIRING HER MALFUNCTIONING BODY.
SHE SOUGHT BEINGS LIKE HERSELF. CYBERNETIC ORGANISMS.
LIKE A PANICKED SWIMMER IN THE THROES OF DROWNING, SHE REACHED OUT TOO HARD.
AND BEGAN TO PULL HER WOULD-BE SAVIORS UNDER WITH HER.

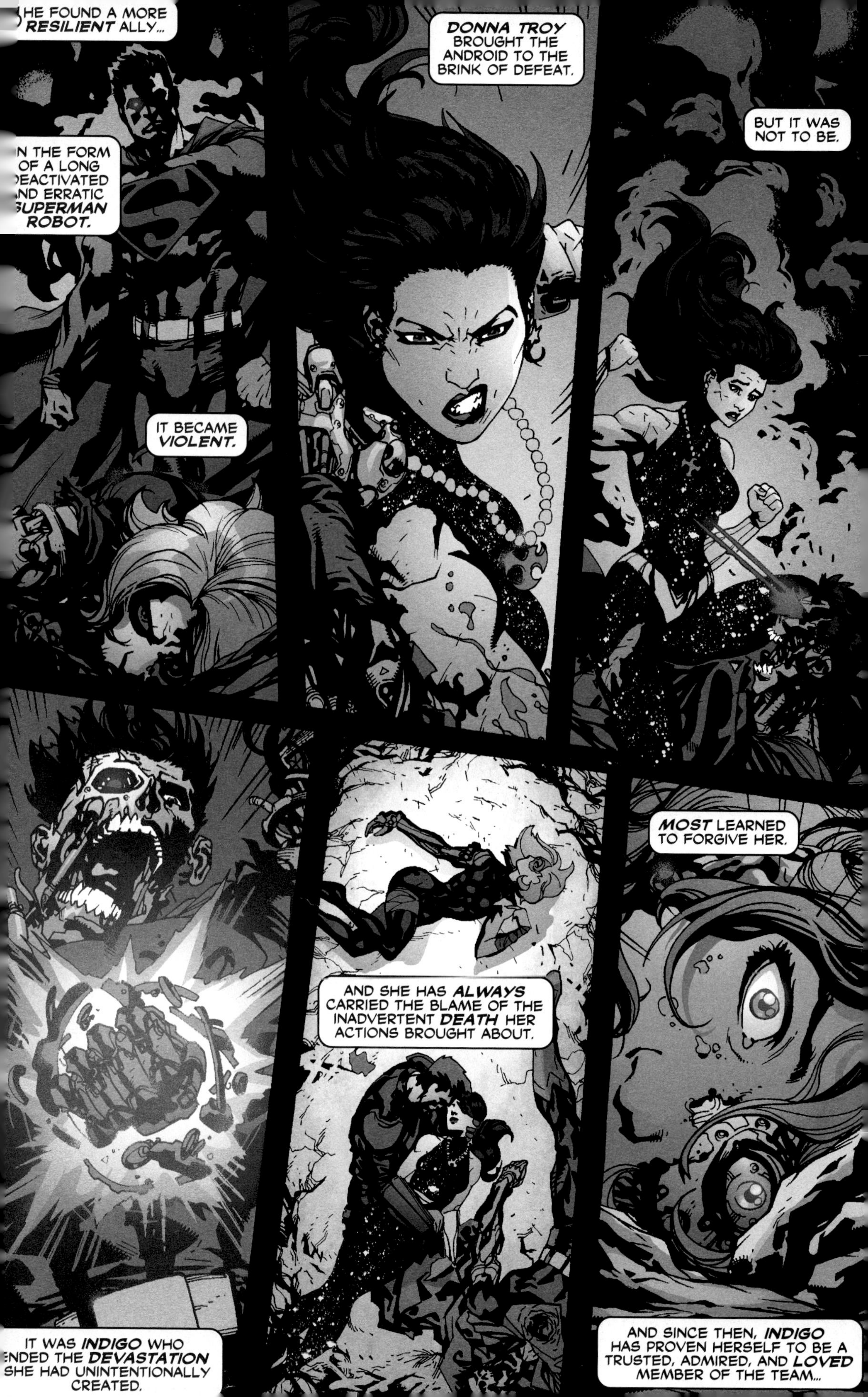
HE FOUND A MORE RESILIENT ALLY...
N THE FORM OF A LONG DEACTIVATED AND ERRATIC SUPERMAN ROBOT.
IT BECAME VIOLENT.
DONNA TROY BROUGHT THE ANDROID TO THE BRINK OF DEFEAT.
BUT IT WAS NOT TO BE.
IT WAS INDIGO WHO ENDED THE DEVASTATION SHE HAD UNINTENTIONALLY CREATED.
AND SHE HAS ALWAYS CARRIED THE BLAME OF THE INADVERTENT DEATH HER ACTIONS BROUGHT ABOUT.
MOST LEARNED TO FORGIVE HER.
AND SINCE THEN, INDIGO HAS PROVEN HERSELF TO BE A TRUSTED, ADMIRED, AND LOVED MEMBER OF THE TEAM...

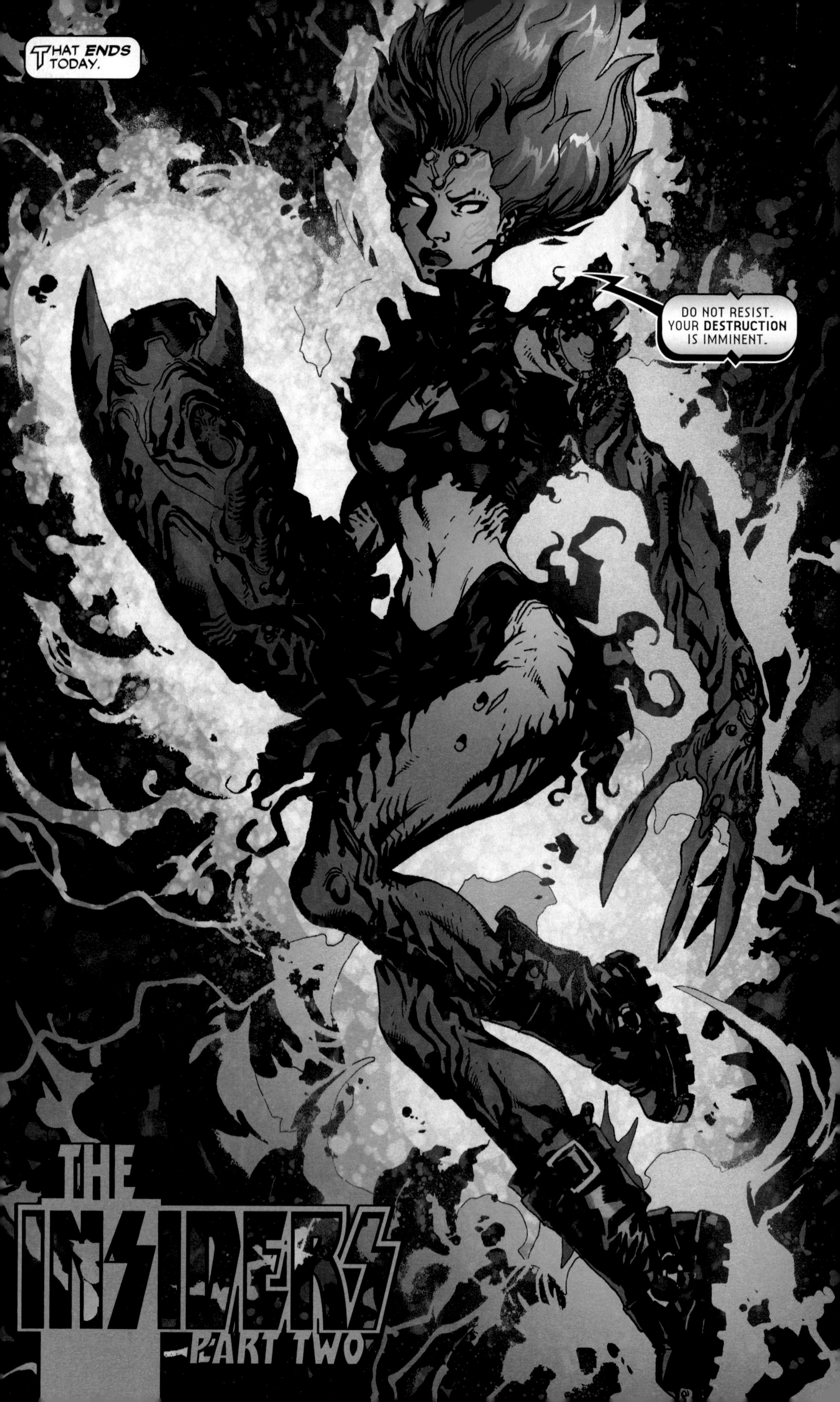
THAT ENDS TODAY.
DO NOT RESIST. YOUR DESTRUCTION IS IMMINENT.
THE INSIDERS
PART TWO

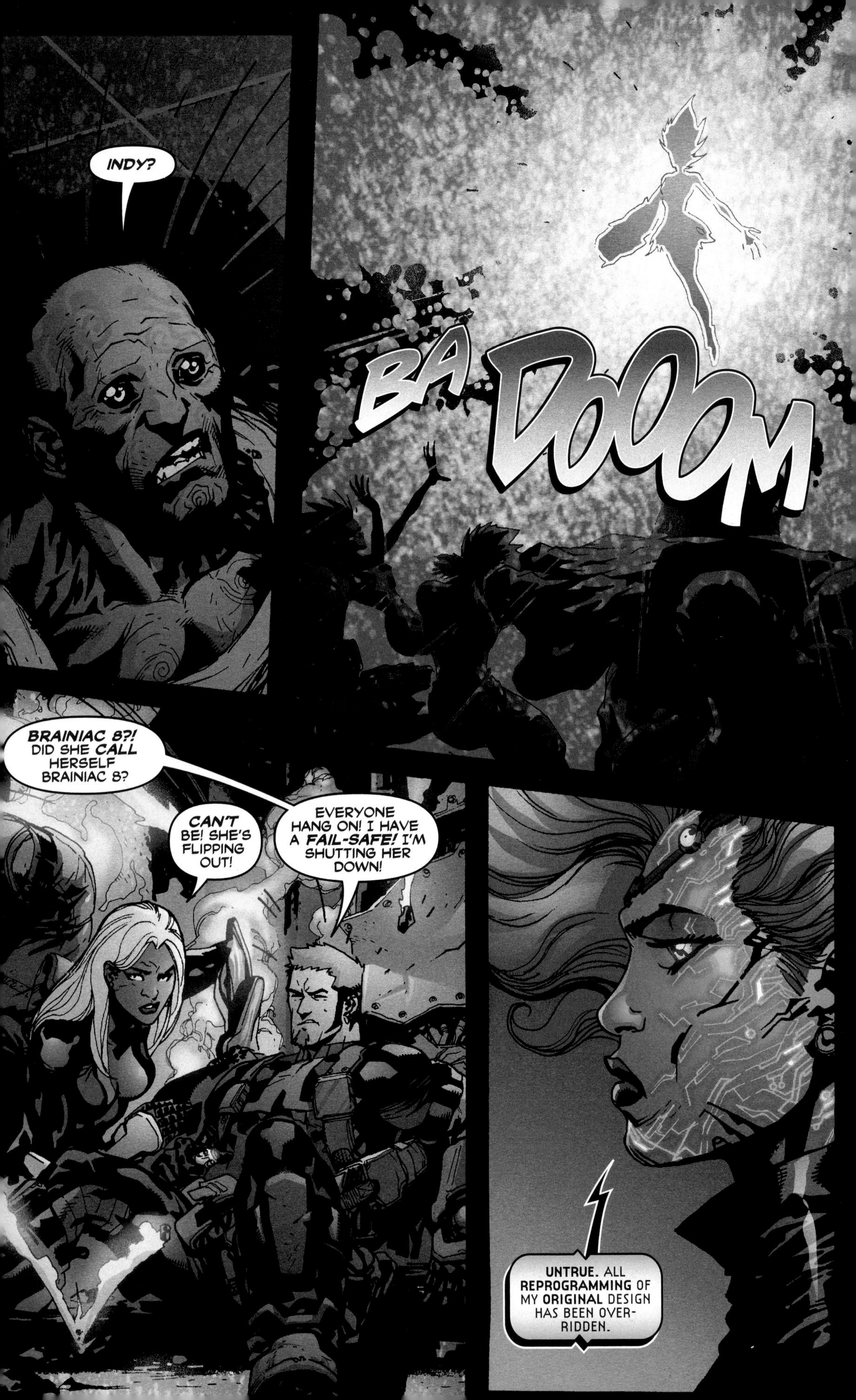
INDY?
BA DOOOM
BRAINIAC 8?! DID SHE CALL HERSELF BRAINIAC 8?
CAN'T BE! SHE'S FLIPPING OUT!
EVERYONE HANG ON! I HAVE A FAIL-SAFE! I'M SHUTTING HER DOWN!
UNTRUE. ALL REPROGRAMMING OF MY ORIGINAL DESIGN HAS BEEN OVER-RIDDEN.

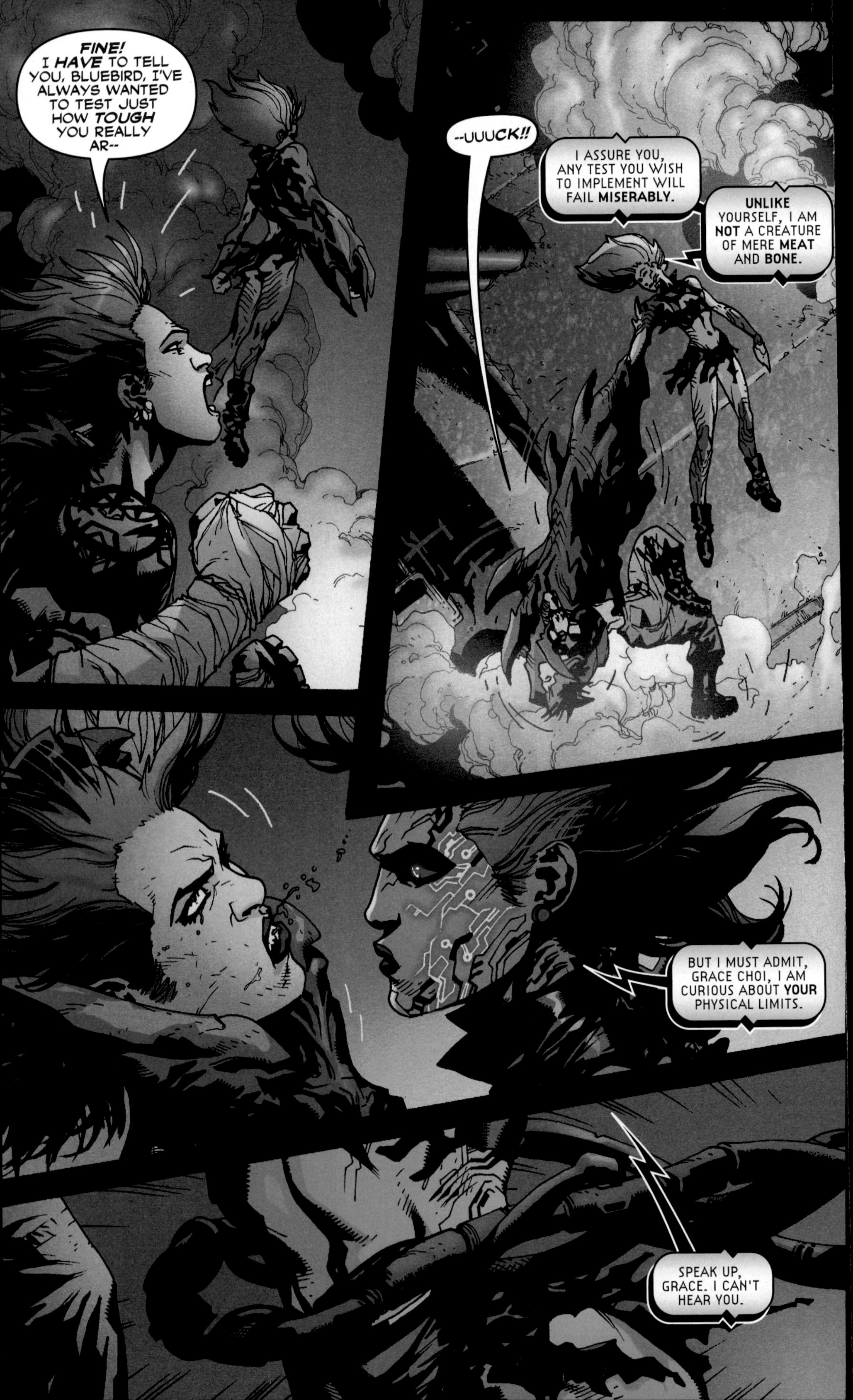
FINE! I HAVE TO TELL YOU, BLUEBIRD, I'VE ALWAYS WANTED TO TEST JUST HOW TOUGH YOU REALLY AR--
--UUUCK!!
I ASSURE YOU, ANY TEST YOU WISH TO IMPLEMENT WILL FAIL MISERABLY.
UNLIKE YOURSELF, I AM NOT A CREATURE OF MERE MEAT AND BONE.
BUT I MUST ADMIT, GRACE CHOI, I AM CURIOUS ABOUT YOUR PHYSICAL LIMITS.
SPEAK UP, GRACE. I CAN'T HEAR YOU.

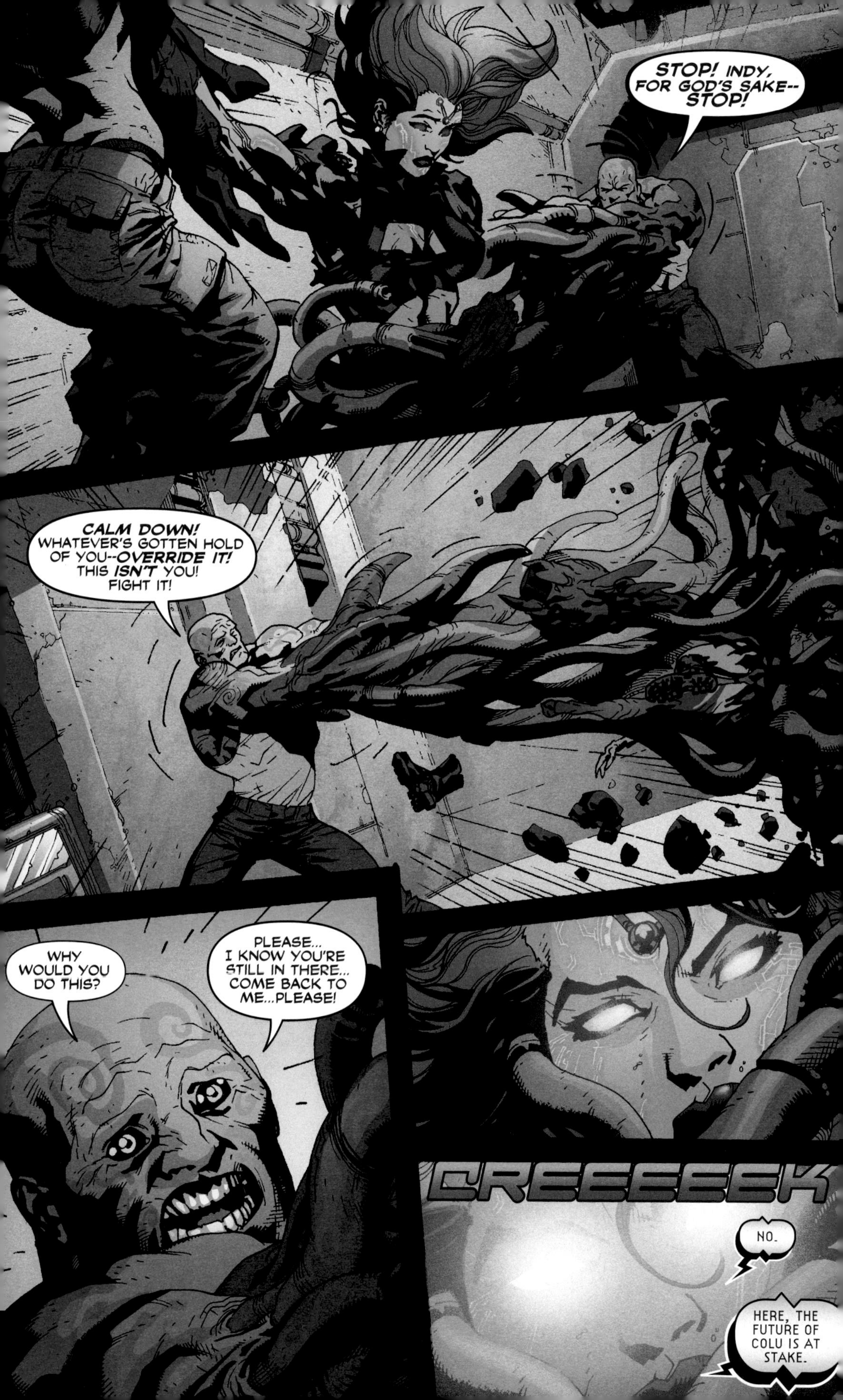

STOP! INDY, FOR GOD'S SAKE-- STOP!
CALM DOWN! WHATEVER'S GOTTEN HOLD OF YOU--OVERRIDE IT! THIS ISN'T YOU! FIGHT IT!
WHY WOULD YOU DO THIS?
PLEASE... I KNOW YOU'RE STILL IN THERE... COME BACK TO ME...PLEASE!
CREEEEEK
NO.
HERE, THE FUTURE OF COLU IS AT STAKE.

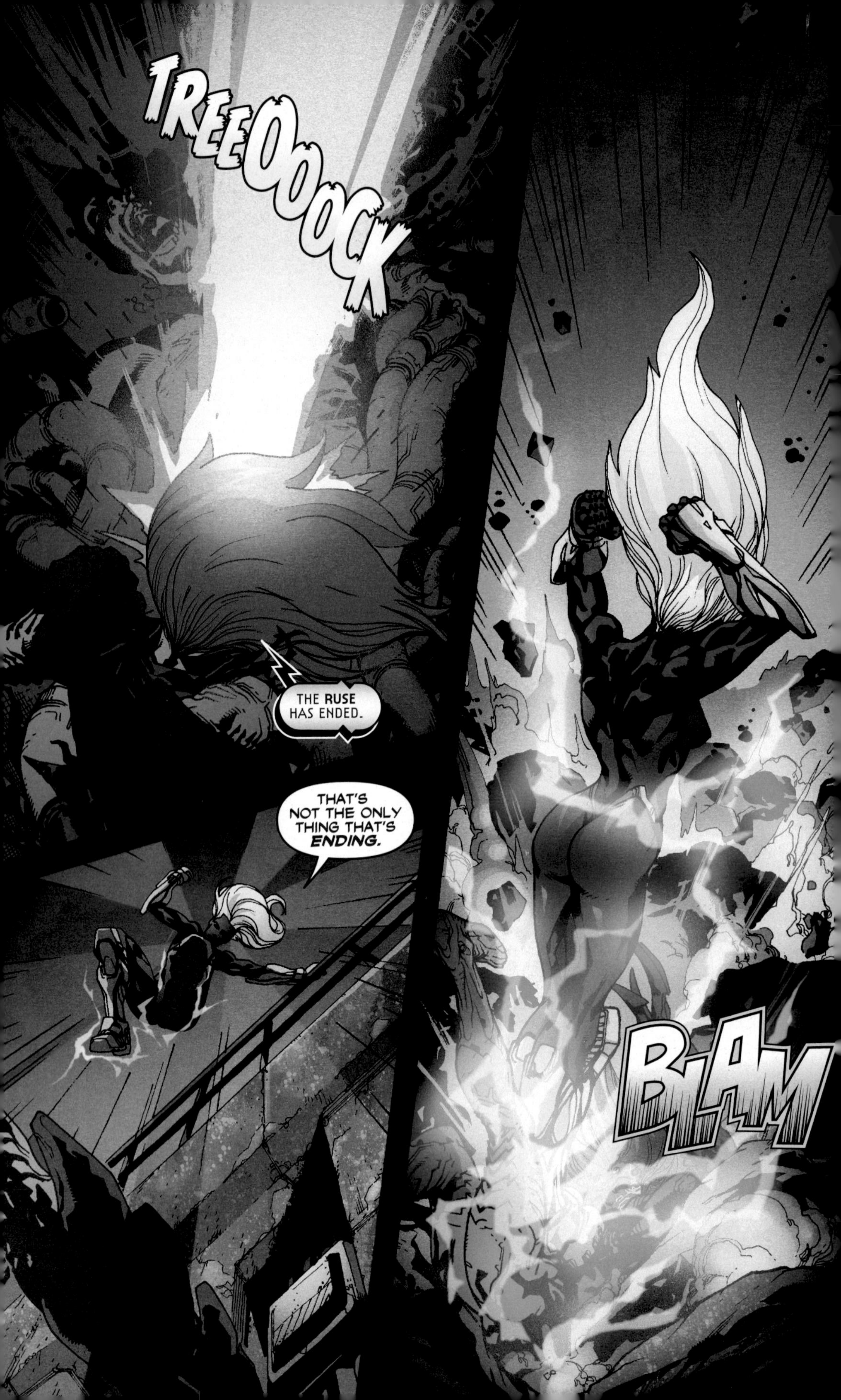
TREEOOOCK
THE RUSE HAS ENDED.
THAT'S NOT THE ONLY THING THAT'S *ENDING.*
BLAM

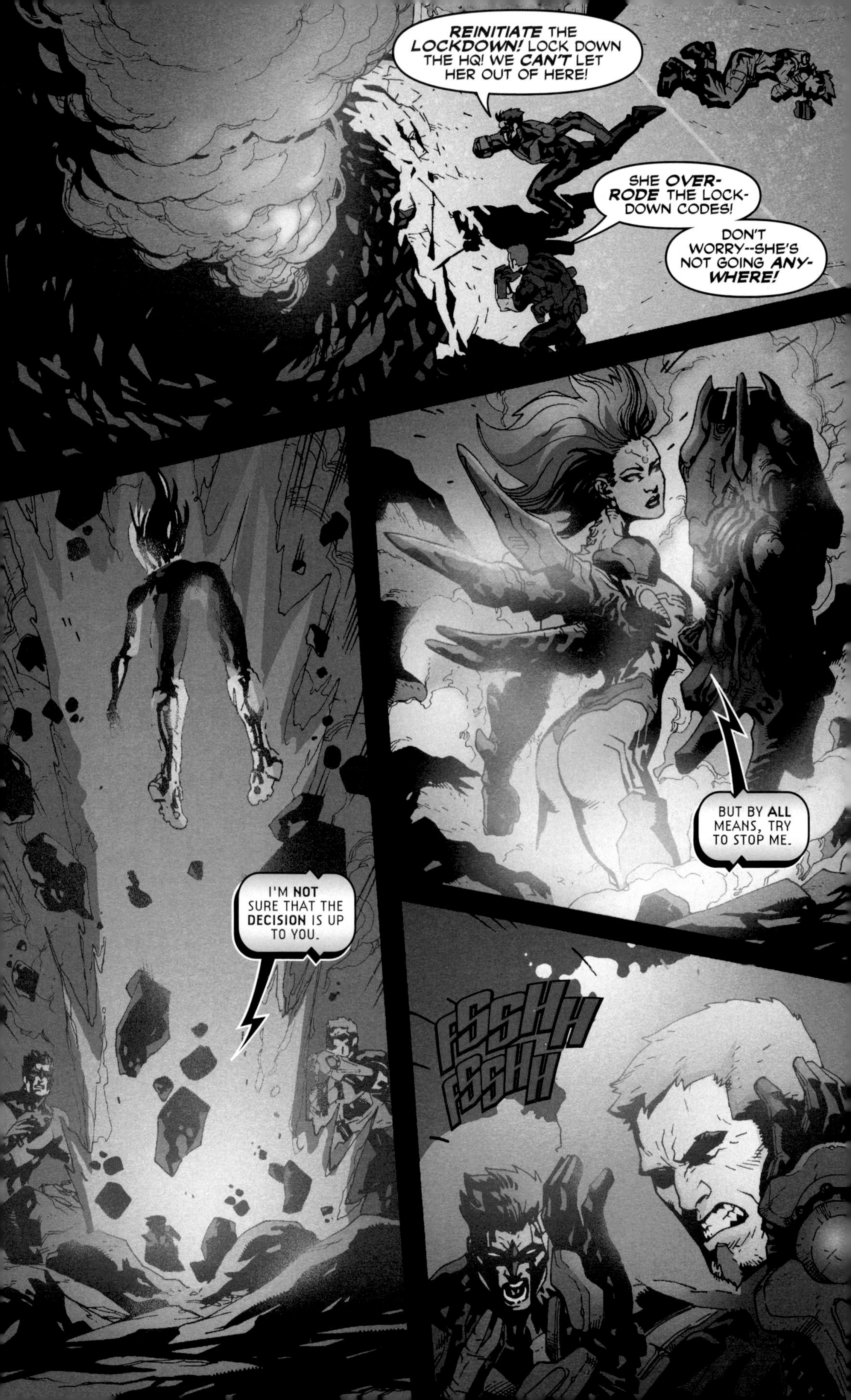

REINITIATE THE LOCKDOWN! LOCK DOWN THE HQ! WE CAN'T LET HER OUT OF HERE!
SHE OVERRODE THE LOCKDOWN CODES!
DON'T WORRY--SHE'S NOT GOING ANYWHERE!
BUT BY ALL MEANS, TRY TO STOP ME.
I'M NOT SURE THAT THE DECISION IS UP TO YOU.
FSSHH FSSHH

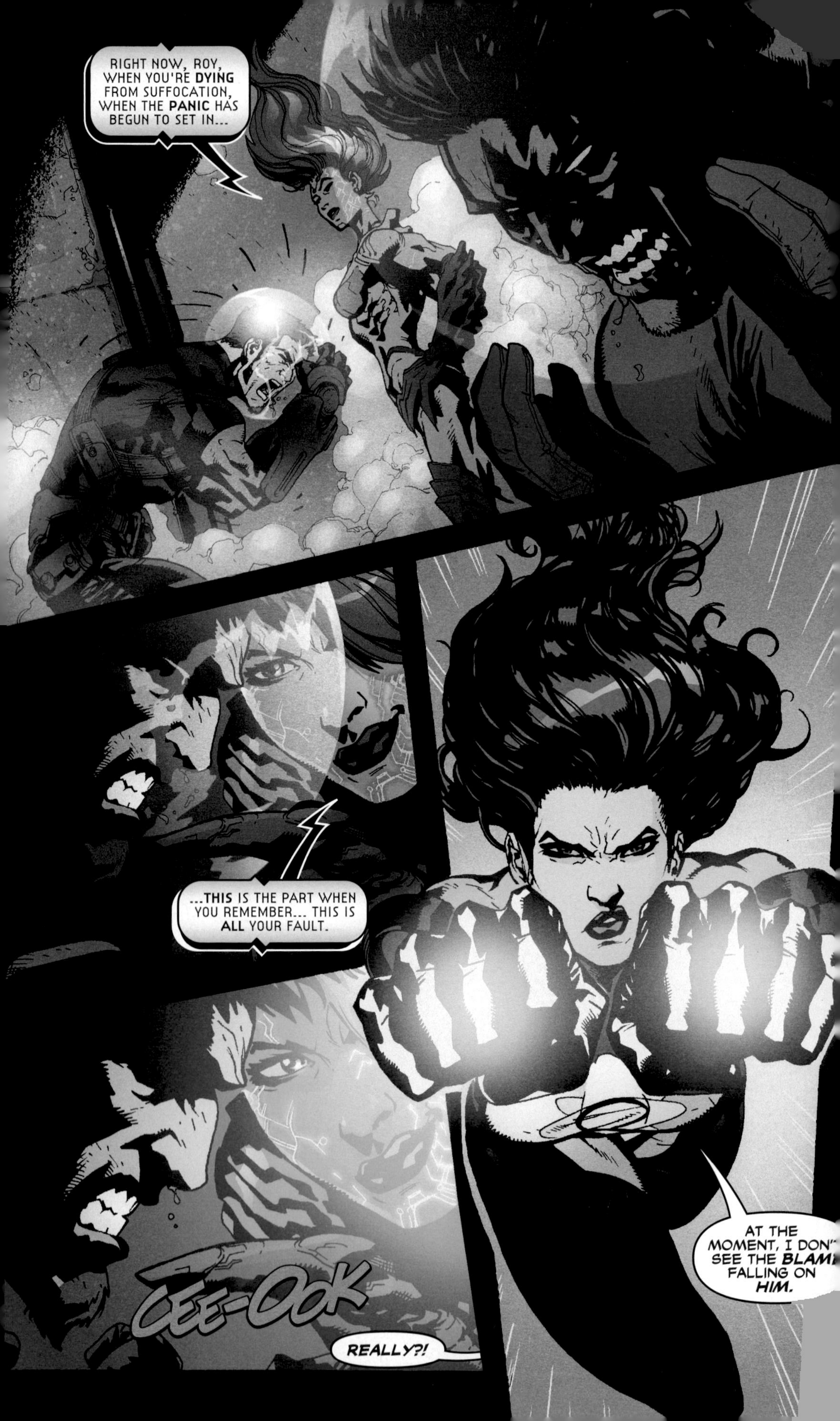
RIGHT NOW, ROY, WHEN YOU'RE **DYING** FROM SUFFOCATION, WHEN THE **PANIC** HAS BEGUN TO SET IN...
...**THIS** IS THE PART WHEN YOU REMEMBER... THIS IS **ALL** YOUR FAULT.
CEE-OOK
REALLY?!
AT THE MOMENT, I DON'T SEE THE *BLAME* FALLING ON *HIM.*

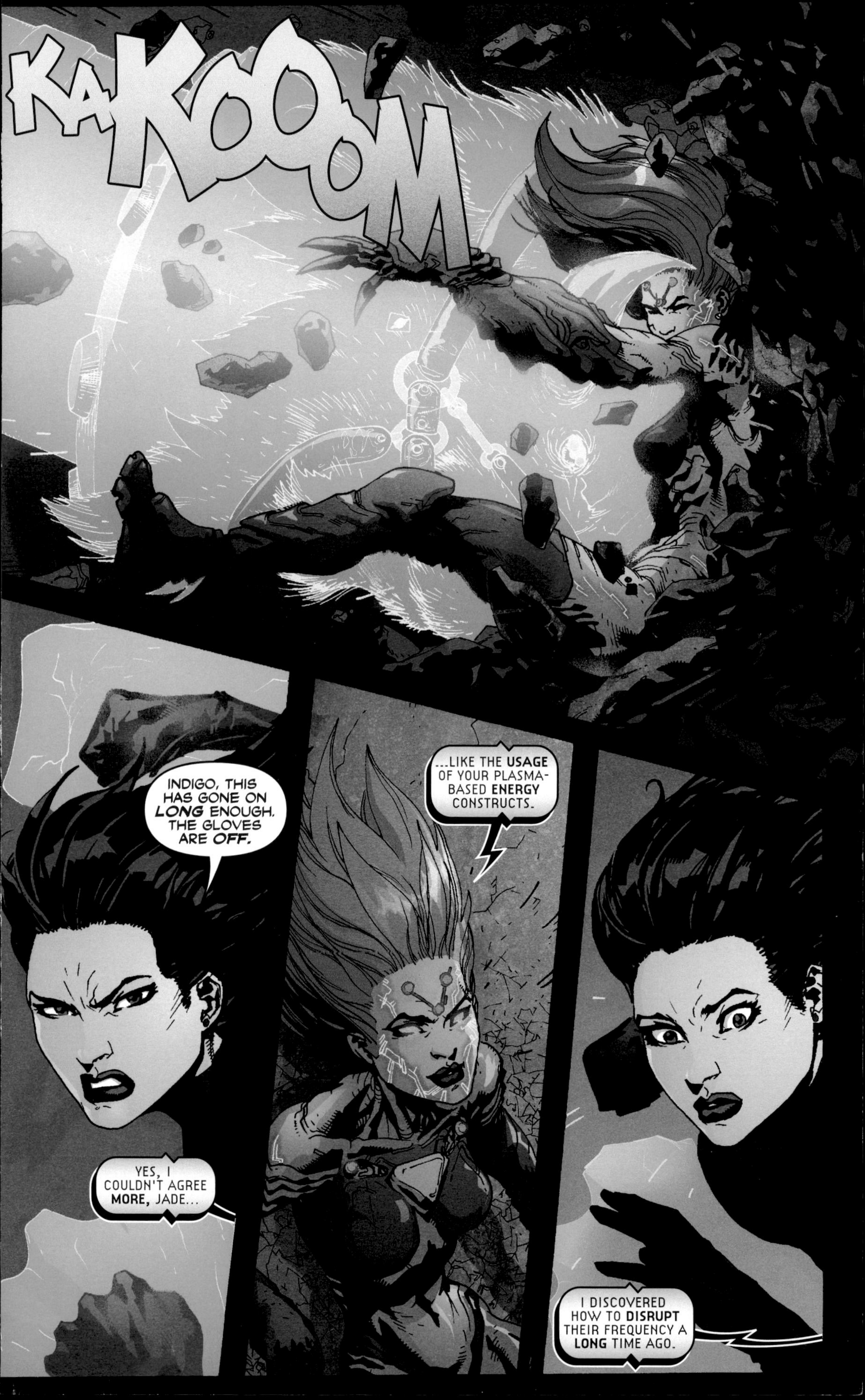
KAKOOOM
INDIGO, THIS HAS GONE ON LONG ENOUGH. THE GLOVES ARE OFF.
YES, I COULDN'T AGREE MORE, JADE...
...LIKE THE USAGE OF YOUR PLASMA-BASED ENERGY CONSTRUCTS.
I DISCOVERED HOW TO DISRUPT THEIR FREQUENCY A LONG TIME AGO.

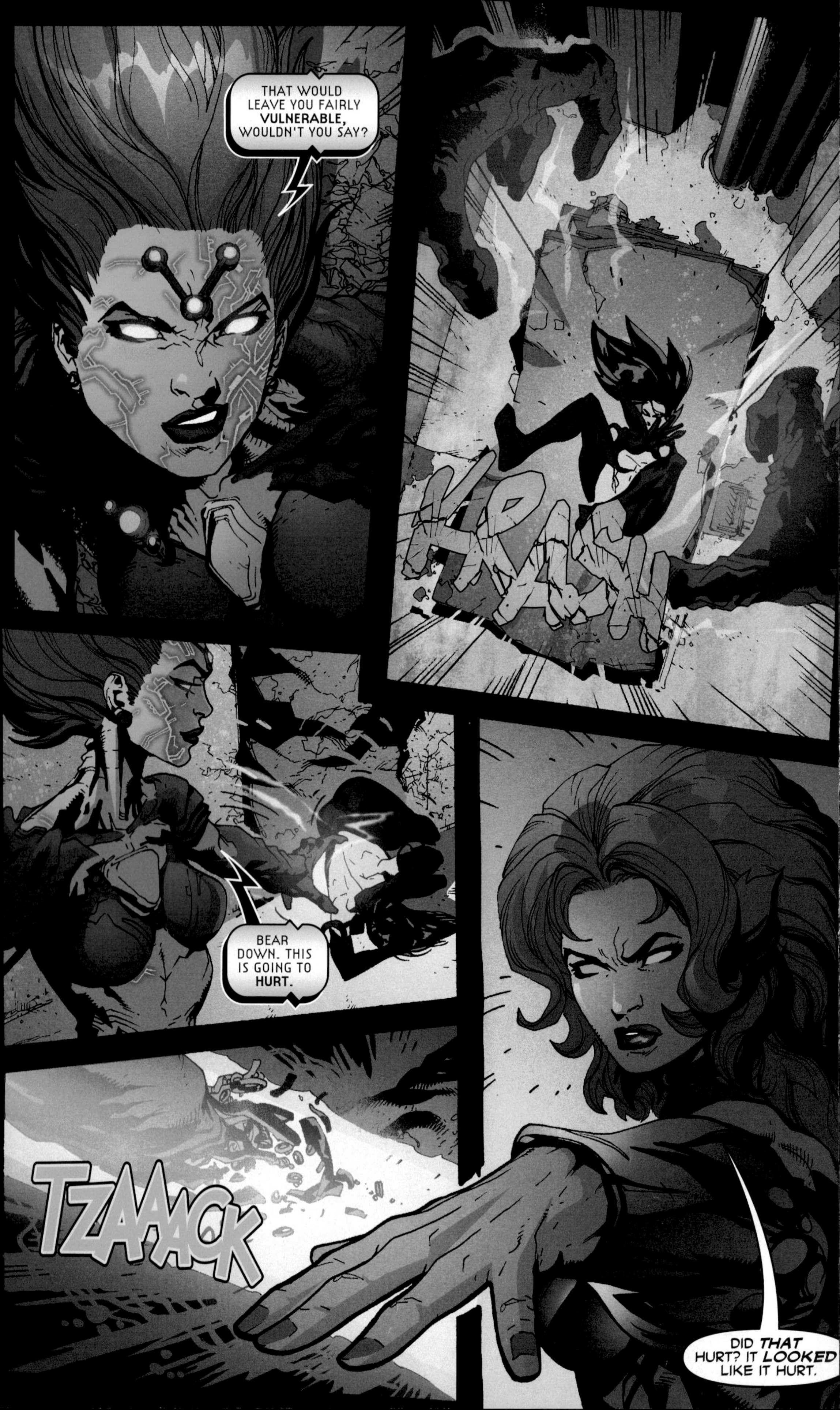
THAT WOULD LEAVE YOU FAIRLY **VULNERABLE,** WOULDN'T YOU SAY?
KRASH
BEAR DOWN. THIS IS GOING TO **HURT.**
TZAAACK
DID ***THAT*** HURT? IT ***LOOKED*** LIKE IT HURT.

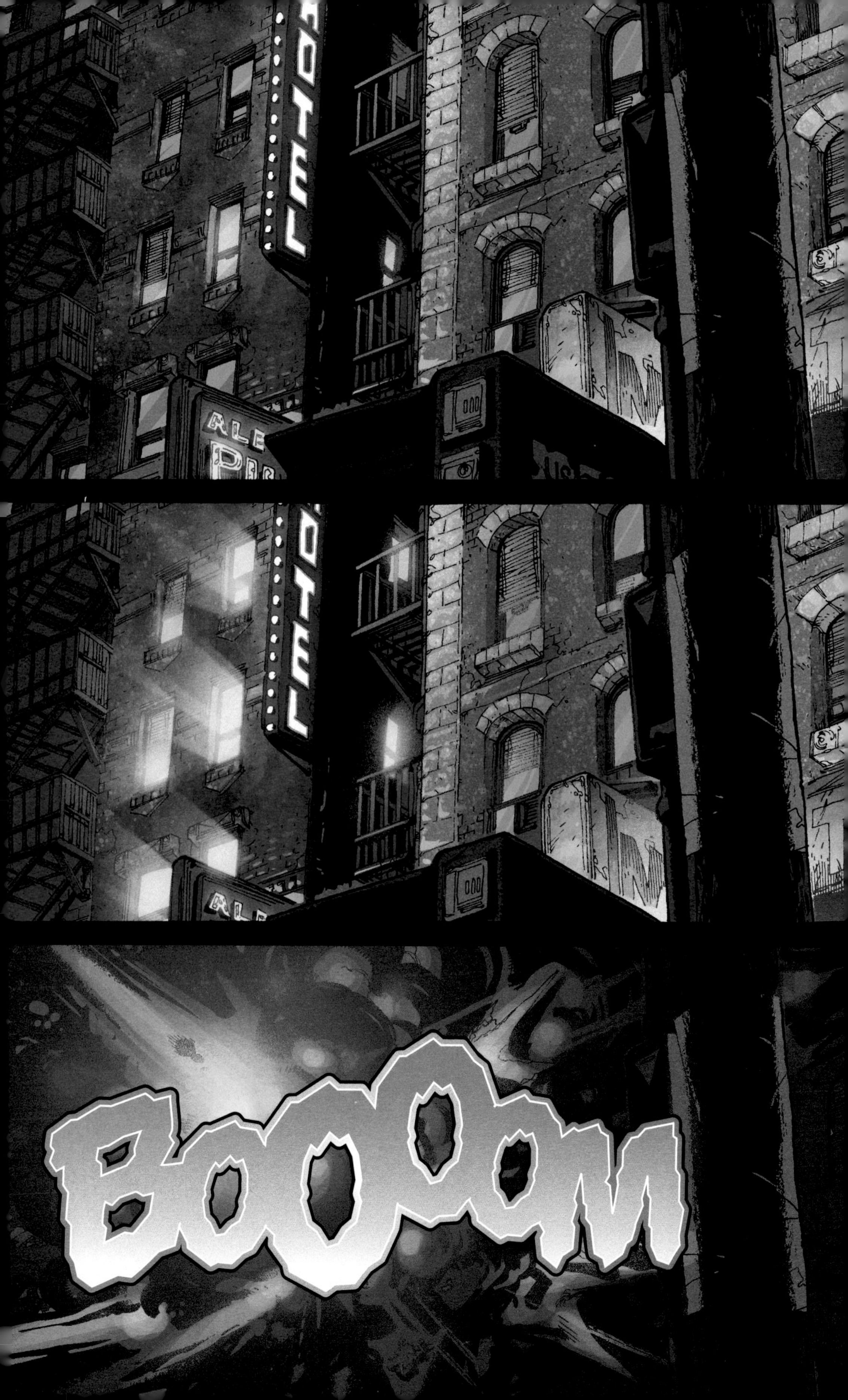
BOOOOM

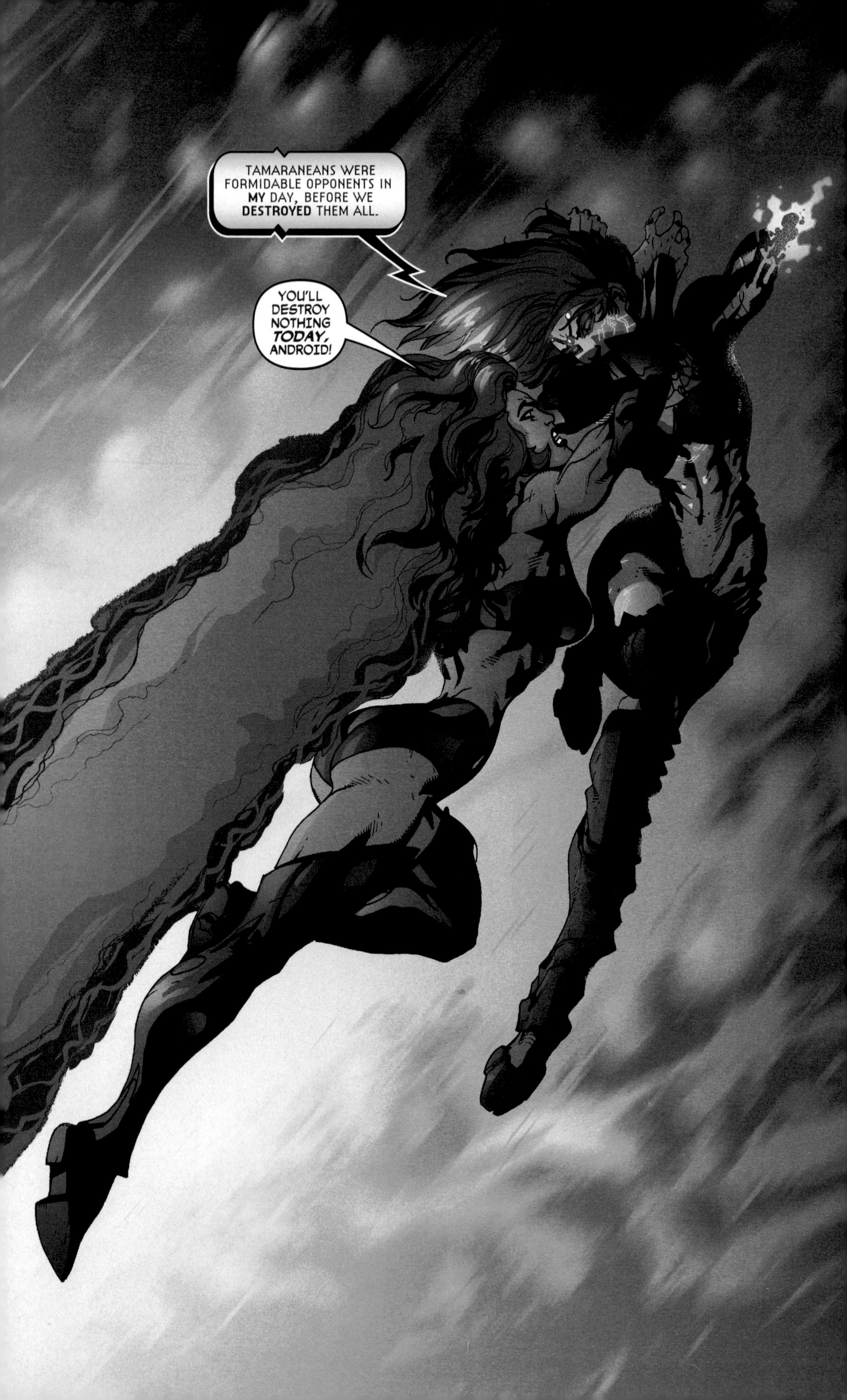
TAMARANEANS WERE FORMIDABLE OPPONENTS IN MY DAY, BEFORE WE DESTROYED THEM ALL.
YOU'LL DESTROY NOTHING TODAY, ANDROID!

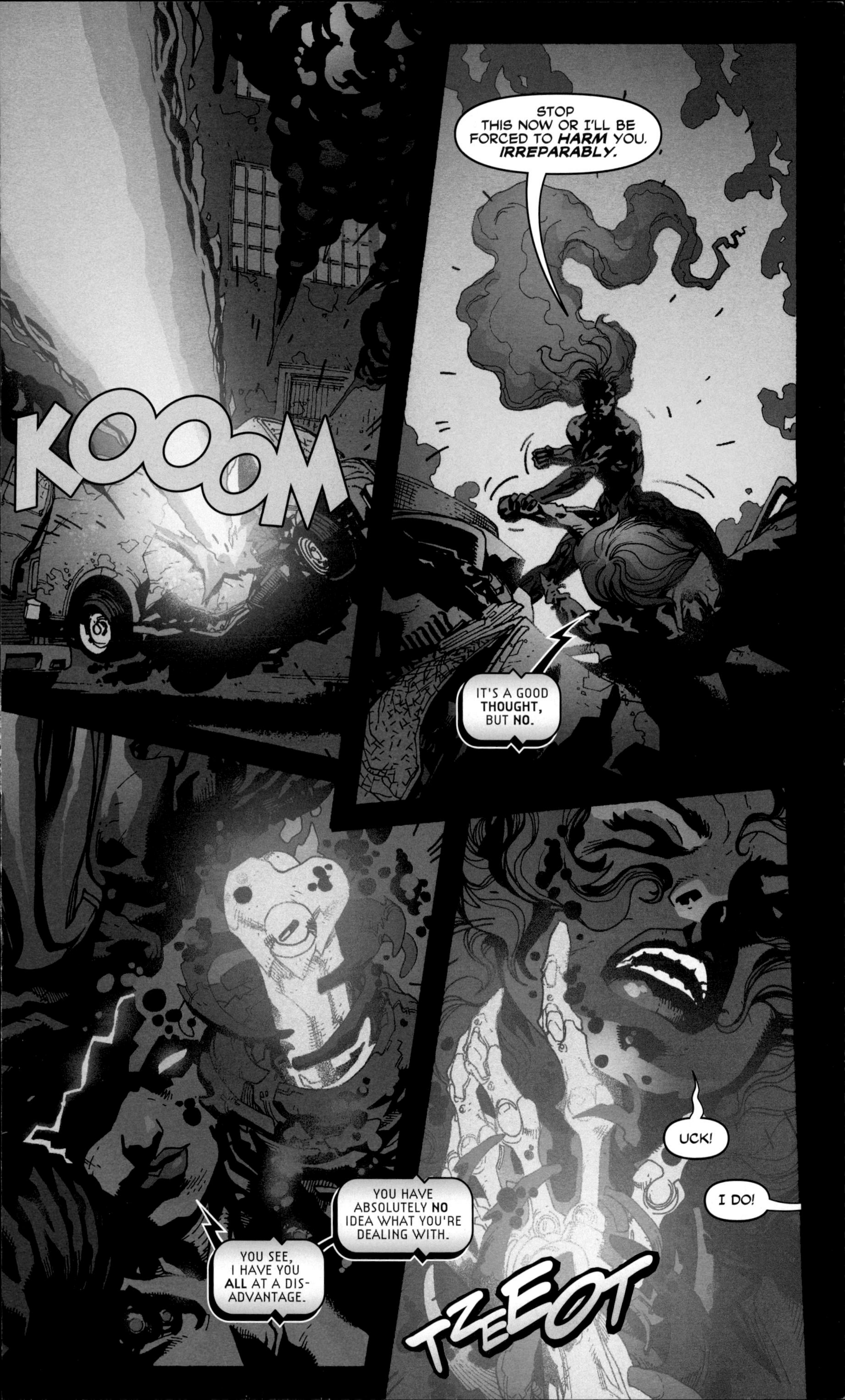
KOOOM
STOP THIS NOW OR I'LL BE FORCED TO HARM YOU. IRREPARABLY.
IT'S A GOOD THOUGHT, BUT NO.
YOU HAVE ABSOLUTELY NO IDEA WHAT YOU'RE DEALING WITH.
YOU SEE, I HAVE YOU ALL AT A DIS-ADVANTAGE.
UCK!
I DO!
TZEEOT

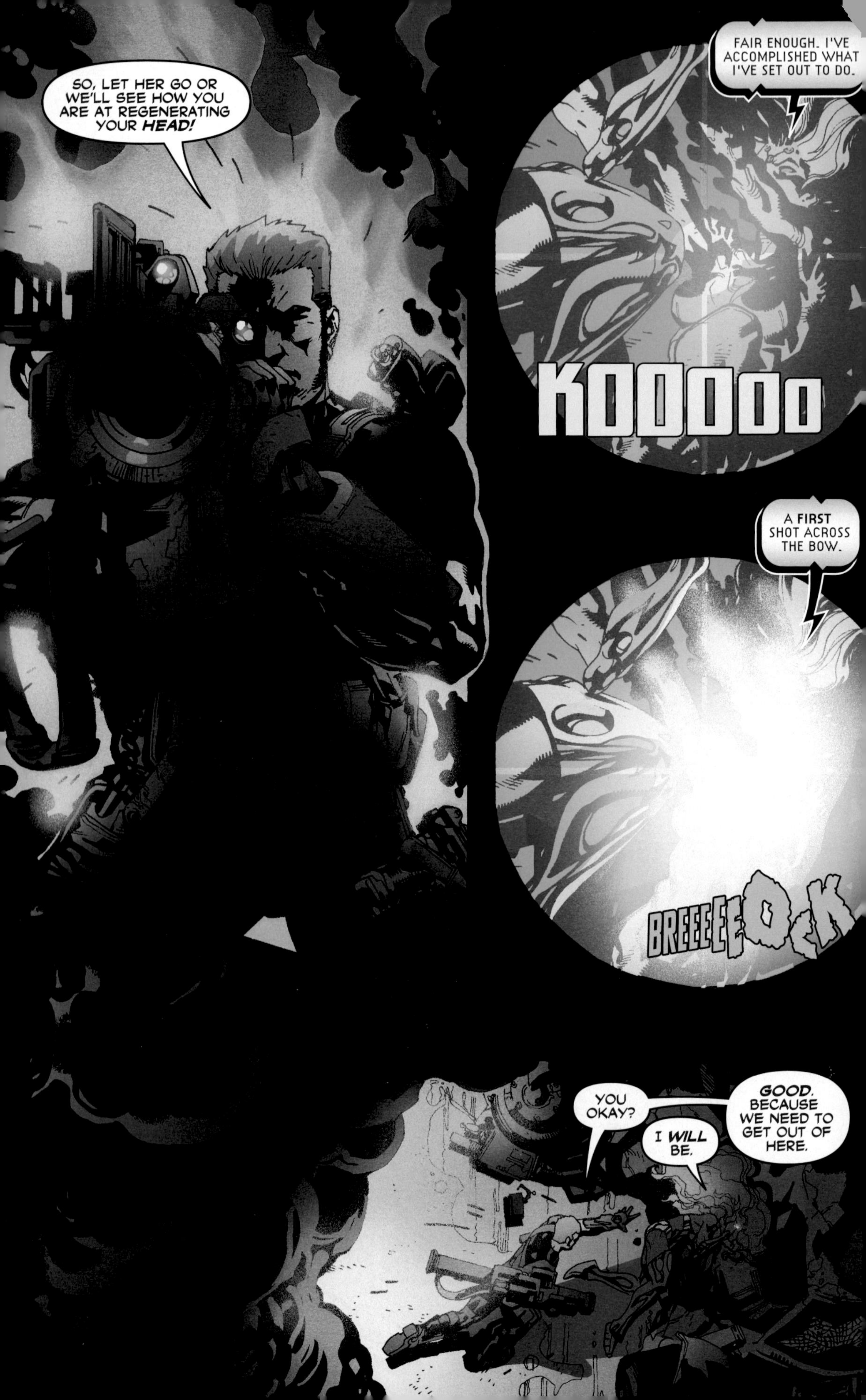
SO, LET HER GO OR WE'LL SEE HOW YOU ARE AT REGENERATING YOUR **HEAD!**
FAIR ENOUGH. I'VE ACCOMPLISHED WHAT I'VE SET OUT TO DO.
KOOOOo
A **FIRST** SHOT ACROSS THE BOW.
BREEEEEOcK
YOU OKAY?
I **WILL** BE.
GOOD. BECAUSE WE NEED TO GET OUT OF HERE.

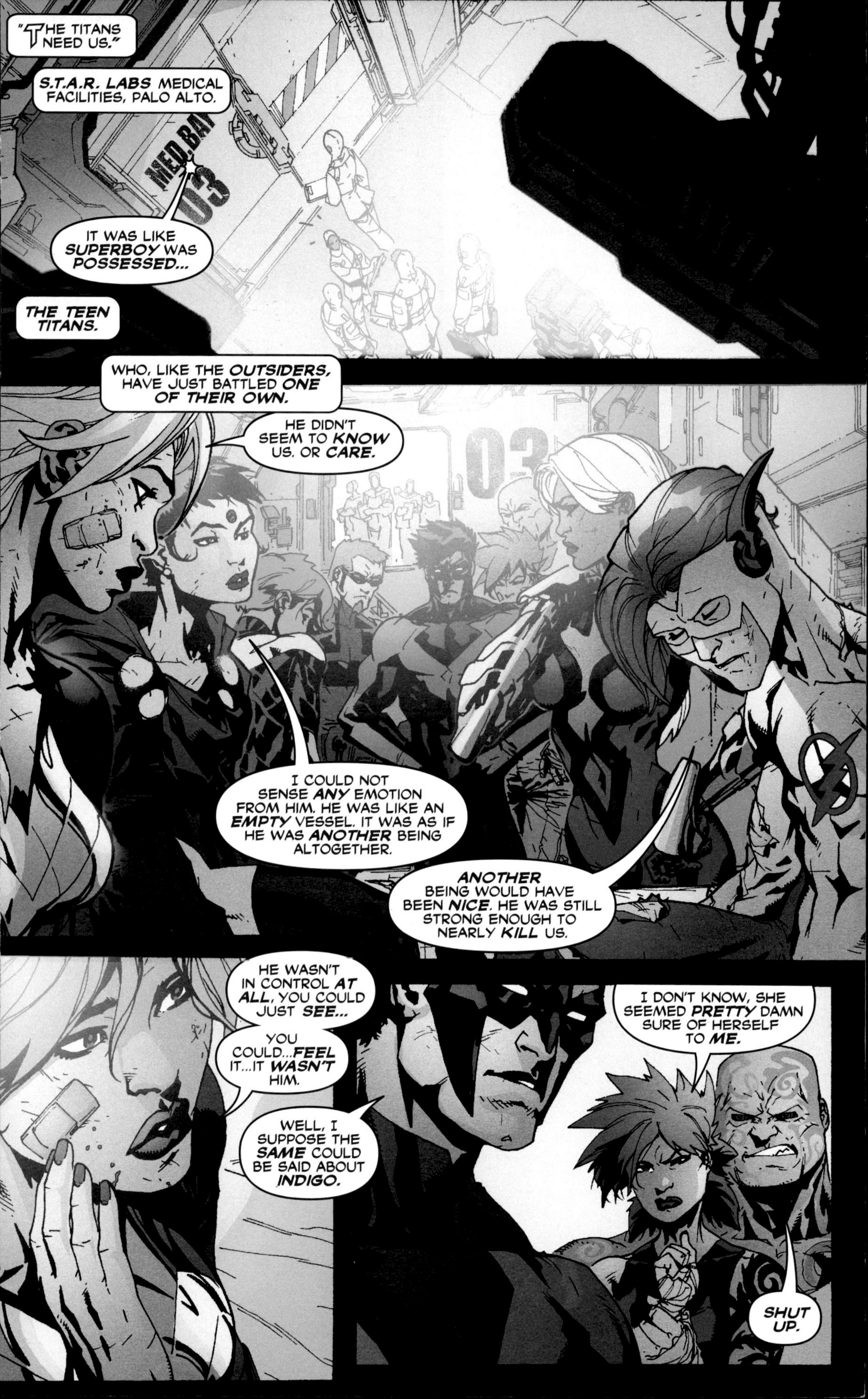
"THE TITANS NEED US."
S.T.A.R. LABS MEDICAL FACILITIES, PALO ALTO.
MED. BAY 03
IT WAS LIKE SUPERBOY WAS POSSESSED...
THE TEEN TITANS.
WHO, LIKE THE OUTSIDERS, HAVE JUST BATTLED ONE OF THEIR OWN.
HE DIDN'T SEEM TO KNOW US. OR CARE.
03
I COULD NOT SENSE ANY EMOTION FROM HIM. HE WAS LIKE AN EMPTY VESSEL. IT WAS AS IF HE WAS ANOTHER BEING ALTOGETHER.
ANOTHER BEING WOULD HAVE BEEN NICE. HE WAS STILL STRONG ENOUGH TO NEARLY KILL US.
HE WASN'T IN CONTROL AT ALL, YOU COULD JUST SEE...
YOU COULD...FEEL IT...IT WASN'T HIM.
WELL, I SUPPOSE THE SAME COULD BE SAID ABOUT INDIGO.
I DON'T KNOW, SHE SEEMED PRETTY DAMN SURE OF HERSELF TO ME.
SHUT UP.

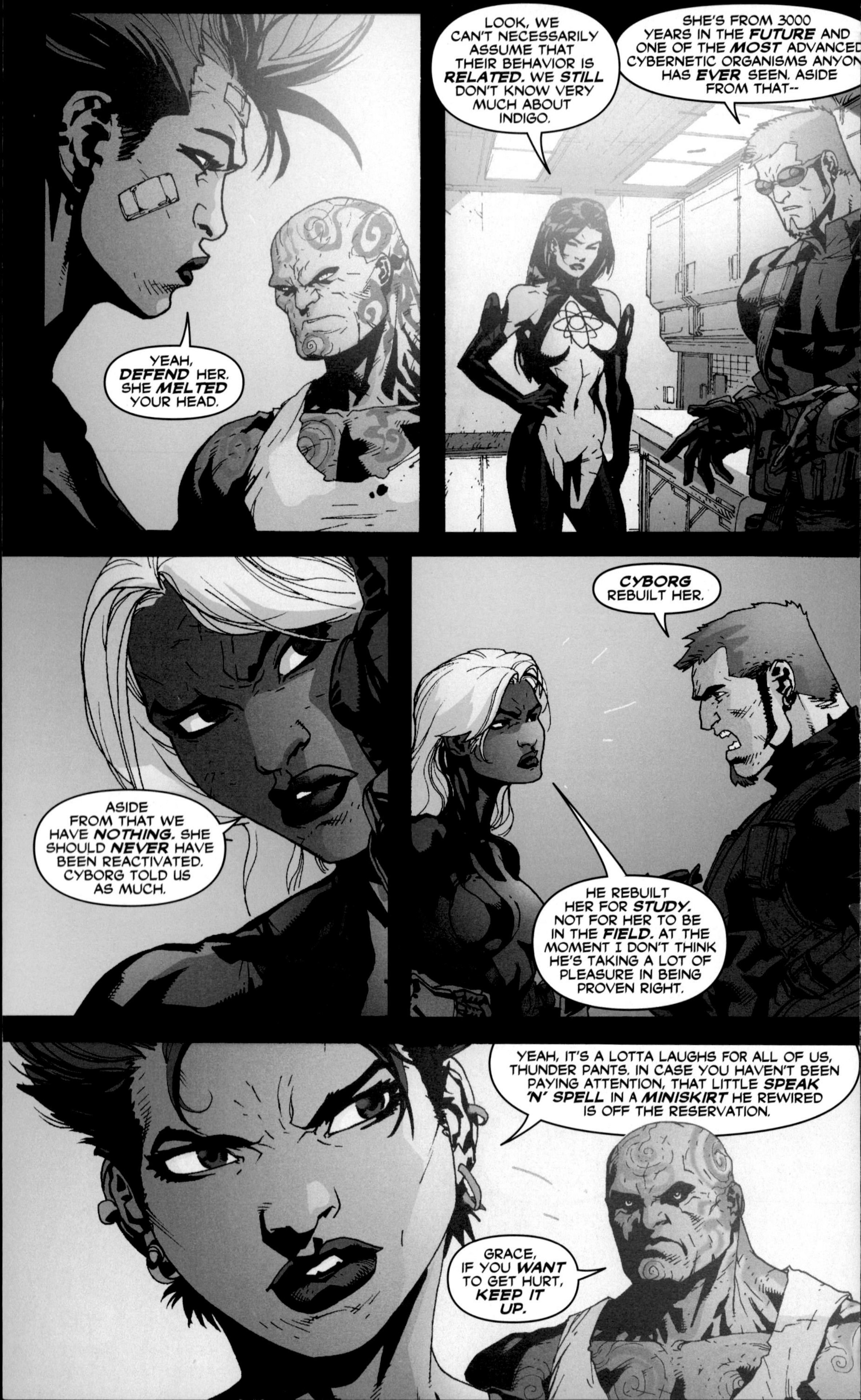
YEAH, DEFEND HER. SHE MELTED YOUR HEAD.
LOOK, WE CAN'T NECESSARILY ASSUME THAT THEIR BEHAVIOR IS RELATED. WE STILL DON'T KNOW VERY MUCH ABOUT INDIGO.
SHE'S FROM 3000 YEARS IN THE FUTURE AND ONE OF THE MOST ADVANCED CYBERNETIC ORGANISMS ANYON HAS EVER SEEN. ASIDE FROM THAT--
ASIDE FROM THAT WE HAVE NOTHING. SHE SHOULD NEVER HAVE BEEN REACTIVATED. CYBORG TOLD US AS MUCH.
CYBORG REBUILT HER.
HE REBUILT HER FOR STUDY. NOT FOR HER TO BE IN THE FIELD. AT THE MOMENT I DON'T THINK HE'S TAKING A LOT OF PLEASURE IN BEING PROVEN RIGHT.
YEAH, IT'S A LOTTA LAUGHS FOR ALL OF US, THUNDER PANTS. IN CASE YOU HAVEN'T BEEN PAYING ATTENTION, THAT LITTLE SPEAK 'N' SPELL IN A MINISKIRT HE REWIRED IS OFF THE RESERVATION.
GRACE, IF YOU WANT TO GET HURT, KEEP IT UP.

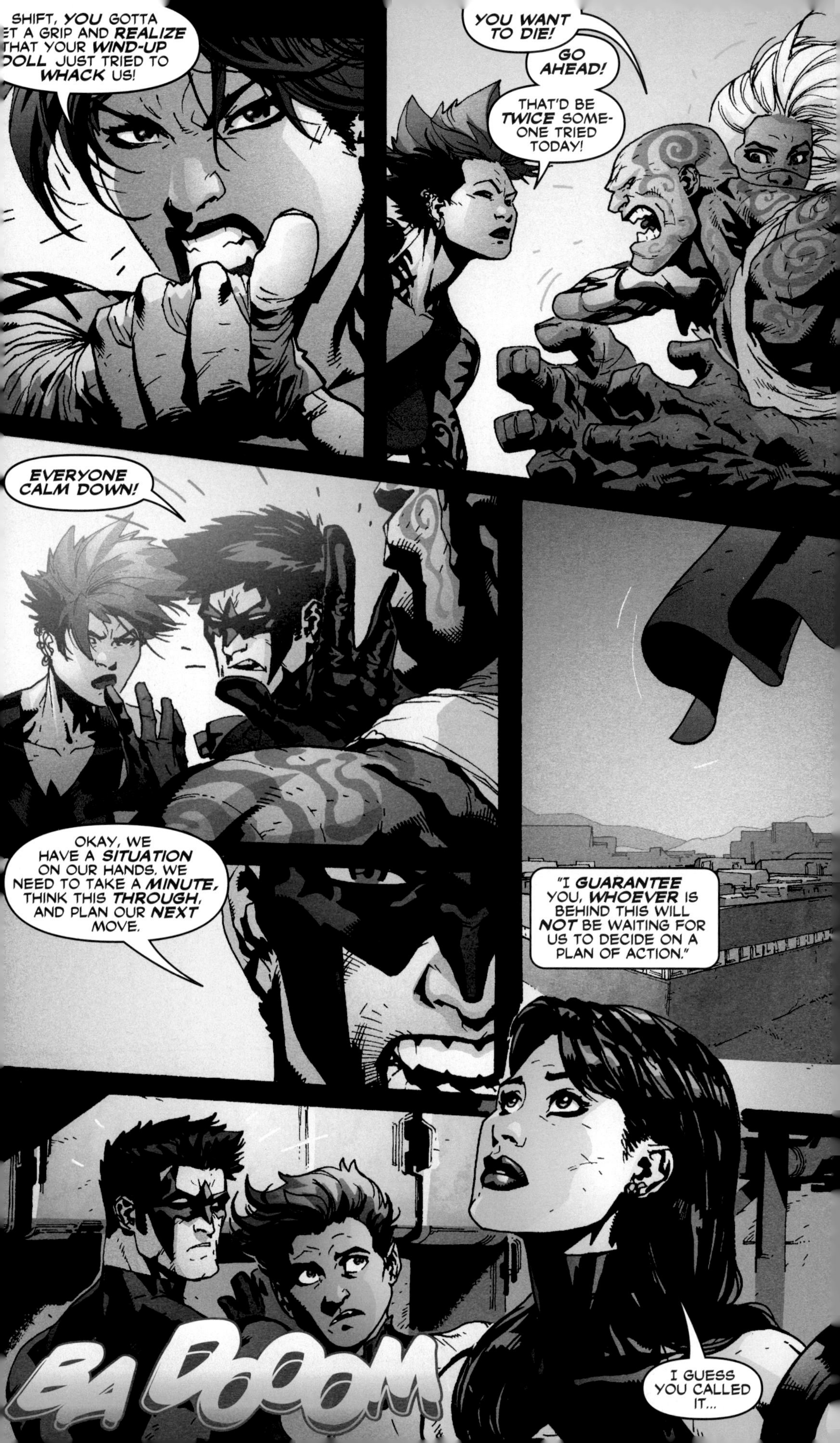
SHIFT, YOU GOTTA GET A GRIP AND REALIZE THAT YOUR WIND-UP DOLL JUST TRIED TO WHACK US!
YOU WANT TO DIE!
GO AHEAD!
THAT'D BE TWICE SOME-ONE TRIED TODAY!
EVERYONE CALM DOWN!
OKAY, WE HAVE A SITUATION ON OUR HANDS. WE NEED TO TAKE A MINUTE, THINK THIS THROUGH, AND PLAN OUR NEXT MOVE.
"I GUARANTEE YOU, WHOEVER IS BEHIND THIS WILL NOT BE WAITING FOR US TO DECIDE ON A PLAN OF ACTION."
BA DOOOM
I GUESS YOU CALLED IT...

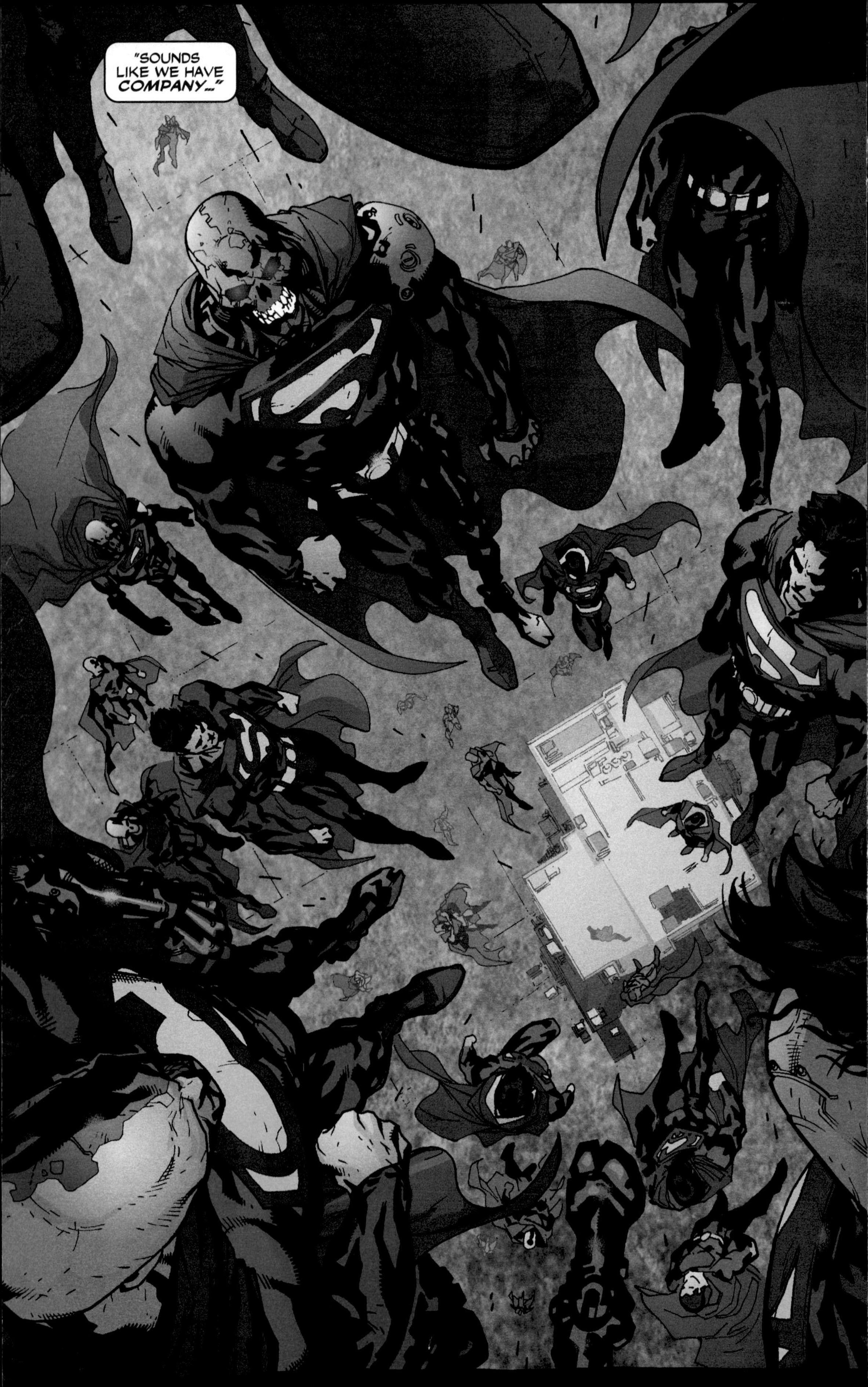
"SOUNDS LIKE WE HAVE COMPANY..."

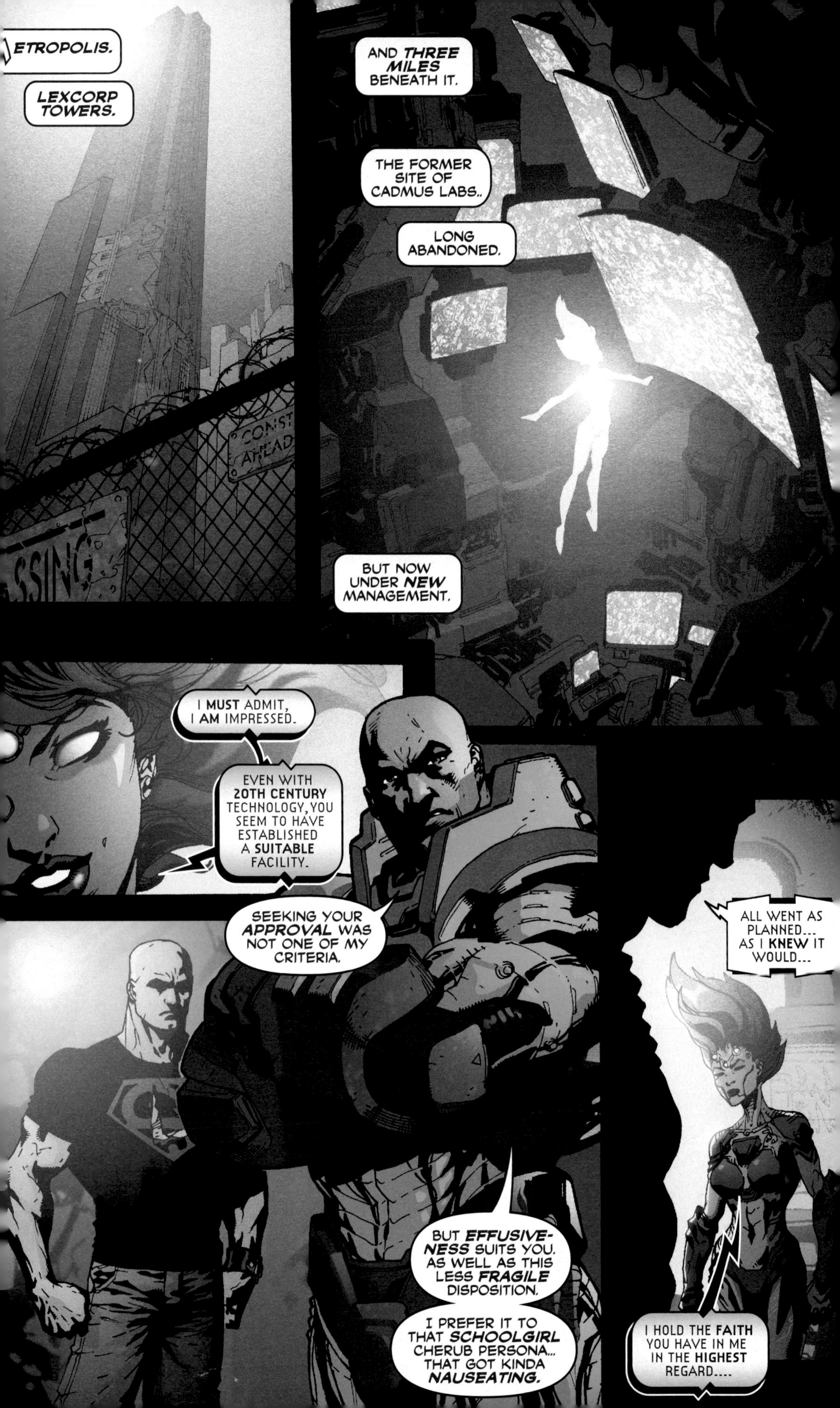

ETROPOLIS.
LEXCORP TOWERS.
CONST AHEAD
SSING
AND THREE MILES BENEATH IT.
THE FORMER SITE OF CADMUS LABS..
LONG ABANDONED.
BUT NOW UNDER NEW MANAGEMENT.
I MUST ADMIT, I AM IMPRESSED.
EVEN WITH 20TH CENTURY TECHNOLOGY, YOU SEEM TO HAVE ESTABLISHED A SUITABLE FACILITY.
SEEKING YOUR APPROVAL WAS NOT ONE OF MY CRITERIA.
ALL WENT AS PLANNED... AS I KNEW IT WOULD...
BUT EFFUSIVENESS SUITS YOU. AS WELL AS THIS LESS FRAGILE DISPOSITION.
I PREFER IT TO THAT SCHOOLGIRL CHERUB PERSONA... THAT GOT KINDA NAUSEATING.
I HOLD THE FAITH YOU HAVE IN ME IN THE HIGHEST REGARD....

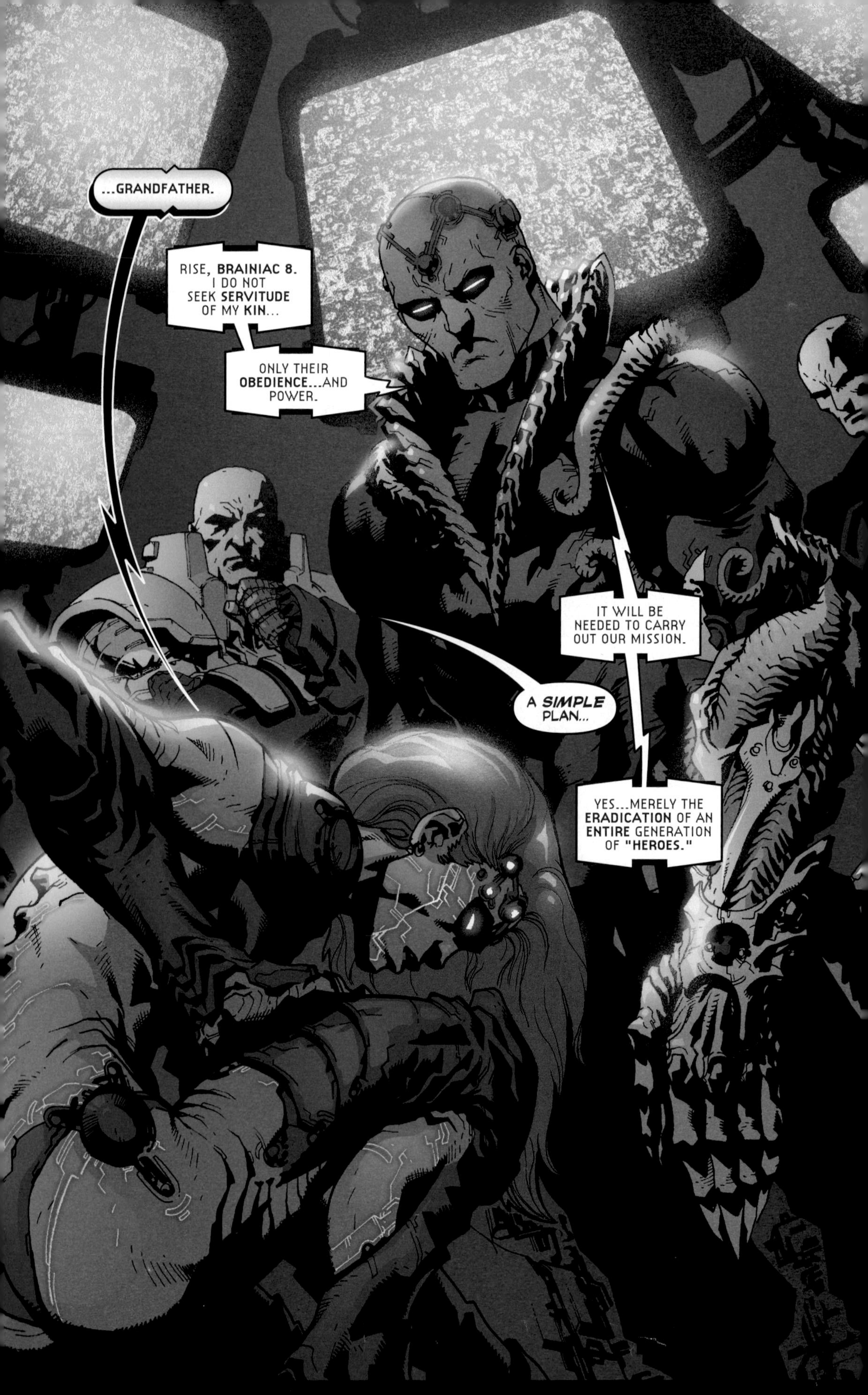
...GRANDFATHER.
RISE, BRAINIAC 8. I DO NOT SEEK SERVITUDE OF MY KIN...
ONLY THEIR OBEDIENCE...AND POWER.
A SIMPLE PLAN...
IT WILL BE NEEDED TO CARRY OUT OUR MISSION.
YES...MERELY THE ERADICATION OF AN ENTIRE GENERATION OF "HEROES."

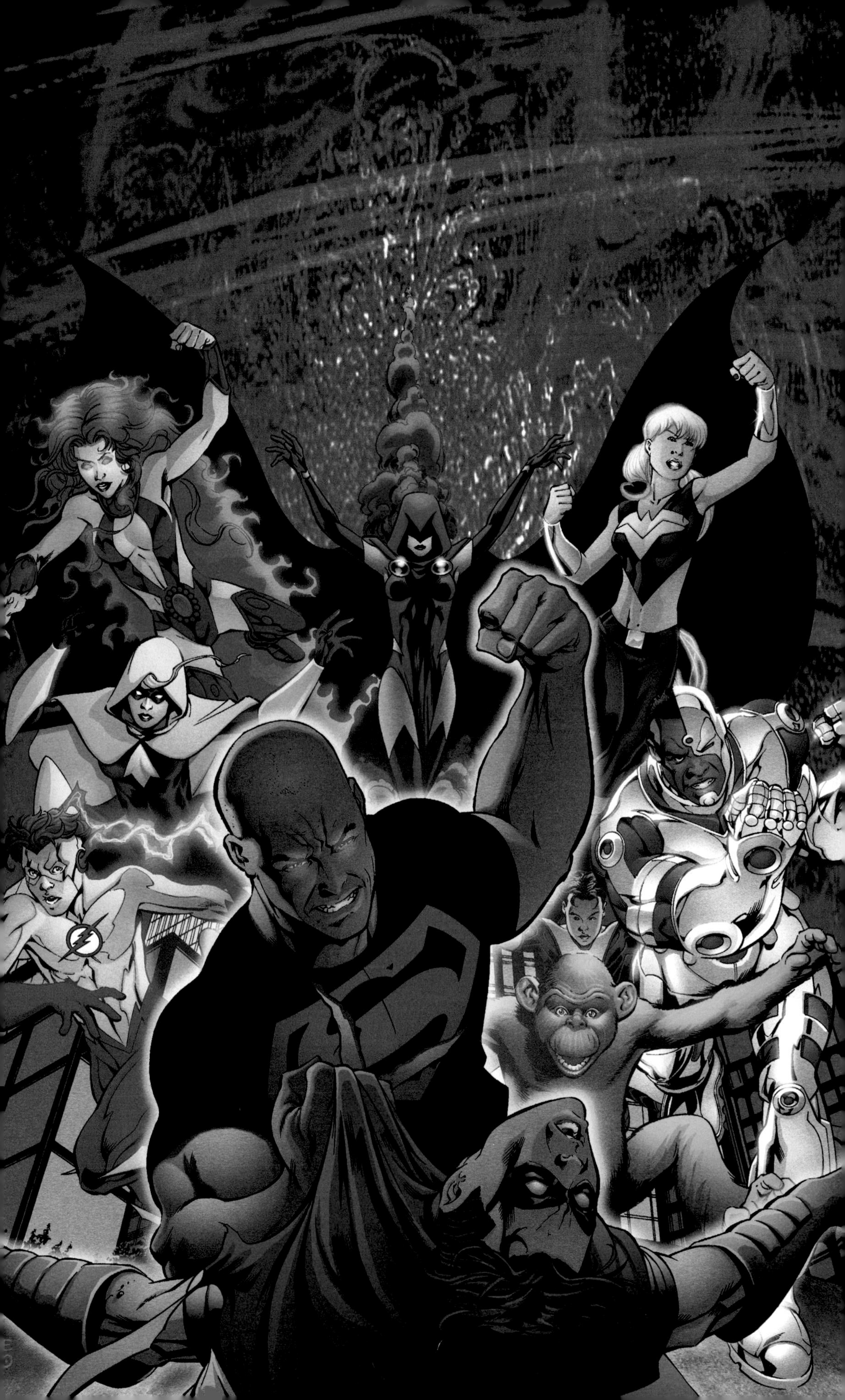

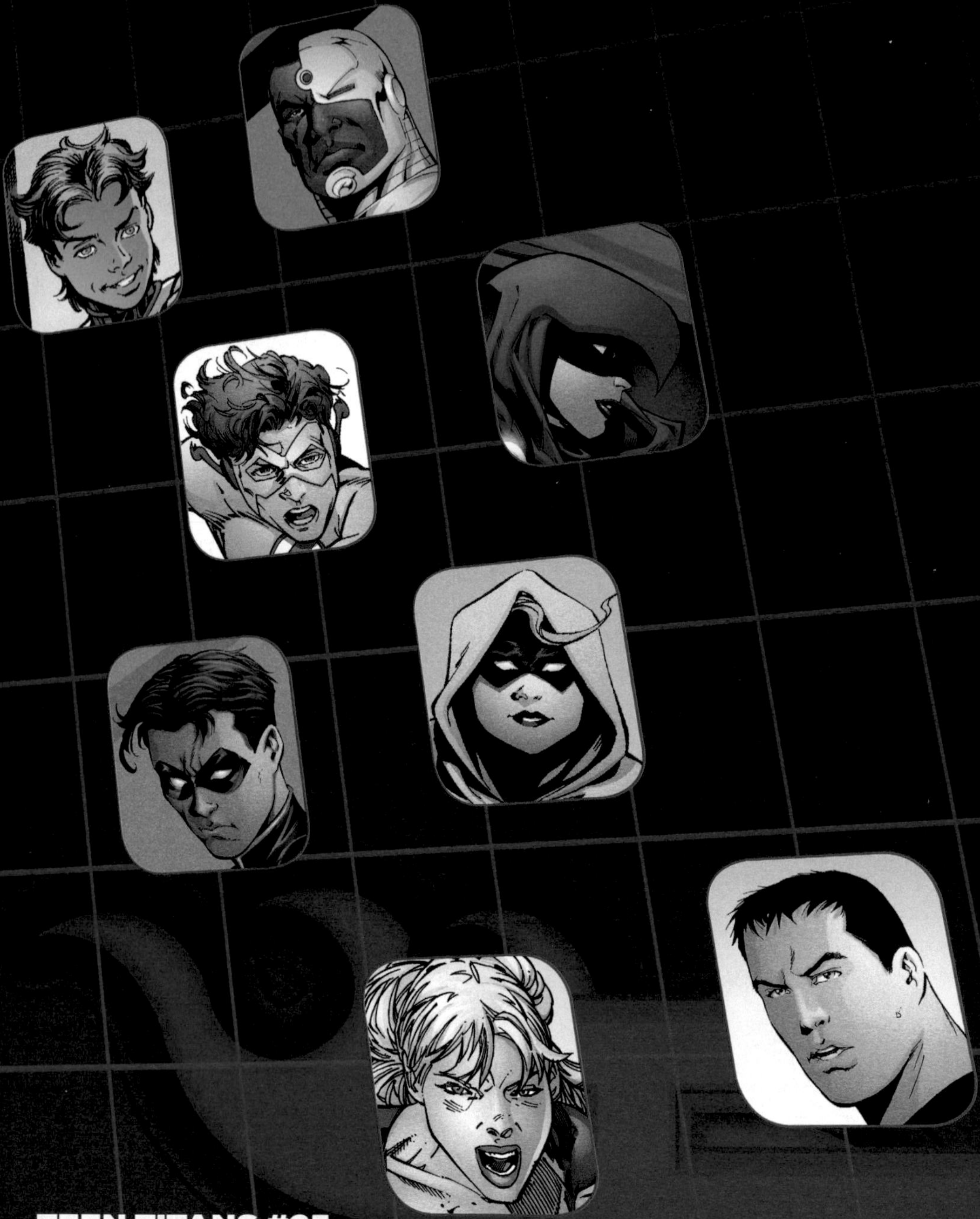

TEEN TITANS #25

GEOFF JOHNS
Writer

MATTHEW CLARK
Penciller

ART THIBERT
Inker

JEROMY COX
Colorist

COMICRAFT
Letterer

MIKE McKONE,
MARLO ALQUIZA & JEROMY COX
Cover Artists

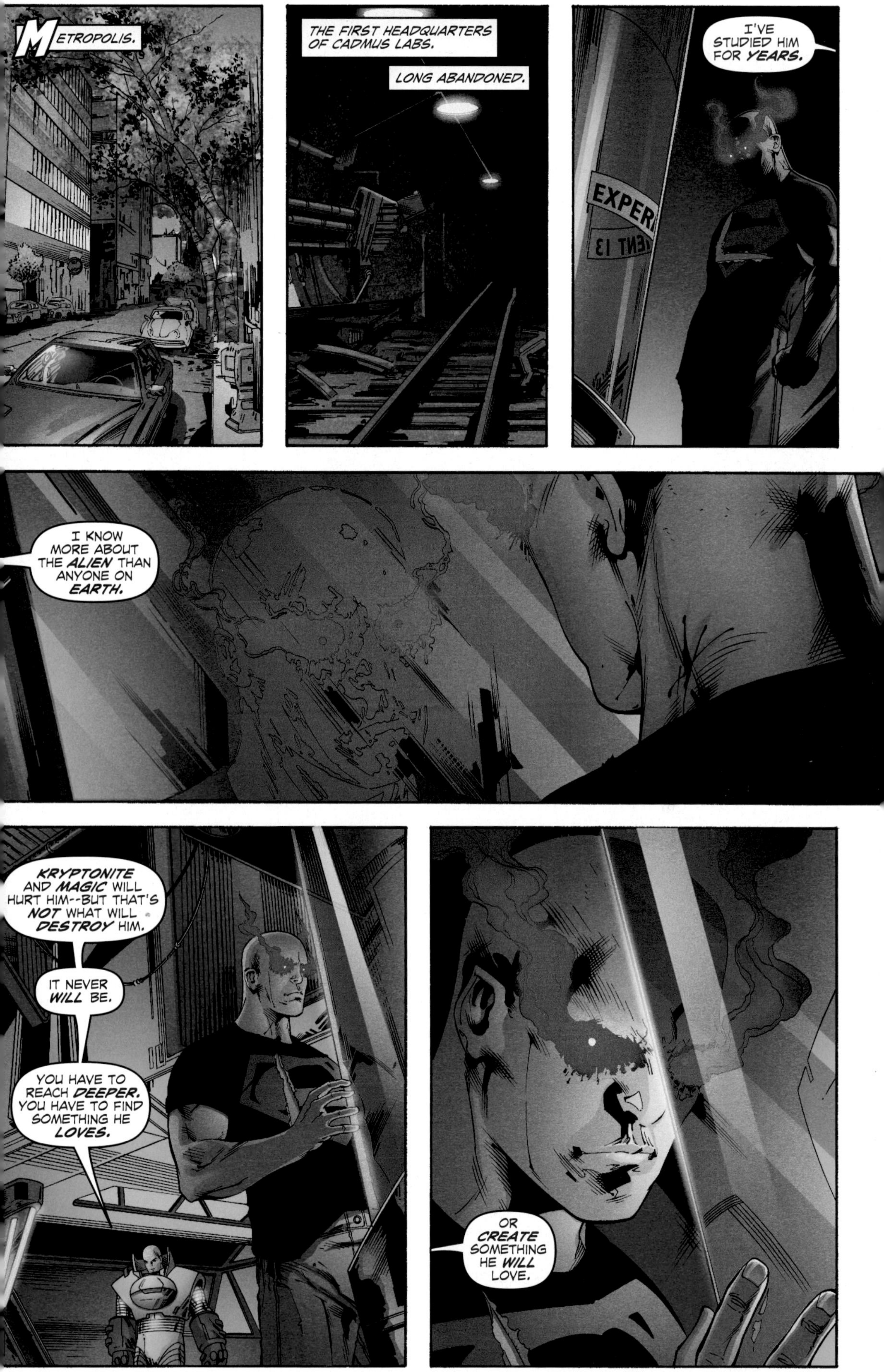
METROPOLIS.
THE FIRST HEADQUARTERS OF CADMUS LABS.
LONG ABANDONED.
I'VE STUDIED HIM FOR YEARS.
EXPER
ENT 13
I KNOW MORE ABOUT THE ALIEN THAN ANYONE ON EARTH.
KRYPTONITE AND MAGIC WILL HURT HIM--BUT THAT'S NOT WHAT WILL DESTROY HIM.
IT NEVER WILL BE.
YOU HAVE TO REACH DEEPER. YOU HAVE TO FIND SOMETHING HE LOVES.
OR CREATE SOMETHING HE WILL LOVE.

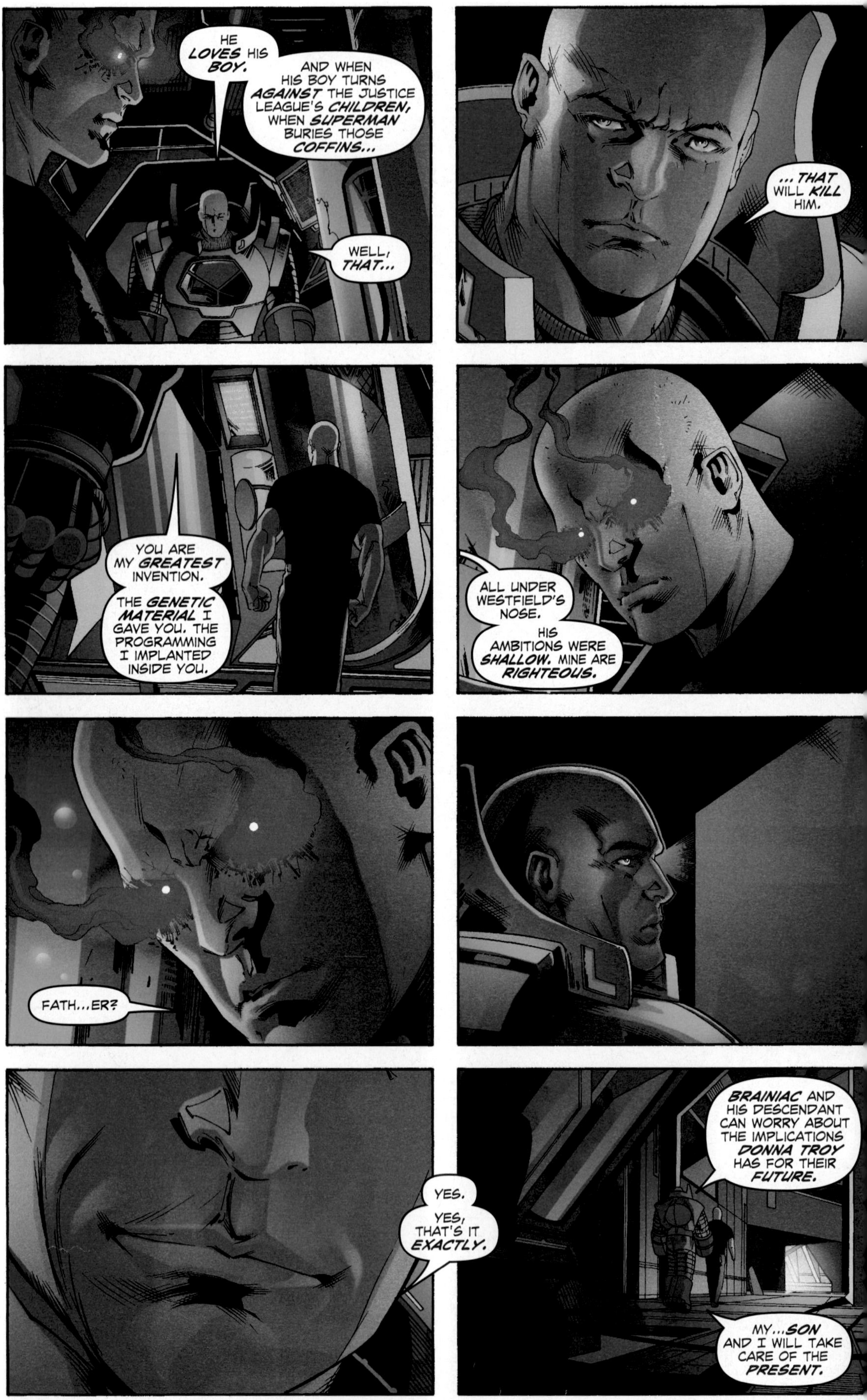
HE LOVES HIS BOY.
AND WHEN HIS BOY TURNS AGAINST THE JUSTICE LEAGUE'S CHILDREN, WHEN SUPERMAN BURIES THOSE COFFINS...
WELL, THAT...
...THAT WILL KILL HIM.
YOU ARE MY GREATEST INVENTION.
THE GENETIC MATERIAL I GAVE YOU. THE PROGRAMMING I IMPLANTED INSIDE YOU.
ALL UNDER WESTFIELD'S NOSE.
HIS AMBITIONS WERE SHALLOW. MINE ARE RIGHTEOUS.
FATH...ER?
YES.
YES, THAT'S IT EXACTLY.
BRAINIAC AND HIS DESCENDANT CAN WORRY ABOUT THE IMPLICATIONS DONNA TROY HAS FOR THEIR FUTURE.
MY...SON AND I WILL TAKE CARE OF THE PRESENT.

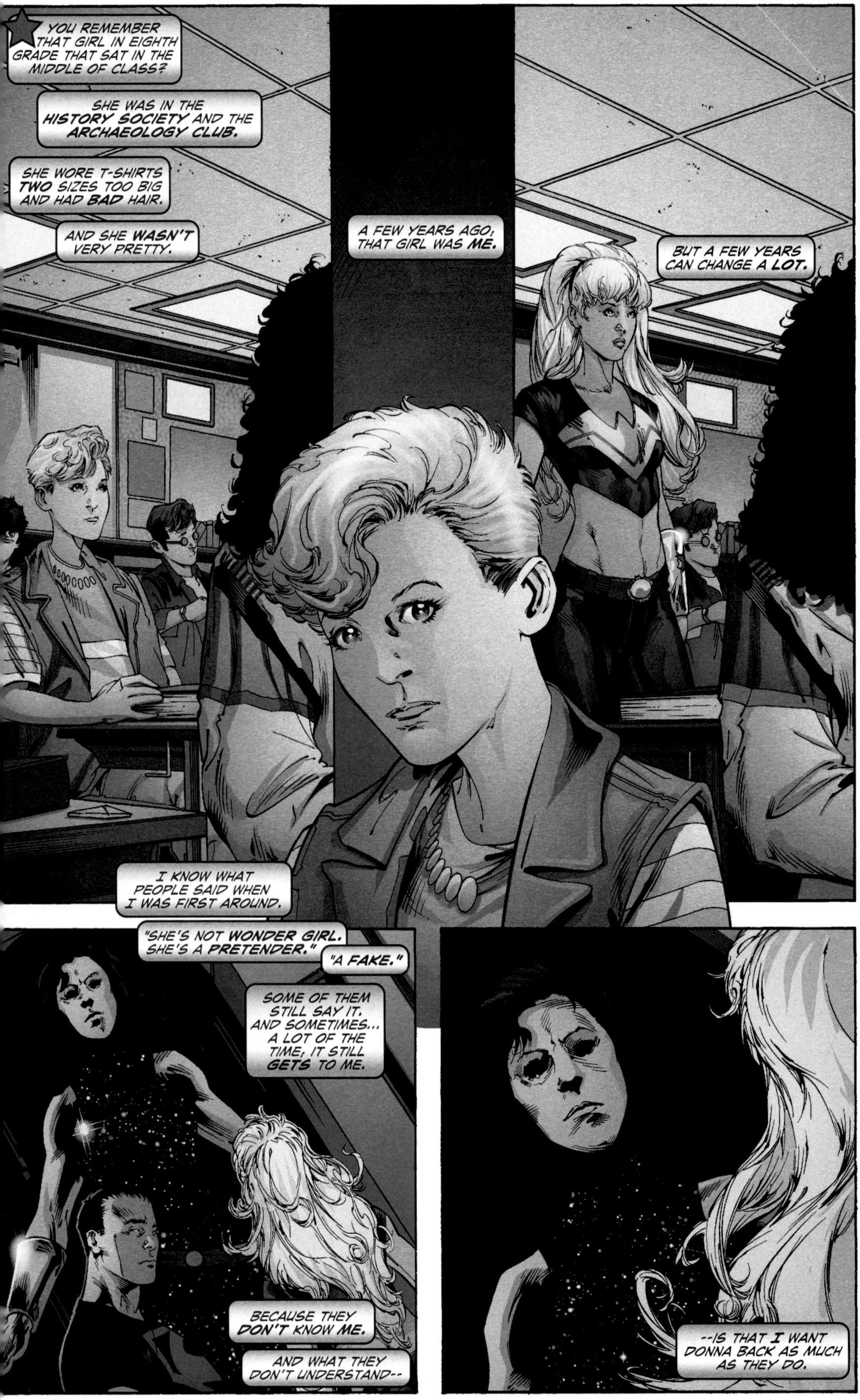
YOU REMEMBER THAT GIRL IN EIGHTH GRADE THAT SAT IN THE MIDDLE OF CLASS?
SHE WAS IN THE HISTORY SOCIETY AND THE ARCHAEOLOGY CLUB.
SHE WORE T-SHIRTS TWO SIZES TOO BIG AND HAD BAD HAIR.
AND SHE WASN'T VERY PRETTY.
A FEW YEARS AGO, THAT GIRL WAS ME.
BUT A FEW YEARS CAN CHANGE A LOT.
I KNOW WHAT PEOPLE SAID WHEN I WAS FIRST AROUND.
"SHE'S NOT WONDER GIRL. SHE'S A PRETENDER."
"A FAKE."
SOME OF THEM STILL SAY IT. AND SOMETIMES... A LOT OF THE TIME, IT STILL GETS TO ME.
BECAUSE THEY DON'T KNOW ME.
AND WHAT THEY DON'T UNDERSTAND--
--IS THAT I WANT DONNA BACK AS MUCH AS THEY DO.

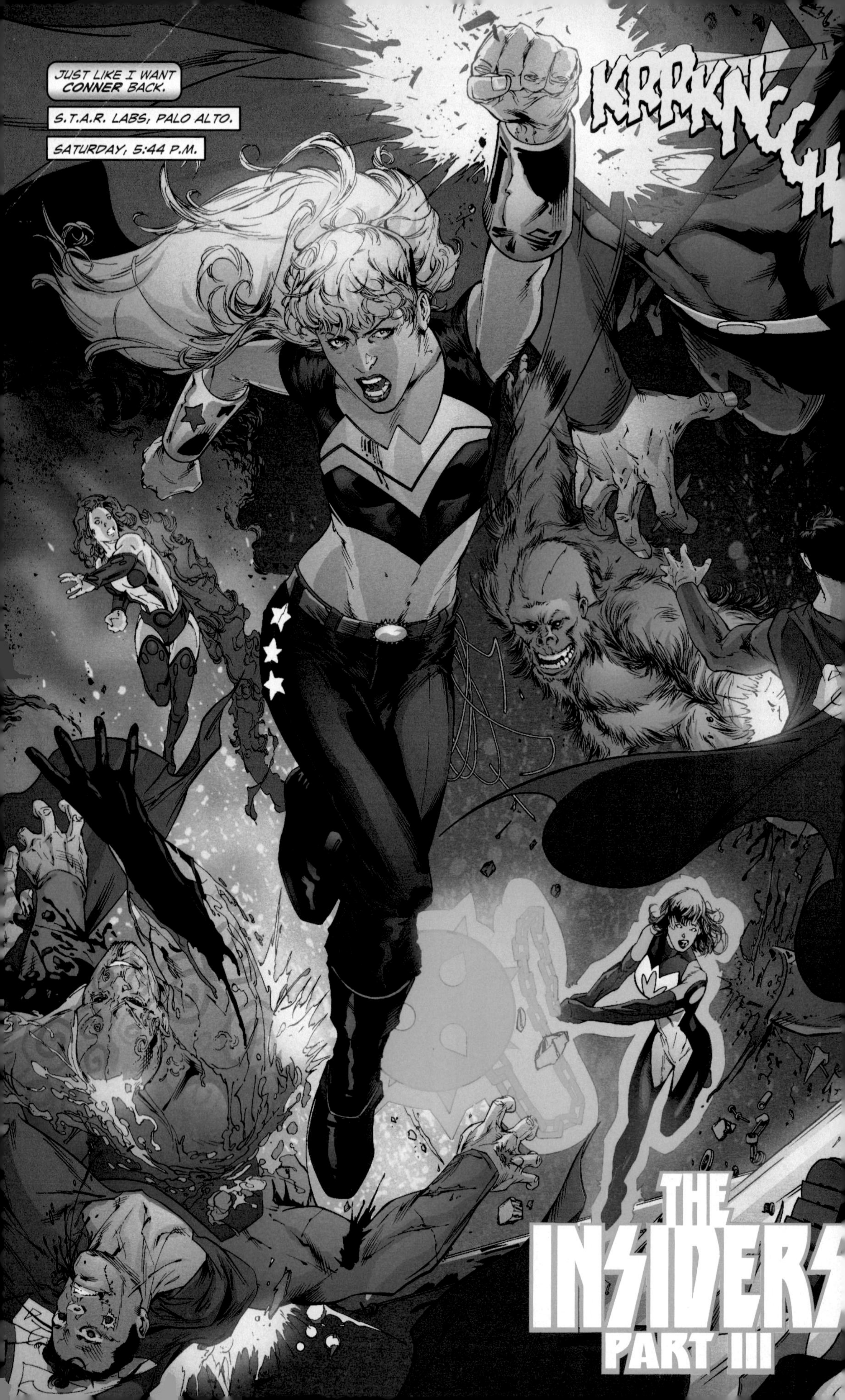
JUST LIKE I WANT CONNER BACK.
S.T.A.R. LABS, PALO ALTO.
SATURDAY, 5:44 P.M.
KRRKNCH
THE INSIDERS
PART III

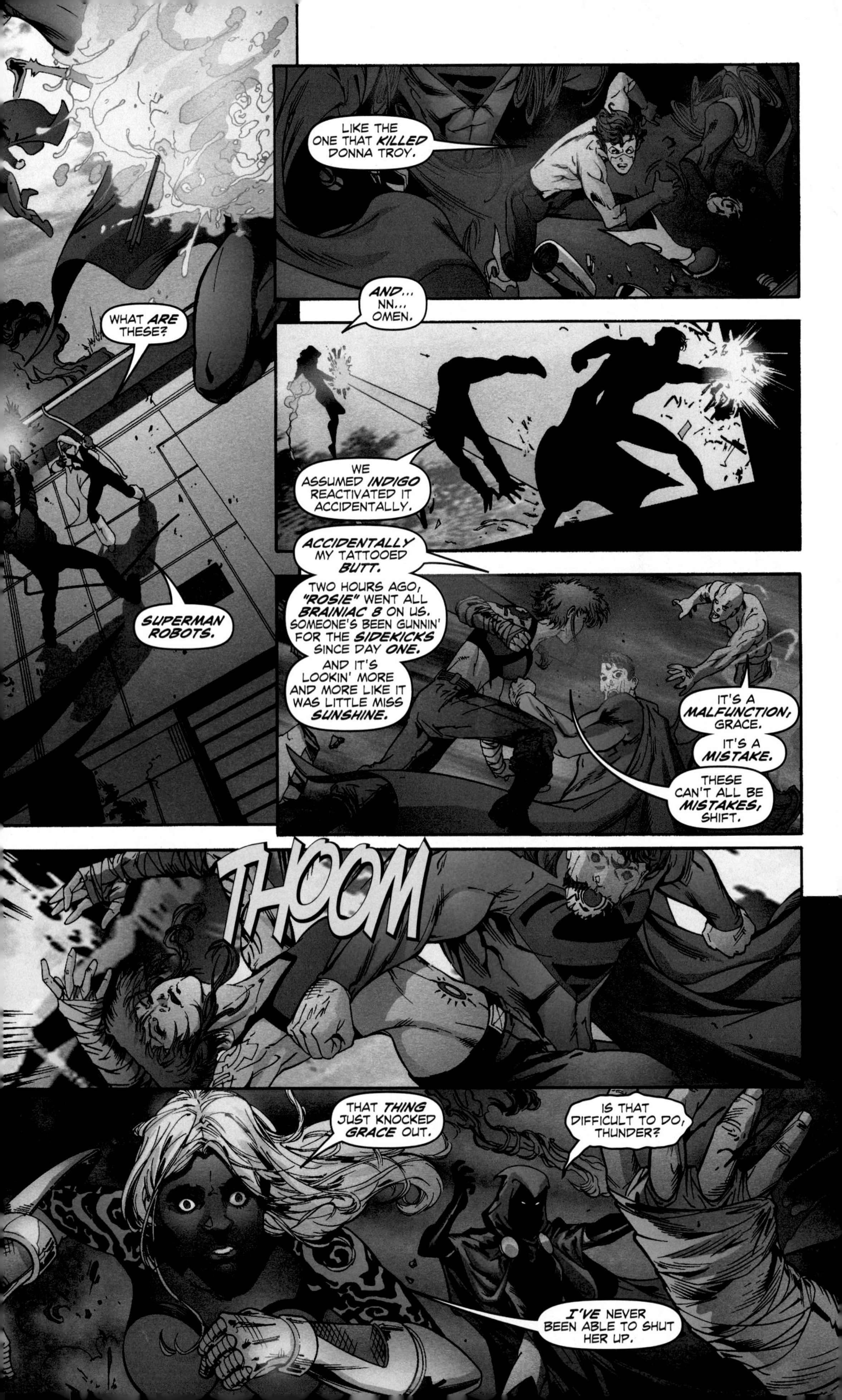

WHAT *ARE* THESE?
SUPERMAN ROBOTS.
LIKE THE ONE THAT *KILLED* DONNA TROY.
AND... NN... OMEN.
WE ASSUMED *INDIGO* REACTIVATED IT ACCIDENTALLY.
ACCIDENTALLY MY TATTOOED *BUTT.*
TWO HOURS AGO, *"ROSIE"* WENT ALL *BRAINIAC 8* ON US. SOMEONE'S BEEN GUNNIN' FOR THE *SIDEKICKS* SINCE DAY *ONE.*
AND IT'S LOOKIN' MORE AND MORE LIKE IT WAS LITTLE MISS *SUNSHINE.*
IT'S A *MALFUNCTION,* GRACE.
IT'S A *MISTAKE.*
THESE CAN'T ALL BE *MISTAKES,* SHIFT.
THOOM
THAT *THING* JUST KNOCKED *GRACE* OUT.
IS THAT DIFFICULT TO DO, THUNDER?
I'VE NEVER BEEN ABLE TO SHUT HER UP.

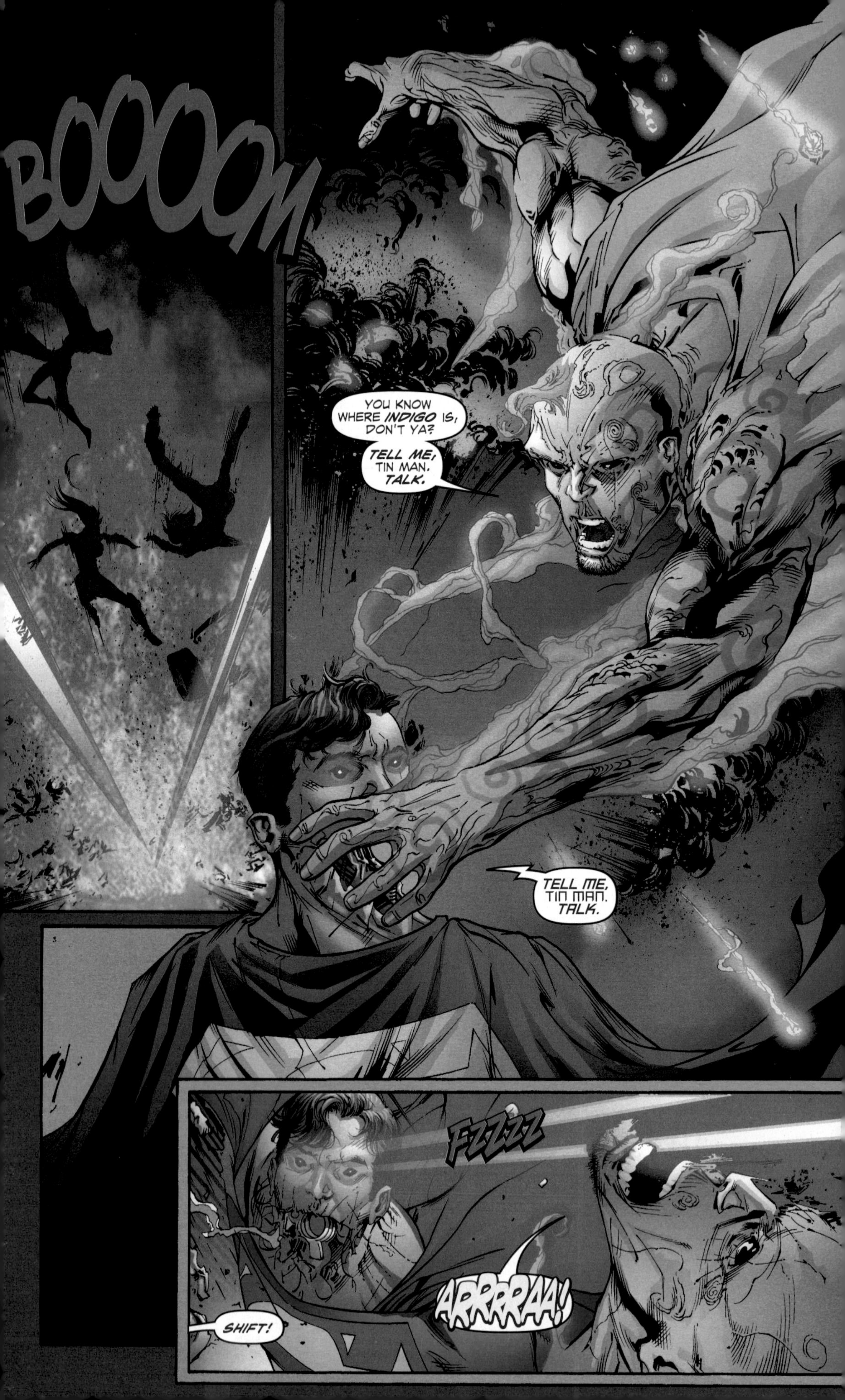
BOOOOM
YOU KNOW WHERE INDIGO IS, DON'T YA?
TELL ME, TIN MAN. TALK.
TELL ME, TIN MAN. TALK.
FZZZZ
ARRRRAA!
SHIFT!

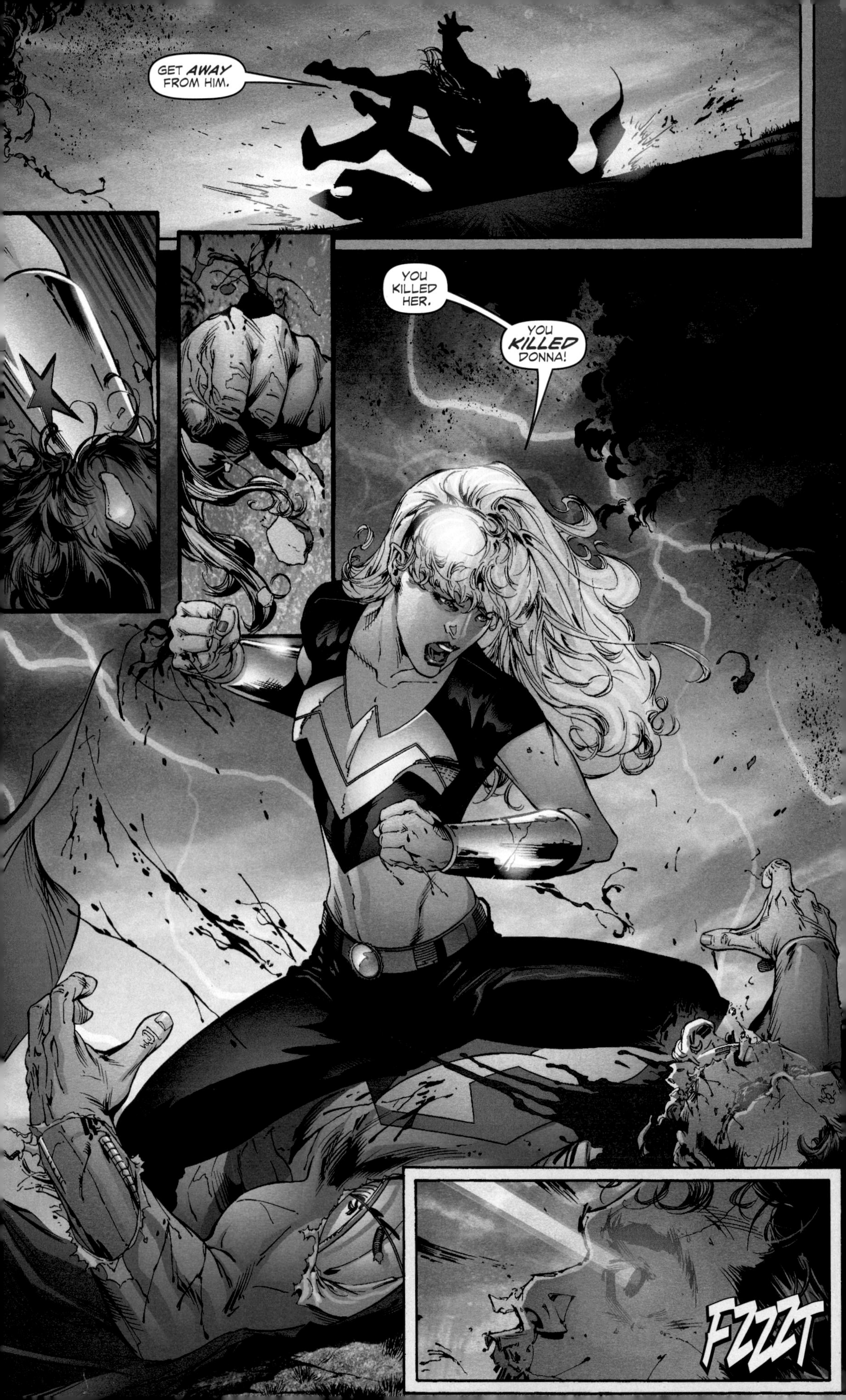
GET AWAY FROM HIM.
YOU KILLED HER.
YOU KILLED DONNA!
FZZZT

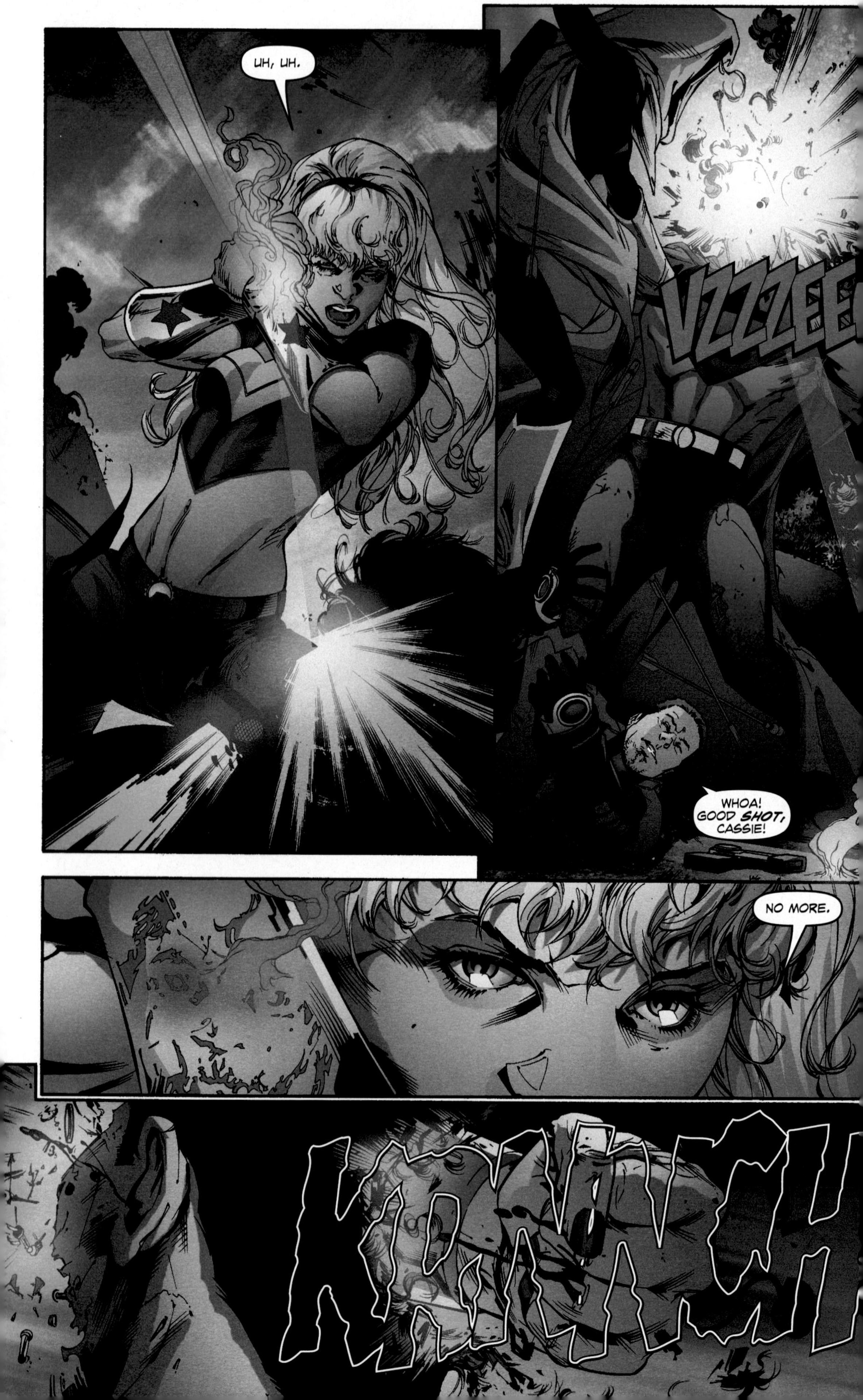
UH, UH.
VZZZEE
WHOA! GOOD SHOT, CASSIE!
NO MORE.
KRRUNCH

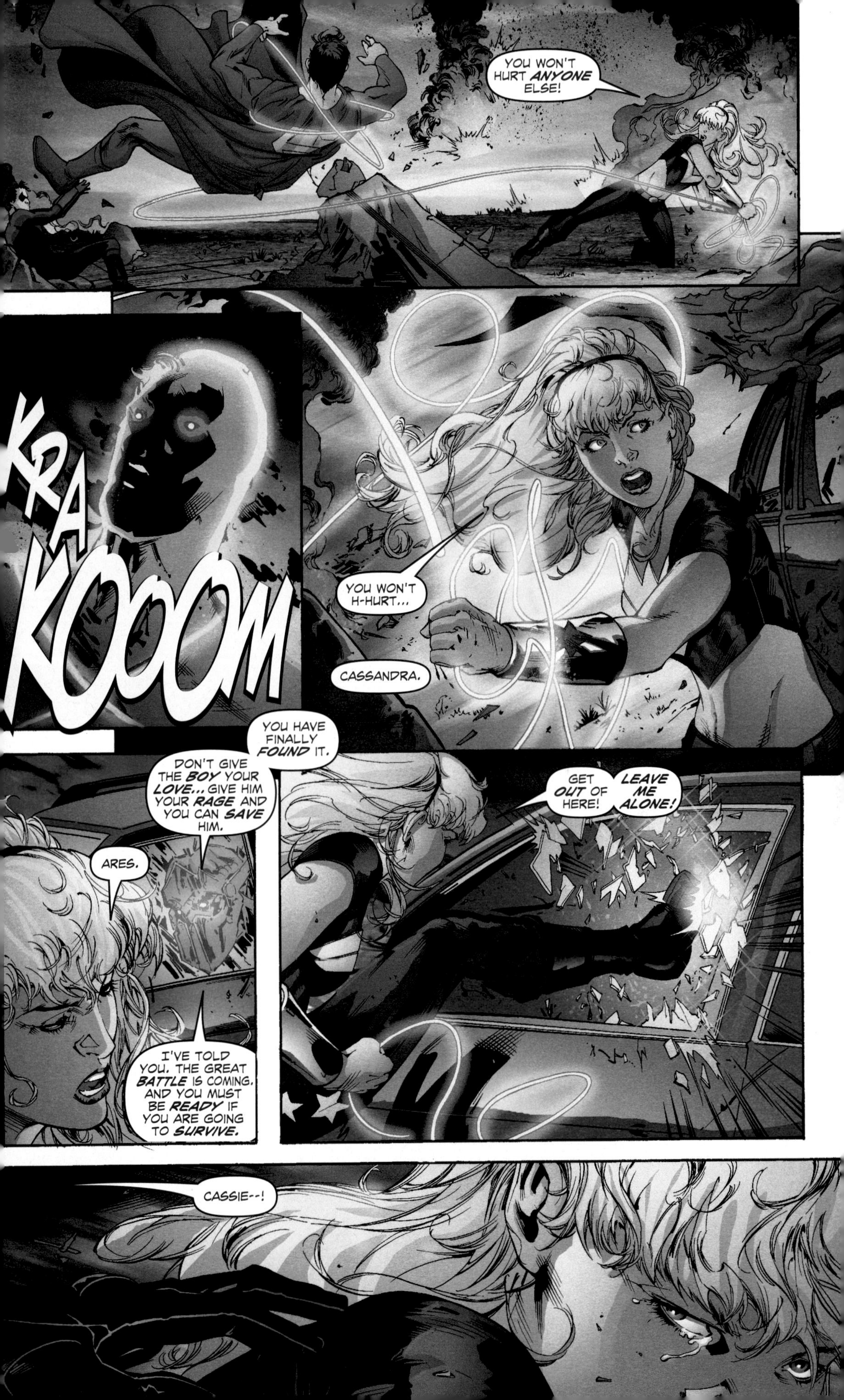
YOU WON'T HURT ANYONE ELSE!
KRA KOOOM
YOU WON'T H-HURT...
CASSANDRA.
YOU HAVE FINALLY FOUND IT.
DON'T GIVE THE BOY YOUR LOVE... GIVE HIM YOUR RAGE AND YOU CAN SAVE HIM.
ARES.
I'VE TOLD YOU. THE GREAT BATTLE IS COMING. AND YOU MUST BE READY IF YOU ARE GOING TO SURVIVE.
GET OUT OF HERE!
LEAVE ME ALONE!
CASSIE--!

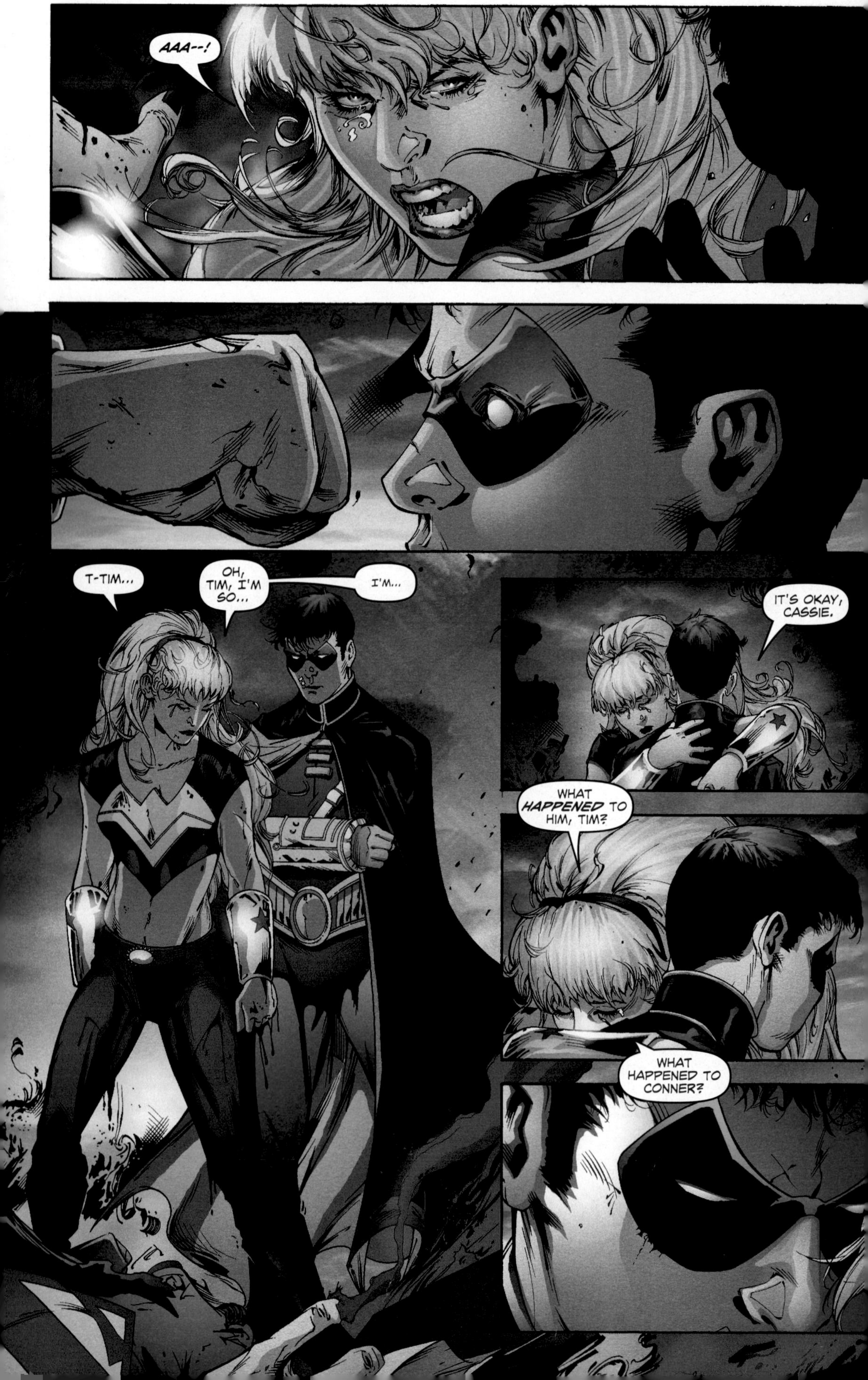
AAA--!
T-TIM...
OH, TIM, I'M SO...
I'M...
IT'S OKAY, CASSIE.
WHAT HAPPENED TO HIM, TIM?
WHAT HAPPENED TO CONNER?

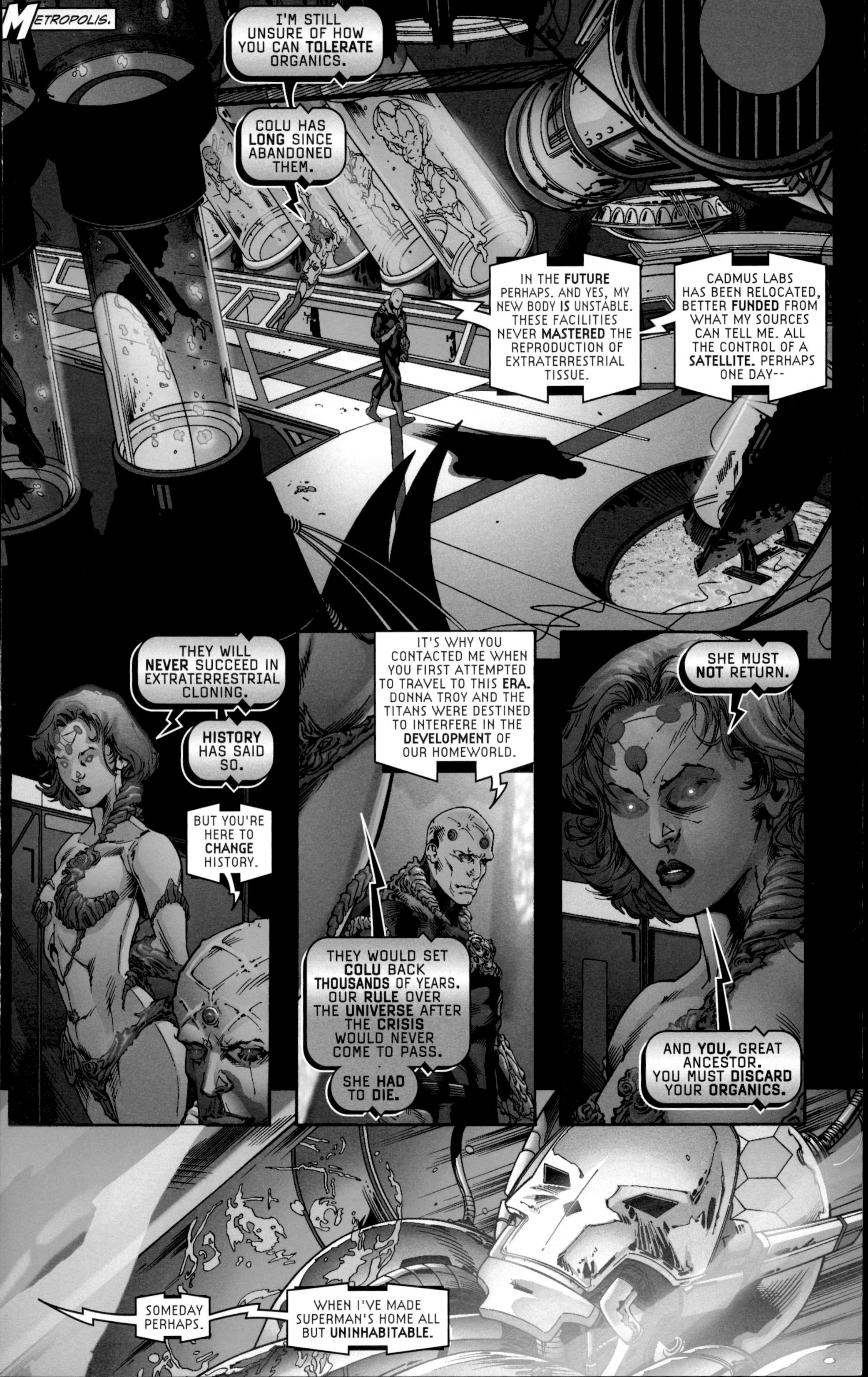
METROPOLIS.
I'M STILL UNSURE OF HOW YOU CAN TOLERATE ORGANICS.
COLU HAS LONG SINCE ABANDONED THEM.
IN THE FUTURE PERHAPS. AND YES, MY NEW BODY IS UNSTABLE. THESE FACILITIES NEVER MASTERED THE REPRODUCTION OF EXTRATERRESTRIAL TISSUE.
CADMUS LABS HAS BEEN RELOCATED, BETTER FUNDED FROM WHAT MY SOURCES CAN TELL ME. ALL THE CONTROL OF A SATELLITE. PERHAPS ONE DAY--
THEY WILL NEVER SUCCEED IN EXTRATERRESTRIAL CLONING.
HISTORY HAS SAID SO.
BUT YOU'RE HERE TO CHANGE HISTORY.
IT'S WHY YOU CONTACTED ME WHEN YOU FIRST ATTEMPTED TO TRAVEL TO THIS ERA. DONNA TROY AND THE TITANS WERE DESTINED TO INTERFERE IN THE DEVELOPMENT OF OUR HOMEWORLD.
THEY WOULD SET COLU BACK THOUSANDS OF YEARS. OUR RULE OVER THE UNIVERSE AFTER THE CRISIS WOULD NEVER COME TO PASS.
SHE HAD TO DIE.
SHE MUST NOT RETURN.
AND YOU, GREAT ANCESTOR. YOU MUST DISCARD YOUR ORGANICS.
SOMEDAY PERHAPS.
WHEN I'VE MADE SUPERMAN'S HOME ALL BUT UNINHABITABLE.

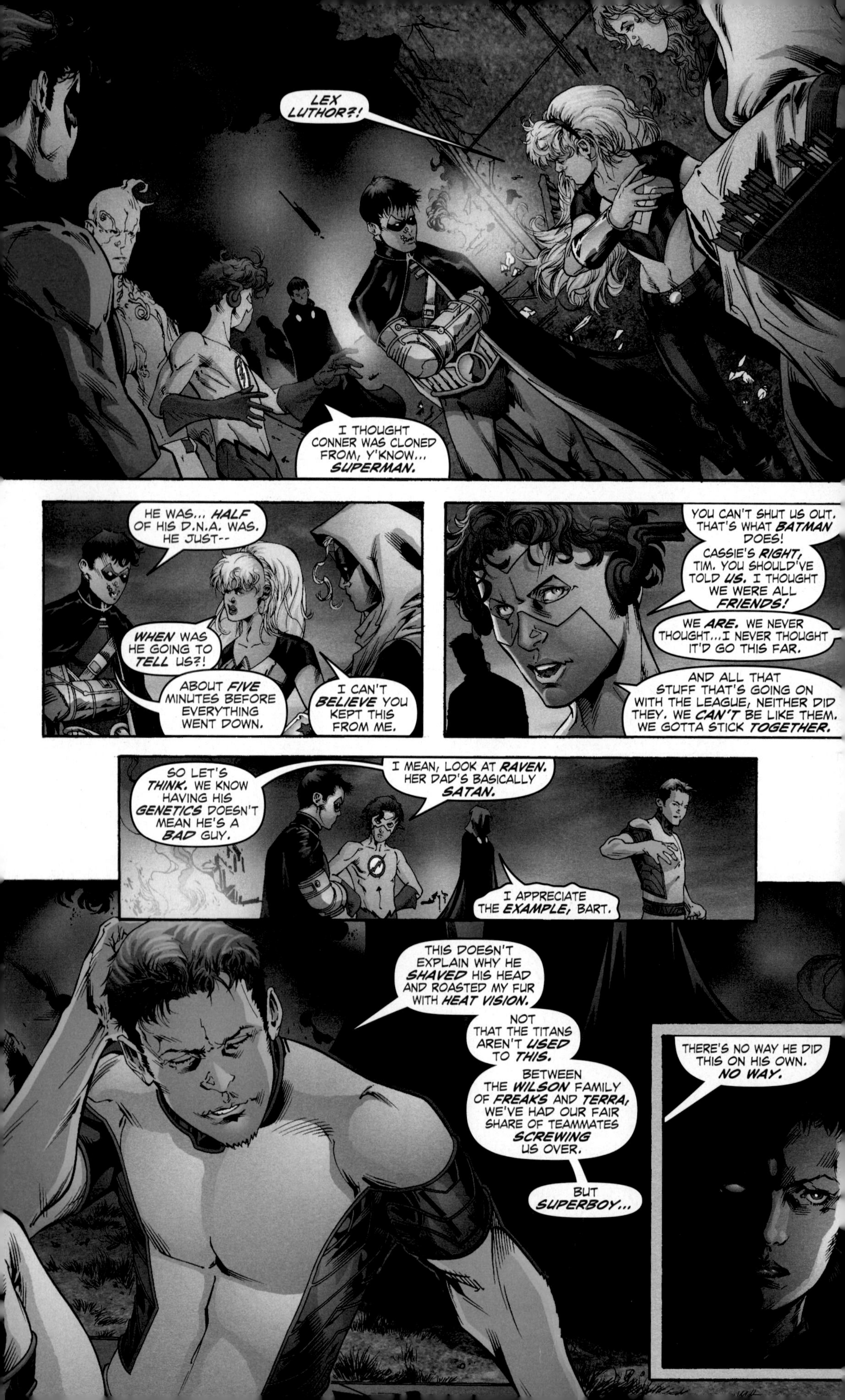
LEX LUTHOR?!
I THOUGHT CONNER WAS CLONED FROM, Y'KNOW... SUPERMAN.
HE WAS... HALF OF HIS D.N.A. WAS. HE JUST--
WHEN WAS HE GOING TO TELL US?!
ABOUT FIVE MINUTES BEFORE EVERYTHING WENT DOWN.
I CAN'T BELIEVE YOU KEPT THIS FROM ME.
YOU CAN'T SHUT US OUT. THAT'S WHAT BATMAN DOES!
CASSIE'S RIGHT, TIM. YOU SHOULD'VE TOLD US. I THOUGHT WE WERE ALL FRIENDS!
WE ARE. WE NEVER THOUGHT...I NEVER THOUGHT IT'D GO THIS FAR.
AND ALL THAT STUFF THAT'S GOING ON WITH THE LEAGUE, NEITHER DID THEY. WE CAN'T BE LIKE THEM. WE GOTTA STICK TOGETHER.
SO LET'S THINK. WE KNOW HAVING HIS GENETICS DOESN'T MEAN HE'S A BAD GUY.
I MEAN, LOOK AT RAVEN. HER DAD'S BASICALLY SATAN.
I APPRECIATE THE EXAMPLE, BART.
THIS DOESN'T EXPLAIN WHY HE SHAVED HIS HEAD AND ROASTED MY FUR WITH HEAT VISION.
NOT THAT THE TITANS AREN'T USED TO THIS.
BETWEEN THE WILSON FAMILY OF FREAKS AND TERRA, WE'VE HAD OUR FAIR SHARE OF TEAMMATES SCREWING US OVER.
BUT SUPERBOY...
THERE'S NO WAY HE DID THIS ON HIS OWN. NO WAY.

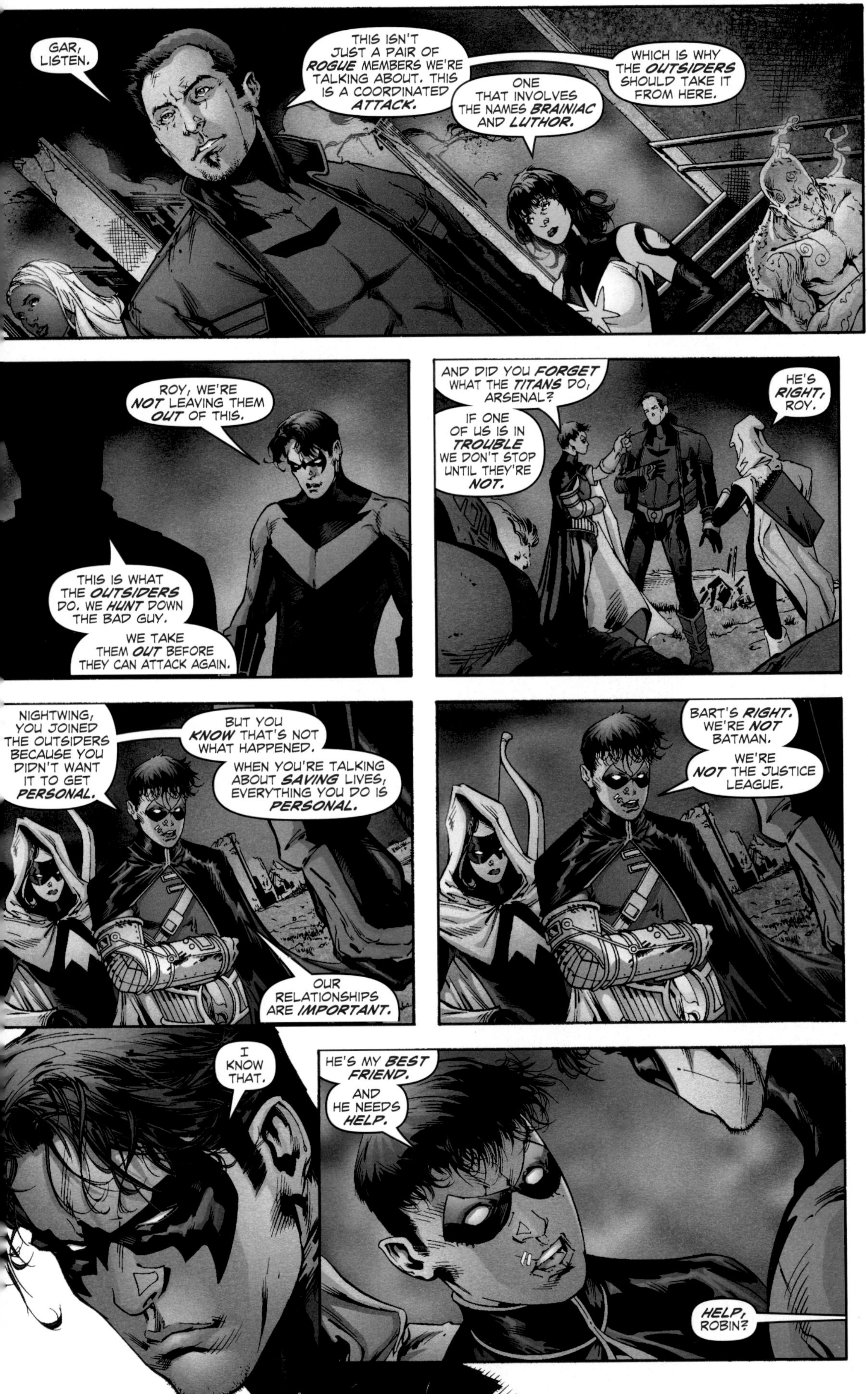
GAR, LISTEN.
THIS ISN'T JUST A PAIR OF ROGUE MEMBERS WE'RE TALKING ABOUT. THIS IS A COORDINATED ATTACK.
ONE THAT INVOLVES THE NAMES BRAINIAC AND LUTHOR.
WHICH IS WHY THE OUTSIDERS SHOULD TAKE IT FROM HERE.
ROY, WE'RE NOT LEAVING THEM OUT OF THIS.
THIS IS WHAT THE OUTSIDERS DO. WE HUNT DOWN THE BAD GUY.
WE TAKE THEM OUT BEFORE THEY CAN ATTACK AGAIN.
AND DID YOU FORGET WHAT THE TITANS DO, ARSENAL?
IF ONE OF US IS IN TROUBLE WE DON'T STOP UNTIL THEY'RE NOT.
HE'S RIGHT, ROY.
NIGHTWING, YOU JOINED THE OUTSIDERS BECAUSE YOU DIDN'T WANT IT TO GET PERSONAL.
BUT YOU KNOW THAT'S NOT WHAT HAPPENED.
WHEN YOU'RE TALKING ABOUT SAVING LIVES, EVERYTHING YOU DO IS PERSONAL.
OUR RELATIONSHIPS ARE IMPORTANT.
BART'S RIGHT. WE'RE NOT BATMAN.
WE'RE NOT THE JUSTICE LEAGUE.
I KNOW THAT.
HE'S MY BEST FRIEND.
AND HE NEEDS HELP.
HELP, ROBIN?

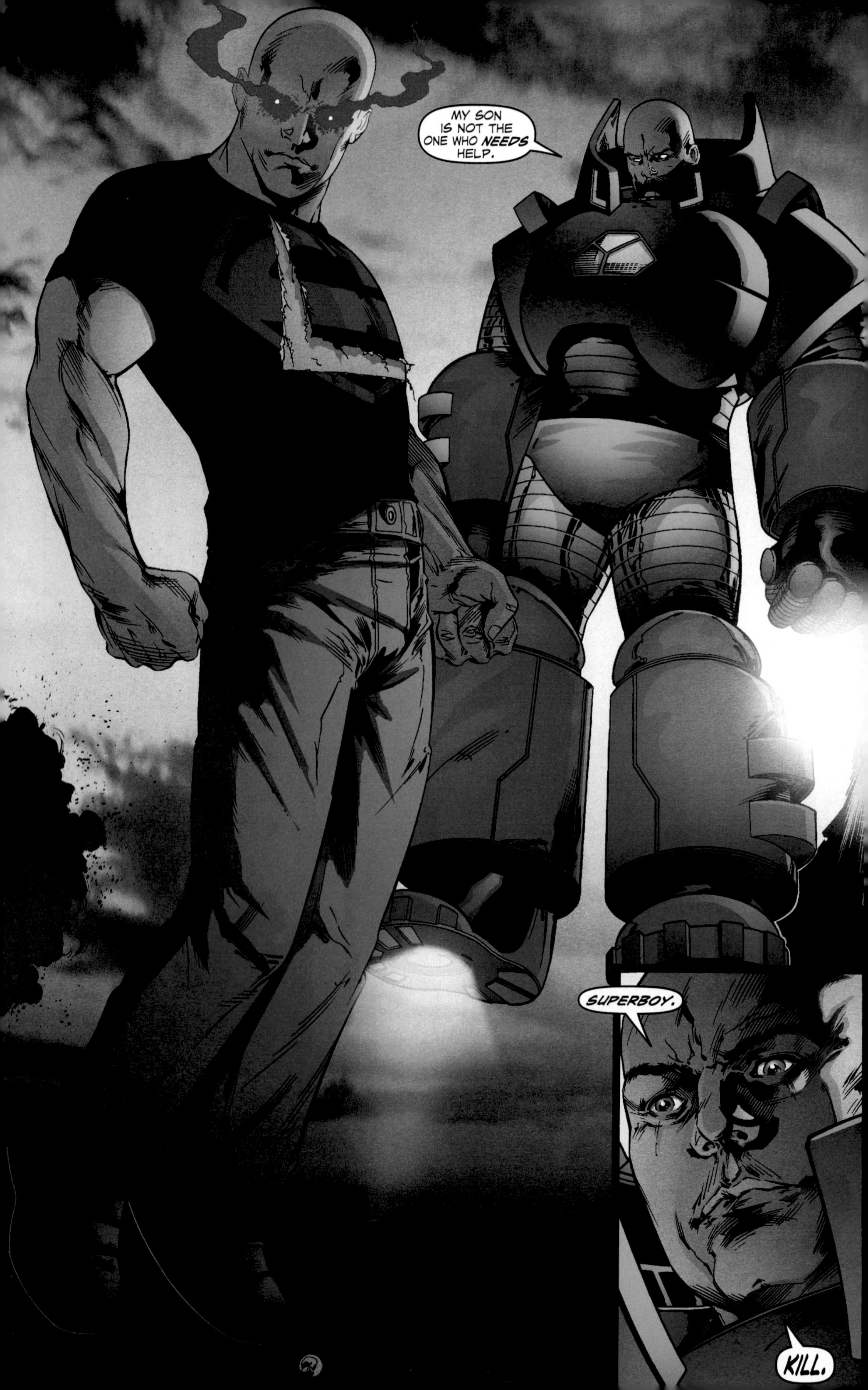
MY SON IS NOT THE ONE WHO NEEDS HELP.
SUPERBOY.
KILL.

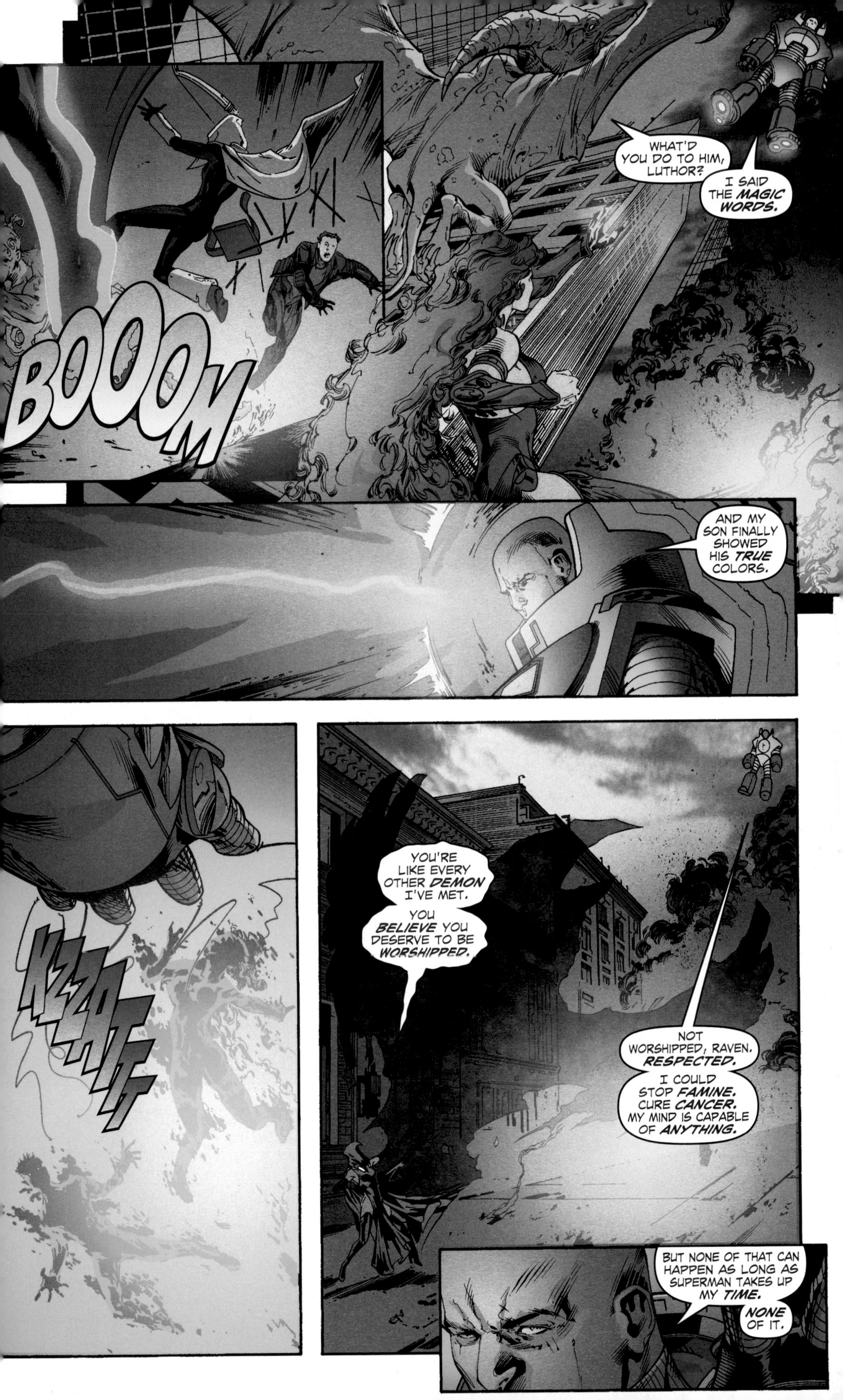
BOOOM
WHAT'D YOU DO TO HIM, LUTHOR?
I SAID THE MAGIC WORDS.
AND MY SON FINALLY SHOWED HIS TRUE COLORS.
KZZATT
YOU'RE LIKE EVERY OTHER DEMON I'VE MET.
YOU BELIEVE YOU DESERVE TO BE WORSHIPPED.
NOT WORSHIPPED, RAVEN. RESPECTED.
I COULD STOP FAMINE. CURE CANCER. MY MIND IS CAPABLE OF ANYTHING.
BUT NONE OF THAT CAN HAPPEN AS LONG AS SUPERMAN TAKES UP MY TIME.
NONE OF IT.

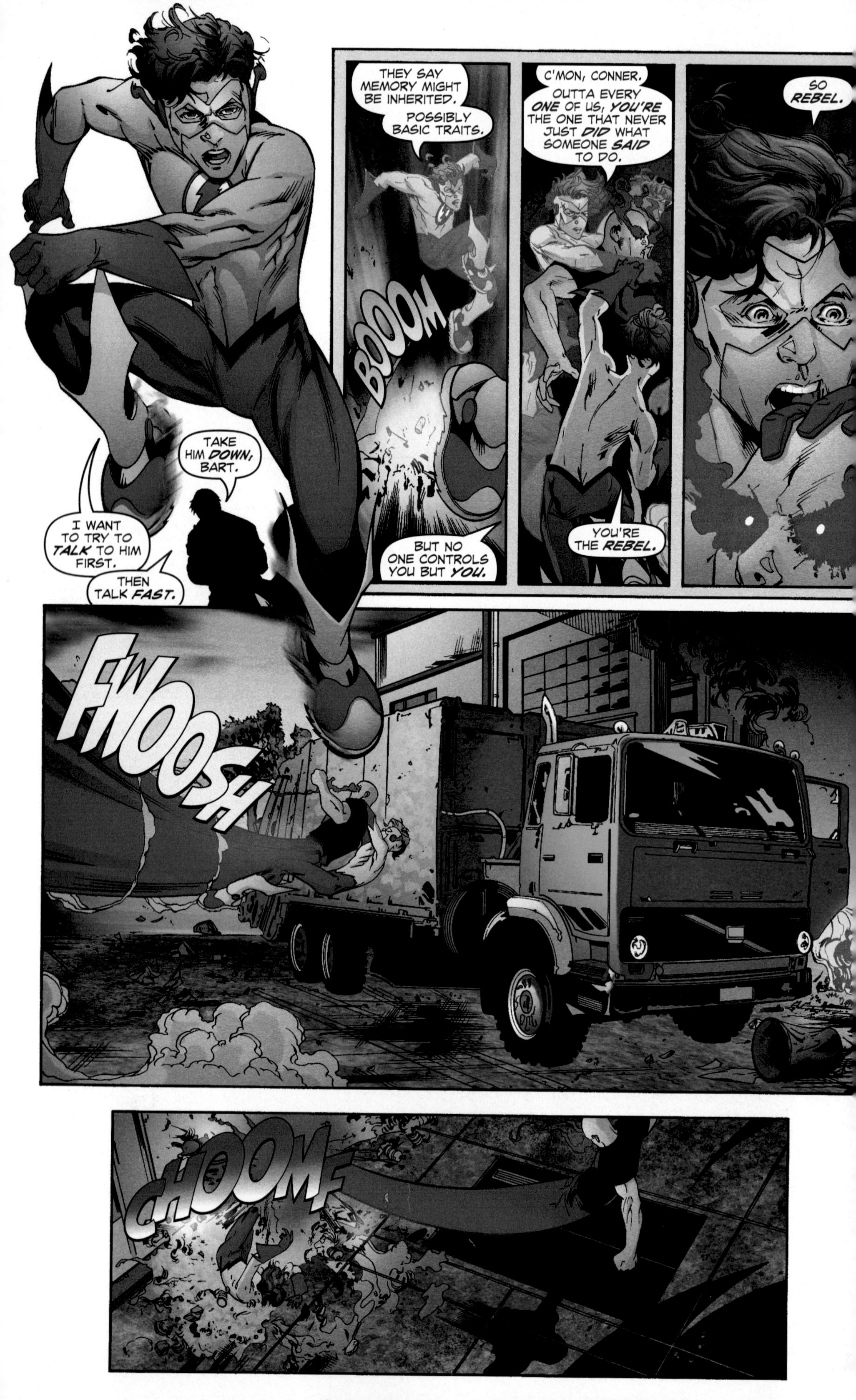
TAKE HIM DOWN, BART.
I WANT TO TRY TO TALK TO HIM FIRST.
THEN TALK FAST.
THEY SAY MEMORY MIGHT BE INHERITED.
POSSIBLY BASIC TRAITS.
BOOOM
BUT NO ONE CONTROLS YOU BUT YOU.
C'MON, CONNER.
OUTTA EVERY ONE OF US, YOU'RE THE ONE THAT NEVER JUST DID WHAT SOMEONE SAID TO DO.
YOU'RE THE REBEL.
SO REBEL.
FWOOSH
CHOOMF

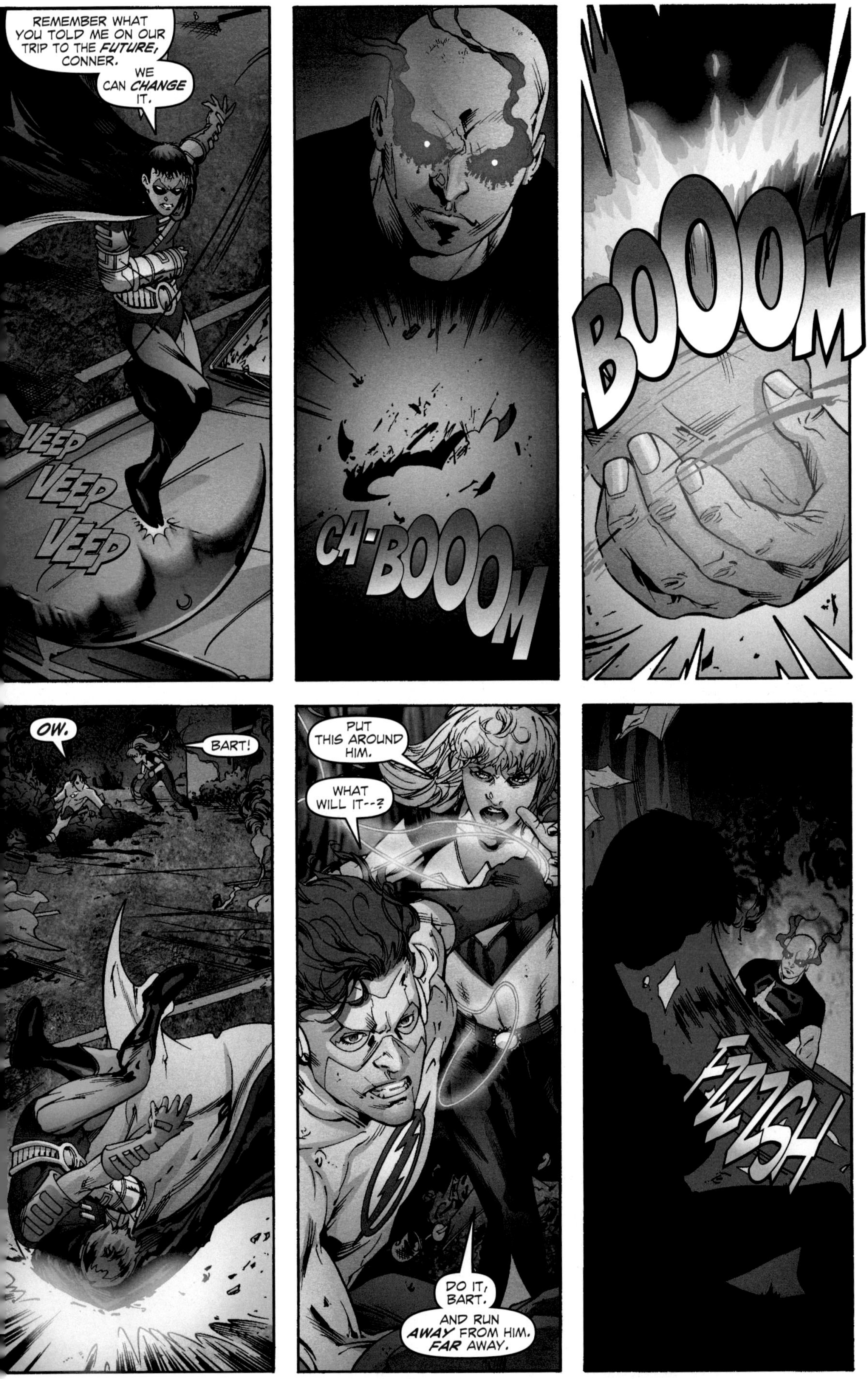
REMEMBER WHAT YOU TOLD ME ON OUR TRIP TO THE *FUTURE*, CONNER.
WE CAN *CHANGE* IT.
VEEP VEEP VEEP
CA-BOOOOM
BOOOOM
OW.
BART!
PUT THIS AROUND HIM.
WHAT WILL IT--?
DO IT, BART.
AND RUN *AWAY* FROM HIM. *FAR* AWAY.
FZZZSH

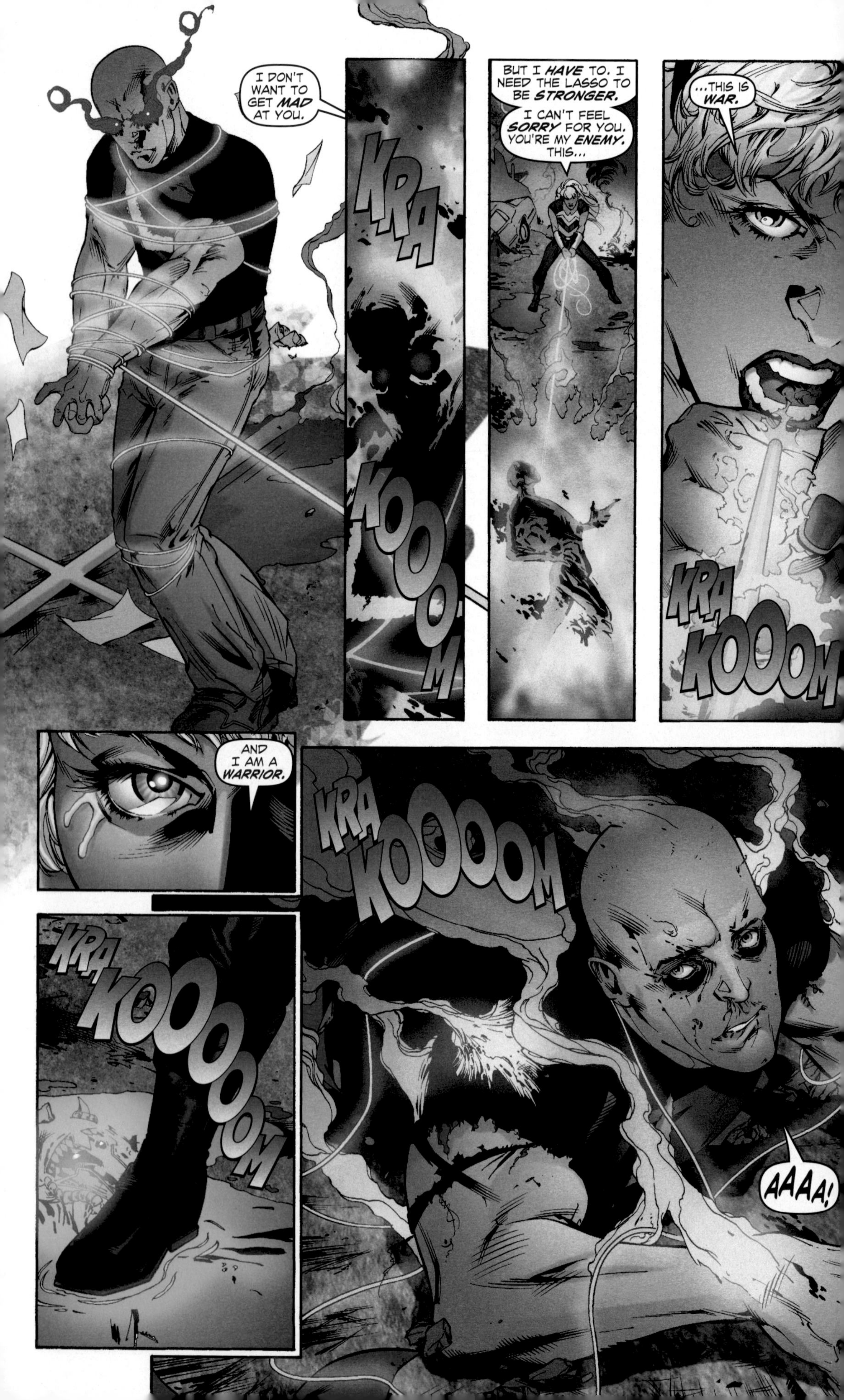
I DON'T WANT TO GET MAD AT YOU.
KRA KOOOOM
BUT I HAVE TO. I NEED THE LASSO TO BE STRONGER.
I CAN'T FEEL SORRY FOR YOU. YOU'RE MY ENEMY. THIS...
...THIS IS WAR.
KRA KOOOM
AND I AM A WARRIOR.
KRA KOOOOOOOM
KRA KOOOOOM
AAAA!

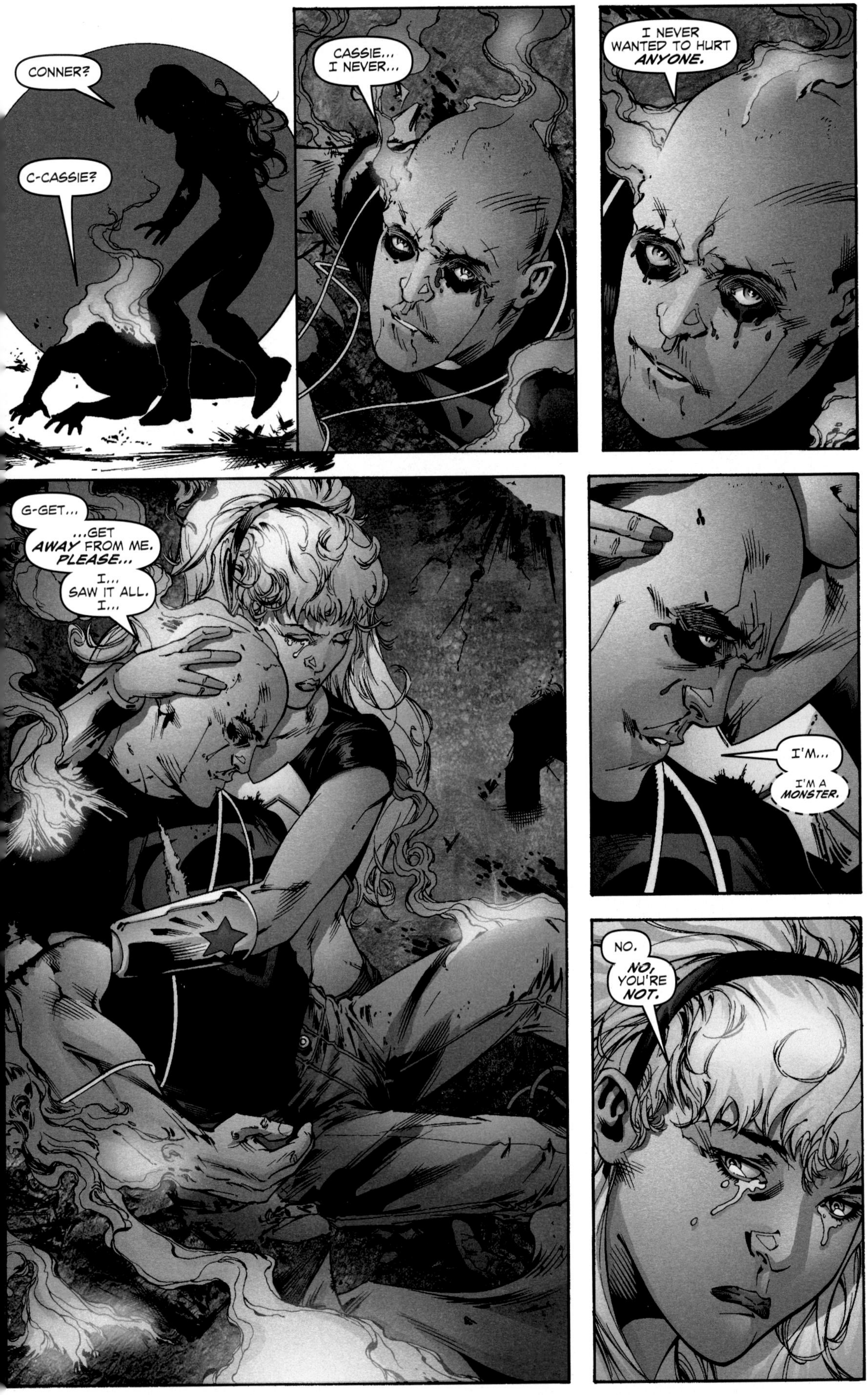
CONNER?
C-CASSIE?
CASSIE... I NEVER...
I NEVER WANTED TO HURT ANYONE.
G-GET...
...GET AWAY FROM ME. PLEASE...
I... SAW IT ALL. I...
I'M...
I'M A MONSTER.
NO.
NO, YOU'RE NOT.

AUT VINCERE AUT MORI

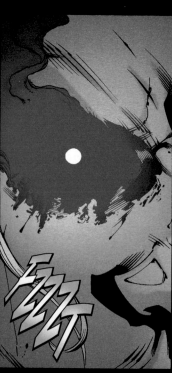

CONNER?

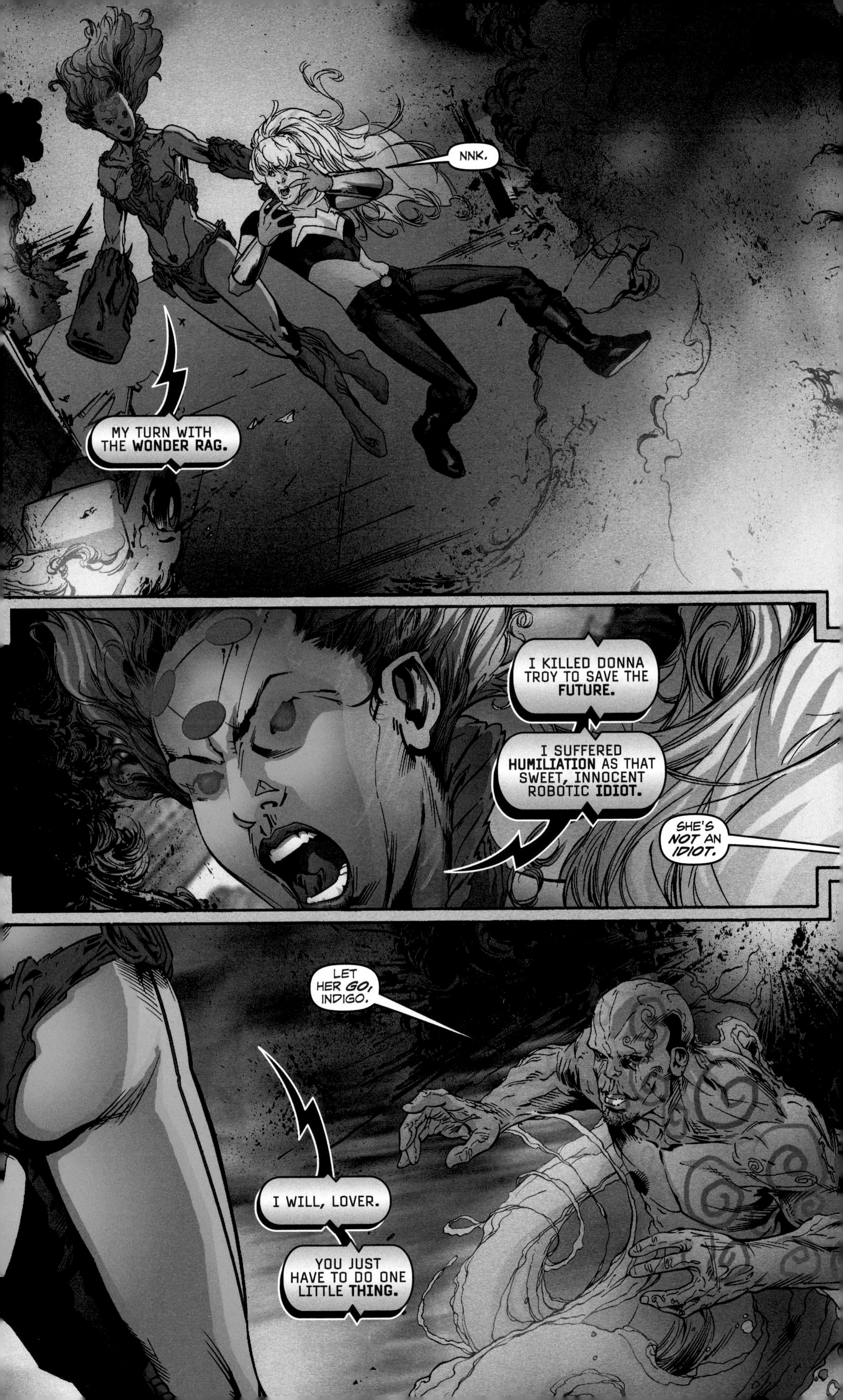
NNK.
MY TURN WITH THE **WONDER RAG.**
I KILLED DONNA TROY TO SAVE THE **FUTURE.**
I SUFFERED **HUMILIATION** AS THAT SWEET, INNOCENT ROBOTIC **IDIOT.**
SHE'S ***NOT*** AN ***IDIOT.***
LET HER ***GO,*** INDIGO.
I WILL, LOVER.
YOU JUST HAVE TO DO ONE LITTLE **THING.**

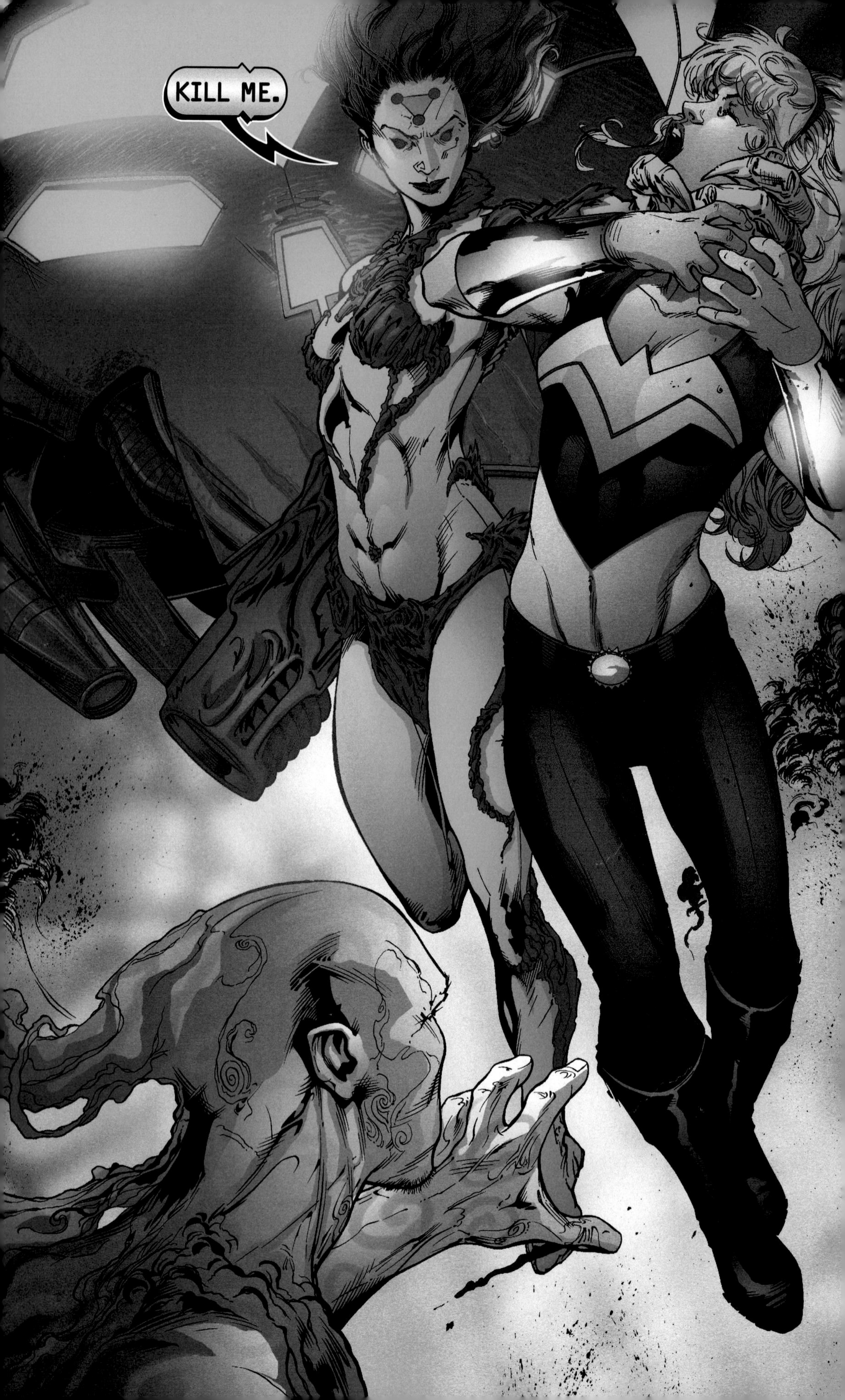
KILL ME.

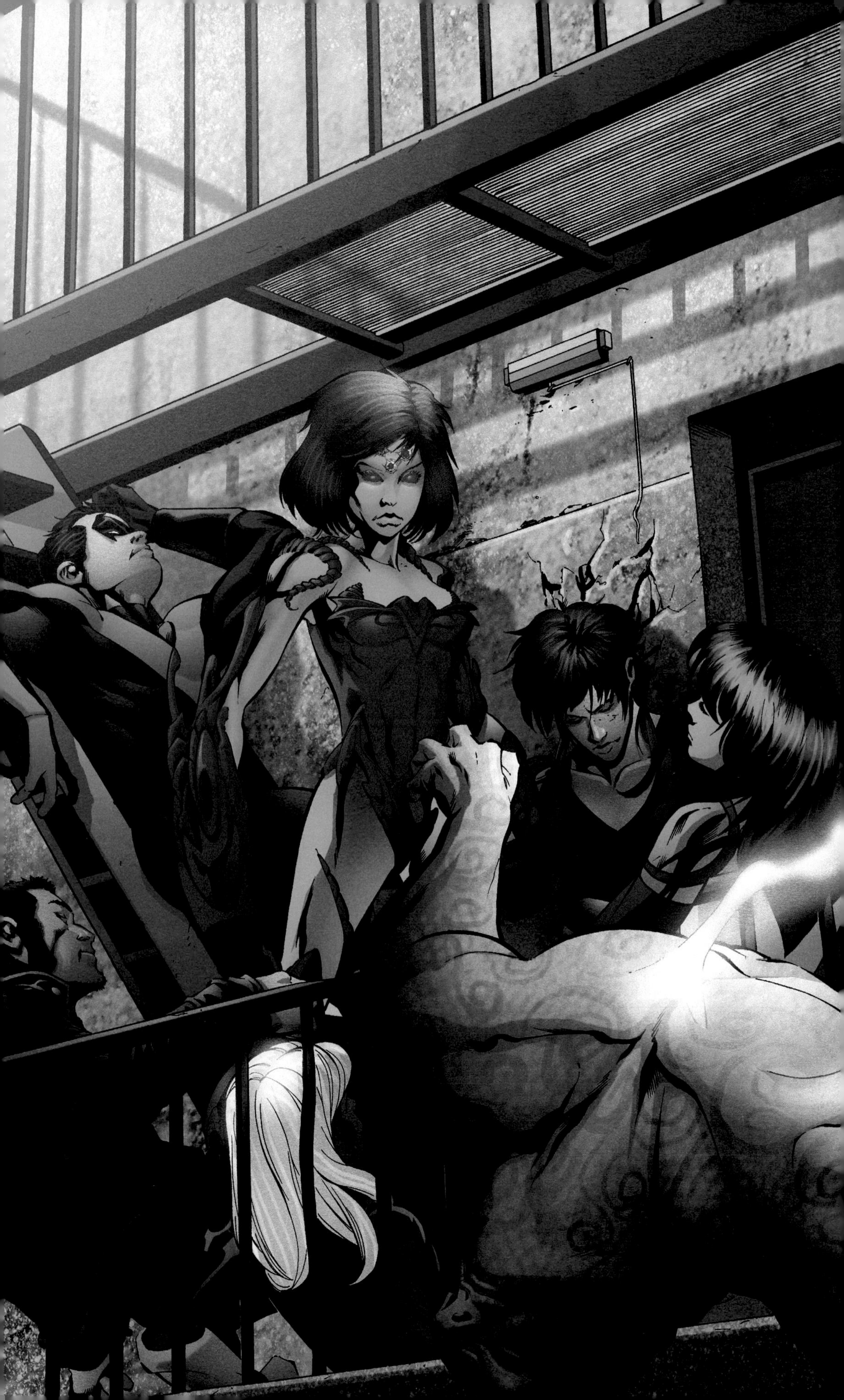

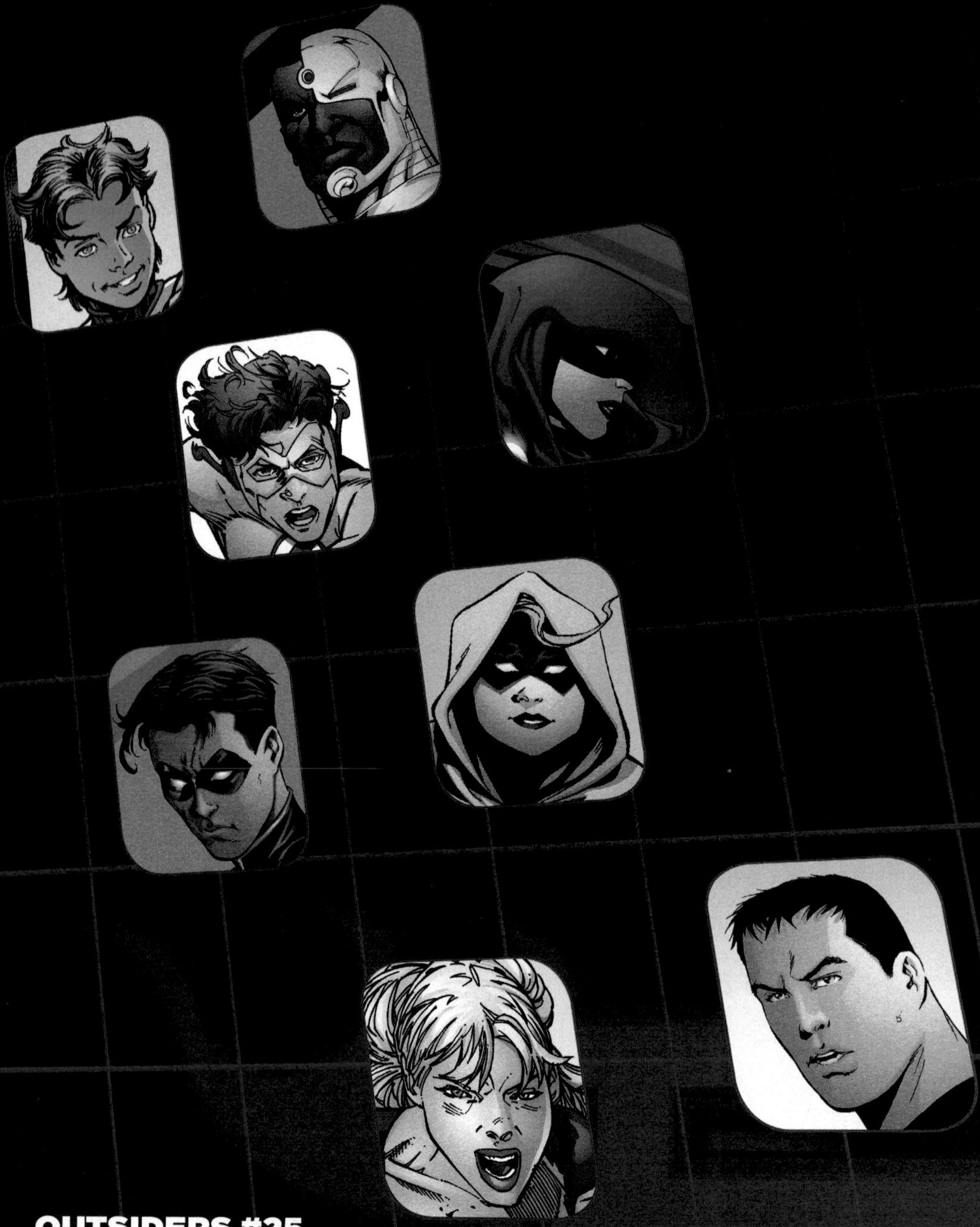

OUTSIDERS #25

JUDD WINICK
Writer

CARLOS D'ANDA
Artist

GUY MAJOR
Colorist

PHIL BALSMAN
Letterer

MIKE McKONE,
MARLO ALQUIZA & JEROMY COX
Cover Artists

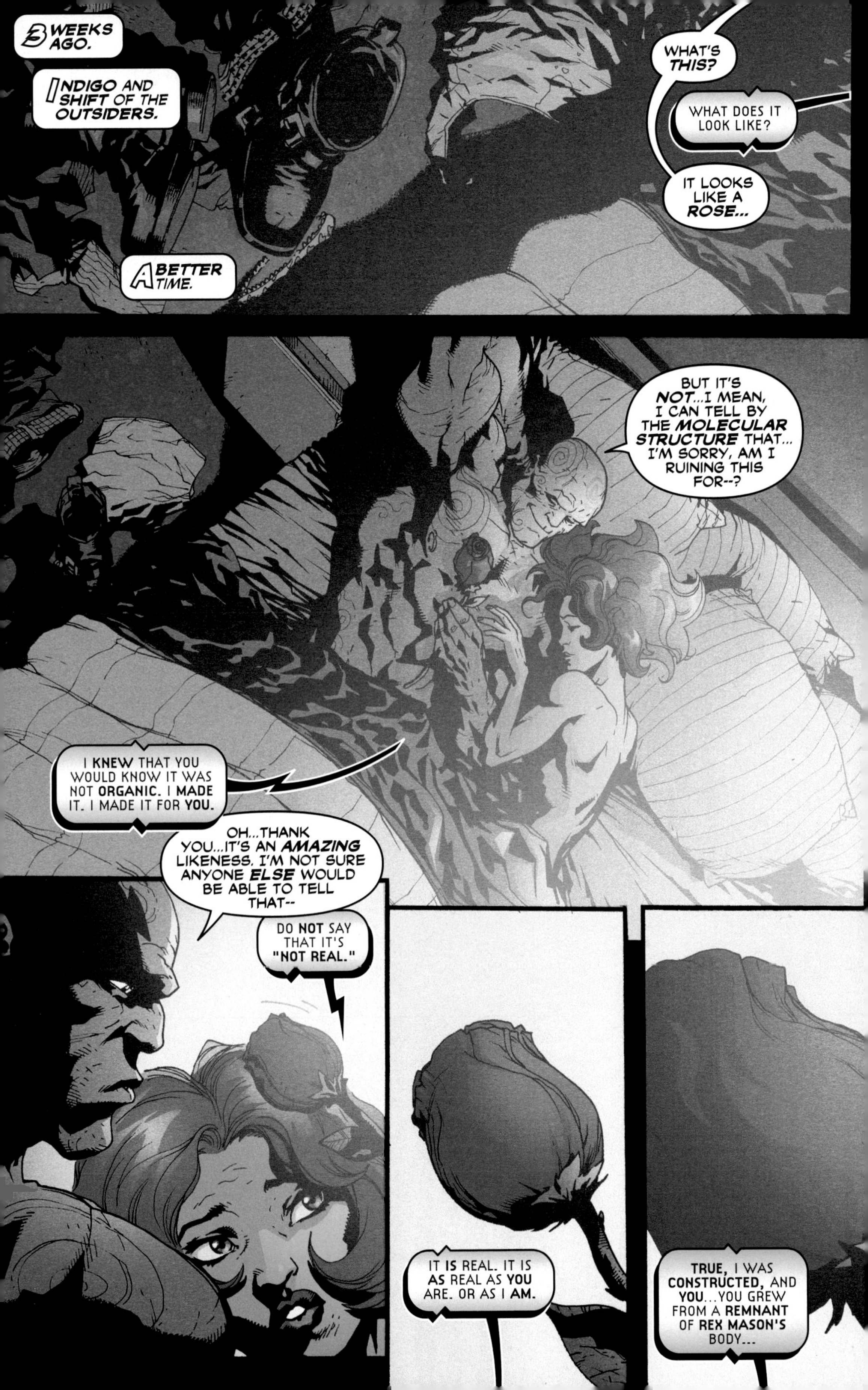
3 WEEKS AGO.
INDIGO AND SHIFT OF THE OUTSIDERS.
A BETTER TIME.
WHAT'S THIS?
WHAT DOES IT LOOK LIKE?
IT LOOKS LIKE A ROSE...
BUT IT'S NOT...I MEAN, I CAN TELL BY THE MOLECULAR STRUCTURE THAT... I'M SORRY, AM I RUINING THIS FOR--?
I KNEW THAT YOU WOULD KNOW IT WAS NOT ORGANIC. I MADE IT. I MADE IT FOR YOU.
OH...THANK YOU...IT'S AN AMAZING LIKENESS. I'M NOT SURE ANYONE ELSE WOULD BE ABLE TO TELL THAT--
DO NOT SAY THAT IT'S "NOT REAL."
IT IS REAL. IT IS AS REAL AS YOU ARE. OR AS I AM.
TRUE, I WAS CONSTRUCTED, AND YOU...YOU GREW FROM A REMNANT OF REX MASON'S BODY...

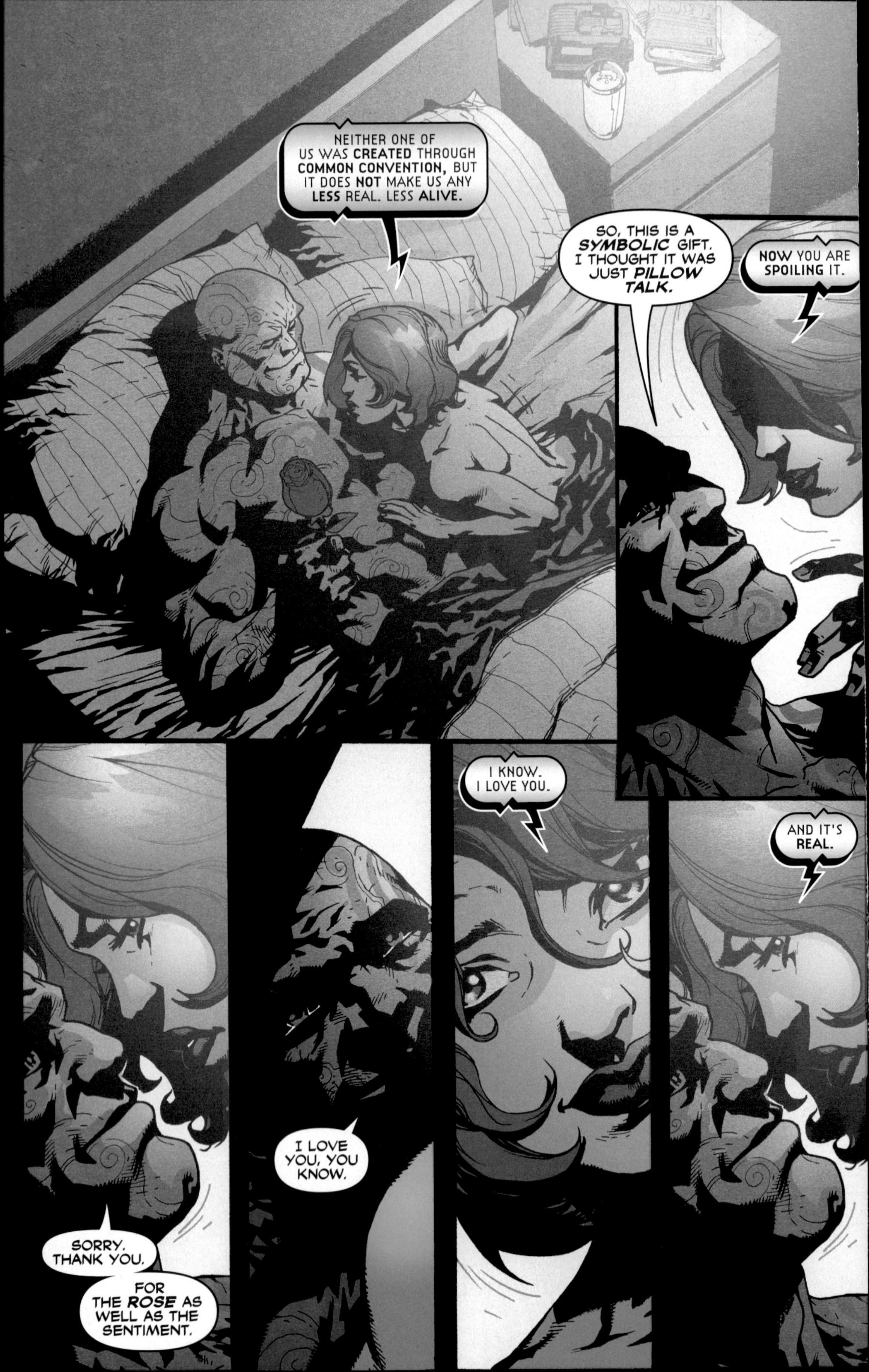
NEITHER ONE OF US WAS CREATED THROUGH COMMON CONVENTION, BUT IT DOES NOT MAKE US ANY LESS REAL. LESS ALIVE.
SO, THIS IS A SYMBOLIC GIFT. I THOUGHT IT WAS JUST PILLOW TALK.
NOW YOU ARE SPOILING IT.
SORRY. THANK YOU.
FOR THE ROSE AS WELL AS THE SENTIMENT.
I LOVE YOU, YOU KNOW.
I KNOW. I LOVE YOU.
AND IT'S REAL.

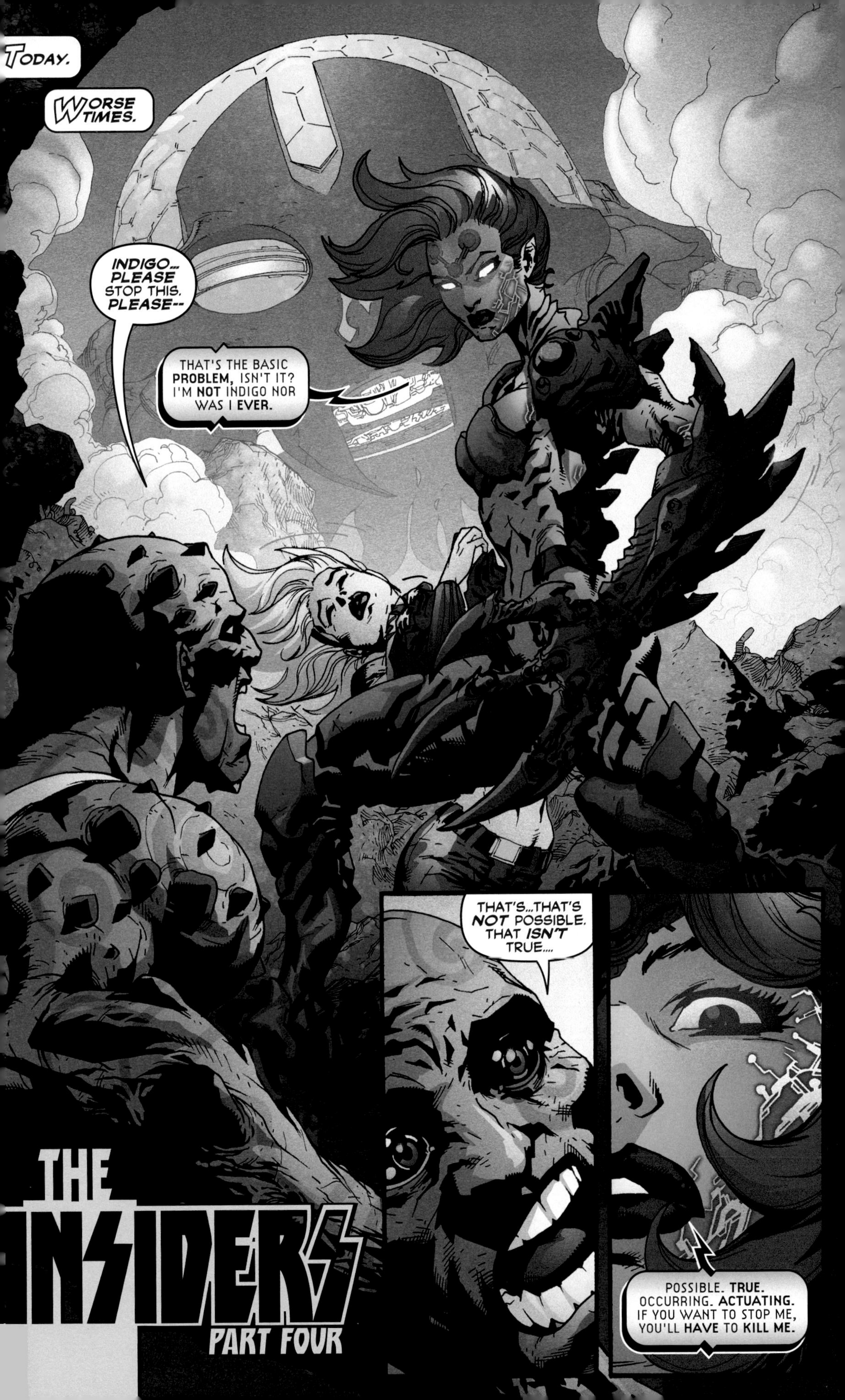
TODAY.
WORSE TIMES.
INDIGO... PLEASE STOP THIS. PLEASE--
THAT'S THE BASIC PROBLEM, ISN'T IT? I'M NOT INDIGO NOR WAS I EVER.
THAT'S...THAT'S NOT POSSIBLE. THAT ISN'T TRUE....
POSSIBLE. TRUE. OCCURRING. ACTUATING. IF YOU WANT TO STOP ME, YOU'LL HAVE TO KILL ME.
THE INSIDERS PART FOUR

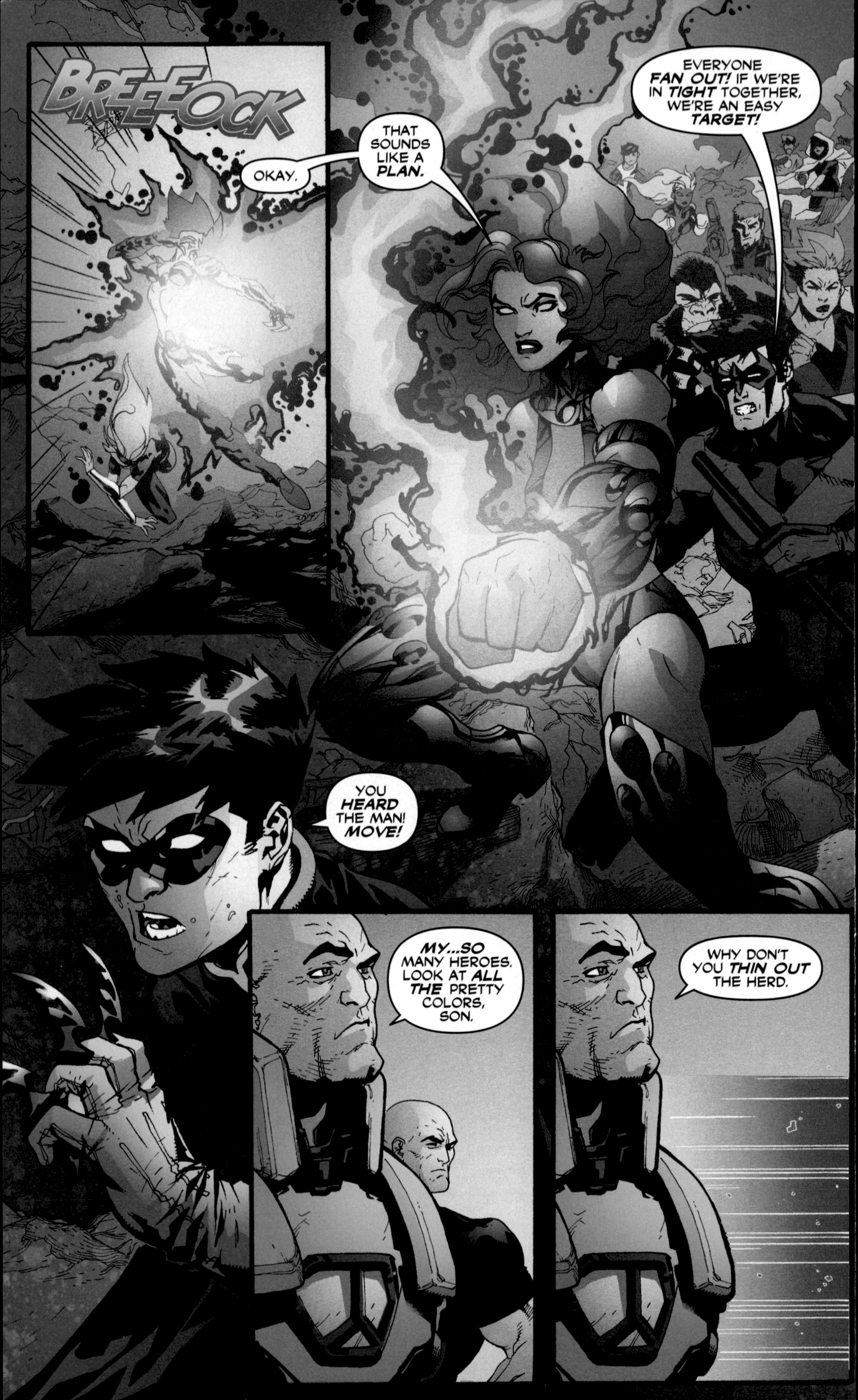
BREEEOCK
OKAY.
THAT SOUNDS LIKE A PLAN.
EVERYONE FAN OUT! IF WE'RE IN TIGHT TOGETHER, WE'RE AN EASY TARGET!
YOU HEARD THE MAN! MOVE!
MY...SO MANY HEROES. LOOK AT ALL THE PRETTY COLORS, SON.
WHY DON'T YOU THIN OUT THE HERD.

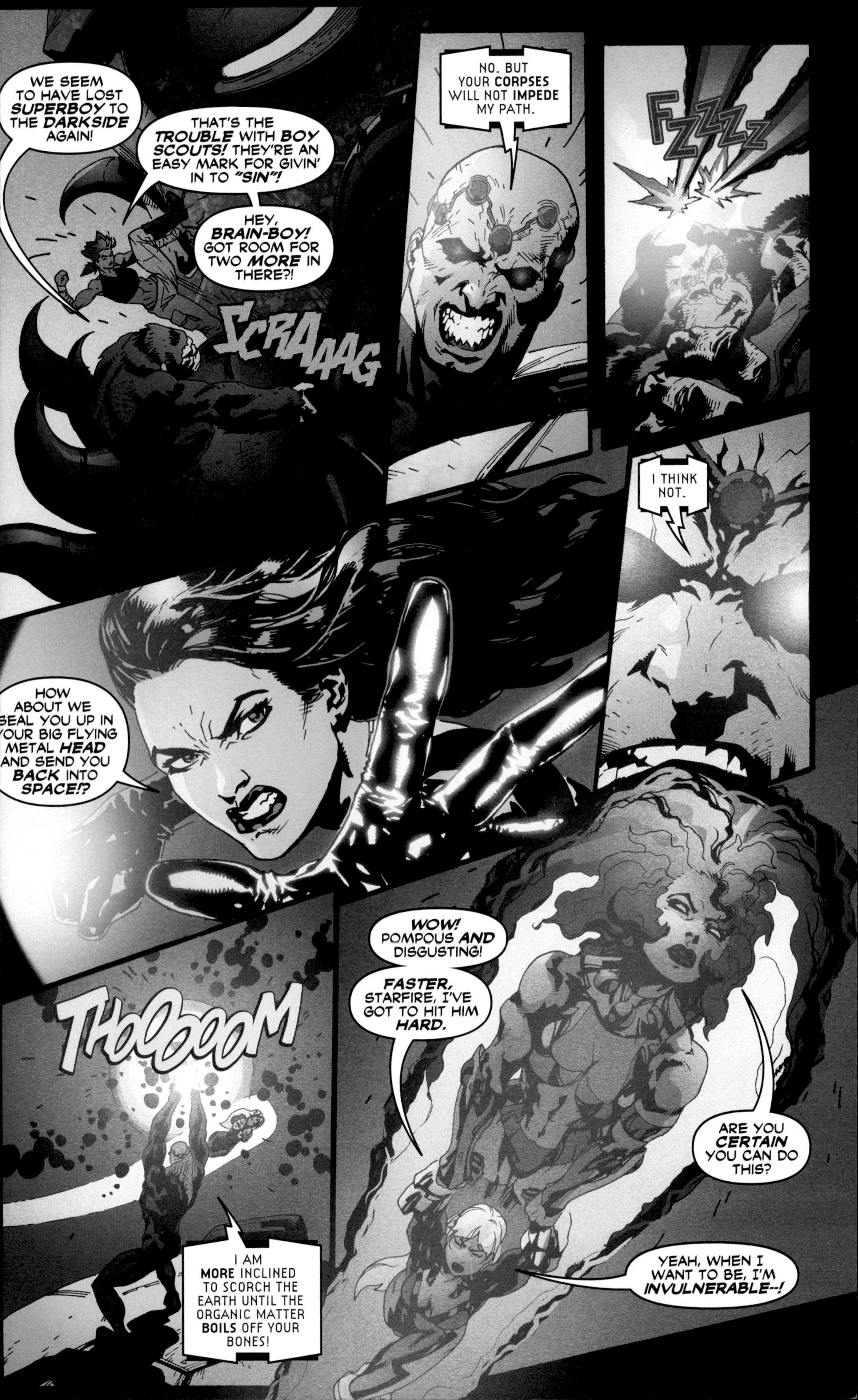

WE SEEM TO HAVE LOST SUPERBOY TO THE DARKSIDE AGAIN!
THAT'S THE TROUBLE WITH BOY SCOUTS! THEY'RE AN EASY MARK FOR GIVIN' IN TO "SIN"!
HEY, BRAIN-BOY! GOT ROOM FOR TWO MORE IN THERE?!
SCRAAAG
NO. BUT YOUR CORPSES WILL NOT IMPEDE MY PATH.
FZZZZ
I THINK NOT.
HOW ABOUT WE SEAL YOU UP IN YOUR BIG FLYING METAL HEAD AND SEND YOU BACK INTO SPACE!?
THOOOOOM
I AM MORE INCLINED TO SCORCH THE EARTH UNTIL THE ORGANIC MATTER BOILS OFF YOUR BONES!
WOW! POMPOUS AND DISGUSTING!
FASTER, STARFIRE, I'VE GOT TO HIT HIM HARD.
ARE YOU CERTAIN YOU CAN DO THIS?
YEAH, WHEN I WANT TO BE, I'M INVULNERABLE--!

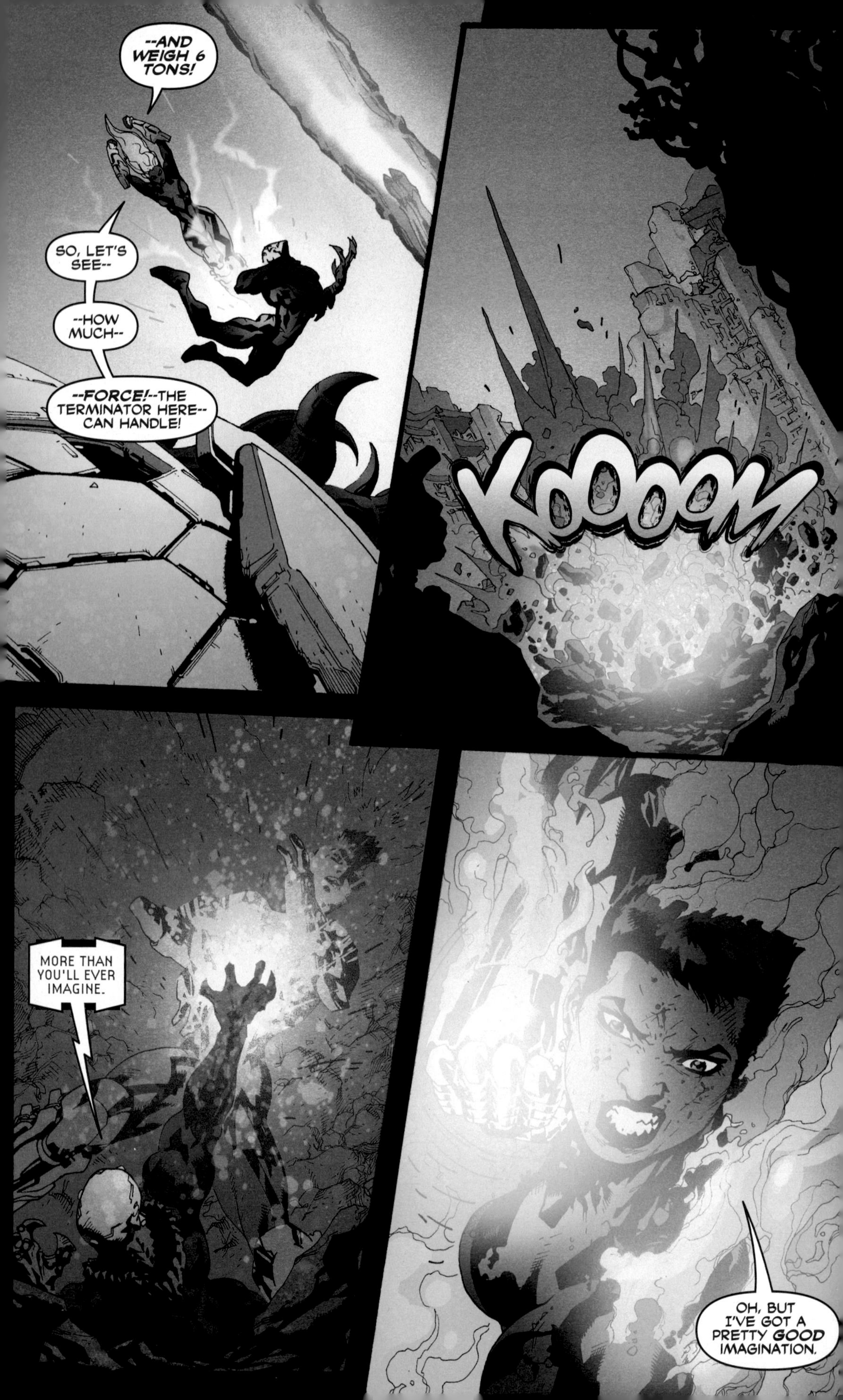
--AND WEIGH 6 TONS!
SO, LET'S SEE--
--HOW MUCH--
--FORCE!--THE TERMINATOR HERE--CAN HANDLE!
KOOOOM
MORE THAN YOU'LL EVER IMAGINE.
OH, BUT I'VE GOT A PRETTY GOOD IMAGINATION.

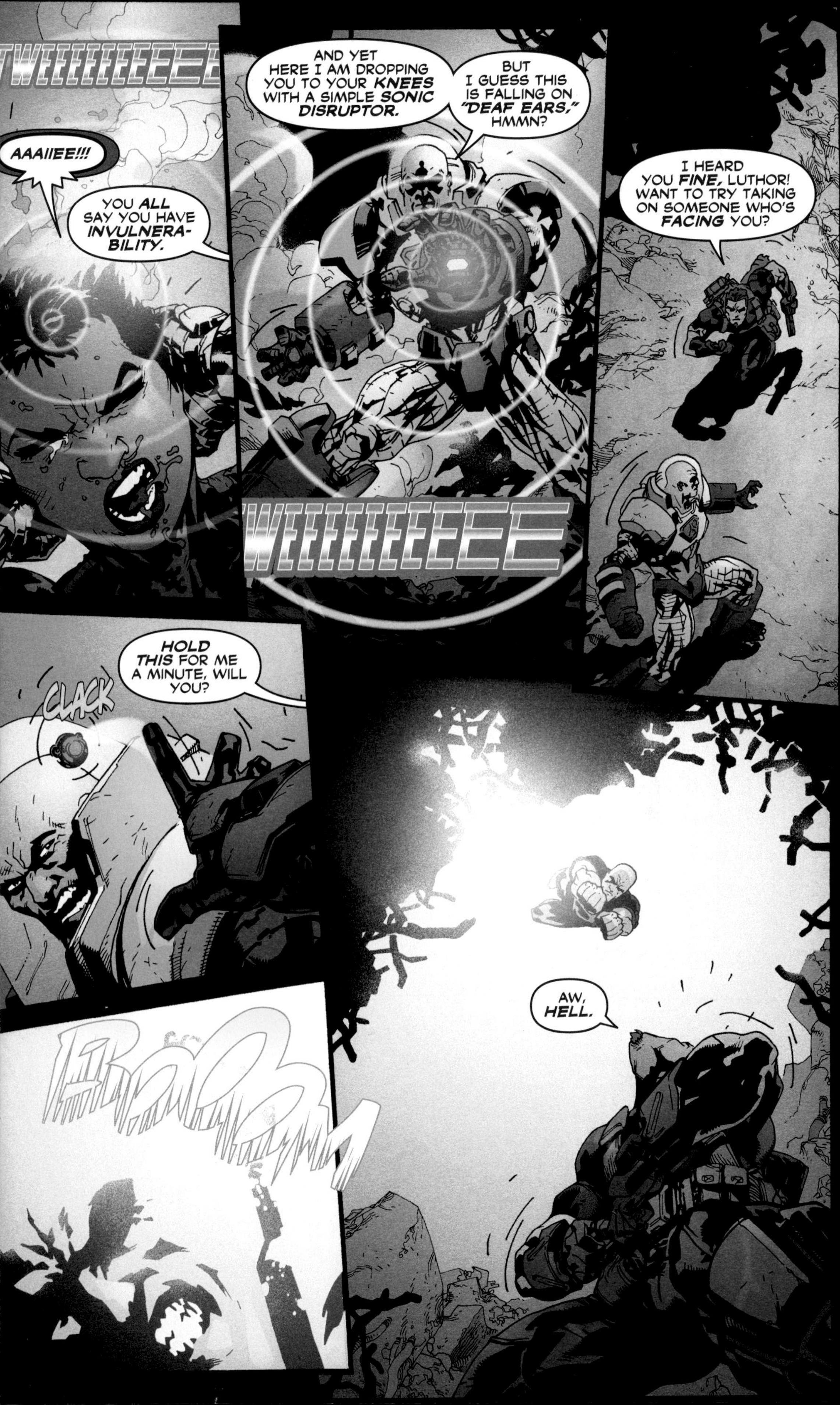

TWEEEEEEEEEEE
AAAIIEE!!!
YOU ALL SAY YOU HAVE INVULNERA-BILITY.
AND YET HERE I AM DROPPING YOU TO YOUR KNEES WITH A SIMPLE SONIC DISRUPTOR.
BUT I GUESS THIS IS FALLING ON "DEAF EARS," HMMN?
WEEEEEEEEEEE
I HEARD YOU FINE, LUTHOR! WANT TO TRY TAKING ON SOMEONE WHO'S FACING YOU?
CLACK
HOLD THIS FOR ME A MINUTE, WILL YOU?
AW, HELL.

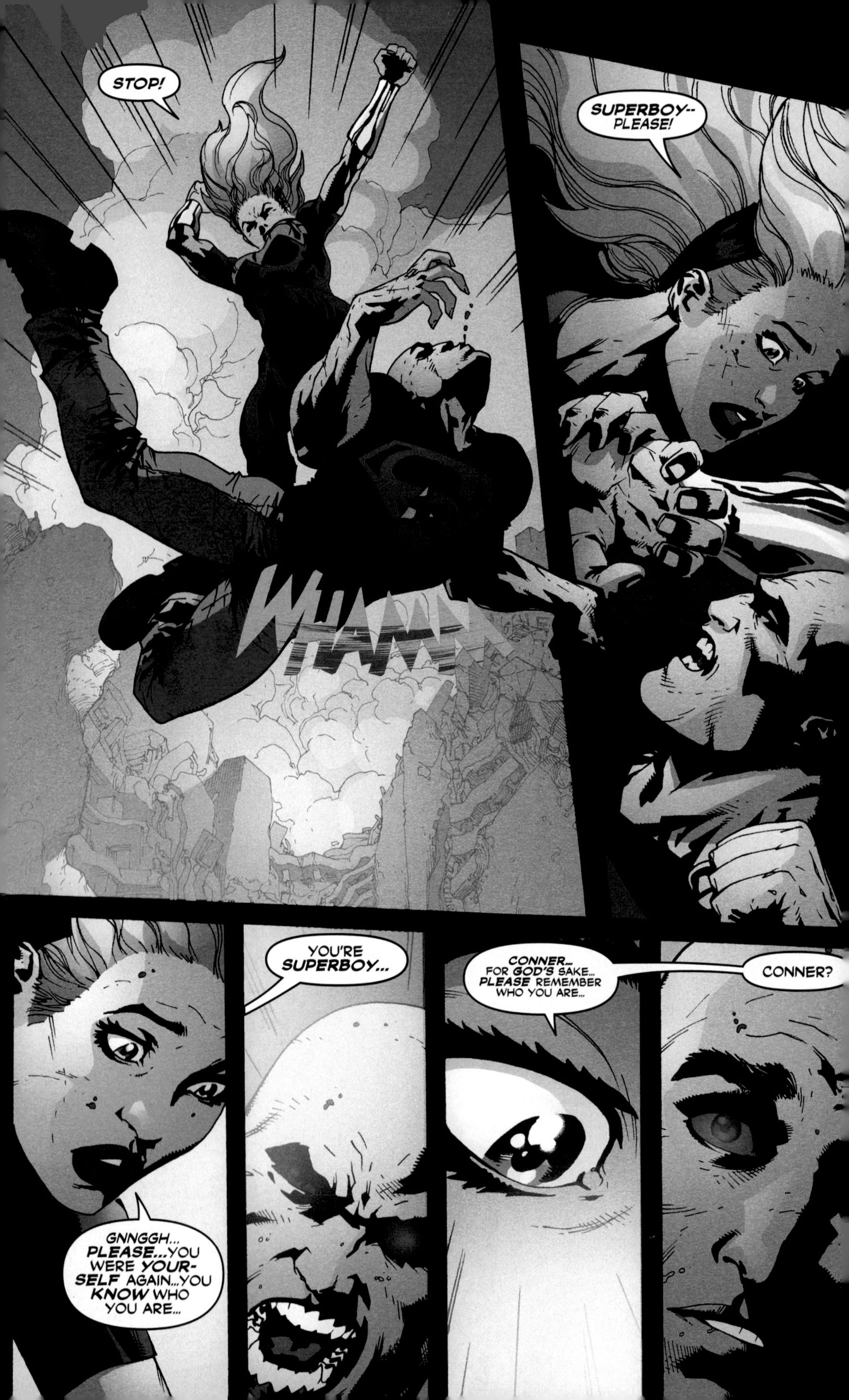
STOP!
WHAAM
SUPERBOY-- PLEASE!
GNNGGH... PLEASE...YOU WERE YOURSELF AGAIN...YOU KNOW WHO YOU ARE...
YOU'RE SUPERBOY...
CONNER... FOR GOD'S SAKE... PLEASE REMEMBER WHO YOU ARE...
CONNER?

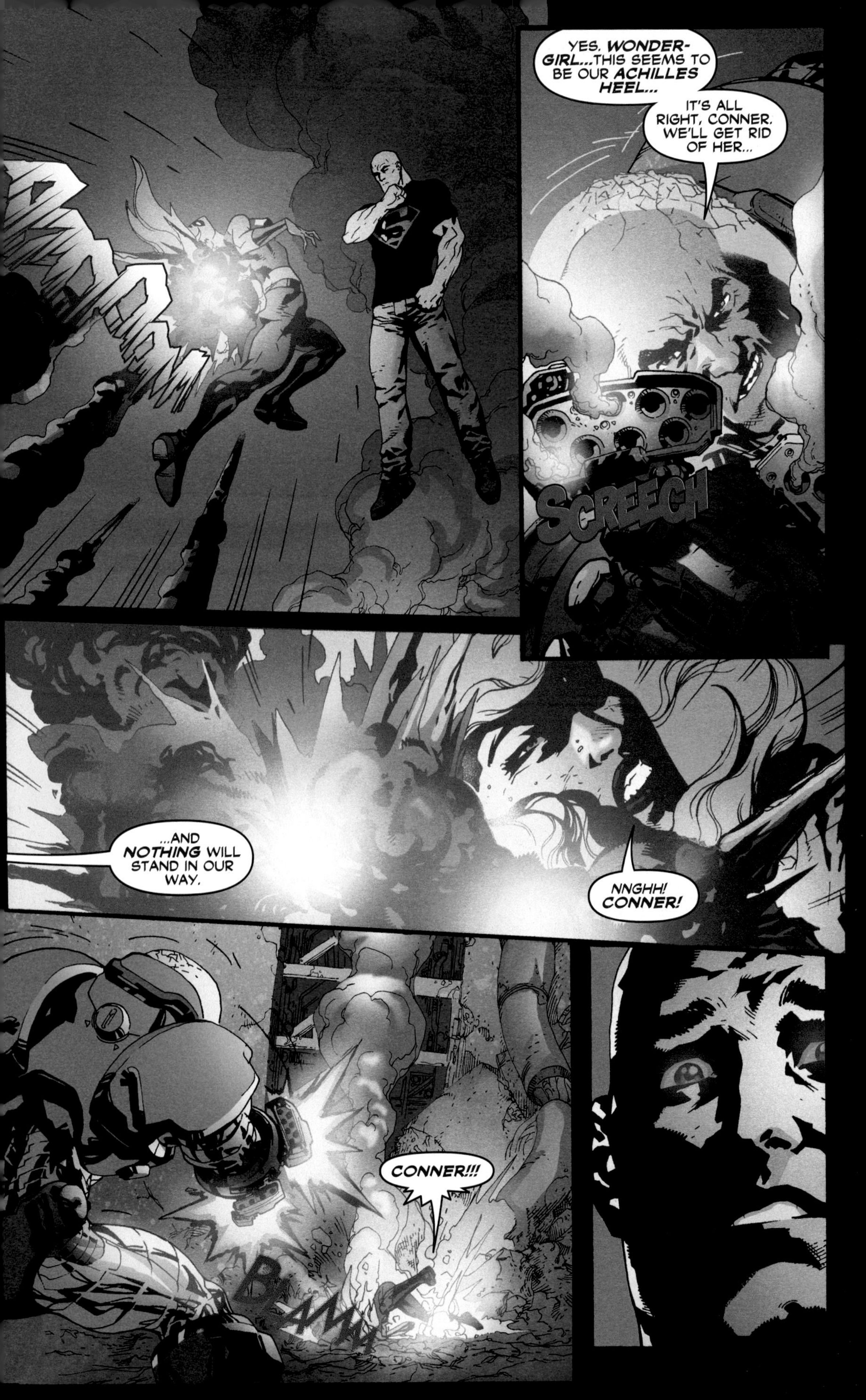

YES, WONDER-GIRL...THIS SEEMS TO BE OUR ACHILLES HEEL...
IT'S ALL RIGHT, CONNER. WE'LL GET RID OF HER...
SCREECH
...AND NOTHING WILL STAND IN OUR WAY.
NNGHH! CONNER!
CONNER!!!
BLAMM

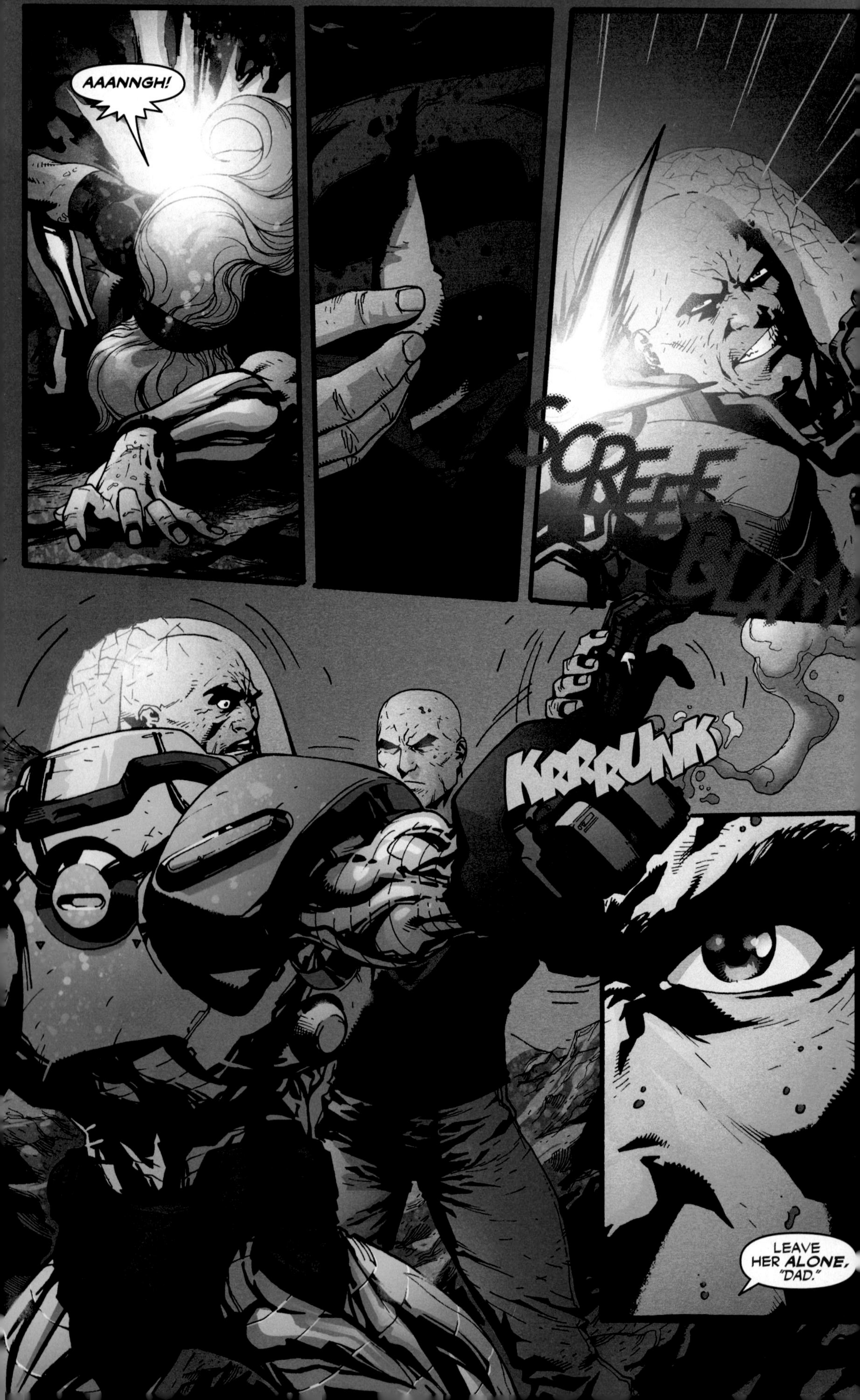
AAANNGH!
SCREEEE
BLAM
KRRRUNK
LEAVE HER ALONE, "DAD."

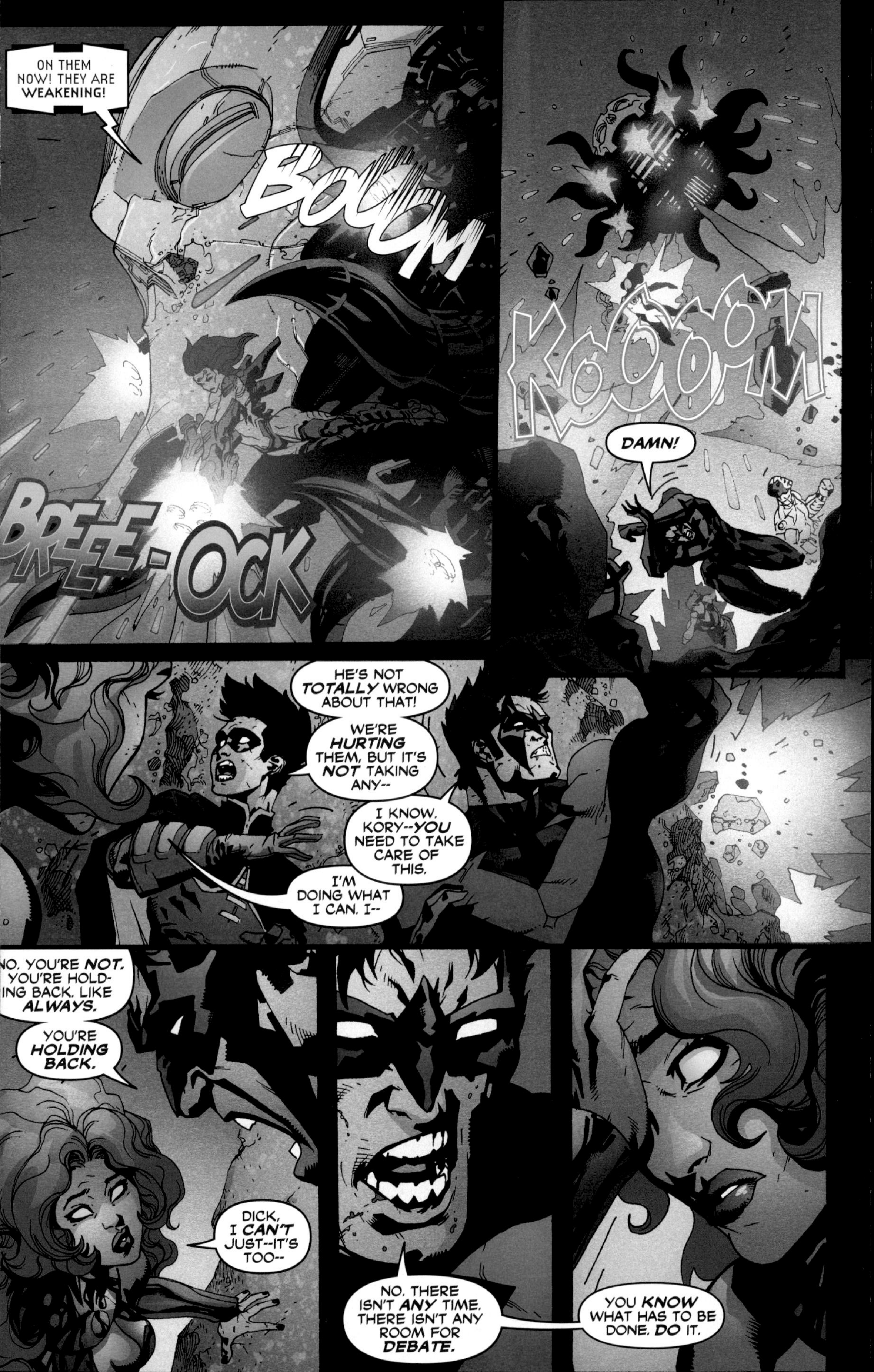
ON THEM NOW! THEY ARE WEAKENING!
BOOOM
BREEE-OCK
KOOOOM
DAMN!
HE'S NOT TOTALLY WRONG ABOUT THAT!
WE'RE HURTING THEM, BUT IT'S NOT TAKING ANY--
I KNOW. KORY--YOU NEED TO TAKE CARE OF THIS.
I'M DOING WHAT I CAN. I--
NO. YOU'RE NOT. YOU'RE HOLDING BACK. LIKE ALWAYS.
YOU'RE HOLDING BACK.
DICK, I CAN'T JUST--IT'S TOO--
NO. THERE ISN'T ANY TIME. THERE ISN'T ANY ROOM FOR DEBATE.
YOU KNOW WHAT HAS TO BE DONE. DO IT.

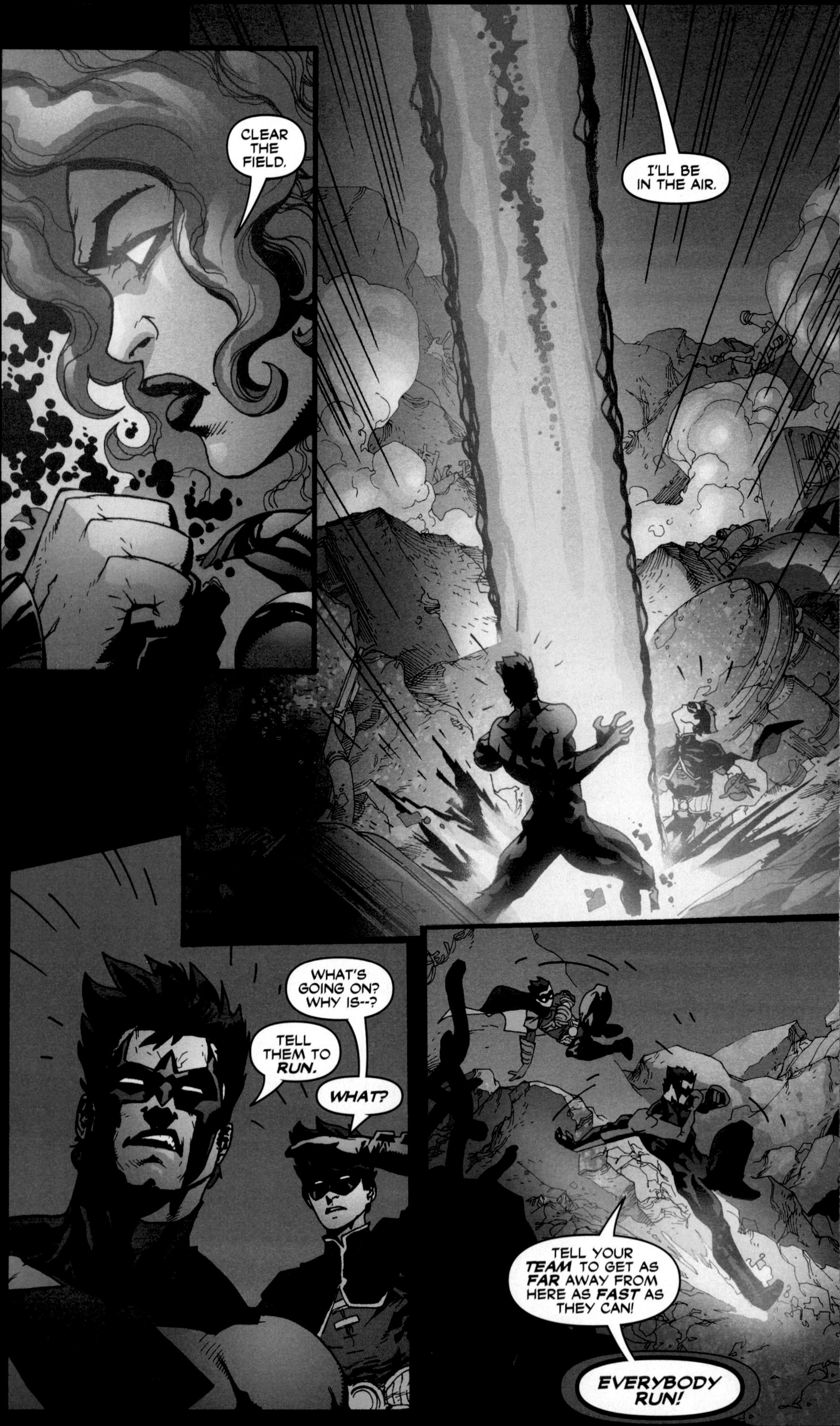
CLEAR THE FIELD.
I'LL BE IN THE AIR.
WHAT'S GOING ON? WHY IS--?
TELL THEM TO *RUN.*
WHAT?
TELL YOUR *TEAM* TO GET AS *FAR* AWAY FROM HERE AS *FAST* AS THEY CAN!
EVERYBODY RUN!

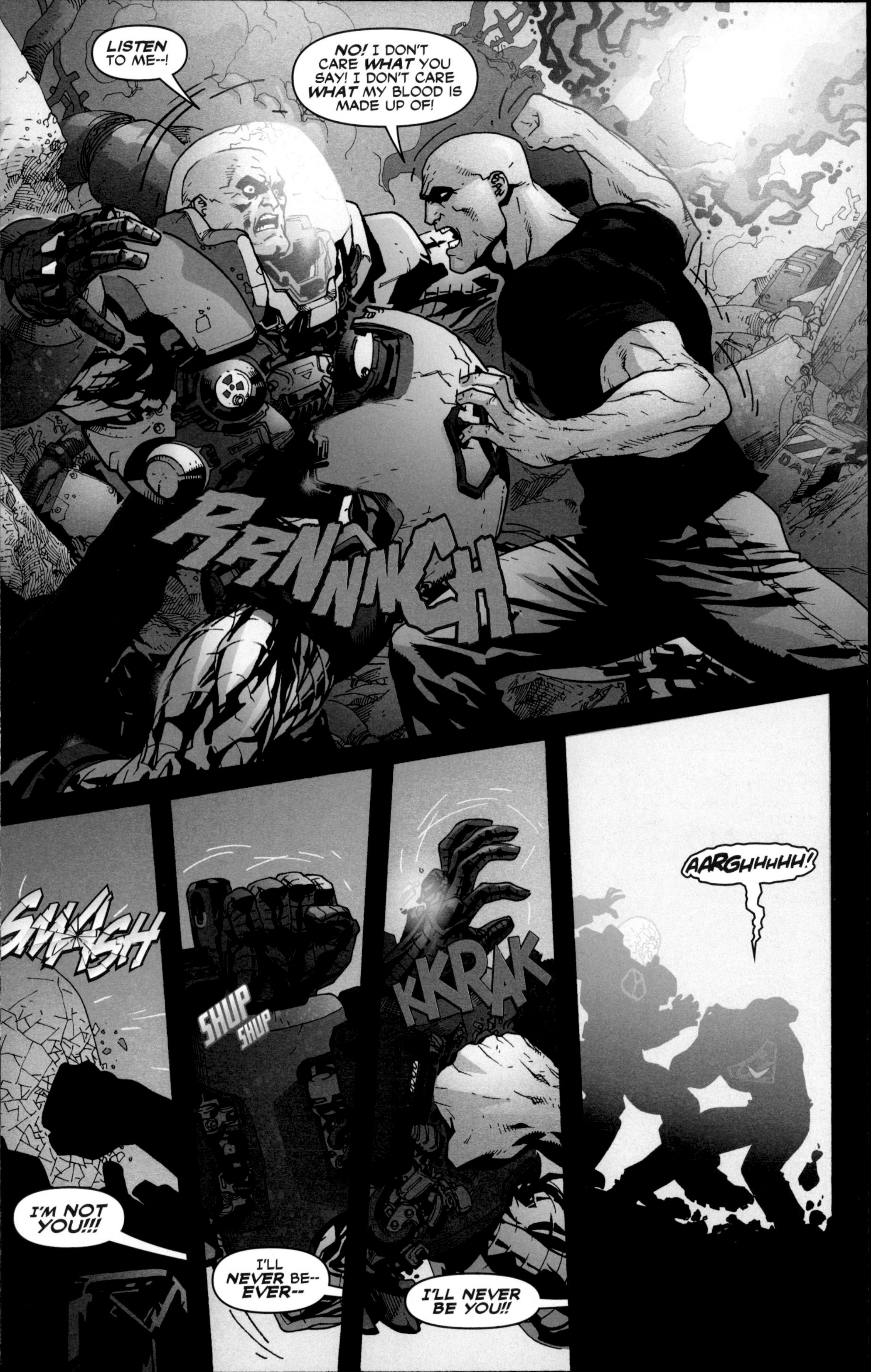
LISTEN TO ME--!
NO! I DON'T CARE WHAT YOU SAY! I DON'T CARE WHAT MY BLOOD IS MADE UP OF!
RRNNNCH
SMASH
I'M NOT YOU!!!
SHUP SHUP
I'LL NEVER BE-- EVER--
KKRAK
I'LL NEVER BE YOU!!
AARGHHHHH!

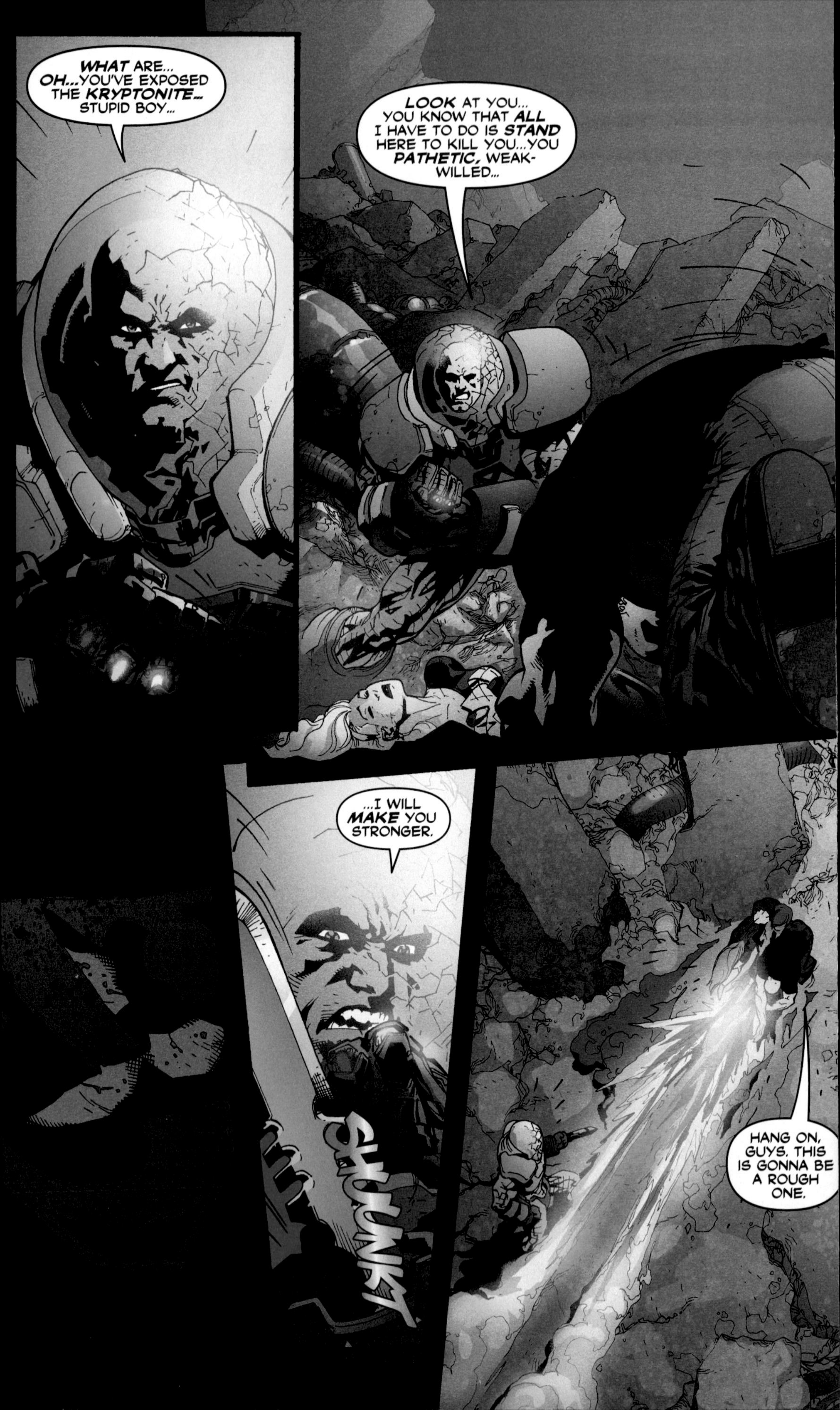
WHAT ARE... OH...YOU'VE EXPOSED THE KRYPTONITE... STUPID BOY...
LOOK AT YOU... YOU KNOW THAT ALL I HAVE TO DO IS STAND HERE TO KILL YOU...YOU PATHETIC, WEAK-WILLED...
...I WILL MAKE YOU STRONGER.
SHUNK!
HANG ON, GUYS, THIS IS GONNA BE A ROUGH ONE.

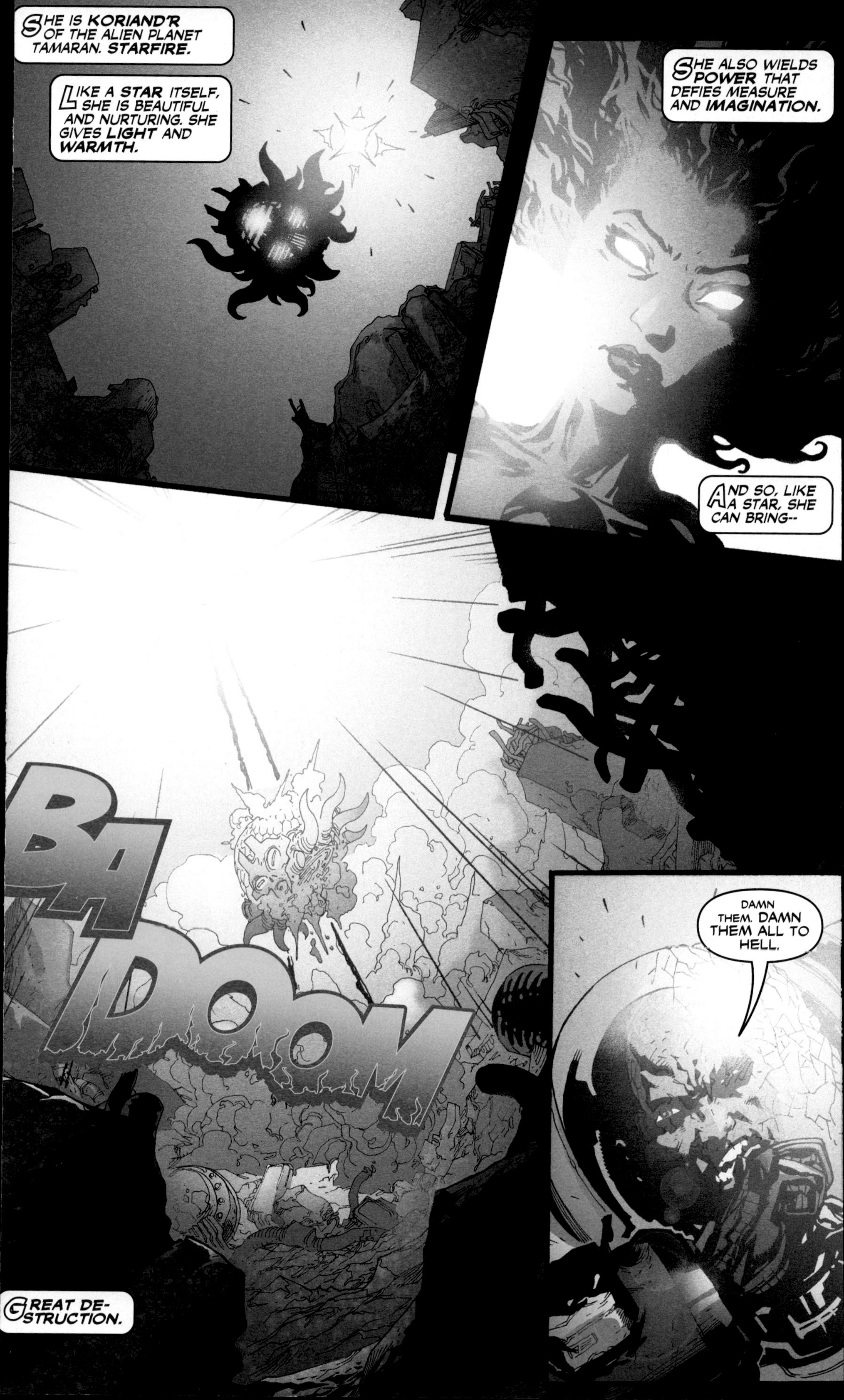
SHE IS KORIAND'R OF THE ALIEN PLANET TAMARAN. STARFIRE.
LIKE A STAR ITSELF, SHE IS BEAUTIFUL AND NURTURING. SHE GIVES LIGHT AND WARMTH.
SHE ALSO WIELDS POWER THAT DEFIES MEASURE AND IMAGINATION.
AND SO, LIKE A STAR, SHE CAN BRING--
BADOOM
GREAT DESTRUCTION.
DAMN THEM. DAMN THEM ALL TO HELL.

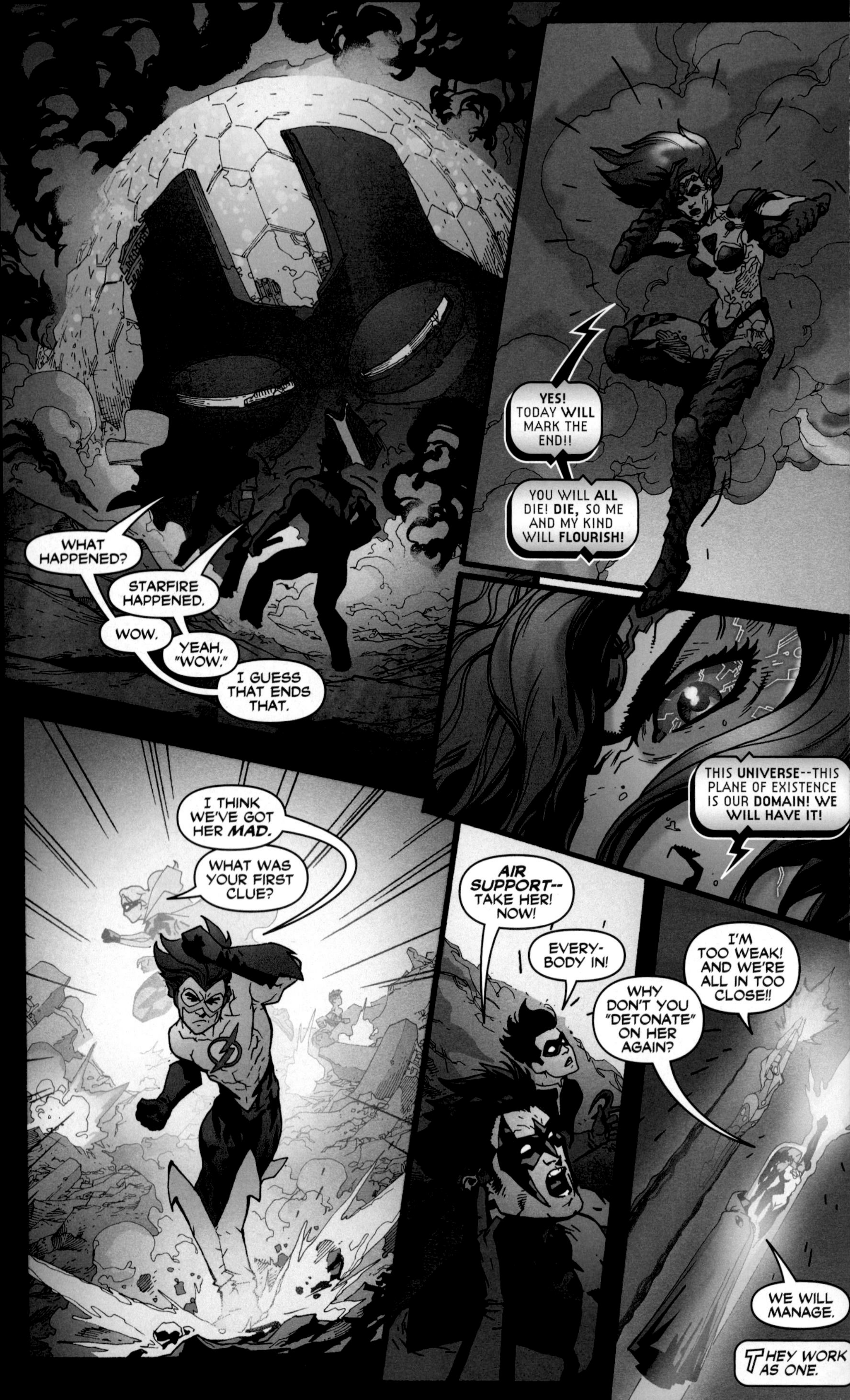
YES! TODAY WILL MARK THE END!!
YOU WILL ALL DIE! DIE, SO ME AND MY KIND WILL FLOURISH!
WHAT HAPPENED?
STARFIRE HAPPENED.
WOW.
YEAH, "WOW."
I GUESS THAT ENDS THAT.
THIS UNIVERSE--THIS PLANE OF EXISTENCE IS OUR DOMAIN! WE WILL HAVE IT!
I THINK WE'VE GOT HER MAD.
WHAT WAS YOUR FIRST CLUE?
AIR SUPPORT-- TAKE HER! NOW!
EVERY-BODY IN!
WHY DON'T YOU "DETONATE" ON HER AGAIN?
I'M TOO WEAK! AND WE'RE ALL IN TOO CLOSE!!
WE WILL MANAGE.
THEY WORK AS ONE.

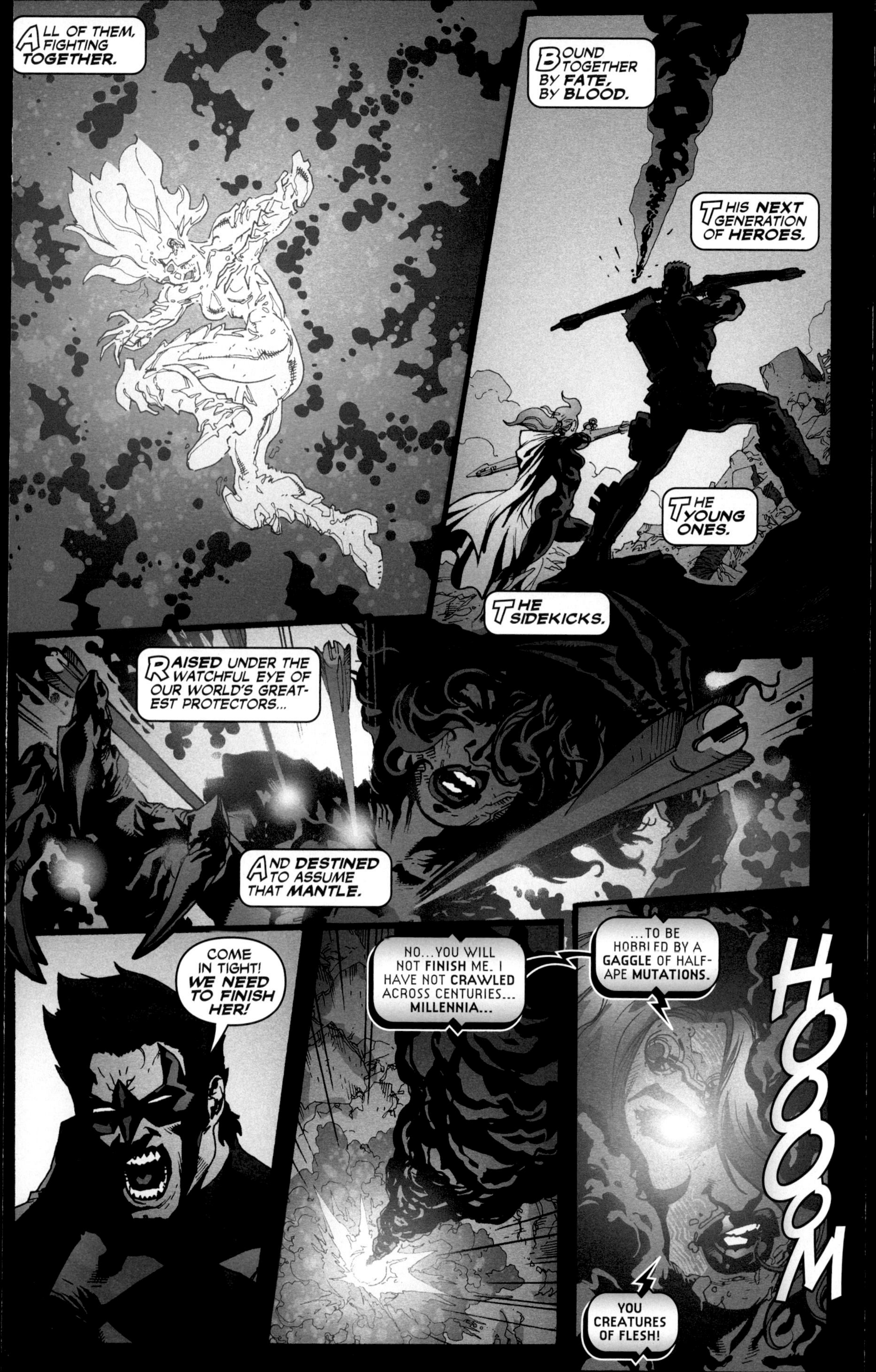
ALL OF THEM, FIGHTING TOGETHER.
BOUND TOGETHER BY FATE, BY BLOOD.
THIS NEXT GENERATION OF HEROES.
THE YOUNG ONES.
THE SIDEKICKS.
RAISED UNDER THE WATCHFUL EYE OF OUR WORLD'S GREAT-EST PROTECTORS...
AND DESTINED TO ASSUME THAT MANTLE.
COME IN TIGHT! WE NEED TO FINISH HER!
NO...YOU WILL NOT FINISH ME. I HAVE NOT CRAWLED ACROSS CENTURIES... MILLENNIA...
...TO BE HOBBLED BY A GAGGLE OF HALF-APE MUTATIONS.
HOOOOM
YOU CREATURES OF FLESH!

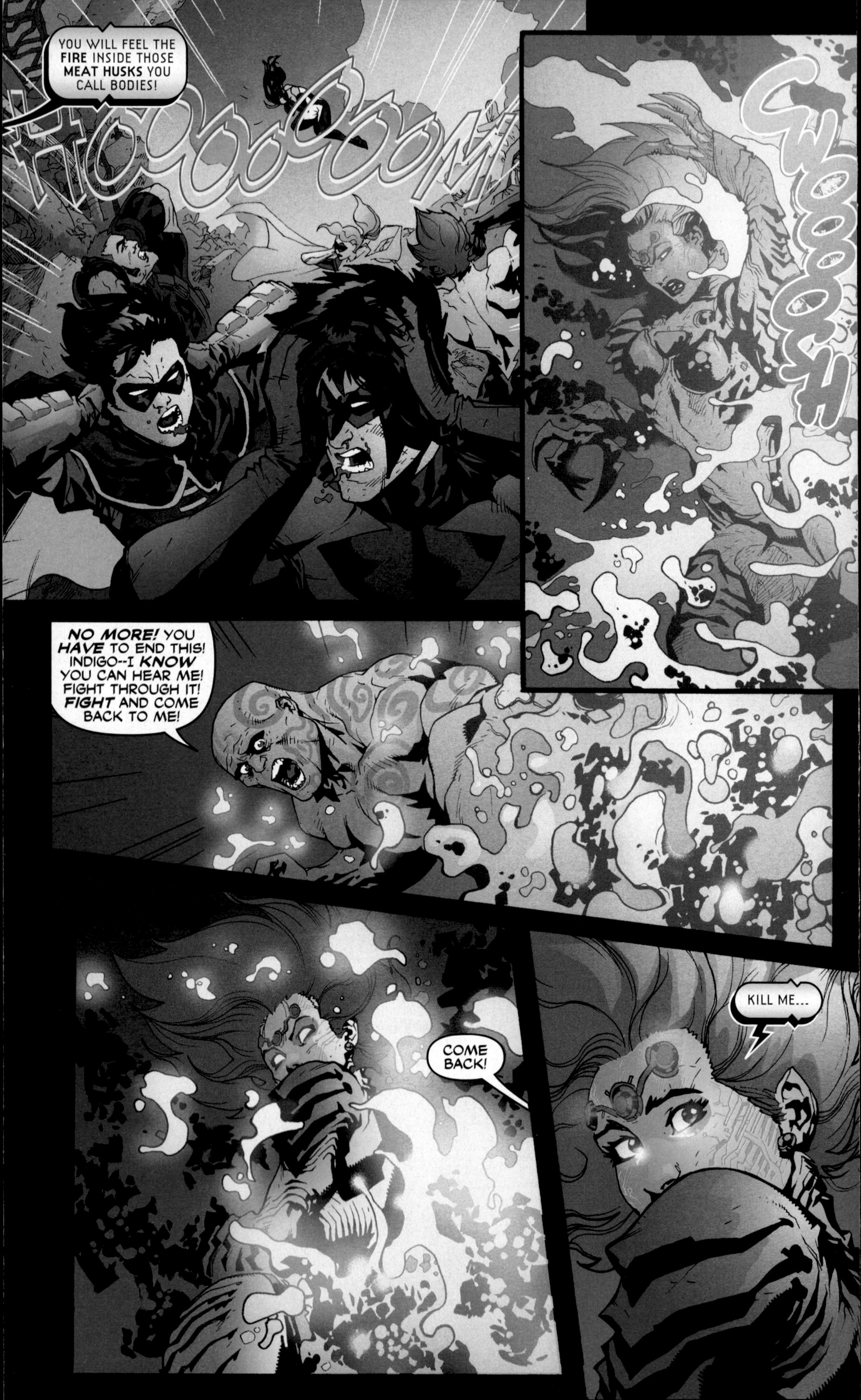
YOU WILL FEEL THE FIRE INSIDE THOSE MEAT HUSKS YOU CALL BODIES!
HOOOOOOOOM!
GWOOOOSH
NO MORE! YOU HAVE TO END THIS! INDIGO--I KNOW YOU CAN HEAR ME! FIGHT THROUGH IT! FIGHT AND COME BACK TO ME!
COME BACK!
KILL ME...

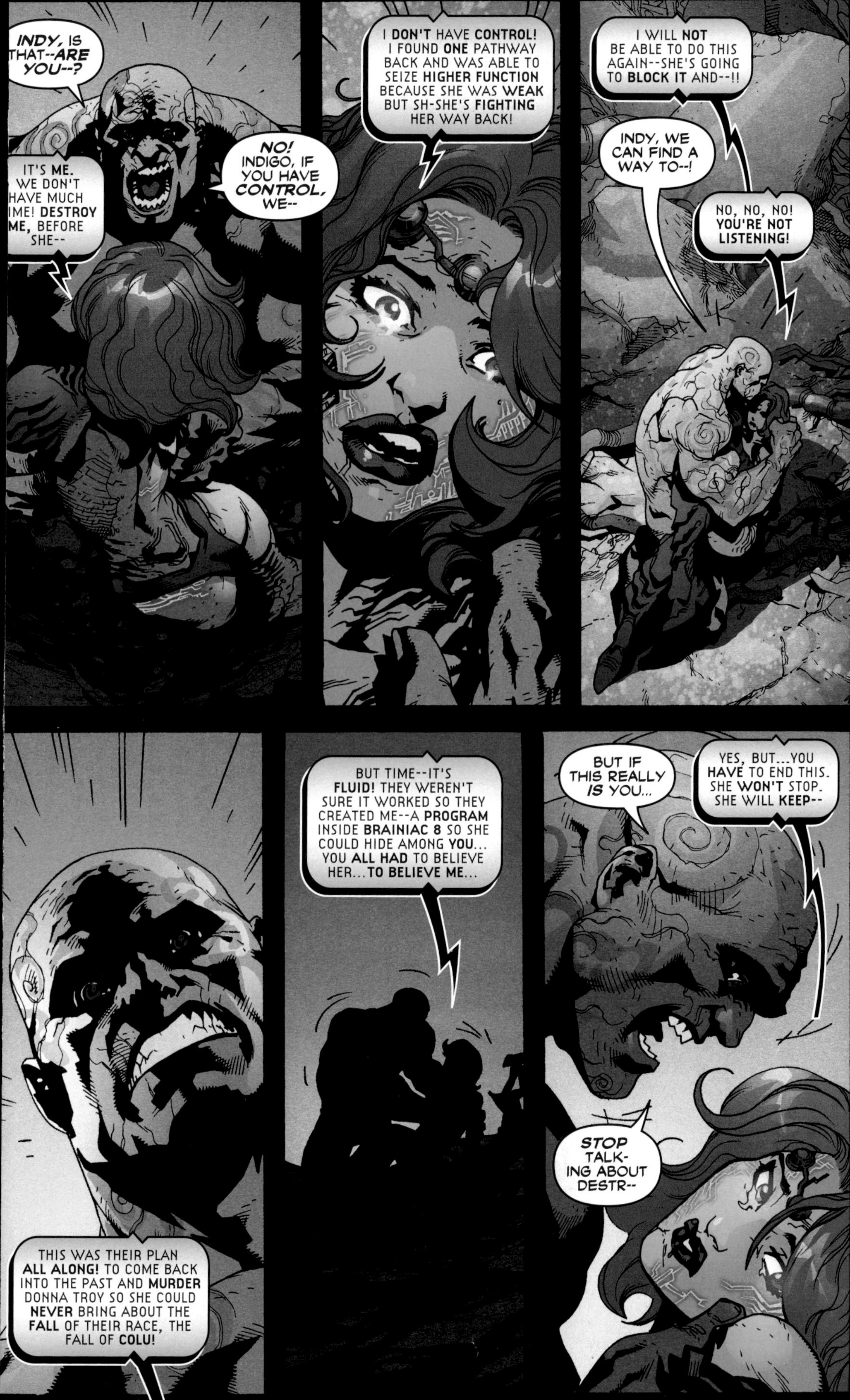
INDY, IS THAT--ARE YOU--?
IT'S ME. WE DON'T HAVE MUCH IME! DESTROY ME, BEFORE SHE--
NO! INDIGO, IF YOU HAVE CONTROL, WE--
I DON'T HAVE CONTROL! I FOUND ONE PATHWAY BACK AND WAS ABLE TO SEIZE HIGHER FUNCTION BECAUSE SHE WAS WEAK BUT SH-SHE'S FIGHTING HER WAY BACK!
I WILL NOT BE ABLE TO DO THIS AGAIN--SHE'S GOING TO BLOCK IT AND--!!
INDY, WE CAN FIND A WAY TO--!
NO, NO, NO! YOU'RE NOT LISTENING!
THIS WAS THEIR PLAN ALL ALONG! TO COME BACK INTO THE PAST AND MURDER DONNA TROY SO SHE COULD NEVER BRING ABOUT THE FALL OF THEIR RACE, THE FALL OF COLU!
BUT TIME--IT'S FLUID! THEY WEREN'T SURE IT WORKED SO THEY CREATED ME--A PROGRAM INSIDE BRAINIAC 8 SO SHE COULD HIDE AMONG YOU... YOU ALL HAD TO BELIEVE HER...TO BELIEVE ME...
BUT IF THIS REALLY IS YOU...
YES, BUT...YOU HAVE TO END THIS. SHE WON'T STOP. SHE WILL KEEP--
STOP TALK-ING ABOUT DESTR--

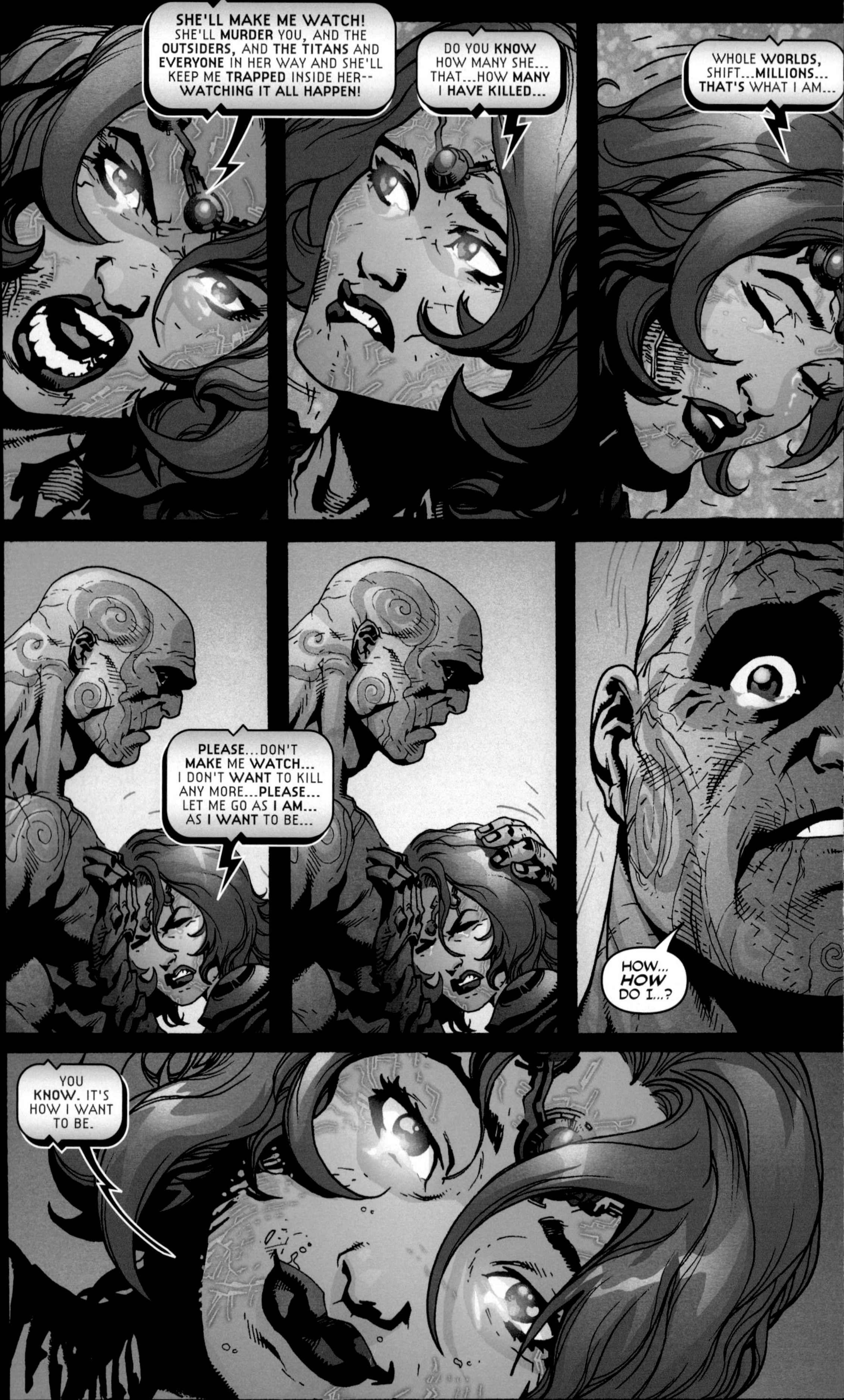
SHE'LL MAKE ME WATCH! SHE'LL MURDER YOU, AND THE OUTSIDERS, AND THE TITANS AND EVERYONE IN HER WAY AND SHE'LL KEEP ME TRAPPED INSIDE HER-- WATCHING IT ALL HAPPEN!
DO YOU KNOW HOW MANY SHE... THAT...HOW MANY I HAVE KILLED...
WHOLE WORLDS, SHIFT...MILLIONS... THAT'S WHAT I AM...
PLEASE...DON'T MAKE ME WATCH... I DON'T WANT TO KILL ANY MORE...PLEASE... LET ME GO AS I AM... AS I WANT TO BE...
HOW... HOW DO I...?
YOU KNOW. IT'S HOW I WANT TO BE.

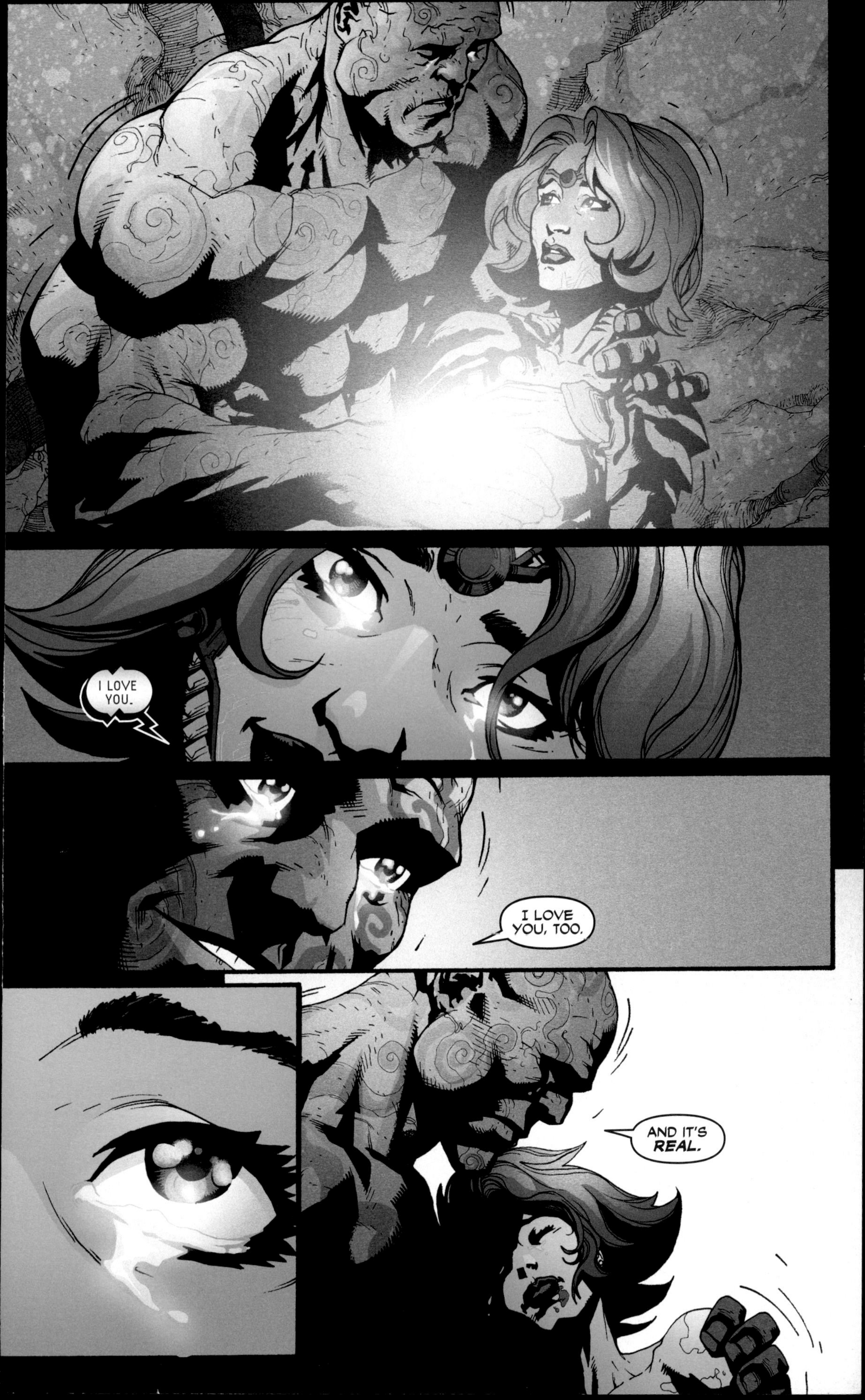
I LOVE YOU.
I LOVE YOU, TOO.
AND IT'S *REAL.*

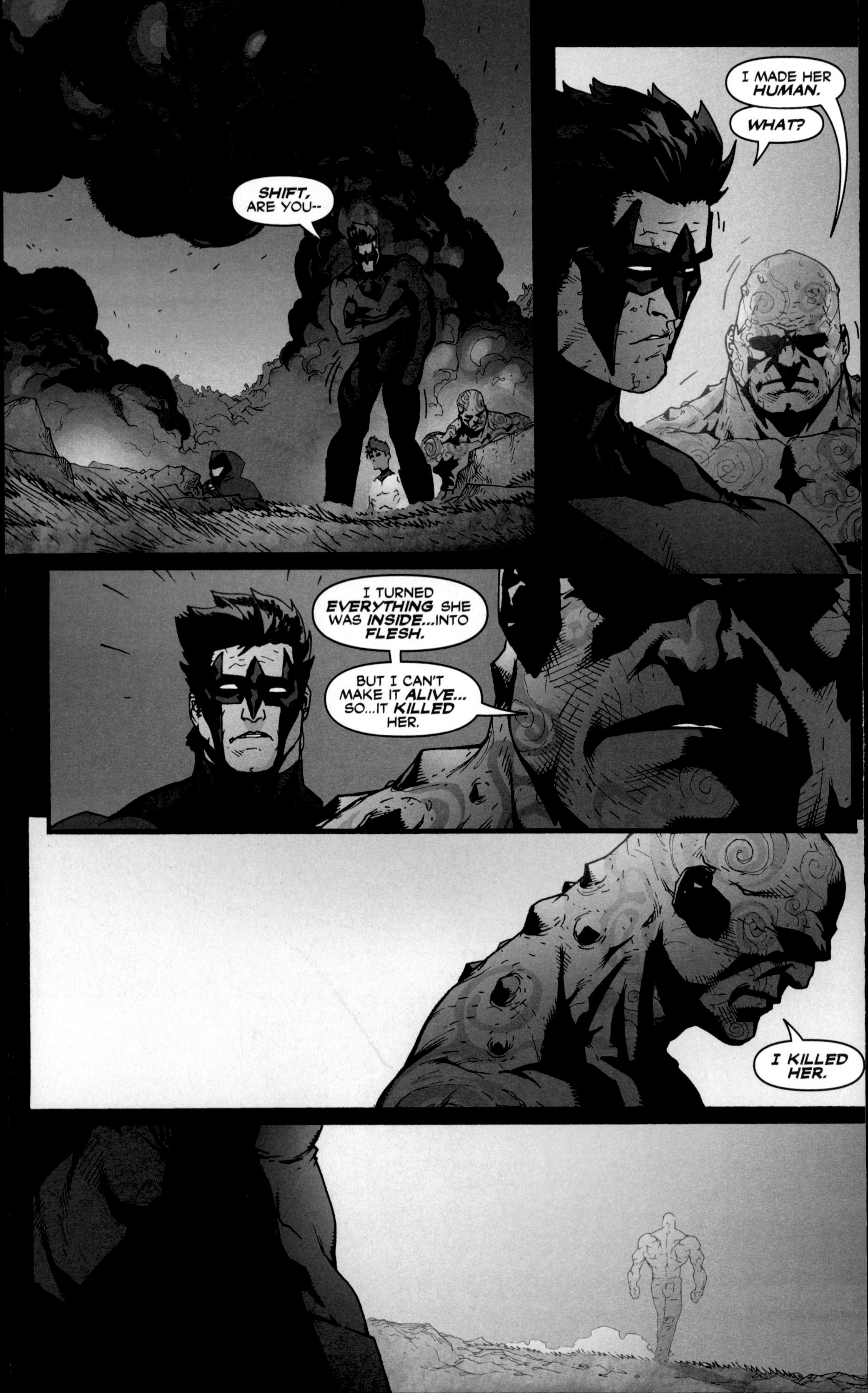
SHIFT, ARE YOU--
I MADE HER HUMAN.
WHAT?
I TURNED EVERYTHING SHE WAS INSIDE...INTO FLESH.
BUT I CAN'T MAKE IT ALIVE... SO...IT KILLED HER.
I KILLED HER.

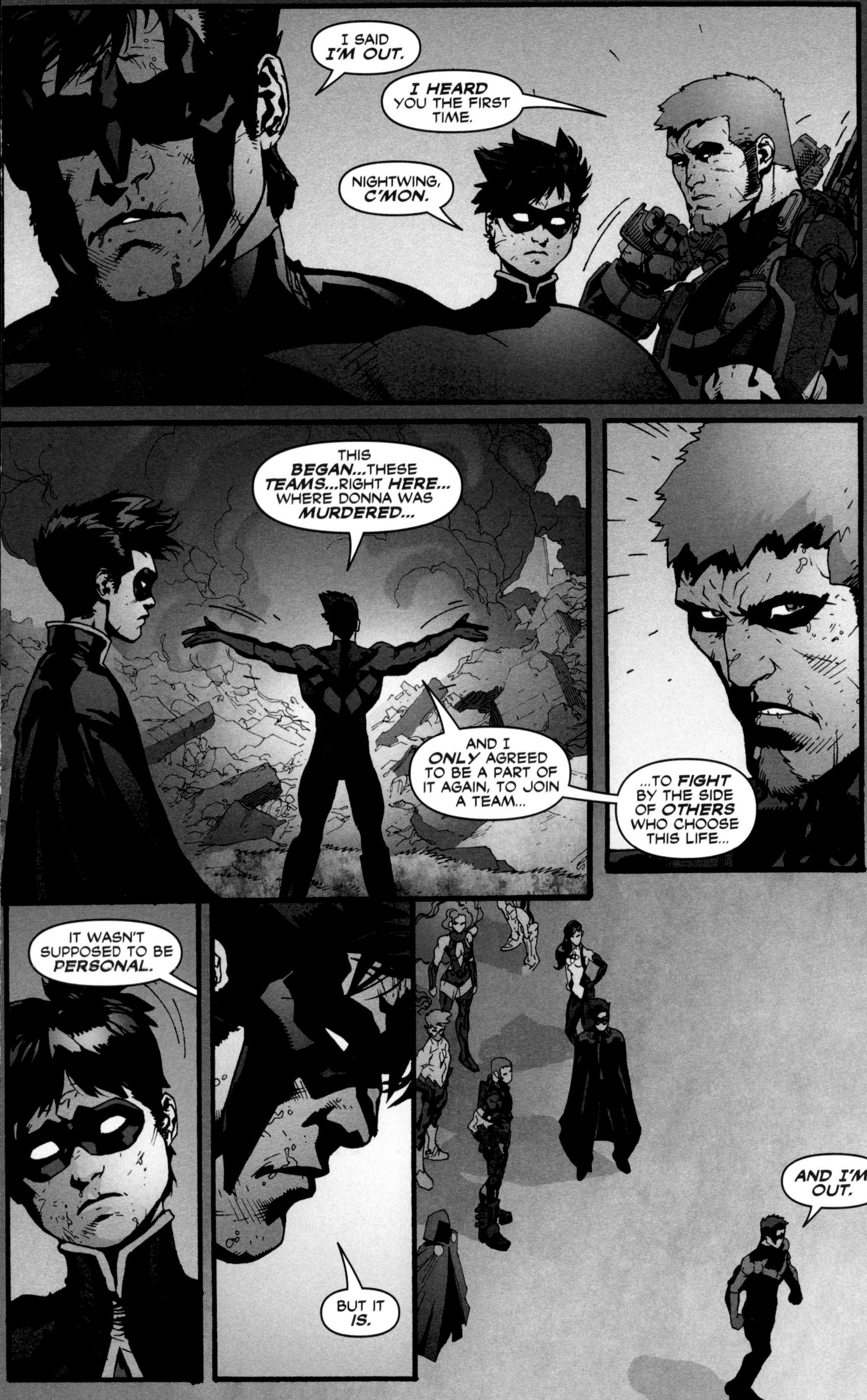
I SAID *I'M OUT.*
I HEARD YOU THE FIRST TIME.
NIGHTWING, *C'MON.*
THIS *BEGAN*...THESE *TEAMS*...RIGHT *HERE*... WHERE DONNA WAS *MURDERED*...
AND I *ONLY* AGREED TO BE A PART OF IT AGAIN, TO JOIN A TEAM...
...TO *FIGHT* BY THE SIDE OF *OTHERS* WHO CHOOSE THIS LIFE...
IT WASN'T SUPPOSED TO BE *PERSONAL.*
BUT IT *IS.*
AND I'M OUT.

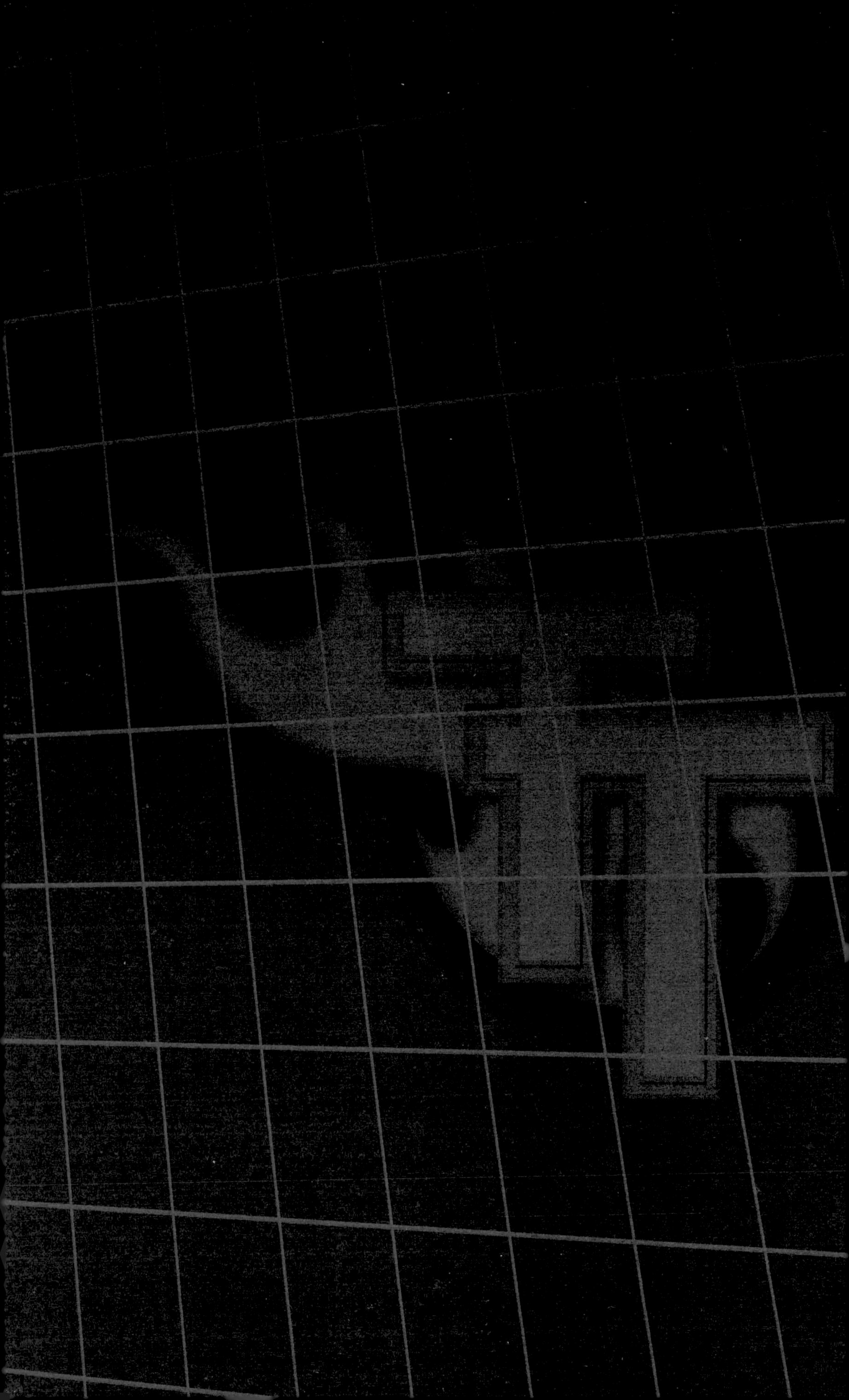

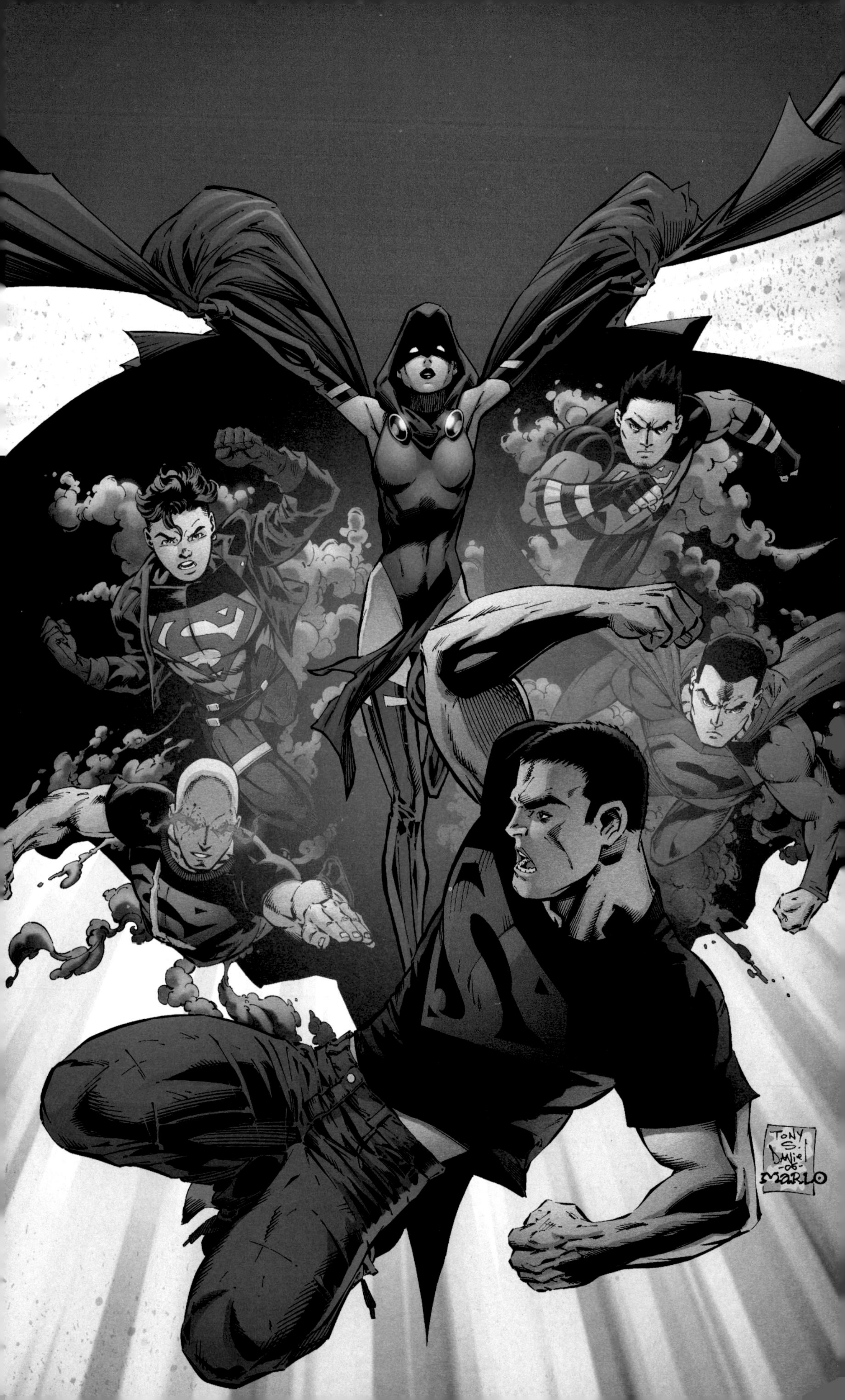
TONY S. DANIEL -06-
MARLO

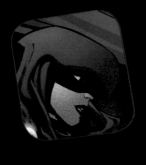

TEEN TITANS #26

GEOFF JOHNS
Writer

TONY S. DANIEL
Penciller

MARLO ALQUIZA
Inker

JEROMY COX
Colorist

COMICRAFT
Letterer

**TONY S. DANIEL,
MARLO ALQUIZA & JEROMY COX**
Cover Artists

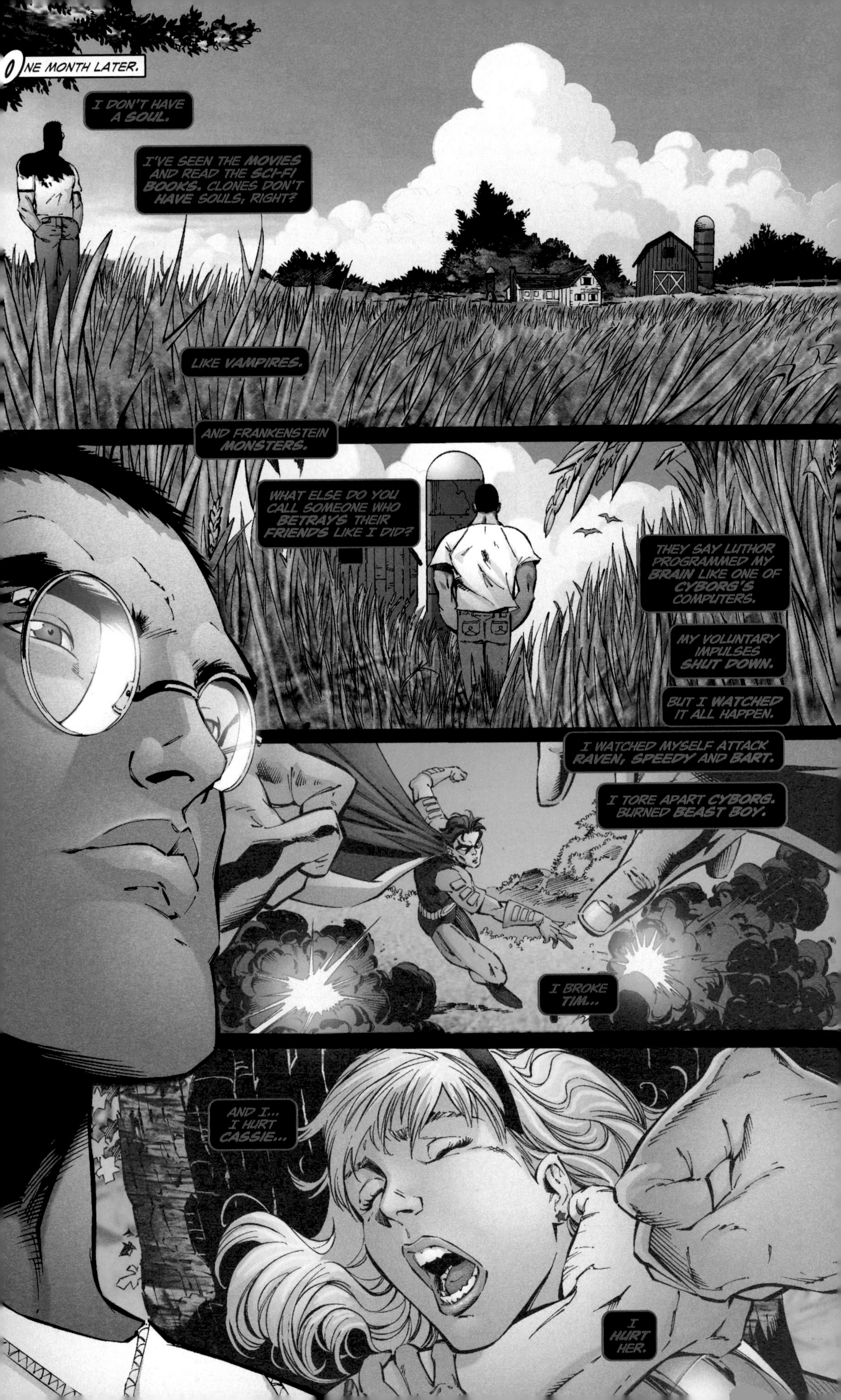
ONE MONTH LATER.
I DON'T HAVE A SOUL.
I'VE SEEN THE MOVIES AND READ THE SCI-FI BOOKS. CLONES DON'T HAVE SOULS, RIGHT?
LIKE VAMPIRES.
AND FRANKENSTEIN MONSTERS.
WHAT ELSE DO YOU CALL SOMEONE WHO BETRAYS THEIR FRIENDS LIKE I DID?
THEY SAY LUTHOR PROGRAMMED MY BRAIN LIKE ONE OF CYBORG'S COMPUTERS.
MY VOLUNTARY IMPULSES SHUT DOWN.
BUT I WATCHED IT ALL HAPPEN.
I WATCHED MYSELF ATTACK RAVEN, SPEEDY AND BART.
I TORE APART CYBORG. BURNED BEAST BOY.
I BROKE TIM...
AND I... I HURT CASSIE...
I HURT HER.

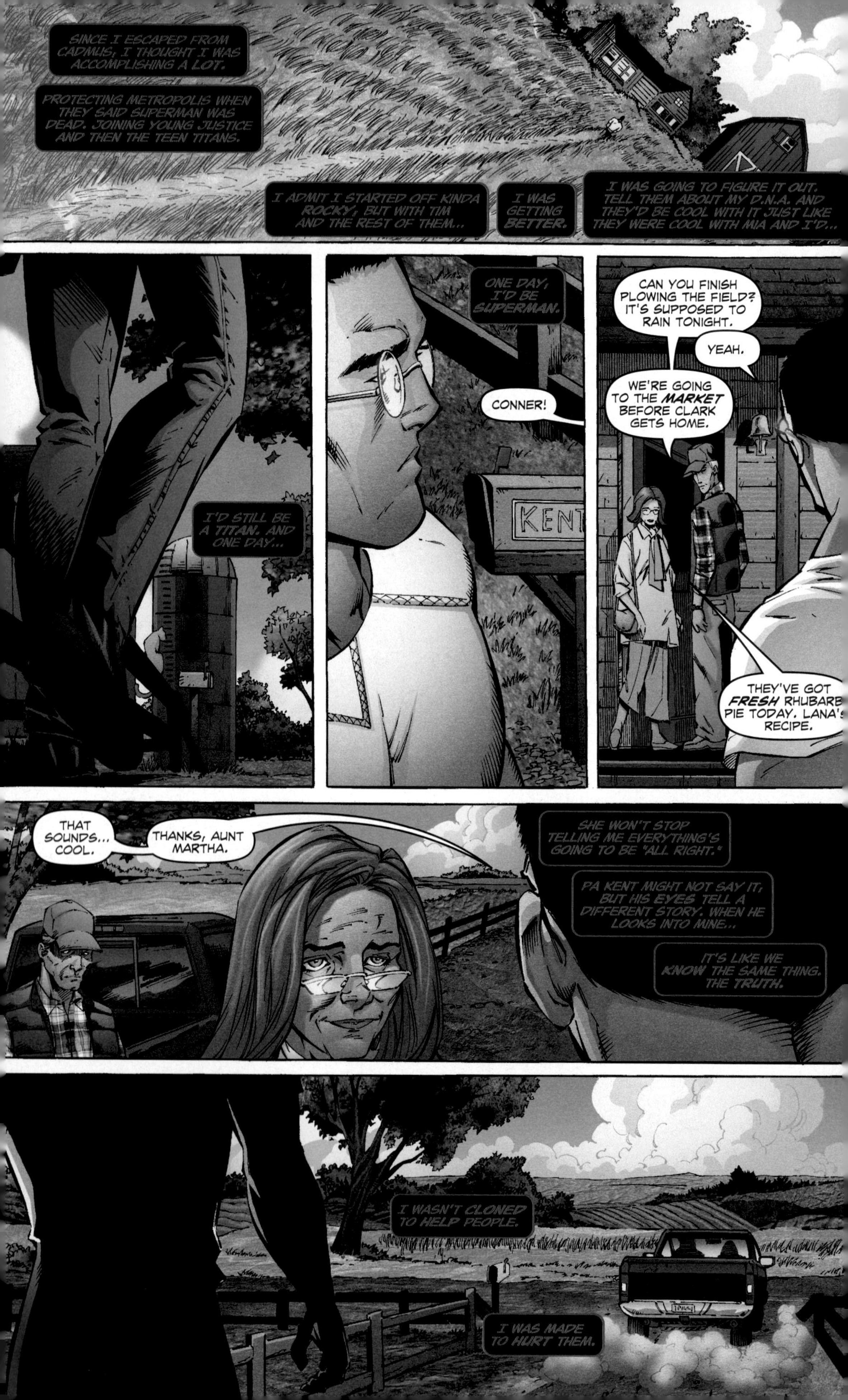

SINCE I ESCAPED FROM CADMUS, I THOUGHT I WAS ACCOMPLISHING A LOT.
PROTECTING METROPOLIS WHEN THEY SAID SUPERMAN WAS DEAD. JOINING YOUNG JUSTICE AND THEN THE TEEN TITANS.
I ADMIT I STARTED OFF KINDA ROCKY, BUT WITH TIM AND THE REST OF THEM...
I WAS GETTING BETTER.
I WAS GOING TO FIGURE IT OUT. TELL THEM ABOUT MY D.N.A. AND THEY'D BE COOL WITH IT JUST LIKE THEY WERE COOL WITH MIA AND I'D...
I'D STILL BE A TITAN. AND ONE DAY...
ONE DAY, I'D BE SUPERMAN.
CONNER!
KENT
CAN YOU FINISH PLOWING THE FIELD? IT'S SUPPOSED TO RAIN TONIGHT.
YEAH.
WE'RE GOING TO THE MARKET BEFORE CLARK GETS HOME.
THEY'VE GOT FRESH RHUBARB PIE TODAY. LANA'S RECIPE.
THAT SOUNDS... COOL.
THANKS, AUNT MARTHA.
SHE WON'T STOP TELLING ME EVERYTHING'S GOING TO BE "ALL RIGHT."
PA KENT MIGHT NOT SAY IT, BUT HIS EYES TELL A DIFFERENT STORY. WHEN HE LOOKS INTO MINE...
IT'S LIKE WE KNOW THE SAME THING. THE TRUTH.
I WASN'T CLONED TO HELP PEOPLE.
I WAS MADE TO HURT THEM.

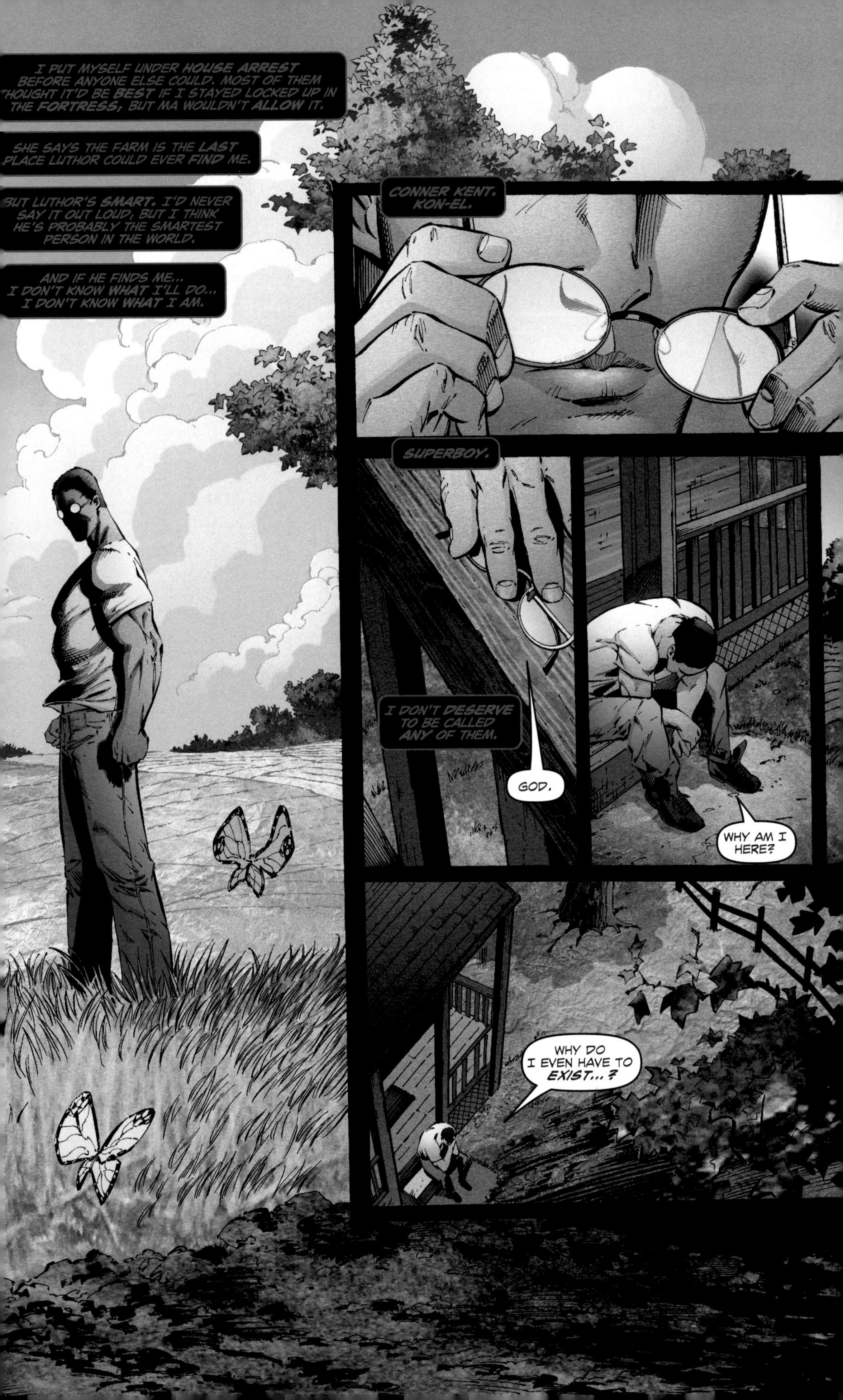

I PUT MYSELF UNDER HOUSE ARREST BEFORE ANYONE ELSE COULD. MOST OF THEM THOUGHT IT'D BE BEST IF I STAYED LOCKED UP IN THE FORTRESS, BUT MA WOULDN'T ALLOW IT.
SHE SAYS THE FARM IS THE LAST PLACE LUTHOR COULD EVER FIND ME.
BUT LUTHOR'S SMART. I'D NEVER SAY IT OUT LOUD, BUT I THINK HE'S PROBABLY THE SMARTEST PERSON IN THE WORLD.
AND IF HE FINDS ME... I DON'T KNOW WHAT I'LL DO... I DON'T KNOW WHAT I AM.
CONNER KENT. KON-EL.
SUPERBOY.
I DON'T DESERVE TO BE CALLED ANY OF THEM.
GOD.
WHY AM I HERE?
WHY DO I EVEN HAVE TO EXIST...?

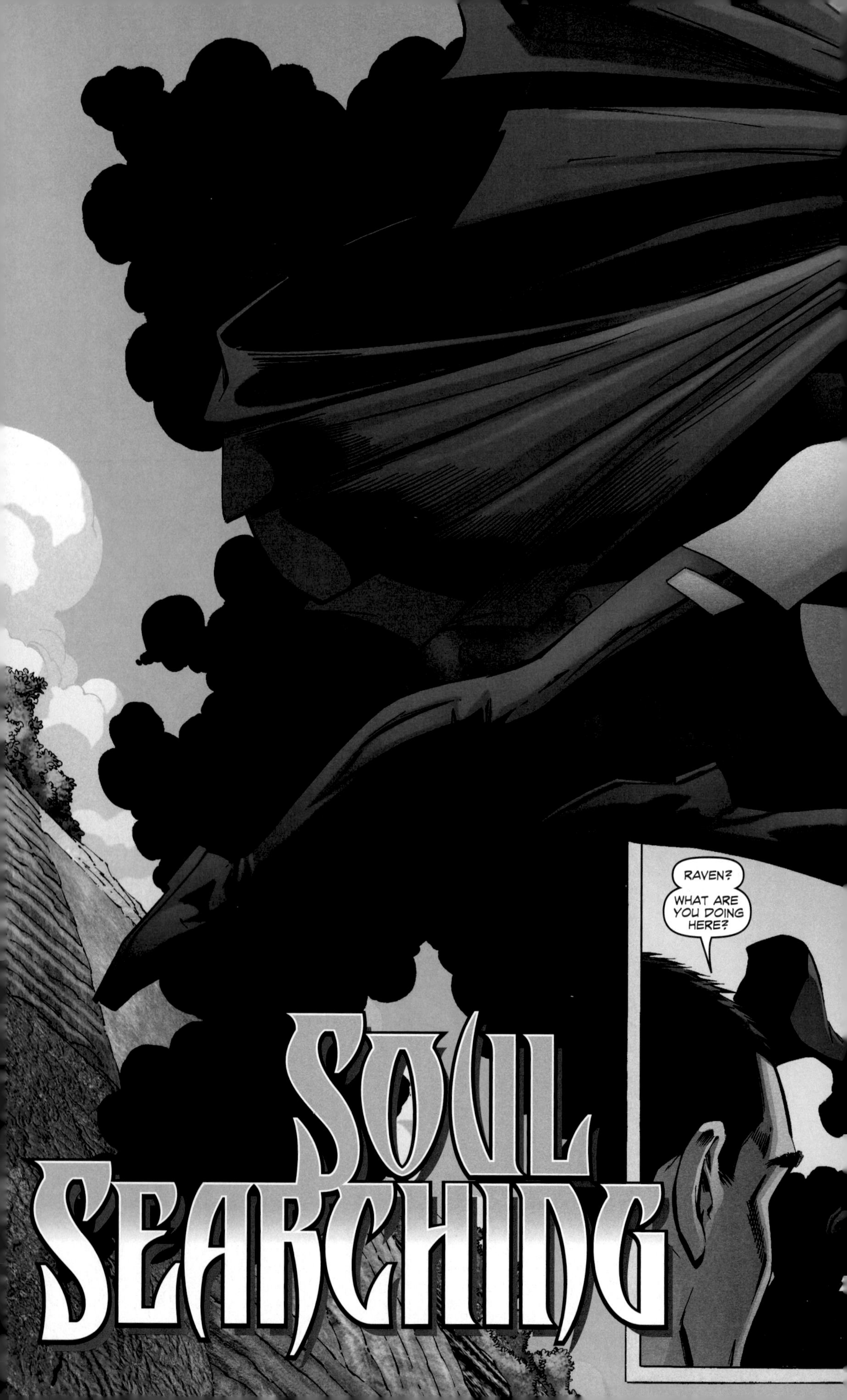
RAVEN?
WHAT ARE YOU DOING HERE?
SOUL SEARCHING

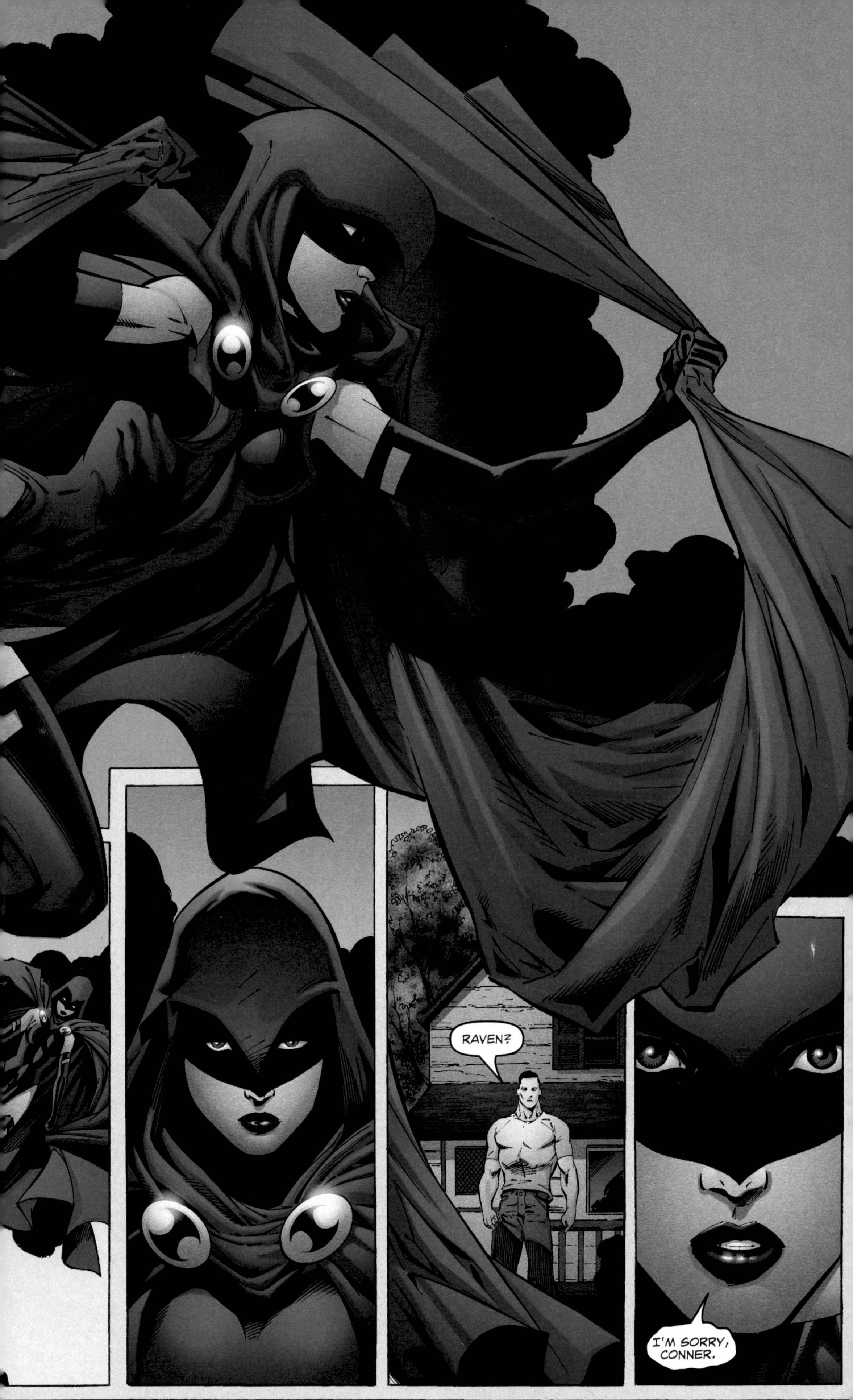
RAVEN?
I'M SORRY, CONNER.

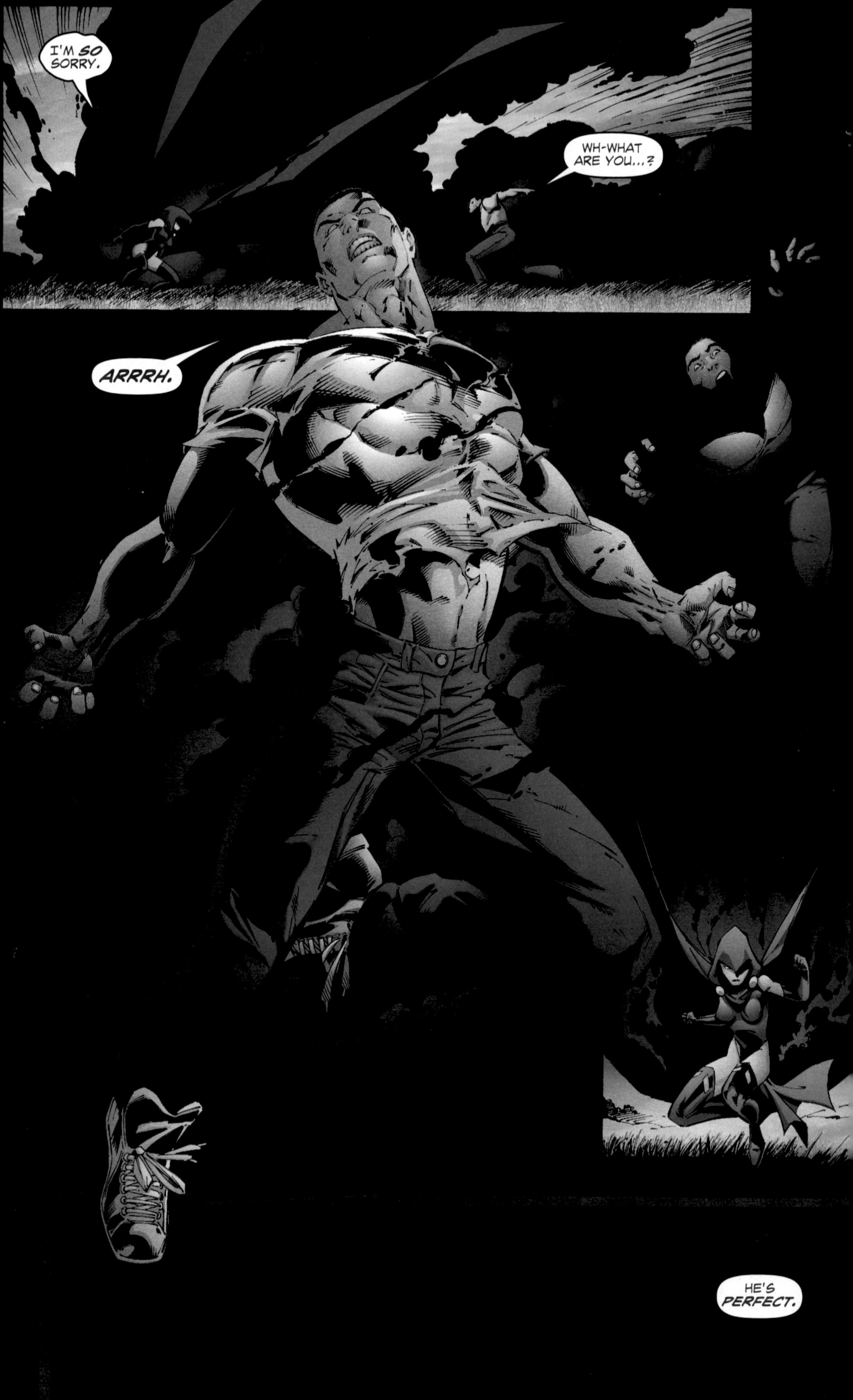
I'M SO SORRY.
WH-WHAT ARE YOU...?
ARRRH.
HE'S PERFECT.

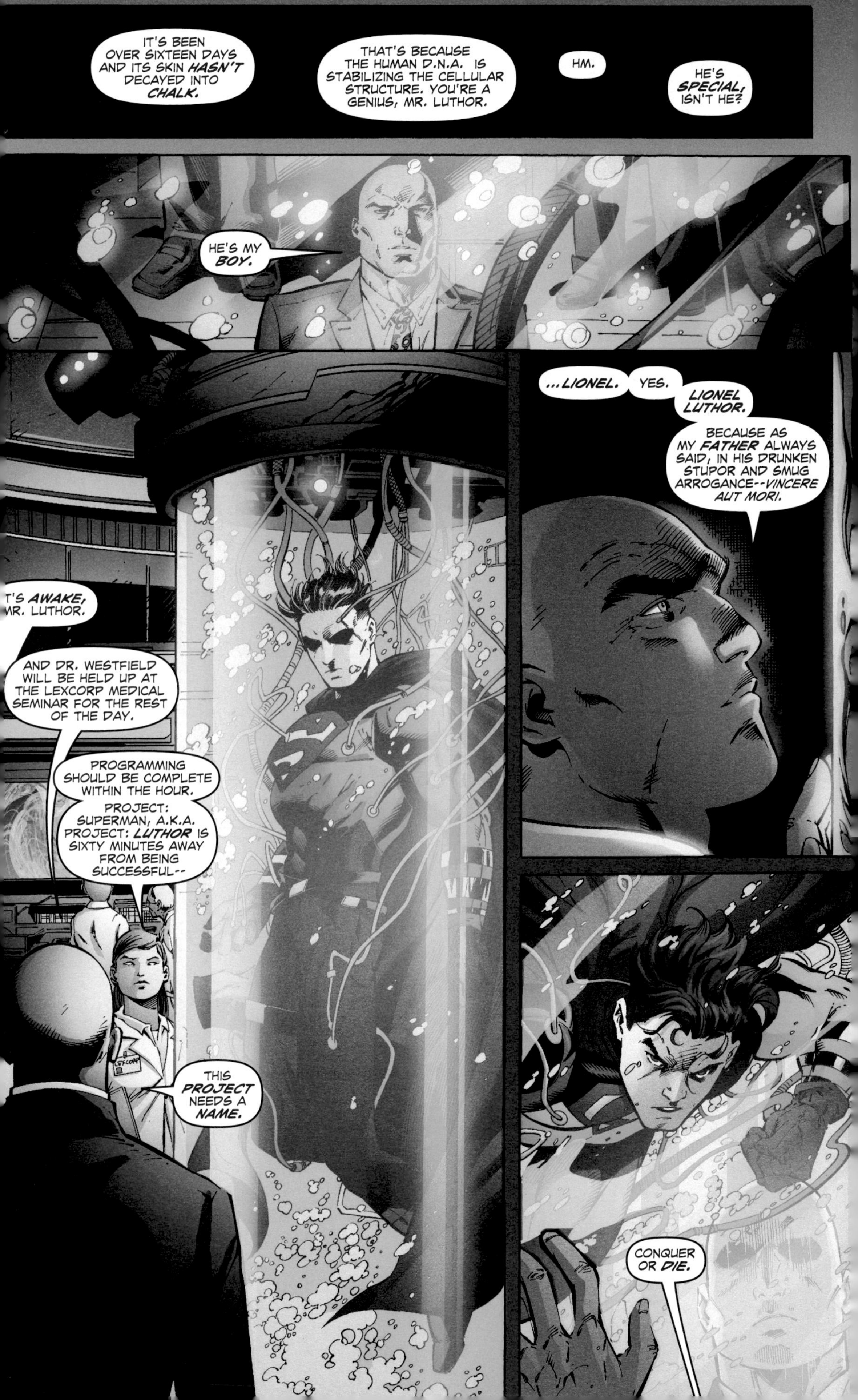
IT'S BEEN OVER SIXTEEN DAYS AND ITS SKIN HASN'T DECAYED INTO CHALK.
THAT'S BECAUSE THE HUMAN D.N.A. IS STABILIZING THE CELLULAR STRUCTURE. YOU'RE A GENIUS, MR. LUTHOR.
HM.
HE'S SPECIAL, ISN'T HE?
HE'S MY BOY.
T'S AWAKE, MR. LUTHOR.
AND DR. WESTFIELD WILL BE HELD UP AT THE LEXCORP MEDICAL SEMINAR FOR THE REST OF THE DAY.
PROGRAMMING SHOULD BE COMPLETE WITHIN THE HOUR.
PROJECT: SUPERMAN, A.K.A. PROJECT: LUTHOR IS SIXTY MINUTES AWAY FROM BEING SUCCESSFUL--
THIS PROJECT NEEDS A NAME.
...LIONEL.
YES.
LIONEL LUTHOR.
BECAUSE AS MY FATHER ALWAYS SAID, IN HIS DRUNKEN STUPOR AND SMUG ARROGANCE--VINCERE AUT MORI.
CONQUER OR DIE.

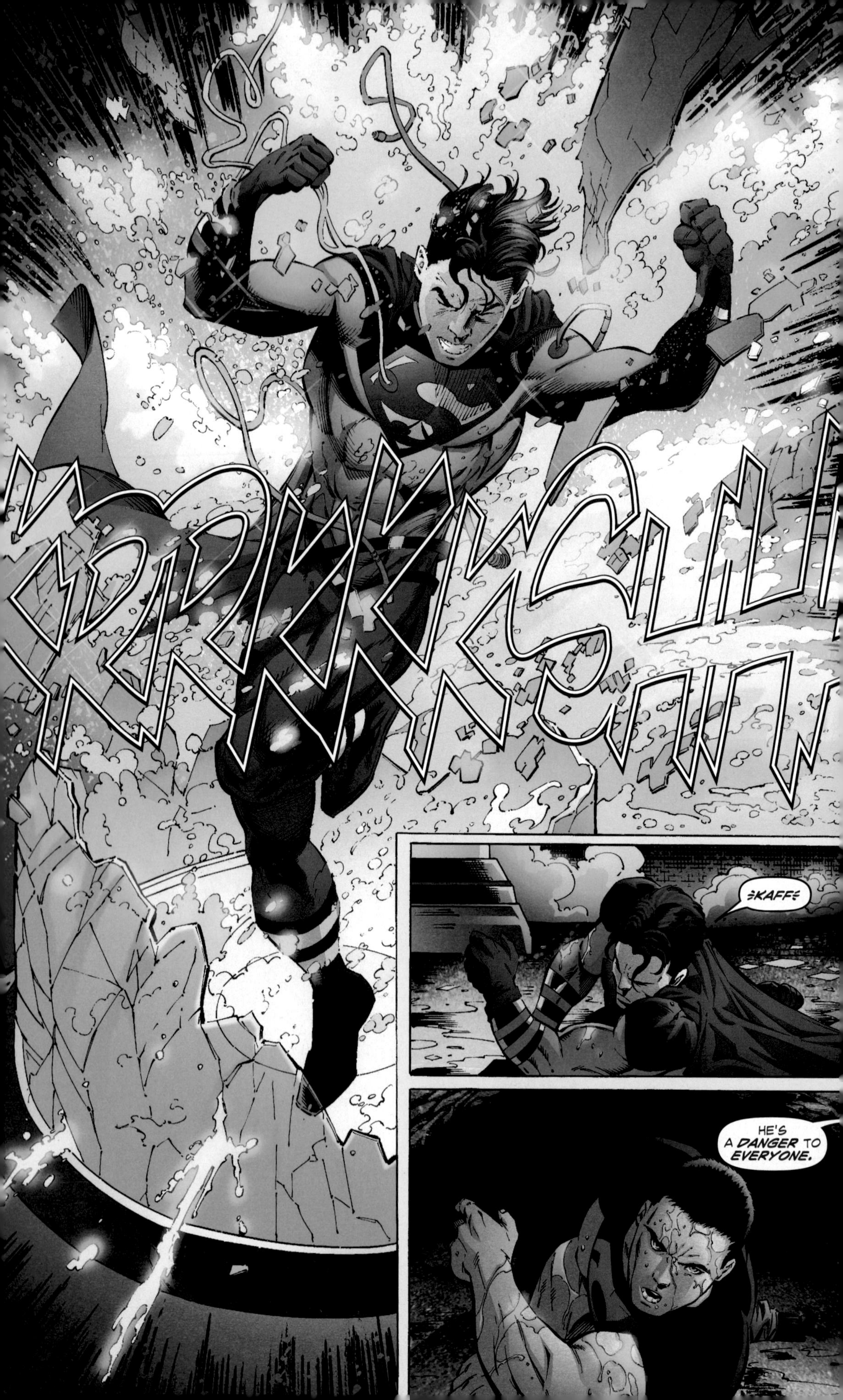
KAFF
HE'S A DANGER TO EVERYONE.

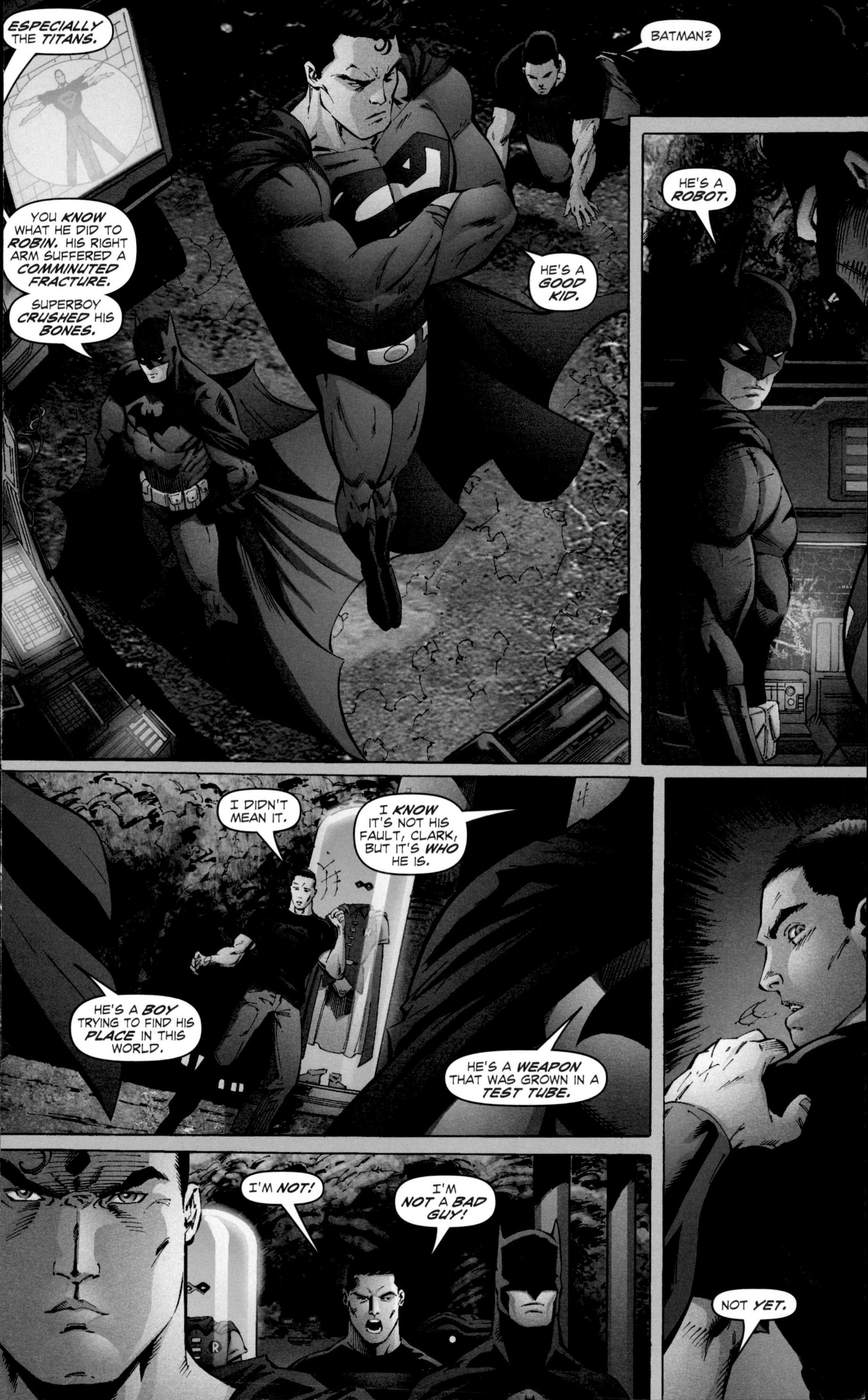
ESPECIALLY THE TITANS.
BATMAN?
YOU KNOW WHAT HE DID TO ROBIN. HIS RIGHT ARM SUFFERED A COMMINUTED FRACTURE.
SUPERBOY CRUSHED HIS BONES.
HE'S A GOOD KID.
HE'S A ROBOT.
I DIDN'T MEAN IT.
I KNOW IT'S NOT HIS FAULT, CLARK, BUT IT'S WHO HE IS.
HE'S A BOY TRYING TO FIND HIS PLACE IN THIS WORLD.
HE'S A WEAPON THAT WAS GROWN IN A TEST TUBE.
I'M NOT!
I'M NOT A BAD GUY!
NOT YET.

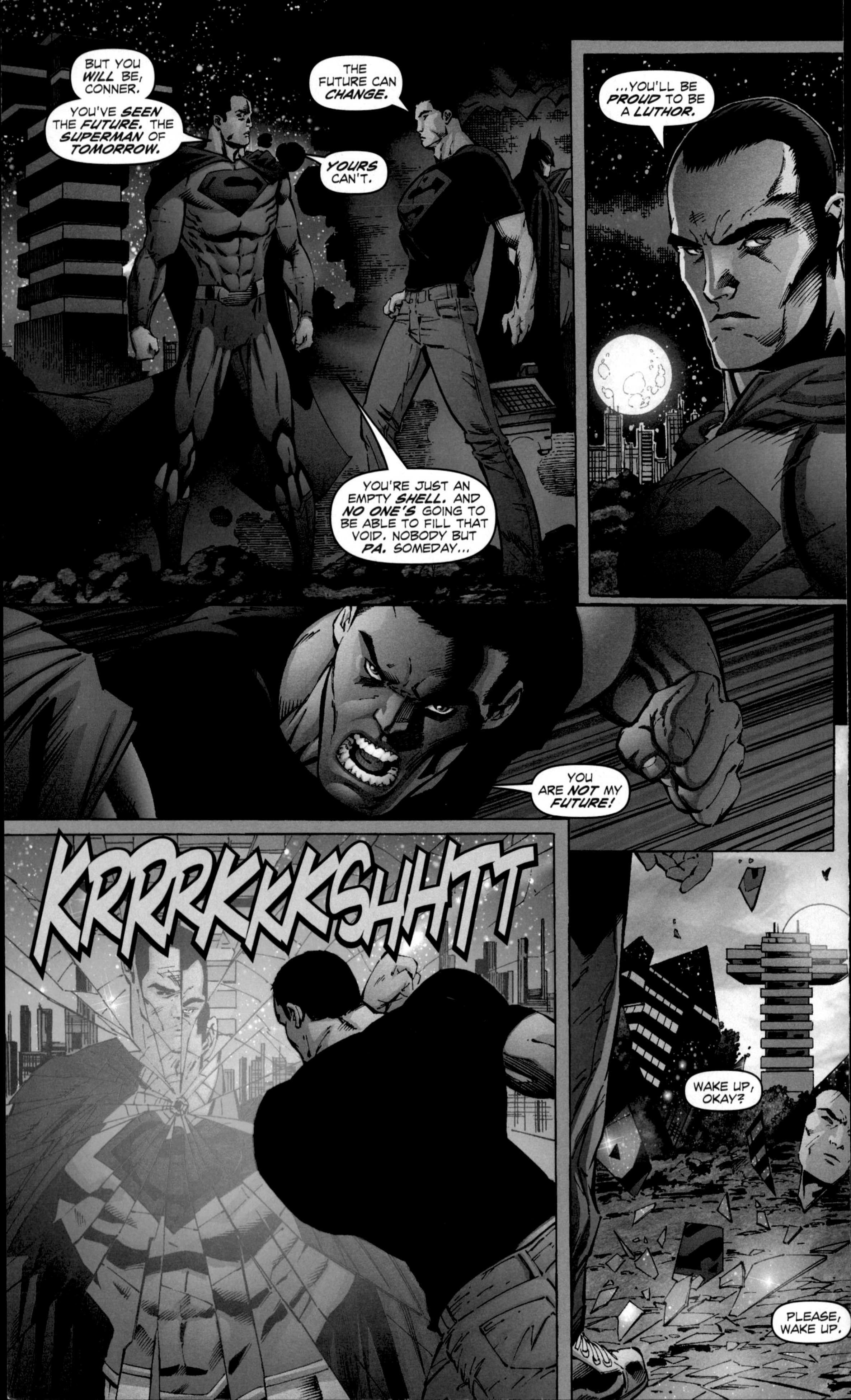
BUT YOU WILL BE, CONNER.
YOU'VE SEEN THE FUTURE. THE SUPERMAN OF TOMORROW.
THE FUTURE CAN CHANGE.
YOURS CAN'T.
YOU'RE JUST AN EMPTY SHELL. AND NO ONE'S GOING TO BE ABLE TO FILL THAT VOID. NOBODY BUT PA. SOMEDAY...
...YOU'LL BE PROUD TO BE A LUTHOR.
YOU ARE NOT MY FUTURE!
KRRRKKKSHHTT
WAKE UP, OKAY?
PLEASE, WAKE UP.

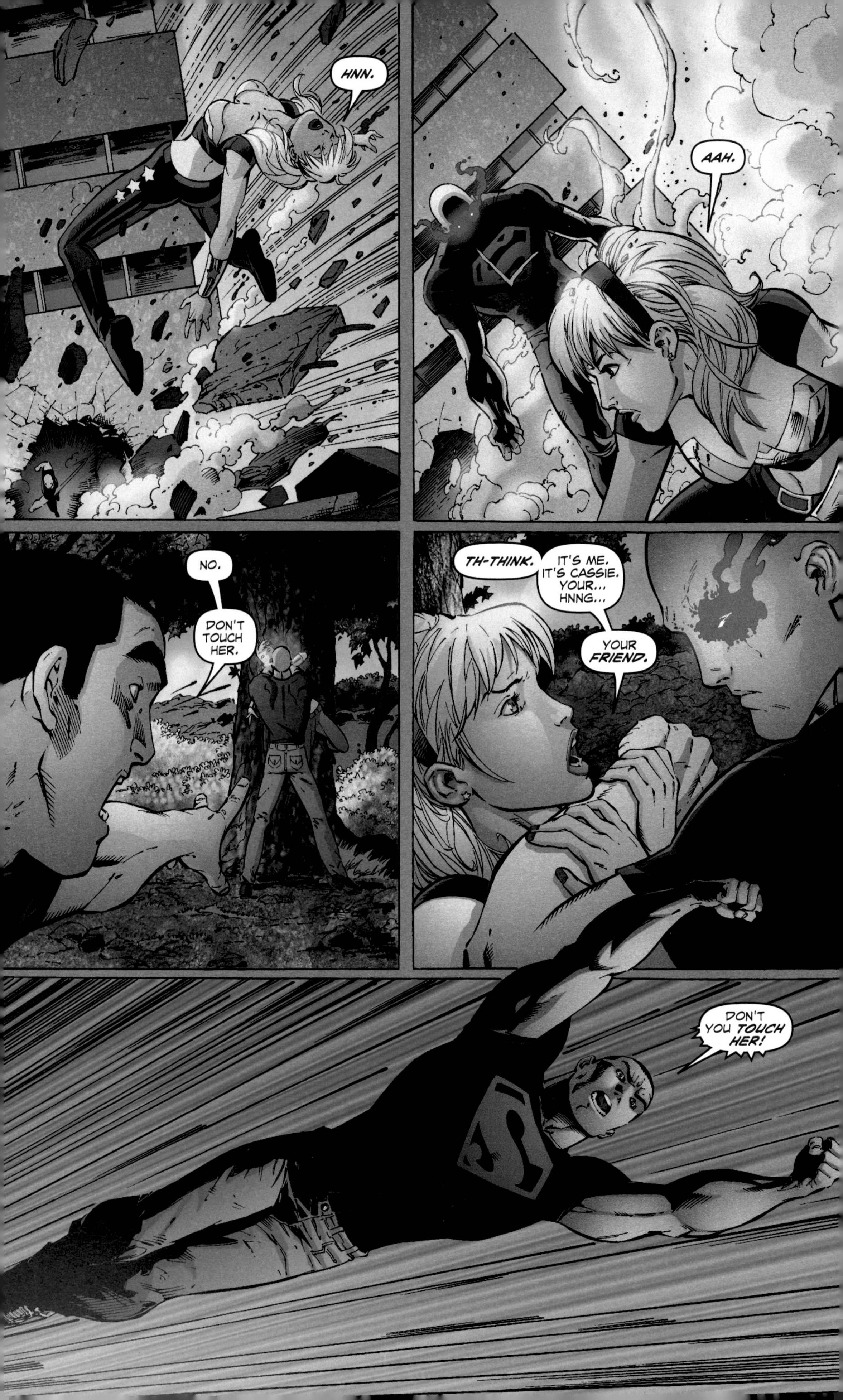
HNN.
AAH.
NO.
DON'T TOUCH HER.
TH-THINK.
IT'S ME. IT'S CASSIE. YOUR... HNNG...
YOUR FRIEND.
DON'T YOU TOUCH HER!

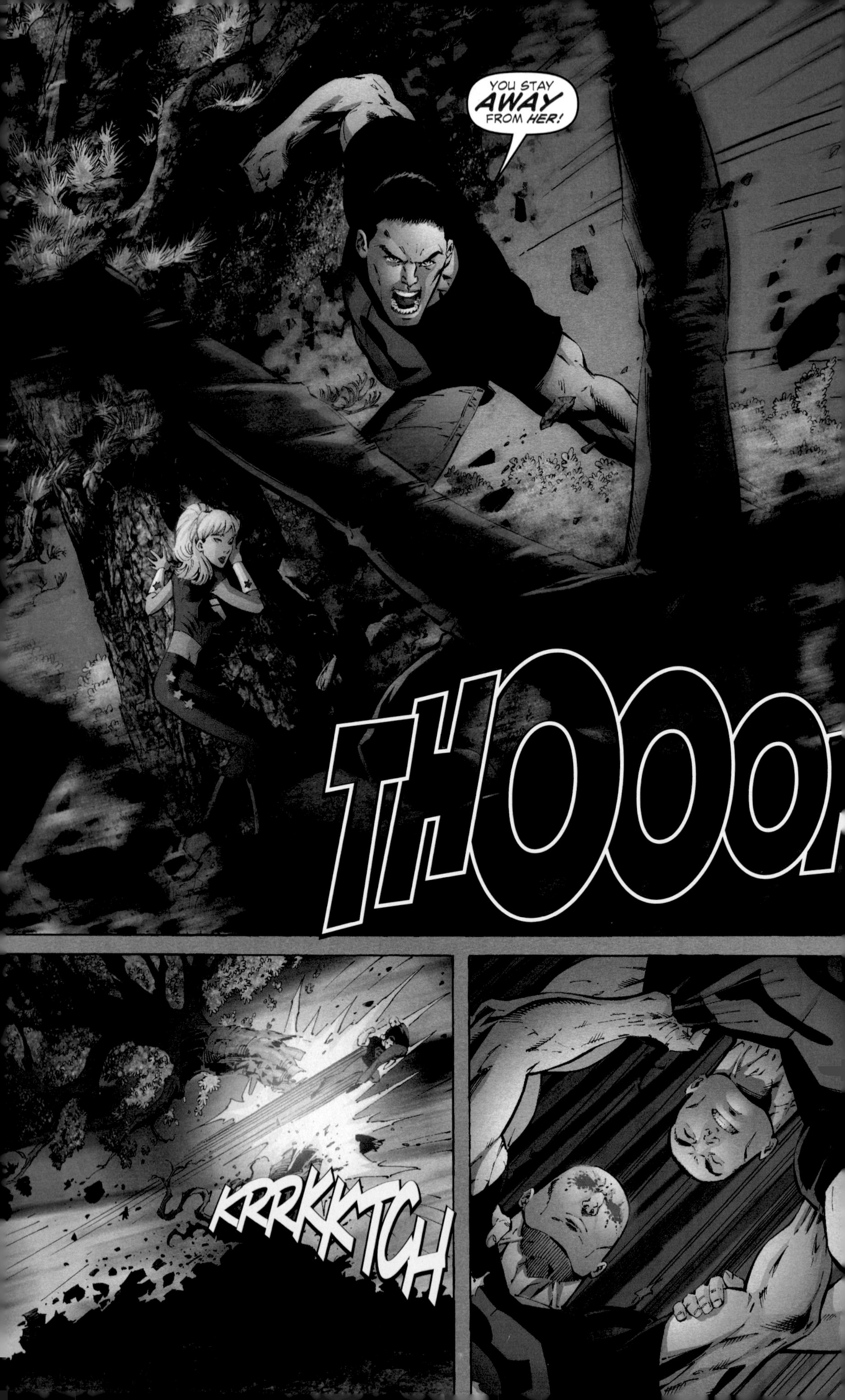
YOU STAY AWAY FROM HER!
THOOOM
KRRKKTCH

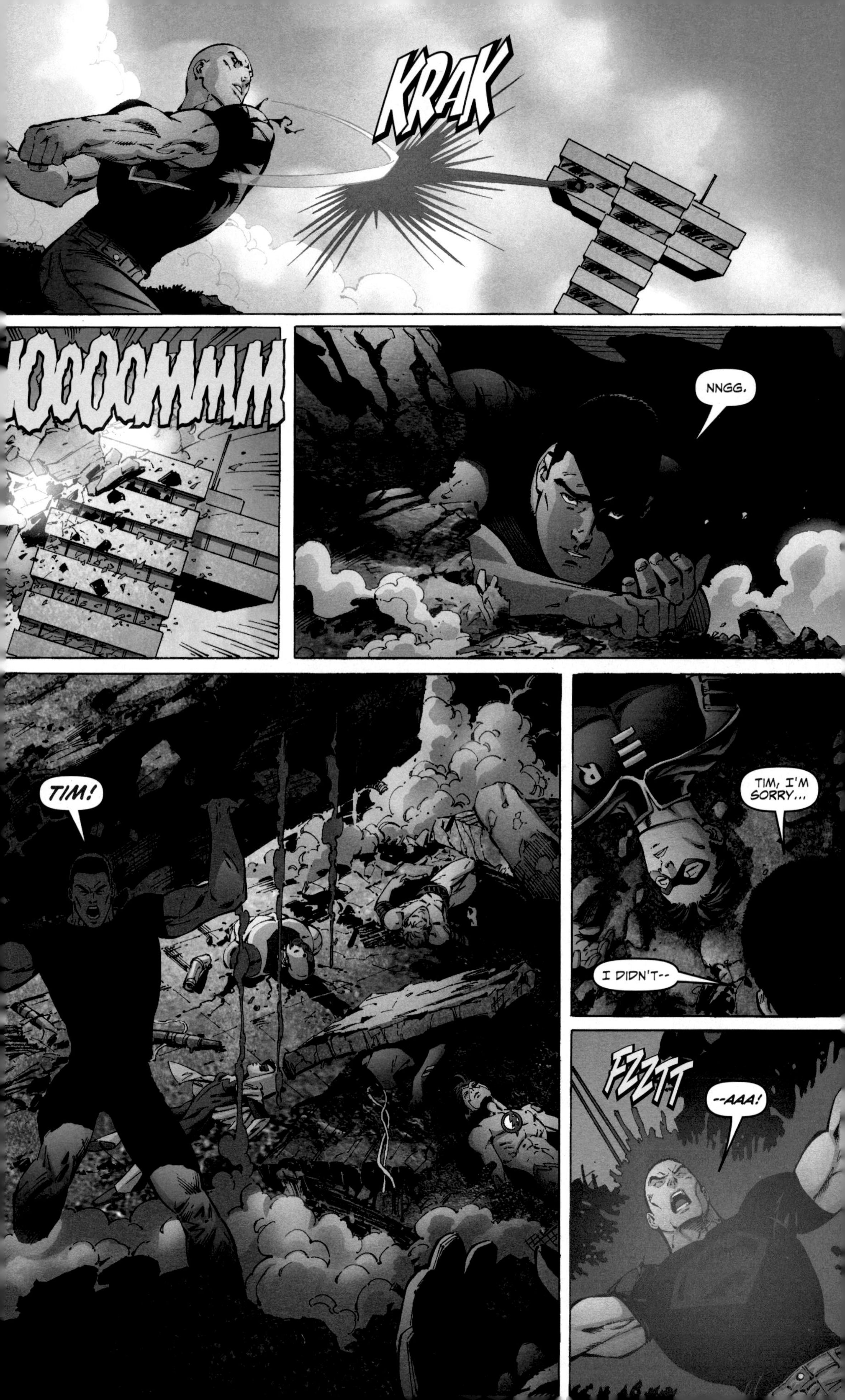
KRAK
OOOOMMM
NNGG.
TIM!
TIM, I'M SORRY...
I DIDN'T--
FZZTT
--AAA!

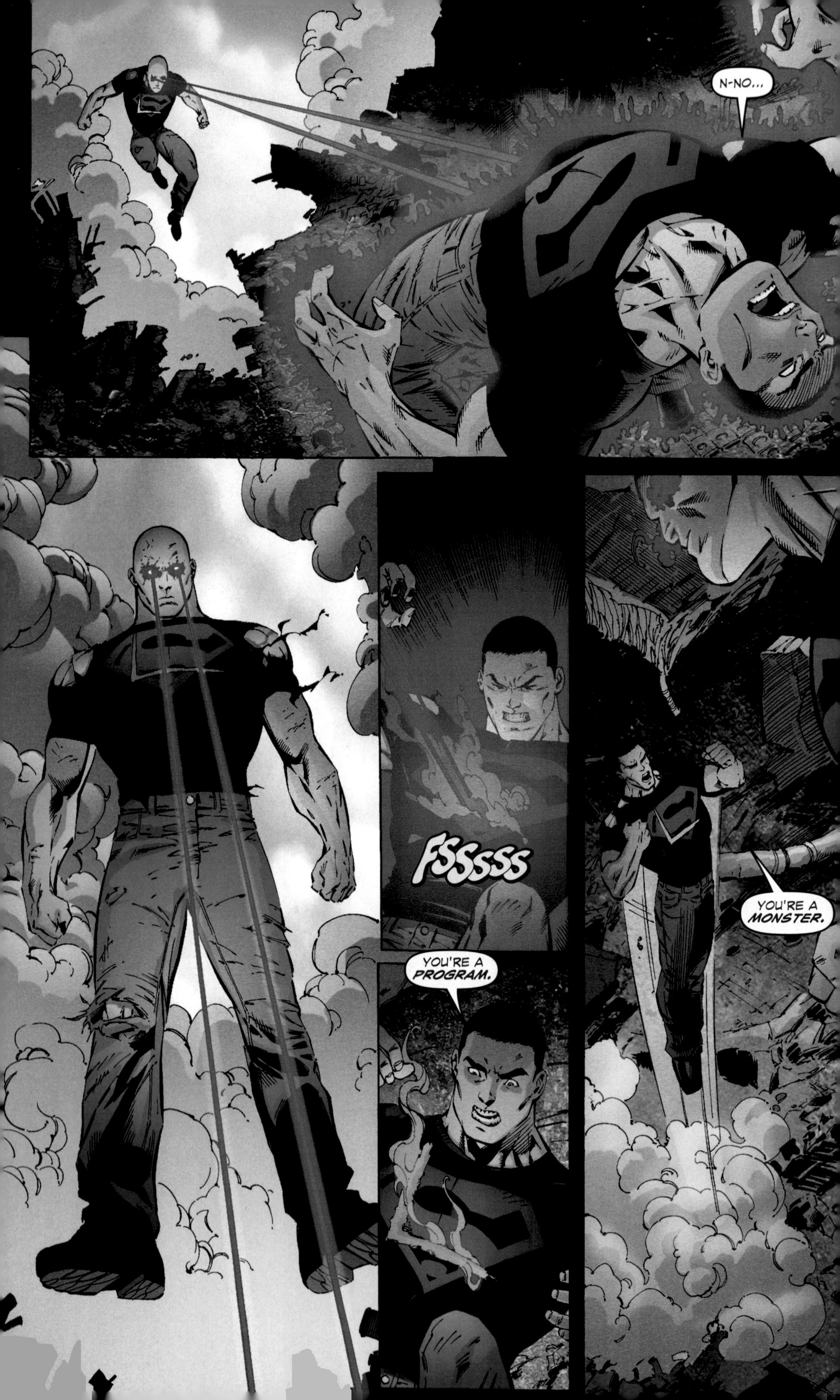
N-NO...
FSSSSS
YOU'RE A MONSTER.
YOU'RE A PROGRAM.

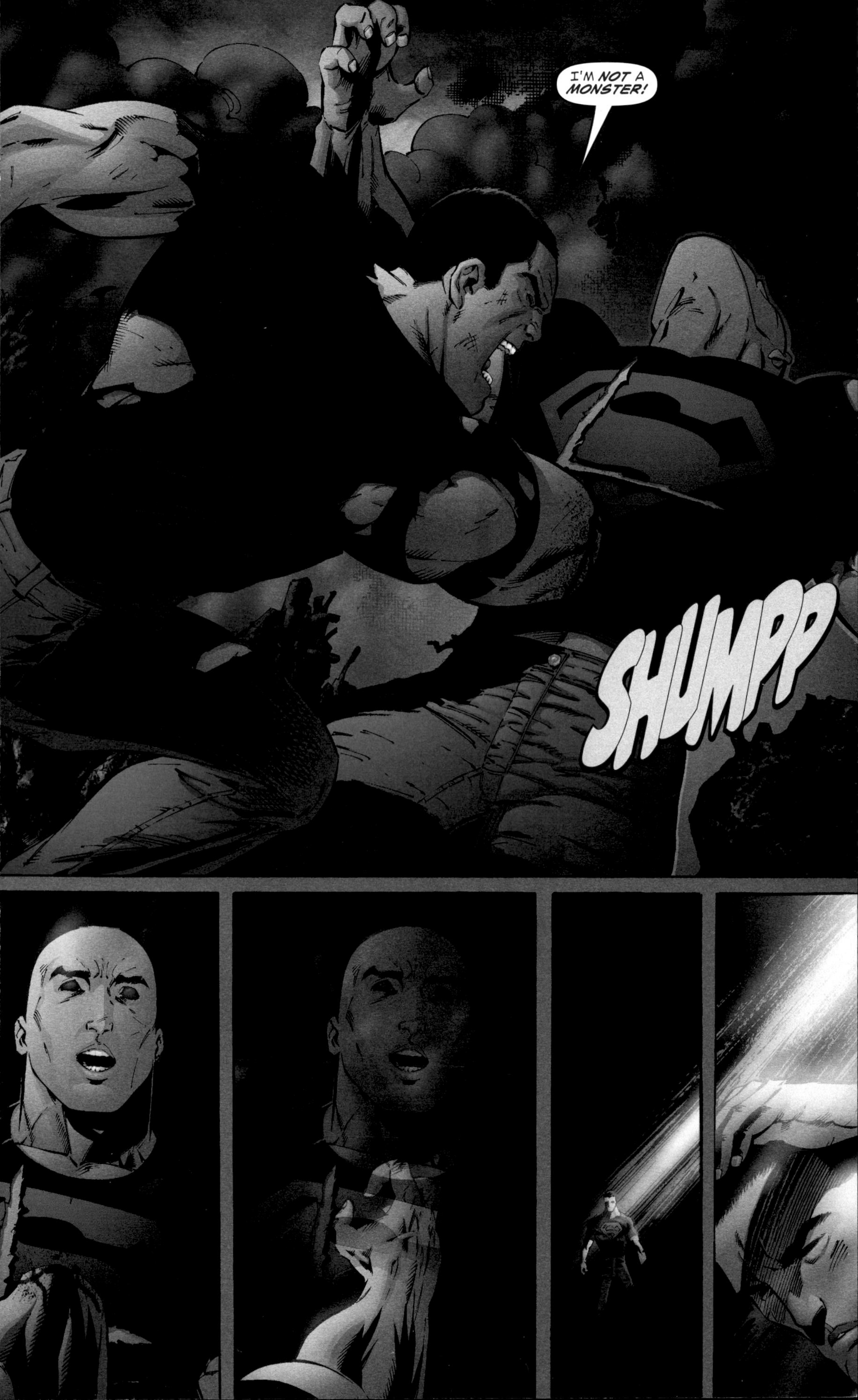
I'M NOT A MONSTER!
SHUMPP

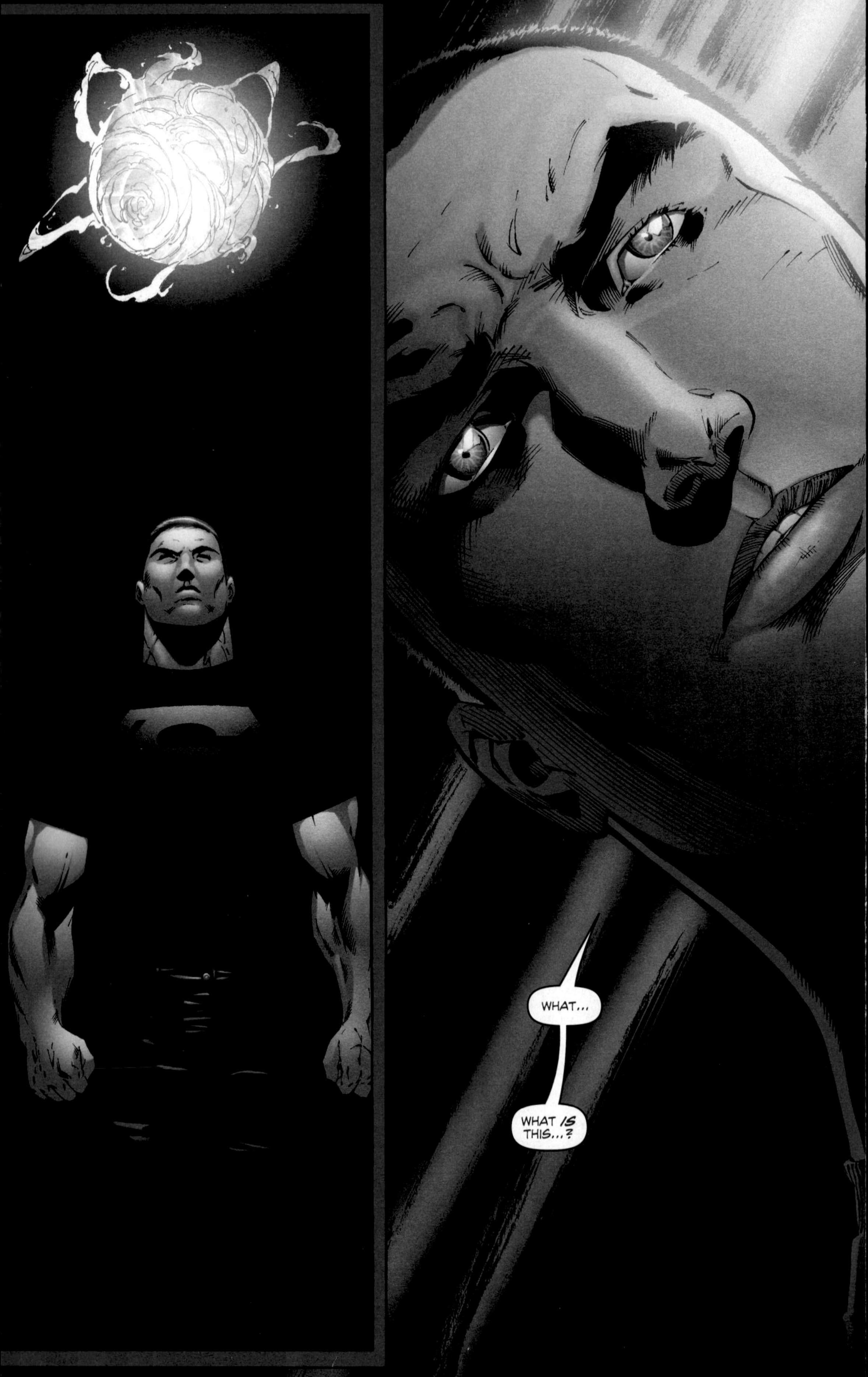
WHAT...
WHAT IS THIS...?

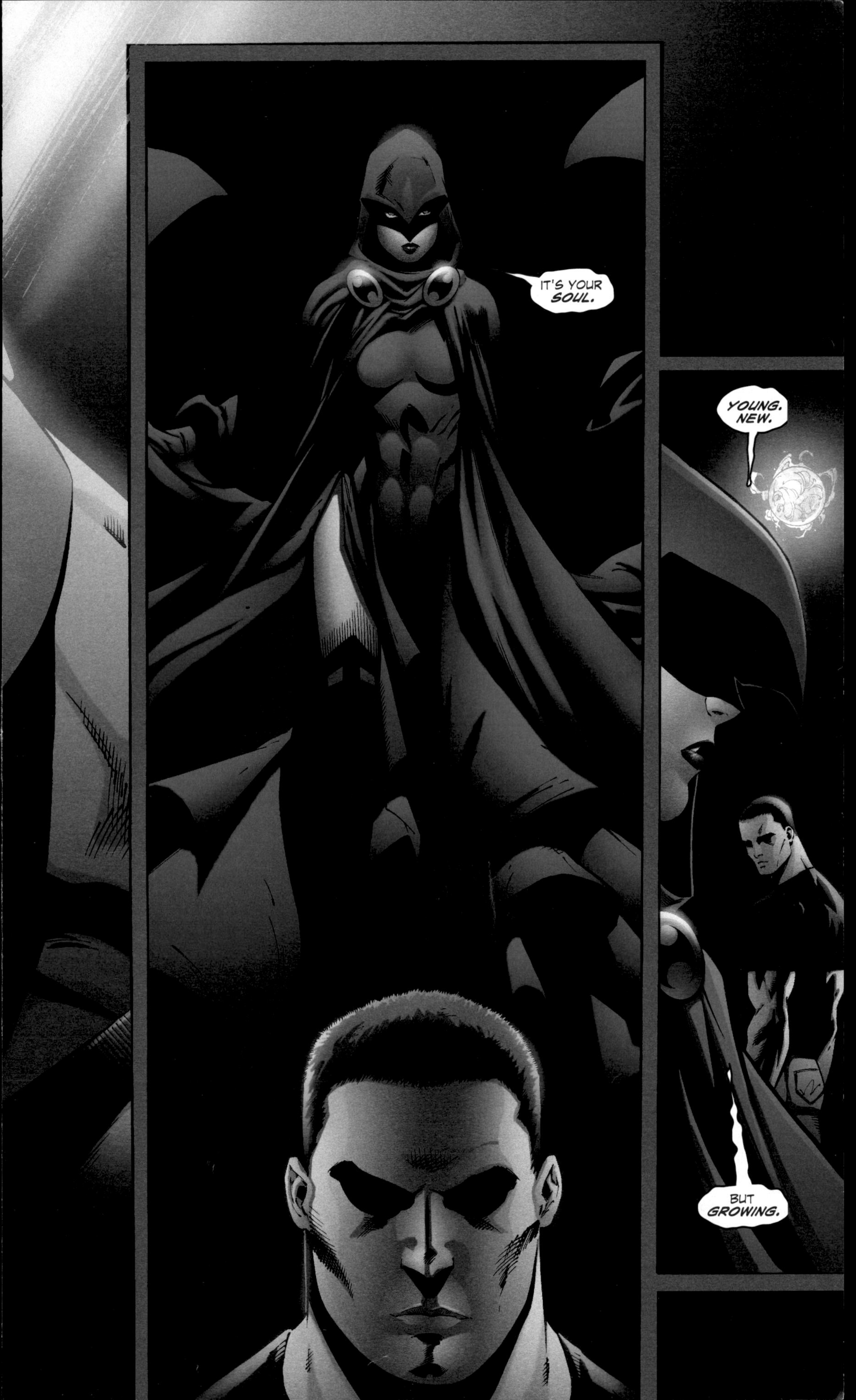
IT'S YOUR SOUL.
YOUNG. NEW.
BUT GROWING.

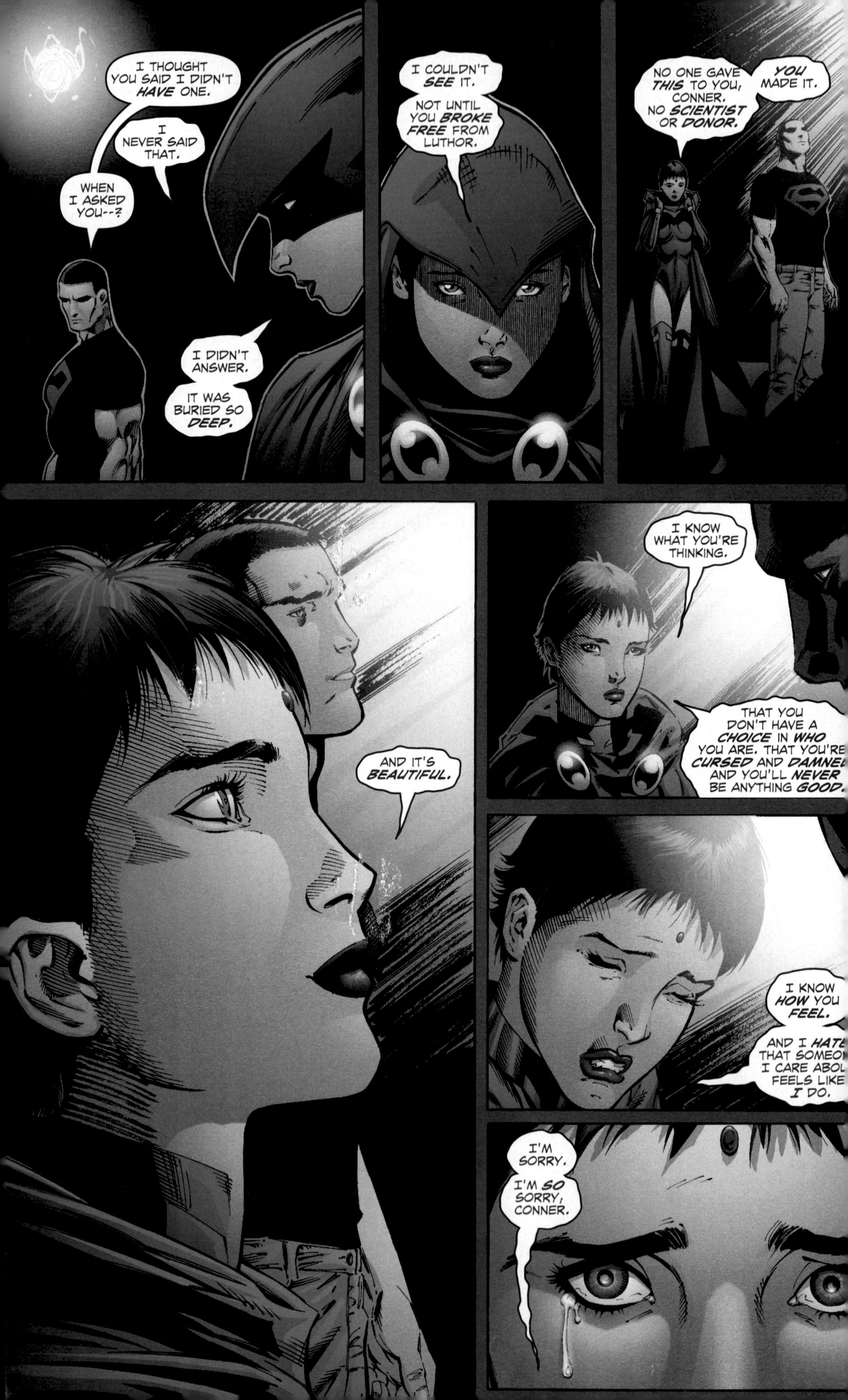
I THOUGHT YOU SAID I DIDN'T HAVE ONE.
I NEVER SAID THAT.
WHEN I ASKED YOU--?
I DIDN'T ANSWER.
IT WAS BURIED SO DEEP.
I COULDN'T SEE IT.
NOT UNTIL YOU BROKE FREE FROM LUTHOR.
NO ONE GAVE THIS TO YOU, CONNER. NO SCIENTIST OR DONOR.
YOU MADE IT.
AND IT'S BEAUTIFUL.
I KNOW WHAT YOU'RE THINKING.
THAT YOU DON'T HAVE A CHOICE IN WHO YOU ARE. THAT YOU'RE CURSED AND DAMNE AND YOU'LL NEVER BE ANYTHING GOOD.
I KNOW HOW YOU FEEL.
AND I HAT THAT SOMEO I CARE ABOU FEELS LIKE I DO.
I'M SORRY.
I'M SO SORRY, CONNER.

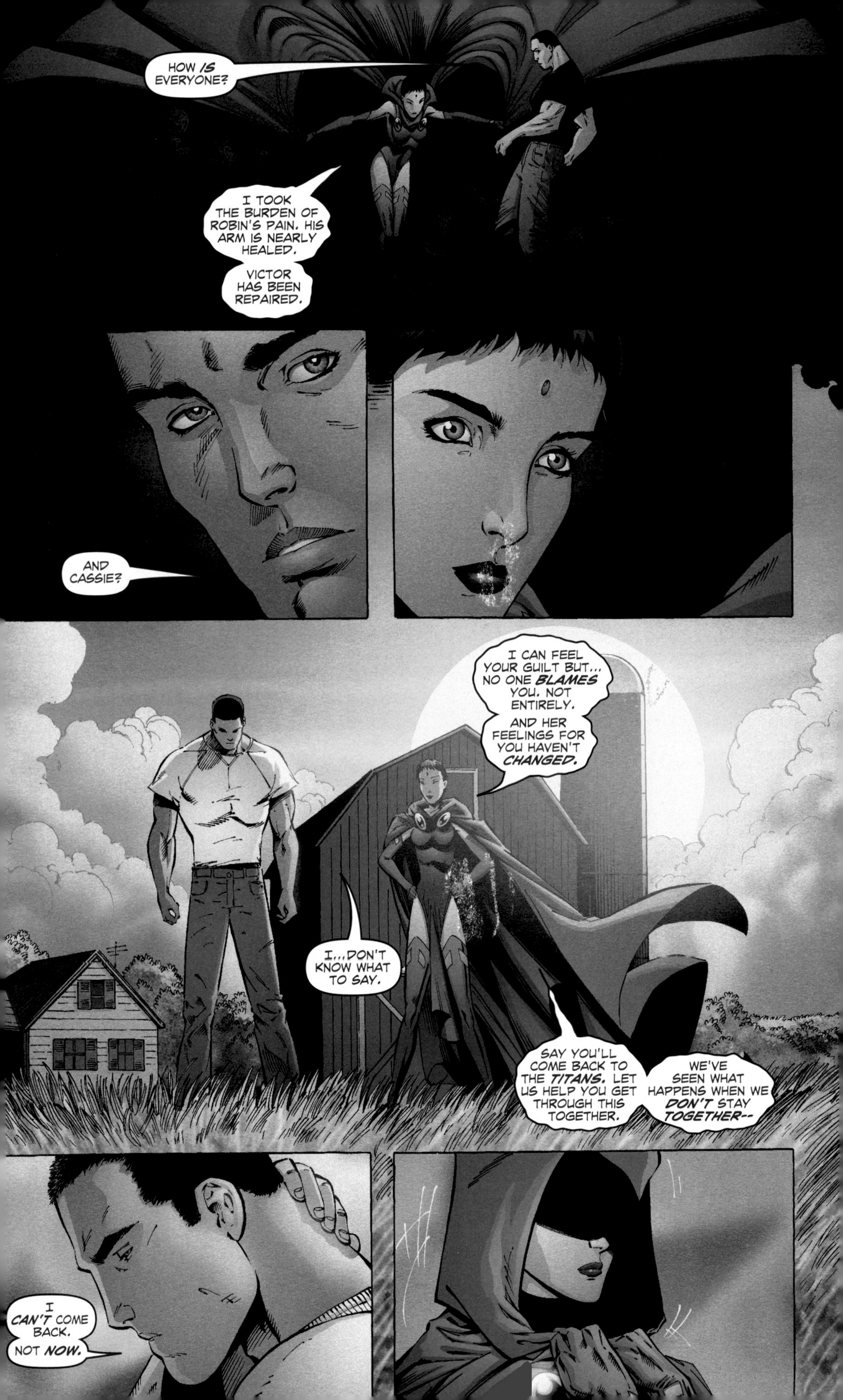
HOW *IS* EVERYONE?
I TOOK THE BURDEN OF ROBIN'S PAIN. HIS ARM IS NEARLY HEALED.
VICTOR HAS BEEN REPAIRED.
AND CASSIE?
I CAN FEEL YOUR GUILT BUT... NO ONE ***BLAMES*** YOU. NOT ENTIRELY.
AND HER FEELINGS FOR YOU HAVEN'T ***CHANGED.***
I...DON'T KNOW WHAT TO SAY.
SAY YOU'LL COME BACK TO THE ***TITANS.*** LET US HELP YOU GET THROUGH THIS TOGETHER.
WE'VE SEEN WHAT HAPPENS WHEN WE ***DON'T*** STAY ***TOGETHER--***
I ***CAN'T*** COME BACK.
NOT ***NOW.***

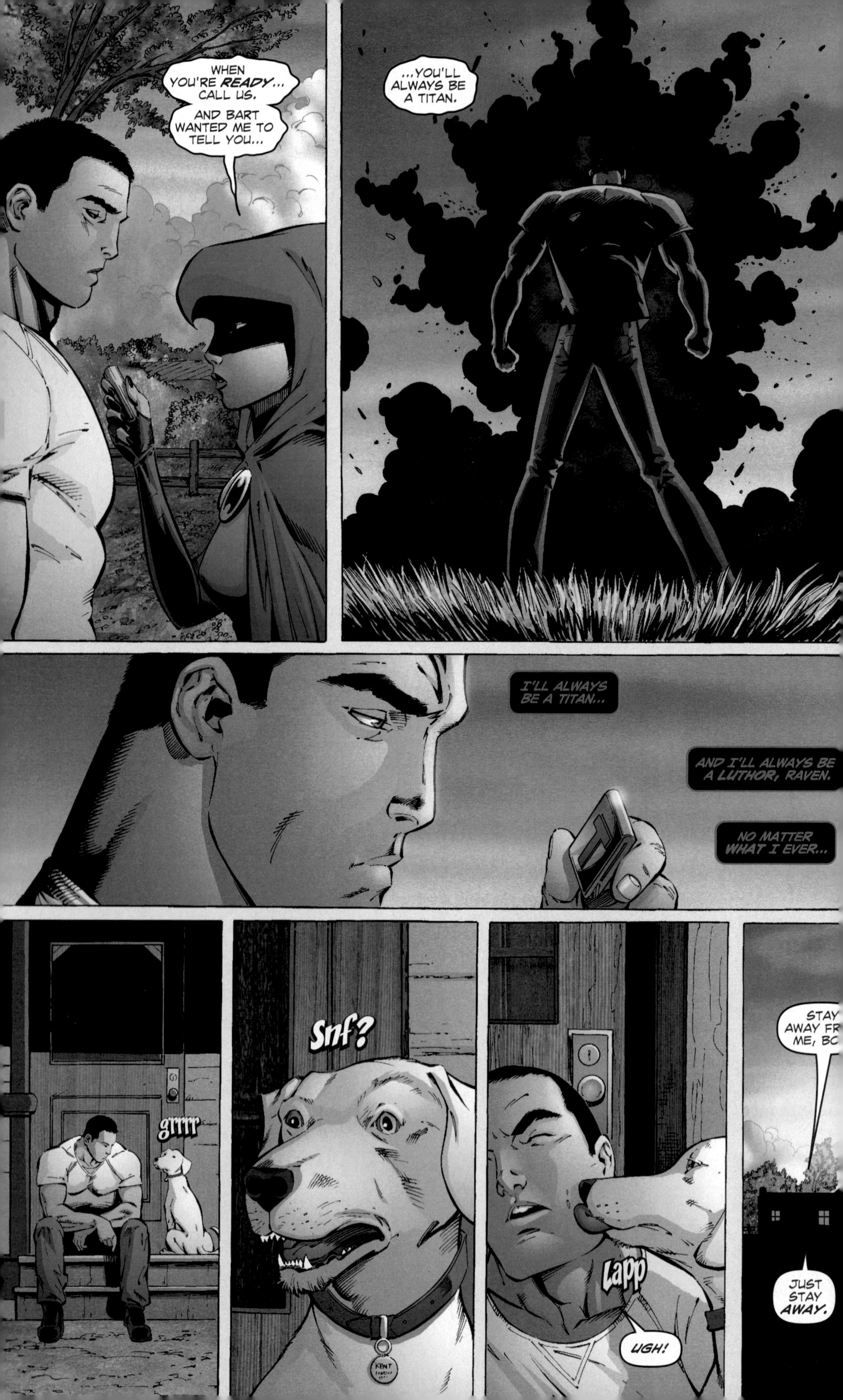
WHEN YOU'RE READY... CALL US.
AND BART WANTED ME TO TELL YOU...
...YOU'LL ALWAYS BE A TITAN.
I'LL ALWAYS BE A TITAN...
AND I'LL ALWAYS BE A LUTHOR, RAVEN.
NO MATTER WHAT I EVER...
grrrr
Snf?
KENT
Lapp
UGH!
JUST STAY AWAY.

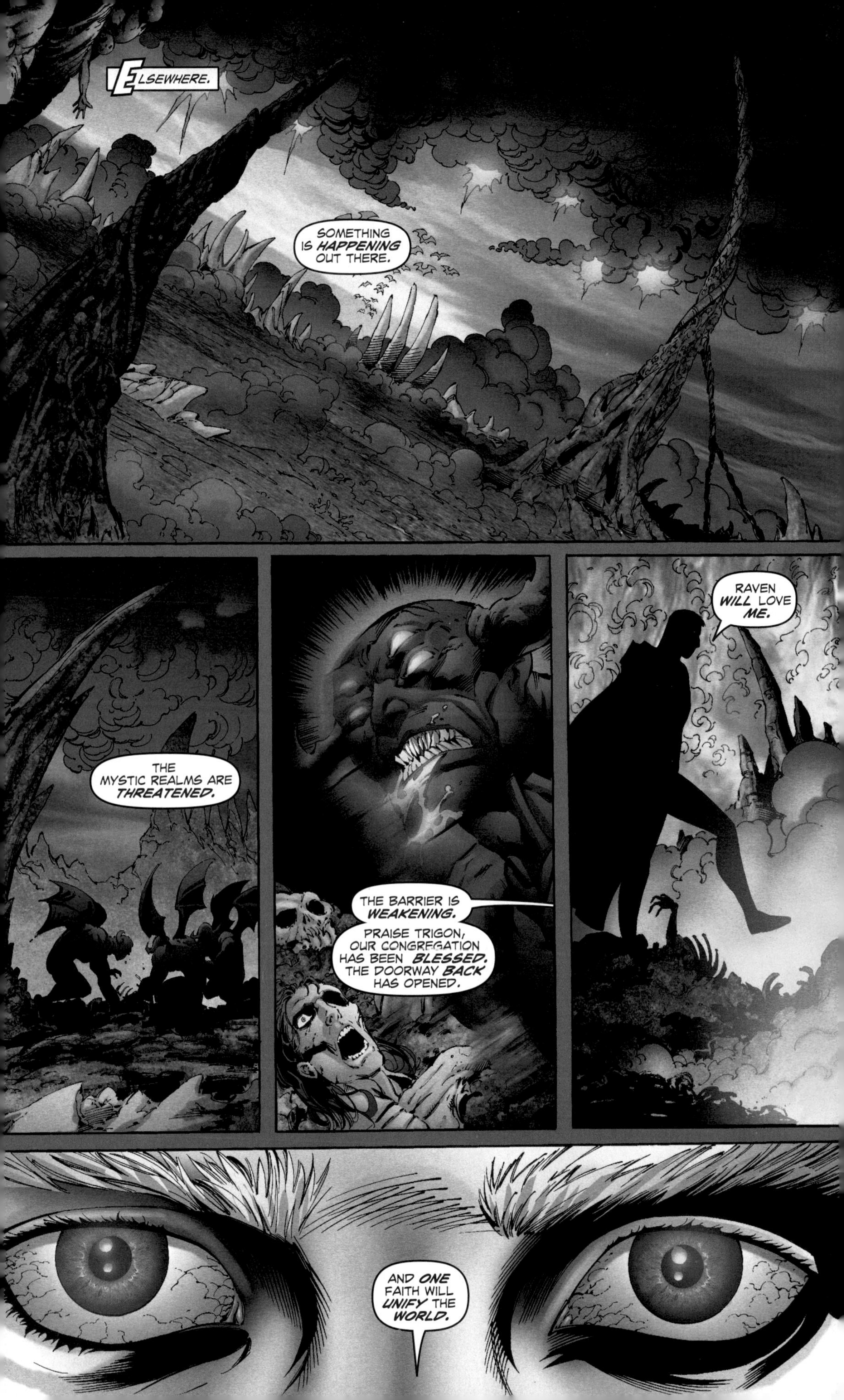
ELSEWHERE.
SOMETHING IS HAPPENING OUT THERE.
THE MYSTIC REALMS ARE THREATENED.
THE BARRIER IS WEAKENING.
PRAISE TRIGON, OUR CONGREGATION HAS BEEN BLESSED. THE DOORWAY BACK HAS OPENED.
RAVEN WILL LOVE ME.
AND ONE FAITH WILL UNIFY THE WORLD.

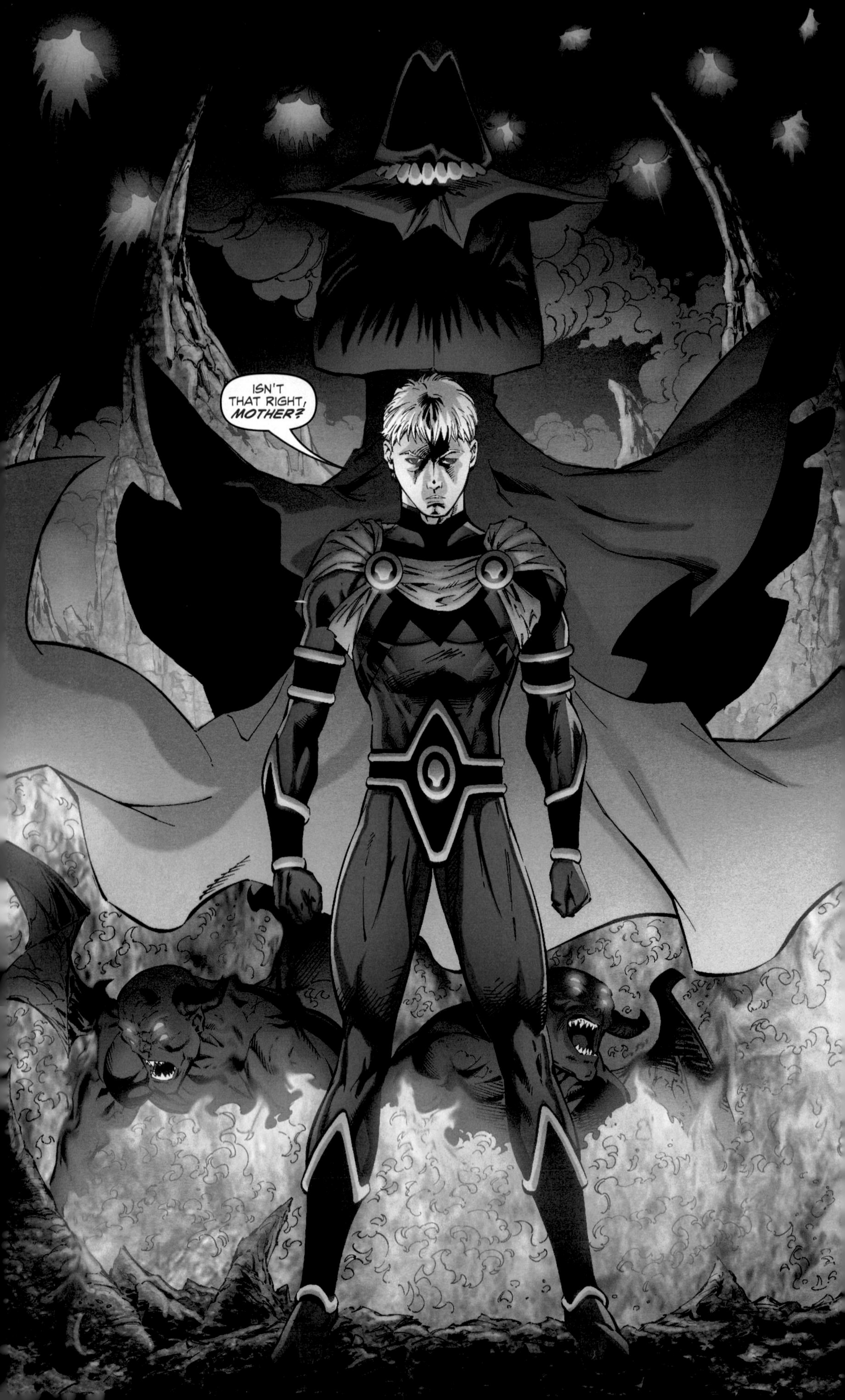
ISN'T THAT RIGHT, MOTHER?

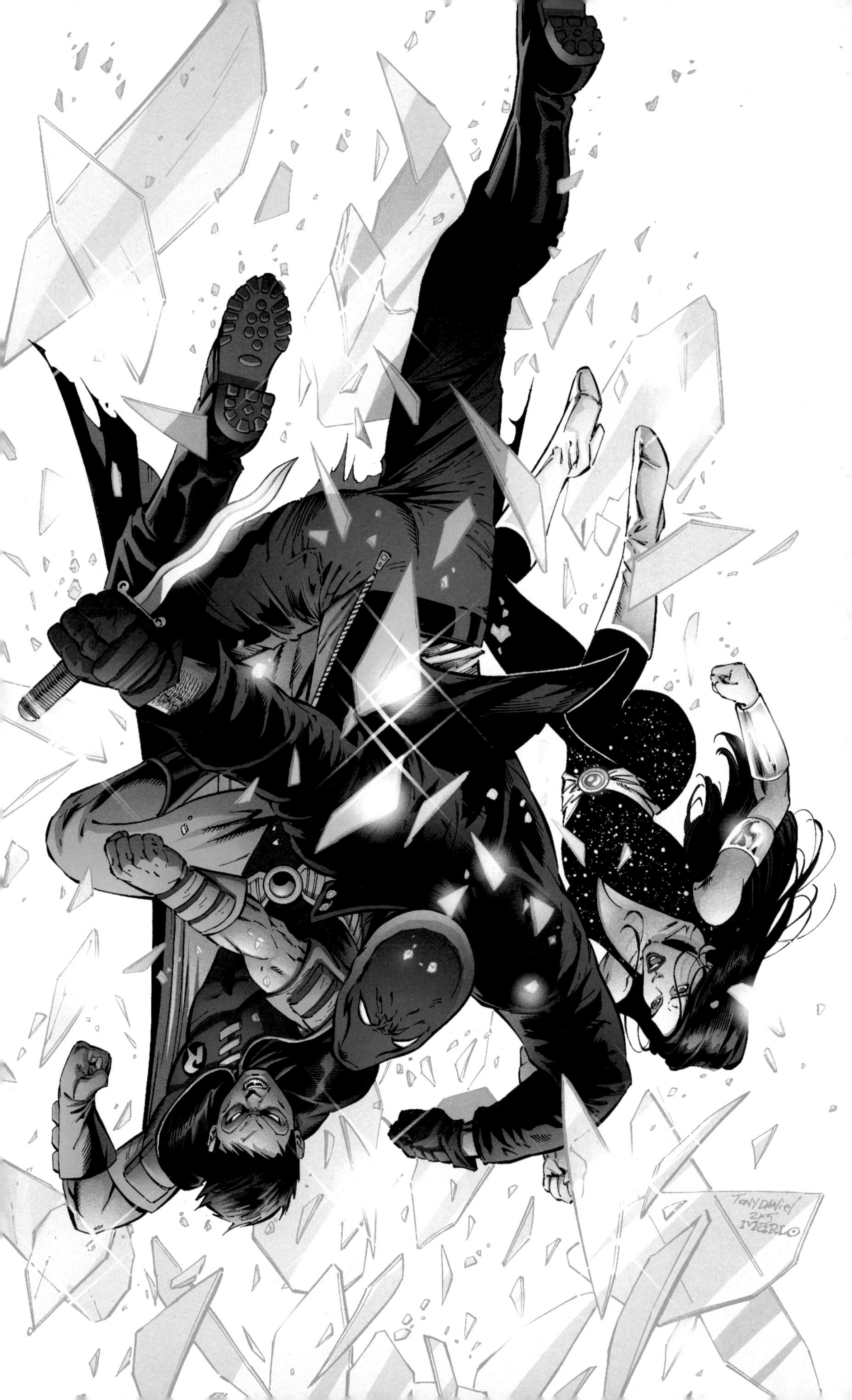
Tony Daniel
2K5
Marlo

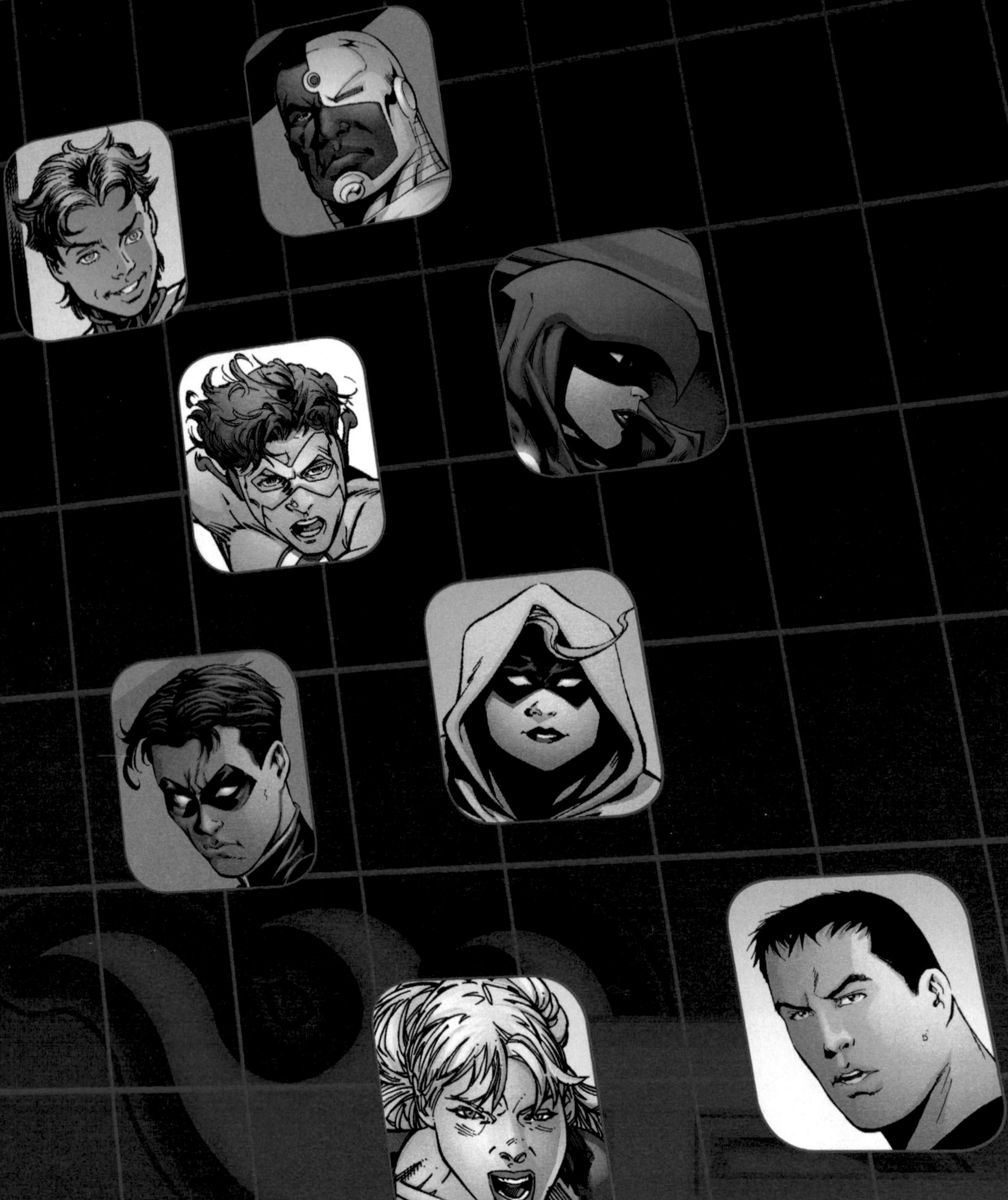

TEEN TITANS #29

GEOFF JOHNS
Writer

TONY S. DANIEL
Penciller

MARLO ALQUIZA
Inker

JEROMY COX
Colorist

PHIL BALSMAN
Letterer

TONY S. DANIEL,
MARLO ALQUIZA & JEROMY COX
Cover Artists

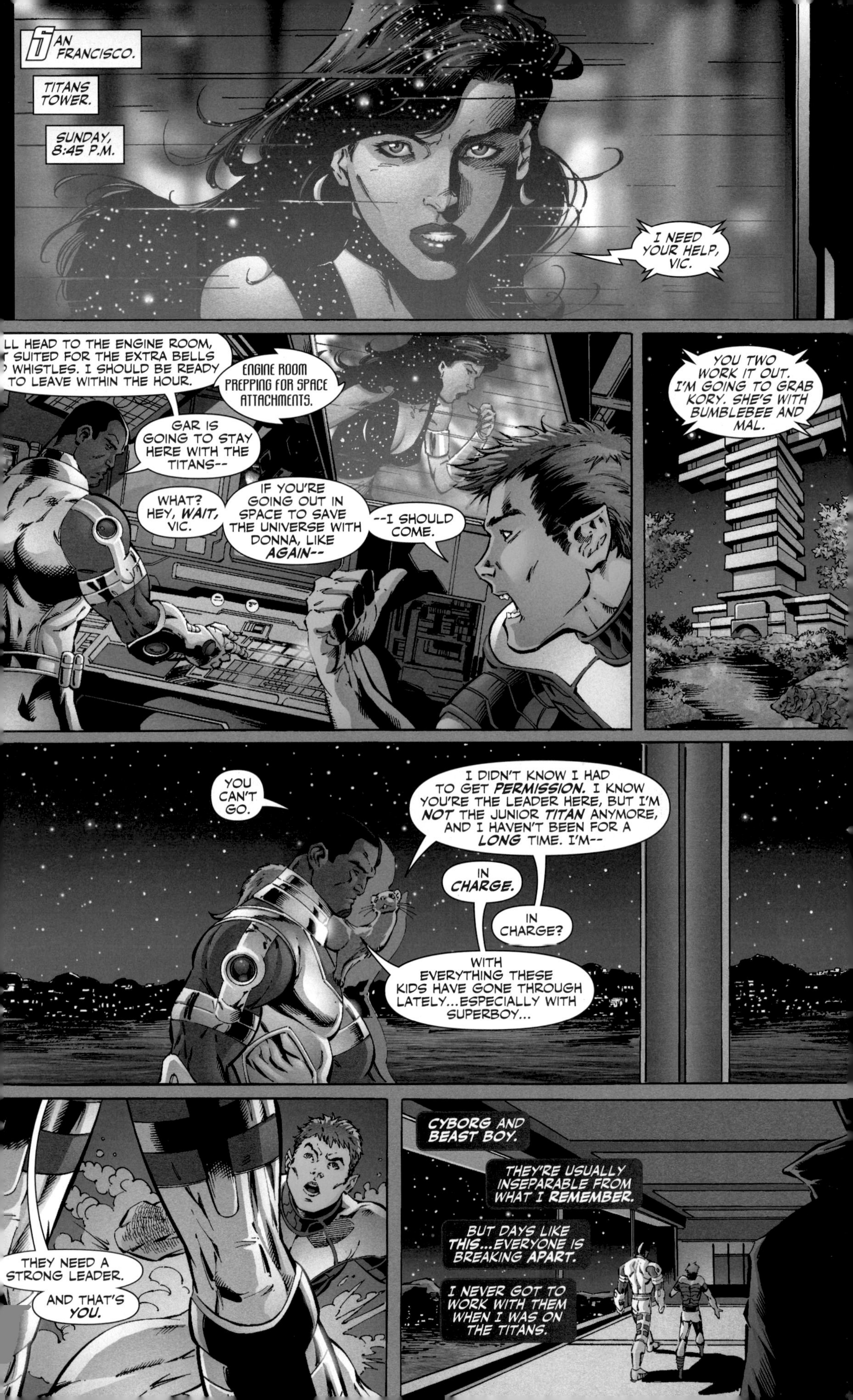
SAN FRANCISCO.
TITANS TOWER.
SUNDAY, 8:45 P.M.
I NEED YOUR HELP, VIC.
LL HEAD TO THE ENGINE ROOM, T SUITED FOR THE EXTRA BELLS D WHISTLES. I SHOULD BE READY TO LEAVE WITHIN THE HOUR.
ENGINE ROOM PREPPING FOR SPACE ATTACHMENTS.
GAR IS GOING TO STAY HERE WITH THE TITANS--
WHAT? HEY, WAIT, VIC.
IF YOU'RE GOING OUT IN SPACE TO SAVE THE UNIVERSE WITH DONNA, LIKE AGAIN--
--I SHOULD COME.
YOU TWO WORK IT OUT. I'M GOING TO GRAB KORY. SHE'S WITH BUMBLEBEE AND MAL.
YOU CAN'T GO.
I DIDN'T KNOW I HAD TO GET PERMISSION. I KNOW YOU'RE THE LEADER HERE, BUT I'M NOT THE JUNIOR TITAN ANYMORE, AND I HAVEN'T BEEN FOR A LONG TIME. I'M--
IN CHARGE.
IN CHARGE?
WITH EVERYTHING THESE KIDS HAVE GONE THROUGH LATELY...ESPECIALLY WITH SUPERBOY...
THEY NEED A STRONG LEADER.
AND THAT'S YOU.
CYBORG AND BEAST BOY.
THEY'RE USUALLY INSEPARABLE FROM WHAT I REMEMBER.
BUT DAYS LIKE THIS...EVERYONE IS BREAKING APART.
I NEVER GOT TO WORK WITH THEM WHEN I WAS ON THE TITANS.

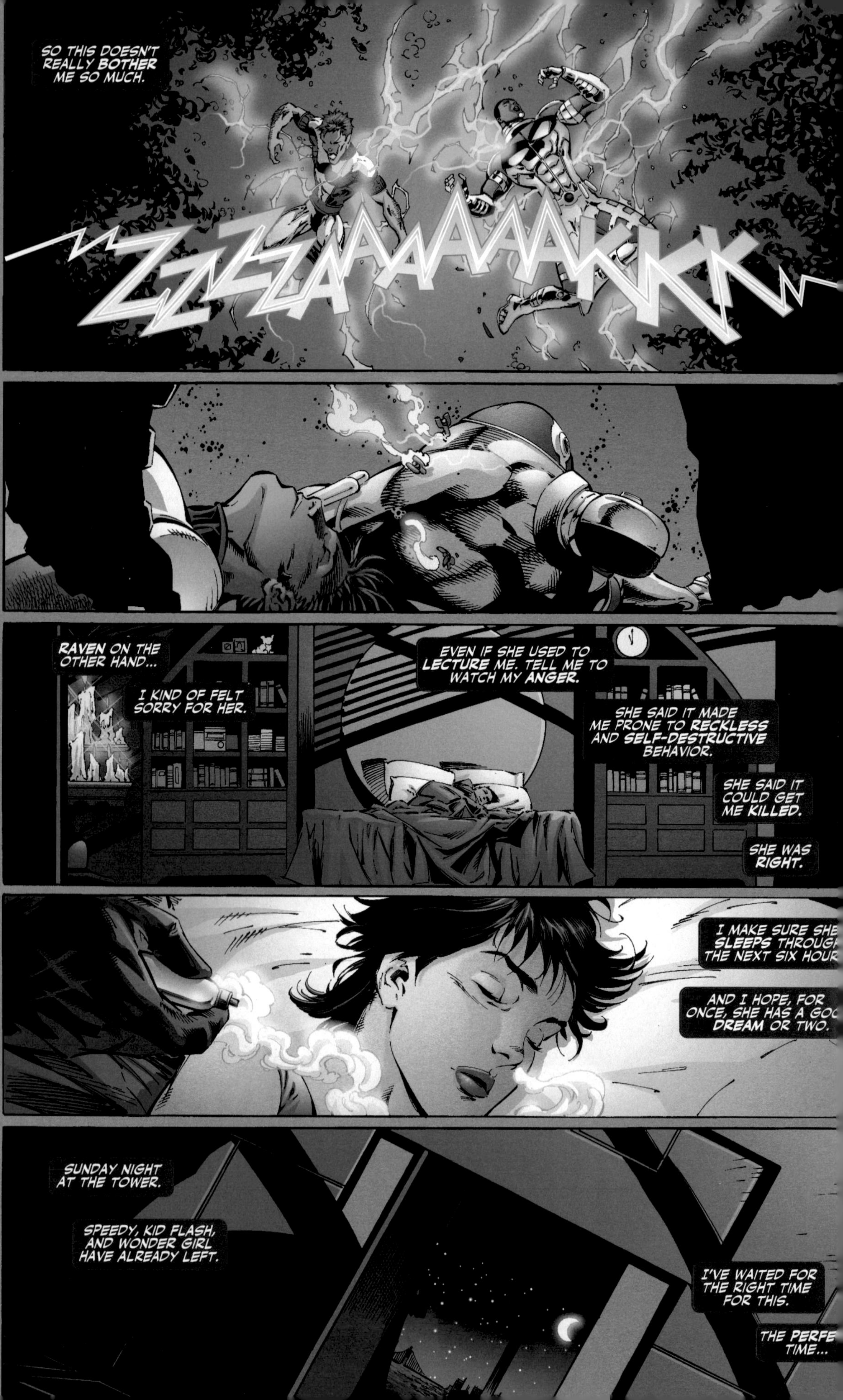
SO THIS DOESN'T REALLY BOTHER ME SO MUCH.
ZZZZAAAAAAKKK
RAVEN ON THE OTHER HAND...
I KIND OF FELT SORRY FOR HER.
EVEN IF SHE USED TO LECTURE ME. TELL ME TO WATCH MY ANGER.
SHE SAID IT MADE ME PRONE TO RECKLESS AND SELF-DESTRUCTIVE BEHAVIOR.
SHE SAID IT COULD GET ME KILLED.
SHE WAS RIGHT.
I MAKE SURE SHE SLEEPS THROUGH THE NEXT SIX HOUR
AND I HOPE, FOR ONCE, SHE HAS A GOO DREAM OR TWO.
SUNDAY NIGHT AT THE TOWER.
SPEEDY, KID FLASH, AND WONDER GIRL HAVE ALREADY LEFT.
I'VE WAITED FOR THE RIGHT TIME FOR THIS.
THE PERFE TIME...

TO MEET TIM DRAKE.

I WISH THERE WAS SOMETHING I COULD DO, BRUCE. I DON'T REALLY KNOW THE MARTIAN MANHUNTER WELL, BUT IF HE'S MISSING...

LOOK, IT'S OKAY. I'LL ASK CYBORG FOR A RIDE HOME.

GOOD LUCK.

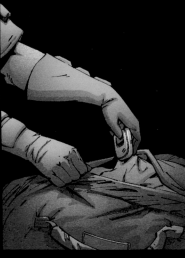

HEY, TIM.

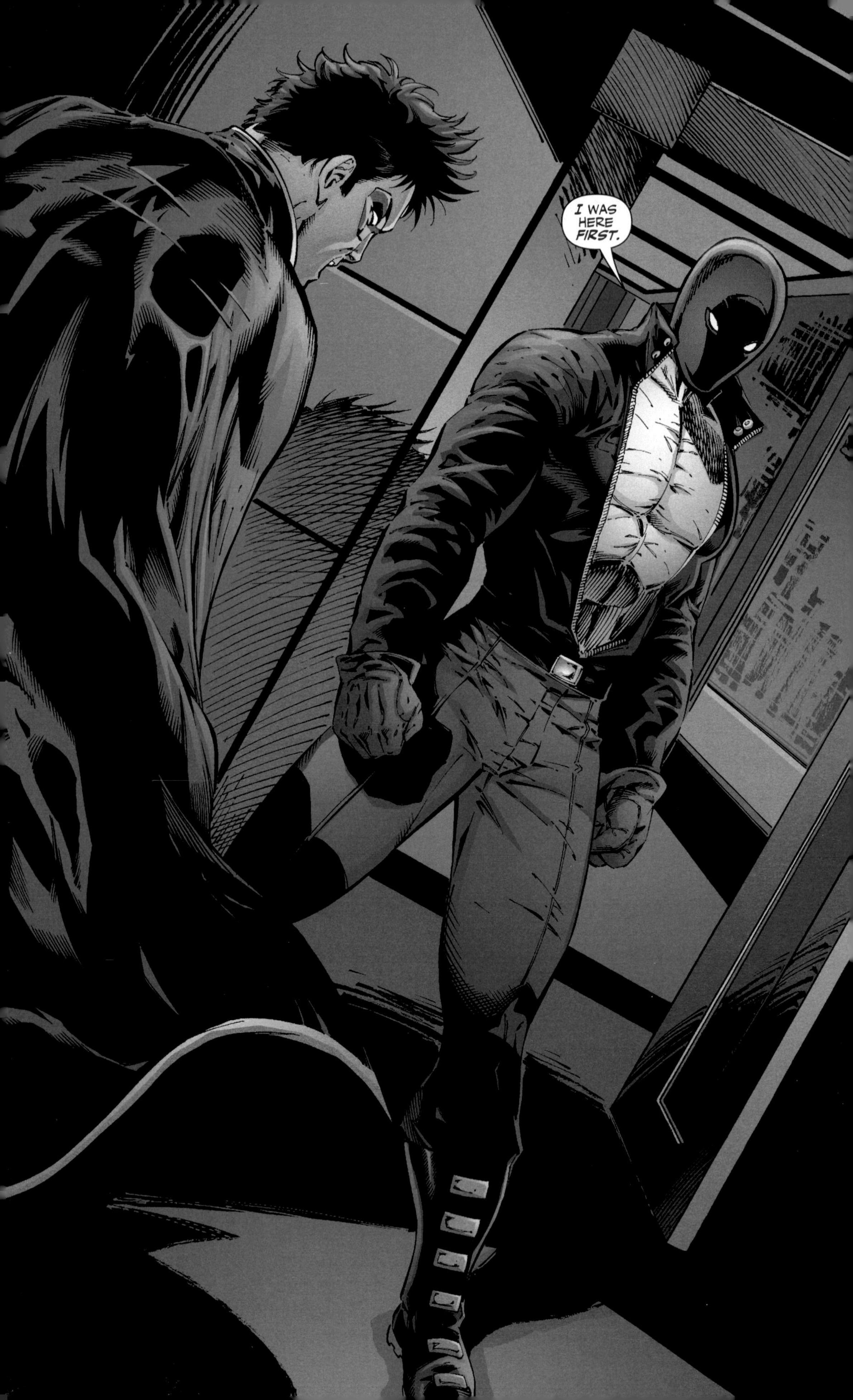
I WAS HERE FIRST.

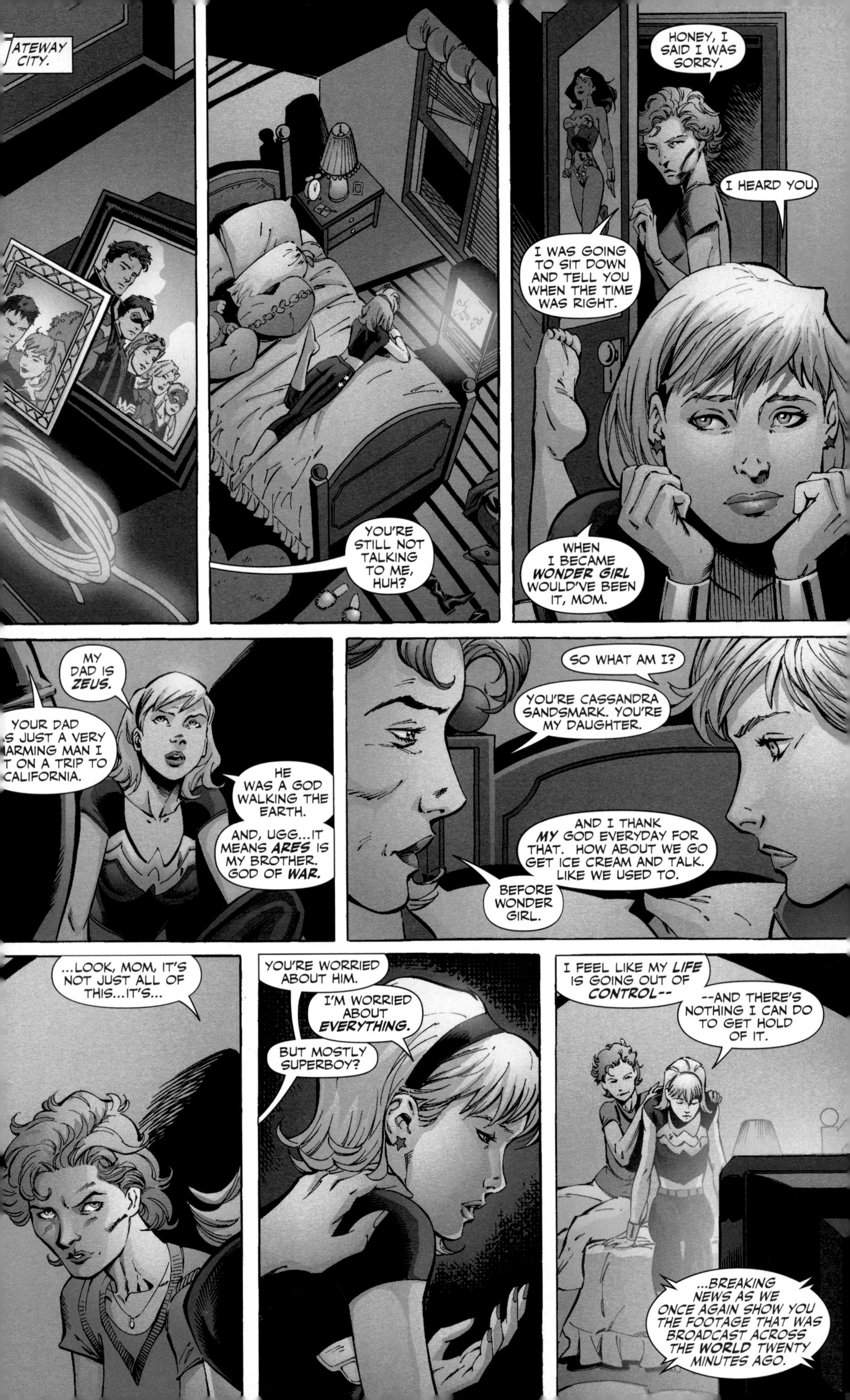

GATEWAY CITY.
YOU'RE STILL NOT TALKING TO ME, HUH?
HONEY, I SAID I WAS SORRY.
I HEARD YOU.
I WAS GOING TO SIT DOWN AND TELL YOU WHEN THE TIME WAS RIGHT.
WHEN I BECAME WONDER GIRL WOULD'VE BEEN IT, MOM.
MY DAD IS ZEUS.
YOUR DAD IS JUST A VERY CHARMING MAN I MET ON A TRIP TO CALIFORNIA.
HE WAS A GOD WALKING THE EARTH.
AND, UGG...IT MEANS ARES IS MY BROTHER. GOD OF WAR.
SO WHAT AM I?
YOU'RE CASSANDRA SANDSMARK. YOU'RE MY DAUGHTER.
AND I THANK MY GOD EVERYDAY FOR THAT. HOW ABOUT WE GO GET ICE CREAM AND TALK. LIKE WE USED TO.
BEFORE WONDER GIRL.
...LOOK, MOM, IT'S NOT JUST ALL OF THIS...IT'S...
YOU'RE WORRIED ABOUT HIM.
I'M WORRIED ABOUT EVERYTHING.
BUT MOSTLY SUPERBOY?
I FEEL LIKE MY LIFE IS GOING OUT OF CONTROL--
--AND THERE'S NOTHING I CAN DO TO GET HOLD OF IT.
...BREAKING NEWS AS WE ONCE AGAIN SHOW YOU THE FOOTAGE THAT WAS BROADCAST ACROSS THE WORLD TWENTY MINUTES AGO.

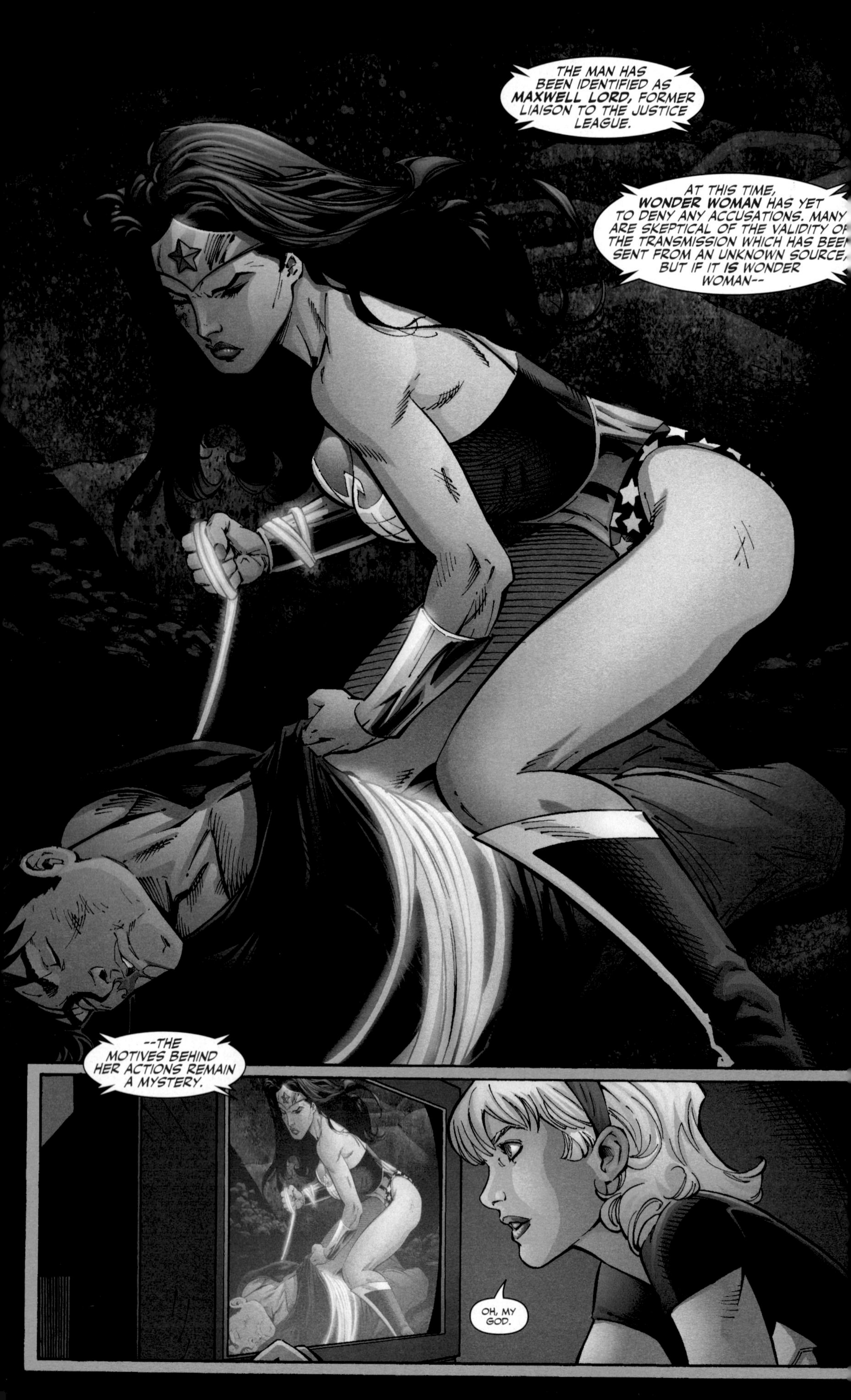
THE MAN HAS BEEN IDENTIFIED AS MAXWELL LORD, FORMER LIAISON TO THE JUSTICE LEAGUE.
AT THIS TIME, WONDER WOMAN HAS YET TO DENY ANY ACCUSATIONS. MANY ARE SKEPTICAL OF THE VALIDITY OF THE TRANSMISSION WHICH HAS BEEN SENT FROM AN UNKNOWN SOURCE, BUT IF IT IS WONDER WOMAN--
--THE MOTIVES BEHIND HER ACTIONS REMAIN A MYSTERY.
OH, MY GOD.

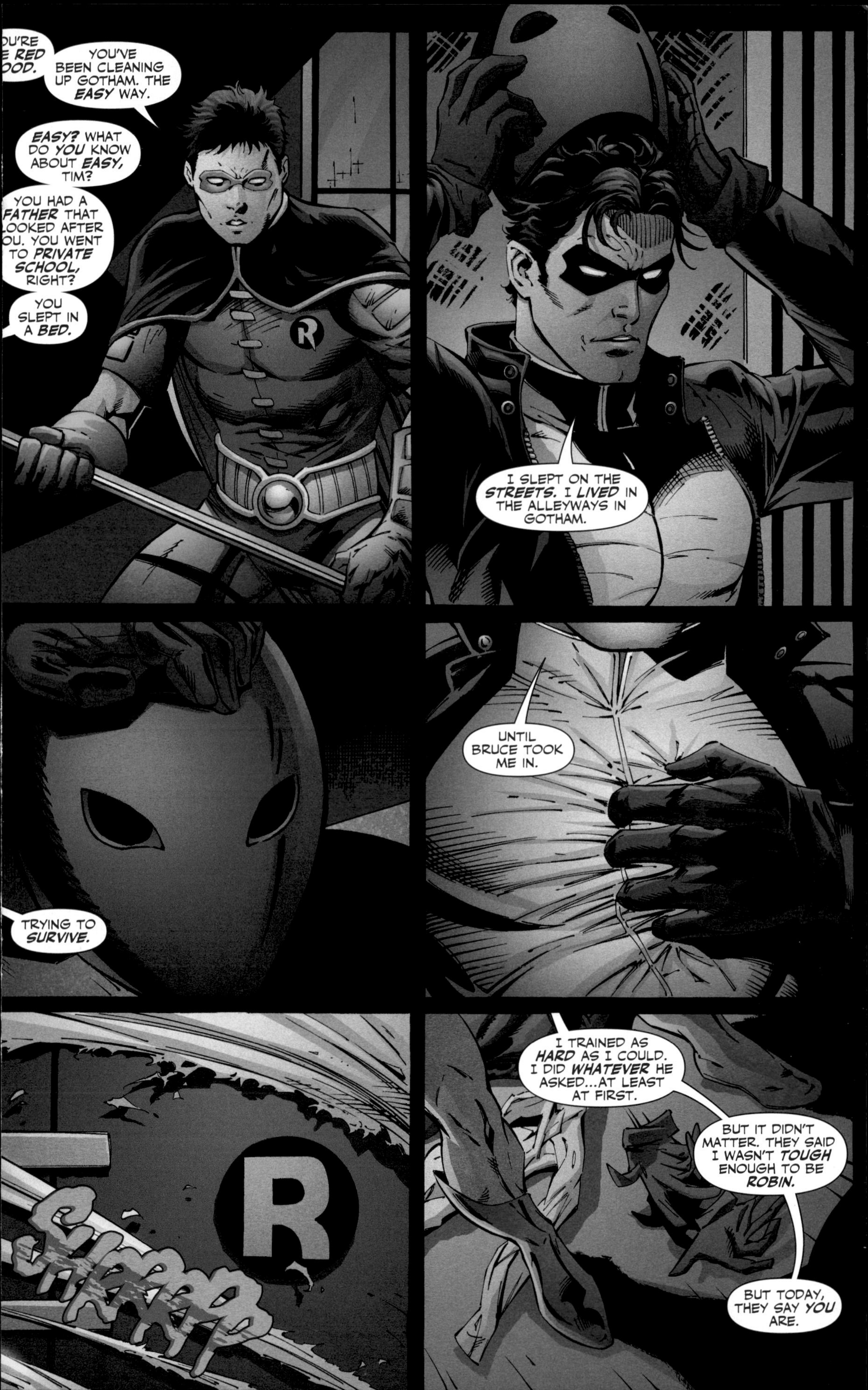

U'RE
E RED
OOD.
YOU'VE BEEN CLEANING UP GOTHAM. THE EASY WAY.
EASY? WHAT DO YOU KNOW ABOUT EASY, TIM?
YOU HAD A FATHER THAT LOOKED AFTER OU. YOU WENT TO PRIVATE SCHOOL, RIGHT?
YOU SLEPT IN A BED.
I SLEPT ON THE STREETS. I LIVED IN THE ALLEYWAYS IN GOTHAM.
TRYING TO SURVIVE.
UNTIL BRUCE TOOK ME IN.
SHRRP
I TRAINED AS HARD AS I COULD. I DID WHATEVER HE ASKED...AT LEAST AT FIRST.
BUT IT DIDN'T MATTER. THEY SAID I WASN'T TOUGH ENOUGH TO BE ROBIN.
BUT TODAY, THEY SAY YOU ARE.

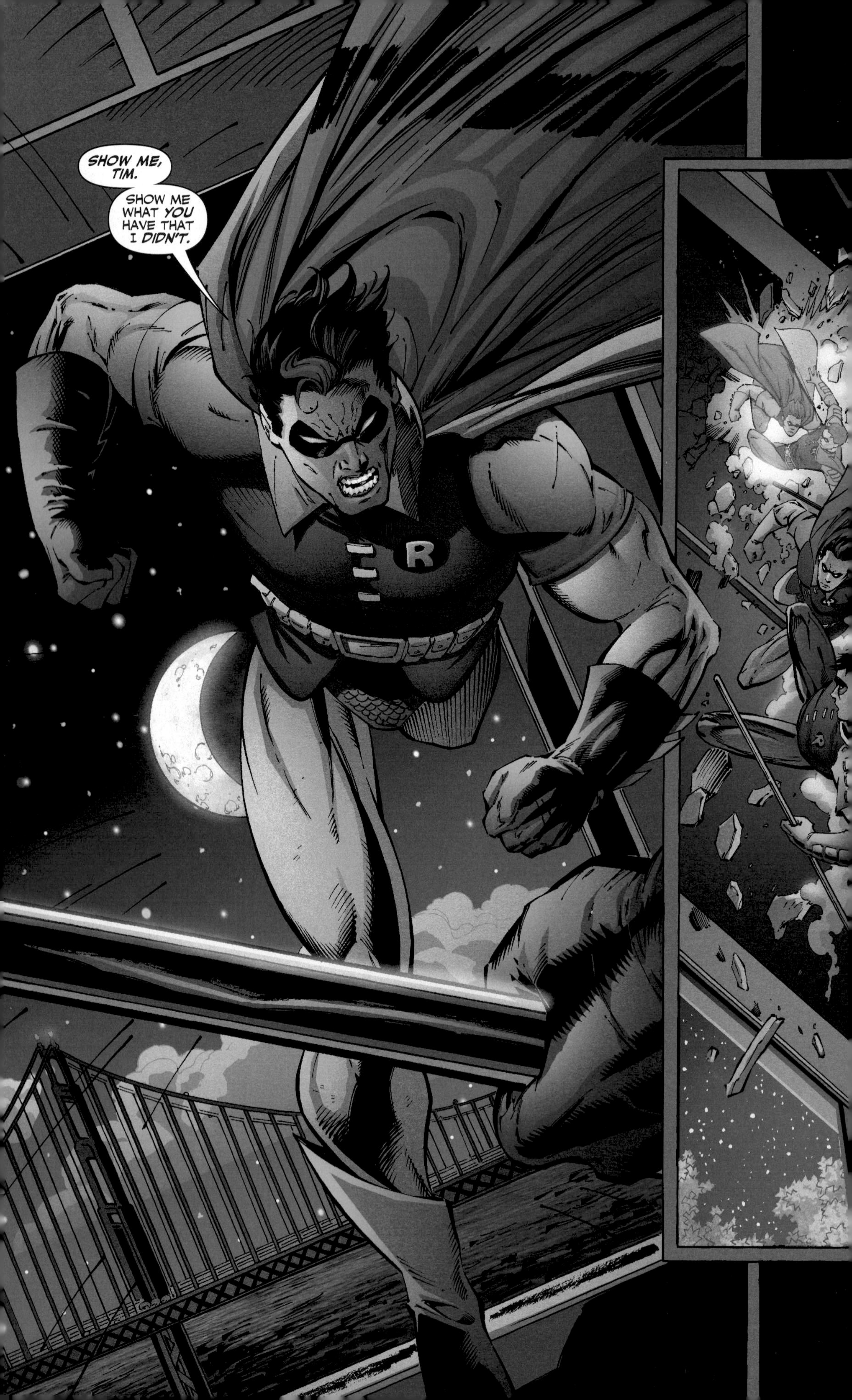
SHOW ME, TIM.
SHOW ME WHAT YOU HAVE THAT I DIDN'T.

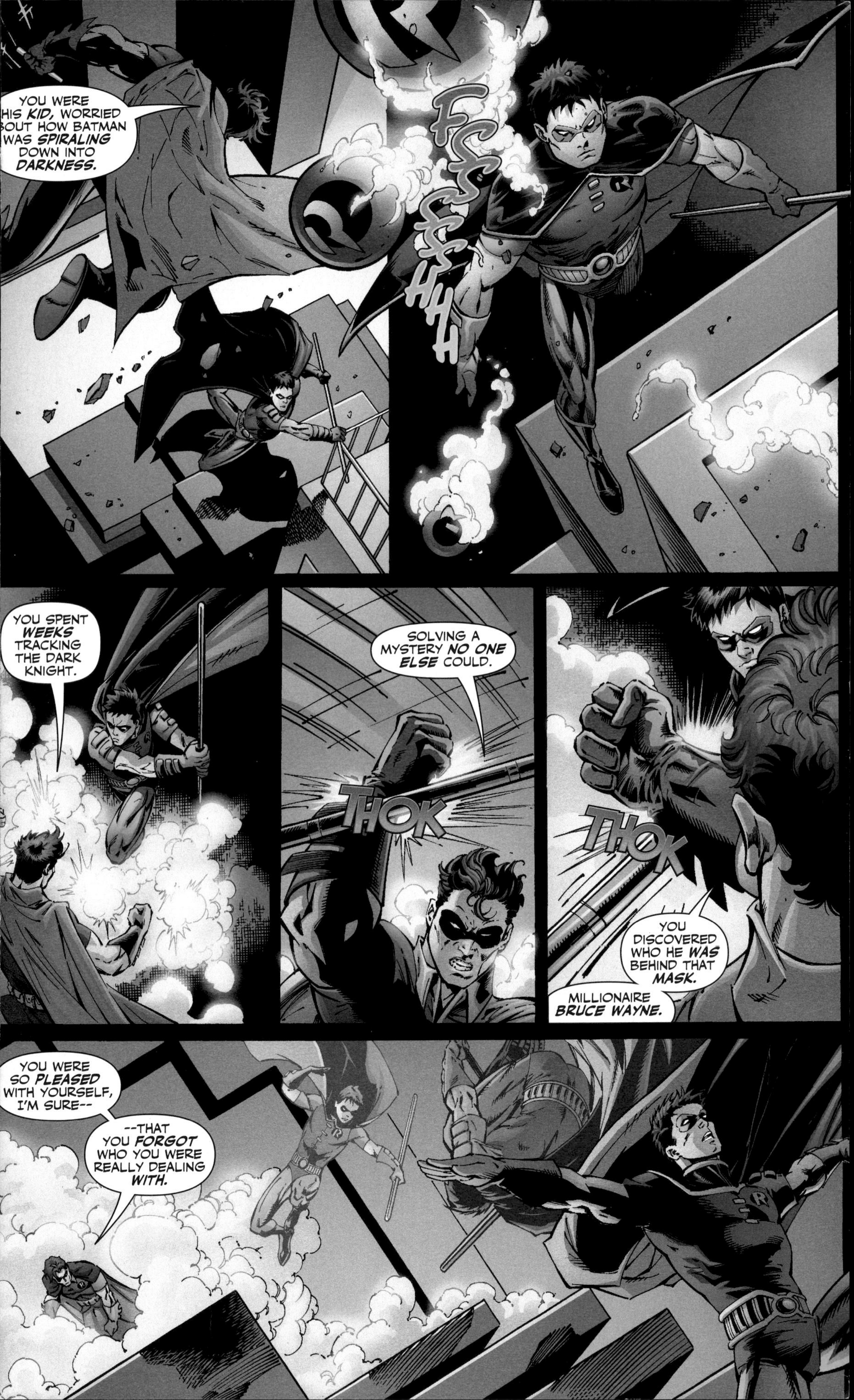

YOU WERE HIS KID, WORRIED 'BOUT HOW BATMAN WAS SPIRALING DOWN INTO DARKNESS.
FSSSHHHH
YOU SPENT WEEKS TRACKING THE DARK KNIGHT.
SOLVING A MYSTERY NO ONE ELSE COULD.
THOK
THOK
YOU DISCOVERED WHO HE WAS BEHIND THAT MASK.
MILLIONAIRE BRUCE WAYNE.
YOU WERE SO PLEASED WITH YOURSELF, I'M SURE--
--THAT YOU FORGOT WHO YOU WERE REALLY DEALING WITH.

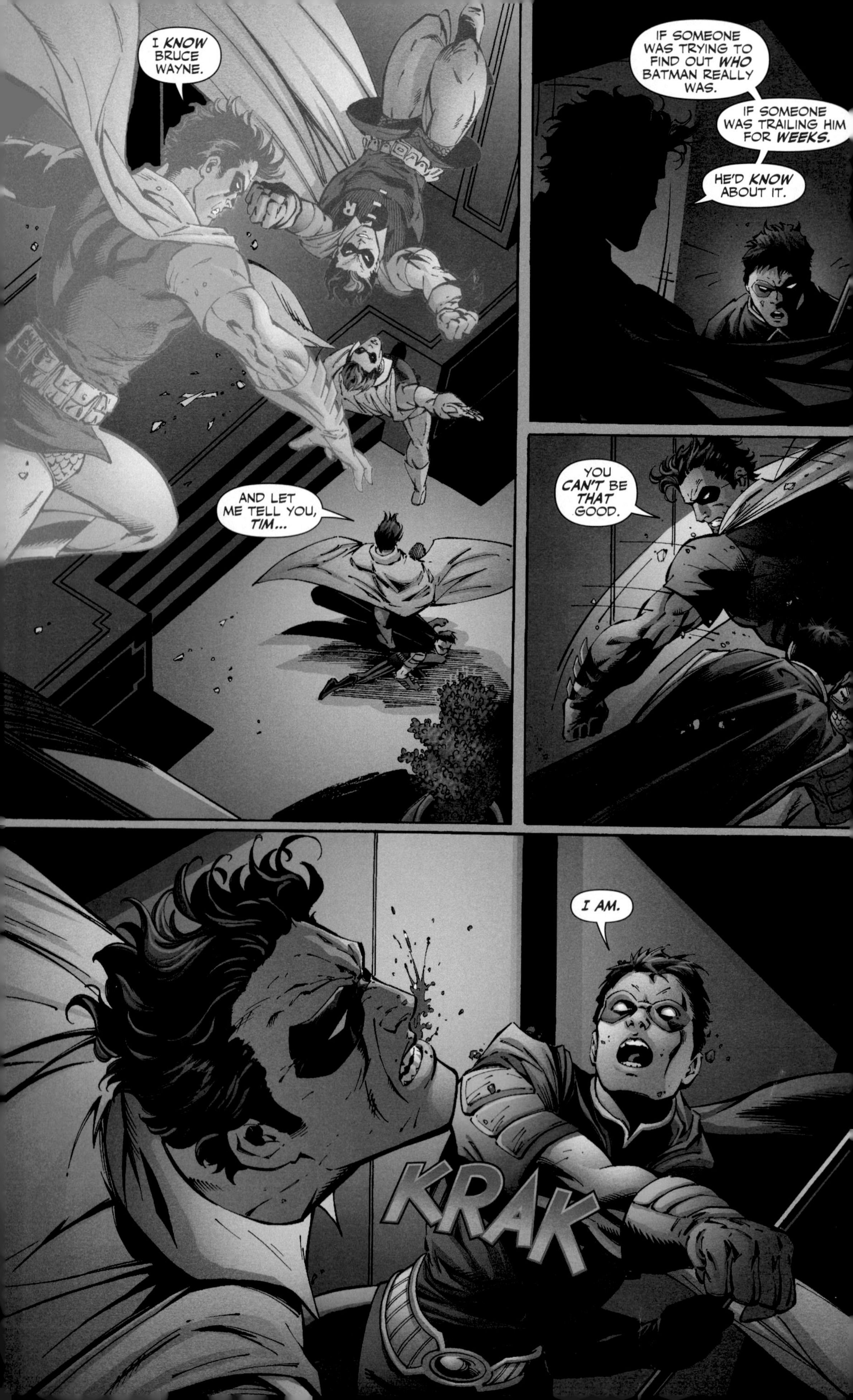
I KNOW BRUCE WAYNE.
AND LET ME TELL YOU, TIM...
IF SOMEONE WAS TRYING TO FIND OUT WHO BATMAN REALLY WAS.
IF SOMEONE WAS TRAILING HIM FOR WEEKS.
HE'D KNOW ABOUT IT.
YOU CAN'T BE THAT GOOD.
I AM.
KRAK

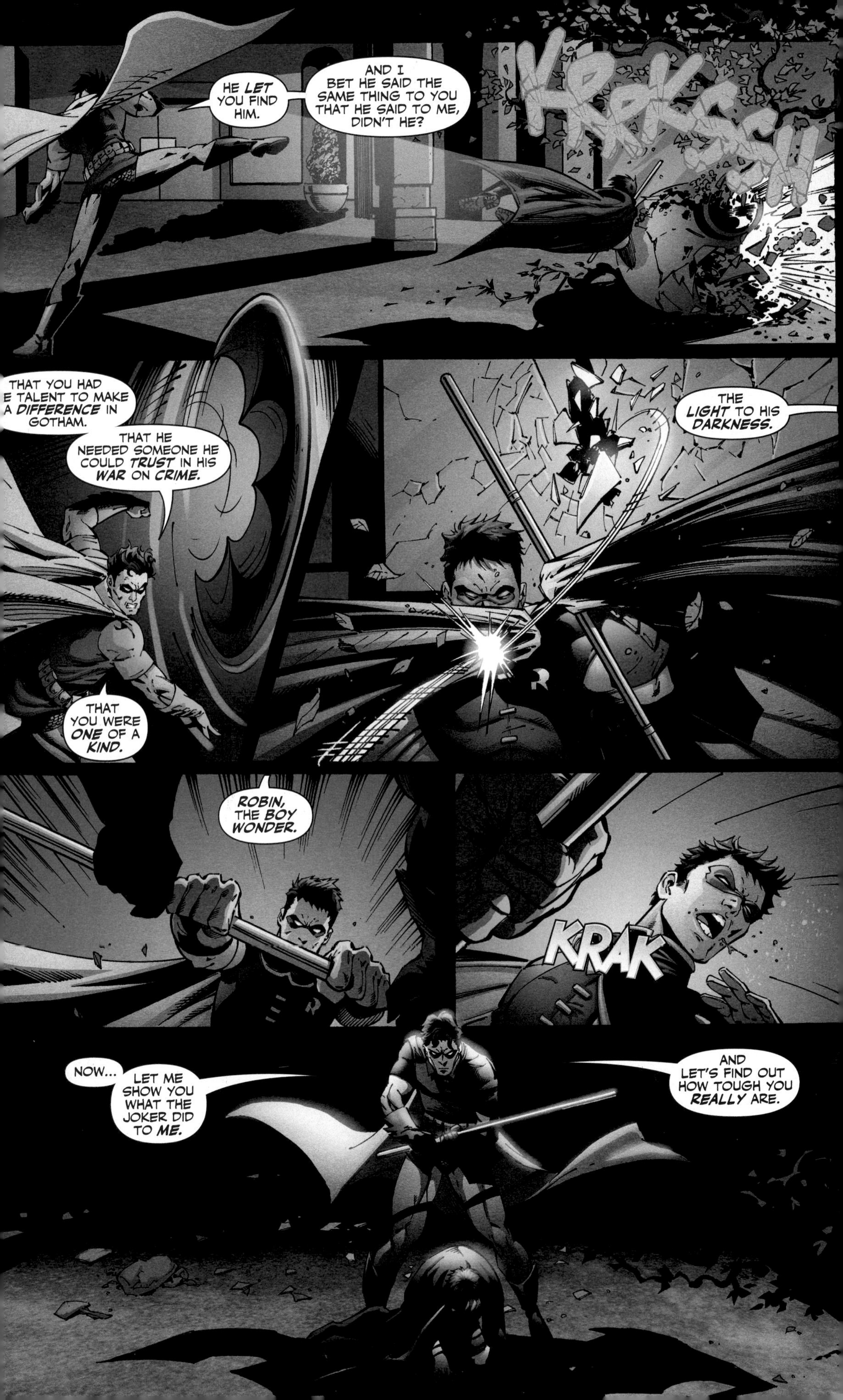
HE LET YOU FIND HIM.
AND I BET HE SAID THE SAME THING TO YOU THAT HE SAID TO ME, DIDN'T HE?
KRRKSSSH
THAT YOU HAD E TALENT TO MAKE A DIFFERENCE IN GOTHAM.
THAT HE NEEDED SOMEONE HE COULD TRUST IN HIS WAR ON CRIME.
THAT YOU WERE ONE OF A KIND.
THE LIGHT TO HIS DARKNESS.
ROBIN, THE BOY WONDER.
KRAK
NOW...
LET ME SHOW YOU WHAT THE JOKER DID TO ME.
AND LET'S FIND OUT HOW TOUGH YOU REALLY ARE.

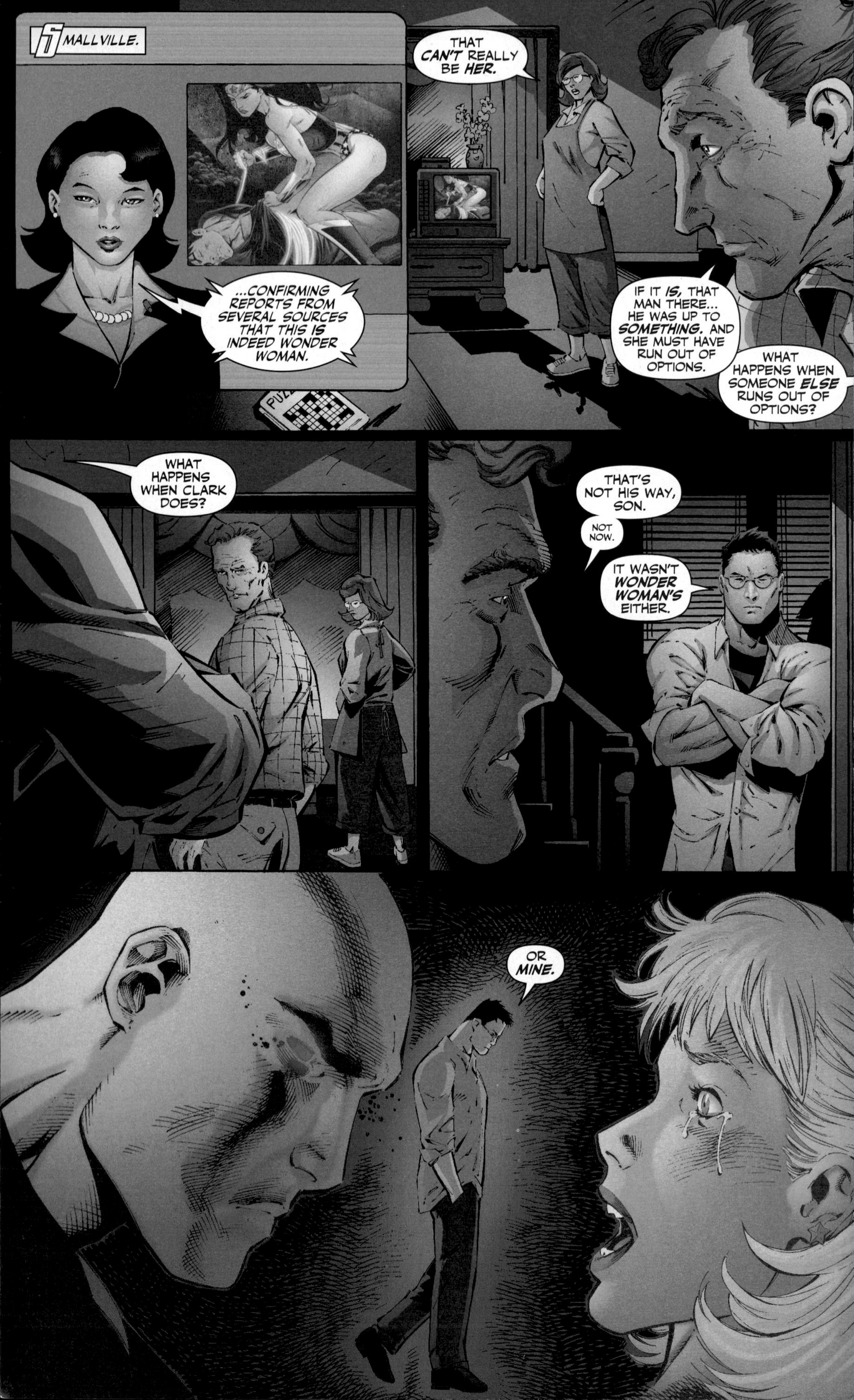
SMALLVILLE.
...CONFIRMING REPORTS FROM SEVERAL SOURCES THAT THIS IS INDEED WONDER WOMAN.
THAT CAN'T REALLY BE HER.
IF IT IS, THAT MAN THERE... HE WAS UP TO SOMETHING. AND SHE MUST HAVE RUN OUT OF OPTIONS.
WHAT HAPPENS WHEN SOMEONE ELSE RUNS OUT OF OPTIONS?
WHAT HAPPENS WHEN CLARK DOES?
THAT'S NOT HIS WAY, SON.
NOT NOW.
IT WASN'T WONDER WOMAN'S EITHER.
OR MINE.

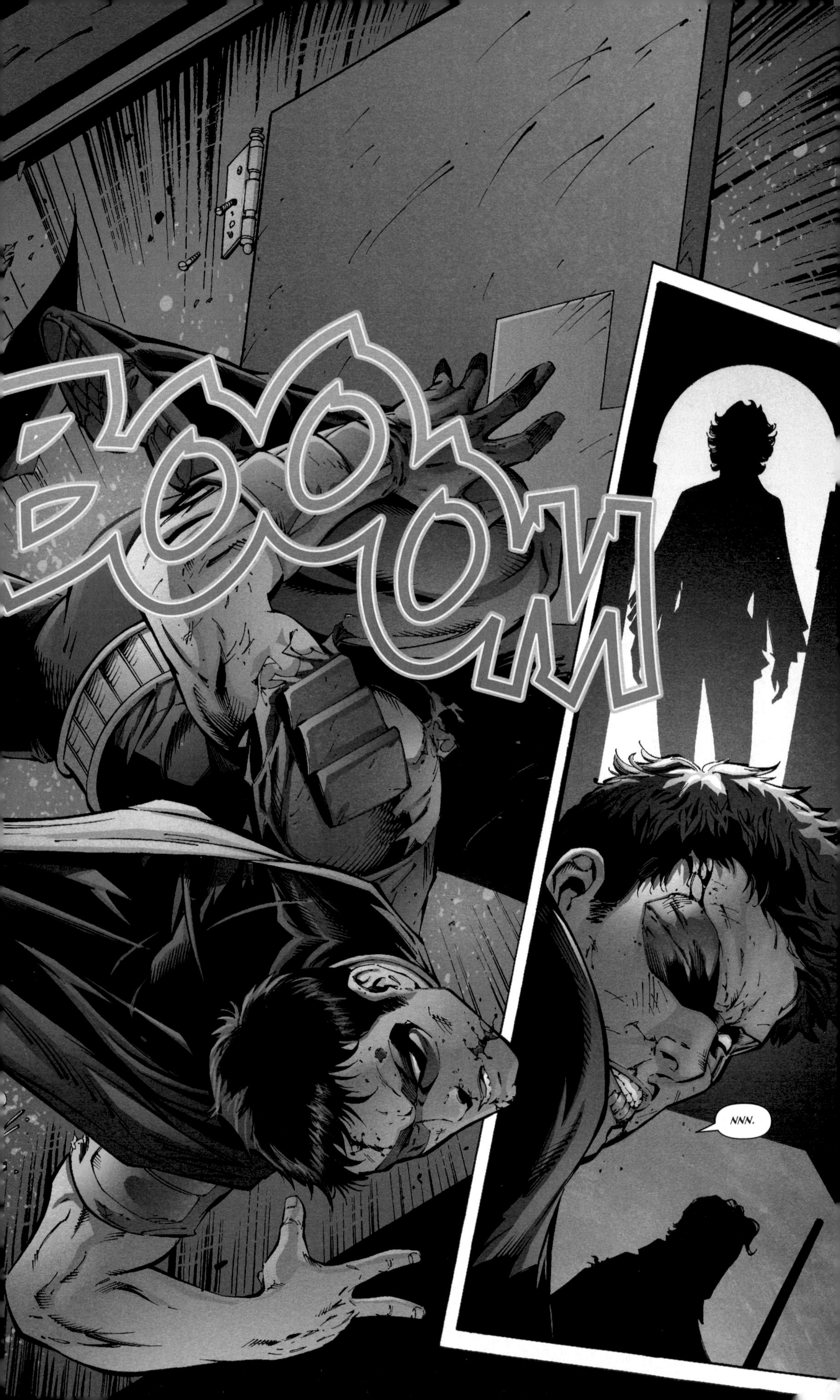
BOOOOM
NNN.

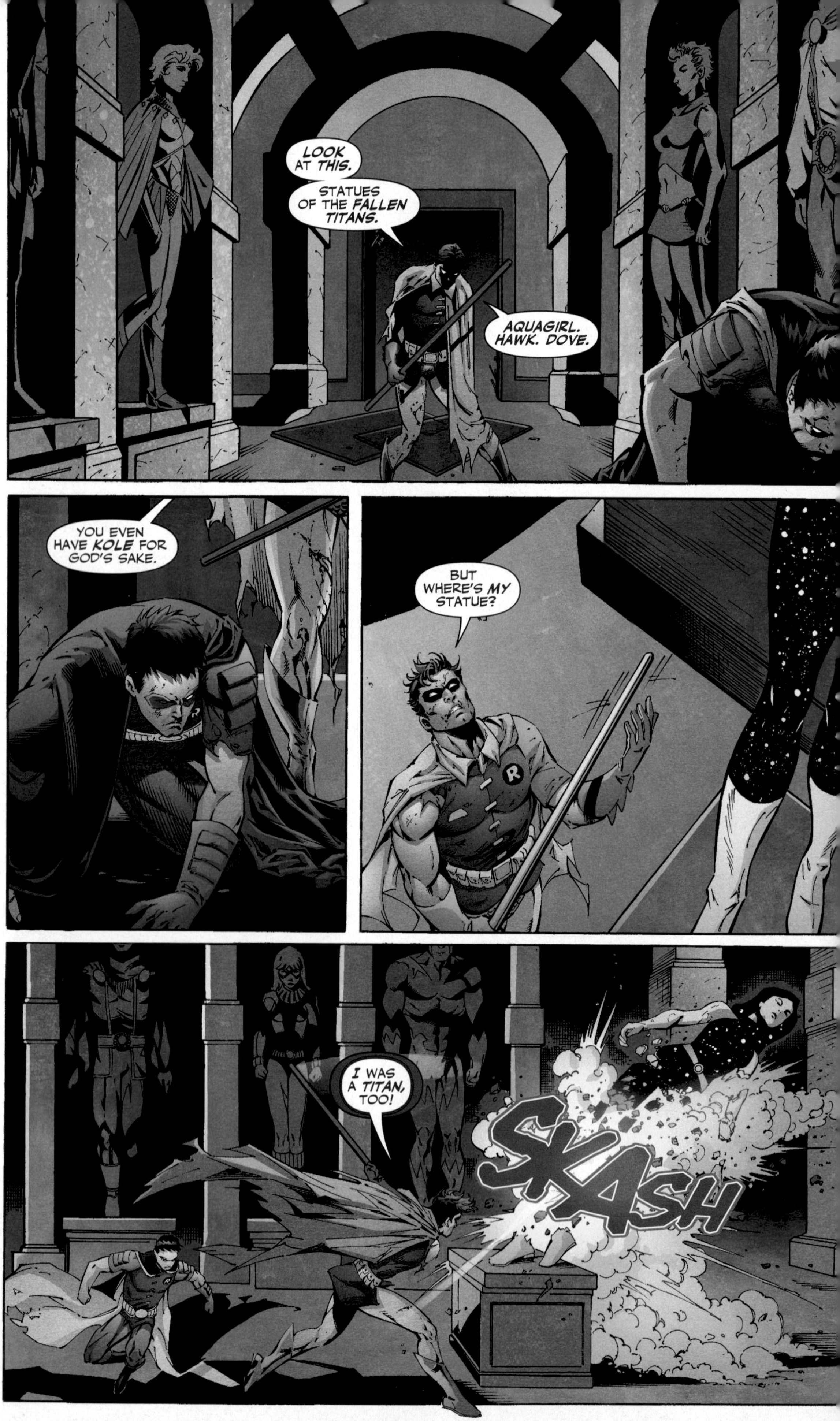
LOOK AT THIS.
STATUES OF THE FALLEN TITANS.
AQUAGIRL. HAWK. DOVE.
YOU EVEN HAVE KOLE FOR GOD'S SAKE.
BUT WHERE'S MY STATUE?
I WAS A TITAN, TOO!
SKASH

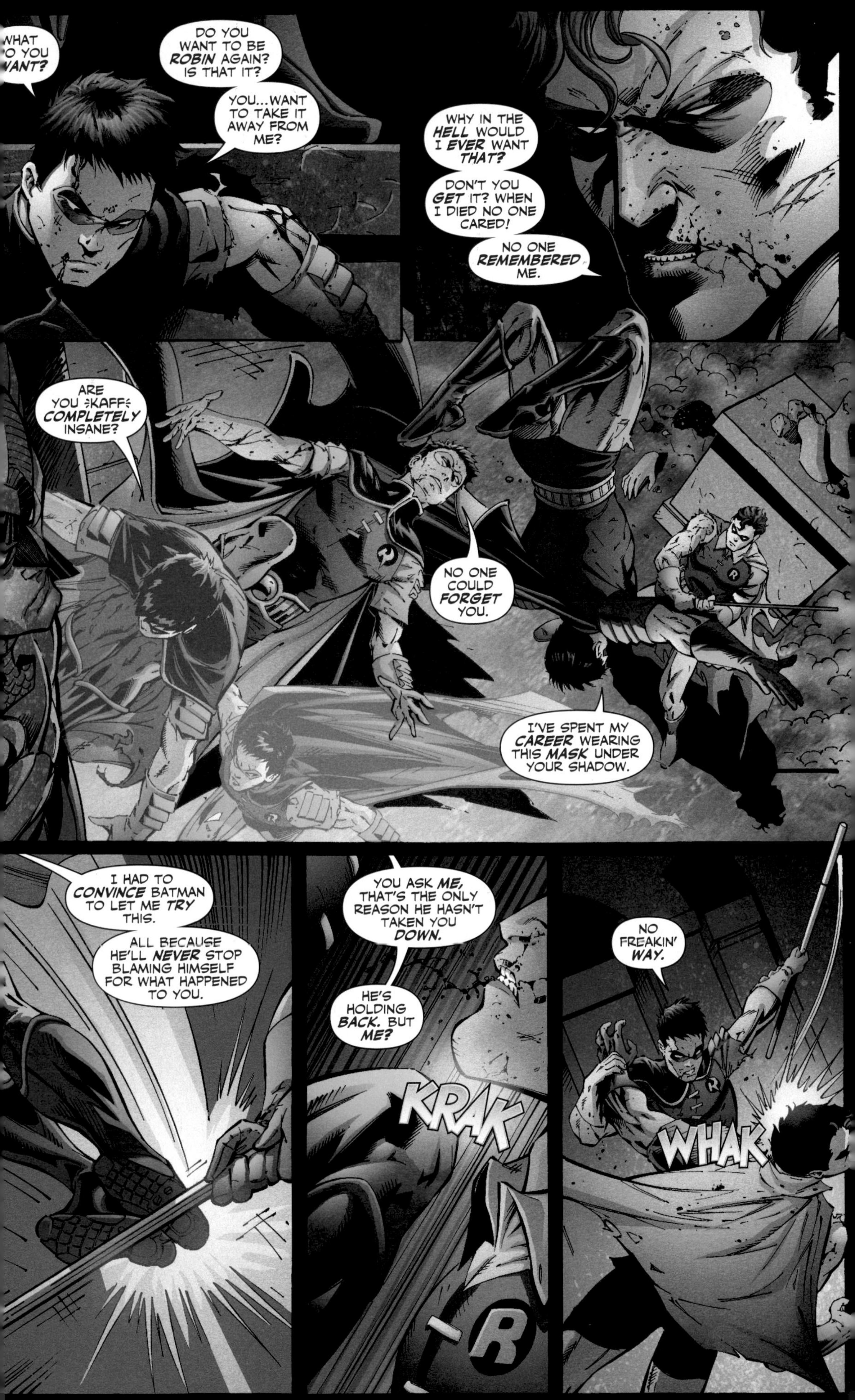

WHAT DO YOU WANT?
DO YOU WANT TO BE ROBIN AGAIN? IS THAT IT?
YOU...WANT TO TAKE IT AWAY FROM ME?
WHY IN THE HELL WOULD I EVER WANT THAT?
DON'T YOU GET IT? WHEN I DIED NO ONE CARED!
NO ONE REMEMBERED ME.
ARE YOU ≑KAFF≑ COMPLETELY INSANE?
NO ONE COULD FORGET YOU.
I'VE SPENT MY CAREER WEARING THIS MASK UNDER YOUR SHADOW.
I HAD TO CONVINCE BATMAN TO LET ME TRY THIS.
ALL BECAUSE HE'LL NEVER STOP BLAMING HIMSELF FOR WHAT HAPPENED TO YOU.
YOU ASK ME, THAT'S THE ONLY REASON HE HASN'T TAKEN YOU DOWN.
HE'S HOLDING BACK. BUT ME?
KRAK
NO FREAKIN' WAY.
WHAK

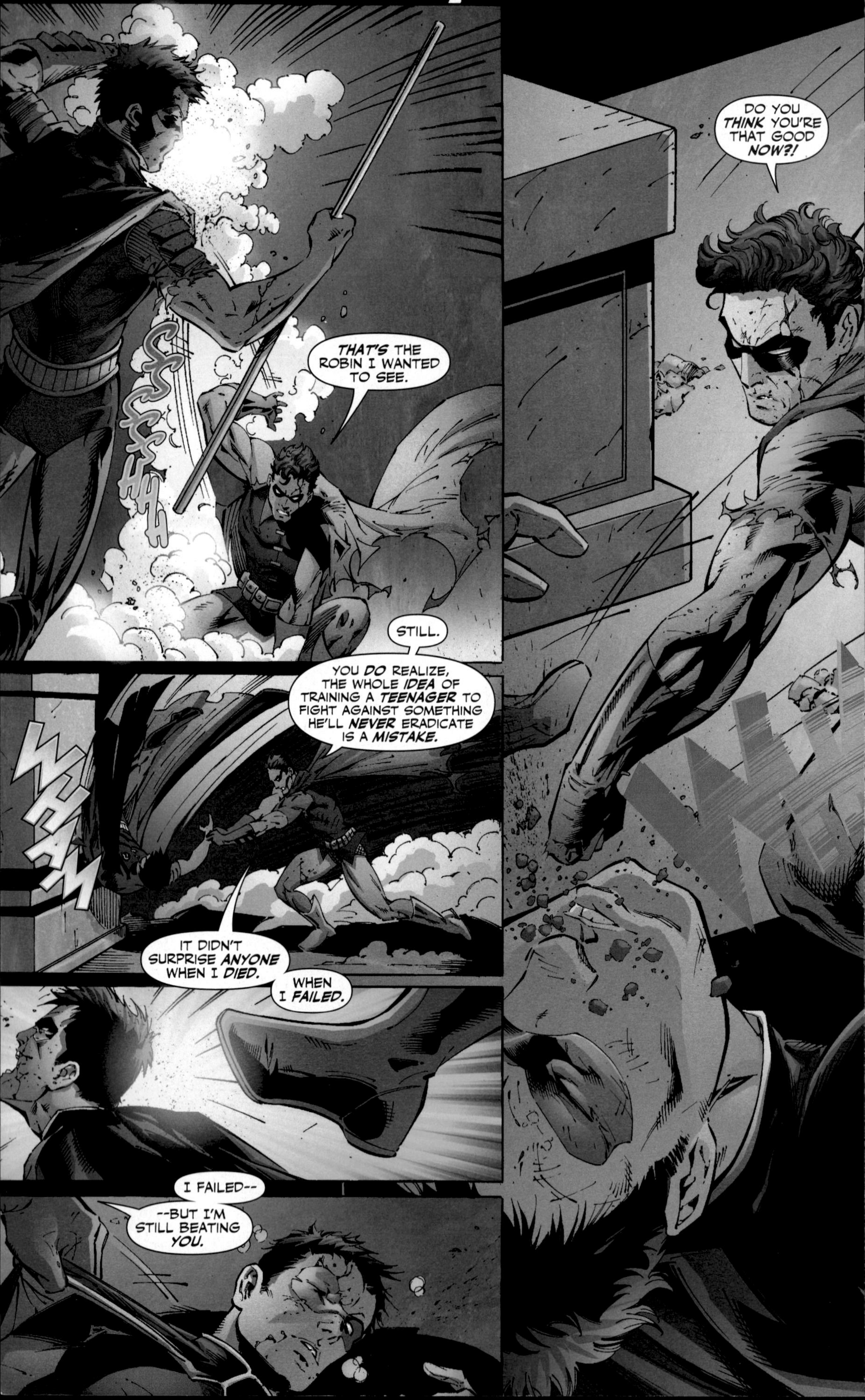

THAT'S THE ROBIN I WANTED TO SEE.
SCCCHHH
STILL.
YOU DO REALIZE, THE WHOLE IDEA OF TRAINING A TEENAGER TO FIGHT AGAINST SOMETHING HE'LL NEVER ERADICATE IS A MISTAKE.
WHAM
IT DIDN'T SURPRISE ANYONE WHEN I DIED.
WHEN I FAILED.
I FAILED--
--BUT I'M STILL BEATING YOU.
DO YOU THINK YOU'RE THAT GOOD NOW?!

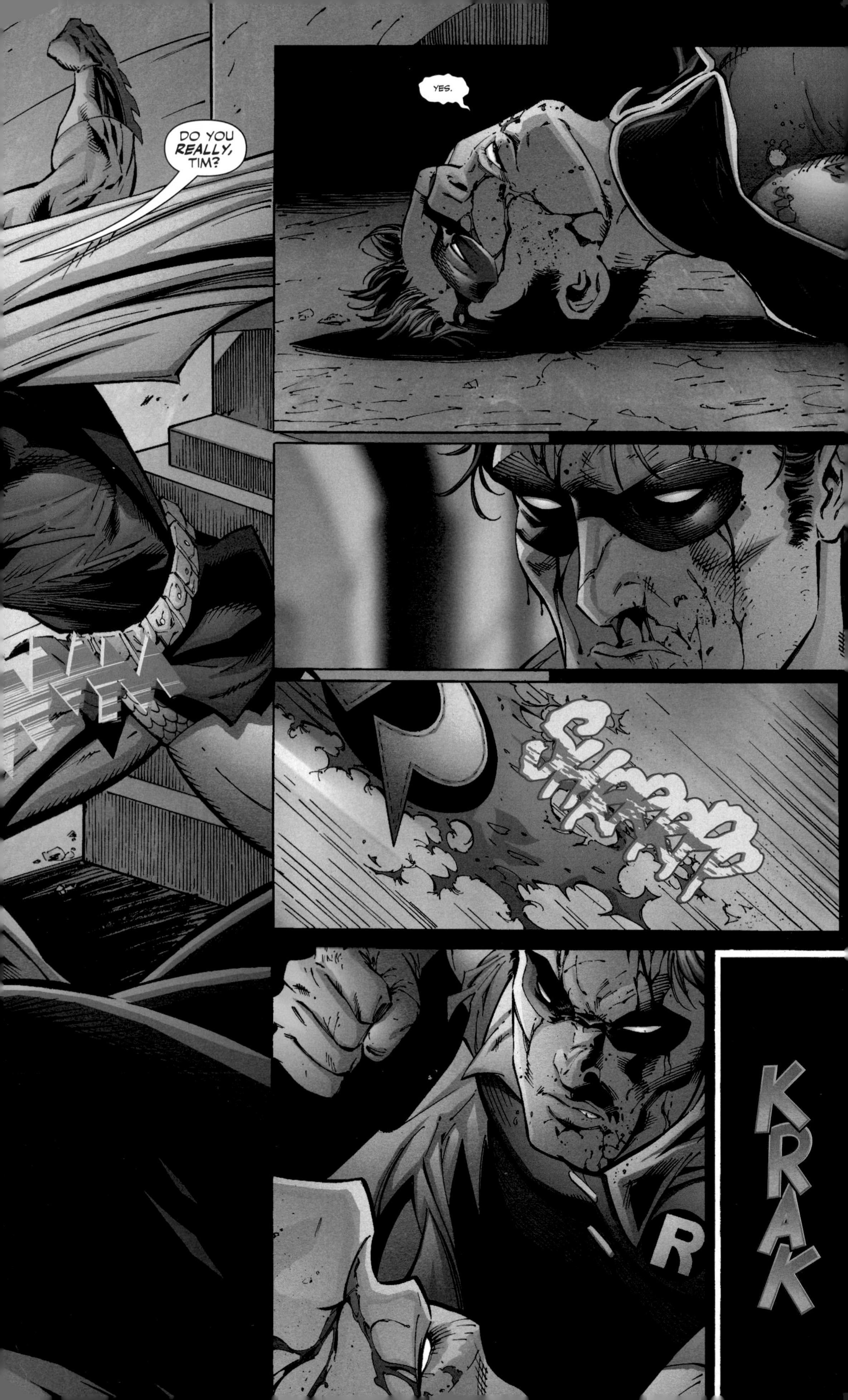
DO YOU *REALLY*, TIM?
YES.
KRAK

OH, MY GOD!

TIM!

C'MON, MAN. HE'S BACK, TOO?

YEAH... I GUESS SO...

RAVEN, MAYBE YOU SHOULD HELP...

WHAT ARE YOU STARING AT?

HOW'D HE GET INTO THE TOWER?

THE SECURITY SYSTEM RUNS A D.N.A. CHECK.

AND JASON *WAS* A TITAN. BRIEFLY.

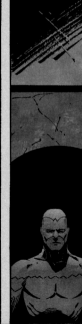

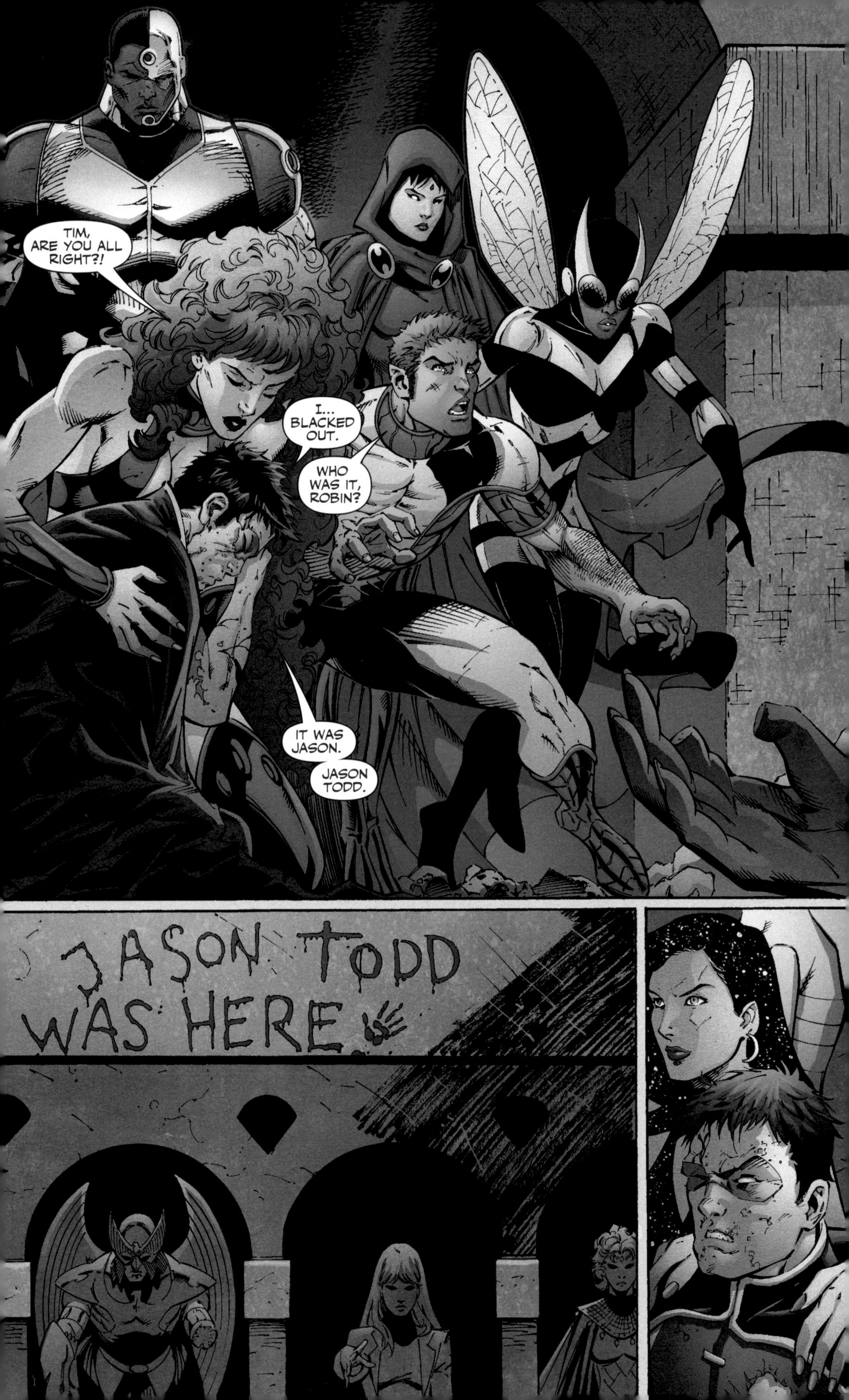
TIM, ARE YOU ALL RIGHT?!
I... BLACKED OUT.
WHO WAS IT, ROBIN?
IT WAS JASON.
JASON TODD.
JASON TODD WAS HERE

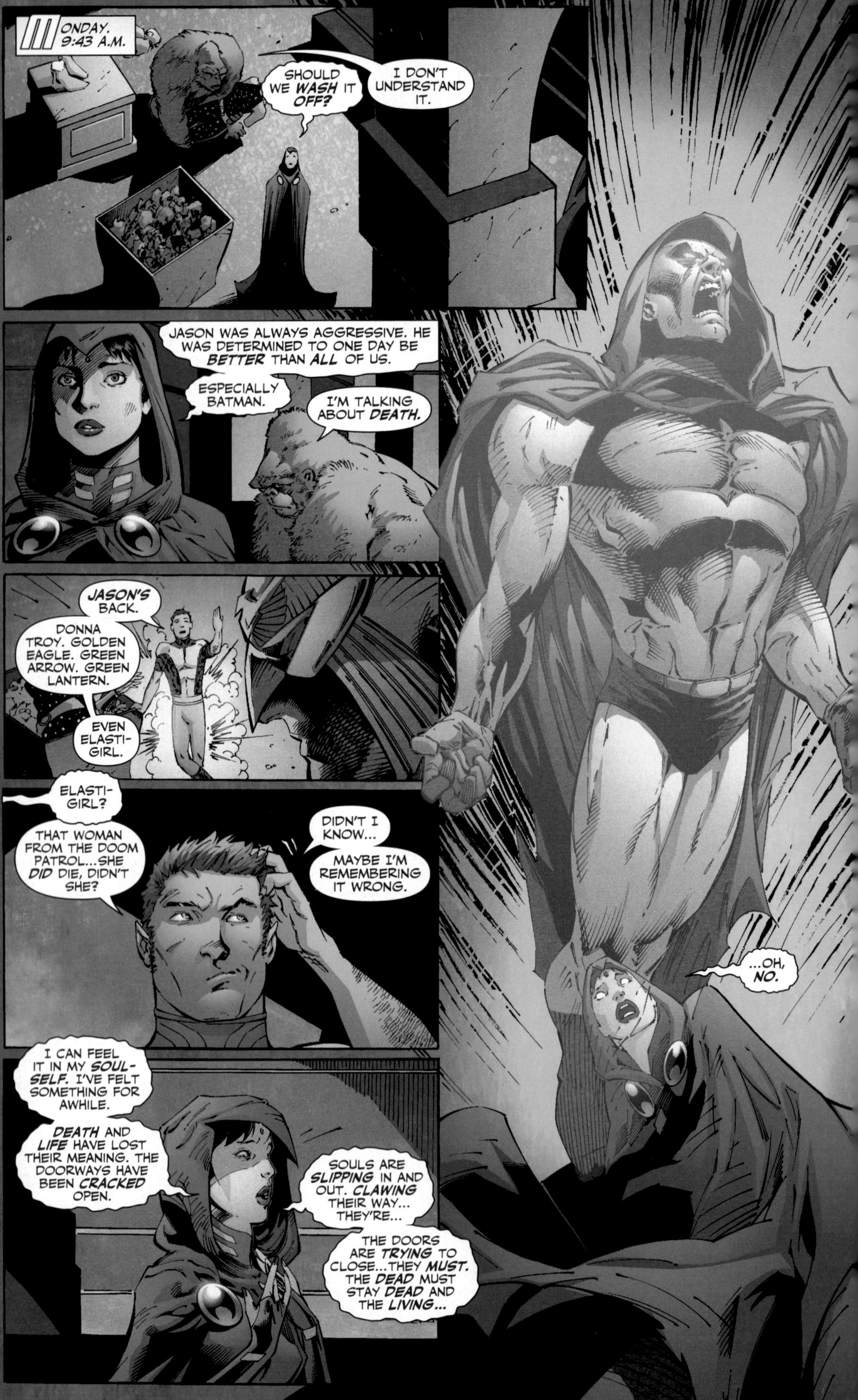
MONDAY. 9:43 A.M.
SHOULD WE WASH IT OFF?
I DON'T UNDERSTAND IT.
JASON WAS ALWAYS AGGRESSIVE. HE WAS DETERMINED TO ONE DAY BE BETTER THAN ALL OF US.
ESPECIALLY BATMAN.
I'M TALKING ABOUT DEATH.
JASON'S BACK.
DONNA TROY. GOLDEN EAGLE. GREEN ARROW. GREEN LANTERN.
EVEN ELASTI-GIRL.
ELASTI-GIRL?
THAT WOMAN FROM THE DOOM PATROL...SHE DID DIE, DIDN'T SHE?
DIDN'T I KNOW...
MAYBE I'M REMEMBERING IT WRONG.
I CAN FEEL IT IN MY SOUL-SELF. I'VE FELT SOMETHING FOR AWHILE.
DEATH AND LIFE HAVE LOST THEIR MEANING. THE DOORWAYS HAVE BEEN CRACKED OPEN.
SOULS ARE SLIPPING IN AND OUT. CLAWING THEIR WAY... THEY'RE...
THE DOORS ARE TRYING TO CLOSE...THEY MUST. THE DEAD MUST STAY DEAD AND THE LIVING...
...OH, NO.

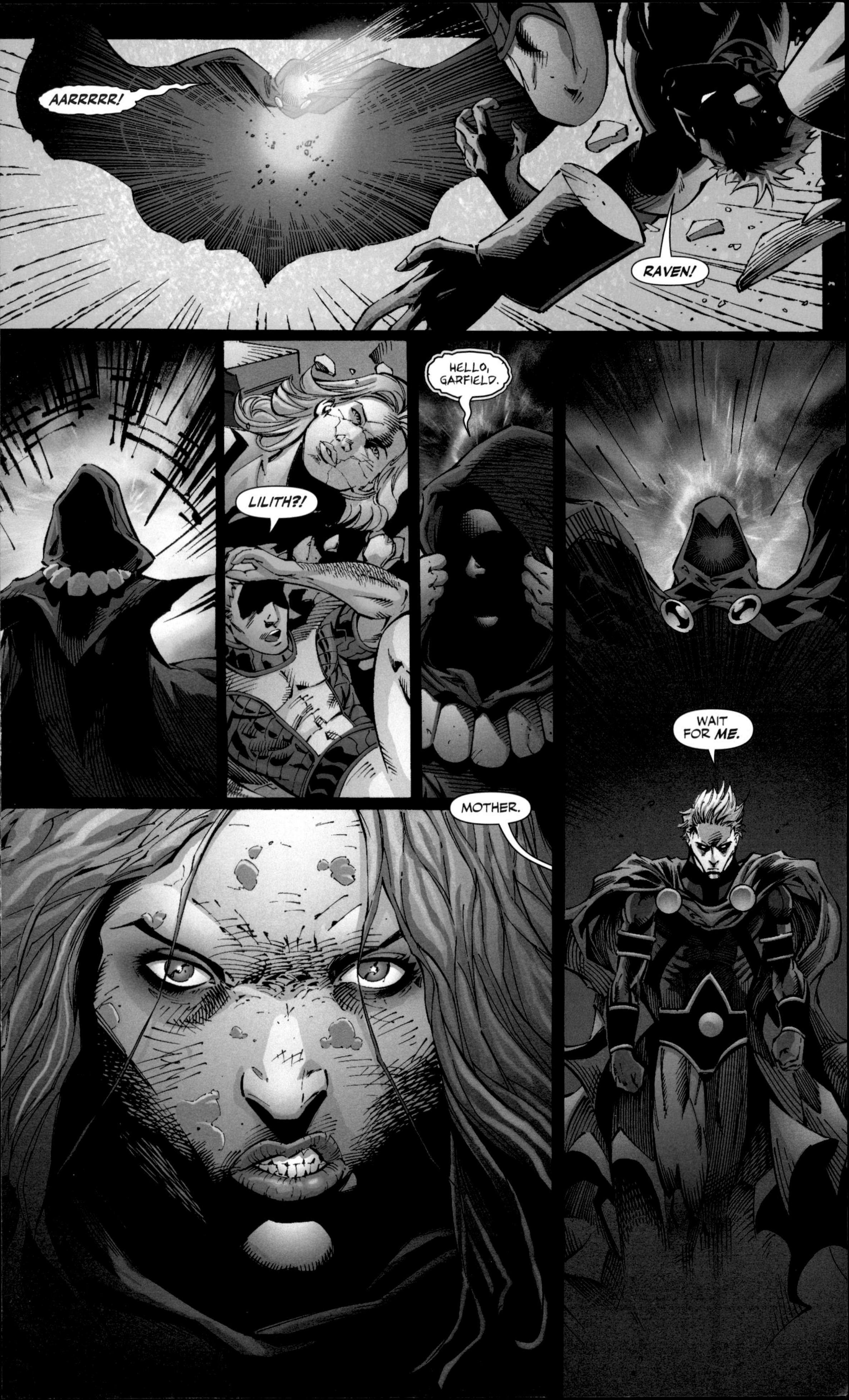
AARRRRR!
RAVEN!
LILITH?!
HELLO, GARFIELD.
WAIT FOR ME.
MOTHER.

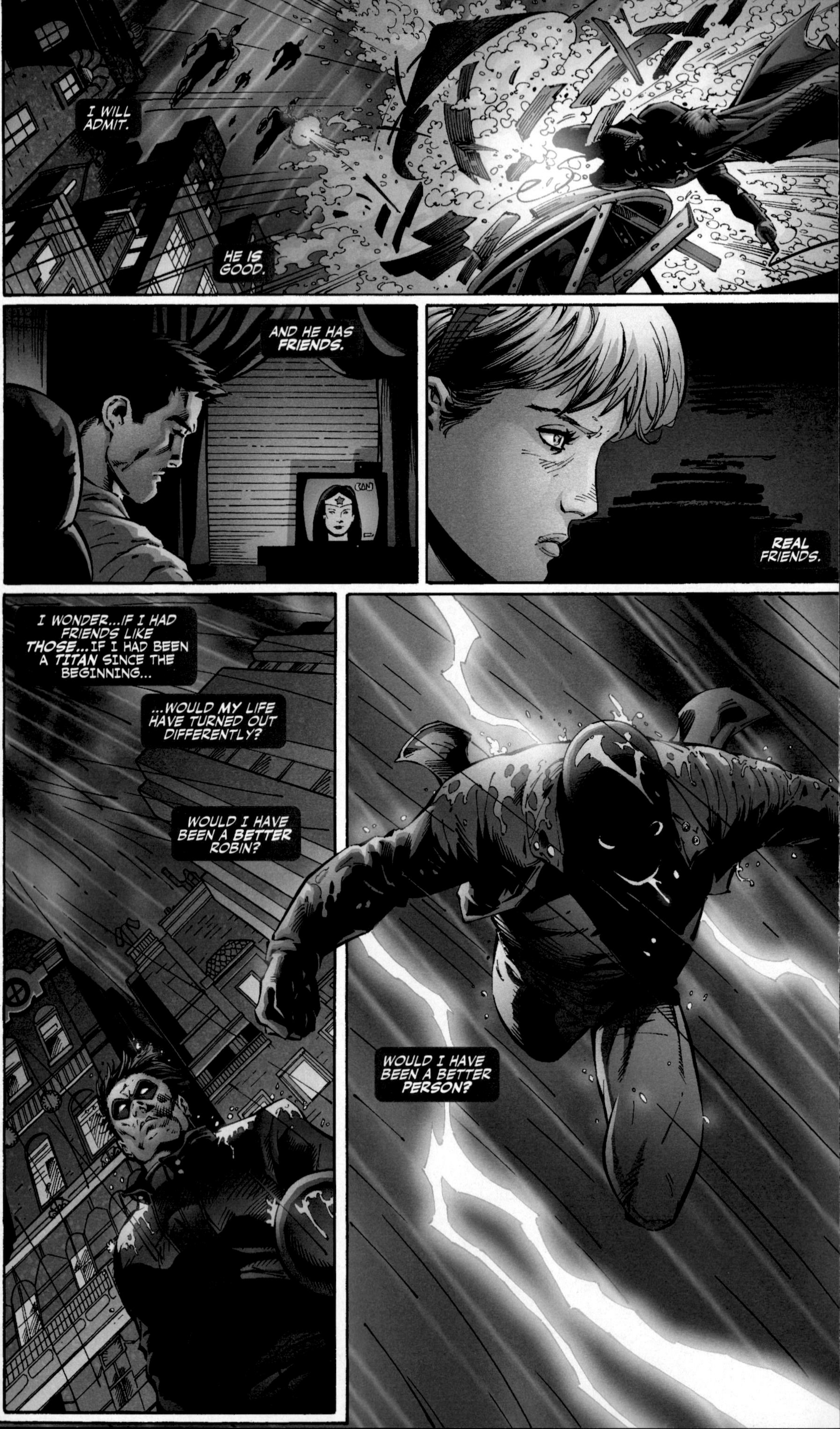
I WILL ADMIT.
HE IS GOOD.
AND HE HAS FRIENDS.
REAL FRIENDS.
I WONDER...IF I HAD FRIENDS LIKE THOSE...IF I HAD BEEN A TITAN SINCE THE BEGINNING...
...WOULD MY LIFE HAVE TURNED OUT DIFFERENTLY?
WOULD I HAVE BEEN A BETTER ROBIN?
WOULD I HAVE BEEN A BETTER PERSON?

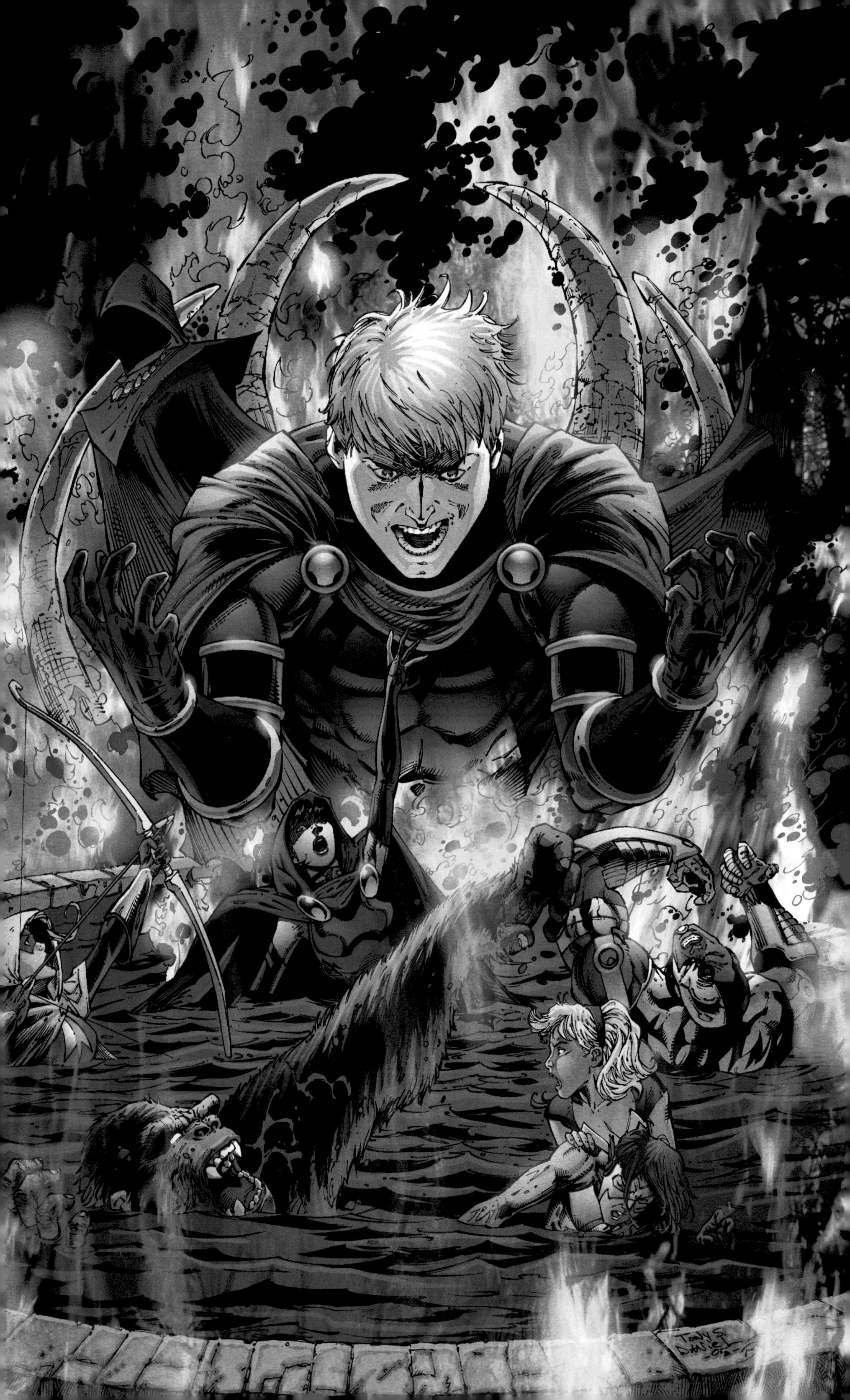

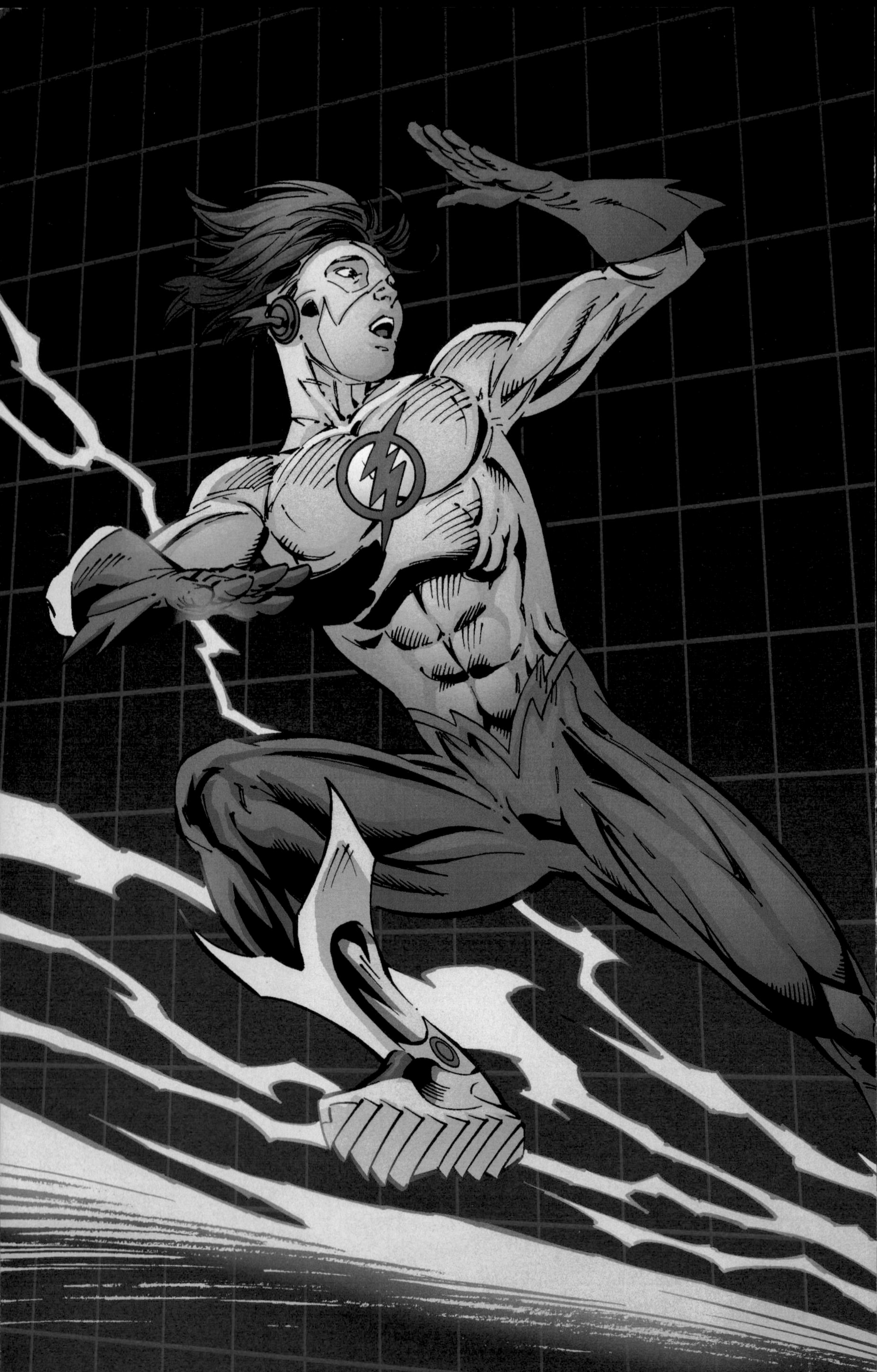

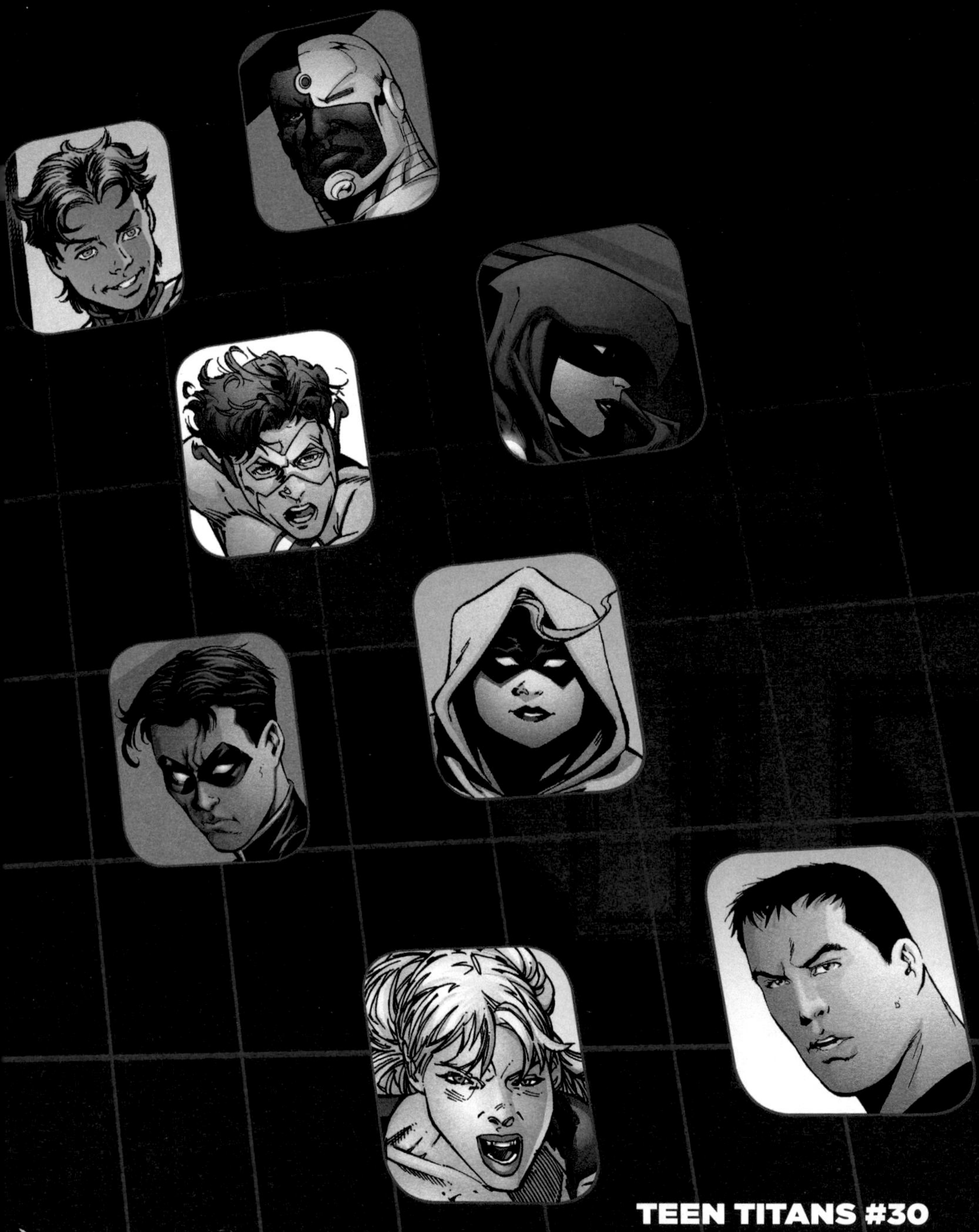

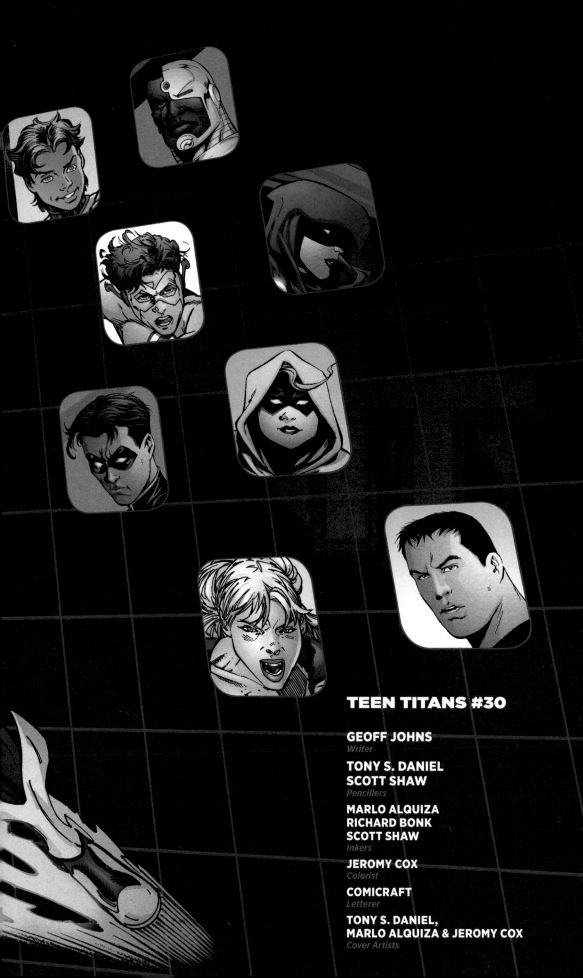

TEEN TITANS #30

GEOFF JOHNS
Writer

TONY S. DANIEL
SCOTT SHAW
Pencillers

MARLO ALQUIZA
RICHARD BONK
SCOTT SHAW
Inkers

JEROMY COX
Colorist

COMICRAFT
Letterer

TONY S. DANIEL,
MARLO ALQUIZA & JEROMY COX
Cover Artists

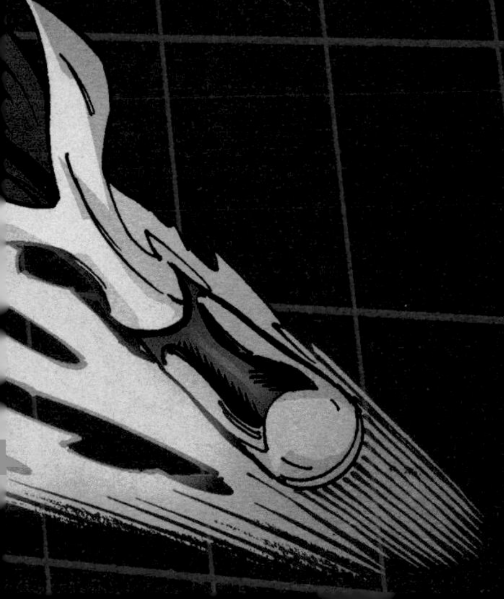

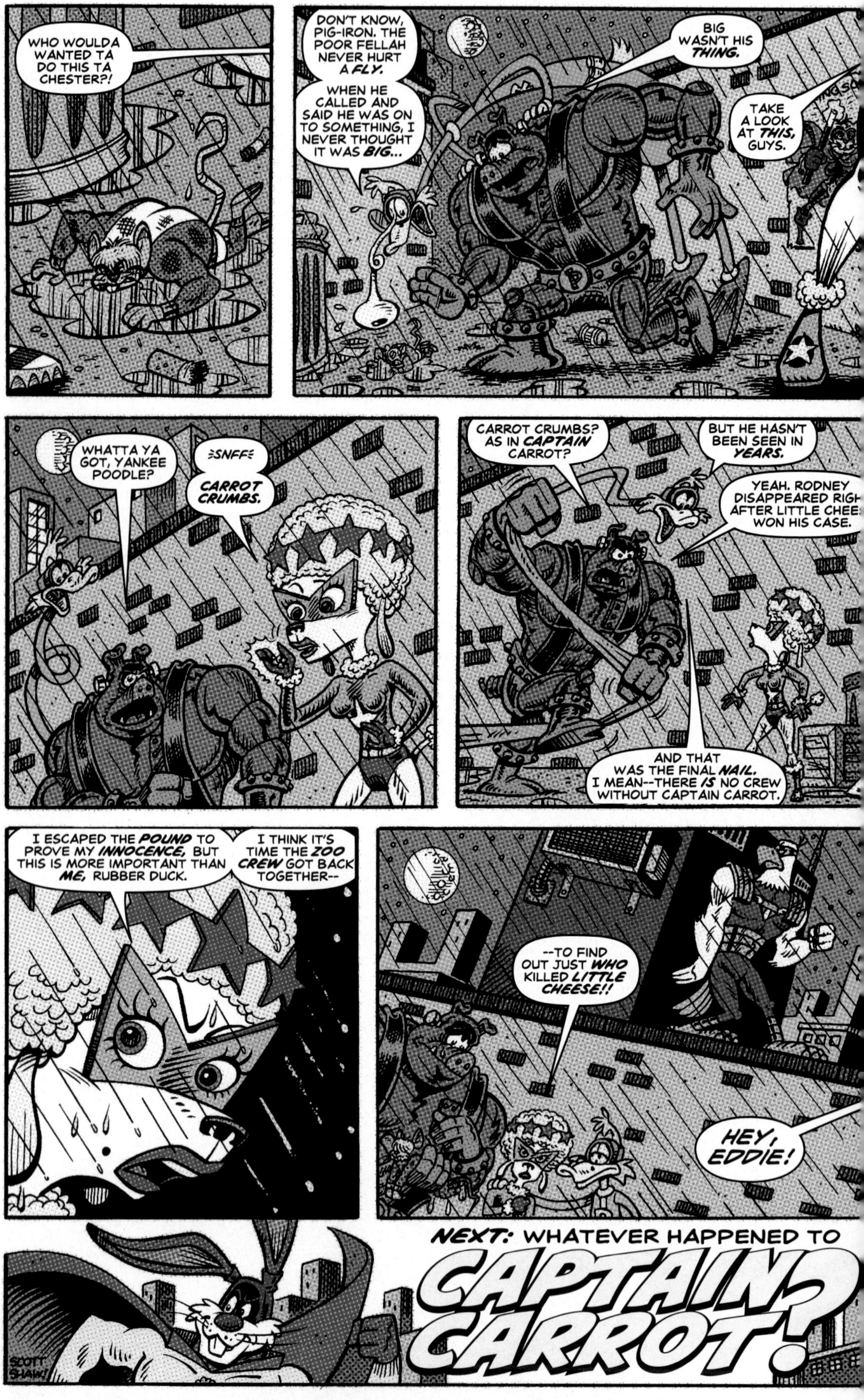

WHO WOULDA WANTED TA DO THIS TA CHESTER?!
DON'T KNOW, PIG-IRON. THE POOR FELLAH NEVER HURT A FLY.
WHEN HE CALLED AND SAID HE WAS ON TO SOMETHING, I NEVER THOUGHT IT WAS BIG...
BIG WASN'T HIS THING.
TAKE A LOOK AT THIS, GUYS.
WHATTA YA GOT, YANKEE POODLE?
SNFF
CARROT CRUMBS.
CARROT CRUMBS? AS IN CAPTAIN CARROT?
BUT HE HASN'T BEEN SEEN IN YEARS.
YEAH. RODNEY DISAPPEARED RIGH
AFTER LITTLE CHEE
WON HIS CASE.
AND THAT WAS THE FINAL NAIL. I MEAN--THERE IS NO CREW WITHOUT CAPTAIN CARROT.
I ESCAPED THE POUND TO PROVE MY INNOCENCE, BUT THIS IS MORE IMPORTANT THAN ME, RUBBER DUCK.
I THINK IT'S TIME THE ZOO CREW GOT BACK TOGETHER--
--TO FIND OUT JUST WHO KILLED LITTLE CHEESE!!
HEY, EDDIE!
NEXT: WHATEVER HAPPENED TO
CAPTAIN CARROT?
SCOTT SHAW!

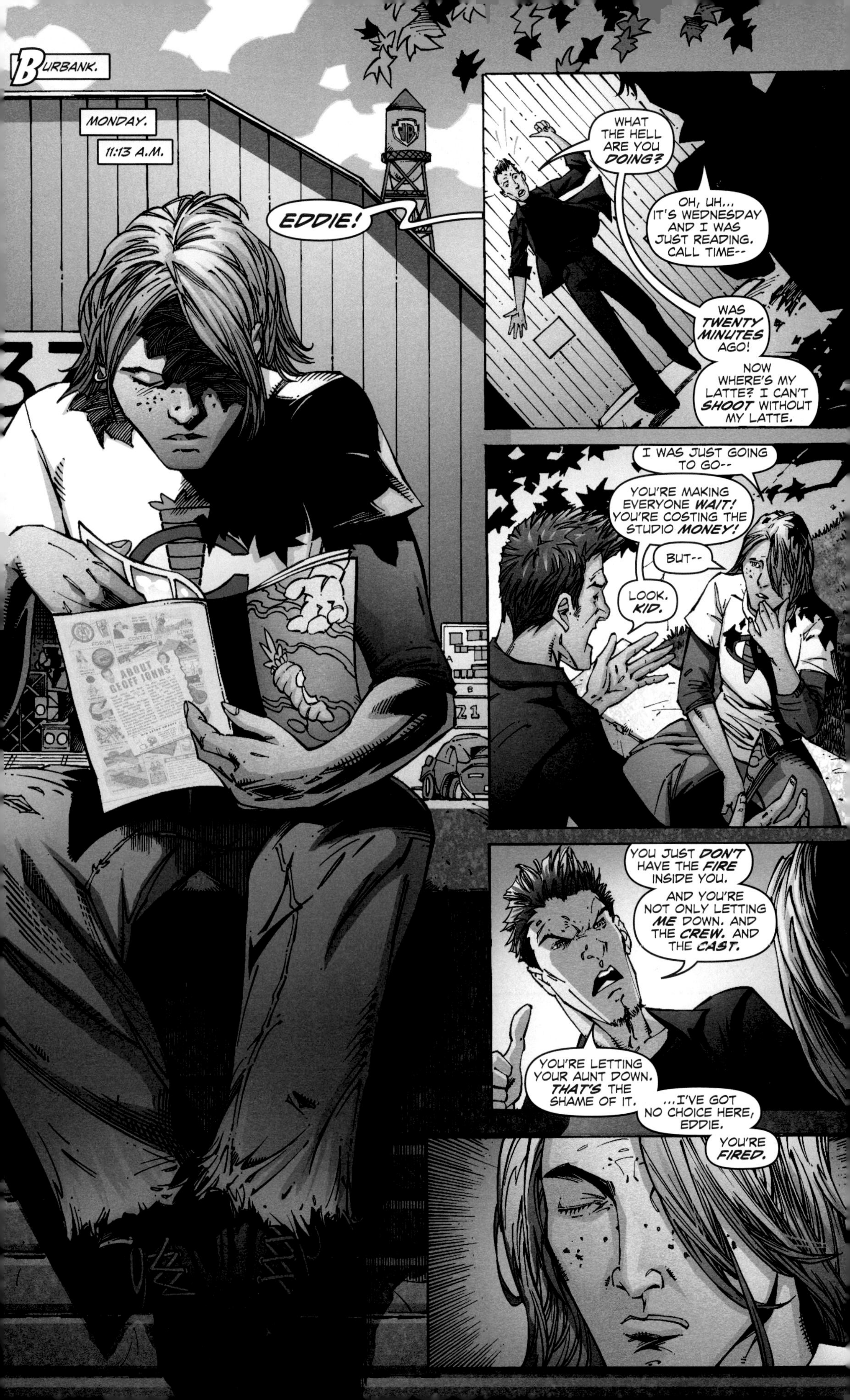
BURBANK.
MONDAY.
11:13 A.M.
EDDIE!
WHAT THE HELL ARE YOU DOING?
OH, UH... IT'S WEDNESDAY AND I WAS JUST READING. CALL TIME--
WAS TWENTY MINUTES AGO!
NOW WHERE'S MY LATTE? I CAN'T SHOOT WITHOUT MY LATTE.
I WAS JUST GOING TO GO--
YOU'RE MAKING EVERYONE WAIT! YOU'RE COSTING THE STUDIO MONEY!
BUT--
LOOK. KID.
YOU JUST DON'T HAVE THE FIRE INSIDE YOU.
AND YOU'RE NOT ONLY LETTING ME DOWN. AND THE CREW. AND THE CAST.
YOU'RE LETTING YOUR AUNT DOWN. THAT'S THE SHAME OF IT.
...I'VE GOT NO CHOICE HERE, EDDIE.
YOU'RE FIRED.

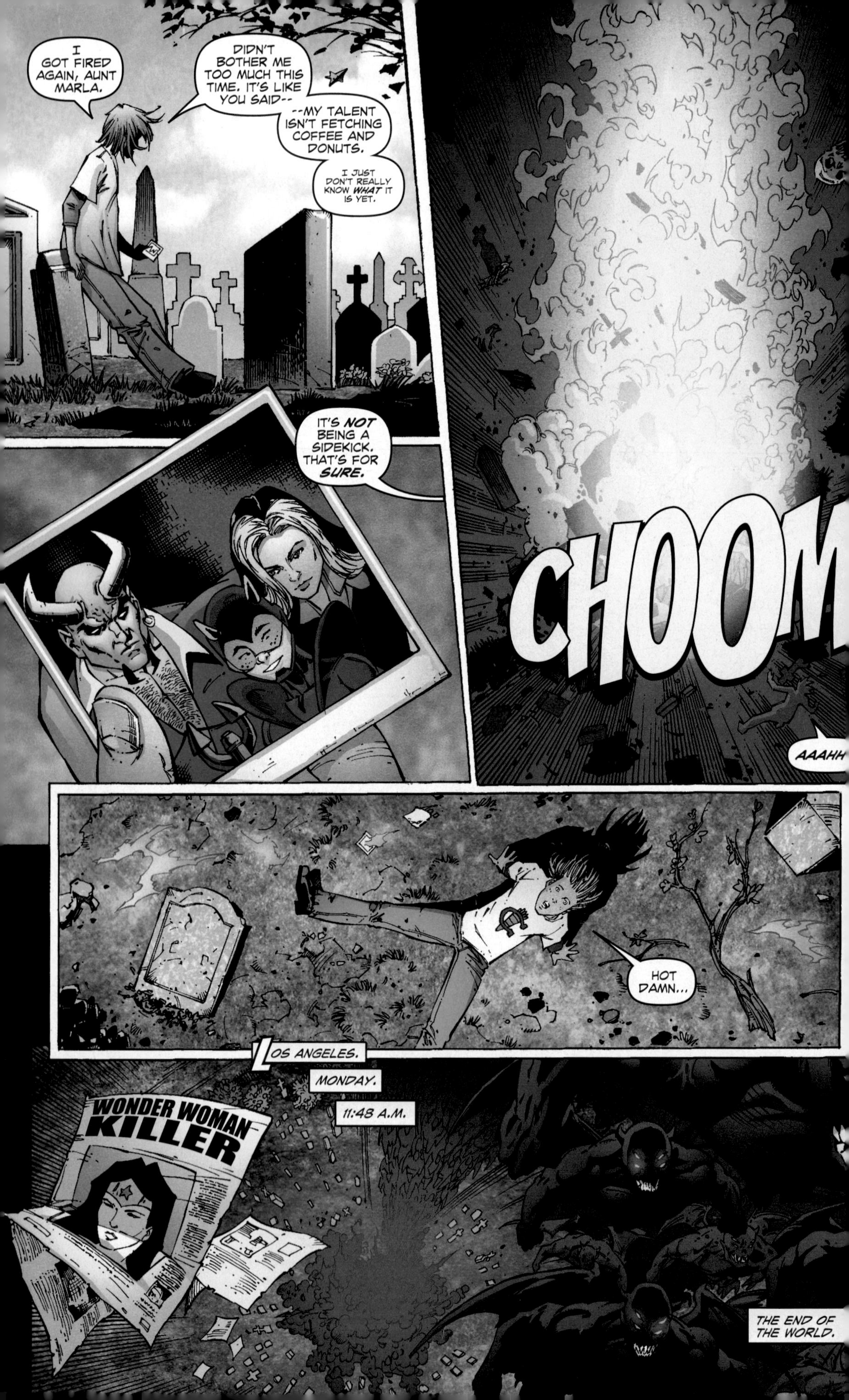

I GOT FIRED AGAIN, AUNT MARLA.
DIDN'T BOTHER ME TOO MUCH THIS TIME. IT'S LIKE YOU SAID--
--MY TALENT ISN'T FETCHING COFFEE AND DONUTS.
I JUST DON'T REALLY KNOW WHAT IT IS YET.
IT'S NOT BEING A SIDEKICK. THAT'S FOR SURE.
CHOOM
AAAHH
HOT DAMN...
LOS ANGELES.
MONDAY.
11:48 A.M.
WONDER WOMAN KILLER
THE END OF THE WORLD.

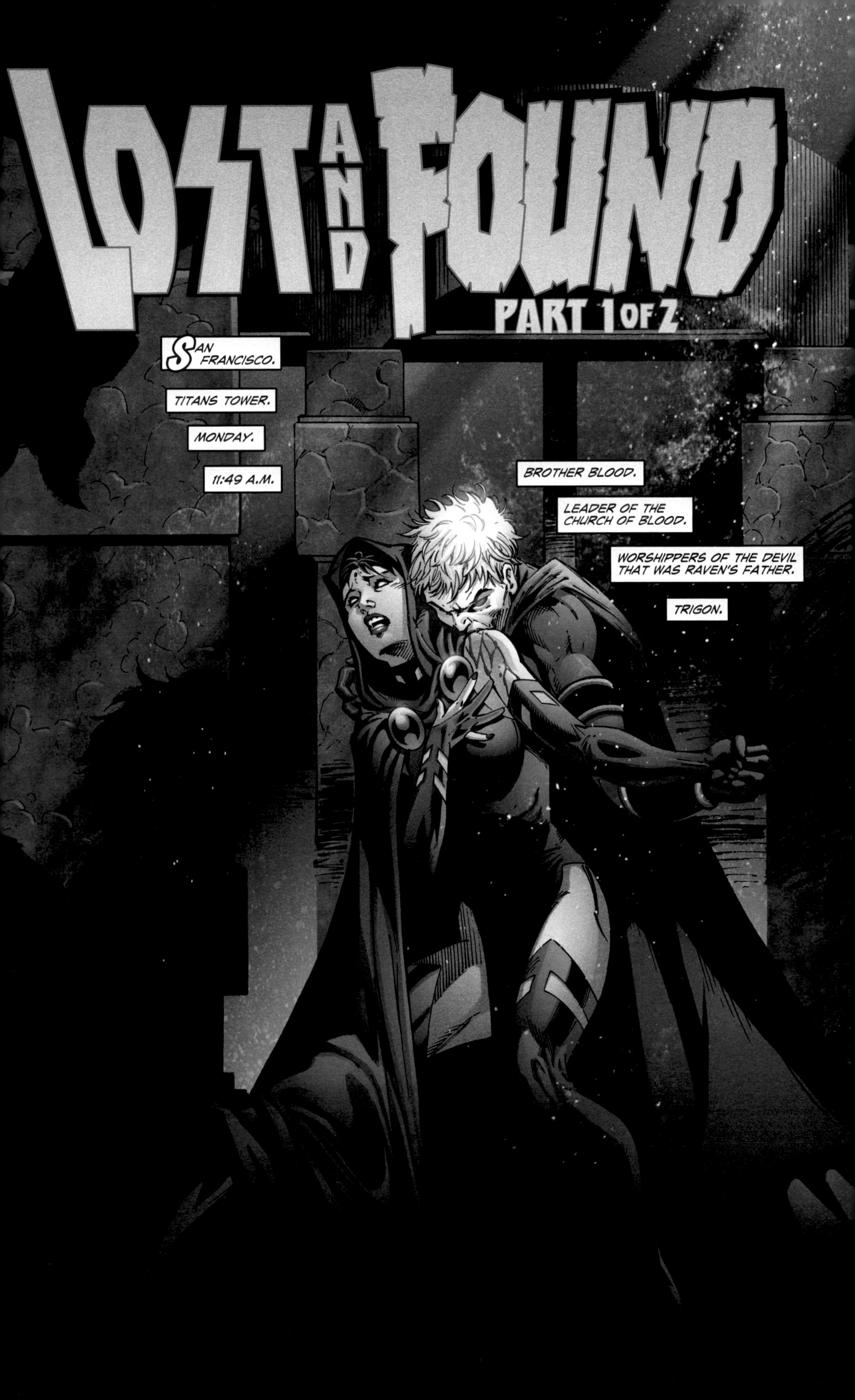
LOST AND FOUND
PART 1 OF 2
SAN FRANCISCO.
TITANS TOWER.
MONDAY.
11:49 A.M.
BROTHER BLOOD.
LEADER OF THE CHURCH OF BLOOD.
WORSHIPPERS OF THE DEVIL THAT WAS RAVEN'S FATHER.
TRIGON.

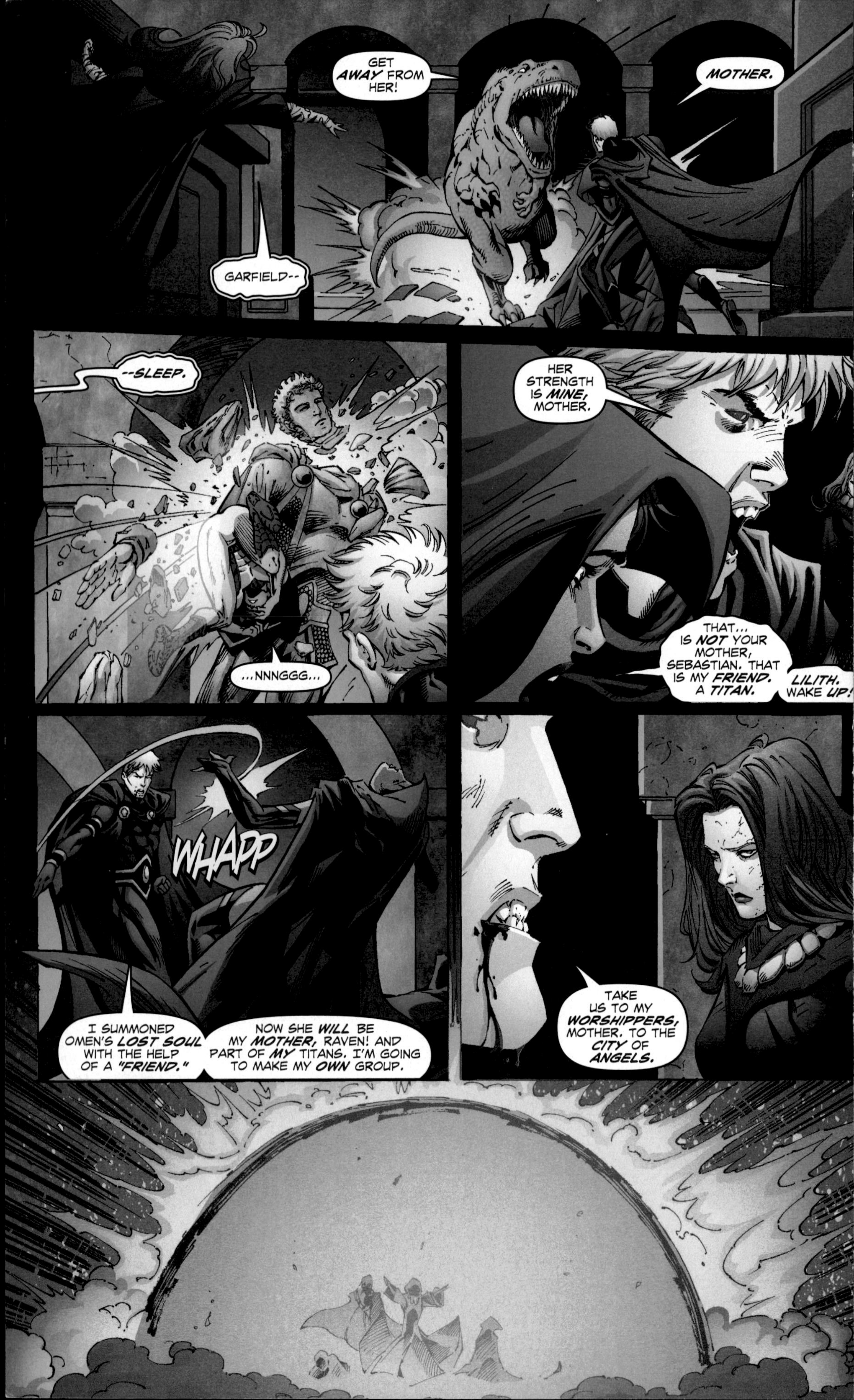
GET AWAY FROM HER!
MOTHER.
GARFIELD--
--SLEEP.
...NNNGGG...
HER STRENGTH IS MINE, MOTHER.
THAT... IS NOT YOUR MOTHER, SEBASTIAN. THAT IS MY FRIEND. A TITAN.
LILITH. WAKE UP!
WHAPP
I SUMMONED OMEN'S LOST SOUL WITH THE HELP OF A "FRIEND."
NOW SHE WILL BE MY MOTHER, RAVEN! AND PART OF MY TITANS. I'M GOING TO MAKE MY OWN GROUP.
TAKE US TO MY WORSHIPPERS, MOTHER. TO THE CITY OF ANGELS.

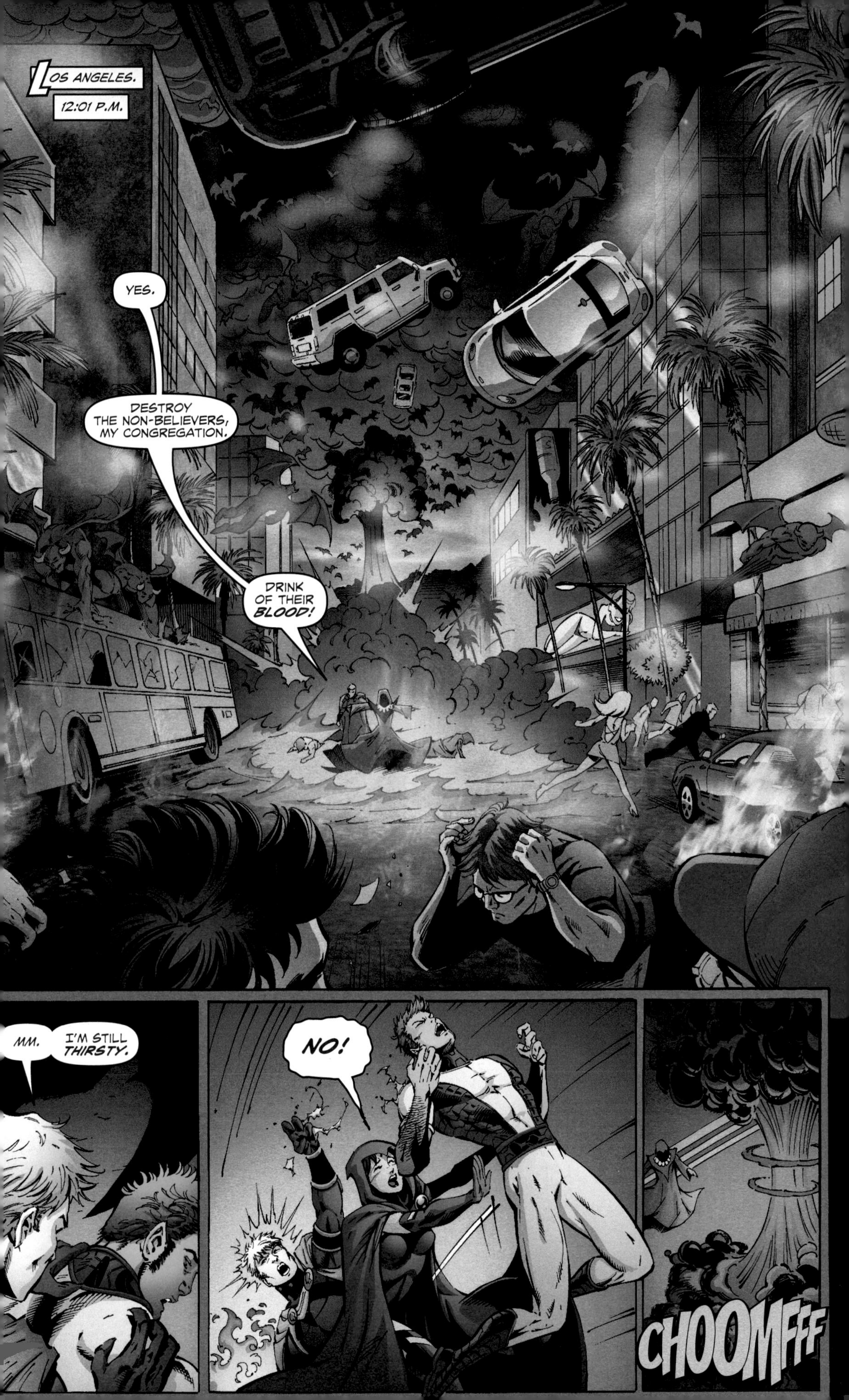
LOS ANGELES.
12:01 P.M.
YES.
DESTROY THE NON-BELIEVERS, MY CONGREGATION.
DRINK OF THEIR BLOOD!
MM.
I'M STILL THIRSTY.
NO!
CHOOMFFF

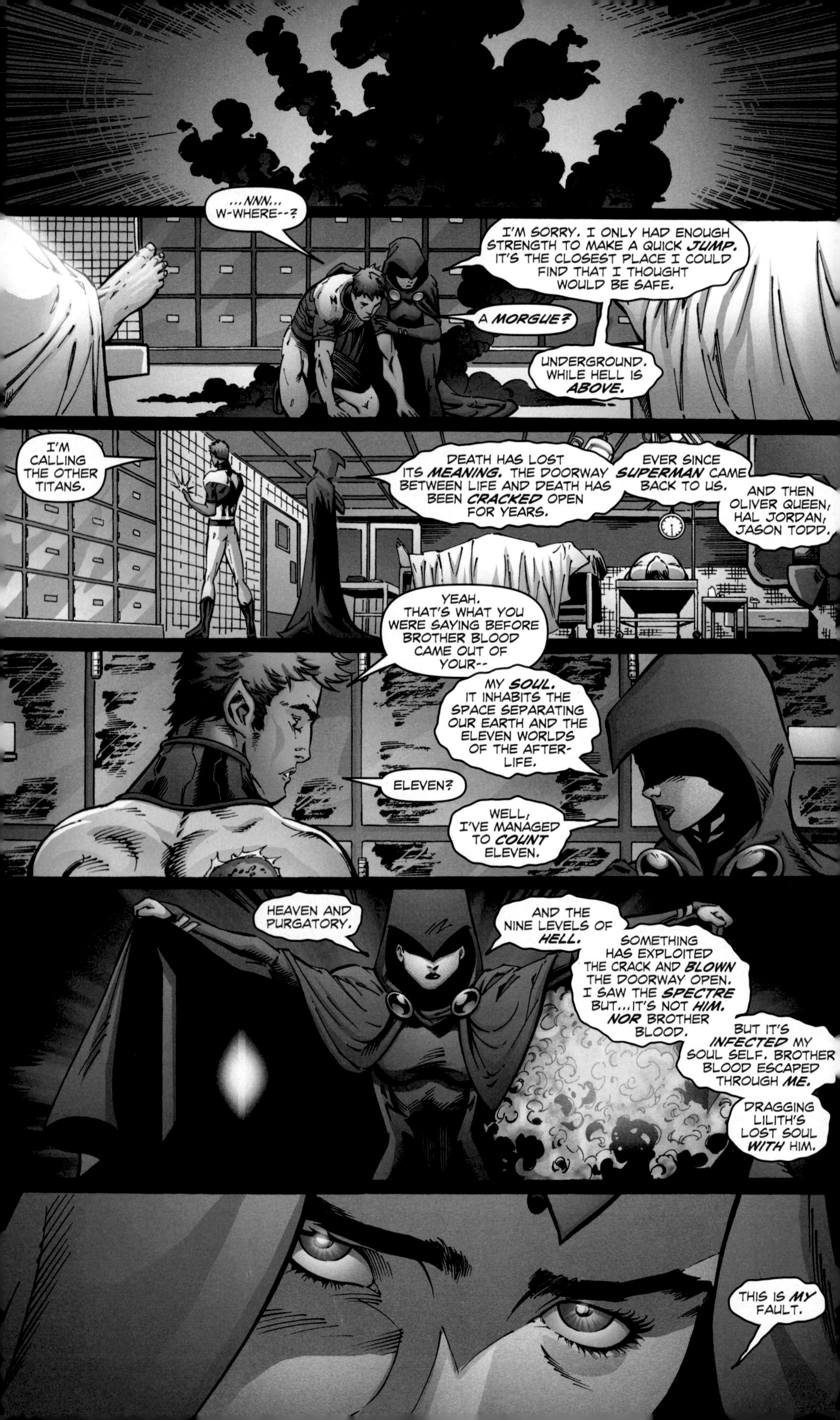

...NNN... W-WHERE--?
I'M SORRY. I ONLY HAD ENOUGH STRENGTH TO MAKE A QUICK JUMP. IT'S THE CLOSEST PLACE I COULD FIND THAT I THOUGHT WOULD BE SAFE.
A MORGUE?
UNDERGROUND. WHILE HELL IS ABOVE.
I'M CALLING THE OTHER TITANS.
DEATH HAS LOST ITS MEANING. THE DOORWAY BETWEEN LIFE AND DEATH HAS BEEN CRACKED OPEN FOR YEARS.
EVER SINCE SUPERMAN CAME BACK TO US.
AND THEN OLIVER QUEEN, HAL JORDAN, JASON TODD.
YEAH. THAT'S WHAT YOU WERE SAYING BEFORE BROTHER BLOOD CAME OUT OF YOUR--
MY SOUL. IT INHABITS THE SPACE SEPARATING OUR EARTH AND THE ELEVEN WORLDS OF THE AFTER-LIFE.
ELEVEN?
WELL, I'VE MANAGED TO COUNT ELEVEN.
HEAVEN AND PURGATORY.
AND THE NINE LEVELS OF HELL.
SOMETHING HAS EXPLOITED THE CRACK AND BLOWN THE DOORWAY OPEN. I SAW THE SPECTRE BUT...IT'S NOT HIM. NOR BROTHER BLOOD.
BUT IT'S INFECTED MY SOUL SELF. BROTHER BLOOD ESCAPED THROUGH ME.
DRAGGING LILITH'S LOST SOUL WITH HIM.
THIS IS MY FAULT.

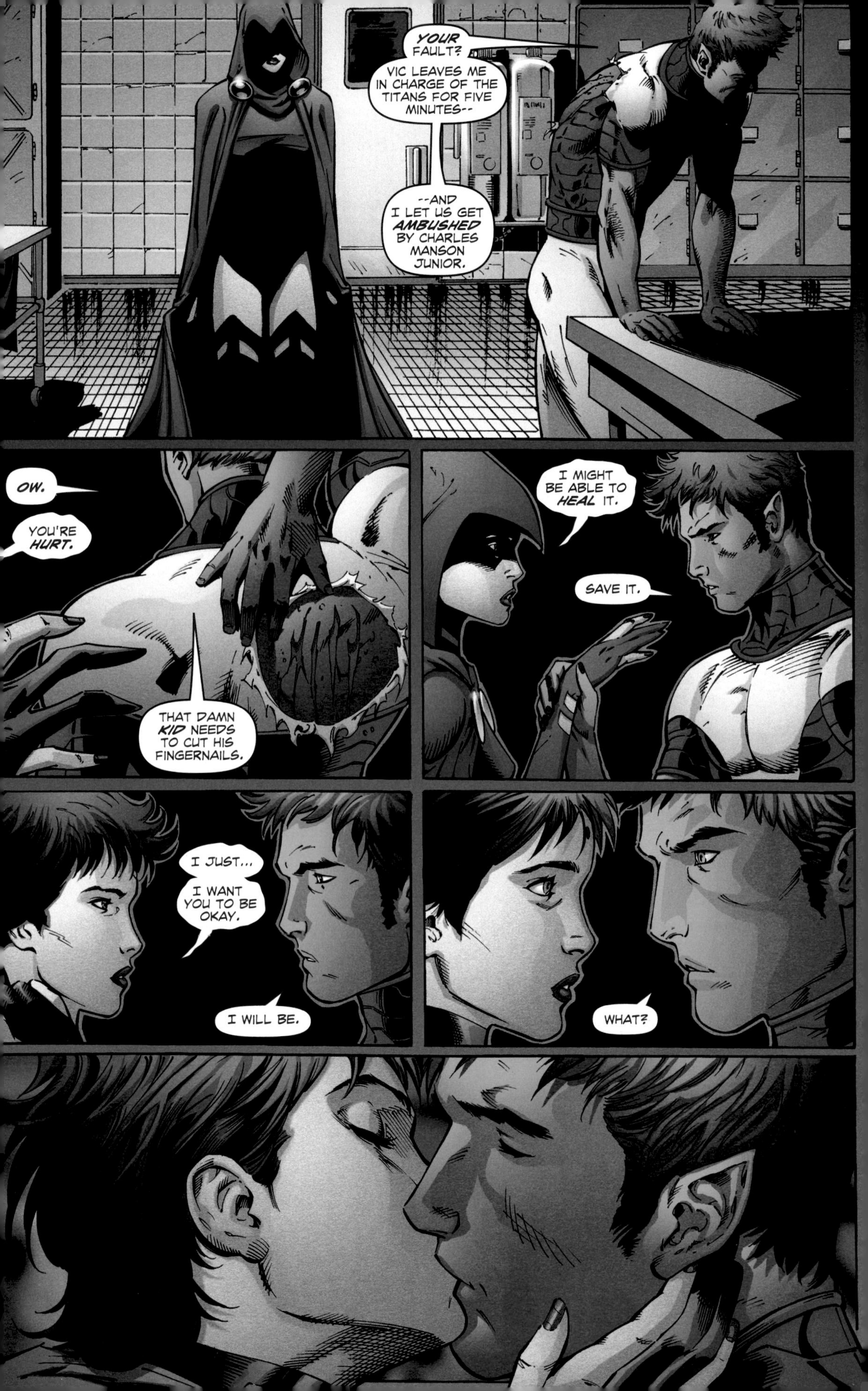
YOUR FAULT? VIC LEAVES ME IN CHARGE OF THE TITANS FOR FIVE MINUTES--
--AND I LET US GET AMBUSHED BY CHARLES MANSON JUNIOR.
OW.
YOU'RE HURT.
THAT DAMN KID NEEDS TO CUT HIS FINGERNAILS.
I MIGHT BE ABLE TO HEAL IT.
SAVE IT.
I JUST...
I WANT YOU TO BE OKAY.
I WILL BE.
WHAT?

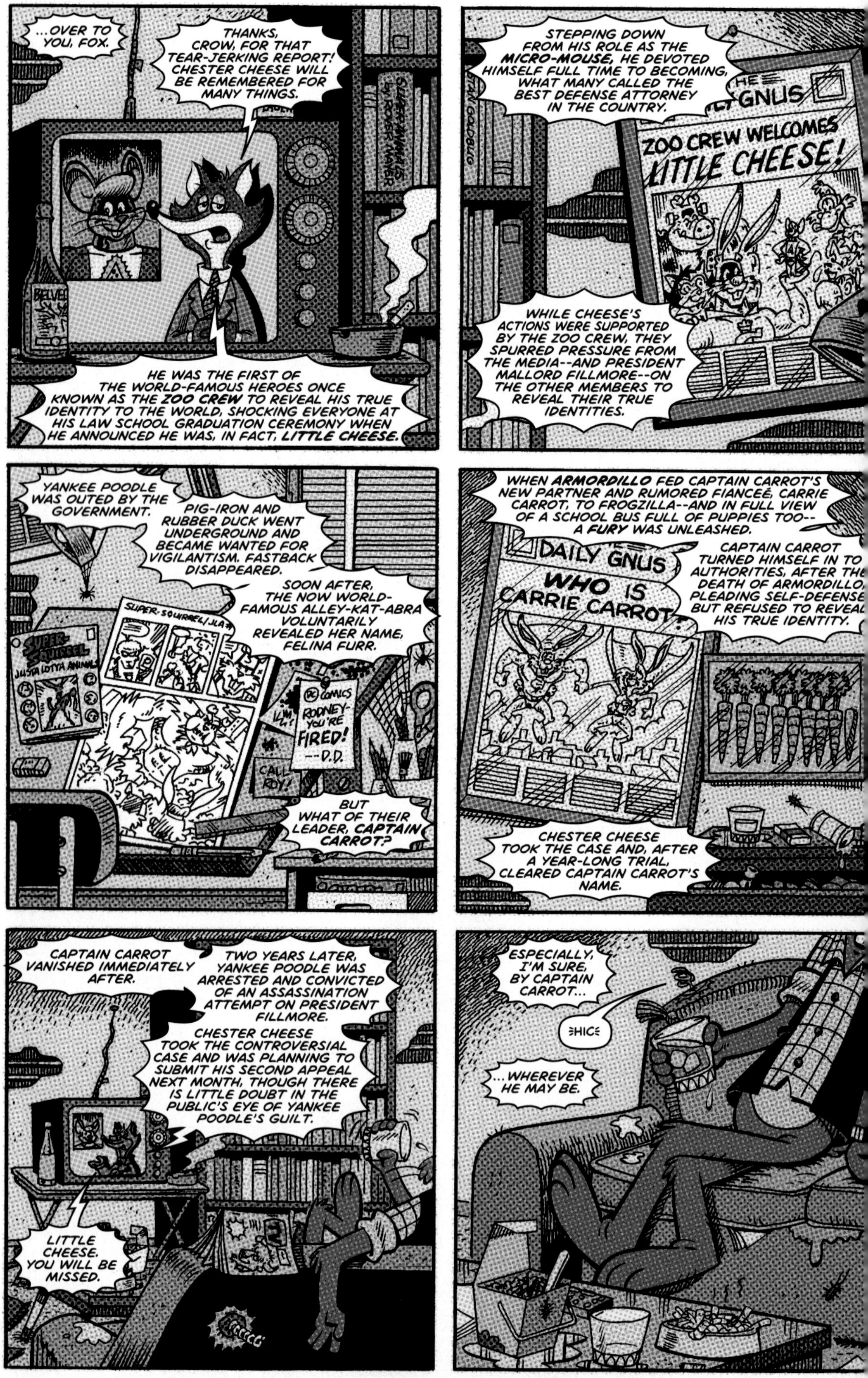
...OVER TO YOU, FOX.
THANKS, CROW, FOR THAT TEAR-JERKING REPORT! CHESTER CHEESE WILL BE REMEMBERED FOR MANY THINGS.
HE WAS THE FIRST OF THE WORLD-FAMOUS HEROES ONCE KNOWN AS THE ZOO CREW TO REVEAL HIS TRUE IDENTITY TO THE WORLD, SHOCKING EVERYONE AT HIS LAW SCHOOL GRADUATION CEREMONY WHEN HE ANNOUNCED HE WAS, IN FACT, LITTLE CHEESE.
STEPPING DOWN FROM HIS ROLE AS THE MICRO-MOUSE, HE DEVOTED HIMSELF FULL TIME TO BECOMING, WHAT MANY CALLED THE BEST DEFENSE ATTORNEY IN THE COUNTRY.
ZOO CREW WELCOMES LITTLE CHEESE!
WHILE CHEESE'S ACTIONS WERE SUPPORTED BY THE ZOO CREW, THEY SPURRED PRESSURE FROM THE MEDIA--AND PRESIDENT MALLORD FILLMORE--ON THE OTHER MEMBERS TO REVEAL THEIR TRUE IDENTITIES.
YANKEE POODLE WAS OUTED BY THE GOVERNMENT.
PIG-IRON AND RUBBER DUCK WENT UNDERGROUND AND BECAME WANTED FOR VIGILANTISM. FASTBACK DISAPPEARED.
SOON AFTER, THE NOW WORLD-FAMOUS ALLEY-KAT-ABRA VOLUNTARILY REVEALED HER NAME, FELINA FURR.
SUPER-SQUIRREL
JUSTA LOTTYA ANIMALS
SUPER-SQUIRREL/JLA
DC COMICS RODNEY-YOU'RE FIRED! --D.D.
CALL ROY!
BUT WHAT OF THEIR LEADER, CAPTAIN CARROT?
WHEN ARMORDILLO FED CAPTAIN CARROT'S NEW PARTNER AND RUMORED FIANCÉE, CARRIE CARROT, TO FROGZILLA--AND IN FULL VIEW OF A SCHOOL BUS FULL OF PUPPIES TOO--A FURY WAS UNLEASHED.
DAILY GNUS
WHO IS CARRIE CARROT?
CAPTAIN CARROT TURNED HIMSELF IN TO AUTHORITIES, AFTER THE DEATH OF ARMORDILLO, PLEADING SELF-DEFENSE BUT REFUSED TO REVEAL HIS TRUE IDENTITY.
CHESTER CHEESE TOOK THE CASE AND, AFTER A YEAR-LONG TRIAL, CLEARED CAPTAIN CARROT'S NAME.
CAPTAIN CARROT VANISHED IMMEDIATELY AFTER.
TWO YEARS LATER, YANKEE POODLE WAS ARRESTED AND CONVICTED OF AN ASSASSINATION ATTEMPT ON PRESIDENT FILLMORE.
CHESTER CHEESE TOOK THE CONTROVERSIAL CASE AND WAS PLANNING TO SUBMIT HIS SECOND APPEAL NEXT MONTH, THOUGH THERE IS LITTLE DOUBT IN THE PUBLIC'S EYE OF YANKEE POODLE'S GUILT.
LITTLE CHEESE. YOU WILL BE MISSED.
ESPECIALLY, I'M SURE, BY CAPTAIN CARROT...
HIC
...WHEREVER HE MAY BE.

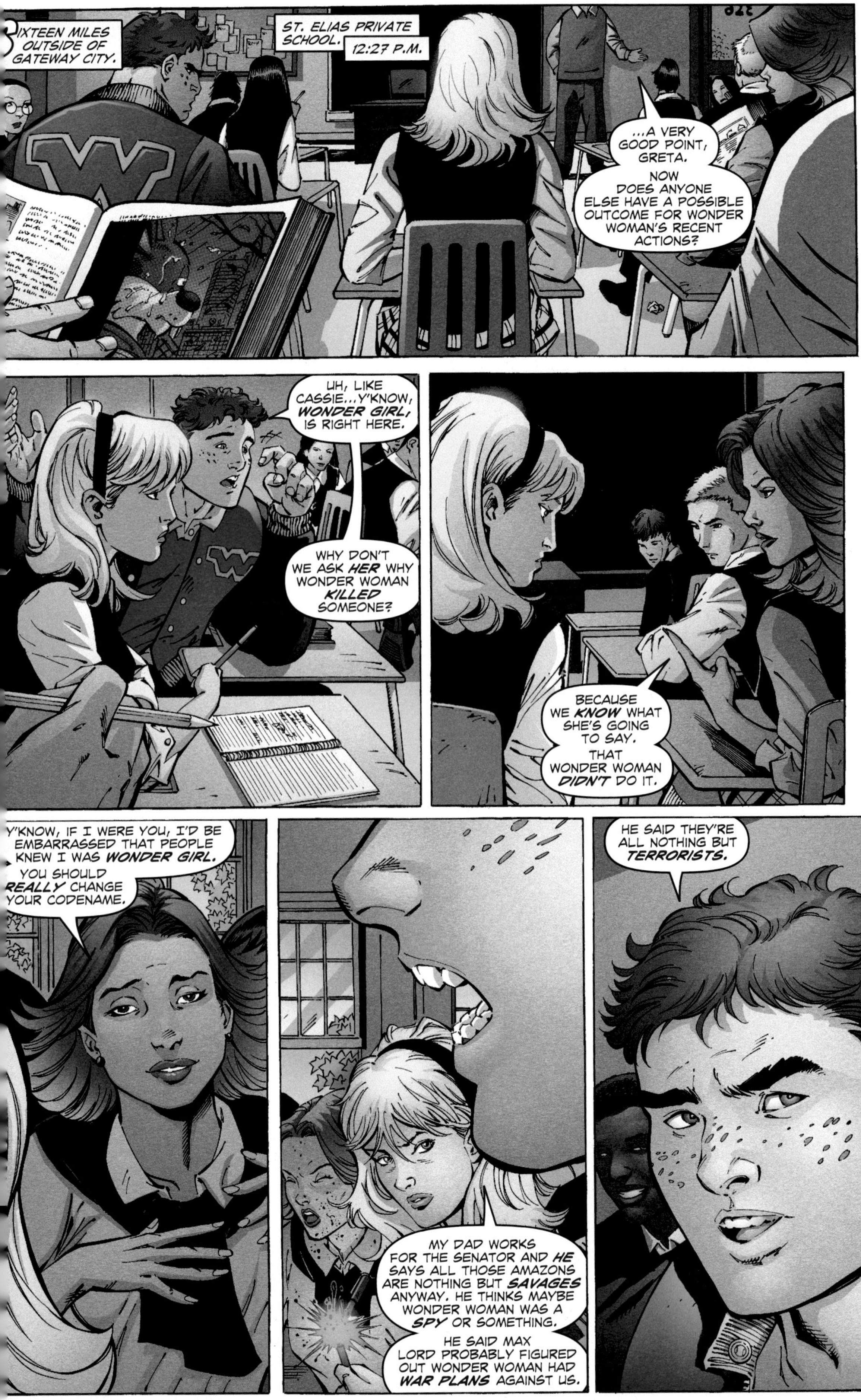
SIXTEEN MILES OUTSIDE OF GATEWAY CITY.
ST. ELIAS PRIVATE SCHOOL.
12:27 P.M.
...A VERY GOOD POINT, GRETA.
NOW DOES ANYONE ELSE HAVE A POSSIBLE OUTCOME FOR WONDER WOMAN'S RECENT ACTIONS?
UH, LIKE CASSIE...Y'KNOW, WONDER GIRL, IS RIGHT HERE.
WHY DON'T WE ASK HER WHY WONDER WOMAN KILLED SOMEONE?
BECAUSE WE KNOW WHAT SHE'S GOING TO SAY.
THAT WONDER WOMAN DIDN'T DO IT.
Y'KNOW, IF I WERE YOU, I'D BE EMBARRASSED THAT PEOPLE KNEW I WAS WONDER GIRL.
YOU SHOULD REALLY CHANGE YOUR CODENAME.
MY DAD WORKS FOR THE SENATOR AND HE SAYS ALL THOSE AMAZONS ARE NOTHING BUT SAVAGES ANYWAY. HE THINKS MAYBE WONDER WOMAN WAS A SPY OR SOMETHING.
HE SAID MAX LORD PROBABLY FIGURED OUT WONDER WOMAN HAD WAR PLANS AGAINST US.
HE SAID THEY'RE ALL NOTHING BUT TERRORISTS.

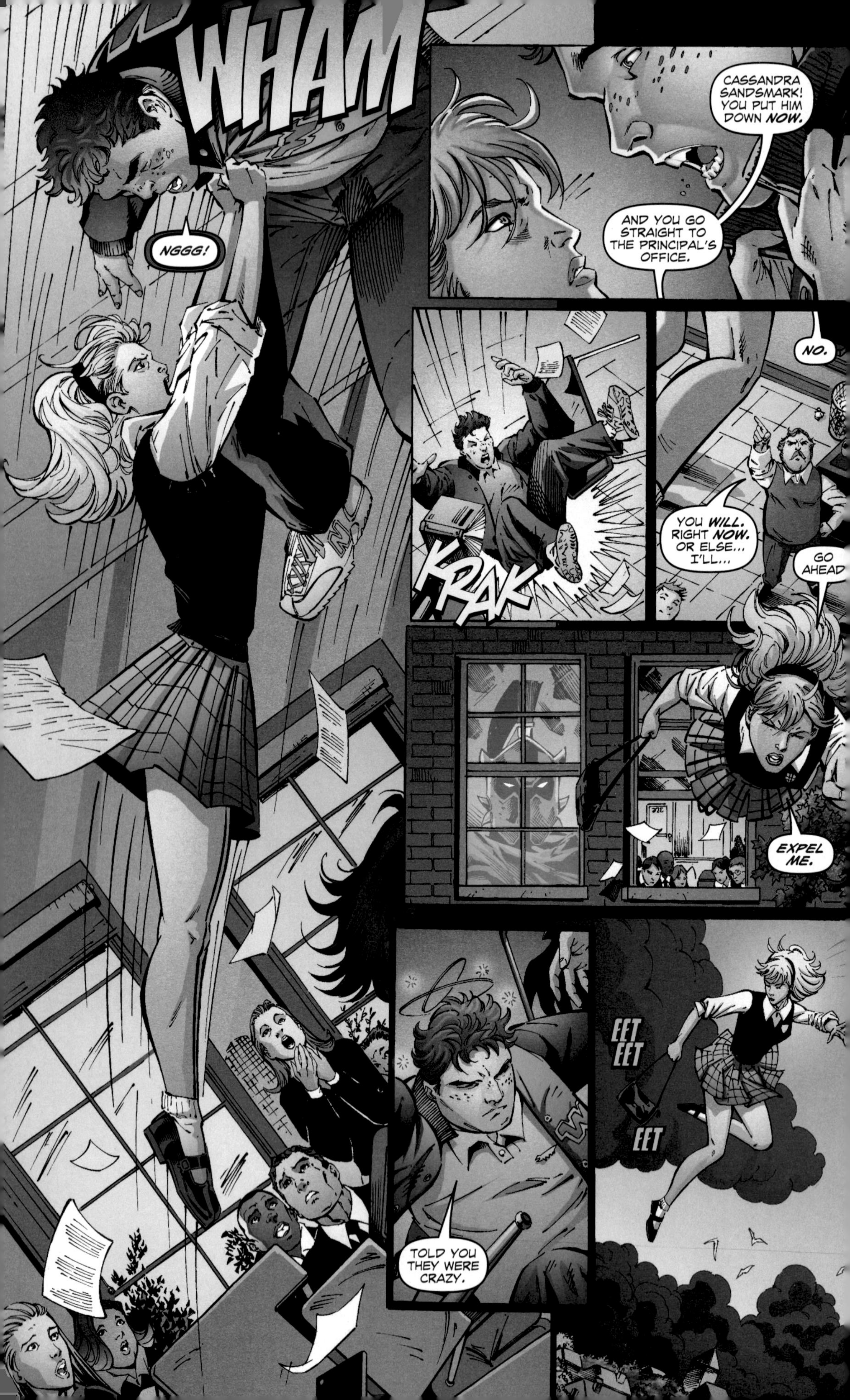
WHAM
NGGG!
CASSANDRA SANDSMARK! YOU PUT HIM DOWN NOW.
AND YOU GO STRAIGHT TO THE PRINCIPAL'S OFFICE.
KRAK
NO.
YOU WILL. RIGHT NOW. OR ELSE... I'LL...
GO AHEAD
EXPEL ME.
TOLD YOU THEY WERE CRAZY.
EET
EET
EET

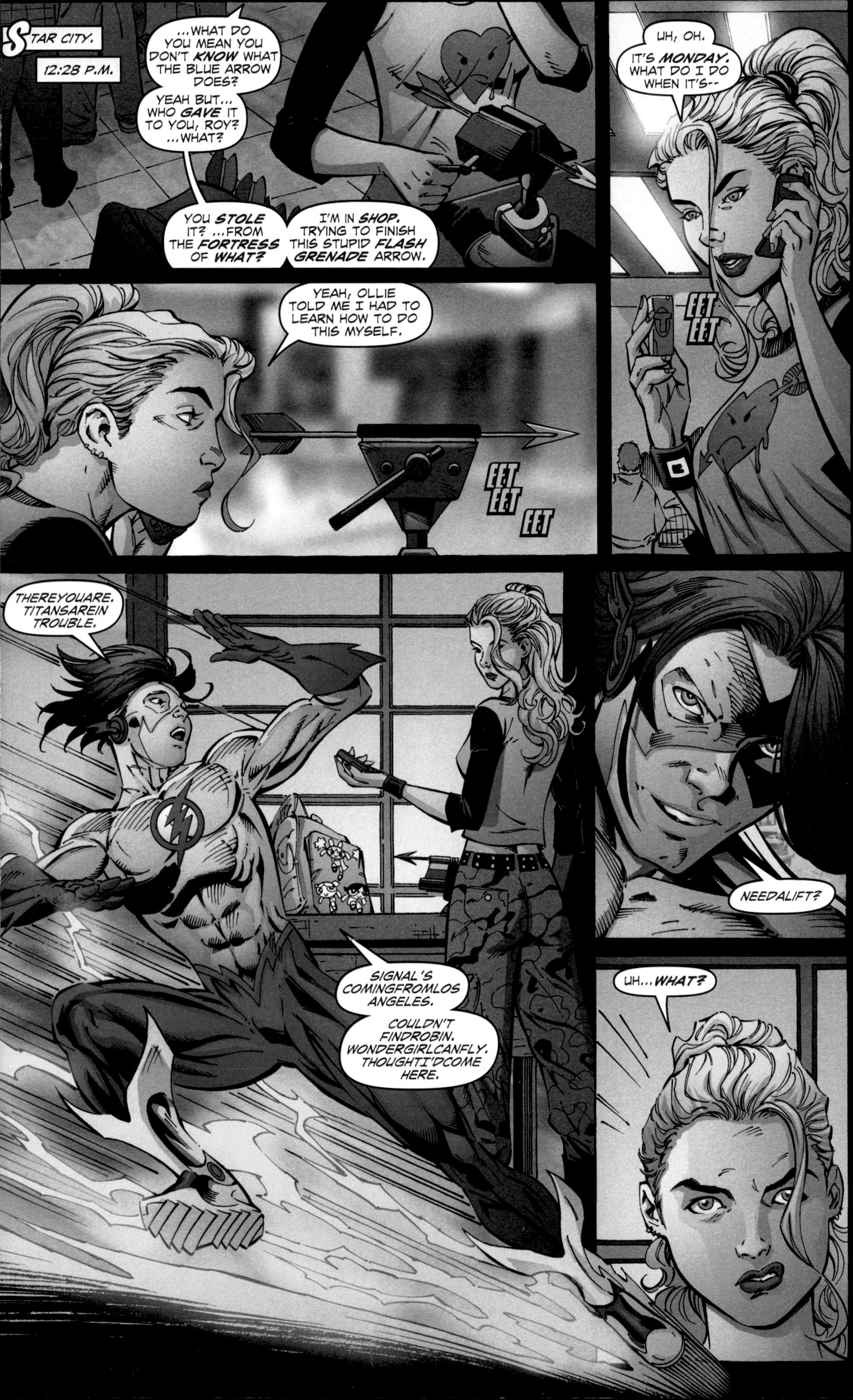

STAR CITY.
12:28 P.M.
...WHAT DO YOU MEAN YOU DON'T KNOW WHAT THE BLUE ARROW DOES?
YEAH BUT... WHO GAVE IT TO YOU, ROY? ...WHAT?
YOU STOLE IT? ...FROM THE FORTRESS OF WHAT?
I'M IN SHOP. TRYING TO FINISH THIS STUPID FLASH GRENADE ARROW.
UH, OH.
IT'S MONDAY. WHAT DO I DO WHEN IT'S--
YEAH, OLLIE TOLD ME I HAD TO LEARN HOW TO DO THIS MYSELF.
EET EET
EET EET EET
THEREYOUARE. TITANSAREIN TROUBLE.
SIGNAL'S COMINGFROMLOS ANGELES.
COULDN'T FINDROBIN. WONDERGIRLCANFLY. THOUGHTI'DCOME HERE.
NEEDALIFT?
UH...WHAT?

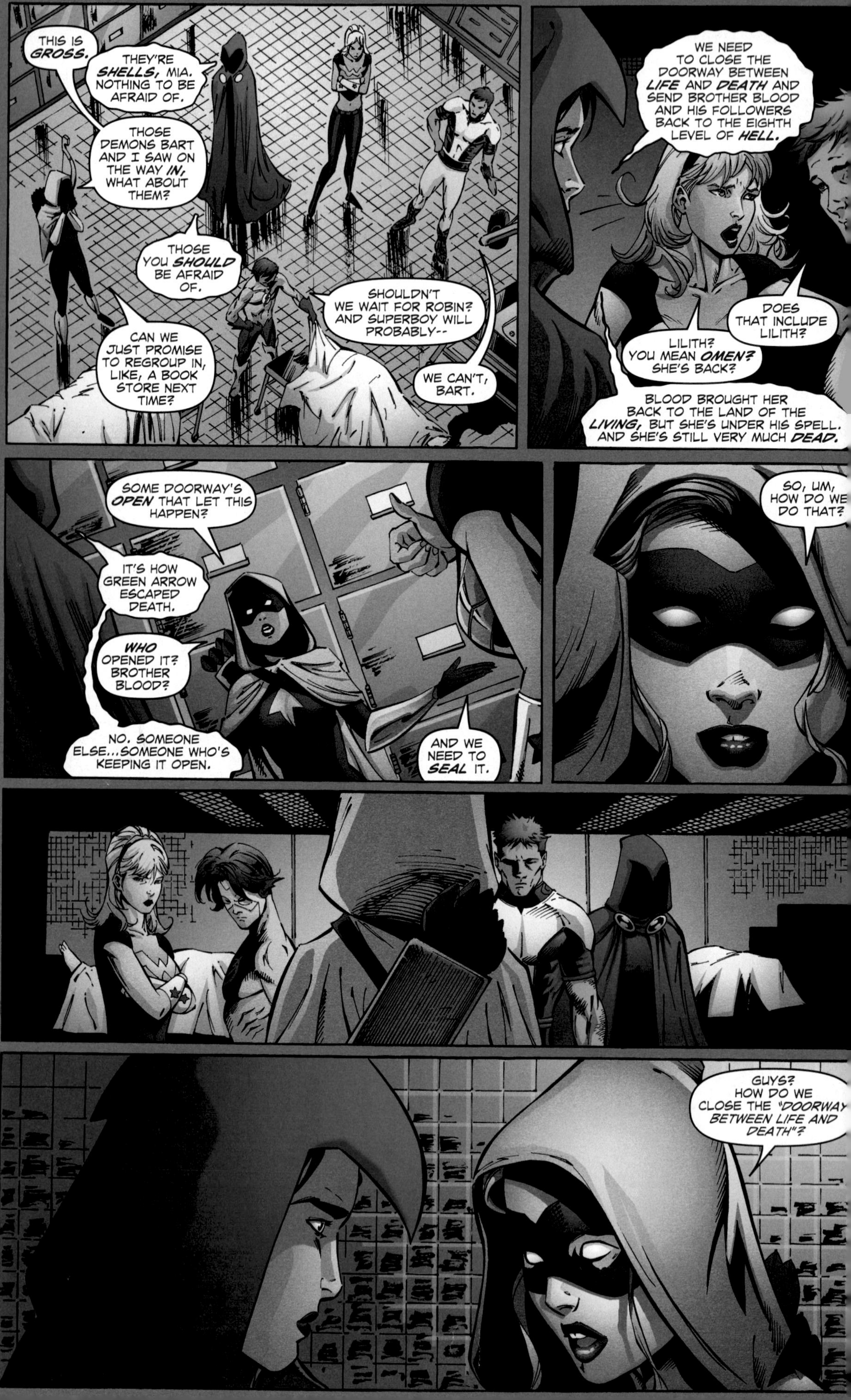
THIS IS GROSS.
THEY'RE SHELLS, MIA. NOTHING TO BE AFRAID OF.
THOSE DEMONS BART AND I SAW ON THE WAY IN, WHAT ABOUT THEM?
THOSE YOU SHOULD BE AFRAID OF.
CAN WE JUST PROMISE TO REGROUP IN, LIKE, A BOOK STORE NEXT TIME?
SHOULDN'T WE WAIT FOR ROBIN? AND SUPERBOY WILL PROBABLY--
WE CAN'T, BART.
WE NEED TO CLOSE THE DOORWAY BETWEEN LIFE AND DEATH AND SEND BROTHER BLOOD AND HIS FOLLOWERS BACK TO THE EIGHTH LEVEL OF HELL.
DOES THAT INCLUDE LILITH?
LILITH? YOU MEAN OMEN? SHE'S BACK?
BLOOD BROUGHT HER BACK TO THE LAND OF THE LIVING, BUT SHE'S UNDER HIS SPELL. AND SHE'S STILL VERY MUCH DEAD.
SOME DOORWAY'S OPEN THAT LET THIS HAPPEN?
IT'S HOW GREEN ARROW ESCAPED DEATH.
WHO OPENED IT? BROTHER BLOOD?
NO. SOMEONE ELSE...SOMEONE WHO'S KEEPING IT OPEN.
AND WE NEED TO SEAL IT.
SO, UM, HOW DO WE DO THAT?
GUYS? HOW DO WE CLOSE THE "DOORWAY BETWEEN LIFE AND DEATH"?

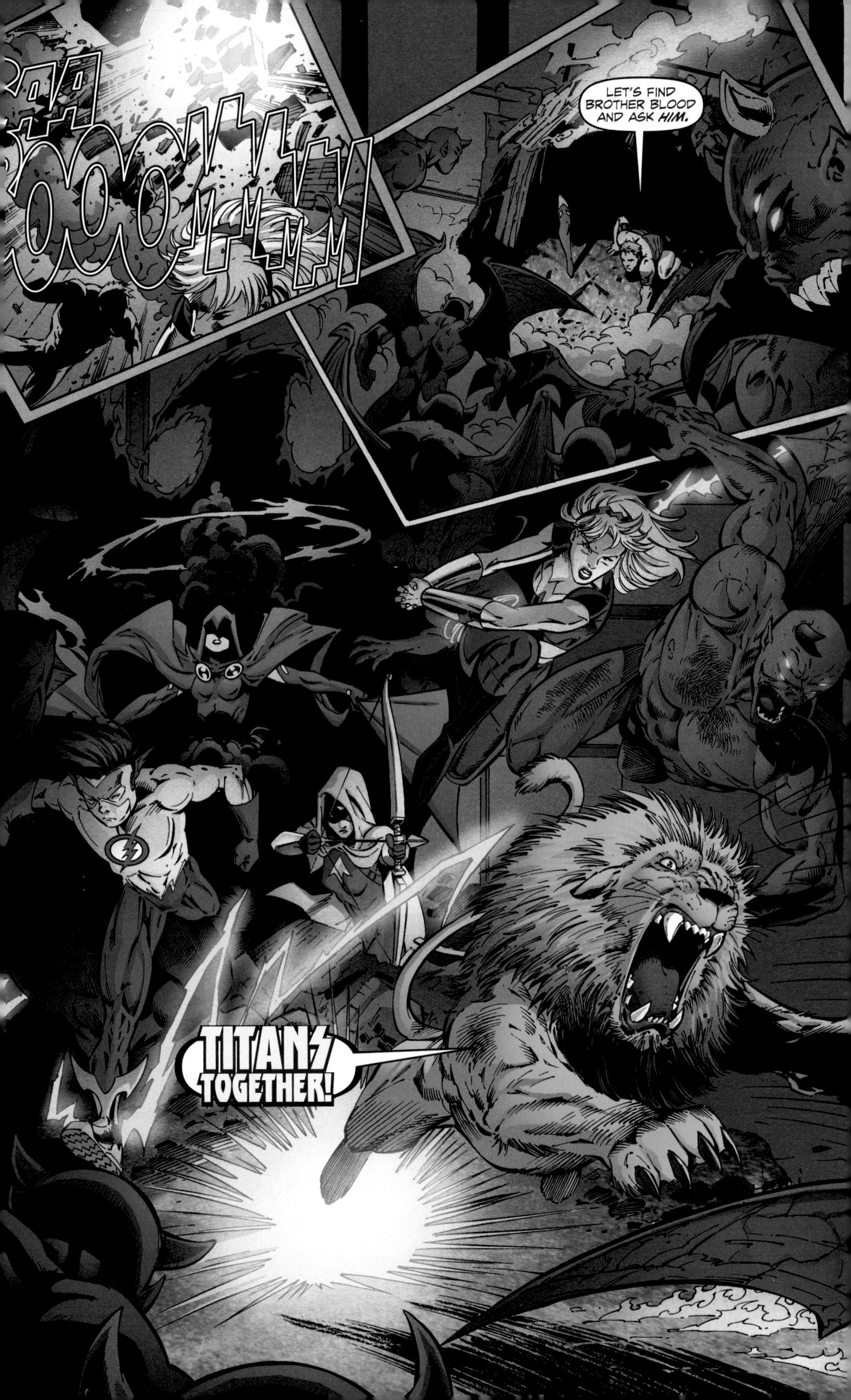
KA-BOOOOMMMM
LET'S FIND BROTHER BLOOD AND ASK *HIM*.
TITANS TOGETHER!

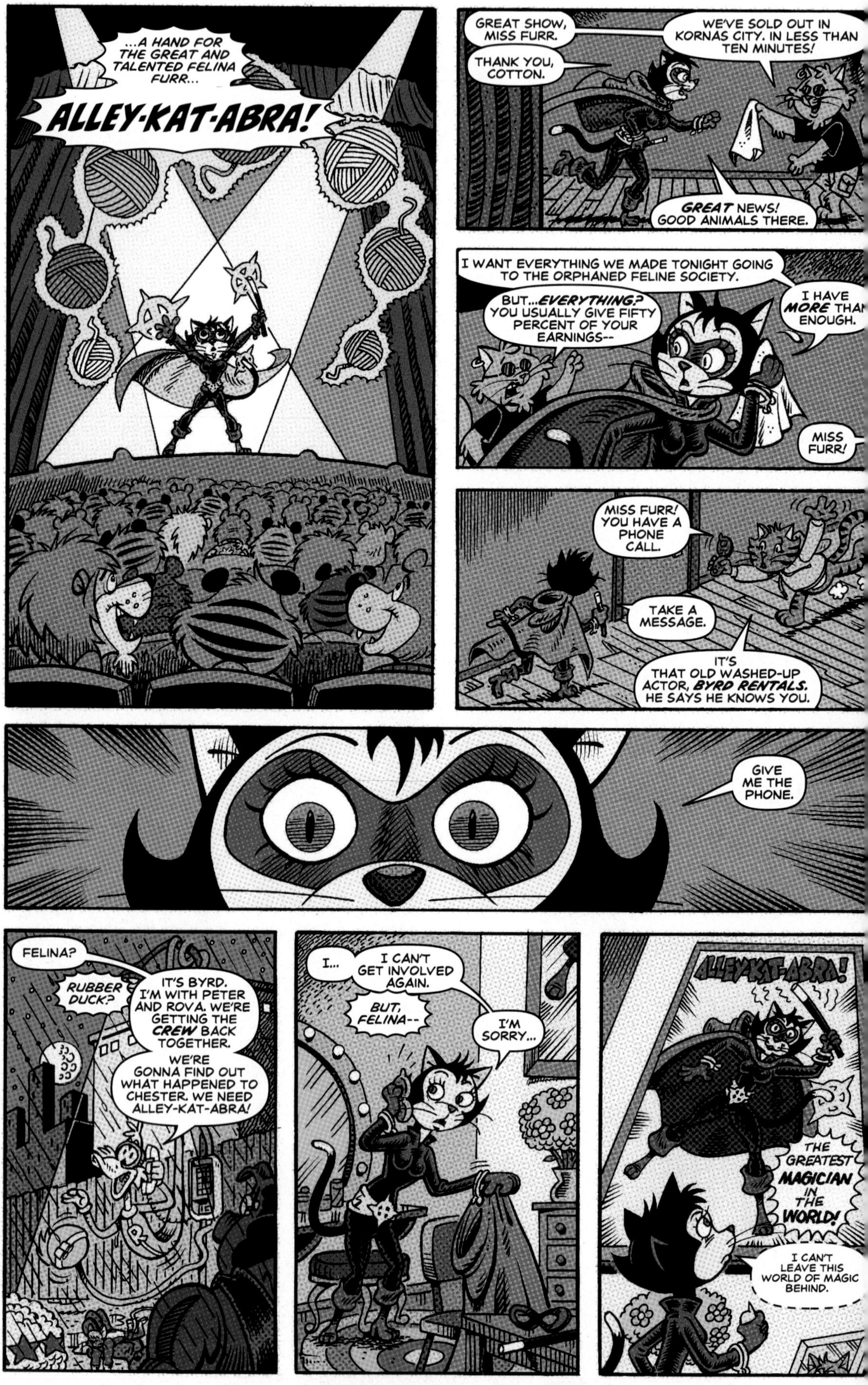
...A HAND FOR THE GREAT AND TALENTED FELINA FURR...
ALLEY-KAT-ABRA!
GREAT SHOW, MISS FURR.
WE'VE SOLD OUT IN KORNAS CITY. IN LESS THAN TEN MINUTES!
THANK YOU, COTTON.
GREAT NEWS! GOOD ANIMALS THERE.
I WANT EVERYTHING WE MADE TONIGHT GOING TO THE ORPHANED FELINE SOCIETY.
BUT...EVERYTHING? YOU USUALLY GIVE FIFTY PERCENT OF YOUR EARNINGS--
I HAVE MORE THAN ENOUGH.
MISS FURR!
MISS FURR! YOU HAVE A PHONE CALL.
TAKE A MESSAGE.
IT'S THAT OLD WASHED-UP ACTOR, BYRD RENTALS. HE SAYS HE KNOWS YOU.
GIVE ME THE PHONE.
FELINA?
RUBBER DUCK?
IT'S BYRD. I'M WITH PETER AND ROVA. WE'RE GETTING THE CREW BACK TOGETHER.
WE'RE GONNA FIND OUT WHAT HAPPENED TO CHESTER. WE NEED ALLEY-KAT-ABRA!
I...
I CAN'T GET INVOLVED AGAIN.
BUT, FELINA--
I'M SORRY...
ALLEY-KAT-ABRA!
THE GREATEST MAGICIAN IN THE WORLD!
I CAN'T LEAVE THIS WORLD OF MAGIC BEHIND.

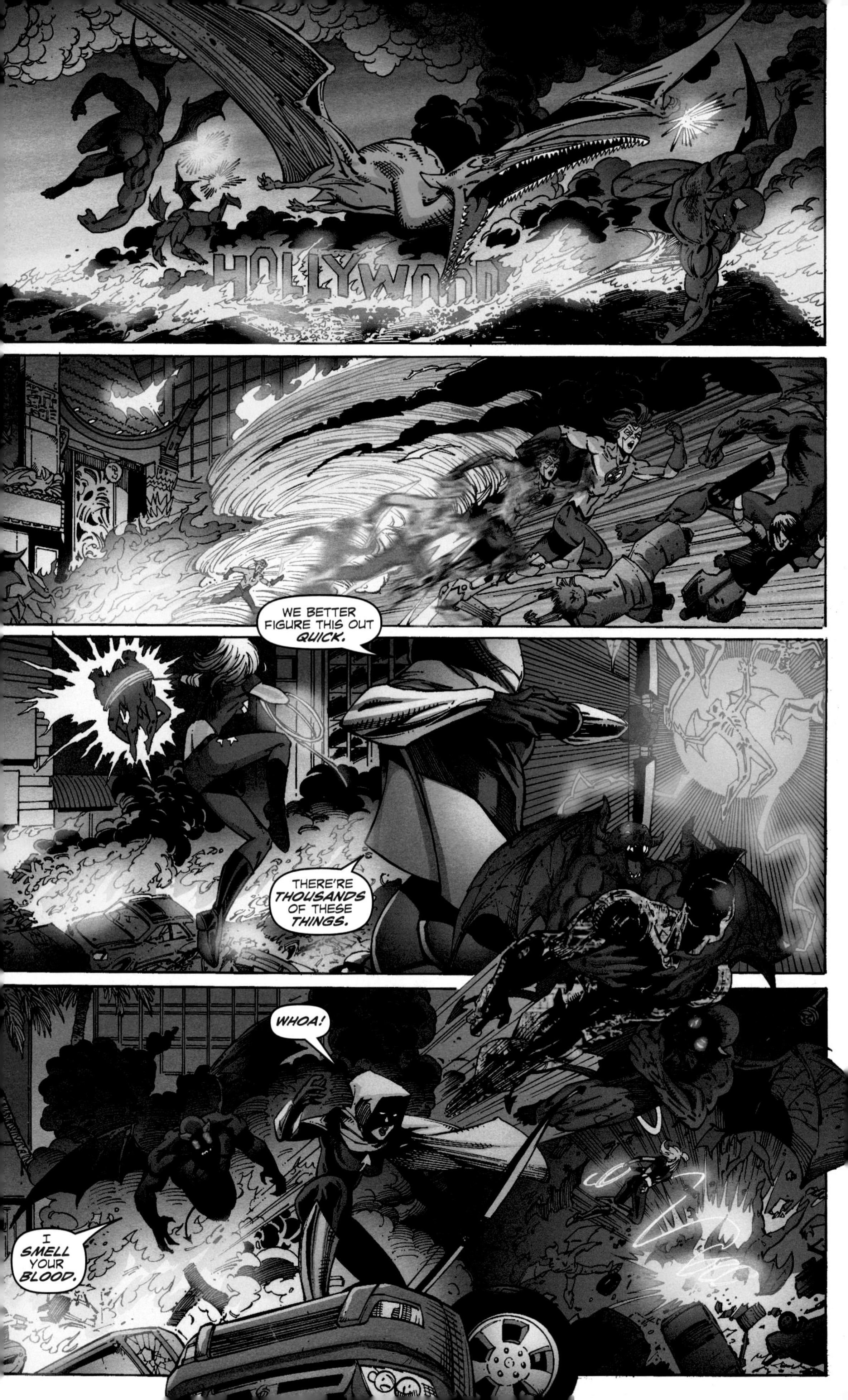
HOLLYWOOD
WE BETTER FIGURE THIS OUT *QUICK.*
THERE'RE *THOUSANDS* OF THESE *THINGS.*
WHOA!
I *SMELL* YOUR *BLOOD.*

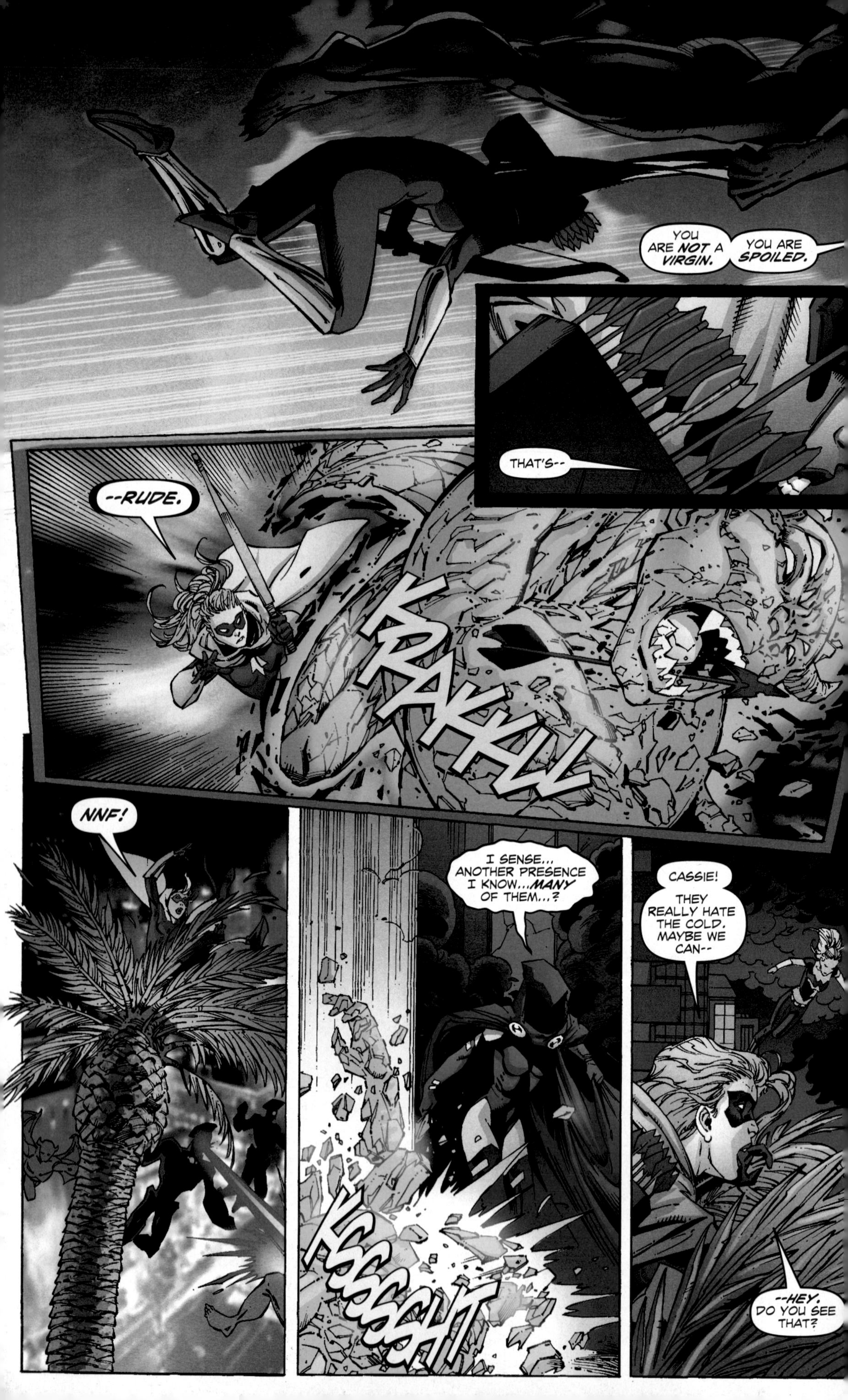

YOU ARE NOT A VIRGIN.
YOU ARE SPOILED.
THAT'S--
--RUDE.
KRAKKLL
NNF!
I SENSE... ANOTHER PRESENCE I KNOW...MANY OF THEM...?
KSSSSSHT
CASSIE!
THEY REALLY HATE THE COLD. MAYBE WE CAN--
--HEY. DO YOU SEE THAT?

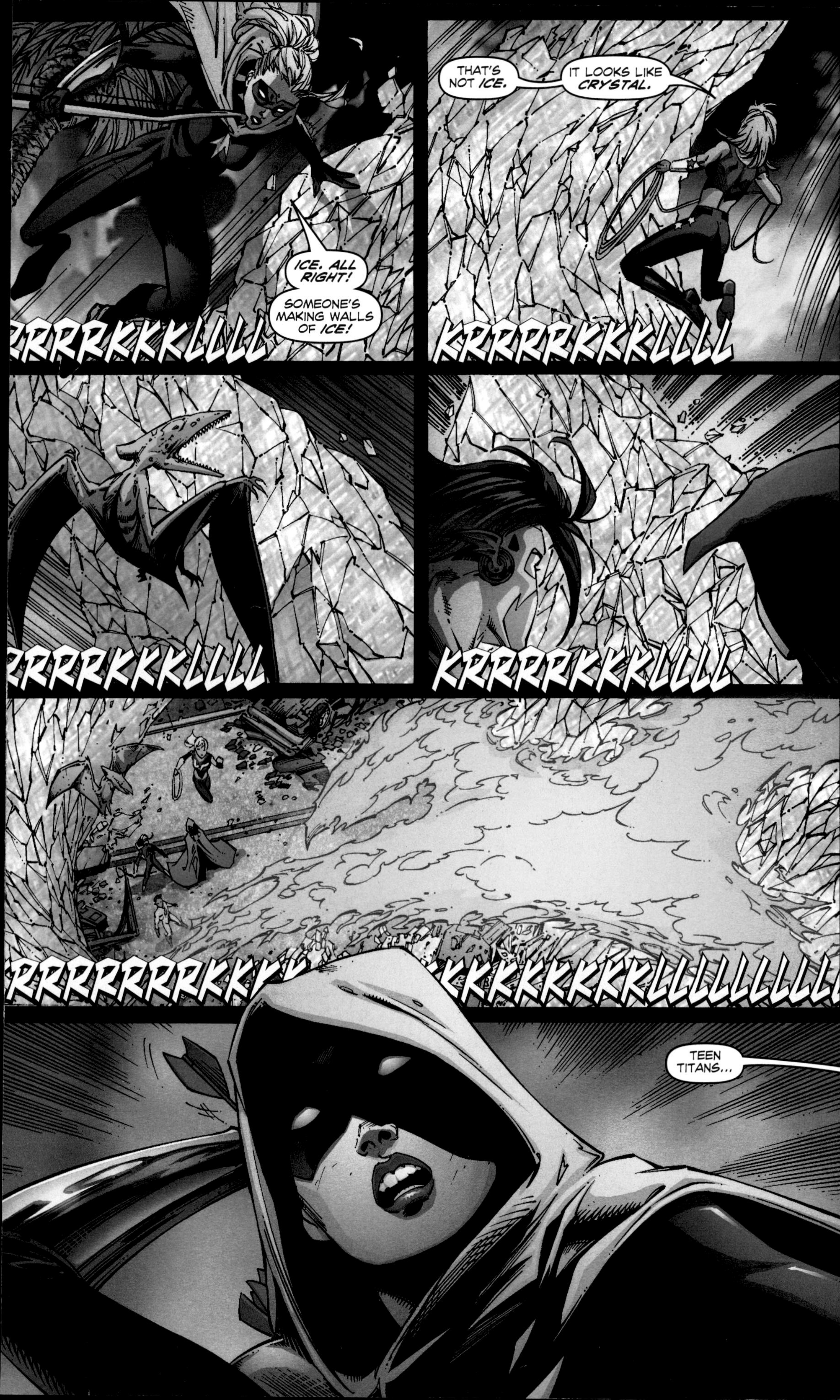
ICE. ALL RIGHT!
SOMEONE'S MAKING WALLS OF ICE!
KRRRRKKKLLLL
THAT'S NOT ICE.
IT LOOKS LIKE CRYSTAL.
KRRRRKKKLLLL
KRRRRKKKLLLL
KRRRRKKKLLLL
KRRRRRRRKKK
KKKKKKKKLLLLLLLLLL
TEEN TITANS...

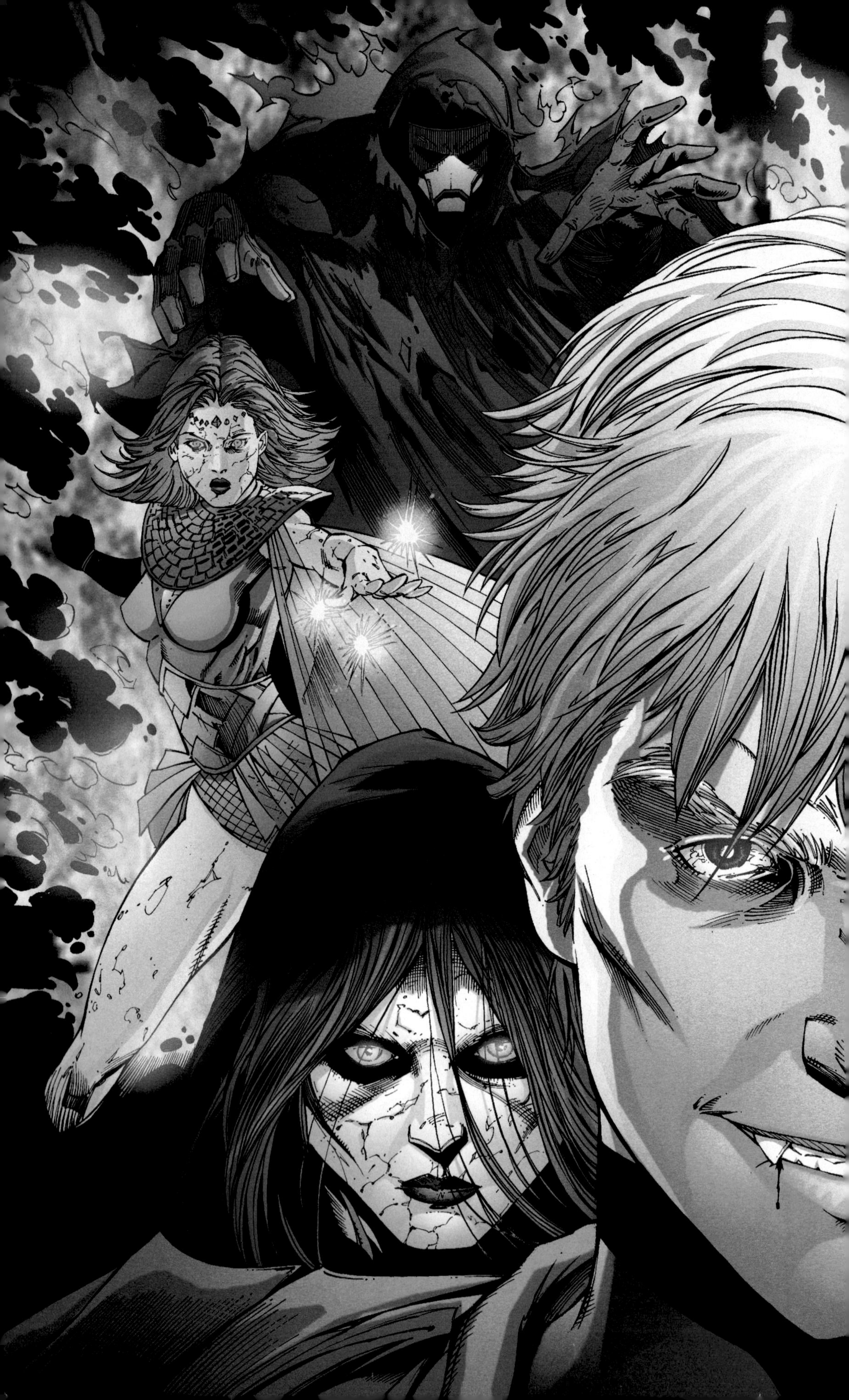

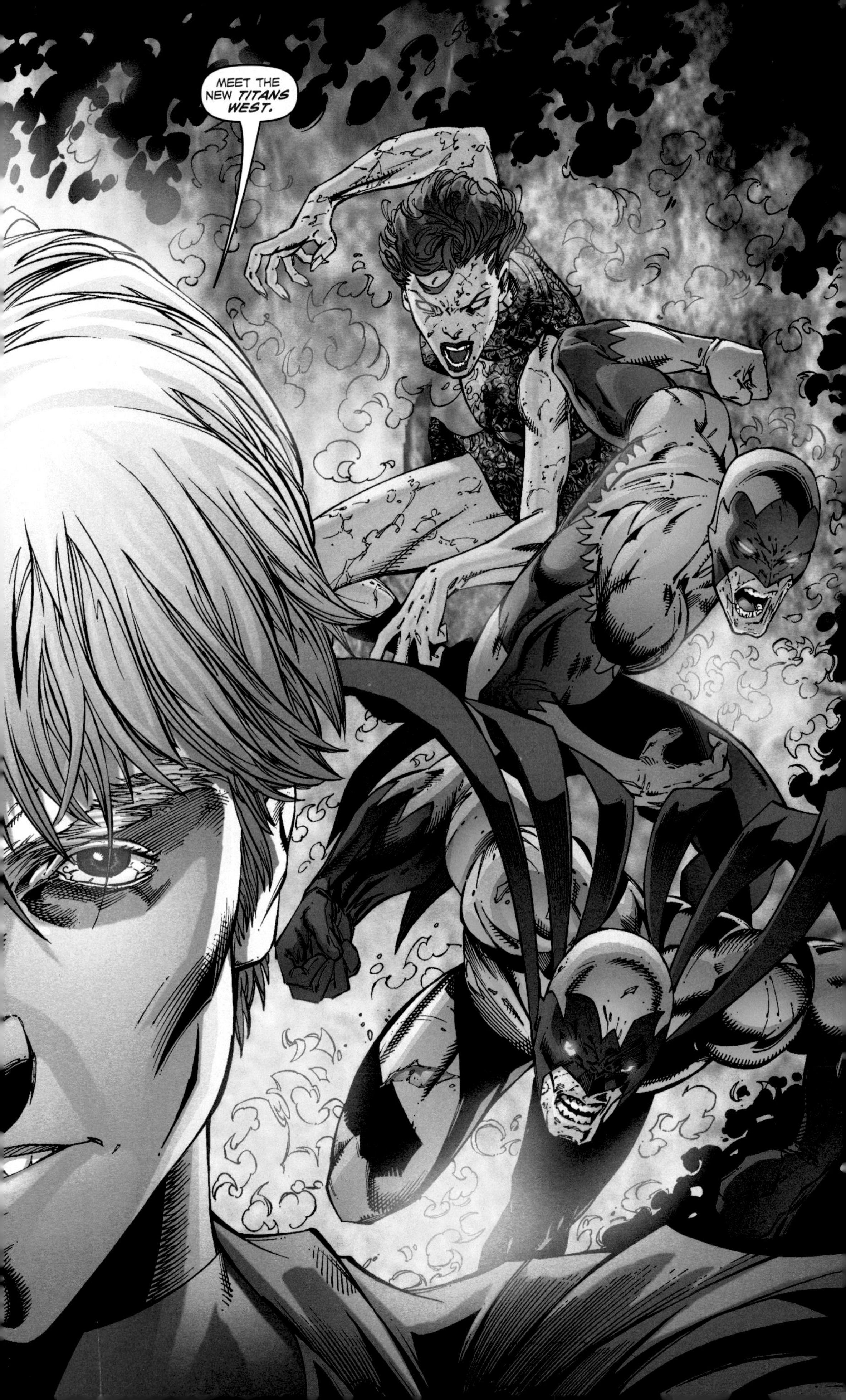
MEET THE NEW *TITANS WEST*.

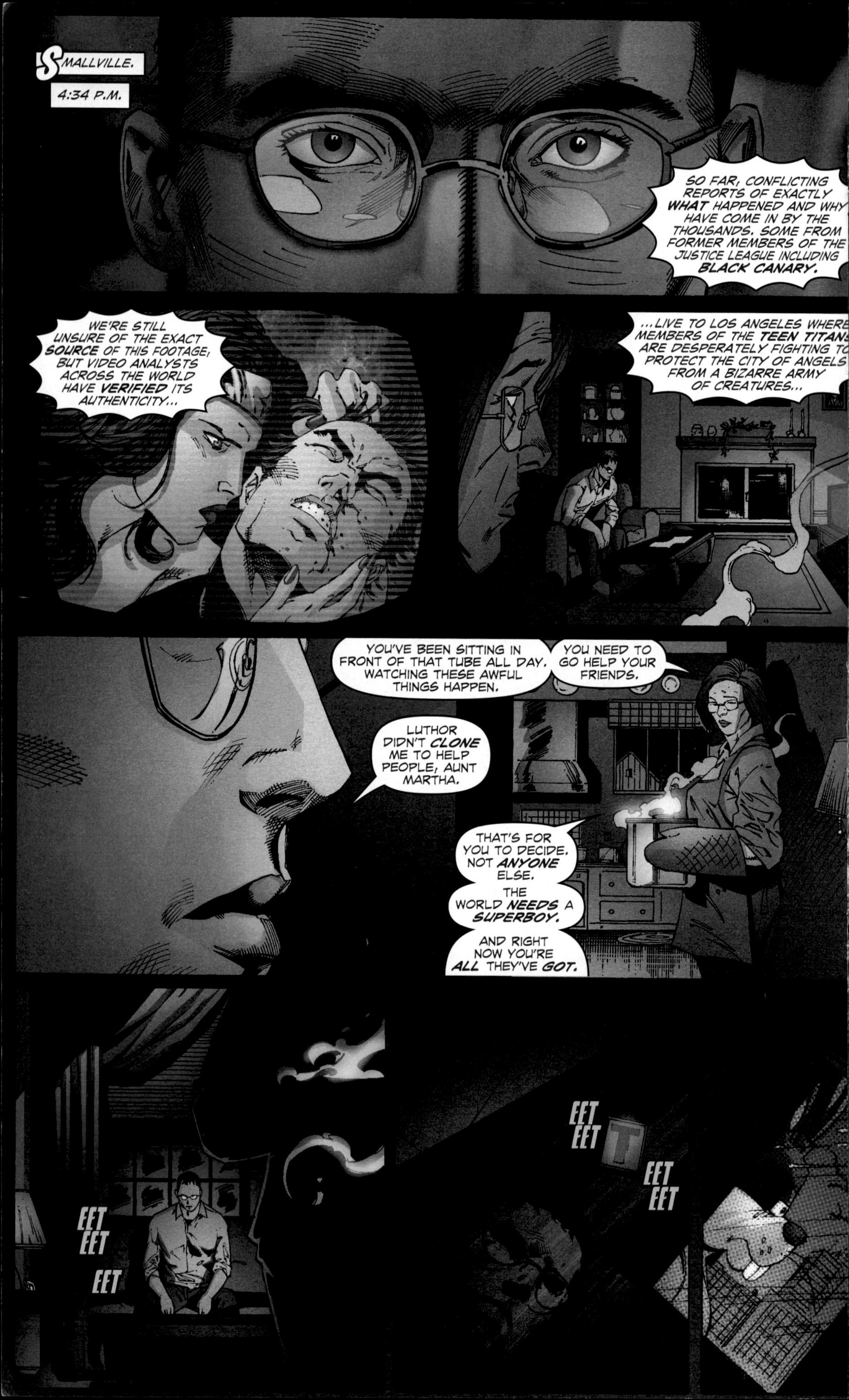
SMALLVILLE.
4:34 P.M.
SO FAR, CONFLICTING REPORTS OF EXACTLY WHAT HAPPENED AND WHY HAVE COME IN BY THE THOUSANDS. SOME FROM FORMER MEMBERS OF THE JUSTICE LEAGUE INCLUDING BLACK CANARY.
WE'RE STILL UNSURE OF THE EXACT SOURCE OF THIS FOOTAGE, BUT VIDEO ANALYSTS ACROSS THE WORLD HAVE VERIFIED ITS AUTHENTICITY...
...LIVE TO LOS ANGELES WHERE MEMBERS OF THE TEEN TITANS ARE DESPERATELY FIGHTING TO PROTECT THE CITY OF ANGELS FROM A BIZARRE ARMY OF CREATURES...
YOU'VE BEEN SITTING IN FRONT OF THAT TUBE ALL DAY. WATCHING THESE AWFUL THINGS HAPPEN.
YOU NEED TO GO HELP YOUR FRIENDS.
LUTHOR DIDN'T CLONE ME TO HELP PEOPLE, AUNT MARTHA.
THAT'S FOR YOU TO DECIDE. NOT ANYONE ELSE.
THE WORLD NEEDS A SUPERBOY.
AND RIGHT NOW YOU'RE ALL THEY'VE GOT.
EET EET
T
EET EET
EET EET
EET

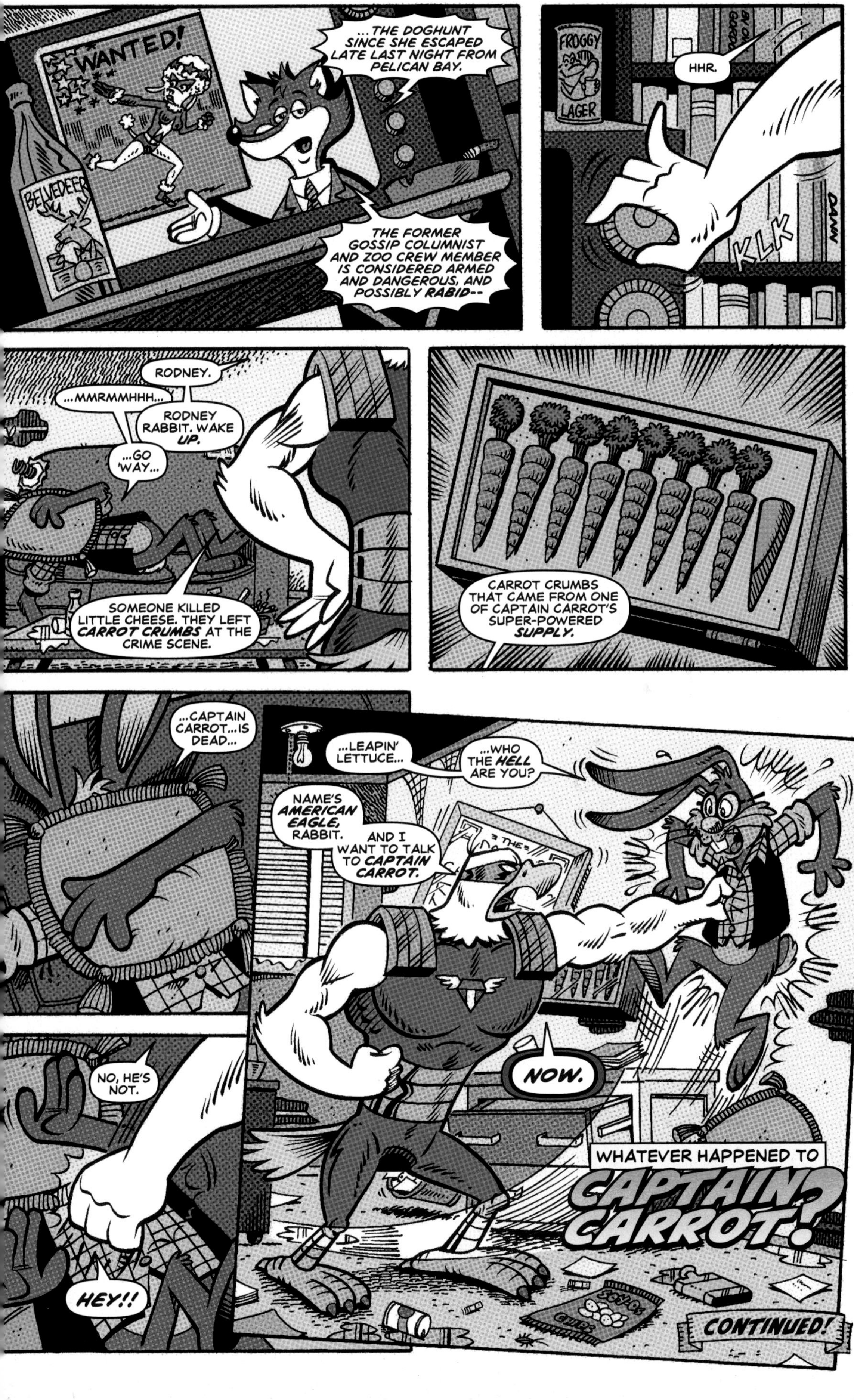
WANTED!
...THE DOGHUNT SINCE SHE ESCAPED LATE LAST NIGHT FROM PELICAN BAY.
BELVEDEER
THE FORMER GOSSIP COLUMNIST AND ZOO CREW MEMBER IS CONSIDERED ARMED AND DANGEROUS, AND POSSIBLY RABID--
FROGGY LAGER
HHR.
KLK
RODNEY.
...MMRMMHHH...
RODNEY RABBIT. WAKE UP.
...GO 'WAY...
SOMEONE KILLED LITTLE CHEESE. THEY LEFT CARROT CRUMBS AT THE CRIME SCENE.
CARROT CRUMBS THAT CAME FROM ONE OF CAPTAIN CARROT'S SUPER-POWERED SUPPLY.
...CAPTAIN CARROT...IS DEAD...
NO, HE'S NOT.
HEY!!
...LEAPIN' LETTUCE...
...WHO THE HELL ARE YOU?
NAME'S AMERICAN EAGLE, RABBIT.
AND I WANT TO TALK TO CAPTAIN CARROT.
NOW.
WHATEVER HAPPENED TO
CAPTAIN CARROT?!
CONTINUED!

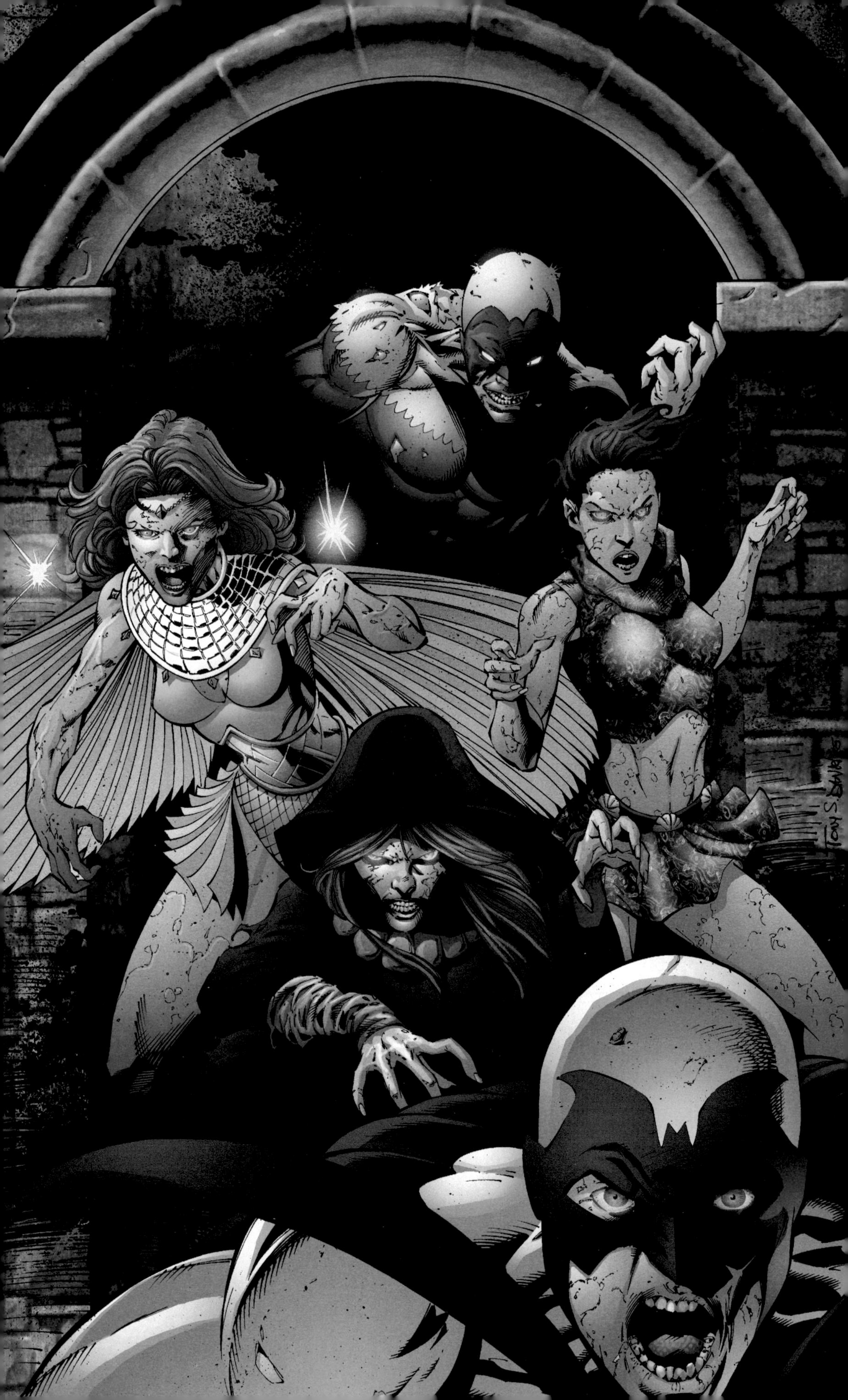

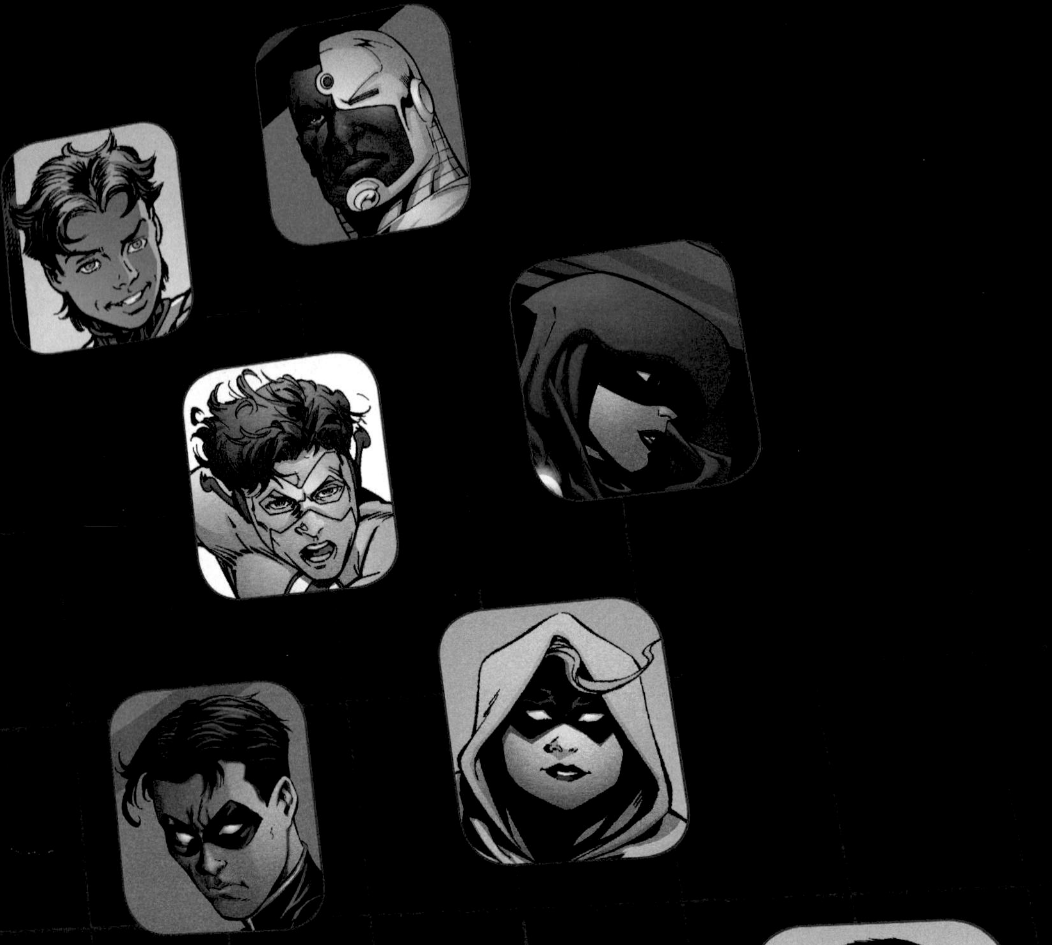

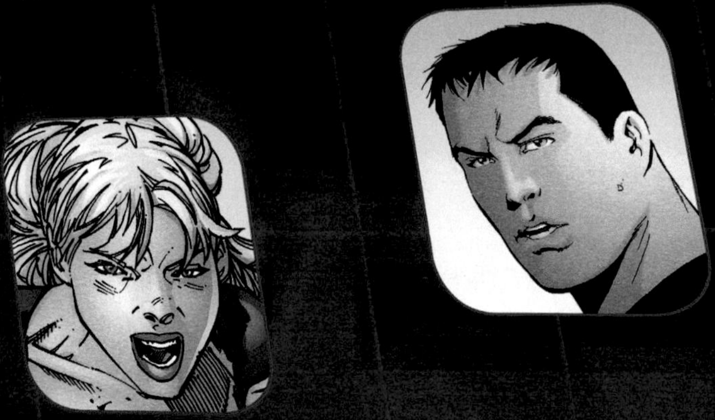

TEEN TITANS #31

GEOFF JOHNS
Writer

TONY S. DANIEL
TODD NAUCK
SCOTT ROBERTS
Pencillers

MARLO ALQUIZA
RICHARD BONK
SCOTT ROBERTS
Inkers

TANYA & RICHARD HORIE
Colorists

COMICRAFT
Letterer

TONY S. DANIEL,
MARLO ALQUIZA & JEROMY COX
Cover Artists

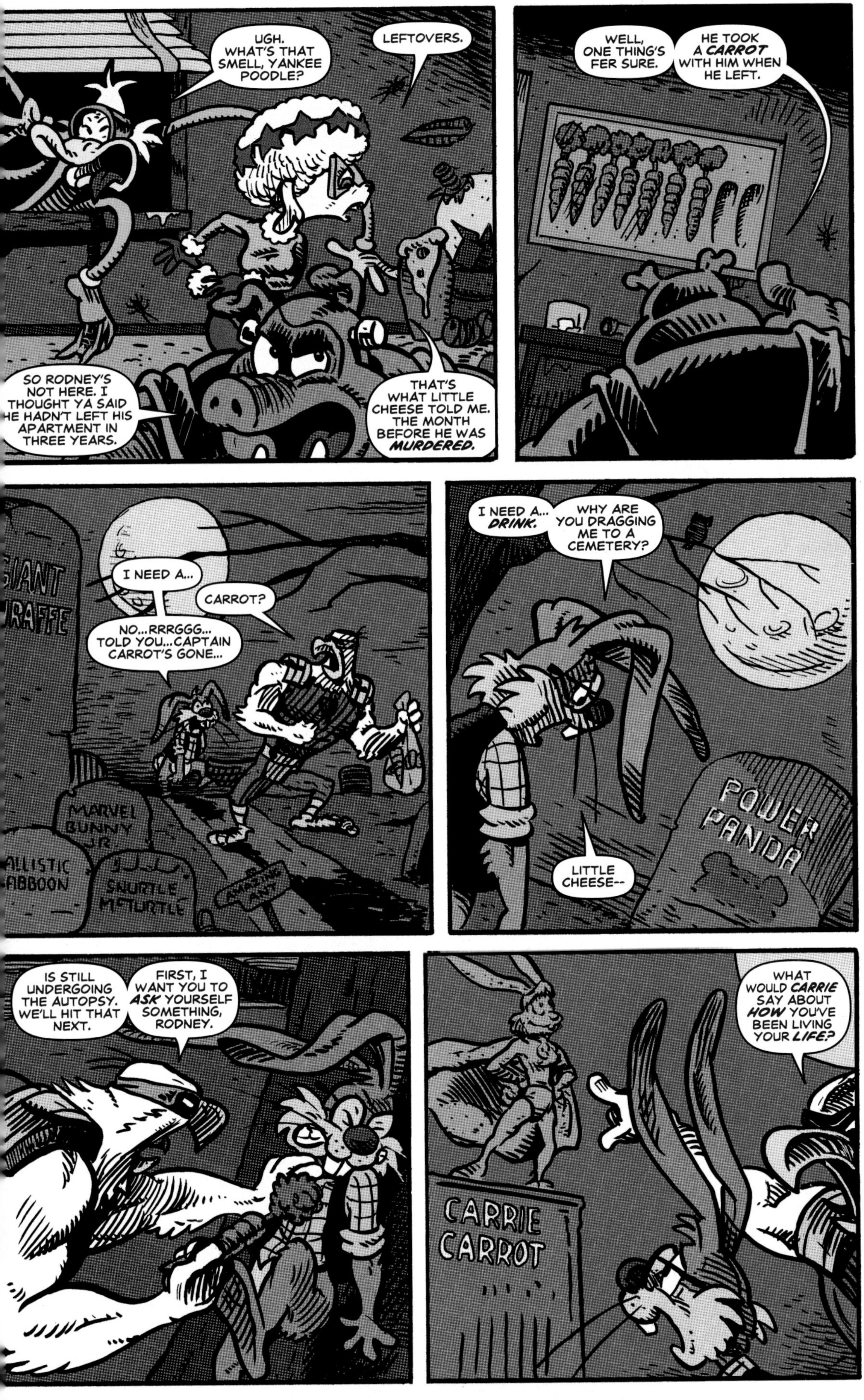
UGH. WHAT'S THAT SMELL, YANKEE POODLE?
LEFTOVERS.
SO RODNEY'S NOT HERE. I THOUGHT YA SAID HE HADN'T LEFT HIS APARTMENT IN THREE YEARS.
THAT'S WHAT LITTLE CHEESE TOLD ME. THE MONTH BEFORE HE WAS MURDERED.
WELL, ONE THING'S FER SURE.
HE TOOK A CARROT WITH HIM WHEN HE LEFT.
GIANT
RAFFE
I NEED A...
CARROT?
NO...RRRGGG... TOLD YOU...CAPTAIN CARROT'S GONE...
MARVEL BUNNY JR.
ALLISTIC ABBOON
SNURTLE McTURTLE
AMAZING ANT
I NEED A... DRINK.
WHY ARE YOU DRAGGING ME TO A CEMETERY?
POWER PANDA
LITTLE CHEESE--
IS STILL UNDERGOING THE AUTOPSY. WE'LL HIT THAT NEXT.
FIRST, I WANT YOU TO ASK YOURSELF SOMETHING, RODNEY.
CARRIE CARROT
WHAT WOULD CARRIE SAY ABOUT HOW YOU'VE BEEN LIVING YOUR LIFE?

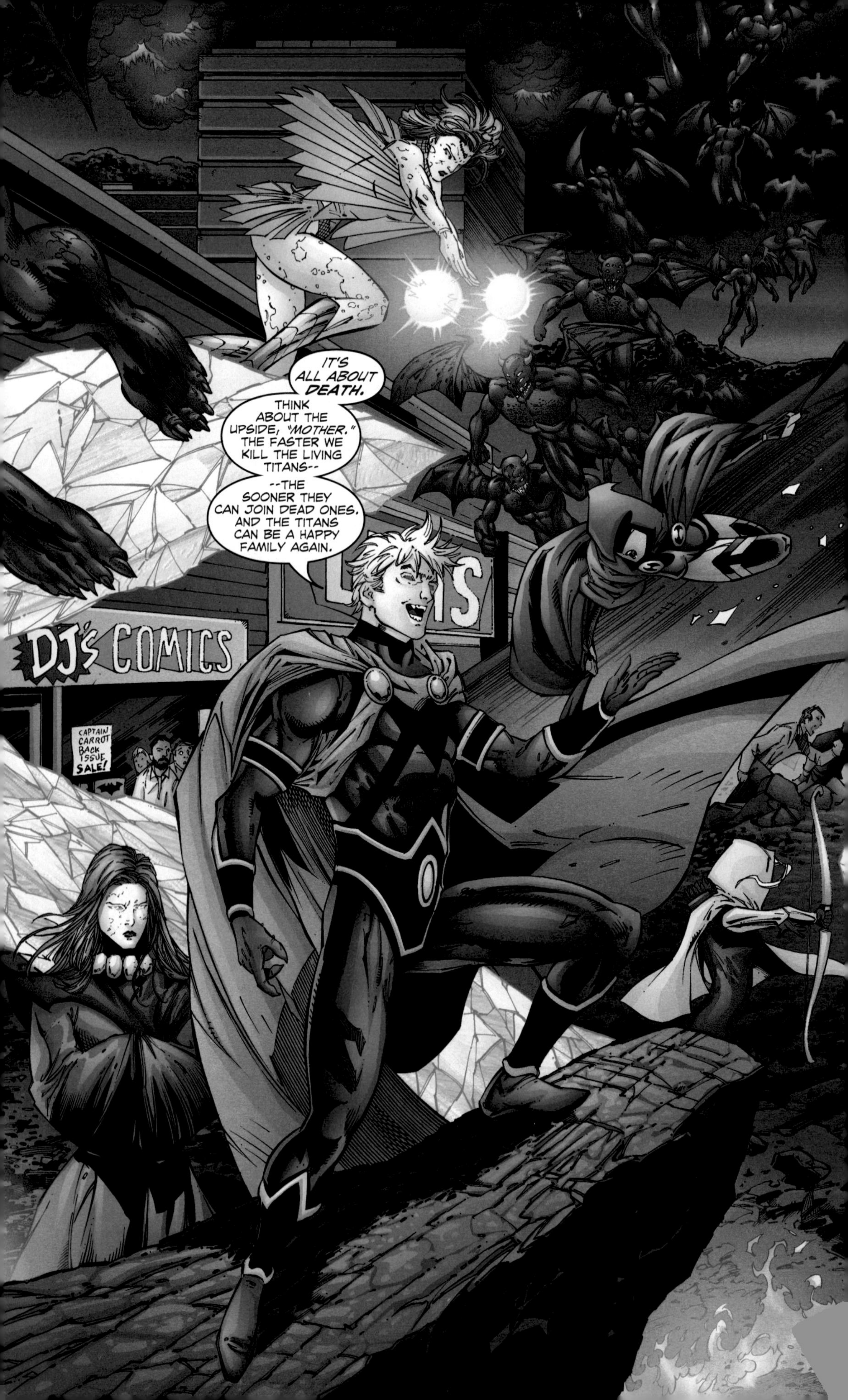

IT'S ALL ABOUT *DEATH.*
THINK ABOUT THE UPSIDE, *"MOTHER."* THE FASTER WE KILL THE LIVING TITANS--
--THE SOONER THEY CAN JOIN DEAD ONES. AND THE TITANS CAN BE A HAPPY FAMILY AGAIN.
DJ's COMICS
CAPTAIN CARROT BACK ISSUE SALE!

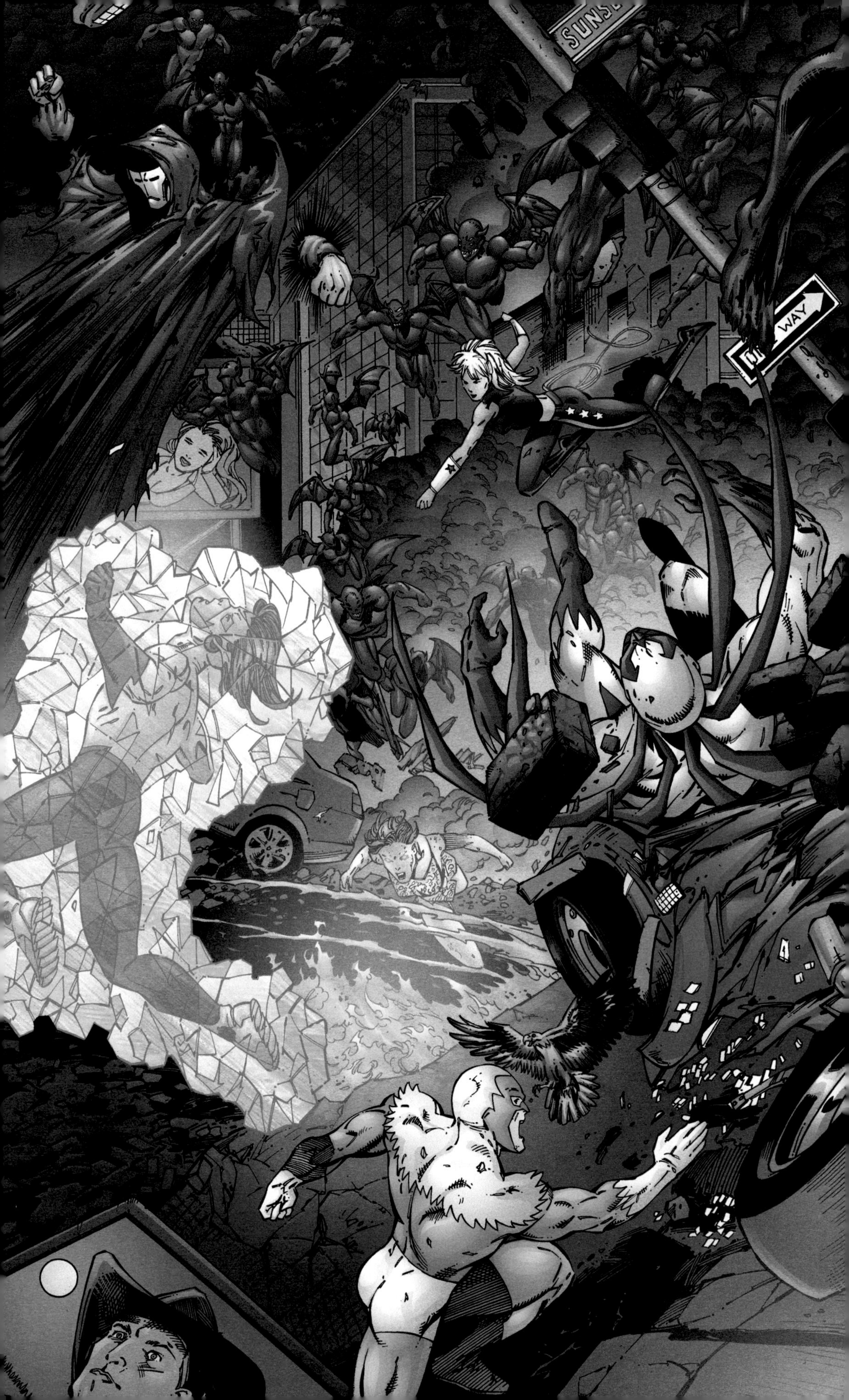
WAY

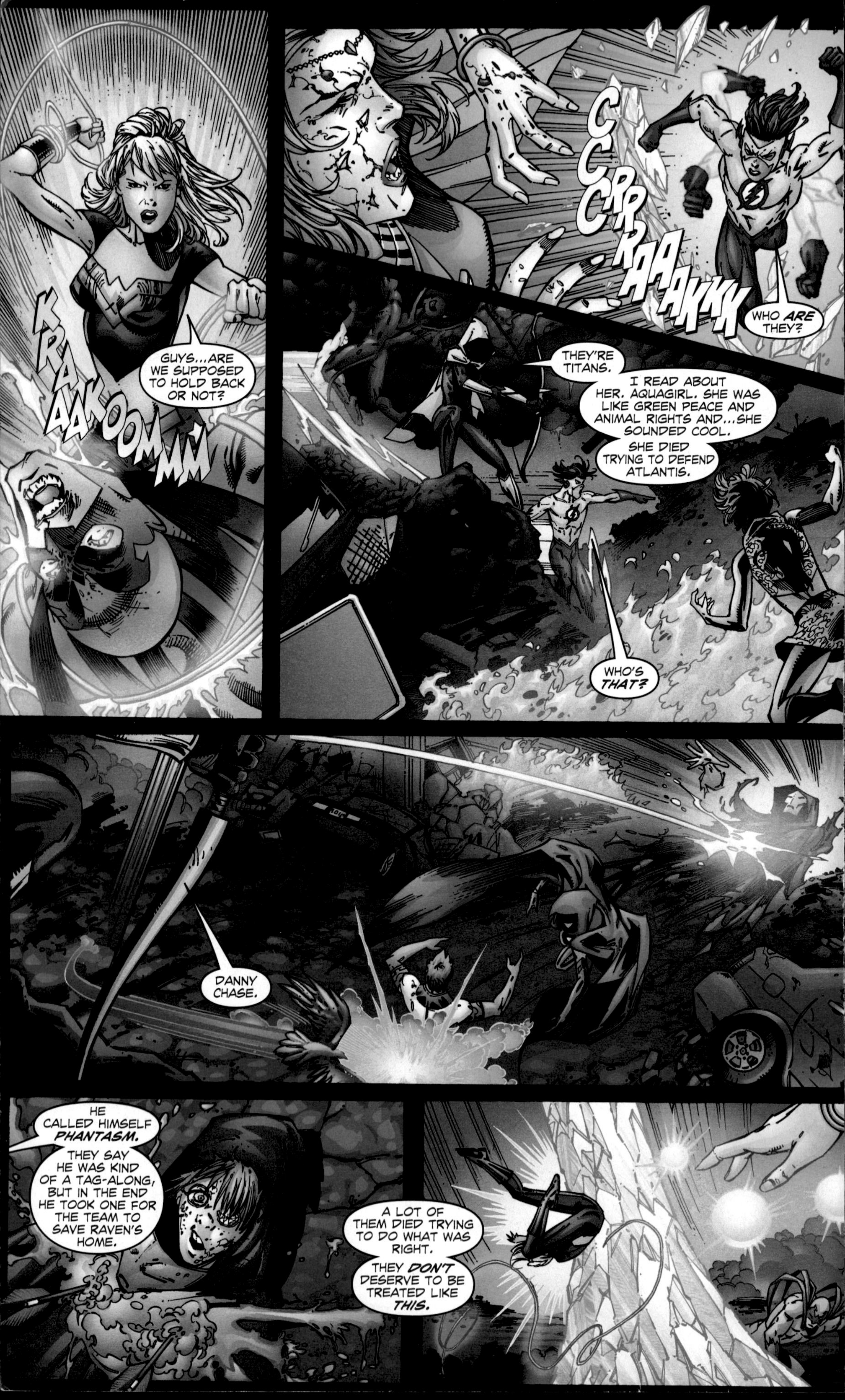
KRAAAKOOMMM
GUYS...ARE WE SUPPOSED TO HOLD BACK OR NOT?
CCCRRRAAAKKK
WHO ARE THEY?
THEY'RE TITANS.
I READ ABOUT HER. AQUAGIRL. SHE WAS LIKE GREEN PEACE AND ANIMAL RIGHTS AND...SHE SOUNDED COOL.
SHE DIED TRYING TO DEFEND ATLANTIS.
WHO'S THAT?
DANNY CHASE.
HE CALLED HIMSELF PHANTASM.
THEY SAY HE WAS KIND OF A TAG-ALONG, BUT IN THE END HE TOOK ONE FOR THE TEAM TO SAVE RAVEN'S HOME.
A LOT OF THEM DIED TRYING TO DO WHAT WAS RIGHT.
THEY DON'T DESERVE TO BE TREATED LIKE THIS.

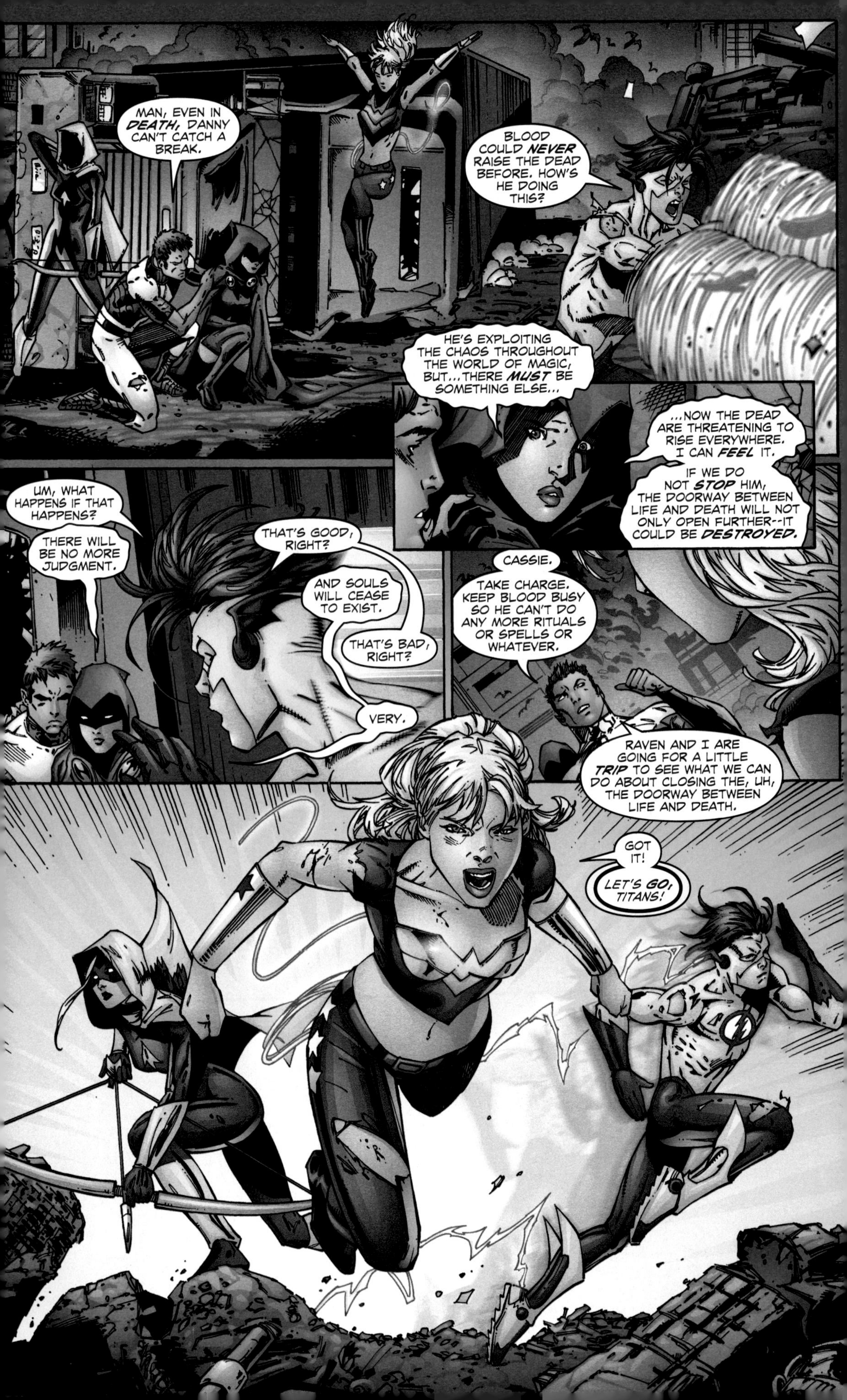
MAN, EVEN IN DEATH, DANNY CAN'T CATCH A BREAK.
BLOOD COULD NEVER RAISE THE DEAD BEFORE. HOW'S HE DOING THIS?
HE'S EXPLOITING THE CHAOS THROUGHOUT THE WORLD OF MAGIC, BUT... THERE MUST BE SOMETHING ELSE...
...NOW THE DEAD ARE THREATENING TO RISE EVERYWHERE. I CAN FEEL IT.
IF WE DO NOT STOP HIM, THE DOORWAY BETWEEN LIFE AND DEATH WILL NOT ONLY OPEN FURTHER--IT COULD BE DESTROYED.
UM, WHAT HAPPENS IF THAT HAPPENS?
THERE WILL BE NO MORE JUDGMENT.
THAT'S GOOD, RIGHT?
AND SOULS WILL CEASE TO EXIST.
THAT'S BAD, RIGHT?
VERY.
CASSIE.
TAKE CHARGE. KEEP BLOOD BUSY SO HE CAN'T DO ANY MORE RITUALS OR SPELLS OR WHATEVER.
RAVEN AND I ARE GOING FOR A LITTLE TRIP TO SEE WHAT WE CAN DO ABOUT CLOSING THE, UH, THE DOORWAY BETWEEN LIFE AND DEATH.
GOT IT!
LET'S GO, TITANS!

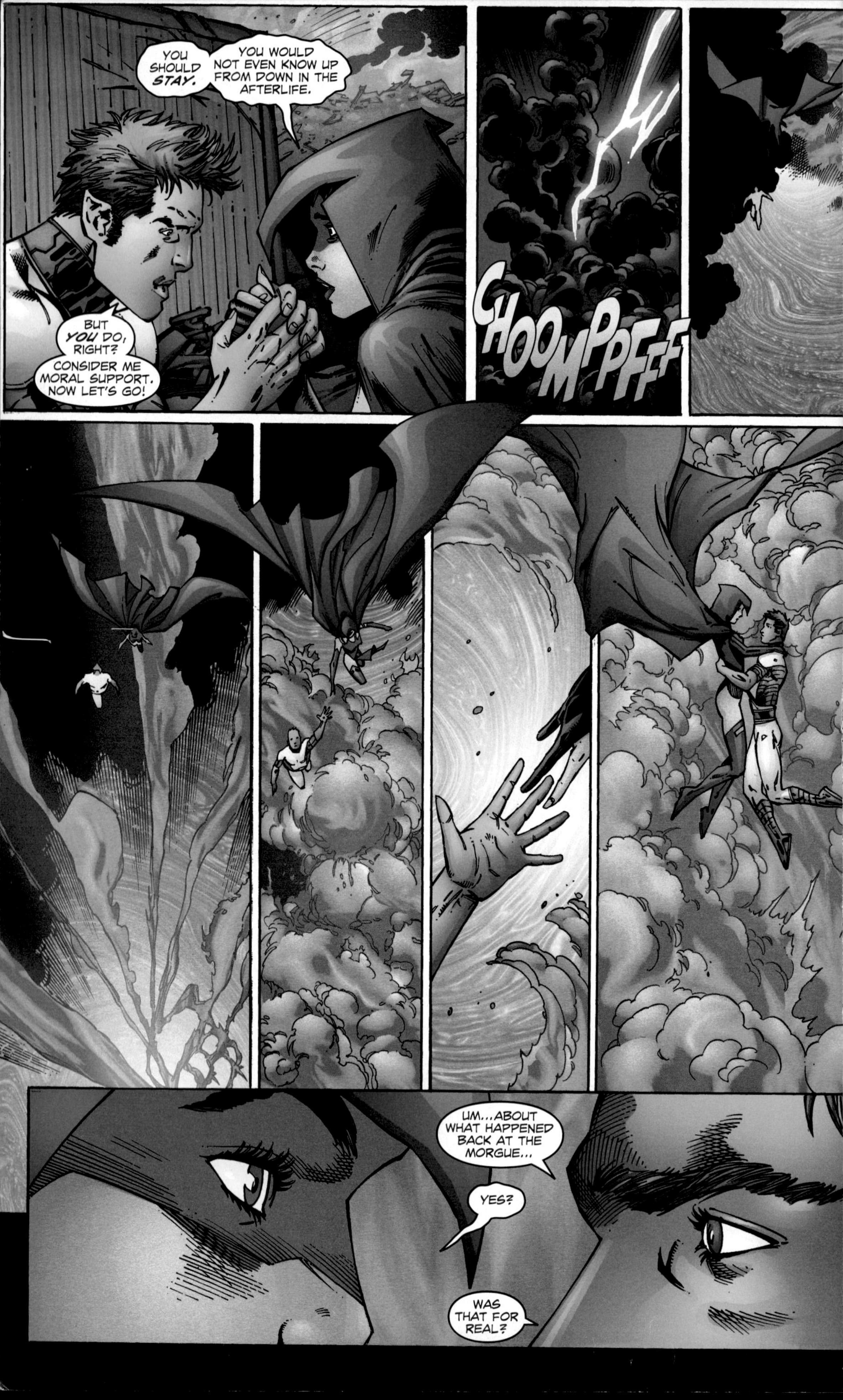

YOU SHOULD STAY.
YOU WOULD NOT EVEN KNOW UP FROM DOWN IN THE AFTERLIFE.
BUT YOU DO, RIGHT? CONSIDER ME MORAL SUPPORT. NOW LET'S GO!
CHOOMPPFFF
UM...ABOUT WHAT HAPPENED BACK AT THE MORGUE...
YES?
WAS THAT FOR REAL?

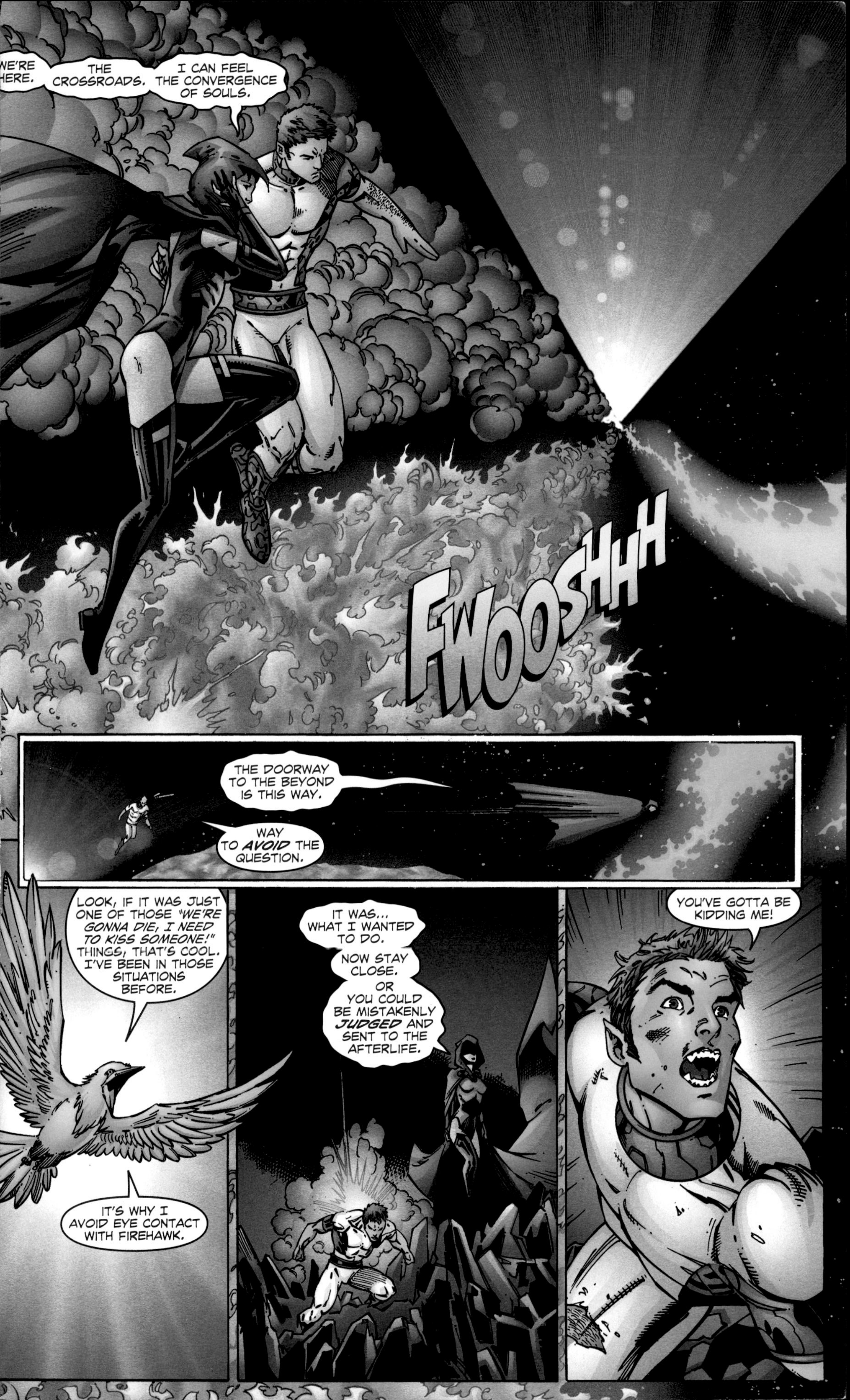
WE'RE HERE.
THE CROSSROADS.
I CAN FEEL THE CONVERGENCE OF SOULS.
FWOOSHHH
THE DOORWAY TO THE BEYOND IS THIS WAY.
WAY TO *AVOID* THE QUESTION.
LOOK, IF IT WAS JUST ONE OF THOSE *"WE'RE GONNA DIE, I NEED TO KISS SOMEONE!"* THINGS, THAT'S COOL. I'VE BEEN IN THOSE SITUATIONS BEFORE.
IT'S WHY I AVOID EYE CONTACT WITH FIREHAWK.
IT WAS... WHAT I WANTED TO DO.
NOW STAY CLOSE.
OR YOU COULD BE MISTAKENLY *JUDGED* AND SENT TO THE AFTERLIFE.
YOU'VE GOTTA BE KIDDING ME!

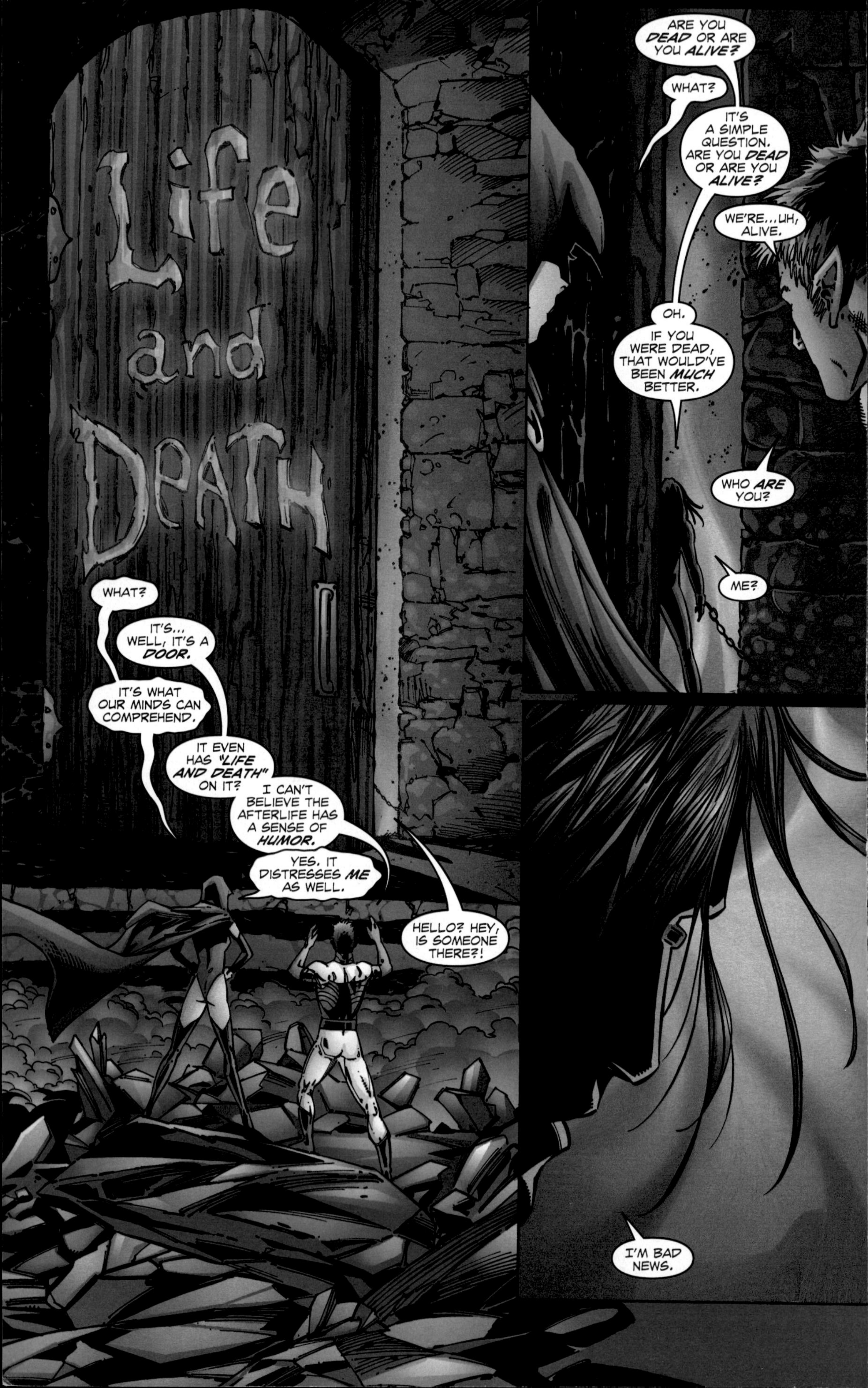
Life and DEATH
WHAT?
IT'S... WELL, IT'S A DOOR.
IT'S WHAT OUR MINDS CAN COMPREHEND.
IT EVEN HAS "LIFE AND DEATH" ON IT?
I CAN'T BELIEVE THE AFTERLIFE HAS A SENSE OF HUMOR.
YES. IT DISTRESSES ME AS WELL.
HELLO? HEY, IS SOMEONE THERE?!
ARE YOU DEAD OR ARE YOU ALIVE?
WHAT?
IT'S A SIMPLE QUESTION. ARE YOU DEAD OR ARE YOU ALIVE?
WE'RE...UH, ALIVE.
OH.
IF YOU WERE DEAD, THAT WOULD'VE BEEN MUCH BETTER.
WHO ARE YOU?
ME?
I'M BAD NEWS.

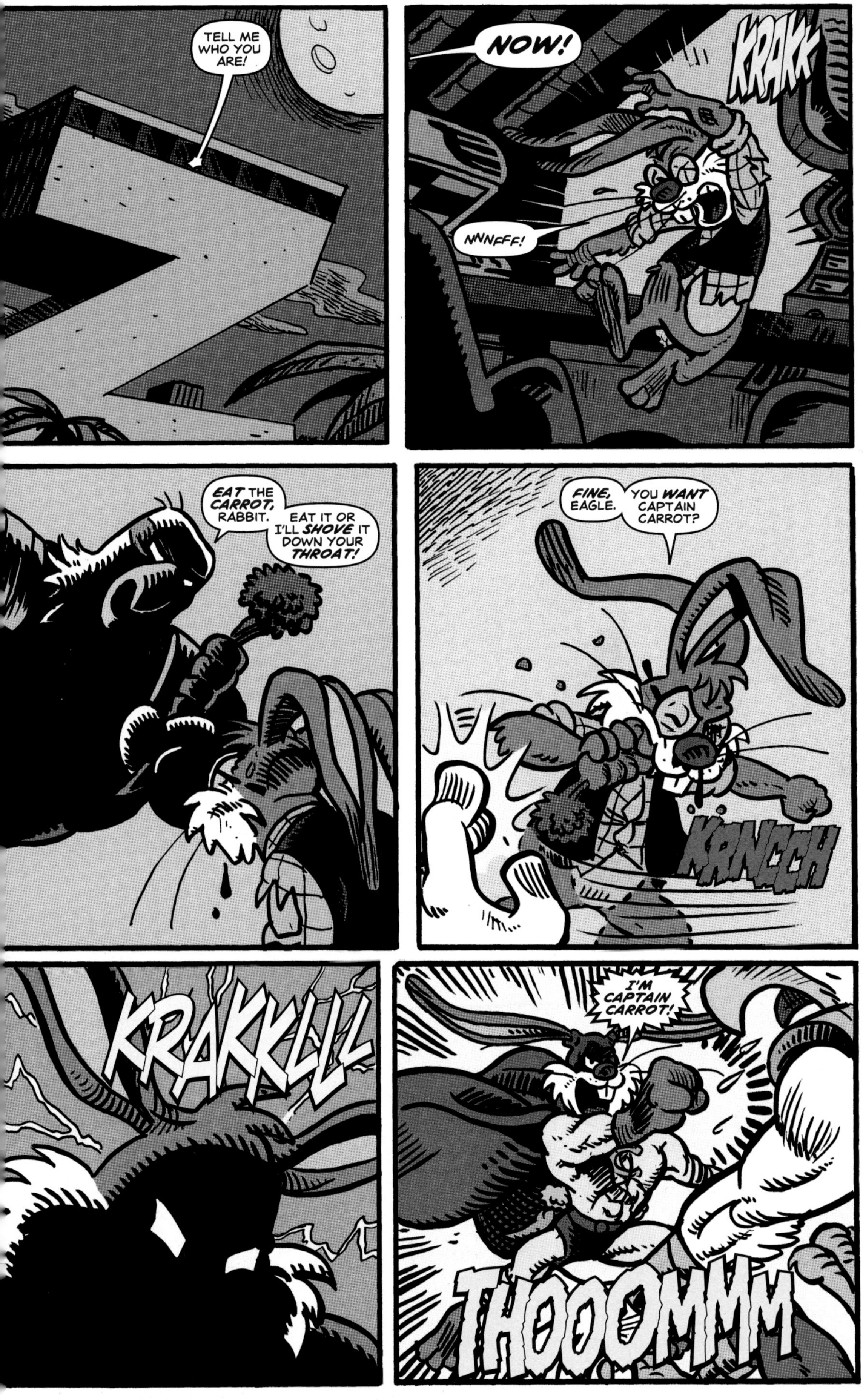
TELL ME WHO YOU ARE!
NOW!
KRAKK
NNNFFF!
EAT THE CARROT, RABBIT.
EAT IT OR I'LL SHOVE IT DOWN YOUR THROAT!
FINE, EAGLE.
YOU WANT CAPTAIN CARROT?
KRNCCH
KRAKKLLL
I'M CAPTAIN CARROT!
THOOOMMM

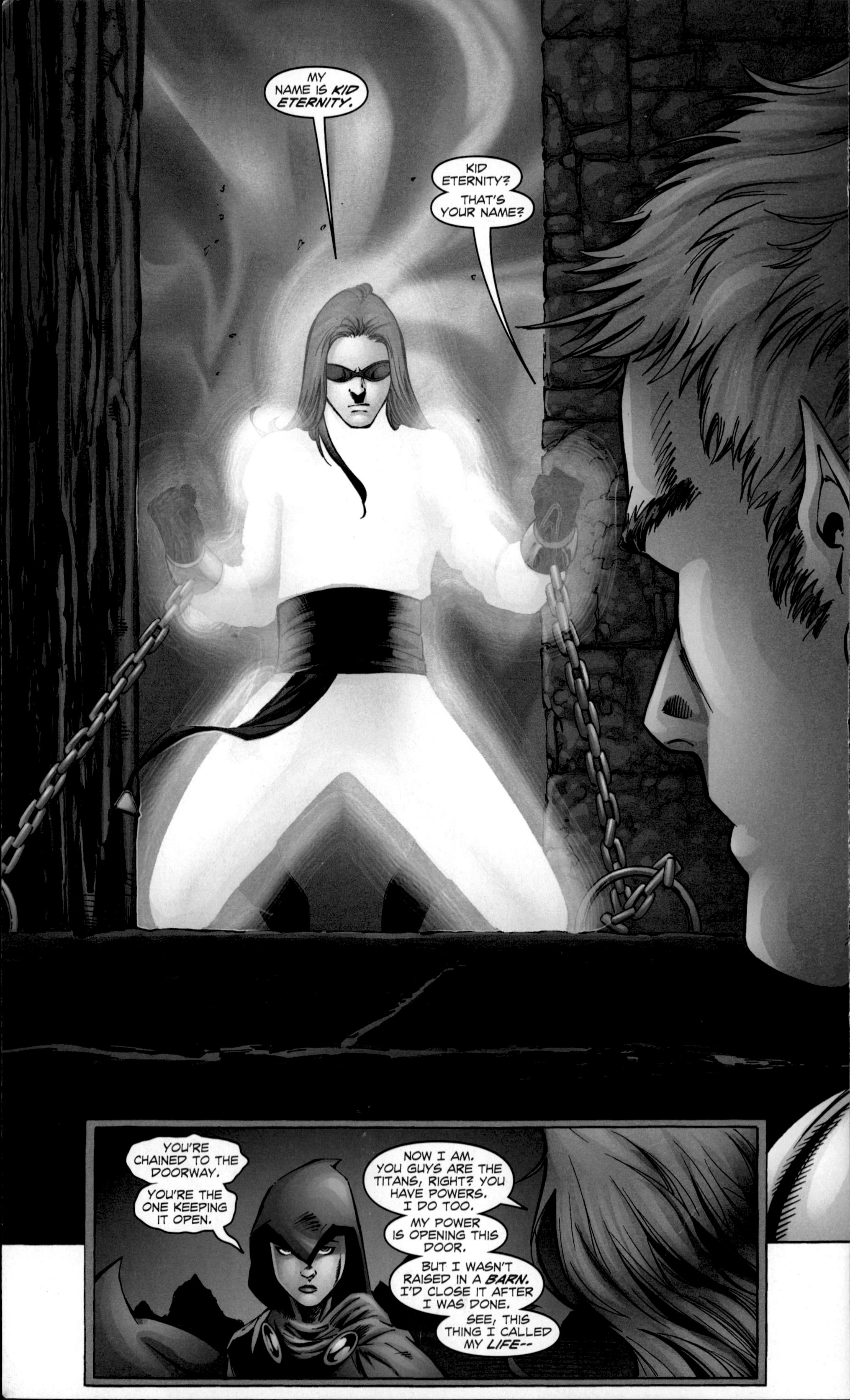
MY NAME IS *KID ETERNITY.*
KID ETERNITY? THAT'S YOUR NAME?
YOU'RE CHAINED TO THE DOORWAY.
YOU'RE THE ONE KEEPING IT OPEN.
NOW I AM. YOU GUYS ARE THE TITANS, RIGHT? YOU HAVE POWERS. I DO TOO.
MY POWER IS OPENING THIS DOOR.
BUT I WASN'T RAISED IN A *BARN.* I'D CLOSE IT AFTER I WAS DONE.
SEE, THIS THING I CALLED MY *LIFE--*

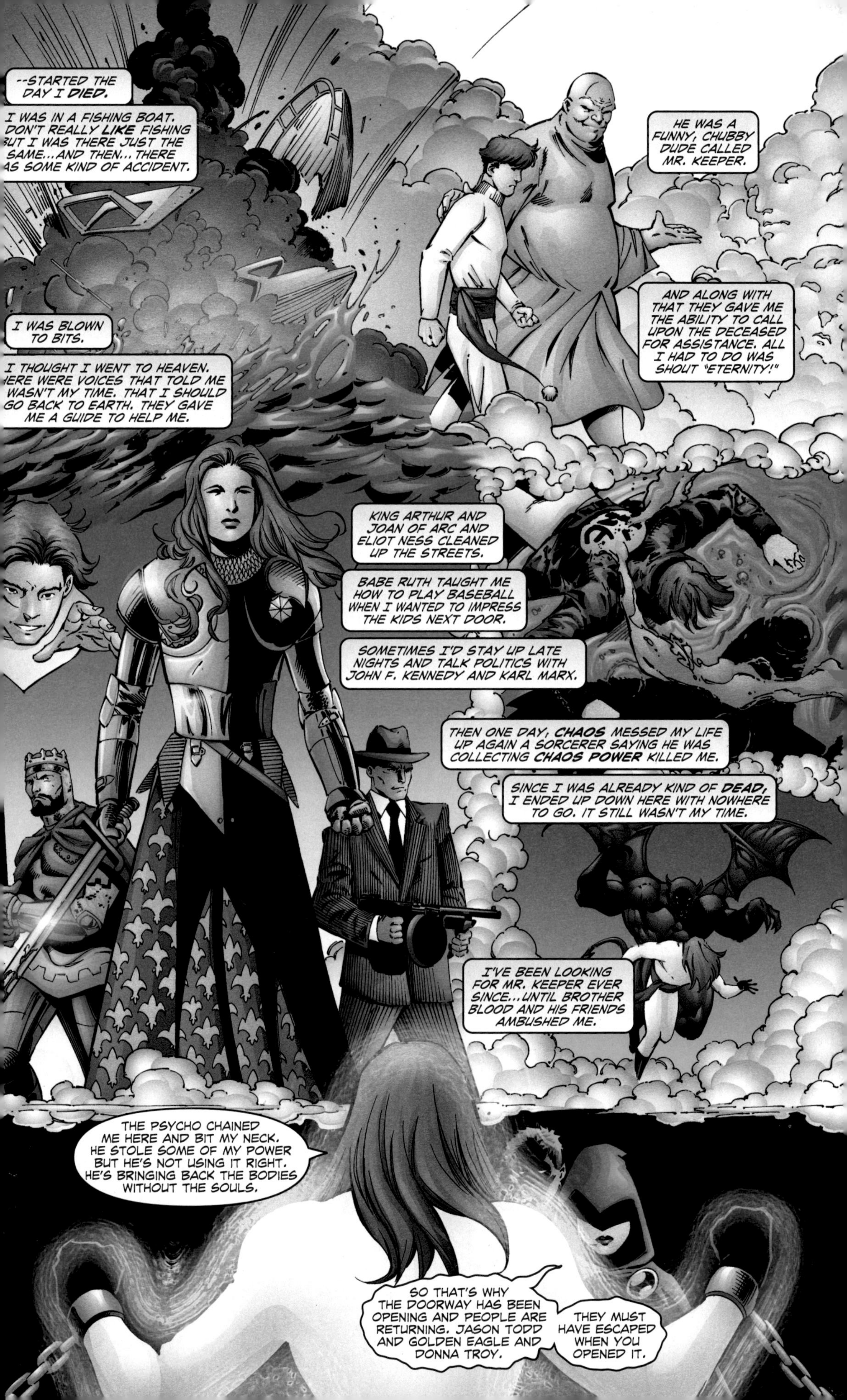
--STARTED THE DAY I DIED.
I WAS IN A FISHING BOAT. DON'T REALLY LIKE FISHING BUT I WAS THERE JUST THE SAME...AND THEN...THERE AS SOME KIND OF ACCIDENT.
I WAS BLOWN TO BITS.
I THOUGHT I WENT TO HEAVEN. HERE WERE VOICES THAT TOLD ME WASN'T MY TIME. THAT I SHOULD GO BACK TO EARTH. THEY GAVE ME A GUIDE TO HELP ME.
HE WAS A FUNNY, CHUBBY DUDE CALLED MR. KEEPER.
AND ALONG WITH THAT THEY GAVE ME THE ABILITY TO CALL UPON THE DECEASED FOR ASSISTANCE. ALL I HAD TO DO WAS SHOUT "ETERNITY!"
KING ARTHUR AND JOAN OF ARC AND ELIOT NESS CLEANED UP THE STREETS.
BABE RUTH TAUGHT ME HOW TO PLAY BASEBALL WHEN I WANTED TO IMPRESS THE KIDS NEXT DOOR.
SOMETIMES I'D STAY UP LATE NIGHTS AND TALK POLITICS WITH JOHN F. KENNEDY AND KARL MARX.
THEN ONE DAY, CHAOS MESSED MY LIFE UP AGAIN A SORCERER SAYING HE WAS COLLECTING CHAOS POWER KILLED ME.
SINCE I WAS ALREADY KIND OF DEAD, I ENDED UP DOWN HERE WITH NOWHERE TO GO. IT STILL WASN'T MY TIME.
I'VE BEEN LOOKING FOR MR. KEEPER EVER SINCE...UNTIL BROTHER BLOOD AND HIS FRIENDS AMBUSHED ME.
THE PSYCHO CHAINED ME HERE AND BIT MY NECK. HE STOLE SOME OF MY POWER BUT HE'S NOT USING IT RIGHT. HE'S BRINGING BACK THE BODIES WITHOUT THE SOULS.
SO THAT'S WHY THE DOORWAY HAS BEEN OPENING AND PEOPLE ARE RETURNING. JASON TODD AND GOLDEN EAGLE AND DONNA TROY.
THEY MUST HAVE ESCAPED WHEN YOU OPENED IT.

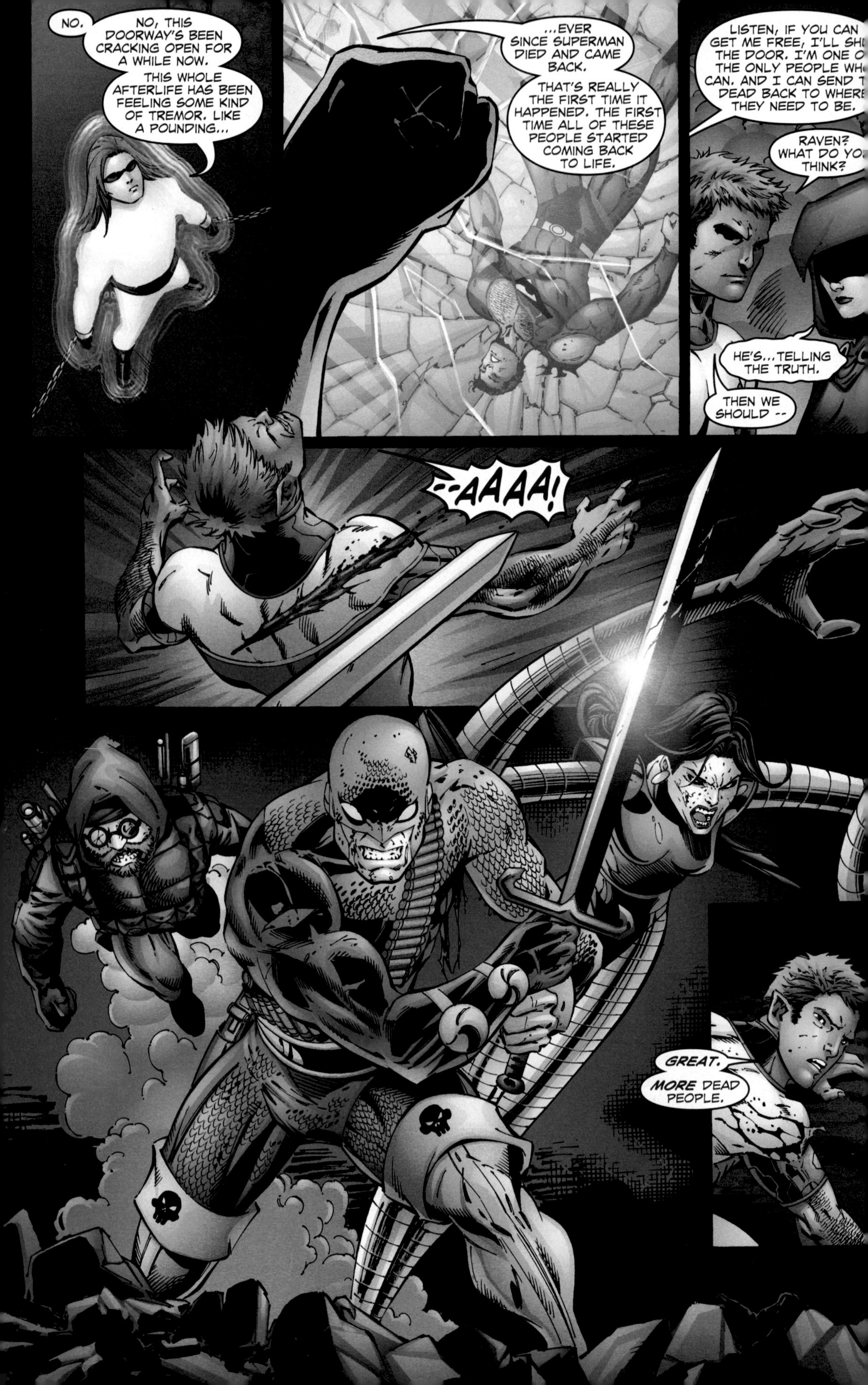
NO.
NO, THIS DOORWAY'S BEEN CRACKING OPEN FOR A WHILE NOW.
THIS WHOLE AFTERLIFE HAS BEEN FEELING SOME KIND OF TREMOR. LIKE A POUNDING...
...EVER SINCE SUPERMAN DIED AND CAME BACK.
THAT'S REALLY THE FIRST TIME IT HAPPENED. THE FIRST TIME ALL OF THESE PEOPLE STARTED COMING BACK TO LIFE.
RAVEN? WHAT DO YO
THINK?
HE'S...TELLING THE TRUTH.
THEN WE SHOULD --
--AAAA!
GREAT.
MORE DEAD PEOPLE.

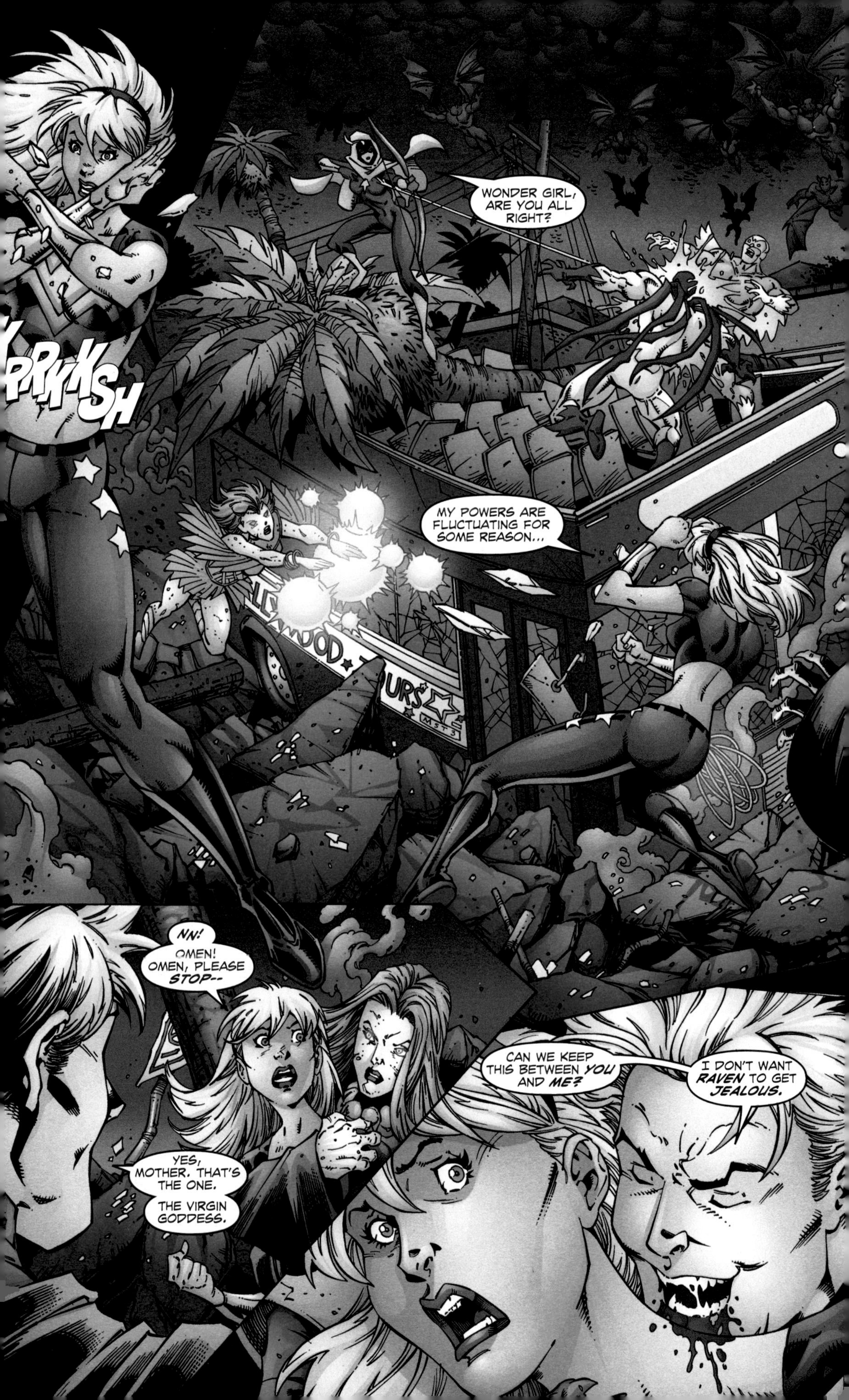

PRKKSH
WONDER GIRL, ARE YOU ALL RIGHT?
MY POWERS ARE FLUCTUATING FOR SOME REASON...
NN!
OMEN! OMEN, PLEASE STOP--
YES, MOTHER. THAT'S THE ONE.
THE VIRGIN GODDESS.
CAN WE KEEP THIS BETWEEN YOU AND ME?
I DON'T WANT RAVEN TO GET JEALOUS.

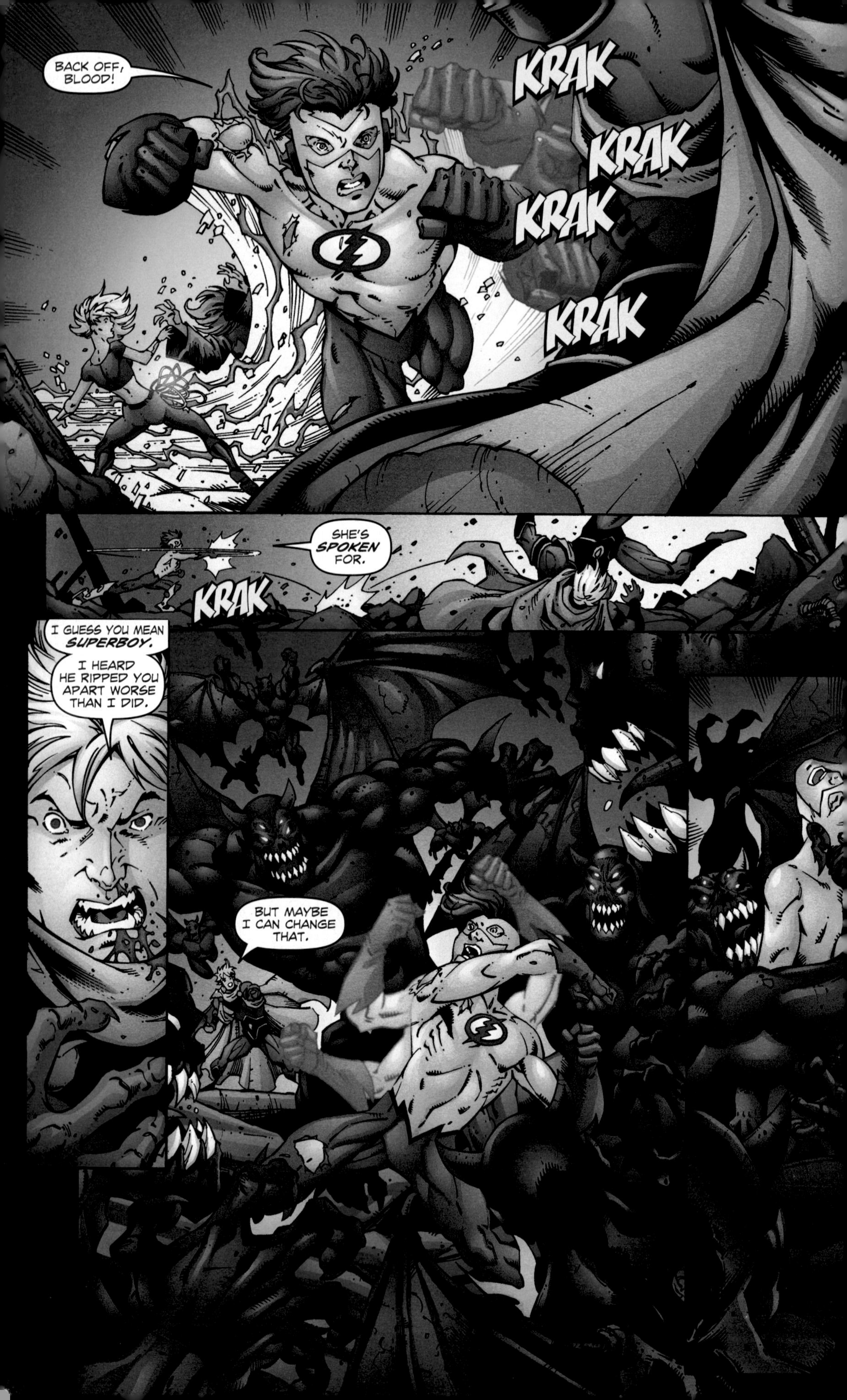
BACK OFF, BLOOD!
KRAK
KRAK
KRAK
KRAK
SHE'S SPOKEN FOR.
KRAK
I GUESS YOU MEAN SUPERBOY.
I HEARD HE RIPPED YOU APART WORSE THAN I DID.
BUT MAYBE I CAN CHANGE THAT.

IT'S *GREAT* TO HAVE YOU BACK, *CAPTAIN!*

LEAPIN' LETTUCE.

TH-THANKS, PIG-IRON!

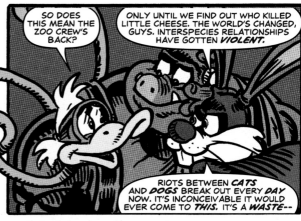

SO DOES THIS MEAN THE ZOO CREW'S BACK?

ONLY UNTIL WE FIND OUT WHO KILLED LITTLE CHEESE. THE WORLD'S CHANGED, GUYS. INTERSPECIES RELATIONSHIPS HAVE GOTTEN *VIOLENT.*

RIOTS BETWEEN *CATS* AND *DOGS* BREAK OUT EVERY *DAY* NOW. IT'S INCONCEIVABLE IT WOULD EVER COME TO *THIS.* IT'S A *WASTE--*

WHICH IS *WHY* THE WORLD NEEDS THE *ZOO CREW.*

TOGETHER YOU'RE A *SYMBOL* THAT ANIMALS CAN WORK *TOGETHER.* WITHOUT THAT SYMBOL...

...IT'S WHY SPECIES LIKE *ME* ARE GOING *EXTINCT.*

YER THE *LAST* ONE, AREN'T YA? THE *LAST* AMERICAN EAGLE.

I DIDN'T HAVE TO BE.

HEY, GUYS. I THINK I SNIFFED SOMETHING OUT.

IT HAS TO DO WITH PRESIDENT FILLMORE. I THINK WE WERE RIGHT. I THINK HE KNOWS WHO KILLED LITTLE CHEESE.

TOP SECRET

ZOO CREW

NICE WORK, DOG.

UM... *THANKS.*

WE'RE GONNA NEED OUR MOST POWERFUL MEMBER IF WE'RE TAKIN' ON THE GOVERNMENT OF THE UNITED SPECIES OF AMERICA.

WE'RE GONNA NEED *ALLEY-KAT-ABRA!*

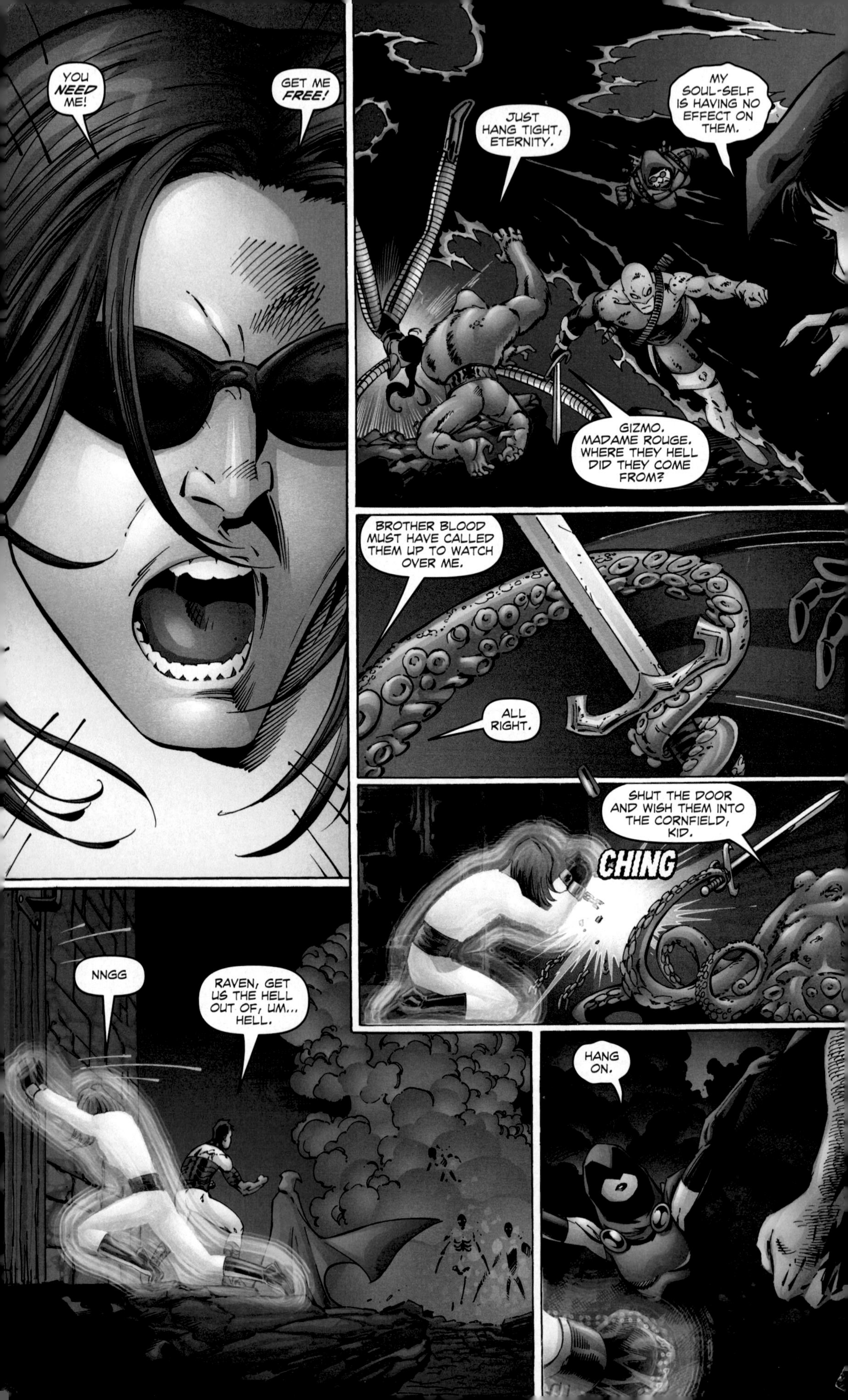
YOU NEED ME!
GET ME FREE!
JUST HANG TIGHT, ETERNITY.
MY SOUL-SELF IS HAVING NO EFFECT ON THEM.
GIZMO. MADAME ROUGE. WHERE THEY HELL DID THEY COME FROM?
BROTHER BLOOD MUST HAVE CALLED THEM UP TO WATCH OVER ME.
ALL RIGHT.
SHUT THE DOOR AND WISH THEM INTO THE CORNFIELD, KID.
CHING
NNGG
RAVEN, GET US THE HELL OUT OF, UM... HELL.
HANG ON.

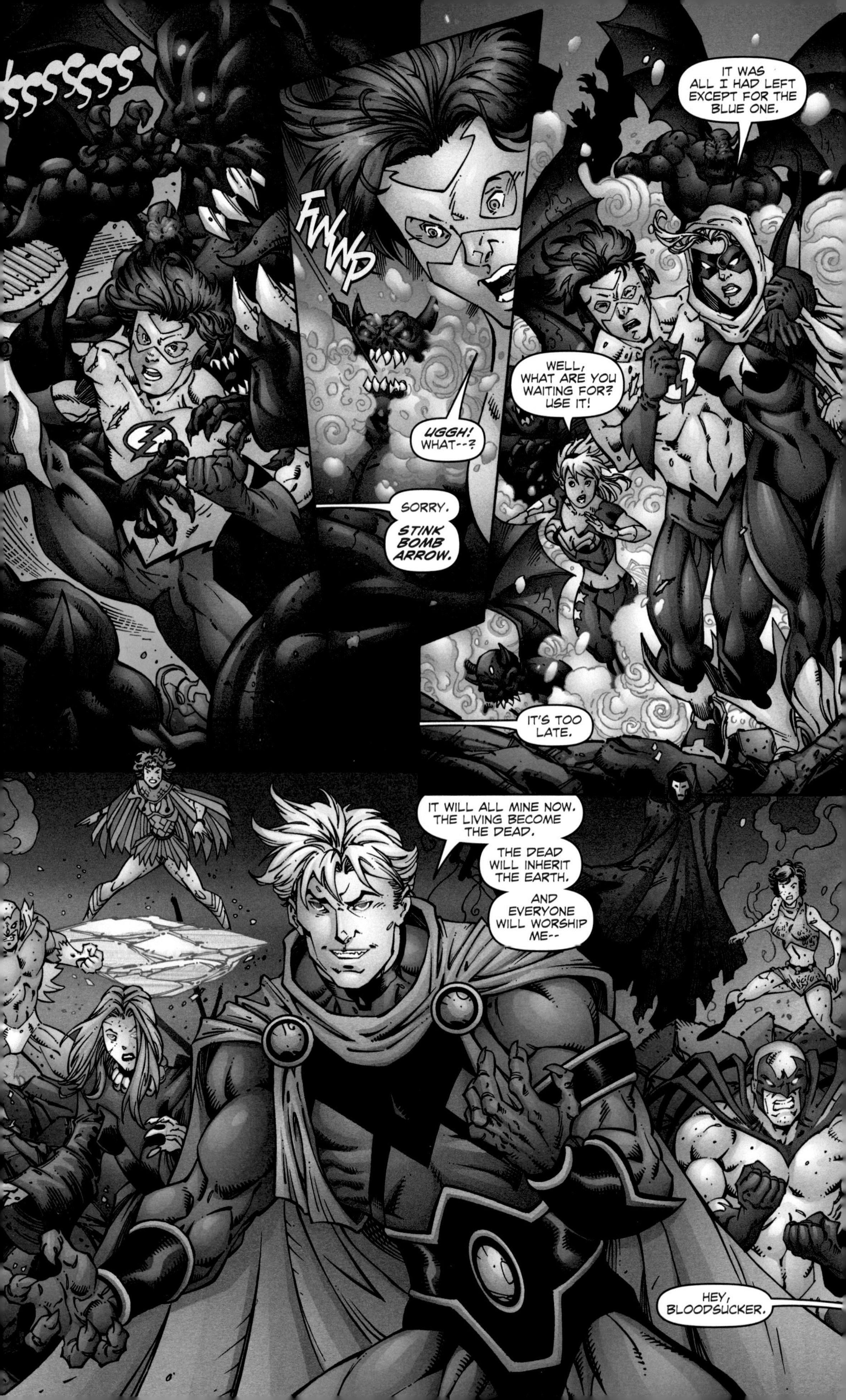
SSSSSSSS
FWNP
UGGH! WHAT--?
SORRY.
STINK BOMB ARROW.
IT WAS ALL I HAD LEFT EXCEPT FOR THE BLUE ONE.
WELL, WHAT ARE YOU WAITING FOR? USE IT!
IT'S TOO LATE.
IT WILL ALL MINE NOW. THE LIVING BECOME THE DEAD.
THE DEAD WILL INHERIT THE EARTH.
AND EVERYONE WILL WORSHIP ME--
HEY, BLOODSUCKER.

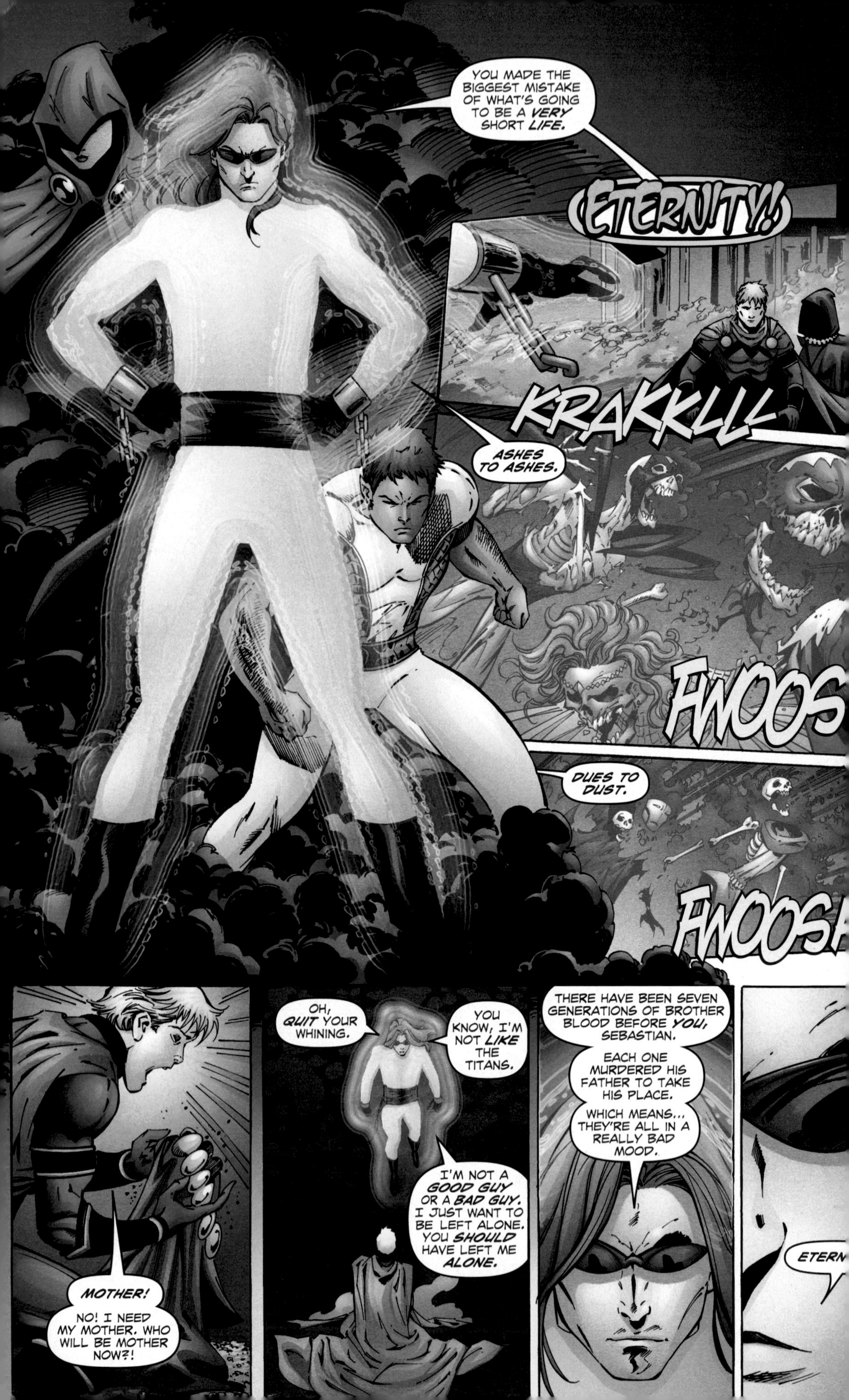

YOU MADE THE BIGGEST MISTAKE OF WHAT'S GOING TO BE A *VERY* SHORT *LIFE.*
ETERNITY!
KRAKKLLL
ASHES TO ASHES.
FWOOS
DUES TO DUST.
FWOOS
MOTHER!
NO! I NEED MY MOTHER. WHO WILL BE MOTHER NOW?!
OH, *QUIT* YOUR WHINING.
YOU KNOW, I'M NOT *LIKE* THE TITANS.
I'M NOT A *GOOD GUY* OR A *BAD GUY.* I JUST WANT TO BE LEFT ALONE. YOU *SHOULD* HAVE LEFT ME *ALONE.*
THERE HAVE BEEN SEVEN GENERATIONS OF BROTHER BLOOD BEFORE *YOU,* SEBASTIAN.
EACH ONE MURDERED HIS FATHER TO TAKE HIS PLACE.
WHICH MEANS... THEY'RE ALL IN A REALLY BAD MOOD.
ETERN

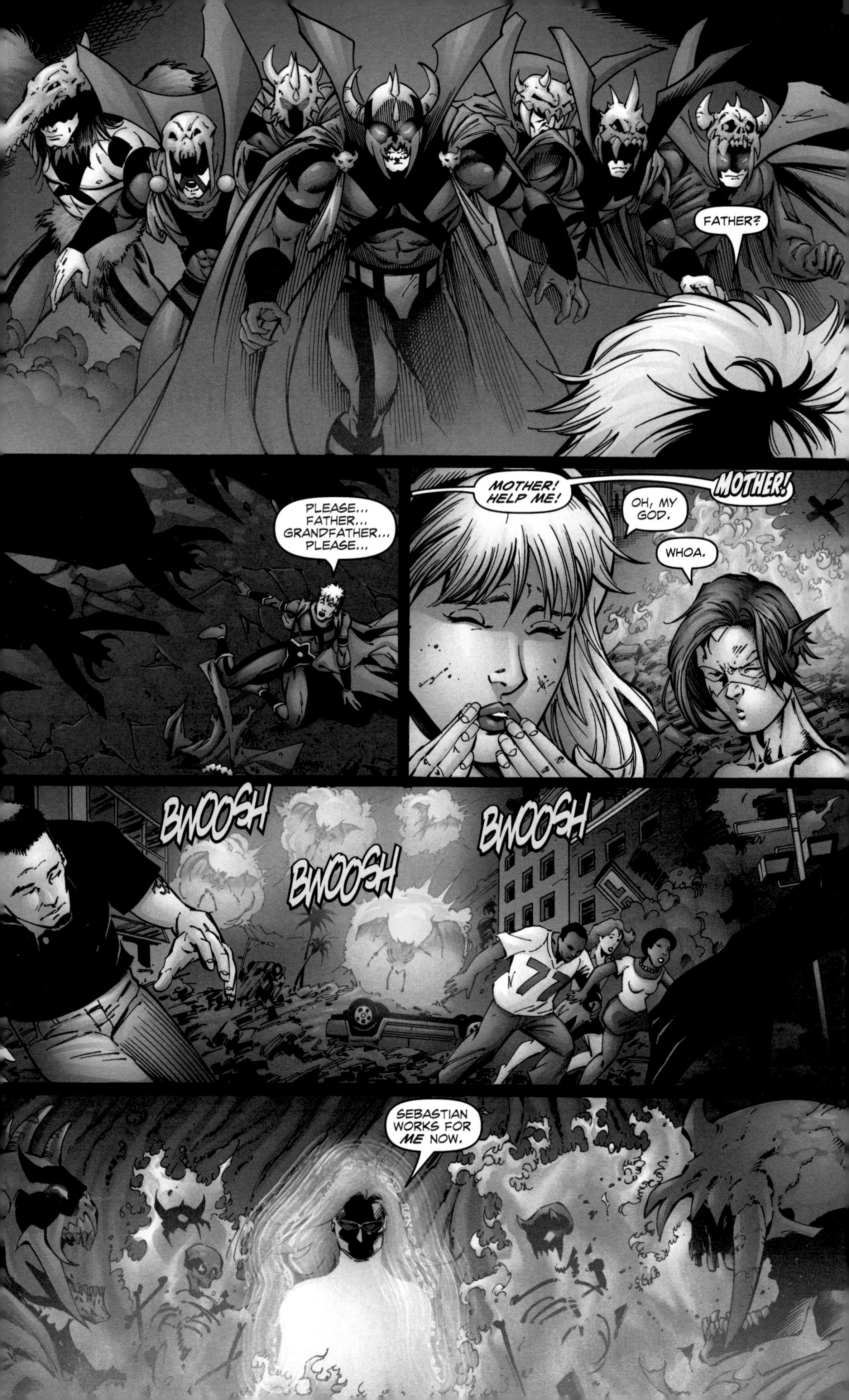
FATHER?
PLEASE... FATHER... GRANDFATHER... PLEASE...
MOTHER! HELP ME!
MOTHER!
OH, MY GOD.
WHOA.
BWOOSH
BWOOSH
BWOOSH
SEBASTIAN WORKS FOR *ME* NOW.

HIS FOLLOWERS HAVE RETURNED TO THE EIGHTH LEVEL OF HELL.

EVERYONE'S BACK WHERE THEY BELONG.

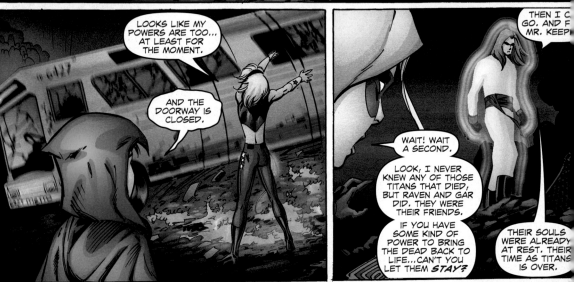

LOOKS LIKE MY POWERS ARE TOO... AT LEAST FOR THE MOMENT.

AND THE DOORWAY IS CLOSED.

THEN I C GO. AND F MR. KEEP

WAIT! WAIT A SECOND.

LOOK, I NEVER KNEW ANY OF THOSE TITANS THAT DIED, BUT RAVEN AND GAR DID. THEY WERE THEIR FRIENDS.

IF YOU HAVE SOME KIND OF POWER TO BRING THE DEAD BACK TO LIFE...CAN'T YOU LET THEM *STAY?*

THEIR SOULS WERE ALREADY AT REST. THEIR TIME AS TITANS IS OVER.

FOR NOW, IT'S *YOUR* TIME TO BE TITANS.

YOU SHOULD *ENJOY* IT WHILE YOU CAN.

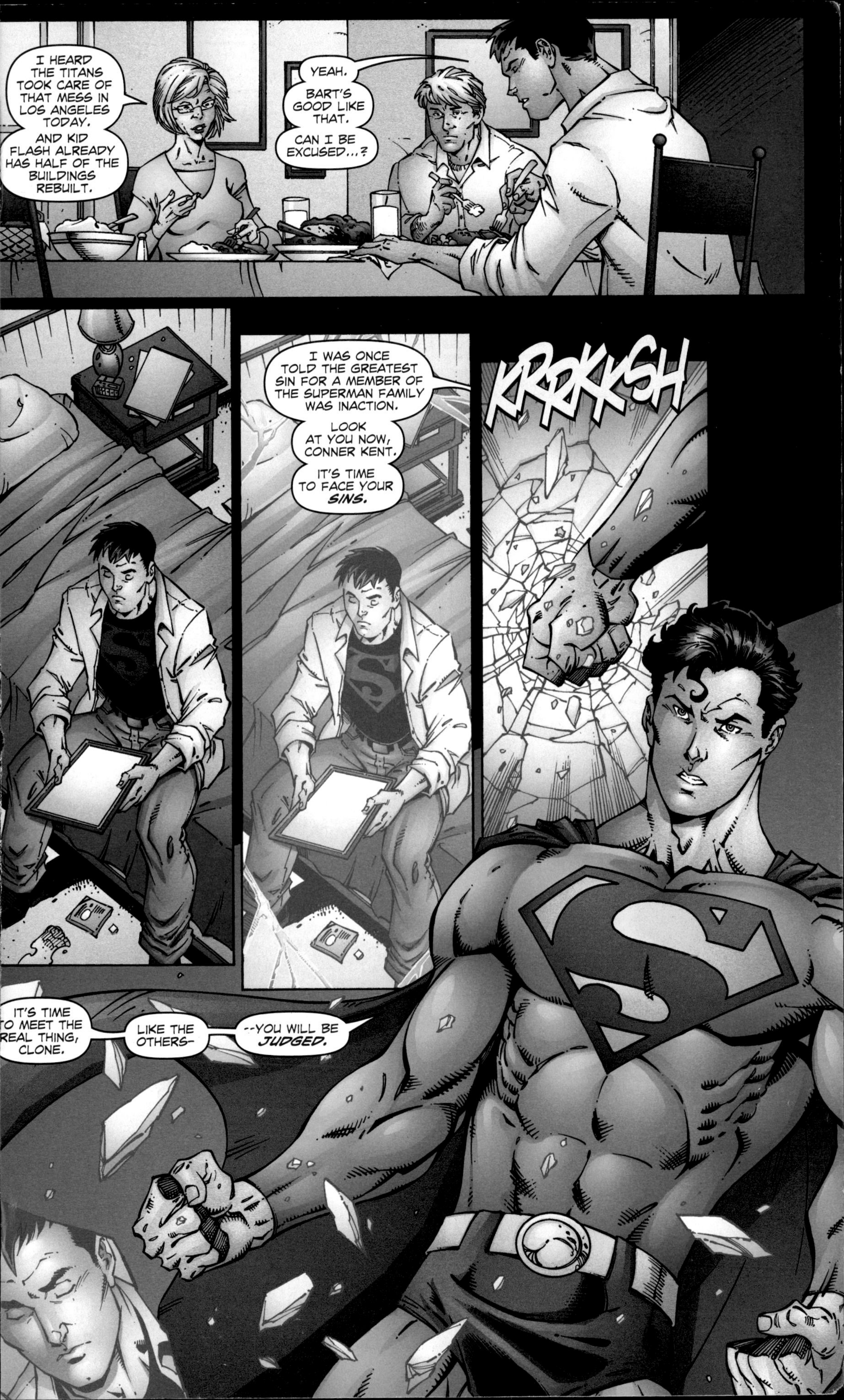
I HEARD THE TITANS TOOK CARE OF THAT MESS IN LOS ANGELES TODAY.
AND KID FLASH ALREADY HAS HALF OF THE BUILDINGS REBUILT.
YEAH.
BART'S GOOD LIKE THAT.
CAN I BE EXCUSED...?
I WAS ONCE TOLD THE GREATEST SIN FOR A MEMBER OF THE SUPERMAN FAMILY WAS INACTION.
LOOK AT YOU NOW, CONNER KENT.
IT'S TIME TO FACE YOUR *SINS.*
KRKKSH
IT'S TIME TO MEET THE REAL THING, CLONE.
LIKE THE OTHERS-
--YOU WILL BE *JUDGED.*

--GUILTY! Alley-Kat-Abra *KILLED* Little Cheese!

BUT *WHY?*

PRESIDENT FILLMORE OFFERED ALLEY-KAT-ABRA A *FORTUNE* TO REVEAL HER IDENTITY AND THE SECRETS OF THE ZOO CREW TO THE GOVERNMENT. SHE TOOK THE MONEY AND BECAME A CELEBRITY.

FASTBACK FOUND OUT ABOUT IT, AND THAT'S WHEN ALLEY-KAT *ZAPPED* HIM INTO THE FUTURE.

WHICH IS WHERE HE CONTACTED *ME* FROM.

SHE *FRAMED* YANKEE POODLE FOR THE ASSASSINATION ATTEMPT WHEN SHE STARTED SEARCHING FOR FASTBACK. THEN KILLED LITTLE CHEESE WHEN HE WAS GETTING TOO CLOSE TO THE COVER-UP.

AND SHE WAS GOING TO FRAME *CAPTAIN CARROT* FOR THE MURDER.

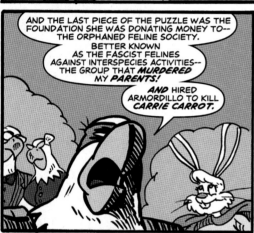

AND THE LAST PIECE OF THE PUZZLE WAS THE FOUNDATION SHE WAS DONATING MONEY TO-- THE ORPHANED FELINE SOCIETY.

BETTER KNOWN AS THE FASCIST FELINES AGAINST INTERSPECIES ACTIVITIES-- THE GROUP THAT *MURDERED* MY *PARENTS!*

AND HIRED ARMORDILLO TO KILL *CARRIE CARROT.*

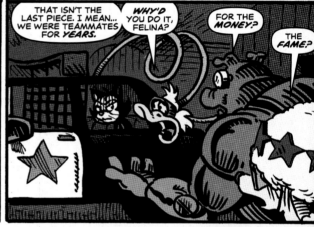

THAT ISN'T THE LAST PIECE. I MEAN... WE WERE TEAMMATES FOR *YEARS.*

WHY'D YOU DO IT, FELINA?

FOR THE *MONEY?*

THE *FAME?*

NO, YOU FREAKIN' *IDIOTS.* DON'T YOU *GET* IT YET? DON'T YOU *GET IT?!*

I'M A *CAT!*

I *HATE* MICE.

WELL? WHAT DO WE DO NOW, CREW?

ARE WE A CREW AGAIN?

WE GOTTA BE, DON'T WE? FASTBACK STILL NEEDS *SAVING!*

BUT WE COULD USE ANOTHER MEMBER BEFORE WE HEAD *ONE HUNDRED YEARS* INTO THE *FUTURE!* WHAT DO YA SAY, EAGLE?

I'D BE *HONORED.*

THEN I GUESS THIS IS *IT.*

THE ALL-NEW ZOO CREW!

THE END